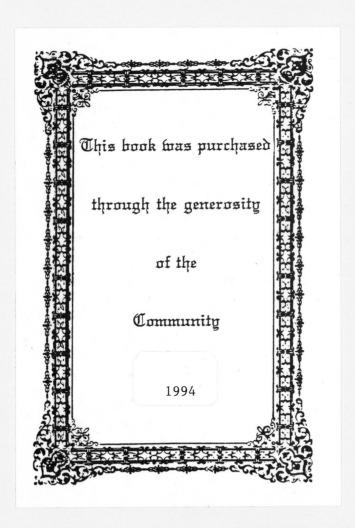

This book was purchased

through the generosity

of the

Community

1994

THE MAKING OF EUROPE

Robert Bartlett

═══

The Making of Europe

CONQUEST, COLONIZATION AND
CULTURAL CHANGE
950–1350

PRINCETON UNIVERSITY PRESS
PRINCETON, NEW JERSEY

Library of Congress Cataloging-in-Publication Data

Bartlett Robert.
    The making of Europe : conquest, colonization and cultural
    change, 950–1350 / Robert Bartlett.
        p. cm.
    Includes bibliographical references and index.
    ISBN 0–691–03298–X
    1. Europe – History – 476-1492.   2. Conquerors – Europe.
    3. Europe – Colonization.   4. Social change.   I. Title.
D200.B27   1993   92–43925
940. 1–dc20

Printed in Great Britain by Clays Ltd, St Ives plc

1 3 5 7 9 10 8 6 4 2

For Penelope

Historia est rerum gestarum narratio.

(Hugh of St Victor, *De sacramentis*, I. prol. 5)

Contents

=====

Maps, Figures and Tables

Maps

Figures

Tables

Plates

====

1. Document of William of Sabina establishing bishoprics in Prussia.
Geheimes Staatsarchiv Preussischer Kulturbesitz, Berlin, Perg. Urk., Königsberg Urk. XLVIII. I. By permission of the Geheimes Staatsarchiv.

2. Carrickfergus castle.
By permission of the Northern Ireland Tourist Board.

3. Albert the Bear as depicted on one of his coins.
By permission of the Märkisches Museum, Berlin.

4. Heavy cavalryman of the thirteenth century.
Paris, Bibliothèque nationale, MS lat. 10136 (*Annales Genuenses*), fol. 141. By permission of the Bibliothèque nationale.

5. A trebuchet of the late twelfth century.
Paris, Bibliothèque nationale, MS lat. 10136 (*Annales Genuenses*), fol. 107. By permission of the Bibliothèque nationale.

6. Peasants enfranchised in return for clearing land.
The Heidelberg MS of the *Sachsenspiegel* (Cod. Pal. Germ. 164), fol. 26v (illustration to *Landrecht* 3. 79. 1). By permission of the Universitätsbibliothek, Heidelberg.

7. Cistercians clearing land.
Cambridge, University Library MS Mm 5 31 (Albert of Stade's reworking of Alexander of Bremen's *Commentary on the Apocalypse*), fol. 113. By permission of the Syndics of Cambridge University Library.

8. The Bremen cog.
By courtesy of the Deutsches Schiffahrtsmuseum, Bremerhaven.

9. Wends and Saxons could not judge or bear witness against each other.
The Heidelberg MS of the *Sachsenspiegel* (Cod. Pal. Germ. 164), fol. 24r (illustration to *Landrecht* 3. 70. 1–2). By permission of the Universitätsbibliothek, Heidelberg.

10. First Wendish coins.
By permission of the Staatliche Museen zu Berlin (Münzkabinett).

Acknowledgements

===

The research on which this book is based has been supported by the University of Michigan Society of Fellows, the University of Edinburgh, the Institute for Advanced Study, Princeton, the Shelby Cullom Davis Center of Princeton University, the University of Chicago, the Alexander von Humboldt Stiftung and the Seminar für mittlere und neuere Geschichte of Göttingen University. The author is grateful to these institutions. Earlier versions of some chapters have been given as talks to university audiences and both the invitations to speak and the comments and criticisms received are much appreciated. Versions of Chapter 3 have appeared in print as *War and Lordship: The Military Component of Political Power, 900–1300* (Fourth Annual Phi Alpha Theta Lecture on History, State University of New York at Albany, 1984) and as 'Technique militaire et pouvoir politique, 900–1300', *Annales: économies – sociétés – civilisations* 41 (1986), pp. 1135–59. Friedrich Lotter gave much help in Göttingen; Patrick J. Geary, William C. Jordan, William I. Miller were kind enough to read the text in typescript and make valuable comments and criticisms; Jon Lehrich provided efficient assistance in the final stages of preparation of the manuscript. The book would not exist without the support, encouragement and occasional stylistic veto of Nora Bartlett.

A Note on References

===

The source of all direct quotations and specific factual statements in the text is given in the Notes. Notes are keyed to significant phrases in the text. To identify a source the reader should thus turn to the appropriate page in the Notes, identifiable from a running heading 'Notes to pp. . . .', and locate the key phrase in italics. Some general bibliography has also been given.

Map 1. *Europe and the surrounding lands in the High Middle Ages*

Introduction

===

Europe is both a region and an idea. The societies and cultures that have existed in this western extremity of the Eurasian land-mass have always been highly diverse, and the case for grouping them together as 'European' has varied from period to period. Since the later Middle Ages, however, there has been enough common ground among the different parts of western and central Europe to make it reasonable to see this region of the world as a whole. When compared with other culture areas of the globe, such as the Middle East, the Indian subcontinent or China, western and central Europe exhibited (and exhibits) distinctive characteristics. In particular, Latin Europe (that is, the part of Europe that was originally Roman Catholic rather than Greek Orthodox or non-Christian) formed a zone where strong shared features were as important as geographical or cultural contrasts.

Some features were basic throughout the Middle Ages: Europe was a world of peasant communities, making a living from pastoral and arable agriculture supplemented by hunting and gathering, with technological and production levels far below those of the present day. Everywhere a small élite of aristocrats dominated and fed itself from the labours of the peasantry. Some were laymen, trained in warfare, proud of family, committed to the continuation of their line; others were clerics or monks, set apart for the Church, avowedly literate and celibate. Lay lords maintained a network of loyalties, alliances and patterns of subordination and domination that made up the political world; clerics and monks were located in a web of institutions and hierarchies with a loose centre in the papal see at Rome. The cultural inheritance of this society was a mixture of Roman, with Latin as its learned language and a partly surviving physical skeleton of roads and cities, Christian, with the pervasive presence of a scriptural, sacramental religion, and Germanic, as witnessed in the names, rites and ethos of the military aristocrats.

The Latin Europe of the early Middle Ages was marked by much greater internal differentiation and by a smaller territorial extent than the Latin Europe of the later Middle Ages. No period of history anywhere can truly be called static or stagnant, but the amount of mobility and cross-regional contact in early medieval Europe was undoubtedly less than that

found in the years after 1000 AD. The new millennium did not mark a
sudden or radical redrawing of the outlines of this society, but from the
eleventh century a period of exceptionally intense creative activity began
within western Europe. The invasions that had marked the earlier period
(Viking, Magyar and Saracen) ceased; and from the eleventh century until
the slump and crisis of the fourteenth and fifteenth centuries stretch the
High Middle Ages, an epoch of economic growth, territorial expansion
and dynamic cultural and social change.

The vitality of European society between the late tenth and early
fourteenth centuries can be seen in many spheres of life. The scale and
speed of production and distribution were transformed: the population
grew, the cultivated area expanded, urbanization and commercialization
restructured economic and social life. Alongside the spread of money, and
of banking and business devices, there developed in some areas a level of
manufacturing activity that had never previously been attained. The same
creativity is found in social organization. In many areas of life fundamental
institutions and structures were given their decisive shape in these centuries:
the incorporated town, the university, central representative bodies, the
international orders of the Roman Catholic Church – all date from this
epoch.

By the year 1300 the European world was relatively densely settled,
productive and culturally innovative. In Flanders tens of thousands of
looms were producing textiles for export; in northern Italy sophisticated
international banking empires were elaborating credit, insurance and investment; in northern France intellectual life of the highest sophistication and
political power of exceptional effectiveness had developed side by side. Just
as this dynamic society had centres, so it had edges, and its internal
dynamism was matched by external or territorial expansionism. In some
senses this phenomenon is obvious and unproblematic. Everywhere in
Europe in the twelfth and thirteenth centuries trees were being felled, roots
laboriously grubbed out, ditches delved to drain waterlogged land. Recruiting agents travelled in the overpopulated parts of Europe collecting
emigrants; wagons full of anxious new settlers creaked their way across the
continent; busy ports sent off ships full of colonists to alien and distant
destinations; bands of knights hacked out new lordships. Yet in this world
of bloody frontiers, raw new towns and pioneer farms, it is not always easy
to delineate the boundaries of expansion. This is partly because 'internal
expansion' – the intensification of settlement and reorganization of society
within western and central Europe – was as important as external expansion;
and hence the problem of describing and explaining these expansionary

movements is not distinct from the problem of describing and explaining the nature of European society itself.

This book approaches the history of Europe in the High Middle Ages from one particular perspective, by concentrating on conquest, colonization and associated cultural change in Europe and the Mediterranean in the period 950–1350. It analyses the establishment of states by conquest and the peopling of distant countries by immigrants along the peripheries of the continent: English colonialism in the Celtic world, the movement of Germans into eastern Europe, the Spanish Reconquest and the activities of crusaders and colonists in the eastern Mediterranean. It asks what developments in language, law, belief and habit accompanied warfare and settlement. In doing so it continually alternates its focus between phenomena that are truly 'frontier', born of the needs of new settlement or military confrontation, and forces and developments that are to be found within the heartlands of the culture, for the expansionary power of this civilization sprang from its centres, even if it may be seen most starkly at its edges. Hence the theme is not only colonial conquest and immigration, the moving edge, but also the foundation of an expansive and increasingly homogeneous society – 'the Making of Europe'.

1. The Expansion of Latin Christendom

He brought masons from far and wide,
Laid the foundations of a church in Troina, soon built it up,
Ceiling and roof were in place, the walls painted with pitch,
Dedicated to Mary the Virgin Mother, endowed with land and tithes,
Richly furnished, raised to be a bishop's seat.

THE SPREAD OF BISHOPRICS 950–1300

Whatever else may have been expanding in the High Middle Ages, there is no doubt about the widening bounds of Latin Christendom, that area of Christendom that recognized papal authority and celebrated the Latin liturgy. Hence one easy preliminary way of measuring expansion is to chart the foundation of bishoprics. While this is not a subtle way of reporting changing spiritual experience, there are several advantages in taking such a clearly defined institution as our measuring block. First, bishoprics were concrete. Each required an individual incumbent, who usually possessed a cathedral church. Both bishop and diocese had names. Thus Latin dioceses can be named, listed, counted and plotted on a map. Every bishopric involved a succession of clerics, a saint, an endowment, a great church, a physical and tangible embodiment of Latin Christendom. Second, bishoprics were usually (and increasingly) territorial. They encompassed not only the prelate in his high church but also a swath of lands, defined ever more exactly and exhaustively. The theory of Latin Christendom was that of a cellular body, and the cells were the dioceses. Every part of Christendom was meant to be in a named and known see, and no part was meant to be in more than one see. Naturally, disputed boundaries and ambiguities were not unknown and in some areas of Europe the territorial diocese took hold only slowly, but the essential truth remains that the dioceses *comprised* Latin Christendom. If small groups of countryfolk ever stated that 'We are not in any bishopric', the immediate response was to condemn this as 'utterly wrong' and to assign them to one. Moreover, these units were relatively – but, in medieval circumstances, remarkably – uniform. The liturgical round, the internal structure and hierarchy, the legal status *vis-à-vis* the papacy – all were fairly standard throughout the wide extent of the western Church. The bishoprics thus provide us with a clear, uniform, measurable unit when we seek to describe the expansion and limits of western Christendom.

It is not only their convenient concreteness that justifies a preliminary description of the expansion of Latin Christendom in terms of the multiplication of its bishoprics, however. The bishop was not only the most easily identified local prelate, he was also an indispensable one. He ordained priests, he confirmed the faithful, he was judge. If bishops disappeared, the Church would soon disappear. As the elementary units of the Church, the bishoprics of the medieval Church are thus a natural as well as a convenient unit of measurement of Christendom.

By the year 1200 there were about 800 bishoprics that recognized the authority of the papacy and celebrated the Latin liturgy. They were very different in size, terrain and social composition. They also varied in age. The Christianity of the Roman empire had been a city-based religion and the oldest bishoprics mirrored the settlement pattern and political map of the ancient civic world. This central core of bishoprics included Italy, France and the Rhineland. The pattern was densest in the Italian peninsula itself, where almost 300 of the 800 bishoprics were to be found, but was also thick in Provence and southern France. The other parts of France and the Rhineland had fewer bishoprics, but they were very regular in their spatial distribution (usually about sixty miles apart) and extended in a comprehensive network from the Atlantic to the Rhine.

These dioceses often had a continuous history going back to the earliest centuries of Christianity. Though some may have experienced a hiatus either during the Germanic invasions of the fifth century or the Viking raids of the ninth and tenth, in these regions it is not uncommon to find sees like Spoleto, whose first reliably reported bishop occurs in the year 353, or Rheims, whose bishop is first mentioned in 314, where a record of at least three bishops per century from *c.* 500 on suggests a continuous line of incumbents.

Quite different in kind were the bishoprics established as Christianity spread, in the fifth, sixth and seventh centuries, into the non-Roman or post-Roman world. Early medieval Ireland and England were not significantly urban and hence a new kind of bishopric was required, one that was not city-based, indeed, one that might be without a fixed seat, adapted to the needs of a people (*gens*) or, in Ireland, a monastic congregation. The early Anglo-Saxon bishoprics thus tended to shift with the varying political patterns and to take their titles from an ethnic group or a region rather than a city. Hence we find 'bishops of the West Saxons' before there were 'bishops of Winchester', 'bishops of the Hwicce' before 'bishops of Worcester'. In this way the institution of the episcopate adapted itself to social conditions very different from those of its birth. Indeed, one of the main features of the ecclesiastical history of the British Isles in the eleventh and twelfth centuries was the re-establishment of the territorial, city-based episcopacy that had come to be the Latin model or norm in place of this early medieval non-urban model.

The eighth and ninth centuries saw some important gains for Latin Christendom, such as the establishment of regular bishoprics in central and southern Germany and, during the reign of Charlemagne, the forcible conversion of the Saxons. Part of the process of securing this conversion was the creation of a network of bishoprics, including Hamburg (831–4), the first diocesan seat east of the Elbe. On the other hand, these centuries also saw spectacular losses for Christendom, as Islamic conquest destroyed the Catholic Visigothic kingdom and submerged and subjugated the bishoprics of the Iberian peninsula.

By the year 900, then, Latin Christendom, as measured by its bishoprics, was limited to three regions: the area of the former Carolingian empire, ruled by Charlemagne's successors and heirs, which contained both the Romanized core of Gaul and Italy and the more recently established German churches; the rump or fringe of Christian Spain along the north coast of the Iberian peninsula from Asturias to the Pyrenees; and the British Isles. These were tight and constrictive boundaries. It seemed, moreover, that even this narrow world might be destroyed. Western Europe can be attacked in three ways: by sea from the north, by sea from the south and by land from the east. In the tenth century it was attacked in all three ways. Viking and Saracen raiders and bands of Magyar horsemen found the rich churches of the West easy prey. Hence the borders of Latin Christendom were not only tight, they were vulnerable. One of the most striking features of the High Middle Ages was the way that this situation was reversed as these borders began to expand on every side.

Eastern Europe in the tenth and eleventh centuries

The first important escape from the constriction which Latin Christendom suffered in the ninth and tenth centuries occurred under the emperor Otto I of Germany. In the year 948 he established, or encouraged the establishment of, a string of bishoprics along his northern and eastern frontiers. East of the Elbe these were to serve the new Ottonian conquests in pagan Slav territory. North of the Eider they were to promote Christianity in what was seen as the client kingdom of Denmark. In 968 Otto crowned years of planning by having his favourite foundation of Magdeburg raised to the status of an archbishopric. It was envisaged as a metropolitan see for 'all the people of the Slavs beyond the Elbe and Saale, lately converted and to be converted to God' and no definite eastern boundaries were assigned to it.

The establishment of an ecclesiastical hierarchy in eastern Europe, as elsewhere, was much influenced by local political considerations. The first was the choice between Byzantine or western forms of Christianity and church authority. From the time when eighth-century popes and Byzantine emperors had quarrelled over whether Illyrium was under the authority of the pope or the patriarch of Constantinople, there had been demarcation disputes in this part of Europe. As relations grew more strained, the disputes took on a sharper tone. The conversion of Bohemia and Moravia in the ninth century had seen the clash of the two brothers, Constantine and Methodius, natives of Thessalonica and inventors of the Slav script, with 'the cohorts of Latins', Bavarian priests from Regensburg and Salzburg. Even today one of the sharpest cultural divisions in the Slavic world is between those peoples who were converted by Germans and those converted by Greeks.

It was, however, Germany which eventually provided the impetus and the model for the creation of West Slav and Magyar churches in the tenth and early eleventh centuries. In the case of Bohemia, the result was a bishopric in Prague, in existence by 973, which was subject to the German archdiocese of Mainz until late in the Middle Ages. Its first incumbents were themselves Germans, and Bohemia, although maintaining a high degree of autonomy and distinctiveness within the Holy Roman Empire, was always tied to that body in a way that Poland and Hungary were not. In these latter countries, in contrast, although German ecclesiastical influence was of the first importance, completely independent hierarchies came into existence at the turn of the millennium. Poland had its own bishopric, Poznań, from 968, but this had originally (in all probability) been subject to Magdeburg. In the year 1000, however, the archbishopric of Gniezno was created, with several other new sees as suffragans; Poznań itself was soon also placed under Gniezno, thus forming a Polish church with a native archbishop. The following year, 1001, the first Hungarian see was established at Esztergom (Gran) and, over the course of the eleventh century, a network of new bishoprics was established by the Hungarian kings along the Danube and east into Transylvania.

Thus, in the space of about sixty years, new churches had been established across a huge part of east-central Europe, the frontiers of the Latin and the Greek churches had been pushed much closer together, and a process had begun that ensured that the Poles, Bohemians and Magyars would look westwards to Germany and to Rome for their cultural and religious models. Despite violent pagan reactions in the eleventh century, these newly established sees survived. East European paganism was already on the defensive.

Scandinavia in the tenth and eleventh centuries

The first Scandinavian sees were those, mentioned above, which were established during the reign of Otto I. These first Danish bishoprics, Hedeby/Schleswig, Ribe and Århus, mentioned in 948 and again in 965, were to have a continuous history from the tenth century. Over the course of the next hundred years the number of Danish bishoprics increased and sees were established on the islands as well as on the mainland of Jutland. English influence was important in developing Denmark's fledgling Christianity; for example, the bishop of Roskilde in the 1020s was an Englishman. In 1060 a territorial network of nine (later eight) bishoprics was organized and, finally, in 1103–4, the Danish church was placed under its own archbishopric, Lund in Scania (now in Sweden but at that time part of the Danish kingdom).

Denmark had the earliest Scandinavian sees and the first fully organized church. The progress of institutional Christianity in Norway, Sweden and Iceland was more fitful, reflecting perhaps the less developed state of royal power in those countries: a strong pro-Christian dynasty was the ideal tool of conversion from the Christian point of view. However, as royal authority consolidated in Scandinavia in the eleventh century, and as the influence of Christian England was flung into the balance, a decisive Christianization took place. The earliest Scandinavian see outside Denmark was Skara in Sweden (*c.* 1014). The chronicler Adam of Bremen mentions the consecration of two bishops in Norway and six in Sweden, as well as nine in Denmark, in the 1060s. Pagan cult continued in some parts of Sweden into the twelfth century, but long before that there already existed a network of Scandinavian bishoprics from Iceland to Uppsala. The process culminated in the mid-twelfth century with the creation of new archbishoprics for Sweden and Norway. In 1164 Uppsala, which a hundred years earlier had been the site of a major temple of regal Thor, warlike Odin and phallic Frey, where sacrificed animals (and, some said, men) hung rotting on the trees of the sacred grove, became the archiepiscopal see of the Swedish church.

Southern Italy in the eleventh and twelfth centuries

The incorporation of eastern and northern Europe into the ecclesiastical framework of the Latin Church occasionally involved violence, but very rarely alien conquest. The West Slav, Magyar and Scandinavian dynasties that introduced Christianity not only survived but even strengthened their positions. Foreign influence there certainly was, from Germany and England, but this influence was largely cultural and did not involve political or military domination.

The situation in the Mediterranean was very different. Here, unlike in the east or north of Europe, Latin Christians encountered cultures that were at least as literate and civilized as their own. While in Poland or Scandinavia there were the bare rudiments of town life – market-places, fortresses, perhaps shrines – the Mediterranean was an area of ancient cities and impressive cultural centres. In the east and the north Latin Christendom was able to spread partly because of its cultural prestige, which drew the rulers of non-literate and non-urbanized Europe to it, but in the Mediterranean the Latins expanded their Church only by force of arms.

One area which saw the creation of a new or newly organized Latin hierarchy in the eleventh and early twelfth centuries was southern Italy and Sicily. This was a region of complex political geography, where the Byzantines, autonomous city-states, Lombard princes and the Muslims of Sicily engaged in continuous and confusing struggle. Over the course of a century, from the time they acquired their first permanent lordship at Aversa in 1030, the Normans were able to impose a new and unified political structure, the kingdom of Sicily, upon this ethnic and cultural diversity. The ecclesiastical counterpart to this political activity was the introduction of Latin bishops, often of north French origin, into Greek sees, the resurrection of dioceses in conquered Muslim regions and, sometimes, the creation of entirely new bishoprics, like Aversa itself (1053) or Catania on the east coast of Sicily, given episcopal status in 1091 and granted to the Breton monk, Ansgar. Ansgar found the church 'greatly neglected, since it had just been snatched from the jaws of an infidel people' and he took care to provide it with all it needed and then, 'joining with him a great body of monks', he installed a strict monastic community there.

Both Greeks and Muslims survived in the kingdom of Sicily, practising their variants of religion with some degree of autonomy, but, from the early twelfth century onwards, the ecclesiastical hierarchy consisted of a network of Latin bishoprics just like those in other parts of Italy, in France,

England or Germany. The Englishmen Richard Palmer and Walter Of-famil, who were archbishops of Messina and Palermo respectively in the second half of the twelfth century, would have found the ecclesiastical structures and liturgical life of Sicily quite familiar.

Spain in the eleventh, twelfth and thirteenth centuries

The story of Sicily in the later eleventh century, that 'reconquest' in miniature, was reflected on the grand scale in the Spain of the Reconquest. The Christian kingdoms of the peninsula, which had been pushed to the very shores of the sea in the wake of the Muslim invasions of the eighth century, began to consolidate and regain territory soon thereafter. The bishopric of Vic in Catalonia, for example, which disappeared from view during the invasions, was re-established in the year 886. By the turn of the millennium there was a little group of bishoprics in Catalonia, including the border town of Barcelona. Four or five hundred miles away, in the north-west of the Iberian peninsula, another group of bishoprics, including the rising star of Santiago, maintained its existence under the aegis of the Leónese–Asturian monarchy. From these toeholds, the Latin hierarchy was able to expand to cover virtually every part of the peninsula in the next three centuries.

The first step occurred in the eleventh century, when a series of bishoprics was created, or given new organizational form, in Castile, in Navarre and in the area to the south of Santiago. The most dramatic gain of this period was Toledo, the ancient ecclesiastical centre of the old Visigothic kingdom, conquered by Alfonso VI of Castile and León in 1085 and soon made the seat of what was to become Spain's largest archdiocese. Alfonso installed as archbishop Bernard, a monk from the prestigious French monastery of Cluny, who had previously served as abbot of Sahagún in León, and, on 18 December 1086, issued a solemn charter of endowment. 'By the hidden judgment of God,' it reads,

this city was for 376 years in the hands of the Moors, blasphemers of the Christian name ... after many battles and numberless slaughter of the enemy, I seized populous cities and strong castles from them, with the help of God's grace. Thus, inspired by God's grace, I moved an army against this city, where my ancestors once reigned in power and wealth, deeming it acceptable in the sight of the Lord if that which the perfidious race under their faithless leader Muhammad took from the Christians, I, Alfonso the Emperor, with Christ as my leader, should restore to the adherents of that faith.

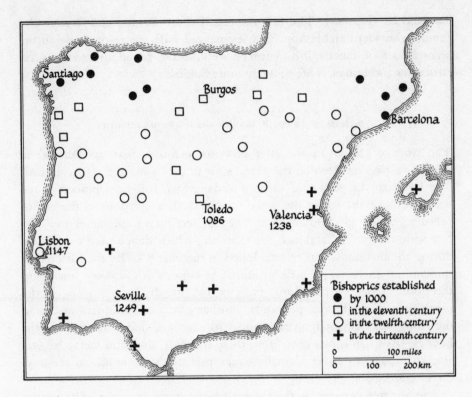

Map 2. Bishoprics established in the Iberian peninsula, ninth to thirteenth centuries

Then, after relating the fall of the city, the appointment of the archbishop and the consecration of the church, 'so that what was until now a dwelling of demons should henceforth be for ever a holy place for heavenly powers and all Christians', the king granted the bishopric a string of villages in the surrounding countryside.

The pace of conquest and ecclesiastical reorganization then increased. In two main pushes, *c.* 1080–1150 and 1212–65, almost the whole of the rest of the peninsula was subjected to Christian kings and organized into Latin dioceses. Lisbon was captured with the help of northern crusaders in 1147; at once 'the episcopal see was restored' and the Englishman Gilbert of Hastings installed as its first bishop; he introduced to his bishopric the liturgical practices of Salisbury. In the late twelfth century the Christian advance faltered for several generations, but the victory of Las Navas de Tolosa in 1212 marked a new impetus. The reigns of Ferdinand III of

Castile (1217–52) and James the Conqueror of Aragon (1213–76) saw Christian occupation of the whole peninsula with the exception of the client state of Granada. Valencia fell to James of Aragon in 1238 and immediately the chief mosque was converted to a cathedral, which was to serve the new bishops until a western-style building was erected in the later thirteenth century. In 1248, after a siege of sixteen months, the Castilians marched into Seville and also turned the chief mosque into the cathedral of the newly formed diocese:

When the noble king Don Ferdinand was settled in the town and his heart was full of joy at the great reward God had given him for his labours, he then began, to the honour and praise of God and St Mary, His mother, to revive the archiepiscopal see, which had of old been abandoned, despoiled and orphaned of its rightful pastor; and a worthy foundation was established in honour of St Mary, whose name this noble and holy church bore . . . and he then gave the archbishopric to Don Ramon, who was the first archbishop of Seville since the king Don Ferdinand won the town.

By the later years of the thirteenth century there were fifty-one bishoprics in the Spanish kingdoms and Portugal. This was quite a dense network: the Iberian bishoprics were only 1.4 times the size of those in anciently converted and densely settled England. The Reconquest thus had, as a natural corollary, the creation of a large new ecclesiastical establishment.

The eastern Mediterranean in the eleventh, twelfth and thirteenth centuries

The best known of all the wars of Christian expansion are the crusades in the eastern Mediterranean, beginning with that remarkable expedition of French and Italian knights and commoners of 1096–9 that marched two thousand miles across largely unknown and unwelcoming lands to storm the Holy City of their faith. Compared with the similar conquests in Sicily and Spain, those in the Levant were less complete and less enduring. Nevertheless, even as the crusaders of the 1090s neared their destination, they began the process of creating a Latin Church in the East. In the wake of the crusaders' conquests, the major cities of Palestine and Syria became the seats of western bishops. Thus in 1099 French archbishops were appointed in the captured cities of Tarsus, Mamistra and Edessa. Daimbert, bishop of Pisa, the papal legate, became patriarch of Jerusalem. Gradually a complete network of patriarchates, archbishoprics and bishoprics filled the Crusader States. The earlier Greek territorial organization was taken as the natural starting point, but it was soon substantially modified by the creation and transfer of sees. The personnel was largely immigrant. The first four Latin patriarchs of Antioch, for example, bore the quintessentially Gallic names Bernard of Valence, Ralph of Domfront, Aimery of Limoges and Peter of Angoulême.

By the 1130s the Latin patriarchates of Antioch and Jerusalem were as extensive as they were ever to be. Thirty or so sees with Latin incumbents extended in an arc from Cilicia to the Dead Sea. Thereafter, the Latin Church on the Levantine mainland was to suffer massive territorial losses, with only partial and temporary recoveries. By the end of the thirteenth century the crusaders had been expelled completely from the mainland and only the series of titular bishops continued as a reminder of this most grandiose aspect of the expansion of Latin Christendom.

The thirteenth century also saw gains for the Latins in the eastern Mediterranean, not, however, from the Muslims but at the expense of the Greeks. In 1191 Richard I of England, *en route* for Palestine, captured Cyprus from its Greek ruler; it eventually came into the hands of a noble family from Poitou, the Lusignans. Within a few decades there is evidence of a Latin hierarchy in Cyprus, with an archbishopric at Nicosia and suffragans at Famagusta, Limasol and Paphos. Numerous Greek sees continued to exist on Cyprus, but under the authority of the Latin archbishop. Another major expansion of the Latin Church took place in the aftermath of the conquest of Constantinople by diverted crusaders in 1204. A Latin empire was erected in its place and, with the Latin empire, came a Latin patriarchate and Latin bishoprics. Their history is often very confusing. Some seem to have existed on paper only. Others had short or intermittent lives, very dependent on the political powers that protected them. Other 'Latin' bishoprics seem to have been simply Greek bishoprics whose incumbents showed a prudent submissiveness to the pope. Nevertheless, the intentions of the Roman Church in relation to its new acquisitions were clear. The church of Athens, for example, seized by the Latins soon after the fall of Constantinople, had a Latin incumbent, Berard, by 1206, who requested and was granted permission to reorganize his new Greek archbishopric on the lines of the church of Paris (*secundum consuetudinem Parisiensis ecclesiae*). A more thoroughly Gallo-Roman model of hegemony would be hard to find. During the period of the Latin empire the cathedral of Constantinople was completely dominated by Venetian clergy. Indeed, in 1205 the Latin patriarch was pressured into swearing an oath 'that no one should be received as a canon of Santa Sophia unless he is a Venetian by birth or has served ten years in a Venetian church'. Although the pope invalidated the oath, the actual composition of the cathedral chapter between 1204 and 1261 was almost as if it had been in force. Of the forty canons whose origins are known, thirty-two were Venetian. The others were Italian and French. This was a colonial church.

In Frankish Greece and the Venetian islands of the Aegean and the eastern Mediterranean bishops of French, Catalan or Italian descent followed each other in regular succession into the later Middle Ages. The Latin expansion in the eastern Mediterranean was more precarious than elsewhere, but it did leave a string of bishoprics obedient to the pope scattered from the frontiers of Albania to Venetian Crete and Lusignan Cyprus. In many ways the Latin hierarchy of the eastern Mediterranean in 1300 looked like the flotsam of a great storm clinging to odd corners of distant shores; but it is worth noting that two centuries before there had been no Latin bishopric east of Italy.

The Baltic region in the twelfth and thirteenth centuries

At the same time as Islam was being attacked and pushed back in the Mediterranean, Christian missionaries and conquerors were penetrating the last stronghold of native European paganism in the lands east of the Elbe and around the shores of the Baltic. Here those West Slav peoples who had not converted, the so-called 'Wends', and their distant linguistic cousins, the Balts (Prussians, Lithuanians and Latvians), along with the Finno–Ugric Livonians, Estonians and Finns, constituted an arc of non-literate polytheism that stretched from the borders of Saxony to the Arctic Circle. This was, in fact, to be the most enduring bastion of European paganism, for it was not until 1386 that the Lithuanian dynasty adopted Christianity (in return for the Polish crown). In this part of Europe the twelfth, thirteenth and fourteenth centuries were marked by evangelization, apostasy and holy war.

The first West Slav people to acquire a Christian bishopric in the twelfth century was the Pomeranians, who lived around the mouth of the Oder. In the wake of their conquest by Boleslaw III of Poland, they became the targets of a mission headed by the German bishop, Otto of Bamberg. Over the course of two visits in the 1120s, despite often violent opposition by adherents of the local deities and the pagan priesthood, he succeeded in destroying temples and idols, building wooden churches and baptizing thousands of Pomeranians. He himself retained a personal jurisdiction over the new-born Pomeranian church, but the year after his death, in 1140, one of his followers was appointed first bishop, with a seat originally at Wolin (Wollin) and later at Kamień (Cammin). Their Christianity stood the

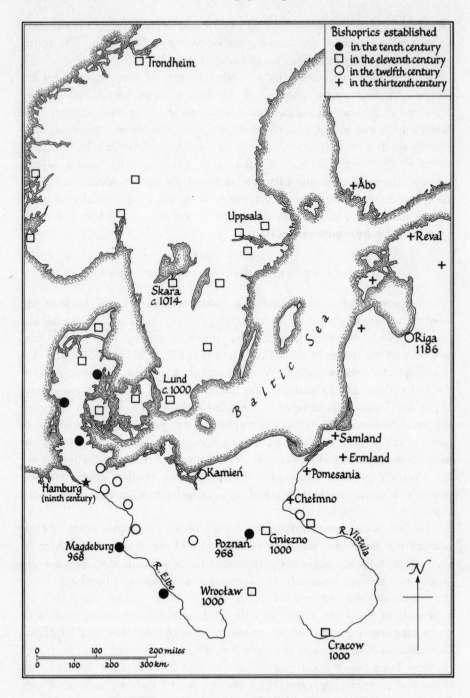

Map 3. Bishoprics north and east of the Elbe, 948 to c. 1300

Pomeranians in good stead a few years later when, during the Wendish Crusade of 1147, a crusading army turned up before their chief city, Szczecin (Stettin). The Pomeranians, with their new bishop beside them, hung a cross from their walls and the crusaders, out-trumped by their own most venerated symbol, went after other prey.

The other new bishoprics founded in Wendish territory in the twelfth century (Brandenburg, Havelberg, Ratzeburg, Schwerin and Lübeck) were established on or near the sites of sees erected by the Ottonians or their successors, the Salians, that had succumbed to pagan Slav reaction. Brandenburg, for example, had been one of the sees founded by Otto I in 948 as a missionary bishopric for his conquests east of the Elbe. During the great Slav rising of 983, however, the bishop was forced to flee, the remaining clergy were enslaved, and the church treasures and the grave of the first bishop were plundered. In the following century and a half Brandenburg went from Slav to German rule and back again repeatedly, but there was never sufficient security to permit the effective re-establishment of the see, though a sequence of titular incumbents was maintained. It was not until the definitive establishment of German rule under the ruthless leadership of Albert the Bear, margrave of Brandenburg (d. 1170), and Henry the Lion, duke of Saxony (d. 1195), that the area between the Elbe and the Oder could be definitively incorporated into the network of Latin bishoprics.

The end of official West Slav paganism came in 1168 when the troops of the Danish king, Valdemar I, stormed the famous temple of Arkona on the island of Rügen. Thereafter the temples were gone and the priests silent. We know little or nothing of the inner life of the Wends after the destruction of their official cult, so it is perhaps presumptuous to talk of conversion, but from the late twelfth century there was no longer a public alternative to Christianity. A network of newly established bishoprics now extended from the Elbe to eastern Pomerania.

The conversion of the other Baltic peoples proved longer, harder and bloodier. While the Wendish peoples had felt increasing pressure, both political and cultural, from the surrounding Christian kingdoms of Germany, Poland and Denmark, and their military and commercial élite was already riddled with Christianity, the Prussians, Estonians and Lithuanians were much less accessible, physically and ideologically. They were numerous, warlike, fiercely committed to their religion; they inhabited highly defensible terrain. It took a century to subdue the Prussians, and the Lithuanians were never conquered.

Early Christian penetration of the Baltic was in the shape of missionary activity. In the wake of the German merchants who sailed from Lübeck to the Dvina, an Augustinian canon named Meinhard came to Livonia and established a mission church. He was formally consecrated bishop around 1186. In Prussia it was the Cistercians who led the way and a missionary from the Polish monastery of Łekno became bishop of Prussia around 1215. In both areas subsequent developments were remarkably similar. In neither region was it possible to maintain an effective missionary bishopric without force; in the mental climate of the age of Pope Innocent III it was natural that force meant the crusade. In both Livonia and Prussia *ad hoc* crusading was found inadequate and was supplemented by the foundation of military orders, the Swordbrothers and the Knights of Dobrzyń (Dobrin) respectively. Eventually, in both cases, the potential of an older and wealthier German military order outdid these new local creations. By 1240 both the Livonian and the Prussian crusades were firmly in the hands of the Teutonic Knights.

Parallel to the introduction of crusading ideology and institutions was the elaboration of an episcopal hierarchy. Papal legates took this matter in hand. During the imprisonment of Bishop Christian of Prussia by the pagans a plan was approved to divide his diocese into four. In 1243 the legate William of Sabina issued a document confirming the division and creating the sees of Chełmno, Pomesania, Ermland and Samland (see Plate 1). Meanwhile, as the conquest of Livonia and the surrounding regions slowly progressed, new bishoprics were created there. In 1251 the missionary Meinhard's old see on the Dvina, now relocated at Riga, was raised to archiepiscopal status and all the other bishoprics of Livonia and Prussia were placed under it. The details of ecclesiastical organization and endowment and the development of real cathedral chapters would obviously still require time, but in the space of two or three generations a new province covering most of the eastern seaboard of the Baltic had been added to the Roman Church. This is what is meant by 'the expansion of Latin Christendom'.

PROBLEMS OF EXPLANATION

Latin Christendom consisted of those churches worshipping in Latin and according to a rite approved by the papacy, usually the Roman rite. One of the striking features of the western Church is, in fact, its insistence on the dominance of one liturgical language and one cultic form. There are a few dubious or borderline cases, where special circumstances allowed other languages or rites within the Roman obedience, but these were few in number and diminished over time. The importance of uniformity and the Roman model is well illustrated by the way the Carolingians sought to enforce the same form of worship in all the churches of their realm and to use Roman manuscripts to provide liturgical models. As the historian Notker put it: 'Charlemagne . . . grieved that the provinces, and even the regions and cities, differed in divine service, namely in their manner of chant', and hence sent to the pope for help. The goals were 'unity' (*unitas*) and 'harmony' (*consonantia*) in the chant and it was to Rome that imperious reformers like Charlemagne looked. Absolute uniformity was, of course, an ideal, but it was an ideal towards which ever closer approximations were made. In the late eleventh century, as the Spanish Mozarabic rite was replaced by the Roman, and the Slavonic liturgy was finally suppressed in Bohemia, the 'Latin' in 'Latin Christendom' gained in meaning.

'Latin' was, in fact, increasingly a term by which adherents of the western Church identified themselves. The crusades and closer, but not necessarily warmer, relations with the Greek and Russian churches made it particularly pertinent. It came to have a quasi-ethnic nuance, as in the phrase *gens latina*, 'the Latin people', and even to spawn abstract nouns parallel to the usage 'Christendom'; for example, when the German princes were debating the choice of a new Holy Roman Emperor in 1125, one chronicler puts into their mouths a concern for the way 'the whole Latin world' (*tota latinitas*) is hanging on their decision. The category 'Latin' thus had a role in the self-description of the people of western Europe and obviously helped lend a kind of conceptual cohesion to groups of very varied national origin and language. Membership of a liturgical community is, however, hardly sufficient in itself as a motor for major military and migratory expansion. 'Latin' was a name which adherents of the Latin rite and Roman obedience applied to themselves, but it is hard to credit the Latin liturgy itself with expansionary power. Indeed, one aspect of the expansion we are discussing seems to be the imposition of that liturgy on Christian regions of divergent tradition by the papacy and other interested groups; and if the spread of the liturgy is conceived of as a consequence of the expansionary movement, it is hard also to have it as a cause.

What seems to be important is not any intrinsic feature of the Latin rite but the fact that it was almost an official liturgy of the Roman Church and hence, eventually, of the Roman obedience. When we turn to the definition of Latin Christendom as an obedience, that is, as a multitude of churches who accepted the authority of the pope, we find an organization with an active executive head, and it is easier to imagine growth springing from the drives of an institution than from liturgical forms. The role of the papacy in the expansionary movement of the High Middle Ages is discussed below in Chapter 10. There attention is focused upon the alliance of papal and aristocratic power, the use of new activist religious orders by the papacy and the remarkable case of the crusades, the best example of a papally orchestrated war of conquest. All these are important, but, even in the last case, it should be clear that orchestration is not the same as playing the instruments: papal directives aroused the crusading armies but they did not give possession of Muslim or pagan fortresses. Even in this, the clearest case of 'Latin Christendom at war', material and lay elements must not be neglected. Moreover, if we recognize the directive role of the papacy from the eleventh century onwards, we must still seek some explanation of why it was just at that period that papal direction became so insistent and so effective. The mere existence of the institution is not enough to account for the rise of the papal monarchy. The papacy is best seen as an enterprising and initiatory institution, but one that made its greatest mark by taking advantage of changes in the world around it. The great popes of the eleventh, twelfth and thirteenth centuries did indeed have a consciously pursued goal of 'extending the bounds of the Church', but they did so in a world where dynamic growth of a material kind was already afoot.

The 'Latins' were also 'Franks'. In the first half of the ninth century the Christian West and the Frankish empire had come close to being coterminous. Apart from the British Isles and the kingdom of Asturias, virtually no Latin Christians acknowledged any overlord but Charlemagne and his son. This world of mixed Roman, Christian and Germanic descent, shaped by the power of ideological warrior-kings ruling from Barcelona to Hamburg and from Rheims to Rome, left a deep imprint on the following centuries. 'Frankish Europe', as we may call it, the lands ruled by the Carolingians, was the heart of the West. In the High Middle Ages this area (to which, with some reservations, England may be added) retained a natural centrality. For processes of growth and development were not uniform throughout Europe, and certain areas can reasonably be classified as central. It cannot be done on the basis of reliable statistics, since they do not exist for this period, but all the indirect evidence suggests that a zone running roughly from south-east England to central Italy would possess a higher concentration of population and higher levels of economic activity than elsewhere. In particular, northern France and northern Italy proved extremely innovative regions. Most of the new religious orders of this period, for example, originated here and spread outwards. Northern France, the birthplace of Gothic architecture, scholasticism and Arthurian romance, gave thirteenth-century civilization much of its distinctive flavour. These areas, it might be argued, formed a 'core' or 'metropolitan region' in relation to the 'periphery' around them.

As the warriors, traders, churchmen and peasants of Frankish Europe conquered and colonized, they took their cult with them. A comparable kind of 'associated expansionism' occurred in the case of the spread of the English language in the period 1500–2000. Few would claim that it is intrinsic features of the language that account for its diffusion; rather, one should look to the naval skills, demographic features, geographical location, etc., of those who just happened to be English-speaking. Similarly, by the eleventh century some Frankish or Latin Christians had developed particular technologies or forms of social organization that gave them an expansionary edge. The spread of Latin bishoprics would then be a consequence of that technologically or socially fuelled expansion. On the other hand, the rhythms and direction of high medieval expansion require a religious explanation too – nothing else can account for the arrival of west European armies in the hill country of Judaea.

The experience of the Celtic world provides another major doubt about simply equating the territorial growth of western society with the multiplication of Latin bishoprics. The case of Ireland is particularly instructive. The country was among the earliest non-Roman societies to be converted to Christianity, by Patrick's missions of the fifth century, and thereafter was itself the centre of missionary activity, as wandering Irish monks evangelized virtually every Germanic people in western Europe. A rich Irish monastic tradition flourished for centuries. There might seem to be no question that Ireland was fully part of Latin Christendom. However, although Christianity was ancient in Ireland, the history of the country in the twelfth and thirteenth centuries seems to be marked by processes very similar to those that were taking place in the areas of northern and eastern Europe being incorporated into Latin Christendom at that same time. The incursion of a feudal cavalry élite, the immigration of peasant settlers, the formation of chartered towns, the introduction of a more widely diffused documentary literacy and coinage – all these aspects of Irish history can be paralleled in other areas experiencing the expansionary wave of the High Middle Ages. A colonial settlement in Munster would have a strong resemblance to one in Brandenburg. Ireland and, to a greater or lesser degree, the other Celtic countries were subject to many of the same processes of conquest, colonization and cultural and institutional transformation as eastern Europe or Spain, but were also an integral part of Latin Christendom from an early date. Despite their being Latin they were the victims, not the bearers, of Latin expansion. It is better to look for a fresh characterization of the process of expansion that includes the Celtic lands rather than be satisfied with the label 'the expansion of Latin Christendom' at the expense of excluding them.

Another aspect of this Irish anomaly is revealed in the way that Ireland was conceptualized by outsiders in the twelfth century. Although the Irish were of ancient Christian faith and shared the creed of Frankish Europe, they exhibited pronounced differences in culture and social organization. The absence of a territorial, tithe-funded church or unitary kingship, the very distinctive system of kinship and the non-feudal, uncommercialized economy struck Latin clergy and Frankish aristocrats as outlandish. When St Bernard described the Irish in the early twelfth century, he wrote of their 'barbarism' and their 'beastlike ways', criticized their marriage customs and their failure to conform to correct ecclesiastical practices, such as the payment of tithes, and concluded by condemning them as 'Christians only in name, pagans in fact'. Native clergy were as outspoken as foreigners and one of the things they sought in this period was the remodelling of the Irish church along lines more like those of the Frankish world. Defined hierarchies of territorial dioceses were introduced into the Celtic lands in the course of the twelfth century. Previously there had, of course, been bishops, but neither diocesan boundaries nor chains of authority had been clear or uniform. Although there are some similarities between this ec-clesiastical remodelling and what went on in Spain or England in earlier centuries, where a growing territorialization and the definition of archdioceses can be found, it is a more extreme case. The native leaders of the twelfth-century reform movement in Ireland were trying to integrate their country into a wider world whose norms were taken as a standard:

Barbarous laws were abolished, Roman laws introduced; everywhere the customs of the Church were received, those that were contrary rejected . . . everything was so much changed for the better that today we can apply to that people the word which the Lord speaks to us through the prophet: 'Them which were not my people, Thou art my people.'

Native reformers therefore thought that the Irish could not be God's people until they had adopted 'Roman laws'. An even sharper line of exclusion was drawn by non-native critics, such as the English prelates who criticized Irish ways or the immigrant warriors and clerics who began to establish lordships in Ireland in the 1170s and 1180s. These observers and intruders made a neat elision. For, while twelfth-century Anglo-Norman incursions into Ireland were motivated, in the words of a contemporary source, by the desire for 'land or pence, horses, armour or chargers, gold and silver . . . soil or sod', the invaders were able to claim 'some show of religion' by portraying the Irish, in the words of St Bernard, as 'Christians only in name, pagans in fact'. They were 'pagans in fact', despite their avowed creed and rituals, because their social order was deviant from the continental western European model. By the twelfth century their economy and social structure looked odd to men from England, France and Italy and this meant that, although the Irish were Christian, they could be described and treated as if they were not. Just as the Christian knights in *The Song of Roland* recognized their counterparts in the chivalrous warriors of Islam and lamented only the fact that they were of the wrong religion – 'If he were Christian, what a knight he would be!' – so, in Ireland, Frankish warriors recognized alien customs even under the cover of a shared religion. When we bear in mind the earlier missionary history of the Irish, the phrase used to justify the planned Anglo-Norman invasion of Ireland is poignant: its purpose was 'to expand the boundaries of the Church'. Not sharing the social patterns of western Europe meant not being part of the Church.

The images of exclusion and otherness available to those who formed and expressed opinions in twelfth-century western Europe included not only the dichotomy Christian/non-Christian, but also that of civilized/ barbarian, and the two polarities were often mutually reinforcing. The Welsh were 'rude and untamed' and hence 'nominally profess Christ but deny him in their life and customs'. The Ruthenians, who 'confess Christ only in name, but deny him in their deeds', were associated with other 'primitive Slavs' and 'wild peoples' of 'uncivilized barbarism'. All this suggests that mere adherence to the Latin liturgy and obedience to Rome were not enough to qualify for full inclusion in the *ecclesia*, that is, in society. As the men of Frankish Europe intruded upon societies around and unlike their own, they found both non-Christians (in eastern Europe and the Mediterranean lands) and local variants of Christianity (notably in the Celtic countries). Their response was to equate the two, if the Christian societies did not have the social and legal characteristics with which they were familiar. The expansion of the High Middle Ages was a matter not simply of Latin Christendom growing, but of the territorial growth of a certain kind of society. It tended to describe itself as Roman and Christian, but also recognized the Celtic lands as alien to it. By the eleventh century 'Latin Christendom' can be used to designate not merely a rite or an obedience but a society.

2. The Aristocratic Diaspora

A good knight by the fame of his valour and by his effort has very often come to great riches and great acquisitions. And many of them have become crowned kings and others have had great riches and great lordships.

One of the more striking aspects of the expansionary activity of the tenth to thirteenth centuries was the movement of western European aristocrats from their homelands into new areas where they settled and, if successful, augmented their fortunes. The original homes of these immigrants lay mainly in the area of the former Carolingian empire. Men of Norman descent became lords in England, Wales, Scotland and Ireland, in southern Italy and Sicily, in Spain and Syria. Lotharingian knights came to Palestine, Burgundian knights to Castile, Saxon knights to Poland, Prussia and Livonia. Flemings, Picards, Poitevins, Provençals and Lombards took to the road or to the sea and, if they survived, could enjoy new power in unfamiliar and exotic countries. One Norman adventurer became lord of Tarragona. A Poitevin family attained the crown of Cyprus.

This period of aristocratic diaspora coincided with the great age of the crusades, and, for many, migration began with the taking of the cross. Nevertheless, this is not the whole story. In some places, notably the British Isles and the Christian kingdoms of eastern Europe, the settlement of aristocratic newcomers took place without a crusading umbrella. In other areas, like Spain or the lands of the pagan Wends, crusading institutions and rhetoric were imported into a situation where land-grabbing by local military leaders was already under way. In southern Italy the Normans did indeed sail to Sicily to oust the Muslims with a papal banner and papal blessing, but they had established themselves in their south Italian base by being ready to fight everyone – Latin, Greek or Muslim – not excluding the pope himself. It is a difficult historical task to determine the relationship between the inflamed religiosity of the First Crusade and the acquisitive expansionism which the lay aristocracy of western Europe had already conspicuously displayed.

Many families engaged in more than one of these expansionary enterprises, crusading or non-crusading. The Joinvilles of Champagne are a well-known example. The name of the house is familiar because its head from 1233 to 1317 was John de Joinville, friend and biographer of St Louis (Louis IX of France). The family was long established in Champagne, first emerging into the historical record in the eleventh century. Based at their castle at Joinville on the river Marne, they were typical Frankish nobles, engaged in the endless small-scale warfare of the time, alternately plundering and endowing the local churches, serving and intermarrying with the great Champenois families such as Brienne, and slowly rising in wealth and prominence. Their story can stand for many.

The earliest lord of Joinville whose activities can be known in any other than a totally fragmentary form is Geoffrey III. He is first mentioned in 1127, in the company of the count of Champagne, and died, after a long life, in 1188. He was seneschal of Champagne, a patron of the new monastic orders and the first member of the family known to be a crusader – he accompanied the count on the Second Crusade of 1147. A crusading tradition soon became ingrained in the family. Geoffrey III's son, Geoffrey IV de Joinville, took part in the siege of Acre in the Third Crusade and died there, surrounded by his Champenois knights, in 1190. His eldest son and heir, Geoffrey V, who was with his father in the Holy Land when he died, was also susceptible to the crusading urge. After spending the 1190s in France – as seneschal of Champagne, an important figure in the complex feudal high politics of that decade – he and his brother Robert both signed themselves with the cross at the great crusading tournament at Ecry in Champagne in 1199. Neither was to return from his passage. Geoffrey was one of the leaders of the crusading army gathered at Venice, but refused to be diverted to Constantinople and set off with the minority to the Holy Land. He died at Krak des Chevaliers in Syria in 1203 or 1204. His brother Robert was carried off by this most fissiparous crusade in yet another direction. He went to southern Italy with his kinsman and compatriot, Walter, count of Brienne, who hoped, before proceeding to the East, to vindicate certain rights to lands and lordship he had acquired there. In the event Walter stayed to fight and die in Apulia, and Robert seems to have shared his fate; he was certainly dead by 1203. Yet another brother became a Templar. The crusades had taken their toll of the Joinville males.

The heir to the Joinville lordship in 1204 was Simon, father of St Louis's biographer. He fought and bargained his way to a confirmation of the hereditary tenure of the seneschalship of Champagne, made two advantageous marriages, one with an heiress from the neighbouring part of the Empire, founded new towns on his domains and twice embarked on

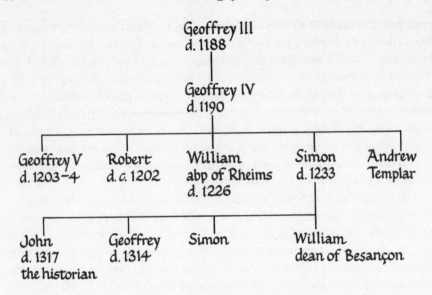

Figure 1. The house of Joinville

crusade, in 1209 against the heretical Albigensians in the south of France and in 1219–20, in the company of John de Brienne, titular king of Jerusalem, in the Damietta campaign in Egypt. By his second wife, Beatrice, daughter of the count of Burgundy, Simon de Joinville left four sons. The eldest, John, inherited the lordship and seneschalship, became an intimate friend of St Louis, accompanied him to Egypt and the Holy Land in 1248–54, and fostered the king's memory after his death in 1270. He saw Louis's canonization in 1297, completed his *Histoire de Saint Louis* in 1309 and died in 1317.

The star of other members of the family was also rising. When John de Joinville departed on crusade in 1248 his younger brother Geoffrey gave a party to send him off. At that time Geoffrey had possession of only one of the Joinville estates, Vaucouleurs. By the time of his brother's return from the Holy Land in 1254, he had made his own fortune. The key to his rise was, as so often, marriage to an heiress, and the key to the marriage advantageous family connections. It can be put in one sentence, though the sentence requires attention: Geoffrey's half-sister's husband was the uncle of the queen of England. The link between the Joinvilles and English royalty was the House of Savoy. This princely house provided the necessary intermediate step between the level of the great seigneurs, like the Joinvilles, and that of a king. Peter of Savoy, the crucial figure in this network, the uncle to Queen Eleanor of England, had received the lands of the earldom of Richmond in 1240. His access to the royal ear gave him influence over the disposal of rich heiresses, and one of the richest was Matilda, granddaughter of Walter de Lacy, lord of Meath. Peter of Savoy had already arranged to have her given to one of his relatives, but the fiancé's early death put her on the marriage market again. At some point between 1249 and 1252 she married Geoffrey de Joinville.

By this single act of patronage the younger son of a Champenois seigneur became lord of a substantial portion of Ireland. His chief centre was the castle of Trim and his scattered lordship extended from the Shannon to the Irish Sea. From 1252 until his retirement from the world to take the Dominican habit in 1308 (he died in 1314), Geoffrey de Joinville, or de Genneville as he is often known, was a dominant figure in Ireland and an important one in England. Like his ancestors, he made the journey to the Holy Land, with his suzerain, the Lord Edward (later Edward I), in 1270, stopping briefly *en route* in Tunis, where his brother's suzerain, St Louis, had just died.

The two younger surviving sons of Simon de Joinville were also well provided for. One, another Simon, received lands from his mother's dowry and augmented them by a good marriage to a Savoyard heiress. Like his brother Geoffrey he served the king of England, though he lived mainly in France. The youngest brother, William, took the traditional path of youngest brothers and entered the Church. His ecclesiastical career was not as spectacular as that of an uncle and namesake who had risen to be archbishop of Rheims, but he accumulated a respectable haul of ecclesiastical benefices in Burgundy and Ireland.

The Joinville family are a perfect example of that adventurous, acquisitive and pious aristocracy on which the expansionary movements of the High Middle Ages were based. Though they left their bones in Syria, Apulia and Ireland, these men were deeply rooted in the rich countryside of Champagne, and agricultural profits were the indispensable foundation for both their local position and their far-flung ventures. As we move from the eleventh century to the twelfth and on into the thirteenth, we see them strengthening their position, endowing religious houses and founding towns, while being drawn ever closer to the great princes of the day – symptomatic is John de Joinville's entry into St Louis's service during the voyage to the East. On the other hand, they retained a purely predatory side. In 1248 John de Joinville stood in the captured city of Damietta, hot in debate on how the Franks 'should divide up what they had won in the city'. Some decades later and 2,500 miles away, his brother Geoffrey met

with the magnates of Meath to agree 'a judgement concerning prey taken
in the marches'. It specified that horses and animals seized by those serving
at Geoffrey's expense should be divided equally between him and his men,
unless the horses were actually taken from Irish enemies who had been
felled by Geoffrey's men with lances. Prisoners were to be at Geoffrey's
disposal. Both John and Geoffrey were leaders of armed men who expected
to live off loot.

The story of the Joinvilles clearly demonstrates the growing strength of
the two most cohesive western European monarchies. Powerful kings such
at St Louis and Henry III could draw the aspiring nobility of regions like
Champagne to them, and competed to do so. Geoffrey de Joinville
certainly did not fight his way to lordship in Ireland by his own wits and
sword-arm, as Robert Guiscard had done in south Italy in the eleventh
century or Strongbow in Ireland itself in the twelfth. His path to power lay
rather through the king's ear and the marriage bed. Nevertheless, the stage
on which the Joinville brothers played their parts had been constructed not
by monarchical power but by the earlier expansion of an international
Frankish aristocracy. John and Geoffrey de Joinville were exemplary and
well-rewarded servants of their respective royal masters, but were also in
the tradition of that violent and self-directing warrior class which had, in
the word of Joinville the biographer's epitaph on his ancestors, 'done great
deeds both this side of the sea and that'.

Another aristocratic family involved in far-flung expansionary enterprises
was the descendants of Robert of Grandmesnil (d. 1050), a landowner and
warrior of the Calvados in Normandy. His family is chronicled by Orderic
Vitalis, a monk of St Évroul, a monastery which had been founded by the
Grandmesnil family and their relatives. Several of Robert's descendants
either voluntarily sought, or found it advisable to seek, the road south, to
southern Italy, where Normans had been carving out lordships for
themselves since the 1030s. They were well received and established marriage ties with the Hauteville brothers, the leaders of the Norman enterprise
in Italy. One son of Robert de Grandmesnil, also called Robert, who had
been abbot of St Évroul until William the Conqueror dispossessed him and
threatened to hang him by his cowl from the nearest tree if he complained,
had a new monastery founded for him at St Eufemia in Calabria; he was
succeeded as its abbot by his sister's son, William. Other sons and grandsons
of Robert of Grandmesnil acquired secular lordships in Italy. One of these,
another William, married Guiscard's daughter and was given extensive
landed estates. The family does not seem to have been ready to acknowledge
an effective superior, however, for William of Grandmesnil rebelled in the

1090s and had to seek refuge in Constantinople in the service of the Byzantine emperor. His son, Robert, restored to favour, quarrelled with Roger II of Sicily over the terms of his military service and was exiled in 1130. Various members of the family were on the First Crusade, though not with an unblemished record: two of them were among the 'rope-trick artists' (*funambuli*), the deserters from Antioch in 1098.

Another grandson of Robert de Grandmesnil had taken a very different direction. Robert, 'of Rhuddlan' as he came to be called, had joined the band of Norman adventurers around Edward the Confessor, king of England. He had been knighted by him and later returned to Normandy. After the Conquest he had followed a kinsman, Hugh of Avranches, across the Channel once more and, when Hugh became earl of Chester, Robert became his chief lieutenant and castellan of Rhuddlan, the forward base against the Welsh in the northern part of the Anglo-Welsh frontier:

This warlike marcher often fought against that restless nation and shed much blood in frequent battles. He pushed back the Welsh by fierce warfare, expanded his territory and founded a strong castle on the hill of Degannwy next to the sea. For fifteen years he ground down the Welsh inexorably and invaded the lands of men who had previously enjoyed liberty and owed the Normans nothing. Through the woods and marshes and harsh mountains he pursued and harried the enemy. Some he slaughtered indiscriminately like beasts, others he bound in chains for long periods or harshly subjected to undue service . . .

Pride and avarice, which control the hearts of everyone in this world of mortal men, drove the marcher Robert to this unrestrained plundering and killing.

'The marcher Robert' (*Rodbertus marchisus*) was eventually killed by Welsh raiders who stuck his head in triumph on the mast of one of their ships. Before this gory end, however, he had built castles far into north Wales, held wide stretches of land there by feudal tenure (*in feudo*) and founded a little borough at Rhuddlan endowed with the rights and customs of the Norman town of Breteuil.

Thus, by the late eleventh century, the grandsons of Robert de Grandmesnil could be found, as lords, lieutenants and warriors, in Wales, in southern Italy, in Constantinople, in Syria. Their vistas were far vaster than those of their grandparent. Such far-flung enterprises were characteristic of the period. From a family drawing its name from Sourdeval in western Normandy, for example, descended Richard de Sourdeval, who came to England under William the Conqueror and is recorded in 1086 in Domesday Book as a Yorkshire landholder; Robert de Sourdeval, who led the besiegers of Catania in Sicily in 1081 and marched to Antioch during the First Crusade; Stephen de Sourdeval, holding lands in the marcher lordship of Brecon around the year 1200; and Hugh de Sourdeval, who acquired estates in the fitzGerald barony of Naas in Ireland and gave his name to Swordlestown – i.e. 'Sourdeval's town' – in County Kildare.

Knights and magnates from France were especially well represented in the crusades and not only participated in new conquests in southern Italy and the British Isles, but also contributed to the Reconquest in Spain. Some of them stayed there: Gaston V of Béarn, who had fought in the Holy Land, campaigned in Aragon and was rewarded with the lordship of Uncastillo, the governorship of Saragossa and half the income of this city; Bertrand de Laon fought for Alfonso I of Aragon and became count in turn of Carrión, Logroño and Tudela; and Robert Burdet went to Spain in about 1110, fought at Tudela and became its castellan and then, in 1128, governor of Tarragona, which he and his descendants ruled for half a century. His wife Sibyl, the daughter of William Capra, a Somersetshire tenant-in-chief, supposedly made the circuit of the walls of Tarragona in the absence of her husband, dressed in a mail coat and carrying a rod of office. A West Country Amazon patrolling a Catalan city was perhaps an unusual sight at any time, but less unusual in the twelfth century than at other periods.

These cases show how far afield French knights ranged. In contrast, the migration of German knights, while substantial and sustained, was more geographically concentrated. Certainly many went on crusade: the crusade historian Röhricht counted well over 500 individuals of whom we have explicit record going from Germany to Outremer in the first century alone of the crusading movement. The presence of Germans could sometimes be decisive. Without the sailors of Cologne and Frisia, for example, the capture of Lisbon in 1147 or Damietta in 1219 would have been far more difficult, perhaps impossible. However, few if any Germans (except those from the half-French border duchies of Lotharingia) established aristocratic dynasties in the East. The vast majority went and returned – or left their bones rather than established their families in the Holy Land. It was only members of the Teutonic Order, a crusading order founded in Acre in 1190, who maintained a permanent German presence in the Crusader States. They had landed possessions along the coast from Acre to Beirut and a headquarters (from 1228 to 1271) at the castle of Montfort or Starkenberg, seven miles inland from Acre. As a military force in the Holy Land, they were surpassed only by the Templars and Hospitallers. Being fighting monks, however, and vowed to celibacy, they did not found new dynasties.

The chief zone of German expansion in the High Middle Ages was eastern Europe. Here German aristocrats established themselves over an immense area. Knights from Saxony could be found in Estonia on the Gulf of Finland, in Silesia along the Oder and throughout Bohemia and Hungary. New family fortunes were made east of the Elbe. Just as the British Isles, the southern part of the Italian peninsula and the eastern Mediterranean witnessed the arrival of aristocrats from the kingdom of France (and Lotharingia, the French-speaking region in the western part of the Holy Roman Empire) in these centuries, so eastern Europe saw knights and magnates pushing eastward from the German kingdom. A comparison of the witnesses in a charter of Barnim I of Pomerania, dating to 1223, and those in a charter of the same prince of 1249 shows how thoroughly the retinue of the 'duke of the Slavs' (*dux Slavorum*) had been Germanized in the intervening quarter-century. German knights like John of Appeldorn, Frederick of Ramstedt and Conrad of Schönwalde were drawn into the retinues of the Pomeranian princes, transforming the culture of the princely court and imprinting themselves upon their new estates. Further up the Oder, Silesia had been open to peaceful German aristocratic penetration since the reign of Boleslaw I (1163–1201), a prince of the Piast family, which had ruled in Poland since the tenth century. Boleslaw had spent seventeen years in exile in Thuringia and brought German Cistercians to found a family monastery on his return. As a thirteenth-century source puts it: 'in those parts any duke or prince who wished to retain German knights or others in his service granted them as fiefs lands in his lordship'. In this way the landed ruling class of the regions east of the Elbe was gradually Germanized. It may even be true to say that, while French aristocratic emigration was more spectacular to contemporaries, that of the Germans had greater long-term consequences for European history.

Thus one must make important geographical distinctions when talking about this expansionary movement of European aristocrats. The line of the Rhine and Danube marked an approximate division between the area of French and German settlement. From Normandy and Poitou, from Saxony and Lotharingia, emigrants streamed outwards to Wales or Apulia, to Livonia and Silesia. There, in their new homes, they had to construct a new future.

CONQUEST LORDSHIPS

The paths for this incoming aristocracy were various. Their entry could be more or less bloody; it could be encouraged or resisted; it could be into a wholly alien or a partly familiar society. At one extreme of this spectrum, there were the invited aristocracies of Scotland, Pomerania and Silesia. At the other extreme, and one of the clearest forms of innovation which arose as a consequence of aristocratic expansion, was the conquest principality of the High Middle Ages, represented by lordships like Brandenburg and Ulster.

The origins of both are traditionally associated with powerful founding figures, but they must also be placed in the general context of frontier conquest and colonization. Colonial ventures are often chain reactions. They bring together unstable and aggressive elements in a situation where all hope to profit and some do so. Splinter expeditions, like that of Cortes in Mexico in the sixteenth century, are common. The Anglo-Norman lordship of Ulster was created by such a tangential freelance movement. In the winter of 1176–7, in the early years of the Anglo-Norman incursion into Ireland, the garrison of Dublin had apparently become restless, and talk was going around about the sloth and lack of enterprise of the commander. At this point the more active and disgruntled members of the Dublin forces were offered the chance of action. The instigator was John de Courcy, member of an Anglo-Norman baronial family (and a distant relative of Robert of Rhuddlan). In midwinter a group of twenty-two knights and 300 footmen under his leadership set off north along the shores of the Irish Sea. The goal of John de Courcy's reckless raid was Ulaid or Ulidia, the eastern part of the province of Ulster. Here various Irish kings had been struggling for supremacy for some time. John and his small force were able to defeat Rory Mac Dunlevy, the local king, and seize Downpatrick in the first battle. From this foothold he was able to build up his principality.

John de Courcy established his power in Ulster between his first conquests in 1177 and his dramatic fall at the hands of Anglo-Norman rivals in 1205 by constant warfare, the construction of castles and the implantation of a body of vassals. In this first respect, endless fighting, his life as lord of Ulidia was not dissimilar to that of any Irish king. He undertook annual raids against various Irish rulers, but was also embroiled with other Anglo-Norman settlers. His allies were heterogeneous. In 1201, for example, he led 'the Foreigners of Ulidia', in alliance with de Lacy and 'the Foreigners of Meath', in a campaign designed to support Cathal Crovderg, one of the claimants to the kingship of Connacht, against his great-nephew, Cathal Carrach. The Connacht succession war saw a confusing medley of such alliances, with Anglo-Normans and Irish on both sides. Descent did not dictate political alignments, and natives and settlers did not form two distinct 'sides'. The goals of much of John de Courcy's warfare were also, in some ways, very traditional. His recurrent raids against Tyrone, for example, do not seem to have had the intention (and certainly did not have the effect) of adding territory to his lordship. A raid in 1197 is typical: after defeating the Cenél Conaill in battle, de Courcy's men 'harried Inishowen and carried great cattle-spoil therefrom'. This world of large-scale cattle raiding is also clearly reflected in grants de Courcy made to St Patrick's, Down, of a tithe of all the animals he captured by raiding or hunting.

Nevertheless, the lordship of Ulster was more than a mounted commando. Within Ulidia itself local power had a rather solid and enduring aspect. The Anglo-Norman military hold on the region was secured by the same kind of castles as had enabled the Normans to dominate England a century earlier: a scattering of motte-and-bailey castles of wood and earth, supplemented by stone keeps at the most important centres. The keep at Carrickfergus is 50 feet square and 90 feet high (see Plate 2) and it remained the core of Anglo-Norman and English power in the region throughout the Middle Ages. De Courcy had a seigneurial administration, of chamberlain, seneschal and constable, a body of vassals, many recruited from north-west England and south-west Scotland, and a penumbra of clerks. He organized and endowed six monasteries in his lordship, founded from or dependencies of English religious houses. He minted silver halfpennies, with his name on one side and that of his adopted patron, St Patrick, on the other. John de Courcy could be described by contemporaries as 'lord of Ulster' (*dominus de Ulvestire*) or even 'prince of the realm of Ulster' (*princeps regni de Ulvestir*). The term *regnum* did not, in medieval usage, imply that its ruler was a *rex* ('king'), but it did suggest an extensive territorial unit whose lord possessed great honour and substantial autonomy. By the time of his fall in 1205 John de Courcy had thus established a new territorial unit in Ireland, a lordship which long survived his disappearance.

The bloody and exhausting business of conquest and settlement required determined and selfish leaders. Such figures cropped up in every part of Europe in the twelfth and thirteenth centuries. They were sometimes men of no great background, but were often, too, already magnates in their own country – already equipped with the resources that so often make further expansion likely. Such a figure was Albert, nicknamed 'the Bear', founder of the line of the Ascanian margraves of Brandenburg (see his depiction on one of his coins, Plate 3).

Brandenburg was a much larger and even more enduring creation than the lordship of Ulster and built on older foundations. In the tenth century the region east of the Elbe and Saale rivers, which formed the boundary of Carolingian Saxony, was divided into several 'marks', frontier regions under the authority of a margrave ('border count'), with unusually extensive military and territorial powers. One such was the Nordmark, established as a separate entity in the 960s and stretching, in theory, from

Elbe to Oder and from Lausitz to the Elde–Peene line. Within this area Slav tribute was enforced, by punitive raids if necessary, some German fortifications were manned by permanent garrisons, and two newly founded bishoprics, Brandenburg and Havelberg, were located. Most of this structure was destroyed in the great Slav uprising of 983, but there continued to be a line of margraves with limited authority on the Elbe and a succession of bishops of Brandenburg and Havelberg, albeit without cathedrals or dioceses.

It was this ghostly framework that was revitalized in the twelfth century. In the middle decades of the century German authority was decisively re-established in the area east of the middle Elbe; the bishops of Brandenburg and Havelberg were able to recover their official seats and begin the planning of new cathedrals. A key figure in this story was Albert the Bear. Albert came from among the highest ranks of the Saxon nobility. His father, Count Otto of Ballenstedt, was richly endowed in north Thuringia and eastern Saxony. He was an experienced fighter in the border wars against the Slavs and had defeated a large raiding party from across the Elbe at Köthen in 1115. Albert's mother, Eilica, was of even more exalted stock, being the daughter of Magnus Billung, duke of Saxony. Albert thus grew up among a powerful aristocratic kindred accustomed to frontier warfare. His early political career was headlong, headstrong and uneasy. He made an alliance with Lothar of Süpplingenburg, successor to the Billungs as duke of Saxony; and, thanks to Lothar's support and in defiance of the Holy Roman Emperor, he gained control of Lausitz, the German frontier region east of the middle Elbe. He was also, because of his maternal descent, himself prepared to put forward a claim to be duke of Saxony. Around 1130 Albert succeeded in alienating Lothar, who had now been crowned king, by seizing the inheritance of Henry of Stade, margrave of the Nordmark. In response, Lothar deprived Albert of Lausitz. It was not until Albert had regained Lothar's favour by supporting him in the Italian expedition of 1132–3 that Albert was again enfeoffed with a major benefice on the frontier. This time it was the Nordmark.

The enfeoffment of Albert the Bear with the Nordmark in 1134 is traditionally regarded as a vital step in the creation of the principality of Brandenburg. Even more important, however, was the final capture by Albert of the town of Brandenburg itself, on 11 June 1157, 'the birthdate of the Mark of Brandenburg':

So, in the year of the incarnation of the Lord 1157, on the 11 June, the margrave, by God's mercy, took possession as victor of the city of Brandenburg and, entering it joyfully with a great retinue, raised his triumphal standard on high and gave due praises to God, who had given him victory over his enemies.

Unlike John de Courcy, Albert the Bear was able to establish his dynasty in his new conquests. His family, the Ascanians, were margraves of Brandenburg for seven generations and by the time of the extinction of the line in 1319 had extended their principality almost 200 miles east of the Elbe.

If we look at the methods employed by the Ascanians to extend their family power in the lands to the Oder and beyond, we see similarities to those employed by John de Courcy in Ireland. This is not surprising. In the twelfth and thirteenth centuries there were some universal requirements for the successful exercise of lordship: castles and vassals were among the most basic. The creation of a feudal military framework was then followed by the conscious development of the area through the encouragement of rural and urban settlement. This was the task of Albert the Bear's great-grandsons, John I (1220–66) and Otto III (1220–67), whose period of joint rule covered the important central decades of the thirteenth century:

After they had grown to be young men they lived together harmoniously as brothers should, the one deferring to the other. This concord enabled them to crush their enemies, raise up their friends, increase their lands and revenues and grow in fame, glory and power. They obtained the lands of Barnim, Teltow and many others from the lord Barnim [of Pomerania] and purchased the Uckermark up to the river Welse. In *Hartone* [unidentified] they acquired castles and advocacies. They built Berlin, Strausberg, Frankfurt, New Angermünde, Stolpe, Liebenwalde, Stargard, New Brandenburg and many other places, and thus, turning the wilderness into cultivated land, they had an abundance of goods of every kind. They were also careful to support religious services, had many chaplains and settled Dominicans, Franciscans and Cistercians within their territories.

The success of the Ascanians hinged on their ability to recruit and reward vassals. Their family became powerful by being able to offer power to other families. One knightly house that followed the Ascanians and won fortune in doing so was that of von Wedel, and a closer look at its members will reveal something of the dynamics of an expansionary aristocracy in a conquest principality.

The earliest mention of the von Wedel family is in a document of 1212. This is a grant by one of the knights of the count of Holstein in favour of the church of Hamburg, and it is ratified by the count, whose officials and retainers witness it. Among them are 'the von Wedel brothers: Henry, Hasso and Reinbern'. Wedel, from which they took their name, is a village in Holstein not far north-west of Hamburg. It was in an area of ancient German settlement, and, though it was not far from the Slav frontier, the Wedels do not seem to have been 'marchers', defined by a frontier role. It is not until 1279, some generations later, that there is evidence for a migration of members of the family eastwards. At this time a Ludwig von Wedel enjoyed the distinction of being excommunicated by the great scholar Albertus Magnus. His offence was intrusion into the property of the Hospitallers along the river Ihna (now in north-west Poland). This area, which the von Wedels were subsequently able to retain in their possession, was some 220 miles east of their home village in Holstein. There is no doubt about the connection between the Holstein family and the eastern migrants, since they shared both an uncommon stock of forenames and the same coat of arms. Ludwig von Wedel was presumably either a younger son of the family seeking to make his fortune or the descendant of one.

The way to make a fortune was not, of course, to launch out into the void. A young and ambitious knight would offer his services to a likely looking prince and hope that his lord would have success and be willing to share some of its profits. The von Wedels appear to have come east to join the service of the dukes of Pomerania, for the excommunication of 1269 mentions Ludwig von Wedel only as an abettor of Duke Barnim I. At this time tensions between Germans and Slavs were subordinate to the process of expansion, and Barnim, though the descendant of pagan Wendish princes, was an energetic founder of towns and a willing recruiter of German peasants and knights. For him what mattered was the development of Pomeranian resources as a basis for the growth of his own dynastic power, not the preservation of national identity. The Wedel lordships of Cremzow and Uchtenhagen both lay in Pomerania (see Map 4). The von Wedels were simply one group among many German retainers drawn to the Pomeranian court.

The original estates of the Wedels in the valley of the Ihna lay in a region of thin settlement whose overlordship was a matter of continual dispute. Polish, Pomeranian and Brandenburg claims competed here. Eventual victory lay with the house of Albert the Bear. The lands along the upper stretches of the Ihna fell into the margraves' hands in the second half of the thirteenth century. One of the things that ensured their success was their ability to recruit retainers, even from their enemies. Within a few years of the excommunication of 1269 the von Wedels – Ludwig and his brothers Henry, Siegfrid, Hasso and Zulis – were vassals of the margrave of Brandenburg. This did not mean that they forfeited their Pomeranian lands

Map 4. Von Wedel estates in eastern Neumark, c. 1270–1325 (after Cramer, 1969)

and ties. Multiple vassalage was a commonplace of the period. It could, indeed, be advantageous in that it did not tie the family's destiny to a single lord. Nevertheless, despite their holdings from the dukes of Pomerania and from the Pomeranian bishop of Kamień (Cammin), the von Wedels were, from 1272, primarily vassals of the margraves, and increasingly important ones.

As the family built up its estates in the Neumark, the 'land beyond the Oder' (*terra transoderana*) of the Ascanians, it faced the same problems as the princely dynasty itself. The only way to secure and exploit new acquisitions was to develop them in an energetic and systematic way. The fundamental task was that of settling the land. The Neumark saw a crop of new villages arise, many of them proudly bearing the names of their owners and creators – Wedel, Altenwedel, Neuwedel, Zühlsdorf and Zühlshagen (from the late-thirteenth-century Zulis von Wedel). Just as the margraves delegated the details of settlement to families like the Wedels, so they, in their turn, sought vassals to aid them. In 1313 Ludolf von Wedel sold to the brothers Dietrich and Otto von Elbe a village south of Schivelbein with the further incentive that 'in addition, if they decide to settle and cultivate the uninhabited woodlands, we promise to them sixty-four *mansi* [peasant farms] with full rights'. The figure of sixty-four *mansi* represents the usual extent of a newly planted village in the Neumark, and hence the arrangement between the Wedels and the Elbe brothers envisaged the creation of entirely new villages in the wilderness that formed part of the grant.

The Neumark was won and held by the sword, and the value of the Wedels to the margraves lay not only in their active exploitation of the agricultural potential of the land but in their ability to supply armed force. Indeed, at the height of their power in the later fourteenth century the family was able to promise to serve 'with a hundred well-armed knights and squires and another hundred armoured crossbowmen'. And in an epoch when the Brandenburg aristocracy came to be legally differentiated by the possession of castles or the lack of them, the Wedels were pre-eminently 'encastled' (*schlossgesessene*). Their earliest recorded castle was Kürtow, which was in their hands before 1300. Shortly thereafter they had temporary possession of Driesen, an important border fortress against the Poles. They naturally built or acquired castles in the centres of their lordships (see Map 4). These were the nails that hammered down their new possessions.

The scope and extent of the power of the von Wedels are shown by the independent role they undertook in the foundation of towns. They created no less than four in the Neumark and the neighbouring part of Pomerania. All can be dated, with some probability, to the first part of the fourteenth century. A document of 1314, in which the brothers Henry and John von Wedel grant privileges to 'their town of Nuwe Vredeland' (Märkisch-Friedland), includes among the witnesses 'the founders and town councillors of the said town'. Such towns were not only symbols of status and witnesses to magnate resources, but also providers of the readiest supply of cash to which a lord could have access. When the von Wedels granted Brandenburg law and various fiscal and jurisdictional privileges to their town of Freienwalde in 1338, they also arranged to receive 100 pounds per annum from the town. Such revenues enabled the Wedels to take the boldest step in their acquisition of land and authority. In 1319 Wedego von Wedel was partner to the purchase of the Land Schivelbein from Waldemar, the last of the Ascanian margraves, for 11,000 marks. It was bought as a job lot: 'the castle and town of Schivelbein, with its people, land, estates, high and low justice, coinage, timber, bridges', etc. It gave the von Wedel family a 'quasi-princely position'.

Within a few generations, the descendants of a knightly family from Holstein had seized the chances offered by the eastern frontier. By moving a few hundred miles eastwards and attaching their fortunes to the rising powers of the area, be they Slav or German in origin, the family had established itself as landed, dominant and indispensable. Its members climbed from among the dependent members of a comital retinue to become leaders of retinues, founders of towns, lords of the land.

NEW CROWNS

The von Wedels were 'quasi-princely'; John de Courcy was a *princeps regni*. There was a step even beyond this. The highest prize was a crown. The eleventh, twelfth and thirteenth centuries were a time when new kingdoms were in the making: Castile, Portugal, Bohemia, Jerusalem, Cyprus, Sicily, Thessalonica. New kingdoms needed new royal dynasties, and it was the restless nobility of western Europe that provided them.

One family with regal aspirations was the house of Montferrat, in north-west Italy, which undertook a spectacular but eventually miscarried series of enterprises aimed at securing new crowns in the East. William the Old, marquis of Montferrat, of an ancient and well-connected line (he was closely related by marriage to both the Capetian kings of France and the Hohenstaufen rulers of Germany), was a hero of the Second Crusade and

returned to Palestine in 1187 only to become one of Saladin's captives at
the great Muslim victory of Hattin. He had five sons, four of whom
pursued secular careers. The oldest, a tall fair-haired man given to heavy
drinking, married the heiress to the kingdom of Jerusalem, but died very
quickly in mysterious circumstances. His posthumous son became King
Baldwin V of Jerusalem (1185–6). Two other sons of William the Old
sought wives and fortunes in Byzantium. One became a victim to the
tangled and lethal politics of Constantinople; but the other, Conrad, made
his way to the Holy Land, defended Tyre against Saladin, married another
heiress to the kingdom of Jerusalem and ruled as king for two years before
he was stabbed to death in the street by the Assassins, an extremist Islamic
sect characterized in western sources as hashish-smoking followers of a
mysterious 'Old Man of the Mountains'. The Muslims feared and admired
Conrad as 'a devil incarnate in his ability to govern and defend a town, and
a man of extraordinary courage'. The last Montferrat brother, Boniface,
was chosen leader of the Fourth Crusade in 1201, led it not to the Holy
Land but to Constantinople and acquired, as his share in the spoils of the
Byzantine empire, the kingdom of Thessalonica, where he settled many
Italian followers. In this way he fulfilled the polite hopes of his court poet
Peire Vidal, who concluded one of his poems addressed to the marquis
with the lines:

> And if things were as I wish and foretell,
> I'd see a crown of gold set on his head.

Boniface died in battle in 1207 defending his new-won crown. His son and
successor, Demetrius, could not maintain his position and was expelled
from Greece in 1224.

The Montferrats were unable to hold on to the crowns that passed
through their fingers. Others had a firmer grasp. One measure of the
importance of the expansion of Frankish aristocrats in the High Middle
Ages is their role in providing ruling dynasties for Europe (see Map 5). Just
as the minor princes of Germany would later provide a useful fund of
kings for the new nationalist monarchies of the nineteenth century, so the
great families of medieval France sent out offspring to sit on distant
thrones. Their success in doing so was remarkable. In the year 1350 there
were fifteen monarchs with the royal title in Latin Christendom. Some
were of common descent, and thus these fifteen individuals represent only
ten ancestral families. If one traces these rulers back in the direct male line
to the eleventh century (or, if that is not possible, as far back as one can), it

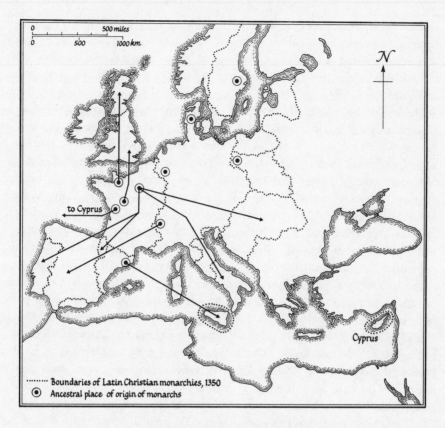

Map 5. Dynastic diffusion in the High Middle Ages

emerges that, of these ten dynasties, five came from the old kingdom of France, mainly from the north (the Île-de-France, Normandy, Anjou and Poitou) but with one important family (the counts of Barcelona) from the south. Another two dynasties came from just east of the kingdom of France proper, one stemming from the comital house of Arlon in Upper Lotharingia, the other from the counts of Burgundy; both regions were culturally French and certainly 'Frankish' in the older sense. Only three families, the Folkunger of Sweden, the Danish royal house and the Piasts of Poland, were not of Frankish descent. If one looks at the rulers of 1350 individually rather than grouping them dynastically, the point is even more striking. Of the fifteen regal monarchs, five were directly descended from the royal house of France, the Capetians. Of the remaining ten, seven descended in the direct male line either from houses of the kingdom of

France or from houses of the French-speaking regions of Lotharingia and Burgundy immediately adjacent to it. This leaves three rulers only, those of the Scandinavian kingdoms and Poland, who represented ancient non-Frankish dynasties. By the late Middle Ages 80 per cent of Europe's kings and queens were Franks.

It might be objected that the importance of German dynasts is underestimated by this analysis. Counting crowned heads in 1350 is a device which excludes many of the big families of Germany – Habsburg and Wittelsbach, who both held the crown at other times, and Wettin – who, in terms of power and ancestry, are comparable to the ruling houses of Scotland or Cyprus. Yet this is, in itself, illuminating. Many ruling dynasties of French origin acquired new kingdoms, that is, kingdoms that were created as part of the expansion of Latin Christendom in the eleventh and twelfth centuries, like Portugal, Naples–Sicily or Cyprus. German expansion in eastern Europe did not produce new colonial kingdoms. Poland, Bohemia and Hungary were already on the map, two as kingdoms, all three as organized Christian polities, by the year 1000. German expansion, under the loose umbrella of the Empire, produced new political units, Brandenburg, for example, or the Wettin lands later to coalesce as Saxony, but no new crowned heads. This is significant for an understanding of the nature of expansion in eastern Europe, where Germans more commonly settled in Christian Slav or Magyar realms than in new German lordships.

The map shows that most ruling families of later medieval Europe traced their ancestry back to Frankish roots. To explain this it is useful to distinguish two periods of Frankish dynastic diffusion. The existence of French dynasties in Naples and Hungary, descendants of St Louis's brother Charles of Anjou, was a consequence of the high political manoeuvring of the late thirteenth and early fourteenth centuries, and the Catalan regime in Sicily was a product of the same set of events, though rather in the nature of a reaction than an action. The crucial context for these new dynasties is the dominant political position of the kingdom of France which it had attained under the Capetian kings of the thirteenth century. The other instances of immigrant Frankish dynasties, however, arose from that Frankish aristocratic diaspora of the eleventh and twelfth centuries which we have already discussed; the political power of the Capetian dynasty was quite irrelevant. The king of Scots in 1350 was the descendant of a Norman family which had benefited from the conquest of England in 1066. The same event, the conquest of 1066, indirectly created the situation which made it possible for Plantagenets to rule at Westminster. The royal dynasties of Portugal and León-Castile descended from two cousins, one belonging to the family of the dukes of Burgundy, one to that of the counts of Burgundy, who had come to the peninsula during that period of intense Frankish, especially Burgundian, influence under Alfonso VI (1065–1109). Alfonso had married a Burgundian wife, Constance, daughter of the duke of Burgundy, and when his wife's kinsmen, Raymond and Henry, turned up in Castile, perhaps as part of a crusading army under the command of the duke of Burgundy, he treated them well. Around 1090 both received royal wives, daughters of Alfonso. Soon after that there is record of Raymond 'of the stock of the Franks' (*de genere Francorum*) exercising high authority in Galicia. Henry, too, obtained comital authority in the region of Braga. He and his son engaged with vigour in warfare against the Muslims, and in 1140 Henry's son assumed the title of king of Portugal. His contemporary on the throne of León-Castile was his kinsman, Alfonso 'the Emperor', son of Raymond of Burgundy. The two Frankish aristocrats had done well over the Pyrenees. Yet another Frankish family, the Lusignans, not only accumulated lands and power in Poitou and England, but also obtained a kingdom in the Mediterranean – to be precise, two kingdoms, Jerusalem and Cyprus. It was Cyprus that they held longest and most securely. They acquired it from Richard the Lionheart, who had conquered it from the Greeks while on his way to Palestine in 1191, and ruled it until 1267, when it passed by marriage to the house of Antioch–Lusignan, a dynasty also of Poitevin descent, which ruled the kingdom for the rest of the Middle Ages.

In this second category, then, one sees the consequences not of the power of the French kingdom, but of the vigour of the Frankish aristocracy of the eleventh and twelfth centuries. The penetration of the British Isles by French knights, the participation of the Burgundian aristocracy in the wars of the Reconquest and the dominance of Franks in the crusading ventures of the eastern Mediterranean had resulted in the establishment of new Frankish dynasties from Scotland to Cyprus. In some cases, we see the creation of new kingdoms by conquest; in others, the grafting of Frankish aristocratic dynasties on to older native ruling families. Dynastic diffusion is one crude measure of the impact of Frankish aristocratic expansionism in the High Middle Ages.

THE NATURE OF ARISTOCRATIC EXPANSIONISM

After the Frankish and Venetian forces sacked Constantinople in 1204, they began to spread out into the surrounding parts of the Byzantine empire,

establishing new lordships and squabbling among themselves. Among the
peoples they encountered were the Vlachs, living dispersed in the Balkans
and, at this time, enjoying a period of particular political success. On one
occasion there was a parley between the leaders of the Vlachs and the
French knight Peter of Bracheux. 'Lord, we wonder greatly at your good
chivalry,' they are reported to have said, 'and we wonder greatly what you
are seeking in this land, and why you came here to conquer lands from
such a distant country. Have you no lands in your own country to support
you?'

The modern historian may well echo the perplexity of the Vlachs and,
like them, seek the drive or motor of the aristocratic expansion in the land-
grabbing of the landless. Obviously, the aristocracy of the aristocratic
diaspora varied very widely in wealth, power and status. There was a gulf
between the counts of Montferrat, negotiating with emperors and marrying
into the royal family of the crusader kingdom, and the landless fighters
who flocked to William the Conqueror in 1066, and explanation of the
behaviour and motives of the former need not necessarily be identical with
that for the latter. Clearly, however, many of these men had no land or
possessed very little in their own country, and the appeal of expansionary
enterprise does seem to be in part the opportunity for the landless to
become landed. The historians of the Norman enterprise in southern Italy
paint a vivid picture of the successful cycle of recruitment and conquest:

A vast crowd of kinsmen, fellow countrymen and also men from the surrounding
regions followed them in the hope of gain and they received them as brothers,
with a willing generosity, and endowed them with horses, arms, clothes and
various gifts. To some they offered broad lands, putting the maintenance of brave
knights before all the riches of this world. Because of this none of their undertakings
failed. Whence the gospel saying seemed to apply to them: 'Give and it shall be
given unto you.' For the more they bestowed the greater their gain.

In the 1040s Richard of Aversa was drawing knights to him by this sort of
generosity – 'What he could carry off he gave and did not keep . . . in this
way the whole land around about was plundered and his knights multiplied
. . . he had had sixty horsemen and now he had a hundred.'

It has been argued that the absence of surnames of European origin
among the Frankish settlers in Outremer suggests 'that these settlers were of
modest origin and had no reason to retain surnames drawn from their
European possessions'; and the point is re-echoed by a chronicler of the
First Crusade: 'Who was poor over there, God makes rich here . . . he who
didn't have a village there has a town here.' In every corner of Europe the

language and images were the same. The first German nobles to establish themselves in Livonia 'were able to acquire honour and property without shame; their satisfaction was so good that they made the journey . . . for their property there became so great and their heirs are still happy with it'. Their contemporaries who carved out lordships and fiefs in Ireland were drawn by similar expectations, expressed here in a piece of recruiting rhetoric:

> Whoever shall wish for land or pence,
> Horse, armour or chargers,
> Gold and silver, I shall give them
> Very ample pay;
> Whoever shall wish for sod or soil
> Richly shall I enfeoff them.

The dream of every footsoldier in these armies was to get on a horse, to make the magical transition from the dusty *pedites* to the galloping *equites*. A successful raid could be the key. According to *The Song of the Cid*, after the hero's capture of Valencia 'those who had been on foot became horsemen'. Another eleventh-century master of predation, Robert Guiscard, was satisfying his followers in the same way in southern Italy. After one night raid in Calabria, 'having seized the spoils of victory, he turned his footsoldiers into knights'. The evidence for a dynamic cycle of plunder, gift-giving, recruitment and further plunder, with crucial breakthroughs to knightly status and landed endowment, is ubiquitous.

The military retinue was one of the basic social organisms of medieval Europe. It consisted of a group of fighting men led by a lord, men who were held together by oaths, camaraderie and self-interest. It had a long ancestry in the Germanic war-band, whose members received gifts as part of 'the heavy traffic in necessary generosity', and, if lucky, land in return for service to their lord. Even if we do not wish to delve as far back as Tacitus's description of lord–follower relations based on the 'fame and glory which stems from having the most numerous and bravest retinue' and the 'means of generosity won from war and rapine', the reciprocity of reward and service is explicit in these words of Beowulf: 'So it was given to me to repay in battle with my bright sword the treasures which he [Beowulf's lord] had granted me; he had given me land, a hereditary estate.'

Land, however, was a special kind of reward and the least common, the scarcest resource and the most highly prized. Retainers and household knights regarded the grant of estate or fief as a goal, and much of the pressure for enfeoffment (the granting of a fief) came from these men, who felt that landed endowment was a necessary prerequisite for marrying and having a family. As early as the eighth century Bede complained that 'there is a general lack of places where sons of nobles or eminent warriors could have property, and so, after they reach the age of puberty landless and unmarried, they are unable to endure celibacy and go beyond the seas, leaving the land which they ought to be defending'. From some centuries later we have a lively account of the household knights (*tirones*) of the French king attempting to persuade their king to enfeoff them at the expense of the Normans: 'O lord king, we have served you unceasingly and have never received enough, except of food and drink. We beg you, drive out and destroy these alien Normans and give us their fiefs and grant us wives.'

Such passages illustrate the enduring structural reasons why enfeoffment was practised. Household knights and retainers grew old and they obviously preferred to envisage old age on their own estates, surrounded by wife and sons, rather than one scrounging scraps in the mead-hall. The fief as defined in the increasingly technical language of the twelfth- and thirteenth-century law books was new (almost by definition), but the estate given as reward for military service was not. That exchange, not some set of legal characteristics, is what gave dynamism to the world of retinues.

The general scarcity of fiefs can be seen in the provisions of such a work as the *Sachsenspiegel*, a German law book written in the 1220s. Between the lines we can sense the existence of continual pressure from the unenfeoffed: there are complex rules about the grant of reversions of fiefs, often multiple reversions; prescriptions about how to treat competing claims to a fief; and a persistent moral thread insisting that the lord *should* grant fiefs and that his men have the right to look elsewhere if he disappoints them. It is a world whose anxious and competitive atmosphere makes clear the relief and joy which would be felt when a fief was finally obtained. 'I have my fief, everyone, I have my fief!' – in the famous words of Walther von der Vogelweide, who was not only one of the great German lyric poets but also an anxious cultivator of patrons.

The scramble for vassals and new fiefs which is so evident in the eleventh century may thus suggest itself as an explanation for the surge of aristocratic expansionism that began in that period. Even as careful and meticulous a scholar as John Le Patourel was willing, in his analysis of 'the Norman Empire', to suggest that 'It may not be necessary to look further for the dynamic which produced the conquests in Britain and in northern France . . . [than] the need for expansion inherent in a developing feudal society.'

And again: 'One source, perhaps the main source, of the dynamic' which produced the Anglo-Norman empire 'was the pressure created by feudalism in the early stages of its development'. The 'pressure' or 'need' which Le Patourel mentions would seem to consist of two main elements: the demand of vassals for fiefs and the desire of lords for fighting men. There was a circularity to this system. The more land one had, the more knights one could enfeoff, and the more knights one had, the easier it was to conquer new lands.

The fact that lords of mounted retinues were in competition with each other does not, however, explain why the whole aristocracy should be on the move outwards. The world of Germanic war-bands and that of the feudal retinue or *mesnie* had losers as well as winners, old men without heirs, families with their backs to the wall, lords whose followers grew fewer year by year. The 'need' for 'expansion' felt by one lord or retinue could surely be met by the absorption or defeat of another. The extinction rate of European aristocracies in the Middle Ages seems, at first glance, to leave plenty of room for newcomers. Of the sixteen families of free lesser nobility in twelfth-century Osnabrück only six survived to 1300, and of seventy knightly families enfeoffed 1125–50 in Eichstätt thirty died out before 1220. Over the century and a quarter between 1275 and 1400 sixteen of the twenty-five chief families of the Namurois (in modern Belgium) disappeared and some of the surviving nine sank in the social scale. One study of the lesser nobles of Forez in southern France revealed an extinction rate of over 50 per cent in a century. Such figures are not perhaps surprising when one considers the high rates of infant mortality and low levels of life expectancy, the violence of aristocratic life and the requirement of celibacy for those who entered the religious or clerical order. They leave space for metabolic as opposed to structural change; that is, there could be intense competitive dynamism within the system but no propensity for the system as a whole to expand, rather like a closed beaker of swirling liquid which itself does not swirl. After all, Irish society in the eleventh and twelfth centuries provides a perfect example of a competitive world of war-bands which manifested no expansionary dynamic flowing beyond the island itself. The competitiveness of the system of military retinues thus might explain its internal dynamics but does not, in itself, adequately account for expansion.

Some of the figures already discussed in this chapter, like Geoffrey de Genneville or John de Courcy, were younger sons, but their families were already well endowed with lands, and neither was forced to seek fortune abroad – both could quite happily have maintained themselves on family estates. It was the lower nobility who might really face the choice between impoverishment and adventure. A classic – perhaps *the* classic – example of the over-breeding, land-hungry lesser nobility is provided by the family of Tancred de Hauteville, the Norman lord whose sons established in southern Italy those conquest principalities which eventually coalesced into the Norman kingdom of Sicily. The chronicler Geoffrey Malaterra, a neighbour of the family in Normandy who followed their steps south, described how Tancred, 'a knight of good family', produced five sons from his first wife and then, after her death, since 'his still green age made continence impossible', remarried and produced seven more. As the twelve sons grew up they received military training and also, presumably, some education in the hard ways of the world:

They saw that as their neighbours grew old their heirs began to quarrel among themselves and that an estate originally granted to one man would, if divided among many, not be sufficient for any. So, in order to avoid a like fate, they took counsel together. By common agreement the first-born, who were stronger and older than the younger brothers, left home first, made their living fighting in various places and, eventually, led by God, came to Apulia in Italy.

The sons of Tancred prospered in southern Italy. They slowly established dominion over the whole of this part of the peninsula and the island of Sicily, and in 1130 Roger, Tancred's grandson, was crowned king of Sicily, thus initiating a new kingdom which was to endure until the time of Garibaldi. The story, as told by Malaterra, and by his fellow monk Orderic Vitalis, stresses the impossibility of supporting twelve sons on the family patrimony. According to Orderic, Tancred told eleven of his sons 'that they should leave their home to win for themselves whatever they needed by their own force of mind and body'. It is indeed hard to imagine any other fate than downward social mobility for a dozen brothers on the family farm.

The Hauteville story can be supplemented by other contemporary statements about aristocratic overpopulation, like Pope Urban II's, as he launched the First Crusade: 'this land you inhabit is everywhere shut in by the sea, is surrounded by ranges of mountains and is overcrowded by your numbers . . . This is why you devour and fight one another.' It might seem that here we glimpse the chief motor of aristocratic expansion. Nevertheless, questions raise themselves. Even in their 'green age' it is unlikely that most Norman knights would produce twelve sons who survived to adulthood. Indeed, it has been calculated that, in the prevailing conditions, the likelihood of a married couple producing sons at all was only 60 per cent. The demography of the French aristocracy in the eleventh century is, and always will be, an unknown, but it is impossible to picture a general rate of reproduction like that of Tancred de Hauteville. If, then, the Hauteville family is demographically as well as militarily and politically exceptional, it would not be reasonable to generalize from their example and argue that the astonishing story of aristocratic migration and conquest in the eleventh century is purely a function of overpopulation.

Certainly, nothing is more plausible than that under-provided military aristocrats would seek fortune abroad. If this is the case, however, there is difficulty explaining why Norman adventurers raised kingdoms in southern Italy while south Italian knights did not make similar inroads into France. At this period parts of the kingdom of France were as politically fragmented as southern Italy and would seem to offer easy pickings – if there were takers. If we do not choose to argue that the Frankish aristocracy was particularly prolific, then we must look again at the idea that opportunities for individual aristocrats at home became increasingly limited. If it is to be convincing, our search for an explanation must isolate something distinctive about the knightly class of post-Carolingian Europe, something that stirred and moved the aristocracy of France and, later, Germany, in a way it had not been stirred and moved before.

Recent work by German and French historians has suggested that the structure of the aristocratic family itself underwent a transformation in the tenth and eleventh centuries. Loosely linked kindreds, for whom maternal and paternal relations might be equally important, and who possessed no enduring genealogical or territorial centre, were, it has been argued, replaced by clearly defined lineages, in which patrimony and primogeniture became ever more important. A single line of male descent, excluding, as far as possible, younger siblings, cousins and women, came to dominate at the expense of the wider, more amorphous kindred of the earlier period. If this picture is credible, it is possible that the expansionism of the eleventh, twelfth and thirteenth centuries was one result. The decline in opportunities for some members of the military aristocracy – notoriously, of course, younger sons – may have been the impetus to emigration. Indeed, one distinguished historian has seen the appeal of Scotland for immigrant knights in the twelfth century in the fact that it was 'a land for younger sons'; while a leading historian of the Crusader States describes the knightly immigration to Outremer as 'the work of younger sons or of young men'. The issue is not simply one of too many sons, as in the Hauteville example, but of a constriction in family structure creating new disabilities.

Certainly the aristocratic dynasties of the thirteenth century had some features that made them more identifiable, more insistent on paternal descent and more restrictive of wider kin-claims than their counterparts of the tenth. They had surnames, drawn from their properties or their castles, that identified them over time. They had heraldic insignia, with increasingly elaborate rules, that identified their family origins, visibly distinguished older and cadet branches and gave preference to male descent. The involvement of the wider kindred in such crucial issues as vendetta and the transmission of property diminished. In twelfth-century England if the deceased were a knight, 'then according to the law of the realm of England, the eldest son succeeds to his father in everything'. In 1185 the duke, bishops and barons of Brittany agreed 'that henceforth in baronies and knights' fees there shall be no division, but the oldest by birth shall have the lordship in its entirety'. It was indeed a practice which brought forth criticism. 'Who made brothers unequal?' asked one twelfth-century author. 'They yield to the singular fortune of one rich son. One has abundance and acquires the whole paternal property, the other laments his empty and impoverished share of the rich paternal inheritance.' In this way the 'house' in the narrow sense – a line of fathers and sons extending through time and focused on hereditary family properties – came into being. The 'narrowing and tightening of the family around the male line' seems well attested.

Whether this 'narrowing' can be empirically linked with the dramatic spread of western European aristocrats into the surrounding regions in the eleventh, twelfth and thirteenth centuries is a more difficult question. The thorough testing of such a hypothesis is a project for the future; it would involve years of meticulous labour, and would, even then, remain speculative, since the genealogies of the aristocracy, even as late as the thirteenth century, can be surmised more often than demonstrated. No conclusive answer is presently available.

'Did not the appearance of new structures of kinship in the aristocracy and the establishment of the feudal system progress at the same pace?' asks one of the pre-eminent historians of the High Middle Ages. Perhaps the key to the aristocratic expansionism of the eleventh, twelfth and thirteenth centuries lies neither in the dynamics of war-bands alone, nor in the structures of kindred alone, but in a fateful conjuncture between the two. The argument has been made that feudal structures demand a more secure territorial basis for the aristocracy and produce a military class 'more firmly rooted in their landed estates', while the eleventh century has been described as a period of 'the reorganization of the Norman knightly class on a territorial basis'. It has also been argued that the transmission of resources intact from generation to generation was a prerequisite for the permanent establishment of feudal military institutions. More important still is the possibility that the landed knightly class of the eleventh century represented not simply new personnel, but a new kind of aristocracy. One can see in the documents of the period the creation of mounted warriors from peasants, as in the Limburg document of 1035 which allows the lord to make his unmarried peasant tenants kitchen-hands or grooms and his married tenants foresters or mounted warriors (*milites*). Even an extinction rate of 50 per cent per century in an expanding economy would not be enough if there were an increasing number of candidates for aristocratic standing. The rise of a class of knights, originally fairly lowly and often without land, combined with the impact of primogeniture and dynasticism, may have overloaded the system to such an extent that expansionary movement abroad was a natural response. Even if Tancred de Hautevilles were mercifully rare, the pressures of a narrowing definition of the family, coupled with the demands of a new knightly class, may suffice to explain the existence of a roving aristocracy. It may have been the younger sons, lamenting their 'empty and impoverished share of the rich paternal inheritance', who took to the roads and the sea-lanes in the eleventh, twelfth and thirteenth centuries. We cannot be certain; but perhaps, by the eleventh century, the Frankish aristocracy, a relatively small military élite organized into strongly patrilineal or dynastic houses and rooted firmly in landed estate, contrasted sharply with the aristocratic kin structures of the surrounding world into which it was beginning to expand.

THE IMPACT ON THE PERIPHERY

Whether the aggressive dynamism of the Frankish knightly class can be explained by feudal tensions or not, there is no doubt that the dissemination of feudal forms of tenure and obligation was one of its consequences. Regions like Ireland, the eastern Baltic, Greece, Palestine and Andalusia, which had not known fiefs, vassals and homage in 1050, became familiar with them in the following centuries. As in southern Italy, 'homage and the fief came in the wake of conquest'. The successful conquerors or warrior-immigrants of the High Middle Ages expected a reward and that reward was typically what they called a fief, a piece of property held by a vassal from a lord in return for prescribed services, usually military. The distribution of fiefs, whether by native rulers trying to attract knightly recruits or by entrepreneurs of conquest like John de Courcy or Albert the

Bear, was part of the process whereby new colonial aristocracies were created.

The *Chronicle of Morea*, for example, a thirteenth-century account of the establishment of Frankish power in Greece, describes the subinfeudation of the Morea: Walter de Rosières received 24 fiefs, Hugh de Bruyères 22, Otho de Tournay 12, Hugh de Lille 8, etc. The crusading orders and local ecclesiastics were also enfeoffed. 'The knights, who had one fief each, and also the sergeants . . . I do not name,' concludes the chronicler. It was this most local level of enfeoffment, however, which was the most important for effective military control. In Brandenburg the margraves' *ministeriales* (originally unfree knights) were allocated fiefs in the lands conquered from pagan Slavs in the twelfth century. The old-settled Altmark, west of the Elbe, provided a pool of knightly retainers who manned the castles and collected the rents in the lands east of the Elbe. In Ireland and Wales the great lordships were granted out by the king of England to magnates, but these then ensured that the process of subinfeudation continued to the local level. Each great lordship owed service calculated in terms of a fixed number of knights: 100 for Leinster, 50 for Meath, 60 for Cork, etc. The Anglo-Norman colony in Ireland was based on the military men planted in the land in this way: 'thus well rooted (*ben . . . aracinez*) were the noble renowned vassals'.

A fief is a legal entity and, as such, is created rather than discovered in nature and has a malleable, conventional form. Yet, given its function of supporting or rewarding a mounted warrior, the knight's fee of the High Middle Ages had to provide revenue within a certain range. Hence there were limits to the number of them that any given ecology could sustain. They varied, of course, as those ecologies varied. Rich farmland could support more fiefs in a given area than poor farmland: knights' fees were composed of ten ploughlands in County Dublin, twenty in County Meath and thirty in inhospitable Westmeath. In an urban and commercial economy, such as that found in the Crusader States, fiefs consisted of money incomes as well as land, typically 400 bezants per annum around 1200.

Despite these variations, it is still possible to give some concreteness to the concept of the fief, for, as Sir Frank Stenton pointed out, though fiefs 'varied in value [and] . . . extent . . . they did not vary indefinitely'. One source of information is the number of fiefs owing knight-service to the king or lord, as listed in surveys or calculated from indirect evidence. England, a kingdom of 50,000 square miles, had approximately 7,500 knights' fees owing such service, an average of a fief for every six or seven square miles. Normandy, which was somewhere around 13,000 square miles, had perhaps 2,500 knights' fees in 1172, one for every five square miles. Champagne, rather smaller than Normandy but appreciably richer, had 1,900 knights' fees. The kingdom of Jerusalem supported about 700, though on a very different economic base from that in northern France. The number of knights' fees within a given area was usually larger than the service owed, since local barons tended to enfeoff more knightly tenants than were required to fulfil obligations to an overlord. The lordship of Leinster in Ireland owed 100 knights to the Crown but the lords of Leinster had created 181 knights' fees there. The former figure represents a knight's fee for every 35 square miles, the latter one every 20 square miles or so. There is also some evidence, not for the number of fiefs owing to the lord, but for the number of knights that a given area could support at need. This figure would obviously be larger. In the mid-twelfth century, for example, the Apulian and Capuan parts of the Norman kingdom of Sicily were surveyed to see how great a military muster they could provide in time of emergency. In area they measured approximately 20,000 square miles; it was estimated that they could provide 8,620 knights, one for every 2.3 square miles. These figures, whatever difficulties of interpretation they present, at least give us an idea of the realm of the possible. Each enfeoffed knight represents a minimum of a few square miles, even of rich Italian countryside, and, in less intensively farmed regions, might require ten times that amount as an ecological basis.

The solidity of a new lordship might depend on the success of the policy of enfeoffment, a point made by the Old French author who described the settlement of the kingdom of Cyprus. 'Now I will tell you,' he wrote

what King Guy did when he had received possession of the island of Cyprus. He sent messages to Armenia, Antioch and Acre and throughout the land, saying that he would give a good livelihood to all those who would come to live in Cyprus ... He gave them rich fiefs ... he enfeoffed 300 knights and 200 mounted sergeants ... and so King Guy settled the island of Cyprus; and I tell you, if the emperor Baldwin had settled Constantinople as King Guy did the island of Cyprus, he would never have lost it.

In this observer's eyes, the crucial difference between the failed Frankish colony in Byzantium and the enduring one in Cyprus was the vigorous promotion of enfeoffment.

It was not only the conquest principalities that saw the imposition of feudal forms. Native dynasties that brought in foreign knights also created a network of fiefs to support them. The immigration of Anglo-French and

Anglo-Norman knights into Scotland at the invitation of the native royal dynasty has been particularly well studied. The forms that feudal tenure took suggest a wholesale and conscious importation: 'early Scottish feudalism, far from appearing undeveloped or only half formed, seems remarkably cut and dried, almost a copybook version of the feudalism of north-west Europe'. In Clydesdale such 'cut and dried' knight's fees were granted to a group of Flemish immigrants. Newcomers might establish new settlements which then bore their name, like the Duddingston (Midlothian) of Dodin and the Houston (Renfrewshire) of Hugh. Sometimes, however, fiefs had to be scraped together from barely adequate landed resources. When David I of Scotland (1124–53), a king who certainly did not lack the will 'to feudalize on a large scale', granted Athelstaneford and other lands to Alexander de St Martin, an immigrant knight of the 1130s, he specified that the property should be held 'in fee and heritage by the service of half a knight, and I shall pay him ten marks of silver a year from my chamber until I am able to make up for him the full fee of one knight'. The radical transformation of Scottish society through the introduction of foreign knights did not escape the attention of contemporaries. One believed that David I's successors were marked by a particular holiness and connected this with the fact that they 'had expelled the Scots, men of vile habits, and brought in knights and enfeoffed them'.

Along with fiefs came the language of feudalism. The vocabulary of all the peoples on the peripheries of Frankish Europe is marked by loan words, often originally from the French, describing the equipment and habits of the immigrant mounted warriors who settled in the eleventh, twelfth and thirteenth centuries. The Hungarian words for 'helmet', 'armour', 'castle', 'tower', 'tournament', 'duke', 'fief' and 'marshal' are all loan words from German, several of them, like 'tournament', having been in turn borrowed by German from French. The Germanic word 'rider' (modern German *Ritter*, 'knight') was used in medieval Ireland (*ritire*) and Bohemia (*rytiry*) for a knight. The Polish and Czech words for fief are direct borrowings from the German *Lehen*. In southern Italy the Normans made the word 'fief', which had been a rarity, common currency. New arrivals brought new terms, reflecting different concepts of social and legal relationships.

The solidarity of the new arrivals depended on the circumstances of their migration. Sometimes groups of lords and vassals were transplanted to a new milieu *en bloc*, like the clusters of Normans in Shropshire after 1066 who turn out to have been already tied by the feudal bond in their home duchy. The Normans who came to southern Italy were interconnected by dense and multiple family and feudal bonds. On a more general level, there might be a common regional origin to give some distinctive cohesion to the new settlers, in the way that the Crusader State of Tripoli was first occupied mainly by southern Frenchmen and that of Antioch by Normans. Of fifty-five noble settlers in the first generation of the kingdom of Jerusalem whose European origins have been traced, twenty-three (over 40 per cent) came from Flanders and Picardy. On other occasions, however, recruitment was on an individual basis and it was only ties to a local dynasty that united the immigrant aristocracy. In Hungary new magnate families came from France, Italy, Spain, Russia and Bohemia, as well as the preponderant Germany, and no coherent immigrant outlook or interest could develop.

The fate of native aristocracies in the face of conquest and immigration was sometimes disastrous. The Irish rulers of the eastern parts of Ireland were completely displaced in the first few generations of settlement. In Valencia a Muslim aristocracy hung on for some decades after the fall of the city in 1238, but disappeared in the risings of the mid-century. In those regions where native dynasties controlled the process of immigration the outcome was normally more balanced. By 1286, for example, five Scottish earldoms were in the possession of Anglo-Norman immigrant families, but eight were still in native hands. In late medieval Hungary descendants of immigrants, as mentioned above, were important, but still constituted only 30 per cent of the magnate class. Here it is a case of grafting rather than dispossession. And even in cases of imported feudalism, room was sometimes left for native fees with different rules of descent: Welsh fees in Wales and Lombard fees in southern Italy were both partible (divisible among more than one heir), while, in contrast, the rule of primogeniture applied in the Norman fees in both regions.

Marriages between incomers and natives were sometimes common. Since there was almost always an imbalance in the immigrant population, with men preponderant by far, intermarriage was usually between immigrant men and native women. Marriage into powerful local families was indeed one way newcomers could establish their position, since they would immediately acquire kin, property and patrons. Sometimes mercenary captains married their employer's daughter, as when Robert Guiscard wedded Sichelgaita, daughter of Gaimar V, prince of Salerno, or Richard fitzGilbert ('Strongbow') Aoifa, daughter of Dermot MacMurrough of Leinster. Similarly, when Pandulf III of Capua wanted to enlist the aid of the Norman leader Rainulf, 'he gave him his sister as wife'. At the highest level there was little in the way of a barrier to intermarriage. Of the wives of the first margraves of Brandenburg, sixteen in number, half were of Slav descent.

The long-term impact of aristocratic immigration was largely determined by issues of manpower. Where the immigrants were few in number it would prove impossible to pursue a policy of expropriation and expulsion. For southern Italy, the meticulous researches of Leon-Robert Ménager have revealed the names of every likely immigrant aristocrat of the eleventh and twelfth centuries: they total 385. Even given the inadequacy of the sources, the picture that emerges is of a small group of Normans and other northern French knights in a population overwhelmingly Lombard, Greek and Muslim. If the colonial aristocrats in this case formed an ethnically distinct minority population, they did not do so for long. Elsewhere the issue was more finely balanced, as in Ireland, where, in the later Middle Ages, it was a critical political question whether the colonial aristocrats would merge with the local population or survive as a sealed élite.

Levels of hostility between incomer and native obviously varied according to the circumstances of the intrusion and the pre-existing cultural differences between the two groups. The barrier between Christian and non-Christian was normally unbridgeable, but the survival of Muslim aristocracies in some places shows that extermination was not the only path. The intrusive aristocracies of the High Middle Ages had differing relationships with and attitudes to indigenous peoples and cultures and could turn out to be an alien and conquering élite, an élite monopolizing power but receptive to native culture or a group mingling with native aristocrats.

One small sign of cultural adaptation is the adoption of toponymic surnames from the new rather than from the old home. This was particularly marked among families lower than the magnate class, since they might have little to be 'of' in their region of origin. As mentioned above, few landed families in the Crusader States had western European toponyms. 'He who was "of Rheims" or "of Chartres" is now "of Tyre" or "of Antioch",' wrote one new settler, 'we have already forgotten the places of our birth.' The knights settled in Sicily took surnames from their new fiefs, while in Frankish Greece the new lords dropped their old names and adopted new, like snakes shedding skin:

The bannerets of Morea, together with the knights, began to raise castles and strongholds, each in his own territory making one of his own; and as soon as they had erected these strongholds, they put aside their surnames, which they had from France, and they assumed the names of the territories which they took.

These are only small signs, and perhaps have a purely linguistic exoticism as their outcome – Simone of Tiberias, Richard of Cephalonia – but names are, after all, tokens of identity.

The eventual linguistic outcome in the colonized areas of Europe depended not so much on the immigration of aristocrats but on the amount of non-aristocratic immigration that accompanied it. This topic will be discussed later, but one may point out here that there seem to be no cases where an immigrant aristocracy alone imposed fundamental linguistic change. Neither the Normans in southern Italy nor the Franks in the eastern Mediterranean established new Francophone regions, even though French was a language of fashion and literature. In England the Norman aristocracy probably had English as a mother tongue in a few generations.

The ties that the newly established aristocracies of the colonized peripheries of Europe maintained with their homelands varied very much in strength and duration. Sometimes an international or transregional aristocracy was created, at least for a time. The barons who held properties in northern France, England and the Celtic countries are a good instance. The de Lacy family, for example, had estates in Normandy as well as acquiring, in the eleventh century, a great baronage centred on the Welsh marches and, in the twelfth, the lordship of Meath in Ireland. The greater lords whom the Scottish kings endowed in their kingdom in the twelfth century almost invariably also held lands in England, and perhaps in France or elsewhere too. Ties between old home and new home were not manifested merely by property-holding. It was often the case that successful colonial aristocrats would share some of their new income with the religious houses of their old home. Thus John de Courcy founded six religious houses in his new lordship of Ulster and each was either a dependency of, or founded by a colony of monks from, a religious house in those parts of England where de Courcy held lands – the north-west and Somerset. Such links could survive even the downfall of the founder. Similar connections can be traced in Wales, where the nineteen Benedictine houses established in the years of conquest (1070–1150) were all initially dependent on houses in England or northern France. The expansionary movement of conquest and land-seeking thus left some long-term traces in both tenurial and monastic geography.

There were, however, difficulties in maintaining such ties permanently. Although the great magnates might move freely from one regional estate-cluster to another, lesser men found it easier to choose to be either resident or absentee, and, if the latter, there were problems maintaining real control of property and strong incentives to cash in their assets. Some of the lesser followers of the de Lacys, who chose not to settle permanently in Ireland, did exactly this with their holdings in Meath, selling them to local men. If property is gradually sorted out in this way, then a time comes when the aristocracy of the newly settled lands can no longer be sensibly termed 'colonial'. After a few generations, in the absence of continued ties with the country of origin, the descendants of immigrants may be as native as the descendants of natives. Alternatively, if the great lords maintain their distant properties but no longer reside in them, a class of absentee lords will be born – a phenomenon 'colonial' in the modern sense of the word. In Ireland both things occurred: at the gentry level an Anglo-Irish landowning class was born, quite distinct from its English counterpart, while at the magnate level much of the soil of colonial Ireland came to be held by absentee landlords, such as the Mortimers and Bigods, who were based in England and visited Ireland rarely if ever.

Links between new and old lands could be broken. In the case of Scotland the Wars of Independence of the late thirteenth and early fourteenth centuries made the casual cross-border ties of the earlier period increasingly difficult. In Spain the creation of trans-Pyrenean estates, which seemed, in the early twelfth century, a very likely outcome of the French participation in the Reconquest, never developed. Already in the 1140s the houses of Béarn and Bigorre were transferring their properties in the Ebro valley to the Templars. The general decline of French involvement in Spain after the mid-twelfth century meant that no permanent links were established of the kind that one sees in some other parts of Europe. The Reconquest became increasingly a Spanish story, and the transplantations we must look at are those between Old and New Castile, Catalonia and Valencia, the Meseta and Andalusia, not those tying the peninsula to the rest of Christian Europe. A symbolic moment is the departure of 'a big crowd of knights from beyond the mountains [i.e. the Pyrenees]' *before* the great Christian victory of Las Navas in 1212.

Questions of geography also played a large part in determining the persistence of links between old and new homes. Expansion into nearby regions that could be reached by land, such as the incorporation of the Mittelmark into the Mark of Brandenburg, usually did not disrupt aristocratic ties, and, as has been pointed out, the knightly class of the Mittelmark was basically provided by that of the adjacent Altmark. Long distances and sea journeys made a big difference. As well as the best-known 'Outremer', the Crusader States, the expansion of the High Middle Ages produced a number of lesser bridgehead societies, like colonial Ireland and the German communities along the Baltic. Commercial and maritime ties with the homeland were easy, but transmarine aristocratic estates were rarer. Most immigrant vassals, like Dietrich of Tiefenau, who was granted the castle of Little Queden (Tychnowy) and 300 holdings in Prussia by the Teutonic Knights in 1236, chose to dispose of their properties in the homeland. Dietrich held lands around Hamelin and on the lower Elbe, which he alienated in the years before this grant. In this sense the special feature of colonial aristocracies, that they were immigrant, settler aristocracies, gradually diminished. Except where an ethnic or religious difference existed between incoming and native populations, colonial aristocracies became, eventually, no different from non-colonial aristocracies, mindful though they might be of their heroic days of conquest and pioneering.

3. Military Technology and Political Power

For who denies that castles are necessary things?

The medieval aristocracy was primarily a military aristocracy and the men who participated in its high medieval diaspora were trained fighters. They possessed a particular set of arms and equipment and had been brought up to fight in a particular way. As a consequence the spread of the Frankish aristocracy entailed diffusion of a military technology – armaments, fortifications and methods of waging war – from its place of origin in the old Carolingian heartlands (to which one may add England after the Norman Conquest of 1066) into other parts of Europe. The expansive power of these aristocrats and the eagerness with which rulers recruited them is partly explicable by the military edge their technique of war gave them.

Within the central parts of north-western Europe there were three main characteristics of warfare in the period 950–1350: the dominant position of heavy cavalry, the ever-expanding role of archers, especially crossbowmen, and the development of a particular kind of fortification – the castle – along with the countervailing siegecraft. Knights, bowmen, castles. It is a picture familiar from the pages of Walter Scott or an MGM epic – and here the romantic novelists and Hollywood had it right. It is only in the picture of power, obligation and purpose which they wove around the technology that they erred.

HEAVY CAVALRY

Already by the tenth century military operations were dominated by heavy cavalry. Over the following centuries the proportion of infantry increased, but their tactical importance never matched that of the mounted fighters until the very end of the period considered here. The cavalry were virtually always numerically inferior, and it may be that their dominance is to be explained on social as much as tactical grounds, but in the armies of 1300, just as in those of the tenth century, the heavy cavalry formed a military élite.

Their military equipment in the early part of our period is portrayed in such valuable pictorial sources as the Leiden Book of Maccabees (tenth century) and the Bayeux Tapestry (late eleventh century). Defensive armament consisted in a conical helmet, a coat of mail (the byrnie or *lorica*) and a large shield; offensive arms included spear, sword and perhaps a mace or club; indispensable for offensive action was the heavy war-horse, or destrier. These men were *heavy* cavalry because they were fully armed and, in particular, because they had the expensive mail coat. Latin sources of the period call such men *armati* – 'armoured men' – or *loricati* – 'men with mail coats'. They were heavy because they were clad in iron. A powerful force was one that was 'all of iron'. The mail coat must often have been the most valuable single object that a knight owned and it is not surprising that they were sometimes pawned by knights in need. At a time when many agricultural implements were still made of wood, when the tool on which human survival turned, the plough, was often still made of wood or only tipped with iron, here were men who were *dressed* in iron. It represented a staggering investment. The full gear of an *armatus* or *loricatus* required approximately 50 lb of iron. When an army such as that raised by Otto II in the 980s included around 5,000 *loricati*, the iron carried by the heavy cavalry alone totalled 125 tons. The figure is all the more striking when we consider that, in this period, a German forge might produce only 10 lb of iron in a smelting process taking two or three days. The economic historian Beveridge wrote:

before the Black Death, wheat was being sold at prices varying with the harvest but ranging about 5 shillings a quarter; steel was being bought for ploughshares and other implements at prices also varying from year to year and ranging about 6 pence a lb, that is to say, at £50 and upwards per ton. Today [1939] a normal price for wheat is about 50 shillings a quarter, and for steel is about £10 a ton. While the price of wheat has multiplied ten times, that of steel has fallen to a fifth; a quarter of wheat will buy fifty times as much steel as once it did. The contrast between the wheat age and the steel age could hardly be better illustrated.

The heavy horsemen of the Middle Ages lived in the wheat age but looked like men of the steel age.

They were heavy cavalry not only because of their armour, but also because of their mounts. Horses required to bear the weight of a fully armed man and to face the rigours of combat had to be specially bred and trained. These destriers are the 'noble horses' frequently mentioned in the sources of the time, which were sought out as booty, dispatched as worthy gifts, traded and exchanged. They were bigger and stronger than the ordinary aristocratic riding horse and they tended to be used only in combat. This implied, naturally, that horsemen would also have other mounts, and the medieval cavalryman is to be pictured as the focal point of a small *equipe* of men and mounts. Both extra destriers and riding horses might be needed. The agreement between Henry I of England and the count of Flanders in 1101, in which the count undertook to supply horsemen, provided that each warrior should have three horses. This is a fairly characteristic number, though some thirteenth-century documents mention horsemen with as many as five mounts. The heavy cavalry were heavy, too, because these horses tended, increasingly, to be protected by trappings and armour.

Heavy cavalry retained its importance throughout the period discussed here, 950–1350. Not all such horsemen were knights. Indeed, one of the most important aspects of the history of this period is the very complex interplay between the purely military and the social meanings of the word 'knight' – *cavalier* and *chevalier*, *Reiter* and *Ritter*. The Latin *miles* did service for both, and the semantics of this term have been investigated minutely by historians. A man described as a *miles* in the early eleventh century was usually simply a heavy cavalryman, a *loricatus*; there was normally no implication of high social status – in fact, sometimes the opposite, for at this time the *milites* were contrasted with the magnates or great nobles. For example, when William the Conqueror deigned to consult his men on the question of his assumption of the crown in 1066, the viscount of Thouars, a man of ancient lineage, commented: 'Never or hardly ever have *milites* been summoned to such a decision!' The *milites* were a rough and rowdy crowd, vital but hardly to be idolized. Already, however, in the eleventh century, in some places, the term had begun to acquire an honorific meaning, a development which was to strengthen and spread over the following centuries. In the eleventh century it was possible to make a man a *miles* by giving him a horse and armour; by the thirteenth century the knight was a member of a closed, hereditary class. Social exclusiveness, religion and romance combined to reshape the meaning of the word.

It is important to be clear, however, that these big changes, which resulted in a new self-description for the aristocracy and, in some part, a new culture and new ideals, had very little effect on the technology of cavalry warfare. In the thirteenth century, just as in the tenth, rather small numbers of horsemen, in mail coats, armed with swords, lances and shields, dominated military activity. With a few minor exceptions, the development in arms, armour and (as far as one can tell) mounts was slight between the figures shown in the Leiden Book of Maccabees or the Bayeux Tapestry and the knights and mounted men-at-arms who fought for Edward I and Philip the Fair at the close of the thirteenth century (for a thirteenth-century depiction see Plate 4).

BOWMEN

Medieval bows were of three kinds: the shortbow, the longbow and the crossbow. The first, the shortbow, was about three feet long and was drawn back to the chest. It was very widely diffused in medieval Europe and was used in warfare by several peoples, notably the Scandinavians. It could be effective in certain circumstances – it helped the Normans win Hastings – but, in terms of range and penetration, it could not compare with the longbow. This was about six feet long and was drawn to the ear. Its origin was in south Wales. Its effects were described in the late twelfth century:

in the war against the Welsh, one of the men at arms was struck by an arrow shot at him by a Welshman. It went right through his thigh, high up, where it was protected inside and outside the leg by his iron cuises, and then through the skirt of his leather tunic; next it penetrated that part of the saddle which is called the alva or seat; and finally it lodged in his horse, driving so deep that it killed the animal.

This is the weapon that was to be taken up by the English kings of the late thirteenth and fourteenth centuries and to lead to the famous victories of the Hundred Years War. Before that time, however, the longbow was extremely localized. The missile weapon that was of central importance in Europe at this time was neither the shortbow, nor the longbow, but the crossbow.

Crossbows are recorded in northern France in the tenth century, but only came into general use after the late eleventh century. The Byzantine princess Anna Comnena described the crusaders' 'barbarian bow, quite unknown to the Greeks', the effect of which was 'diabolical' (*daimonios*). Her opinion was echoed by the concerned clergy of the West. The Lateran Council of 1139 ruled: 'We forbid henceforth, under pain of excommunication, the employment against Christians and Catholics of that deadly art, so hateful to God, of crossbowmen and archers.' Such reservations had little effect. By the end of the twelfth century large groups of mounted crossbowmen were among the most effective and fearful of a prince's instruments of war. In 1241, when the German king Conrad IV was preparing to face the threat of Mongol invasion, he drew up a short list of emergency measures to be taken by the princes. On this list of five measures there was room for the curt injunction: 'Let them have crossbowmen.'

Crossbows were effective because, despite their slow rate of fire, they had a frightening penetrating power. Among the corpses excavated from the battlefield of Visby in Gotland (1361) are some whose skulls contain five or six crossbow bolts inside the skullcase – that is, bolts that had penetrated both whatever head protection the peasant soldiers of Gotland had and also the bone. Nor were mail coats and helmets any defence. The knightly leaders of the cavalry were vulnerable too. Louis VI of France was wounded by a crossbow bolt, Richard the Lionheart killed by one. Some incidents of the English civil war of 1215–17 show the impact of the weapon. Several leaders of the baronial revolt were killed by crossbowmen, who shot them from the shelter of castle walls. When the baronial garrison at Rochester surrendered in 1215, King John was willing for the captured men-at-arms to be ransomed, 'except for the crossbowmen; the crossbowmen, who had killed many knights and men-at-arms in the course of the siege, he ordered to be hanged'. This unenviable eminence was a consequence of their military importance. At the decisive battle of Lincoln in 1217 it was the 'death-bringing shafts' of the royal crossbowmen, 250 in number, that decided the battle by killing the barons' horses, 'slaughtering them like pigs'.

Crossbowmen were pariahs – lumped together, in clerical sources, with mercenaries and heretics – but pariah professionals. Although hated and feared they were well remunerated. Around the year 1200, foot crossbowmen earned twice as much as ordinary footsoldiers in France. Rulers often made special arrangements to secure their services. Land might be held *per arbalisteriam*, that is, in return for service as a crossbowman. A German soldier held a large farm in Silesia 'for which he serves with a crossbow, as is specified in his charter'. Expenditure of wages for crossbowmen, and for the purchase of crossbows and tens of thousands of bolts, recurs continually in the princely financial records of the thirteenth century. Here was one of the major military developments of the period 950–1350; a new weapon rose to prominence, not only spreading moral shock, but also creating a new professional corps and offering new opportunities to rulers.

This same period saw an even more significant military development, the emergence and evolution of a new kind of fortification.

CASTLES

Because they were not all lords of castles, Hugh of Abbeville became more powerful than the rest of his peers. For he could do what he liked without fear, relying on the protection of the castle, while others, if they tried anything, were easily overcome since they had no refuge.

The passage above refers to the founder of the line of the counts of Ponthieu, emerging from among a group of rivals in the last decades of the tenth century. As is very explicitly stated here, a decisive factor in his success story was the possession of a castle. It gave him the edge. All over Europe in the tenth and eleventh centuries such struggles were being fought out. The men who came out on top were those who could make effective use of castles, men like Frederick of Swabia, who, in the often quoted words of his kinsman Otto of Freising, 'dragged a castle at his horse's tail'.

The encastellation of Europe which took place between the tenth and the thirteenth centuries was a development of quite fundamental military and political importance, and it is worth trying to be precise when analysing the distinctive novelty of the castle. This is not easy. There had been fortifications in Europe for millennia and they had taken many different forms. No one set of criteria will differentiate absolutely sharply the fortresses of the early Middle Ages from the castles of the High Middle Ages. There will always be areas of ambiguity and overlap. Nevertheless, if we are content with a characterization of the difference that covers most cases, we can say that the castles which covered Europe in the tenth to twelfth centuries were distinguished by two features – they were small and they were high.

The smallness of the castle can be strikingly illustrated by some sites where a castle was raised within an earlier and larger fortification. The Norman castles erected in England after the conquest provide good examples. At Old Sarum the Norman castle stands in the middle of an earlier earthwork that is about thirty-five times as large as the castle. The same contrast can be seen elsewhere. In the Auvergne the smaller castles of the new millennium were often erected within the boundaries of the older communal fortifications, which could be twenty times their size. In north Germany the great Saxon fortifications of the eighth century had very large diameters. One, Skidrioburg, was about 1,000 by 800 feet. There is a great difference between defensive sites like this and those raised later in the same area. Around 980, when the new forms of castle building were

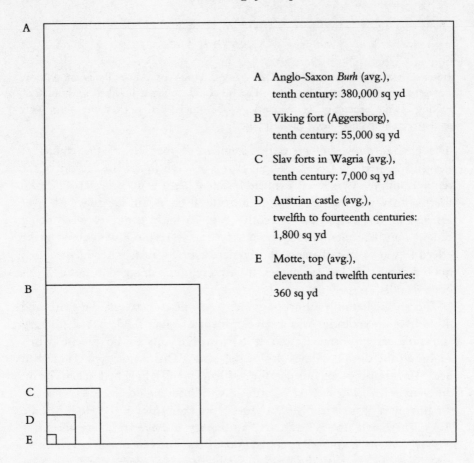

A   Anglo-Saxon *Burh* (avg.),
    tenth century: 380,000 sq yd

B   Viking fort (Aggersborg),
    tenth century: 55,000 sq yd

C   Slav forts in Wagria (avg.),
    tenth century: 7,000 sq yd

D   Austrian castle (avg.),
    twelfth to fourteenth centuries:
    1,800 sq yd

E   Motte, top (avg.),
    eleventh and twelfth centuries:
    360 sq yd

Figure 2. Areas of selected medieval fortifications

developing, the bishop of Oldenburg erected a castle at Nezenna in
Holstein. This measured between 50 and 150 feet in diameter. The contrast
in size reflects a contrast in function. Skidrioburg was a large communal
fortress intended for the defence of a whole community. Nezenna was an
episcopal – that is, a seigneurial – fortification, for the protection of a lord,
the bishop, and his followers, his clerks and his *milites*. (See Figure 2 for
other examples.)

Because they were small, seigneurial rather than communal, castles
involved less work and thus could be raised in much greater numbers than
the larger defences of earlier times. The eleventh and twelfth centuries

form the age of the new castles, as is witnessed by the Newcastles, Châteauneufs and Nienburgs still scattered across the face of Europe. In England around 1100 there may have been as many as 500 castles, all of them built in the previous fifty years. This represents an average of a castle every ten miles. Comparable figures can be cited for parts of northern France. In regions where military pressure was intense, like the English–Welsh or Saxon–Slav borders, the density of fortification was even greater. This was a veritable militarization of society.

The most distinctive physical feature of castles, their height, was in part a consequence of their size. They were not intended to oppose truly massive earth ramparts to the attacker. They were not places of refuge for whole communities and hence did not have large reserves of manpower for defence. Castles were intended to be defensible by a few and the way to ensure this was to make them small but high. The height gave them both inaccessibility and dominance of their surroundings. Inside a castle, a garrison was hard to get at but could also command everything within sight: 'the keep is a queen, looming aloft, mistress of all she surveys'.

One simple way to gain height was to plant the castle on a hill or mountain spur. A whole class of castles, including notably the *Hohenburg* of central and southern Germany, is characterized by this kind of site. In the absence of a hill, it was still possible to build one, and so the eleventh and twelfth centuries saw western Europe gradually covered with mottes, artificial mounds raised to form the heart of the castle. The British Isles, France and northern Germany contained hundreds of mottes in this period, averaging around 100 feet in diameter at the base, only 30 feet at the top. The small site at the top of the motte was intended to take a tower. This was another way of gaining height. Once the high ground was gained, either on a natural or on a man-made hill, the tower was the final touch, taking the defenders out of reach yet simultaneously presenting them with a platform from which to observe or throw missiles.

The tower, which, especially in the early period and in seigneurial (as distinct from royal and princely) castles, was very small, was the last defence and the toughest. It represented the furthest development in that process of concentration of defence which was the essence of the story of the castle. In the endless castle warfare described in Suger's *Life of Louis the Fat* (early twelfth century) it is the tower which is the ultimate objective: at Crécy the king 'occupied the castle and seized the strong tower as if it were a peasant's hut'; at Le Puiset the leader of the defenders, 'since the walled castle was not safe enough refuge for him, withdrew into the motte, that is the upper wooden tower'; at Mantes 'the king, clad in armour, rushed in, sped through the castle to the tower, and surrounded it'. The arming of the tower, with men, weapons and provisions, was a message of intent quite as unmistakable as the arming of a modern warhead.

The small and relatively simple castles of the tenth and eleventh centuries offered opportunities. It has already been pointed out that anyone willing to take advantage of the new form of fortification might be able to outstrip rivals, to pull himself above his peers, to win or expand his lordship. There is a nice illustration of this in the text *De diversitate temporum* of Alpert of Metz, which describes the struggles of the lords of the lower Rhine in the early eleventh century. 'There is a marsh,' he wrote, '200 paces from the Meuse, within which was a little hill, very hard to reach . . . For anyone eager for a change in things (*studenti novis rebus*) it offered the chance to build a castle.' 'New things' (*novae res*) was the standard medieval term for revolutionary change and this passage shows how contemporaries perceived the castle as an innovative force in the tenth and eleventh centuries, reshaping the rules of both military and political life.

As the quotation from Alpert shows, one aspect of these changes was geographical. Men went about the country with their eyes open for certain kinds of sites. They wanted places that 'offered the chance to build a castle' and these sites might be the ones which otherwise had little to offer – a hill in a marsh attracted the attention of the castle-builders in the early eleventh century; perhaps for the first time men had use for such a site. Of course, many castles were built to control well-settled areas or were raised in towns (often at the cost of some destruction of a previous settlement), but one important aspect of the spread of castles was a reorientation away from the settled areas. This comes out strongly in accounts of the castle-building undertaken by Henry IV of Germany in the 1060s and 1070s. 'He sought out high hills, fortified by nature, in uninhabited places, and built castles there,' wrote the Saxon clerk Bruno. The king derived unexpected benefit from this reconnaissance of rough terrain. When faced by revolt in 1073, Henry was able to escape 'through the wild woods, which he had travelled through often while seeking out sites for castles'. The new opportunities and needs of castle-building had turned Saxony inside out for the king. Not the settled farming areas, but the bleak forests and hills were the zones of promise in his eyes. Examples could be multiplied – Okehampton castle up on the edge of Dartmoor, brooding over its attendant settlement down below; the ancestors of the Landgraves of Thuringia carving out a 'clearance lordship' for themselves around their castle of Schauenburg, high in the Thüringer Wald – but enough has been said to give some idea of the impact of castles at this time.

The small, high fortification of the tenth and eleventh centuries was a technical innovation and would have been so even without the development of a whole new stage of castle-building, using stone. It is worth considering the two developments separately, for although the evolution of the castle can be traced naturally from the earth-and-wood motte-and-baileys of the eleventh century through to the stone castles of the thirteenth, the two stages required different technical resources and had different political consequences.

The technological development of the stone castle over the course of the eleventh, twelfth and thirteenth centuries can only be summarized here. Stone castles were built in the tenth century but remained extremely rare until the twelfth. They represent an entirely new stage in fortification. The great stone castles of the later twelfth and thirteenth centuries are a quite different military and political phenomenon from that rash of earth mounds and wooden towers that had spread over Europe earlier. They were much more expensive and took far longer to build. Motte-and-baileys could be raised quickly – the Normans built two in 1066 in the two weeks between their landing and the battle of Hastings – but castles like Dover (late twelfth century) or the Edwardian castles of Wales were built over a course of decades. Expenses mounted. Over the period 1168–89 Henry II spent around £6,500 on Dover. His average expenditure on castles was around £700 p.a. In the reign of his son John this went up to £1,000 p.a., and in the reign of John's son, Henry III (1216–72) it went up again to £1,500 p.a. The great castle-builder, Edward I, outdid them all and spent around £80,000 in twenty-seven years on his Welsh castles alone. In Edward's reign, for purposes of comparison, a knight on campaign earned 2 shillings per day (i.e. £1 in ten days).

The greater stone castles of the thirteenth century, with their tall keeps and their rings of concentric walls, their elaborate gatehouses and sophisticated defences, could not be stormed or burned simply by showing the vigour of a Louis the Fat. The development of fortification required a similar development in siegecraft. The same period that sees the spread and refinement of the stone castle, the twelfth and thirteenth centuries, witnesses also the evolution of siege machines and siege techniques. The tension-based artillery of the tenth and eleventh centuries – basically giant catapults or bows – was supplemented by an artillery weapon using counterweights, the trebuchet, which was in use in England, France, Italy and Germany by the early thirteenth century (see Plate 5). The French engineer and architect, Villard de Honcourt, described how to construct one and drew sketches. The largest machines of this type were capable of throwing projectiles of

500 lb almost 300 yards. This same period also saw increasing refinement in undermining skills, the regular employment of sappers and engineers and the proliferation of a menagerie of 'rams', 'cats' and other machines of attack. Siegecraft became a science. In 1181 the besiegers of the walled town of Haldersleben were able to capture it by damming the local river and flooding the town.

THE SPREAD OF FRANKISH ARMS

The main features of the military technology of the 'central area' of western Europe in the period 950–1350 were thus an enduring emphasis on heavy cavalry, the rise of firepower, especially that of the crossbowmen, the development of castles at first of earth and wood, later of stone, and the corresponding improvement of siege machines.

When we turn to consider the political consequences of this technology, a very important chronological and geographical distinction must be drawn. The military technology described above developed earlier in some regions than in others. The motte-and-bailey castle, for example, arose in northern France or the Rhineland in the early eleventh century and was imported to England only after 1050. Crossbowmen, too, were employed on the continent before crossing the Channel. Like England, Saxony seems to have adopted some forms of the new technology, notably the castle, later than northern France or western Germany. Overall, however, the most important distinction seems to be between those areas that had heavy cavalry and castles by around 1100 and those that did not. A sketch map of military techniques in non-Mediterranean Europe around the year 1100 would show three zones. The first would be the region already described, including northern France, Germany and England. In this zone warfare centred around heavily armoured cavalry, castles, siegecraft and, increasingly, bowmen. There were two other zones. One of them was the zone where footsoldiers predominated. This included Scotland, Wales and Scandinavia. Here men fought on foot with spears and bows, axes and swords. When the king of England imposed a military quota on the Welsh principality of Gwynedd in 1247 he expected 1,000 footmen and 24 well-armed horsemen. The proportions speak for themselves. The final zone was a region of cavalry, but of light, not heavy, horsemen. Eastern Europe, including the lands of the West Slavs, the Balts and the Hungarians, made up the largest part of this zone, but warfare in Ireland seems to have been similar, in its basic outlines, too. The Irish horsemen were notably the lightest in Europe, having neither stirrups nor true saddles and acting as mounted spearsmen or javelineers, but the eastern Europeans too employed a lighter cavalry than that of Germany or France. One German observer noted with interest how the Slavic Pomeranians had only one horse apiece and carried their own arms – no spare destriers, no squires.

The situation in the Mediterranean region was rather different. Frankish armies did indeed bring their armaments and tactics with them into this area. Castles were built and powerful siege machinery employed in the Crusader States, Sicily and Spain. The heavy cavalry of the westerners was remarked upon by Greek and Muslim observers. One Muslim source noted how, at Damascus in 1148, 'the infidel cavalry waited to make the charges, for which it is famous'. In Spain the high saddle and long stirrups of the Christian knights were recognized as admirably suited to the shock charge. The minstrel Ambroise depicts a Muslim emir, describing the European knights of the Third Crusade, saying: 'nothing can withstand them since they have such armour, so strong, solid and secure'. The crossbow, too, was a distinctive arm of the westerners in the Mediterranean region, and in Spain, just as in northern Europe, crossbowmen enjoyed tax exemptions and generous grants of property.

Nevertheless, the contrast between western and non-western forces in the Mediterranean was less striking and the westerners' superiority less clear-cut than in non-Mediterranean Europe. Frankish armies here encountered indigenous societies and civilizations with an ancient tradition of stone fortification and elaborate siegecraft. Both Muslim and Greek armies included armoured cavalry, and the Muslims used the composite bow ('fitted together with glue', as Fulcher of Chartres observed) to good effect. Military outcomes reflected this closer balance of forces. Eventually the Muslims were able to throw the Christians out of Palestine and Syria and as late as 1200 they were on the offensive in Spain. In the thirteenth century the Greeks recovered much of the territory they had lost during the Fourth Crusade. Only at sea did the westerners attain and preserve an enduring and decisive advantage in the Mediterranean.

In non-Mediterranean Europe, however, in both the zones just mentioned, that of footsoldiers and that of light cavalry, there were striking contrasts to the 'central region' of France, Germany and England. There the chiefs would certainly wear mail, but armour was unusual. There would be no forces 'all of iron'. Though they had fortified sites, there were no castles in the specific sense we have described; and, while the south Welsh had longbowmen and the Scandinavians men with the short bow, crossbowmen were unknown. Our picture of non-Mediterranean

Europe in the year 1100, then, is of a world of knights and castles, of crossbows and siege machines, which gradually shaded off into a different world to the north and east. One of the most central developments of the twelfth and thirteenth centuries was the expansion of this world of knights and castles into that other world. The diffusion of the new technology had profound political repercussions; it transformed Celtic, Scandinavian and eastern European society.

Military technology spread in three, closely related ways. The first was conquest. The knights and castle-builders and crossbowmen of the central western European area used their military might to extend their lordship into the lands of the east and the west. Norman expansion in the British Isles and German conquests in eastern Europe both involved the arrival of new military methods and new weapons in the conquered areas. The second way the technology spread was a direct consequence of the first. As the aggressive forces threatened the supremacy of native rulers and aristo-cracies, so these countered in the most effective way – by imitation. By the mid-thirteenth century the rulers of, for instance, Wales or Pomerania had become virtually indistinguishable from their foes in armament and methods of waging war (as in much else). The third path of military diffusion was a variant of the one just mentioned. Many rulers in the Celtic world, in the north and in the east of Europe adopted the military techniques and organization prevalent in England, France and Germany not simply as a desperate defensive measure, but as part of a conscious, intentional policy of developing their power and, as a subsidiary means to this goal, of increasing the resources of the peoples they ruled. In these ways, by conquest, by defensive imitation and by planned development, the techniques and methods of England, France and Germany gradually reached the whole of the Latin West – and some of the pagan peoples beyond – over the course of the twelfth, thirteenth and early fourteenth centuries.

A perfect example of the first two methods of diffusion, conquest and imitation, is provided by the history of the eastern Baltic. The establishment of German power in the region in the early thirteenth century is described by the chronicler Henry of Livonia. Henry is renowned for the detail of his observations on military matters and the interest he showed in weapons and warfare, and his account makes it clear that the German colonies in the eastern Baltic (the area then known as Livonia) depended for their existence upon their superiority in military technology and techniques.

The first German missionary among the Livonians, Meinhard, who came to the area in the 1180s in the wake of German traders, was a shrewd, even calculating evangelist. After the Livonians had suffered a savage raid by the Lithuanians,

Meinhard accused the Livonians of foolishness because they had no fortifications. He promised that castles would be built for them if they decided to become and be considered sons of God. They agreed and promised, and confirmed on oath, that they would receive baptism. So, the next summer, stonemasons were brought from Gotland.

Soon, stone castles, built by foreign masons, were rising in Livonia for the first time. Mortared stonework, as distinct from earthworks reinforced with drystone facing, was a complete novelty in the region. Meinhard had observed the military superiority of his own people, the Germans, and had tried to use it as an incentive in his attempt to convert the pagan Livonians. As it turned out, he was defrauded. Once the Livonians were in possession of their new castles, they reverted to paganism.

This story, which is recorded in the very first pages of Henry of Livonia's *Chronicle*, introduces a subject which recurs constantly throughout the work – the superior military technology of the Germans and its slow seepage to the enemy. Stone castles were only one part of this edge. The Germans also had more armour. This gave them both physical and psychological advantages. When heavily outnumbered by the Lithuanians, the German knight Conrad, 'with his horse and himself well-armoured, like a knight, attacked the Lithuanians with the few Germans who were present. But they were frightened by the brightness of their armour and God sent fear into them and they gave way before them on every side.' This 'brightness of armour' (*nitor armorum*) had a terrifying effect upon the enemy. When one group of German knights 'charged through the centre of the enemy, they terrified them with their armoured horses'. The advantage of armour was not only in inspiring fear, of course. Henry of Livonia noted the particular vulnerability of the native peoples. In one battle 'the unarmoured enemy were wounded everywhere by flying arrows'. Henry was quite explicit about the contrasts he observed: the Estonians 'were unarmoured, for they are not accustomed to use armour as much as other peoples do'.

The vulnerability of unarmoured or lightly armoured local fighters was compounded by the superiority of the Germans in missile weapons. The crossbowmen among the Germans made a decisive difference. They could defend a fortress or a ship; they could fight in the field; they were invaluable in assaults on enemy fortifications. On one occasion a hostile army bypassed a fortress simply because of the crossbowmen they encountered. This was in 1206, when the Russians descended the river Dvina and came to the fort of Üxküll, recently built by the Germans. 'Some of them were seriously wounded by the crossbowmen . . . From this they knew that there were Germans in the fort and they went on down the river . . . the Russians were ignorant of the art of the crossbow.'

The Germans also possessed superiority in siegecraft. In their attack on the fortress of Mesoten in 1220,

some of them built a tower, others put up paterells [throwing machines], others shot with crossbows, others built 'hedgehogs' [mobile protective shelters] and began to dig at the rampart from below. Others carried up wood, filled the ditch with it and pushed the tower across it, while others began to dig beneath its shelter . . . At last the large machine was put up and great rocks were cast at the fort. The men in the fort, seeing the size of the rocks, were seized with great terror.

This combination of siege towers, mining and ballistic weapons was extremely powerful. The heavy throwing machines were particularly frightening. Native ways of waging war contained no ready response. At the siege of Fellin, 'the Germans built a machine, and, by hurling stones night and day, they broke down the fortifications and killed innumerable men and animals in the fort, since the Estonians had never seen such things and had not strengthened their houses against such attacks'. 'Since the Estonians had never seen such things' – the phrase encapsulates the gap in military technology between the core area of western Europe, France, Germany and England, and the geographical peripheries. It was the existence of this gap that enabled a small number of Germans to impose their lordship over far larger native populations in the eastern Baltic. However, Henry of Livonia's *Chronicle* not only tells of the victories of the Germans; it also recounts the effort of the local peoples to fight back. As they fought back, they learned from their enemies.

It was not easy for the native peoples to acquire the technology of their enemies, and some of their early attempts were so unsuccessful as to seem slapstick. During the siege of Holme in 1206, for example, 'the Russians also made a little machine like that of the Germans, but not knowing the art of throwing rocks, they hurled them backwards and wounded many of their own men'. After such abortive beginnings, the native peoples acquired working knowledge of both ballistic machines and the crossbow early in the 1220s, that is, about a generation after the first German attacks. The way these skills spread is partly to be explained by the military demands of the local situation. If the Germans (or the Danes, who also invaded at this time) wished to establish hegemony in the region, they had to use local people. They needed them not only as agricultural producers, paying tribute and tithe, but also as military auxiliaries. There were not enough foreigners to support an autonomous military establishment. Yet, if the native forces were to be effective auxiliaries, they had to have at least some contact with the superior techniques of warfare of their German leaders. In this way, the seepage of technical knowledge began.

The way the Oeselians (an Estonian people) acquired siege machines demonstrates the transfer of technical knowledge through such channels. The Oeselians, one of the toughest and most ferocious peoples with whom the invaders had to deal, were preparing large-scale resistance in the 1220s, and their preparations included sending missions to another local people, who had already become possessed of knowledge of siege weapons through their alien conquerors:

Some of them went into Warbole to study the technique of the paterell, the machine which the Danes had given to the people of Warbole, who were their subjects. They returned to Oesel and began to build paterells and other machines and taught others. Each of them made his own machines.

Soon they had instructed the other Estonians and the Russians in this art. The use of siege machines, which Henry terms 'the German technique' (*ars Theutonicorum*) in his *Chronicle*, has become also 'the Oeselian technique' (*ars Osiliarum*) by the last pages of his work.

German military techniques spread in other ways. Especially in the early days, the invaders needed local forces not only in the form of subject auxiliaries, but also as independent allies. One of the most tempting inducements they could offer a potential ally was a gift of some new tools of war. Thus the bishop of Riga, the leader of the Germans in Livonia, sent gifts of armoured horses or military advisers to nearby Russian rulers. The neighbouring king of Kukenois (Kokenhusen) received 'twenty strong men, armoured and mounted, knights, crossbowmen and masons to strengthen his fortress'.

The natives not only encountered the new weapons as the tools of their masters or the gifts of allies. They could also take them from the bodies of their enemies. Many native fighters acquired mail coats from German corpses. When fortresses were taken, armour, horses and crossbows would fall into their hands. Some fortifications were strengthened by the Germans, but then fell back under native control. They would now be harder to recapture. All in all, by the 1220s the Germans were facing enemies, in some areas, who fought with weapons and techniques more and more like their own.

Two points are clear from this story. First, the Germans possessed military superiority based upon heavy cavalry, stone castles, crossbows and siege machines (in addition to their edge in shipbuilding). Second, the technical gap was not so immense that the natives could have no hope of ever catching up. The situation had some similarities with later colonial experience in America and Africa, but the technical edge enjoyed by the invaders was, in this case, not so overwhelming.

A comparable pattern of events can be observed in Wales and Ireland in the twelfth and thirteenth centuries. Here, as in the eastern Baltic, the initial penetration of the country was made possible by the invaders' military advantages. The castle, for example, was introduced into Wales and Ireland by the invaders, and the classic first step of the Anglo-Norman adventurers who arrived in Wales and Ireland in the twelfth and thirteenth centuries was the erection of a central castle. 'After the Normans had conquered the English in battle,' wrote one twelfth-century observer in reference to Wales, 'they added this land to their dominions also, fortifying it with innumerable castles.' The process is conjured up vividly in the native Welsh chronicle, the *Brut y Tywysogion*:

the king sent to Gilbert fitz Richard, who was brave, renowned and powerful, and a friend to the king – and he was a man eminent in all his actions – to ask him to come to him. And he came. And the king said to him: 'You were always,' said he, 'seeking of me a portion of the territory of the Britons. I will now give you Cadwgan's territory. Go and take possession of it.' And then he gladly accepted it from the king. And then, gathering a host, along with his comrades he came to Ceredigion. And he took possession of it and built in it two castles.

In such ways Wales experienced the impact of the castle as an instrument of conquest, as England had done half a century before, as Ireland was to do half a century later. In Ireland heavily armoured Anglo-Normans faced opponents who were without such protection: 'The Foreigners and the Irish of Teamhair [Tara] joined unequal combat: shirts of thin satin were about the sons of Conn and the Foreigners were a single phalanx of iron.' When the O'Connors attacked Athenry in 1249 and 'saw the terrible mail-clad cavalry coming towards them out of the town, prodigious fear and terror seized them at the sight and they were routed'.

Yet, as in Livonia and other parts of eastern Europe, the technical advantages of the invaders were not vast and did not last for ever. Although one twelfth-century Welsh author wrote of the Anglo-Normans building castles 'after the manner of the French', by the end of that century the Welsh princes were themselves using siege machinery and constructing stone castles. Osmotic processes, such as intermarriage, hospitality, service as hostage, exile and temporary alliance, broke down the barriers between invaders and indigenous populations. Advantages in the art of fortification and in armour, not to mention non-technological advantages (greater wealth, larger population), enabled an Anglo-Norman aristocracy, backed, in some cases, by peasant settlement, to make inroads into Wales and Ireland but not to subdue and replace native society. Wales between the late eleventh and the late thirteenth centuries was thus a 'half-conquered' country. The fate of Ireland was similar, but permanent. Both countries had clearly experienced the impact of an alien military technology which was effective enough to establish new colonial powers but not so superior that it could sweep the board.

The success of the Anglo-Norman invaders was limited, and one of the reasons for this was that their techniques of warfare were not always and in all circumstances superior. Heavy cavalry, for example, was well suited to 'champaign country' – broad rolling plains or the like – but in the mountains of Wales or the bogs of Ireland a man in a mail coat on a charger might well be inappropriate technology. On one occasion an Anglo-Norman leader in Ireland is depicted as urging his men to hurry out of a valley, where they were in danger of attack:

> Lords barons all,
> Let us pass through this valley promptly
> So that we may be on the hill,
> On the hard field and in open ground.

Difficulties of terrain often muffled the impact of the heavy cavalry of western Europe, not only in Wales and Ireland but also in eastern Europe. The death of William of Holland in 1256 is also instructive. He had attacked the Frisians, 'uncouth, uncivilized and unconquered men', who wore light armour and fought on foot with javelin and axe, and they had cunningly lured him into a frozen marsh. William, 'sitting on a huge war-horse, covered in iron, and wearing mail coat and helmet', fell through the ice and thrashed around in the chilly water until the Frisians finished him off.

Despite such limitations, it is right to see the central area of western Europe, as defined above, as possessing clear military advantages. In most cases, armoured cavalry, castles, siege machines and crossbowmen were powerful and desirable. This is demonstrated most clearly in those cases where rulers of geographically peripheral areas consciously fostered the adoption of new military methods. This is the third of the methods mentioned above whereby military techniques spread.

If native rulers encouraged the transformation of their own society, they could maintain their power against external threats. It was a kind of inoculation. It was a process which took place in several countries – Scotland, the West Slav principalities of Pomerania and Silesia and the Scandinavian countries – and it involved various related changes. A native aristocracy would have to be won over and transformed or else rendered harmless; foreign immigration would be encouraged; a new aristocracy might be created; relations with external powers might be fundamentally modified.

Scotland is a classic example of a country that transformed itself, under the direction of its native dynasty, by a policy of deliberately invited immigration. This involved a complete transformation of the military and political framework within which the Scots operated. The story of how this came about can be told by looking at three successive phases in the perennial sequence of Scots invasions of northern England. In the reign of Malcolm III (1058–93), in 1138 and again in 1174 Scots armies plundered Northumberland. In the anguished reports of English chroniclers of all three periods there is, of course, the common note of misery; there are also, however, significant differences, which point to a process of military and political change.

When Malcolm III's lightly armoured fighters came south in the late eleventh century, they came to burn, to plunder and to enslave. A successful raid was a great step forward economically, replenishing their stock and their labour force. 'The young men and the young women and whoever seemed suitable for work and toil were driven bound before the enemy . . . Scotland was filled with English slaves and handmaidens, so that even now no little village, nor even homestead, is without them.' One of the pious works of Malcolm's English wife, Queen Margaret, was the relief and ransoming of such slaves.

The English, faced with this threat, had two options. One was to make for the most defensible settlement. A secure site like Durham became completely crammed with refugees when the Scots moved south. We have a description of the scene in 1091, when, much to the discomfort of our clerical source, herds of livestock filled the churchyard and the monks' services could hardly be heard above the cries of babies and the laments of their mothers. But not everyone was near enough to such a superb defensive spot, nor was there room for all. The alternative was to go off into the wild, where uplands and forests might offer some protection. In 1091 'some hid themselves in hiding places in the woods and hills'. In 1070 the Scots pretended to return to Scotland in order to lure the refugees out of their hiding places and back into their villages, so that they could plunder them. If it was not possible to take refuge in the dales or get to a centre like Durham, the only recourse was to run to the church, where stone walls and the power of the saint offered at least something. Around 1079 King Malcolm's men approached Hexham:

The men of Hexham were aware of the king's anger, but what could they do? They had not the numbers to resist, a fortification to flee to, nor the help of any allies. The one and only hope of them all was the power of the saints, a power they had often felt. So they assembled in the church.

At this time the north of England had virtually no castles. Not that whole populations could have been brought inside a castle, but a locally based military power would certainly have impeded and threatened any invaders. In their absence, the populace would 'trust in the protection of that peace brought by the presence of the most holy body'. (Other medieval observers noted that regions without castles required particularly active vindictive and protective saints.)

The situation changed rapidly – indeed, it was already changing during the reign of Malcolm III. The changes took place on both sides of the border. First, after the Norman Conquest, castles began to arise all over the north of England. As early as 1072 one was built at Durham. It was not intended to protect peasants' livestock or crying babies but as a place 'where the bishop and his men could maintain themselves secure from attackers'. Newcastle was built in 1080, Carlisle in 1092. In the early decades of the twelfth century the bishop of Durham founded a castle at Norham on the Tweed 'to check the raids of brigands and the invasions of the Scots'. Second, however, important developments took place in Scotland itself. The sons of Malcolm III, especially David I (1124–53), saw the military strength of their neighbours and rivals to the south and began a deliberate policy of planting Anglo-Norman knights and barons in Scotland as their vassals. In sharp contrast to Wales and Ireland, the 'Norman conquest' of Scotland was by invitation only. The kings of the Scots could now call not only upon lightly armed native forces, but also upon the newcomers – heavy cavalry and castle-builders. One of the most famous of the historical sources that illustrate this process is the charter of 1124 recording King David's grant of Annandale, in south-west Scotland, to Robert Bruce, an Anglo-Norman aristocrat and ancestor of the later Scottish king. Here was created, on the borders of the dissident province of Galloway, a large fief, with motte-and-bailey castles, held by a Norman baron in close connection with the king. The advantages of the process in

the king's eyes are as obvious as the threat that would be felt by the native
aristocracy and the men of Galloway. Already, in 1124, this charter is
witnessed by Anglo-Norman immigrants, not by native magnates.

When we turn to consider the Scottish invasion of 1138, the political and
military results of the spread of the new technology of war into both the
north of England and Scotland are clear. In some ways, the raids of that
year were simply plundering, slaving raids of the kind familiar to King
David's father: 'The men were all killed, the maidens and widows, naked,
bound with ropes, were driven off to Scotland in crowds to the yoke of
slavery.' Nevertheless, things were changing. It may not indicate any more
than one man's personal attitudes, but King David returned his share of the
slaves. It was the 'Picts' – that is, the native Scots – who were singled out
by the chroniclers for the brutality of their enslaving. For the Scots army
of 1138 included not only the 'Picts', and the men of Galloway, renowned
for such habits as braining babies on doorposts, but also a substantial
number of the newly introduced Norman knights. The Scots army of 1138
was beginning to look more like the armies of Anglo-Norman England.

The methods of warfare had also changed since the 1070s. The encastellation of northern England meant that the invaders had to face new difficulties. The knights in the English castles could sally out and harass the Scots.
They had to be neutralized. Long sieges might be necessary. On one
occasion, King David besieged Wark castle for three weeks 'with crossbows
and engines'. The castles were the new targets and tools of war. They
presented not only new difficulties, but also new opportunities. For
Malcolm III, in the late eleventh century, the question of 'seizing'
Northumberland could hardly arise. He could burn, he could plunder, he
could enslave. He might manage to exact tribute or blackmail or take
hostages. But as soon as his men returned to Scotland his power became
only the power of threat. After the north was encastellated, however, the
seizure of the area became a real possibility – it meant capturing and
holding the castles. A few years before the invasion of 1138, David I had
done just that: 'with a great army he occupied and held five castles'. The
five included Carlisle, Newcastle and Norham – the very places built to
guard against the Scots. Paradoxically, the fortifications raised to defend
against invasion had made a real and more enduring conquest that much
more likely. The castles provided a handle to possession.

The strains and tensions of a kingdom faced with the military and
political process described above were highlighted on the battlefield near
Northallerton, where, in 1138, the 'battle of the Standard' was fought
between the Scots under King David and the English and Norman forces

of the north of England. The battle was preceded by a fierce quarrel on the Scottish side. The king and his own Norman and English advisers decided to place in their front line 'as many armoured knights and archers as were there'. Immediately the men of Galloway protested: 'Why, O king, are you afraid and why do you fear those iron coats you see afar? . . . We have conquered mail-clad men.' One of the Scots earls then boasted: 'O king, why do you agree to the wishes of these foreigners when not one of them, with their armour, will be before me in battle today, although I am without armour?' This prompted one of the king's Normans to call the earl a bluffer, and the only way the king could calm the situation down was by conceding to Galwegians the right to form the vanguard.

Here on the very field of battle, the tensions created by the spread of new methods of war raised themselves. The divisions would have been highly visible. The front ranks of the Scots were formed of the Galwegians, 'unarmoured and naked', bearing spears and cowhide shields; behind them were the troops under the king's son, composed of knights and archers; the king's own bodyguard was made up of English and French knights. They would have resembled their opponents more than their own front ranks.

In the battle of the Standard the Galwegians attacked bravely and fiercely, uttering their war-cries, but were halted by the solid ranks of armoured knights facing them and the showers of arrows – 'northern flies bubbling up from the caves of the quivers, pouring out like heavy rain'. As they writhed 'as full of arrows as a hedgehog of spines', their leaders dead, the rest of the Scottish army began to falter. Soon the English advanced, the Scottish king's knights dragged him from the field, and the whole Scottish army fled, to be hunted and harried to the border by the local populations they had so long plundered and raided. King David must have wished that he had more of the foreign knights and barons, that the process of military change had gone further and faster.

His grandson, William the Lion (1165–1214), continued the policies of King David. 'He cherished, loved and held dear people from abroad. He never had much affection for those of his own country.' When he invaded England in 1173–4 he was attempting to acquire Northumberland, where he had hopes of 'lordship in castle and keep'. He began a war of sieges. His siegecraft was not perfect (one machine killed some of his own men, in an incident similar to that described above in a distant Baltic siege thirty years later), but the war was recognizably the same kind of war as took place in contemporary France or Germany. Alongside his unarmoured native levies, he had his own knights and many Flemish mercenaries. When we read of the fight at Alnwick, where the king was captured, we hear of how the

Scots king is *pruz* and *hardi* – the classic chivalric terms of praise – how knights of Scotland are *mult bons vassaus* ('fine vassals') and how they fight the English knights with a kind of mutual respect until they are forced to surrender and await ransom; one of the duels between the Scottish and English knights is described as follows:

William de Mortimer greatly distinguished himself on that day. He sweeps through the ranks like a mad boar. He deals a succession of great blows and takes as good as he gives. He found himself up against a resolute knight, Lord Bernard de Balliol . . . he brought him and his charger to the ground, and he put him on parole as is customary with a knight. Lord Bernard shows himself to advantage and incurs no censure. At the end of the battle he will be praised who smites best with the sword and does the most fighting.

The only thing that distinguishes the Scottish and English knights here is the fact that they are on opposite sides. According to one account, King William at first mistook the English attackers for some of his own men returning from plundering; this is a clear indication of how similar in appearance the heavy cavalry of the two sides had become. The point was completely taken by the Galwegians. For them the English and Norman immigrant aristocracy were as much the enemy as the men south of the border. As soon as they heard of King William's capture at Alnwick, they rose, destroyed all the new castles that had been built in Galloway and killed all the newcomers they could find. It was an action that reveals the savagery of the struggle generated within Scotland by the impact of a new aristocracy – even an aristocracy invited by the dynasty – bearing a new technique of war. Nevertheless, the future lay with the incomers. In the thirteenth century a Scots force of armoured men and crossbowmen asserted Scottish authority over the 'unarmoured and naked' Manxmen. By the fourteenth century descendants of Norman knights ruled Scotland as kings.

The process that took place in Scotland between the eleventh and fourteenth centuries is paralleled in other countries. Pomerania, for example, which was the home of a lightly armoured, slave-raiding and politically decentralized people in the late eleventh century, transformed itself over the course of the twelfth and thirteenth centuries. As the native dynasty invited in numerous German knights, granted them land and availed itself of their military services, it strengthened its own hold and ensured that Pomerania, like Scotland, would be able to survive pressure from other powers. The charters of the Pomeranian princes in the first half of the thirteenth century, as the number of German knights among the witnesses grows year by year, remind us of documents like the grant of Annandale discussed in Chapter 2 above – a record distant in time and place but shaped by the same general forces and requirements.

In the Scandinavian kingdoms, as in Scotland, military change was accomplished without alien conquest. The Danish civil wars of the 1130s mark the introduction of German heavy cavalry and siege techniques into Scandinavia: Saxons built siege machines at Roskilde in 1133, and three hundred German *milites . . . fortissimi* took part in the battle of Fotevik in the following year; but this introduction of foreign military personnel and technique was securely under the aegis of native rulers. Though there was fierce struggle between innovators and traditionalists, Scandinavian dynasties and aristocracies preserved their power and their independence throughout the period of military transformation.

The recruitment of Norman knights by the kings of Scotland, or of German knights by the rulers of Pomerania or Denmark, can be explained on two complementary levels. One, the more general, is that the employment of foreign fighters had certain attractions for any medieval prince. None of them was interested in the development of a national state, but all were eager to secure and expand their military power. The obvious way to do this was to recruit fighting men and reward them. There was no good reason why recruitment should be limited by political boundaries and, indeed, there were some clear advantages to be gained from enlisting warriors from other domains. Such men would be, initially at least, entirely dependent on the prince they served. They would have no local aristocratic or territorial ties to complicate their loyalties or to provide them with the capacity to be rivals. They would be mobile and keen to prove themselves and win their rewards. It is not surprising, then, that the military retinues of many great lords of the Middle Ages had a strong component of foreign soldiers. In areas such as Scotland or the West Slav lands, however, these general considerations were reinforced by specific ones: here the incomers brought superior techniques of war. This explains the coming of the Anglo-Normans to Scotland and the role of German *hospites* in Poland, Bohemia, Hungary and other parts of eastern Europe in the twelfth to fourteenth centuries. In the words of one Hungarian cleric: 'As immigrants come from various lands, so they bring with them various languages and customs, various skills and forms of armament, which adorn and glorify the royal household and quell the pride of external powers. A kingdom of one race and custom is weak and fragile.'

It would be simplistic, of course, to try to explain the political map of Europe in 1300 solely in terms of the impact of a particular military

The Making of Europe

technology. Other factors often made a decisive difference. Not to mention underlying demographic and economic forces, there are many political and cultural considerations to be weighed. The early dynastic unity of Scotland, as contrasted with Wales and Ireland, was vital. In eastern Europe the date of conversion to Christianity shaped the political fortunes of peoples – those who converted early (by 1000) survived into the later Middle Ages as kingdoms, while the others did not. As one might expect, the military interacted with the political rather than determined it. Nevertheless, one central strand is formed by the story of how heavy cavalry, castles and superior ballistics diffused from their heartland between the Loire and the Rhine to the courts and retinues of Irish kings and Lithuanian dukes.

4. The Image of the Conqueror

—————

The charter of the sword – what better one is there?

As the military aristocracy of western Europe extended its lordship outwards in the eleventh, twelfth and thirteenth centuries, its members created not only conquest states and colonial societies, but also representations of themselves and their enterprises. These images of conqueror and conquest are enshrined in the histories and charters that their clerical brothers and cousins drew up and in the songs and stories that the aristocracy composed and enjoyed. Written memorials of this kind record the words and gestures of famous conquerors. They elaborate a terminology and rhetoric of expansionary violence. Mythic motifs recur: the first coming of the conquerors; the figure of the heroic military pioneer, perhaps a poor knight or noble, who took the gamble of foreign conquest; the superhuman exploits of the new men. What emerges from such records is the self-image of the conqueror.

The conqueror was a man with a special set of drives, certain patterns of emotion. Those classic image-makers, the early chroniclers of the Norman conquest in southern Italy (Geoffrey Malaterra, William of Apulia, Amatus of Monte Cassino), do not ascribe Norman success to numbers or to technical advantages, but to a series of psychological characteristics. The Normans formed a small island of northerners in a sea of Lombards, Greeks and Muslims, but they had mental qualities that gave them an edge. First was their energy (*strenuitas*). This is a theme particularly prominent in the pages of Malaterra, who writes of the energy of the Hauteville clan, the leaders of the Norman enterprise; of Norman chiefs who are 'energetic in arms'; of men who 'obtained the favour of all through their energy'; of a pre-battle harangue in which the Normans are urged 'be mindful of the much praised energy of our ancestors and our race, which we have maintained unto the present'; and of Greek fear of subjugation 'by the energy of our men'. Robert Guiscard's invasion of the Byzantine mainland in 1081 showed his 'great daring and knightly energy'.

As well as being vigorous, the Normans are courageous, the 'toughest of soldiers' (*fortissimi milites*), according to Malaterra, who always 'fight bravely' (*fortiter agentes*). The text of Amatus of Monte Cassino survives only in a later French translation, but there is perhaps a case to be made that the French captures much of the spirit – and perhaps the terminology – of the early days of the Norman venture. He describes 'knights of great prowess' (*fortissimes chevaliers*) who dominate southern Italy from their centre at Aversa – 'the city of Aversa, full of chivalry' (*plene de chevalerie*) – and relates how 'the honour of the Normans grew each day and the knights of great prowess multiplied each day'. 'To tell the truth,' he writes disarmingly, 'the boldness and prowess (*la hardiesce et la prouesce*) of these few Normans was worth more than the whole multitude of the Greeks.' He praises their 'courage' (*corage*), 'boldness' (*hardiesce*) and 'valour' (*vaillantize*) and has even the Byzantine emperor speaking of 'the boldness and strength of this people of Normandy'.

For these pro-Norman chroniclers the arrival of the Normans represented a quite new force on the scene, the coming of a people distinguished, above all, by military prowess – 'the people of Gaul, more powerful than any people in the force of arms', as William of Apulia put it. During the Sicilian campaign of 1040, when the Normans served as mercenaries of the Byzantines, the bravest of the Muslims of Messina routed the Greek contingent: 'Then it was the turn of our men. The Messinese had not yet experienced our prowess and attacked fiercely at first, but when they realized they were being pressed much harder than usual, they turned tail in flight from this new race's warfare.' This 'new race' changed the rules and expectations of warfare.

Part of the change was towards a new cruelty, brutality and bloodthirstiness, for savagery was as important a part of the image as vigour and valour. The 'ferocious Normans', as William of Apulia called them, had a reputation. To the local Lombard princes they seemed 'a savage, barbarous and horrible race of inhuman disposition'. It was an image that was carefully cultivated. An incident which demonstrates the calculated brutality of the Norman leaders occurred during a dispute between Normans and Greeks over booty. A Greek envoy came to the camp. One of the Normans standing nearby fondled his horse's head. Then, suddenly, 'so that the envoy should have something terrifying to report back to the Greeks about the Normans, he struck the horse in the neck with his naked fist, knocking it half-lifeless to the ground with one blow'. The insolent and hair-raising destruction of the envoy's horse (he was immediately given an even better one) was intended to convey a message: the Normans do not shrink from bloodcurdling violence. An even more remarkable piece of planned terror took place after the Norman leader Count Roger defeated the men of Palermo at some distance from their town, in 1068. The Muslims had brought with them in their baggage messenger pigeons, which now fell into the Normans' hands. Roger had them released to fly back to Palermo, where the women and children waited for news. They bore accounts of the Norman victory. The accounts were written in the blood of the dead Muslims.

The purpose of this suddenly unleashed savagery, a controlled use of the uncontrollable, was to win submission. It is not depicted as simple anarchy or brutal self-expression. The violence was intended to alert the local population to the presence of new players on the scene, players who were determined to be winners. In another passage from William of Apulia we read of Robert Guiscard's first irruption into Calabria:

> Everywhere the Norman race had a renowned name,
> But, not yet having experienced their power,
> The Calabrians were terrified at the arrival
> Of such a ferocious leader. Robert, supported
> By many soldiers, commanded looting and fire
> To be made everywhere in the land which they assailed. It was to be devastated
> And everything done which might bring fear to the inhabitants.

Likewise, when he besieged the city of Cariati, it was 'so that its fall should strike terror into the other cities'. The rationale is clear: there must be 'something terrifying to report about the Normans'. Surrounded on all sides by enemies far more numerous, only a reputation for 'innate military ferocity' could tip the balance.

The goal of terror was wealth and lordship; and just as the Normans and their memorialists were clear-headed about their own violence, so they spoke unabashedly about their acquisitiveness:

They spread here and there through various parts of the world, in various regions and countries ... this people set out and left behind small fortune in order to acquire a greater. And they did not follow the custom of many who go through the world, and enter the service of others, but, like the ancient knights, they wished to have everybody subject to them and under their lordship. They took arms and broke the bond of peace and performed great feats of war and knighthood.

With these words Amatus sketches out a picture of a wandering military breed, whose goals were wealth and domination. Malaterra strikes the same note: 'The Normans are a crafty race, they always revenge wrongs done to them, they prefer foreign fields to their own in the hope of gain, they are greedy for booty and power.' 'Greedy for lordship' is the phrase Malaterra uses to describe the Hauteville clan. Count Roger, one of its most successful members, has 'an inborn desire for lordship'.

The series of images and the complex of emotions and qualities that marked representations of the conquering Normans in southern Italy in the eleventh century were not limited to that historical context. Other writers who dealt with the activities of the expansionary aristocracy also played with these terms and images. Orderic Vitalis, the chronicler of the Normans at the high point of their expansionary movement, uses the word *strenuus* and its cognates 142 times. The mixed army of Normans, English, Flemings and Germans that besieged Lisbon in 1147 is depicted as receiving the following eulogy from its ally, the king of Portugal: 'We know well and have learned by experience that you are tough and vigorous and men of great industry.' The Normans' self-praise, of course, put such eulogies into the shadow. Their leader at Lisbon, Hervey de Glanville, is reported as saying:

Who does not know that the Norman race refuses no effort in the continual exercise of its power? Its warlikeness is ever hardened by adversity, it is not easily upset by difficulties nor, when difficulties have been overcome, does it allow itself to be conquered by slothful inactivity, for it has learned always to shake off the vice of sloth with activity.

In another passage from the same account of the capture of Lisbon, words are put into the mouths of the Muslims besieged in the city: 'It is not poverty that is driving you,' they say to the Frankish army, 'but inner ambition.' This 'inner ambition' (*mentis . . . ambitio*), a psychological striving that surpassed simple economic need, is also hinted at in another passage in Orderic Vitalis. After the failure of the Norman campaign against the Byzantines in 1107, one of the army supposedly says to their leader, Bohemond, the son of Robert Guiscard: 'No hereditary right drew us to this daring attempt . . . but desire to rule in the domains of another persuaded you to undertake such a difficult task . . . and desire for gain enticed us.'

The energy, brutality and appetite for domination described by the western chroniclers appear also in the characterization of the western European conquerors by Muslim and Greek observers, and the fact that the image was taken on board by their enemies suggests that the western European military aristocrats really did exhibit perceptible differences of behaviour. The image is, of course, a representation, a carefully presented self, but it was no mere literary topos. The psychology of the conquerors, their self-image, the self they presented, the selves that their clerical cousins depicted and the selves that their enemies perceived form an interlocking network.

Naturally, the image is less favourable when recorded by those who suffered from the violence and vigour, but it is recognizably the victims' version of the same array of attributes that the Norman historians give us. Memorialists of the Norman conquest of southern Italy like Amatus of Monte Cassino recurrently associate the Greek enemies with unwarlikeness and femaleness. In the very first encounter of Normans and Greeks, for example, the northerners 'see that they are like women', and in one harangue their leader says: 'I will lead you against feminine men' (*homes feminines*). What is striking about this contrast between the manly energy of the Normans and the effeminacy of the Byzantines is that it clearly corresponded to a difference between the social psychology of the two groups that the Greeks themselves recognized – though of course they did not put it in the same words.

Anna Comnena, daughter of the Byzantine emperor Alexius (1081–1118), in her *Alexiad*, paints a famous portrait of the western knights, including Normans from Sicily, who marched through Constantinople on their way to the Holy Land. Her father, the emperor, she writes, heard of the imminent arrival of 'countless Frankish armies': 'He was alarmed at their approach, for he was acquainted with their unchecked passion, their instability of mind . . . and how, as they were always gaping for wealth, they would casually disregard their agreements at the slightest excuse.' Their impetuousness and unpredictability were linked, however, with a manic irresistibility: 'the Celtic race [as she often termed the westerners] is, in any case, extremely reckless and impetuous, but when they have occasion, they are irresistible'. Their greed was part of the same complex of conquest characteristics: 'The Latin race is, in any case, avaricious, but when they intend to overrun a country, they are unbridled and know no reason.' Western armies showed a berserk readiness to grapple with their enemies:

The Celtic race is independent, does not seek counsel and never employs good military order or skill, but whenever battle and war occur, there is a baying in their hearts and they cannot be held back. Not only the soldiers but also their leaders fling themselves irresistibly into the midst of the enemy ranks.

As Anna Comnena notes, the martial competitiveness of the western leaders was of one cloth with that of their fighting men – the implicit distinction between skilful generals eyeing the battle from a distance and soldiers grappling in the mêlée did not apply. As the Muslim emir Usamah ibn Munqidh, another non-western observer of the crusaders, put it: 'Among the Franks no quality is more highly esteemed in a man than military prowess.' 'Each of the Celts,' wrote Anna, 'desired to surpass the others'; and it was personal, physical violence that was the key to success in this competitive military society. Robert Guiscard, she noted, 'had a heart full of passion and anger and among his enemies he expected that either he would drive through his opponent with his spear or himself be destroyed'. His son, Bohemond, for whom Anna felt fascination as well as loathing, 'was harsh and savage . . . and his very laughter made others shudder'. The rage and bombast exhibited by Tancred, Bohemond's nephew, showed him 'acting like his race'. These men are recognizably the rough heroes depicted by the Norman chroniclers. Anna Comnena would have acknowledged the justice of Malaterra's epithets for Guiscard: 'in everything he was the boldest and most daring striver after great things'.

The Greeks looked at the westerners and saw an irrational, barbaric drive for power – 'bloodthirsty and warlike men', in the words of the historian Michael Attaleiates. The Muslim gentleman Usamah wrote of 'the Franks . . . animals possessing the virtues of courage and fighting, but nothing else'. Vigour, boldness, brutality and greed: this was the Faustian brew that made up the conqueror. They were ingredients with a long future ahead of them.

CONQUEST AND THE IMAGINATION: TIME, MEMORY, THE PAST

The victorious and often dramatic advance of western military power in the High Middle Ages, which took small conquering élites to Palestine, to Greece, to Andalusia, to Ulster, to Prussia, and the outward migration of rural and urban settlers that accompanied it, produced an outlook of confident expectation. The Frankish warriors came to see themselves as men 'to whom God has given victory as a fief'. They anticipated an expansionary future and developed what can only be called an expansionary mentality. The experience of successful conquest and colonization imprinted itself upon the minds of princes, lords and clerics, so that they came to expect or anticipate that the future would see more new lordships created by force, more planned clearance and settlement, ever more income from tribute, taxes, rent and tithes.

A sure sign of this confidence about further expansion is the existence of many prospective, speculative or anticipatory grants and titles. There was a futures market among the medieval aristocracy. The tone is caught very well by the title that Robert Guiscard, the Norman conqueror of southern Italy, bore from 1059: 'By the grace of God and St Peter, duke of Apulia and Calabria and, with their help, future duke of Sicily'. Frequently documents were drawn up which carefully allocated the as yet only envisaged conquests. In 1150, for example, the king of Castile and the count of Barcelona made an agreement 'concerning the land of Spain which the Saracens hold at present', and by its terms the count was to hold Valencia and Murcia, when acquired, in return for homage to the king. In this case the division of the spoils was a little premature, for within a decade the Almohads had rolled down from the Moroccan hills and the Christians were engaged in desperate defensive warfare. The count of Barcelona's descendants did not attain their goals of 1150 until the 1230s and 1240s. An expansionary mentality does not, of course, guarantee expansion. Nevertheless, the frequency of such grants argues for a generalized expectation among both lay and ecclesiastical aristocrats that there would be future expansion.

The military orders were particularly avid recipients of such prospective grants, in all three theatres in which they fought – the eastern Mediterranean, the Iberian peninsula and the Baltic. The crusading prince Raymond III of Tripoli granted the Hospitallers rights over the Muslim city of Homs in 1185, even at the very time when Saladin was gradually closing his grip on the Crusader States. The Spanish kings regularly made speculative grants to the orders and also to individual churches. When Raymond Berengar IV of Aragon-Catalonia made substantial grants to the Templars in 1143, he specified: 'I concede to you quit and free a tithe of whatever I will be able to acquire justly with God's help and I concede to you a fifth of conquered Saracen land.' In the late eleventh century Sancho Ramírez of Aragon granted to a French monastery a tithe of the tribute paid to him by the Muslims of Ejea and Paradilla and added: 'when God in his holiness gives those villages to holy Christendom, the mosques of both villages will be made into churches for God and St Mary of Sauve-Majeure'. The expansion of Latin Christendom was clearly not only visible to contemporaries but seen as a process with a future. In one instance in the Baltic region the crusading knights seem to have been slightly too avid. Henry of Livonia recounts how the Swordbrothers, the military order established to pursue the crusade in Livonia (the eastern Baltic region), sought from the bishop of Riga 'a third part of the whole of Livonia and also of the other lands and peoples in the area which were not yet converted but which the Lord would in the future subject to holy Christendom through them and the other men of Riga'. The bishop was not in agreement: 'a man cannot give what he does not possess', he argued, and the knights had to be content with a third of the lands already acquired only. More often, however, local potentates were quite happy to give what they did not possess. They believed, along with William the Conqueror, that 'that man will certainly conquer the enemy who can bestow not only what is his own but also what belongs to the enemy'.

Prospective grants were also common in Ireland and Wales. Kings of England would grant a baron 'all the lands and holdings which he has acquired or which in future he will be able to acquire from our Welsh enemies' or 'all the lands he can conquer from the Welsh the king's enemies'. Large-scale speculative grants were made of lands ruled by Irish kings. On one notorious occasion Connacht was granted to an Anglo-Norman lord and to the native king of Connacht on the same day. On a much more local scale lords made grants like that of Nicholas de Verdon of tithes 'from two knight's fees in the first castlery that I shall establish in my land of Uriel' or the knight Roelinus of 'all the churches . . . and tithes . . . of all my conquest that I have acquired or will be able to acquire in Ireland'. The Normans in Italy were similarly optimistic. Their leader in the mid–eleventh century, William Iron Arm, offered to share with the prince of Salerno 'the land already acquired and that yet to be acquired'. When Robert Guiscard and his brother Roger resolved their differences, the agreement was that Roger should have half of Calabria, 'which had been acquired or which was to be acquired, as far as Reggio'. Prospective conquest reached even into the dream world. A monk of Benevento dreamed of two fields full of people, one larger and one smaller. A helpful exegete explained: 'The people are those whom God's majesty has subjected to Robert Guiscard; the larger field is that of the people who shall be subject to him, but are not yet.' The dream logic here provided quite literally new fields for conquest.

The conquerors and colonizers who spread outwards from western Europe into the continental peripheries in the High Middle Ages thus looked forward to an expansionary future. When they looked back they saw formative periods of conquest and settlement. The conquerors recognized that their right lay in conquest and was not aboriginal, and indeed, celebrated that fact. For the descendants of a conquest aristocracy the conquest became mythologized as a founding moment and a defining breach in time. William of Apulia expressed his purpose in writing *The Deeds of Robert Guiscard* in the following words:

As a poet of modern times, I will undertake to proclaim the deeds of men of
   modern times.
My purpose is to tell under whose command the Norman people
Came to Italy, how they came to stay there
And under which chiefs they attained victory in the land.

The moment of the taking of possession of the land became a point of
orientation around which memory and the past were organized. 'Oh, time
so longed for! Oh, time remembered among all others!' wrote one French
cleric of the seizure of Jerusalem by the crusaders in 1099, and it was not
unknown for later writers in the kingdom of Jerusalem to date events from
'the liberation of the city', but this was only the most extreme example of a
heroic *Landnahme*. The elaborate dating of the capture of cities in the
chronicle records underscores the dramatic new beginning that conquest
was deemed to represent. The margrave of Brandenburg's capture of his
titular city was recorded in the following words: 'in the year of the
incarnation of the Lord 1157, on 11 June, the margrave, by God's mercy,
took possession as victor of the city of Brandenburg'. Similar triumphal
entrances and fresh starts are found in Spanish historiography:

It was the day of the translation of St Isidore of León, who was archbishop of
Seville, in the [Spanish] era one thousand, two hundred and eighty-six, when it
was the year of the incarnation of our lord Jesus Christ one thousand, two hundred
and forty-eight, when the noble and fortunate king Don Ferdinand entered into
this noble city of Seville.

Those who were present at these new beginnings were rapidly
mythologized and given special standing in the collective memory. Jurors
in a lawsuit of 1299 in Ireland could refer back a hundred years to the
actions of 'Roger Pipard, a conqueror at the first conquest of Ireland',
while when Geoffrey de Genneville, the lord of Meath, ratified his barons'
privileges in the last quarter of the thirteenth century, he did so after
'hearing and understanding the charters and records of my magnates of
Meath and their ancestors, those, namely, who first came into Ireland with
Hugh de Lacy to his conquest'. Participation in the conquest could indeed
be the basis of special status, as in the Greek Morea (the Peloponnesian
peninsula), conquered by Frankish knights in the aftermath of the Fourth
Crusade of 1204, where there was a specially privileged group of 'barons of
the conquest'. These were descendants of those who had been enfeoffed at
the time of 'the acquisition of the Principality'. They had the right to
dispose of their fiefs by testament, whereas other, less privileged fiefs
escheated to the lord on failure of direct heirs. There is a case of one

rebellious vassal, as a punishment, having his fief converted from one status to the other, 'so that, in future, he could not hold it as of conquest' (*tenir de conqueste*). In its very name, this privileged baronial tenure continually recalled the founding moment of conquest and the peers who had participated in it. 'The law of the Morea,' as one expert put it, 'is dominated by the fact of the conquest.'

Memories of such expeditions of conquest might provide a foundation charter for a rough aristocratic egalitarianism. If the formative stage of a policy were represented as a dangerous enterprise in which all participants alike shared risks and gambled on rewards, then descendants of the conquerors could resist monarchical pressure by appealing to that primitive joint venture. The Frankish Morea produced just such a vision. When he was imprisoned by the Byzantine emperor and being pressed to cede his territories, William de Villehardouin, prince of the Morea, expressed this precise if tendentious conception:

Now this land of Morea, my lord, I do not hold as my patrimony, nor as land inherited from my grandfathers to hold it with the power to give it away and make a gift of it. The land was conquered by those nobles who came here to Romania from France with my father as his friends and comrades. They conquered the land of Morea by the sword and they divided it among themselves by the weights upon the scales; each was given according to his rank, and afterwards all of them together elected my father . . . and made him commander . . . Therefore, lord basileus, I do not have the power to give away one jot from the land which I hold, for my progenitors won it by the sword in accordance with our usages.

Exactly parallel arguments emerged in other conquest states and lordships. 'My ancestors came with William the Bastard and conquered their lands with the sword,' objected the earl Warenne when challenged by Edward I's *quo warranto* judges. 'The king did not conquer and subject the land by himself, but our forebears were sharers and partners with him.' When the same king challenged the regalian status of the earl of Gloucester in his Welsh lordship of Glamorgan the earl responded 'that he holds these lands and liberties by his and his ancestors' conquest'.

Conquests produced a 'law of conquest' which was more elaborate than a mere law of the jungle. When the Christians took possession of Jerusalem in 1099 they seized the houses in the city by a regulated right of conquest:

After the great massacre, they entered the houses of the citizens, carrying off whatever they found in them. Whoever first entered the house, whether he were rich or poor, was not to be harmed by anyone else in any way, but took, held and possessed the house or palace and whatever he found in it as if his very own. They established this rule to be held between them.

In the twelfth century the Muslim emir, Usamah, describes how the Christians captured a city and then 'took possession of the houses, and each one of them put the sign of the crucifix over one house and planted over it his flag'.

A strong awareness of the conquest as a rupture naturally implied the image of a time before the conquest, before the arrival of the conqueror, when the land had other possessors and occupants. This consciousness of dispossessed precursors is reflected in the use in charters of such phrases as 'in the time of the Irish' in Ireland, 'in the time of the Moors' and 'in the time of the Saracens' in Spain or 'in the time of the Greeks' in Venetian Crete. On at least one dizzying occasion, the phrase 'in the time of the Saracens' was used in a prospective grant: after its conquest from the Muslims, the count of Barcelona was to hold the city of Denia (south of Valencia) 'with all its appurtenances and with all that demesne that the Saracens might have in the time of the Saracens'. Here the men who drafted the charter not only looked to the future but saw themselves in the future looking back at the past – which was, of course, their own present.

The picture that etched itself into the minds of the conquerors and new settlers thus contained a strong image of what might be loosely called 'those days' – the days before the new and current dispensation. Naturally a vital question was the status of legal rights claimed from 'those days'. Men pondered whether the conquest had created a jural *tabula rasa*, an entirely new start, or whether possessions and privileges from before the dramatic moment of fissure might still have some validity in the new age. In Ireland, for example, the exact legal significance of the conquest was important in defining property rights. Churches that predated the coming of the Anglo-Normans were anxious to secure confirmations of the lands and grants they had received before the crucial moment, which was variously termed 'the coming of the English', 'the conquest of Ireland by the English', 'the coming of the Franks into Ireland', 'the arrival of the English and the Welsh in Ireland' (this from a Henry fitz Rhys!) or, most precise of all, 'the first arrival of Earl Richard [Strongbow] in Ireland'. In 1256 the bishops of the province of Tuam and their tenants complained 'that they are impleaded concerning lands which they and their predecessors have held peacefully in the time of the lord Henry, the king's grandfather [i.e. Henry II], and from the conquest by the English and even before their arrival in Ireland'. The royal ruling on the issue brushed aside the relevance of tenure before the conquest:

On this subject it is provided and ordained that if any plaintiff bases his plea upon the seisin of his ancestors before the time of Henry the king's grandfather and before the conquest by the English and makes no mention of seisin in the time of the king's grandfather or after the time of the conquest, he shall fail in his case and lose his right by that very fact.

Establishing the exercise of a right 'since the conquest' was a winning argument in Irish legal affairs. It was the limit of legal memory. Similarly, in Wales, royal attorneys dismissed claims based on the charters of the native princes with the sweeping argument that 'the land of Wales is a land of conquest . . . and through this conquest all the liberties and possessions of everyone were annulled and joined and annexed to the Crown of England'. Even in those lordships where native dynasties were not conquered but themselves presided over the implantation of a new aristocracy and a social transformation there was a strong awareness of a fissure in time. When one of the dukes of Mecklenburg, a descendant of pagan Slav princes who had successfully weathered the storm of German aristocratic, burgess and peasant immigration in the thirteenth century, came to confirm the liberties of his vassals, he did so by endorsing 'the right that their fathers and ancestors have enjoyed since the new plantation'. The 'new plantation' (*novella plantacio*) was the 'fresh start' in the history of the region, strongly etched in the minds of those who came after.

THE LITERATURE OF CONQUEST

Conquest and colonization could thus be represented as a dramatic and formative process and often appeared to participants (or victims) as a distinct, fateful and perhaps heroic story. The very first generation of settlers told tales of their arrival in the new land, portrayed the villains and heroes of the early years and picked out certain moments for mythic treatment. Hence a body of tale, legend and memory was generated, part of which is recoverable because it was transmitted in writing. The conquerors and immigrants produced a literature of conquest.

The corpus of representations of conquest that were spawned in the High Middle Ages in prose and verse sometimes played a formative part in literary history. French prose, for example, begins as a literature of conquest. Its very earliest examples are two works written in the decade after 1210.

One is Robert of Clari's French prose account of the Fourth Crusade, which opens with the words: 'Here begins the history of those who conquered Constantinople and afterwards we shall tell you who they were and for what reason they went there.' Equally an example of explanatory conquest literature is Geoffrey de Villehardouin's *Conquest of Constantinople*, composed by one of the leaders of that expedition, and couched in heavily apologetic mode. From approximately the same period comes the vernacular translation of William of Tyre's *Chronicle* describing the establishment and the history of the Crusader States, a work which, along with a French continuation which may be even earlier, was known to contemporaries as 'The Book of Conquest' (*Livre dou conqueste*).

Within twenty years of the coming of the Anglo-Normans to Ireland in 1169 Gerald of Wales had composed his *Conquest of Ireland* (*Expugnatio Hibernica*), a highly partial account of how his relatives had 'stormed the ramparts of Ireland'. As a member of one of the leading families involved in the venture, Gerald could draw on the memories of his uncles and cousins, who had been battling in Ireland for twenty years. Their 'noble deeds could promise each of them an eternal memorial of praise', he wrote; and this history is a family epic of conquest, comparable in many respects to the works written by the historians of the Norman venture in southern Italy in the eleventh and twelfth centuries. As a pendant to Gerald's work stands another heroic account of the same deeds, but in a different genre, that of French rhymed chronicle rather than Latin history. The *Song of Dermot and the Earl*, as it has been christened, is written in 3,500 rhyming octosyllabic lines. It has many of the trappings of so-called oral literature, such as apostrophizing the audience ('Lord barons . . . know that . . .'), protesting the truth of its story ('sanz mentir', 'de verite', etc.), in particular through the invocation of a source ('solum le dist de mun cuntur', 'Cum nus recunte le chanson') and repeating lines ('They sent everywhere for physicians / To heal the sick: / To heal their wounded / They sent everywhere for physicians'). Its exact date of composition and its author are debated questions, but the *Song* was probably put into its present form in the first quarter of the thirteenth century, though drawing on good information from the 1170s.

Curiously, the establishment of a German colony in the eastern Baltic, which began a few decades after the Anglo-Norman incursion into Ireland, is also recorded in both the Latin prose of a clerical chronicler and a rhymed vernacular account. The Latin account, equivalent to Gerald's in that respect, is Henry of Livonia's *Chronicle*, which records the establishment of the Germans in Livonia year by year from the last decades of the twelfth century to 1227. Unlike Gerald, Henry had a discernible sympathy for the native people and considered himself as much a missionary as a colonist. He criticizes the harshness of the German lay judges 'who exercised their office more to fill their purses than with respect to God's justice'; and he gives long and sympathetic treatment to the visit of the papal legate, William of Sabina, who 'exhorted the Germans not to place a yoke of intolerable weight upon the shoulders of the neophytes, but rather the yoke of the Lord, light and sweet'. The birth pangs of the new colony in Livonia, and its subsequent history, are also recorded in rhyming German couplets in the *Livländische Reimchronik*, written late in the thirteenth century, probably by a member of the Teutonic Order. The existence of parallel Latin and vernacular texts for both the Irish and Livonian enterprises gives a particular richness to the evidence when we examine the self-representation of a colonial society in the early days of its establishment.

All conquest literature seeks to explain to the conquerors 'why we are here'. The *Song of Dermot* does this in highly personalized terms. The Irish king Dermot steals away the beautiful wife of his rival O'Rourke, with her connivance, and O'Rourke, 'to avenge his shame' (*sa hunte . . . venger*), allies himself with O'Connor, the High King, to attack Dermot. Many of Dermot's tributaries abandon their lord at this moment: the author of the *Song* castigates these men for their *traisun* and labels them *felun* and *traitur*. Betrayed and exiled, Dermot seeks refuge in England, complaining that 'wrongfully my own people have cast me out of my kingdom'. With the consent of the king of England, a body of Anglo-Norman knights and barons agrees to help Dermot. Shortly thereafter the English land in Ireland and begin the task of subduing the traitors. The story of the abduction of the beautiful Devorguilla and the need for revenge was a theme that would have moved the feudal aristocracy whether or not they knew the plot of the *Iliad*. The portrayal of the first Anglo-Normans in Ireland as knightly adventurers, helping a 'courteous king' regain his inheritance from traitors, was one that the colonists could stomach. In addition, there is a more prosaic sense in which the poem legitimizes the English colonial aristocracy, for it contains a detailed account, over a hundred lines in length, of the distribution of lands to the first generation of settlers:

> Earl Richard then gave
> To Maurice fitzGerald –
> The Naas the good earl gave
> To fitzGerald with the whole honour.
> This is the land of Offelan

Which belonged to the traitor MacKelan.
He gave him Wicklow too
Between Bray and Arklow.
This was the land of Killmantain
Between Dublin and Wexford.
Twenty fiefs in Omurethy
The noble earl also
Gave to the warrior
Walter de Ridelesford.

This account of the subinfeudation of Leinster and Meath is a foundation charter and has even been described, perhaps over-enthusiastically, as 'a sort of original Domesday Book of the first Anglo-Norman settlement'.

The *Expugnatio Hibernica* of Gerald of Wales similarly answers the questions, who were the first Anglo-Normans in this island, and what are the roots of our colony? His partisanship is very specific, however, and not all invaders are heroes. He is the champion of a group within the conquering élite, the first wave, who came mainly from south Wales, and, in particular, of course, his own family. The text itself reveals the strain between this predilection for the fitzGeralds and the need to keep a wary eye on the chances of royal patronage – the work was dedicated to Richard the Lionheart of England and contains a eulogy of Henry II. In a passage with the rubric 'Praise of his family' (*Generis commendatio*), Gerald writes: 'O family, O race! Always suspect for your numbers and inborn energy (*innata strenuitas*). O family, O race! Capable by yourself alone of conquering any kingdom, if envy, begrudging them their vigour (*strenuitas*), had not descended from on high.' We can hear in this passage the grating discontent of a conquest aristocracy which felt itself bridled by the less than whole-hearted support it received from the English Crown. Despite – or because of – the tensions it expresses, the *Expugnatio* was a successful work. It survives in fifteen medieval manuscripts (excluding excerpts) and in the fifteenth century was translated into both English and Irish, the English version circulating quite widely in Ireland (six manuscripts). The work clearly continued to serve as a popular origin tale for the colony. Indeed, in the translation included in the revised version of Holinshed's *Chronicles* in 1587, it maintained this function into the Elizabethan and Stuart periods.

The situation in Livonia was different from that in Ireland, because there the colonists were Christian and the native peoples pagan. The author of the *Livländische Reimchronik* begins his poem not with a geographical or historical description of Livonia or the German crusades, but with the

Creation and Incarnation. For him this is the proper starting point. The wars undertaken by German knights in the thirteenth century did not appear as an episode in national history, but were part of the long process by which 'God's wisdom made Christendom wide' – the abstract and corporative nouns *kristenheit* and *kristentuom* are common. This explains why the poet selects Pentecost and the missions of the apostles for mention in the early lines of the poem. The conquest of Livonia, 'where no apostle ever came', is certainly a distinctive part of the story of the spread of the worship of Christ, but it is a *part*. In keeping with this emphasis, the German merchants and knights who came to Livonia in the late twelfth and thirteenth centuries are consistently referred to as 'Christians' (*die kristen*), and their opponents – although the poet distinguishes their various tribes precisely – can be generally characterized as 'pagans' (*die heiden*) and the abstract or collective *heidenschaft* counterposed to *kristenheit* and *kristentuom*. Although the *Reimchronik* is, in essence, a triumphalist epic of bloody wars, its framework is that expressed in the opening lines: 'now I will let you know how Christianity came to Livonia.'

Blended into the wider perspective of Christianization are the epic heroism and grim irony of Middle High German warrior literature. A raid on Jersika (Gercike) is described in the following jaunty manner: 'They came to Jersika early in the morning, broke into the castle and struck down many powerful men, so that they called "alas" and "alack". They woke many who were there sleeping and broke their heads. That was a knightly expedition!' Another passage describes how the Lithuanians 'slew many a powerful man who could well have defended himself if his luck had not run out', a classic example of that indirection and doom-ladenness so familiar in Germanic epic from *Beowulf* to the *Nibelungenlied*. The tale is one of endless fighting, punctuated carefully by reference to the succession of the masters of the Teutonic Order. The pagans can be heroes too, and fate for both Christian and pagan is hard: 'So you could see many an undismayed hero, powerful and distinguished, from both the Christians and the pagans, fall into grim death; the snow there was red with blood.'

Not all the memorials of conquest are pure triumphalism. While some did indeed speak for the conquering lay aristocracy, others, like the *Chronicle* of Henry of Livonia, voiced the concern of a missionary church. But it is clear that such work as the *Expugnatio Hibernica*, the *Song of Dermot and the Earl*, Henry of Livonia's *Chronicle* and the *Livländische Reimchronik* are colonial literature. They were written by immigrants, and the vernacular poems were in a language that had not been spoken in the area of composition a few generations before. The literary models on which they drew, the Latin prose history and the rhymed vernacular chronicle, were western European, French or English, not indigenous. They speak with varied voices, but they all have colonial accents. Like the image of the demonic personality presented by the Norman myth-makers and the dream of the new start in the conquered land propagated in law and legend, the eulogistic literature of conquest provided imaginative validation of conquest states and colonial societies. Here were the charters of the conquerors and colonizers.

NAMING

The final gift of conquest to the western European aristocracy was a name. For it was in the process of the dramatic expansionary enterprises of the eleventh, twelfth and thirteenth centuries that a shorthand term was popularized that had the connotation of 'aggressive westerner'. That term was 'Frank'.

The use and usefulness of the term are illustrated in the *De expugnatione Lyxbonensi*, a rousing account of the capture of Lisbon in 1147 by a crusading army of seamen and pirates from north-west Europe. The anonymous author, probably a priest from East Anglia, begins his story immediately by stressing the diversity of the fleet that mustered for the expedition: 'peoples of various races, customs and languages assembled at Dartmouth'. He then goes on to specify the main contingents: under the command of a nephew of the duke of Lower Lotharingia there were the men 'from the Roman Empire' – mostly, we later learn, inhabitants of Cologne; under a Flemish lord, the Flemings and the men of Boulogne; and, in four divisions headed by Anglo-French knights and English towns-men, were the men of the English ports. Subsequent references make it clear that the fleet also included Bretons and Scots. One of the reasons for the severity of the code of regulations which was adopted to govern the fleet was this ethnic and cultural heterogeneity.

The author of the account is continuously aware of these ethnic divisions. As is usual with such categories, they are not purely neutral. Ethnic characterization accompanied ethnic labelling: the Flemings are 'a fierce and untameable people'; the Scots have kept the regulations, 'even though no one would deny that they are barbarians'. Again, as is to be expected, the author's own ethnic group – 'our men, that is, the Normans and the English' – is eulogized. 'Who does not know that the Norman race refuses no effort in the exercise of continuous courage?'

The strength of these ethnic divisions is patent throughout the campaign. At every point there are quarrels and jealousies between the different groups. But this is not the whole story. There are two circumstances when something beyond diversity is described. First, the author sometimes wishes to employ a term that will apply to all the members of the expedition. He does have such a term: 'Franks'. 'Two churches were constructed by the Franks,' he writes, 'one by the men of Cologne and the Flemings, the other by the English and the Normans.' The 'Franks' in this passage are from three different kingdoms and speak three different languages (nor, it should be noted, did these political and linguistic divisions coincide). Nevertheless, this heterogeneous group of knights, sailors and their womenfolk, gathered from the ports of the Rhineland, the North Sea and the Channel, could plausibly and conveniently be termed 'Franks'.

Another person who found such a generic label useful was Affonso I of Portugal. Though, as discussed in Chapter 2, he was himself the son of an immigrant Frankish noble, a Burgundian who had prospered in the Iberian peninsula, he used the term as a handy description of these 'others'. If the anonymous author is accurate in his record, the king referred to this mixed German, Flemish, French, Norman and English fleet as 'the ships of the Franks'. After concluding written terms with them, he notified all of 'the agreement between me and the Franks' and promised them possession of Lisbon and its lands, if it fell, 'to be held according to the honourable customs and liberties of the Franks'.

Thus there are two closely related circumstances in which the general label 'Frank' was convenient. One was when a member of a body composed of various ethnic groups from western Europe wished to employ a label for the whole of this body; another when someone who conceived of himself as outside of that body (even if such externality was subjective, as in Affonso's case) wanted to give a group name to the foreigners. Thus both as self-appellation and as designation by others, 'Frank' was associated with the 'Frank away from home'. It was a term which had originated in a precise ethnic name but grew in the eleventh and twelfth centuries to refer to western Europeans or Latin Christians in general, especially when on the road or at sea.

The classic enterprise which stimulated the use of this term was the crusade, the 'Deeds of the Franks' as its earliest chronicler called it, and it seems to have been the First Crusade that gave the term a general currency. Prior to that period, of course, it already had a long history, first as an ethnic designation, later in association with a particular polity, the 'realm of the Franks' (*regnum Francorum*). The generalization of the name to cover all westerners was a fairly natural result of the virtual equivalence of the Carolingian empire and the Christian West in the ninth century and, also logically enough, seems to have been used in this way first by non-westerners. The Muslims denominated the inhabitants of western Europe *Faranǧa* or *Ifranǧa*. Tenth-century Muslims wrote of the land of the Franks as chilly but fertile, with inhabitants distinguished both by their bravery and by their lack of personal hygiene.

The Byzantines had plenty of contact, often frosty, with western powers and they, like the Muslims, seem to have labelled any westerners 'Franks' (φραγγοι). A particularly revealing exchange took place in the middle of the eleventh century, at the height of the quarrel between Michael Cerularius, patriarch of Constantinople, and the papacy. Cerularius had written a general letter to the western clergy, which had been translated into Latin. The address of the translation read: 'to all the chiefs of the priests and the priests of the Franks' – clearly the original Greek must have used a form of φραγγοι. The irascible cardinal Humbert of Silva Candida wrote an offended reply: 'You say you are writing to all the priests of the Franks . . . but not only the Romans and the priests of the Franks but also the whole Latin Church . . . calls out to contradict you.' Humbert seems to think the phrase 'the priests of the Franks' is intended as an ethnic circumscription, a meaning certainly not present in the original. It is not so much the contrast between 'the priests' and 'the whole . . . Church' that should be emphasized here, but the cardinal's assumption that the term 'Frank' limits, rather than being equivalent to, the term 'Latin'. He was writing at a time when this equation was made in the East but not yet in the West.

It seems to be the case that the vast and polyglot armies of the First Crusade picked up the term 'Frank' as a self-appellation from the non-westerners who already employed it in this general way. Eleventh-century Byzantine writers customarily referred to Norman mercenaries as 'Franks', and there was a natural case for applying the name to the western knights, including Normans, who arrived in Constantinople in 1096. The Muslims used the term so generally that Sigurd I of Norway, who came to the Holy Land in 1110, could be described as 'a Frankish king'. The crusaders were aware that this was their general appellation. 'The barbarians are accustomed to call all westerners Franks,' wrote Ekkehard of Aura; while the chaplain Raymond of Aguilers, attached to the household of Raymond of Toulouse on the First Crusade, made a careful distinction between the term as used by the crusaders themselves, with the meaning 'men from northern France' and the term as used in a general sense by 'the enemy'. Much later, in the thirteenth century, the same usage prevailed: 'all the people who live beyond the sea name all Christians "Frank", taking the term in a broad sense', wrote a Dominican observer of the Mongols, Simon of Saint Quentin. It was this 'broad sense' that westerners on the First Crusade came to be willing to apply to themselves.

As an expedition that brought together many different ethnic and linguistic groups and took them thousands of miles from their homelands, the crusade was clearly a forcing house for new identities. The crusaders were certainly 'pilgrims', but also 'pilgrim Franks'. The participants on the First Crusade equated 'our Franks' with 'the pilgrim knights of Christ', saw their triumphs as redounding 'to the honour of the Roman Church and the Frankish people' and gloried in how Jesus had brought victory to 'the pilgrim Church of the Franks'. When Baldwin I was crowned in Jerusalem in 1100, he thought of himself as 'first king of the Franks'. The name symbolized the desired transcendence of local and ethnic rivalries and rang down the years as the rallying cry of western Christian unity. Enmired in the quarrels and backbiting of the Third Crusade, the minstrel Ambroise looked back nostalgically to the solidarities of a hundred years earlier:

When Syria was recovered in the other war and Antioch besieged, in the great wars and battles against the Turks and miscreants, so many of whom were slaughtered, there was no plotting or squabbling, no one asked who was Norman or French, who Poitevin or Breton, who from Maine or Burgundy, who was Flemish or English . . . all were called 'Franks', be they brown or bay or sorrel or white.

The new generic term was not only of value on crusade, however, for it was also a convenient label for the migratory population spreading outwards from the central parts of western Europe whatever direction it was heading. Franks were, of course, particularly Franks when they were strangers, for the term was of limited reference when applied to the homelands of western Europe. Thus in the second half of the twelfth century we find mention of 'men living in Constantinople . . . whom they [the Greeks] called Franks, immigrants (*advene*) from every nation', while a settlement of colonists in Hungary was called 'the village of the immigrant Franks' (*villa advenarum Francorum*). The Celtic world also felt the impact of the Franks. Welsh chroniclers refer to the incursions of *Franci* or *Freinc* from the late eleventh to the early thirteenth centuries, and the Anglo-Norman enterprise in Ireland was, as we have seen, termed 'the coming of the Franks' (*adventus Francorum*).

For the rulers of the Celtic lands the Franks were not only rivals to be confronted but also models to be emulated. The O'Briens of Munster expressed their claim to dynastic supremacy by calling themselves 'the Franks of Ireland'. In Scotland the name had a similar resonance. Here the native dynasty presided over a radical reshaping of the bases of its own power in the twelfth century, which transformed the Scottish monarchy into a polity much more like its neighbours to the south. As part of this reorientation the Scottish kings assumed a new identity – as 'Franks'. 'The more recent kings of the Scots,' observed one early-thirteenth-century chronicler, 'regard themselves as Franks (*Franci*) in stock, manners, language and style, they have pushed the Scots down into slavery and admit only Franks into their household and service.' In the twelfth and thirteenth centuries to be a Frank implied modernity and power.

The term can be found at every edge of Latin Christendom. The trans-Pyrenean settlers who came into the Iberian peninsula in the late eleventh and twelfth centuries were Franks and enjoyed 'the law of Franks'. We know that Affonso I of Portugal approved the grant of specific privileges for foreign immigrants (the *forum Francorum*) and this would explain his familiarity with the concept when dealing with the crusading fleet in 1147. After the fall of Constantinople to the westerners in 1204, they established an empire in its place that could be called 'New Francia', and when Greeks submitted on terms to the new conquerors they might bargain for the right to be treated as 'privileged Franks' (φραγκοι εγκουσατοι). In eastern Europe immigrant settlements in Silesia, Little Poland and Moravia were endowed with 'Frankish law' or might use field measurements 'of the Frankish type'.

The term 'Frank' thus referred to westerners as settlers or on aggressive expeditions far from home. It is hence entirely appropriate that when the Portuguese and Spaniards arrived off the Chinese coasts in the sixteenth century, the local population called them *Fo-lang-ki*, a name adapted from the Arabic traders' *Faranǧa*. Even in eighteenth-century Canton the western barbarian carried the name of his marauding ancestors.

5. The Free Village

═══

It profits the commonwealth greatly to invite people from
various regions by the grant of liberties and good customs to
settle unpopulated places.

THE DEMOGRAPHIC BACKGROUND

The question of why Latin Christendom expanded in the High Middle
Ages leads naturally and simply to the question of whether its population
was increasing. Of course, population growth is neither a necessary nor a
sufficient condition for the expansion of a culture area; for technical and
organizational advantages, along with such intangibles as cultural prestige
and aggressive drives, can result in the dissemination of a culture without
much in the way of demographic change – the partial westernization of
Japan, for example, has taken place with absolutely negligible western
settlement. But the situation in medieval Europe was clearly different.
Migration certainly played a part in this expansion, and we are thus
justified in asking, at a very simple level, whether the population of Europe
was growing in this period and, if so, how fast and with what effects.

The historical evidence available to answer questions about population
trends in Europe varies from period to period. There are three epochs: the
last century or so, when national censuses and registration of births,
marriages and deaths make the application of sophisticated statistical
techniques pertinent and fruitful; the period between the sixteenth and the
nineteenth centuries, when local registration of baptisms, burials and marriages and the existence of many state-wide fiscal records enable detailed
analyses to be conducted, though sometimes only on a local scale or very
approximately; and, lastly, the ancient and medieval periods, when, generally speaking, the only figures available are rare, local, partial and
chronologically discontinuous. The High Middle Ages falls clearly into this
most intractable era of demographic history.

In these circumstances, analysis of the trends in the medieval European
population must be approached in a spirit of humility. Such figures as are
available must be used, of course, but they will never result in a statistical

demographic history. Moreover, in the absence of dependable statistical series, indirect or impressionistic evidence has to be squeezed as far as it can be. The nature of the evidence thus makes the task of the historical demographer of the High Middle Ages different in kind from that of his or her counterpart studying industrial Europe.

One need not be too pessimistic, however. The indirect or impressionistic evidence does all point in the same direction and it seems to indicate that the High Middle Ages was a time of growth in the European population. There is no doubt, for example, that towns were growing in number and size. In England alone 132 new planned urban settlements were established in the twelfth and thirteenth centuries. While the walls of Florence begun in 1172 enclosed 200 acres, those begun just a century later in 1284 enclosed more than 1,500 acres. By 1300 it is not impossible that some of the big western European cities were approaching a population size of 100,000. This dramatic urbanization is not absolutely unequivocal evidence but it makes easy sense against a background of demographic growth. Similar evidence for the clearance of new agricultural land points in the same direction. Everywhere the net of settlement and territorial organization – parish, lordship and bailiwick – was growing denser. Whole zones of Europe, especially in the east of the continent, experienced planned settlement on a large scale. And the economic indicators, such as prices, wages, rents and fineness of currency, though often hard to interpret, generally point to an expanding population. The 'strong inflationary pressures' of the thirteenth century, for example, have been explained by the fact that 'the increased population put pressure on the agricultural resources'.

The most dramatic exception to the general dearth of large-scale statistical sources in Europe in the period studied here is in the case of England. Domesday Book of 1086 and the Poll Tax returns of 1377 are both national in scope and survive virtually complete. They have proved sufficiently tempting to induce several historians into submitting to 'the lure of aggregates', the attempt to reach population figures for an entire kingdom. Naturally part of the attraction of these sources is that they relate to the same area (approximately) at an interval of 300 years. For our purposes, they are particularly alluring, since they date from early in the process of expansion and from soon after its end. Especially if one is willing to speculate on the size of the population a generation or two before the 1377 figures, that is, before the impact of the Black Death of 1348, one has the prospect of creating something like a 'before-and-after' picture. However, it may be that these sources are inadequate for such a reconstruction.

There is no doubt that both sources are fairly difficult to deal with. Neither of them is a census. The deduction of a possible population figure from either involves the introduction of guesswork. Domesday Book, for example, records a total population of 268,984. This is not the population of England in 1086. But there is room for doubt as to exactly what it is. Darby, in his magisterial study, lists some of the omissions that need to be rectified: the urban population, the inhabitants of the northern counties not covered by Domesday Book, etc. In addition, of course, there are likely to be simple mistakes and undercounting in the rural population of the areas that were covered. Moreover, and most important, the recorded population includes only heads of households, not individuals. Hence, in order to attain total population figures, this number must be multiplied by household size – the notorious and controversial 'multiplier'. Darby gives six different calculations, based on multipliers of 4, 4.5 and 5, and counting slaves either as individuals or as heads of households. The results range from 1.2 million to 1.6 million. It is safe to take the former figure as the minimum possible population for England in 1086. The maximum, however, is less certain. Postan pointed out that the population recorded in Domesday Book may not represent the heads of all households, but only those holding full peasant tenancies. An indeterminate number of landless men and subtenants would then have to be added to the total – perhaps increasing it by a half. If one takes Darby's maximum figure of 1.6 million and adds this hypothetical 50 per cent, the new maximum is 2.4 million.

The Poll Tax returns of 1377 present some similar problems. They record a population of 1,361,478 individuals of over fourteen years of age. In order to deduce the total population of England at its fourteenth-century peak from this figure, one must postulate (1) the level of evasion, (2) the proportion of the population under fourteen and hence exempt from tax and (3) the relation between this decimated post-plague population and the much higher population that must have existed before the coming of the plague. Each of these estimates can be no more than an educated guess. There is a general consensus that about a third of the English population died in the Black Death. There had been several recurrences between 1348 and 1377, however, and some would argue that the 1377 population might even have been as little as half that of the pre-plague peak. If we accept reduction by a third or by half as the extreme parameters, one can then feed in different calculations of the rate of evasion (including exemption and lost records) and the proportion of the population under fourteen. The latter figure, judging by the known capacities of the human animal and comparison with the age structure of other populations, was very likely between 35 per cent and 45 per cent. The evasion level is the most difficult to estimate, but a figure of 20 per cent to 25 per cent has been suggested and seems realistic. Very much lower figures are not plausible. On the basis of these guesses, one can construct a range of possibilities. If the evasion rate was low (20 per cent), the proportion of children low (35 per cent) and the loss from plague only one third, extrapolation from the 1377 figures produces a fourteenth-century peak of just under 4 million. If one makes the opposite assumptions of high levels of evasion, a child population of 45 per cent of the total and a reduction from pre-plague levels by a half, one reaches a peak figure of over 6.5 million (see Table 1).

Table 1. *Possible figures for the peak population of medieval England (in thousands, rounded)*

Recorded pop.	Evasion rate	Adult pop.	Per cent children	Total in 1377	Plague loss	Peak pop.
1,360	25%	1,813	45%	3,297	50%	6,594
1,360	20%	1,700	35%	2,615	33%	3,923

These calculations thus produce minima and maxima of 1.2 million and 2.4 million for 1086 and 4 million and 6.6 million for the fourteenth-century peak. It might be thought that figures with such a margin of error are useless. However, first, they establish without doubt that the trend of population was upwards in the twelfth and thirteenth centuries. They thus corroborate the circumstantial evidence. Second, they can serve to establish a range of possible growth rates. If one takes the lowest possible figure for 1086 and the highest possible for the fourteenth century, one can establish the highest possible growth rate in the intervening period; if one takes the highest possible for 1086 and the lowest for the later period, one has the lowest possible growth rate. These rates can then be compared with those for other historical periods. The results of such an operation are shown in Table 2.

As can be seen, the range of possible growth rates for England in the twelfth and thirteenth centuries, 0.2 per cent to 0.68 per cent, corresponds roughly with the range of growth rates for the period between the mid-sixteenth and mid-eighteenth centuries, when England was still

Table 2. *Demographic growth rates for various historical periods*

Growth rate (% per annum)	Historical example	Growth rate (% per annum)	Historical example
− 0.07	England 1650–1700	**0.68**	**England 1080–1330 (max. assumption)**
0.20	**England 1080–1330 (min. assumption)**	0.80	Modern developed world
0.27	England 1700–1750	0.81	England 1750–1800
0.35	England 1541–1741	1.33	England 1800–1850
0.48	England 1600–1650	2.50	Modern under-developed world
0.62	England 1550–1600		
0.62	England 1541–1871		

pre-industrial, but surviving records are much fuller. Considering the long-term trends and the sustained nature of the growth, one can reasonably claim that population grew in the High Middle Ages at much the same rate as it grew, overall, in the sixteenth, seventeenth and early eighteenth centuries. Of course, there must have been enormous variation in time and place. Sometimes the population would fall; sometimes it might rise faster than the maximum suggested. A fortunate survival of local records from Taunton in Somerset, for example, demonstrates a growth in population between 1209 and 1348 at a rate of 0.85 per cent. In the area around Nice the number of households increased from 440 to 722 between 1263 and 1315, a growth rate of 0.95 per cent.

There are many unresolved issues in the demographic history of the Middle Ages. It is not at all clear whether the growth that took place in the period after the eleventh century began, or accelerated, at that time or whether it was the culmination of centuries of growth at this level. Nor is there an entirely satisfactory model that would integrate the components of fertility, such as birth rates and levels of nuptiality and mortality, with the constraints of production, such as farming techniques, or social structure, such as family patterns and property rights. Nevertheless, at the back of our minds when we seek to understand the dynamics of expansion in the High Middle Ages, we can postulate long-term growth of a pace quite comparable with that of the early modern period, with its rapid urbanization and emigration.

PATTERNS OF MIGRATION

In the High Middle Ages the population of Europe was not only growing, it was moving. Some of this movement was over short distances, as the new towns were filled with migrants from nearby villages, or rural colonists established daughter hamlets or farmsteads a walking distance from their original homes. Also, however, there were movements of population, by land and by sea, that took settlers hundreds or even thousands of miles from their birthplaces, sometimes into environments that were climatically or culturally utterly strange to them. Historians label the period between the fourth and sixth centuries the *Völkerwanderungszeit*, the 'migration period', but, in terms of numbers of migrants and long-term effects, the migratory movements of the High Middle Ages merit the appellation even more fully.

The spatial patterns of migration in this period were complex, but, nevertheless, the overall redistribution of the European population is clear. As population grew, there was a movement of people outwards from the western central European core into the continental peripheries that adjoined it on all sides, the Celtic lands, the Iberian peninsula, scattered parts of the Mediterranean and, especially, Europe east of the Elbe. 'Expansion' is a metaphor but also, from the point of view of population dynamics, a literal truth. However many mercenaries or scholars moved from the peripheries of Latin Christendom to its centres, they were greatly outnumbered by the rural and urban population moving in the opposite direction, outwards – from England to Ireland, from Saxony to Livonia, from Old Castile to Andalusia.

Emigration was not, of course, uniform in scale and direction in every part of Christendom. Some areas were more deeply affected, others less involved. One important distinction of scale was between immigration by sea and by land, for really large-scale transmarine migration, so significant for the New World in modern times, does not appear to have taken place in medieval Europe. Transmarine colonies were indeed established, notably in the Holy Land – *Outremer*, 'the land across the sea', as it was termed – and in the eastern Baltic and in Ireland. But in these areas the immigrants usually formed only a small minority, comprising a secular and ecclesiastical aristocracy, a class of urban burgessess and a sprinkling of rural farmers. It was the areas of contiguous territorial expansion, such as the Iberian peninsula and the lands east of the Elbe, that saw immigration on a scale large enough to produce that sharpest of all cultural fissures, fundamental linguistic change. It was the settlement of tens of thousands of German urban and rural immigrants in the twelfth and thirteenth centuries, the so-called *Ostsiedlung*, that led to the Germanization of the lands east of the Elbe and the establishment of German-speakers in places like Berlin and Lübeck, which later became symbols of the German world. One likely explanation for this contrast between areas of thick settlement and the thinness of immigrant populations in 'Outremers' like Livonia or Syria is the fact that one has to pay a fare to cross the sea. Although land transport was slow and arduous and it was far more expensive to transport goods by land than by sea, individual migrants or migrant families, whether on foot, mounted or with a cart, could make their way cheaply and quite independently along the land routes. Sea travel immediately involved higher costs.

Expansionary migration characterized the twelfth and thirteenth centuries especially, but began earlier in some areas. In the Iberian peninsula Christian settlement followed Christian conquest as early as the ninth and tenth centuries, but it was the fall of Toledo in 1085 that really quickened the pace – that was the moment, according to Muslim writers, when 'the power of the Franks first became apparent'. The Aragonese acquired the Ebro valley in the first half of the twelfth century, the Castilians moved down into Andalusia in the mid-thirteenth, and the Portuguese were in permanent possession of the Algarve by 1249. As the Christian kings occupied the Muslim parts of the Iberian peninsula, a permanent preoccupation was the settlement of the lands they had acquired. Sometimes this was necessary because of an exodus of the former Muslim population; sometimes new planned settlement took place in previously unoccupied regions. Most of the settlers came from within the peninsula itself, but others drifted down from southern France. The Templar estates between Tudela and Saragossa had, in the mid-twelfth century, tenants with indicative names like Raymond Gascon, William of Condom, Martin of Toulouse and Richard of Cahors. There was room for them. The total amount of land involved in the Reconquest was massive – around 150,000 square miles – and the Iberian kingdoms remained relatively empty lands. Nevertheless, migration into the newly conquered areas reshaped the human geography of the peninsula in this period.

The *Ostsiedlung*, the settlement of Germans east of the Elbe and Saale rivers, the traditional eastern limit of German settlement, was of even vaster scale. The process began gradually in the first half of the twelfth century, notably in eastern Holstein, where Lübeck was founded (for the first time) in 1143. In the second half of the century German settlement extended into Brandenburg, perhaps to Mecklenburg and – it is at least mentioned as a possibility – to Silesia in 1175, when Duke Boleslaw I granted freedom from 'Polish law' to the Cistercians of Lubiąż (Leubus) for 'any Germans who till the monastery's lands or are settled by the abbot to live on them'. The same period witnessed some German settlement in Bohemia and Transylvania. Then, in the thirteenth century, the whole of eastern Europe became covered with German-speakers, from Estonia to the Carpathians. Some were farmers, some merchants, some miners. Their arrival changed the map of Europe permanently and has had historical ramifications of the first importance down to the present.

In comparison with the settlements of the Reconquest and the *Ostsiedlung*, other movements were certainly less dramatic. They were, however, of significance for the regions involved and serve as further confirmation of the impression that here we are witnessing a truly general or continental phenomenon. For just as immigrant farmers moved into the valley of the Tagus or the forests of Silesia, the Celtic lands – Wales, Ireland and Scotland – were receiving new colonial populations from England and, to some extent, from northern France, while in the eastern Mediterranean some settlement took place in the wake of the crusades. In all these cases we see the movement of population from the central core of western Europe outwards.

As an example of this outward-moving flow we may take the Flemings, the inhabitants of the low-lying county of Flanders on the North Sea coast. Flanders is a region that can reasonably be classified as 'central' in the framework of medieval Europe, located, as it is, between England, France and Germany on busy shipping routes. It witnessed the early growth of a centralized feudal principality, had the most important cluster of commercial and manufacturing towns north of the Alps and probably attained a higher population density than any region of comparable size outside Italy. Even after the crises of the fourteenth century Flanders had sufficient vitality to produce a distinctive culture of its own, that misleadingly called 'Burgundian'.

In the High Middle Ages, Flemings spread throughout Europe. Many of them were peasant settlers but there were also Flemish knights, soldiers and artisans to be found in every corner of Latin Christendom – and beyond: a Raymond the Fleming was 'chief guardian and keeper of the city gate' in Constantinople in 1081. The Norman Conquest of England in 1066 involved so many Flemings that when, shortly after the conquest, William I issued a writ protecting the lands of the archbishop of York, he threatened sanctions against any malefactor 'French or Flemish or English'. Military adventure in England continued to attract the Flemings and they played an important role as mercenaries in the civil wars and rebellions of the twelfth century. In the great rebellion of 1173–4, for instance, one of the rebel leaders, the earl of Leicester, 'embarked on a venture with Flemings and French and men from Frisia'. The king of Scots, who joined the rebels, was interested in recruiting Flemings from Flanders 'and their fleet, fifties and hundreds of those sturdy people'. One contemporary observer rather looked askance at these plebeian recruits and pictured them coming 'to get for ourselves the wool of England that we so much desire'. 'The truth is,' added our chronicler, 'that most of them were weavers, they do not know how to bear arms like knights, and why they had come was to pick up plunder and the spoils of war.'

Other Flemish fighting men were interested in a more substantial reward and succeeded in establishing themselves as respected landowners in their host countries. A small group of them, for example, were settled as knightly tenants by Malcolm IV of Scotland (1153–65) in Upper Clydesdale. They had characteristic names like Wizo and Lamkin, which they imprinted on their property (Wiston, Lamington). Other Flemings, like Freskin and Berowald the Fleming, held land yet further north, in Moray and Elgin, and Earl David, brother of King William the Lion and lord of Garioch (Aberdeenshire), addressed one of his charters to 'French and English and Flemings and Scots'. Two of the most important aristocratic families of medieval Scotland, Douglas and Moray, were of Flemish descent.

Other Flemings settled in towns. They have been described as forming 'an important element in the early burgh population' in Scotland, and in Berwick they had their own centre, the Red House, held from the king of Scots. There was certainly a colony in Vienna, where, in 1208, Duke Leopold VI of Austria granted certain privileges to 'our burgesses, whom we call Flemings, whom we have settled in our city of Vienna'. All the big cities of the Ostsiedlung had inhabitants whose ultimate origins are revealed by the surname 'Fleming'.

It was particularly as peasant settlers with an expertise in drainage that the Flemings (like their neighbours the men of Holland) were welcomed. Before the year 1000 they had already begun to protect and reclaim land by means of dikes and drainage ditches, and Count Baldwin V of Flanders (1036–67) was praised for 'rendering uncultivated land fertile by your care and industry'. In the next century this expertise was tapped by lords outside

Flanders. In 1154 Bishop Gerung of Meissen 'placed energetic men immigrating from Flanders in a certain uncultivated and virtually uninhabited place' to found a village of eighteen peasant holdings (*mansi*). Five years later Abbot Arnold of Ballenstedt sold to Flemings some hamlets near the Elbe that had previously been occupied by Slavs. They reorganized the hamlets into one village of twenty-four *mansi*, which was subject to Flemish law (*iura Flamiggorum*). The involvement of Flemings in settlement east of the Elbe was so characteristic that one of the two standard forms of peasant holding or *mansus* there was known as 'the Flemish *mansus*'. Even today village names like Flemmingen, area names like Fläming in Brandenburg and also, it has been suggested, traces of Netherlandish dialect show the imprint of Flemish peasant colonization east of the Elbe. The first Germanic settlers in Transylvania, the unsettled eastern part of the kingdom of Hungary, who arrived there in the 1140s or 1150s at the invitation of King Geza, were referred to in twelfth-century documents as Flemings. Although some scholars are of the opinion that this term had become generalized and meant only 'colonist', others believe, with some plausibility, that it was ethnically specific, and may even have referred to Flemish settlers coming not directly from Flanders, but from the new Flemish villages in eastern Germany.

A large colony of Flemings was also settled in south Wales by Henry I of England in about 1108. The impact they made upon the Welsh is recorded in the native chronicle, the *Brut*:

a certain folk of strange origin and custom . . . were sent by King Henry to the land of Dyfed. And that folk seized the whole cantref [territorial division] of Rhos . . . after having completely driven thence the inhabitants. And that folk, as is said, had come from Flanders, their land, which is situated close to the sea of the Britons, because the sea had taken and overwhelmed their land . . . after they had failed to find a place to live in – for the sea had overflowed the coast lands, and the mountains were full of people so that it was not possible for everyone to live together there because of the multitude of the people and the smallness of the land – this folk begged and beseeched King Henry that they might obtain a place to live in. And then they were sent to Rhos, driving thence the rightful inhabitants, who have lost their rightful land and their rightful place from that day to this.

The passage is not absolutely exact – the 'mountains' of Flanders are a feature of the Welsh chronicler's mental landscape rather than actual Flemish topography – but the essentials are there: a relatively small and overpopulated land threatened by the sea, which sent out migrants to distant and culturally alien milieux.

The Flemish colony in south Wales, centred in the region of Rhos in south Pembrokeshire, preserved its cultural particularity for many generations. It possessed distinctive names, like those borne by Wizo, 'the chief of the Flemings' who passed through Worcester on his way from Flanders to Pembrokeshire in 1112, and the Freskin son of Ollec recorded in the royal records of 1130, recognizably Flemish place names, like Wiston (compare the identical name in Clydesdale), and even special divinatory practices. The Flemish language was spoken in Pembrokeshire until at least 1200. Hostility between the implanted colony and the native Welsh was unremitting. Mutual raids and killings marked the whole of the twelfth century and went on into the next. In 1220 the Welsh prince Llywelyn ap Iorwerth 'gathered a mighty host to attack the Flemings of Rhos and Pembroke' and 'traversed Rhos and Deugleddyf for five days, inflicting a great slaughter on the people of the land'. The acute observer Gerald of Wales, writing in 1188, said of the Flemings:

they are a brave and sturdy people, mortal enemies of the Welsh, with whom they engage in endless conflict; a people skilled at working in wool, experienced in trade, ready to face any effort or danger at land or sea in the pursuit of gain; according to the demands of time and place quick to turn to the plough or to arms; a brave and fortunate people.

Here, in a more sympathetic mode, is the perception we have already encountered of the Flemings as weavers rather than knights. Gerald is perhaps more accurate in seeing them as equally fighters, traders and artisans – or possibly pastoralists, since the Pembrokeshire Flemings certainly raised flocks of sheep. One of the striking features of the Flemings was indeed their versatility: knights, mercenaries, weavers, traders, peasant settlers.

In 1169 the Anglo-Normans came to Ireland. This, at any rate, is the usual description historians give that event. To one Irish annalist, however, what happened was 'the coming of the fleet of the Flemings'. A large contingent of Pembrokeshire Flemings joined the initial mercenary group who involved themselves in Ireland and, over the following decades, many won land and settled, as they had already done in England, Wales and Scotland. In this way the expansionary movements of the High Middle Ages spread the Flemings throughout Christendom. It is possible to find a Gerard Fleming settled in Palestine in the 1160s, a Michael Fleming as sheriff of Edinburgh around 1200 and a Henry Fleming as bishop of Ermland in Prussia in the late thirteenth century. The Flemings exemplify in microcosm the vast demographic expansion of the period.

THE LEGAL FRAMEWORK

Obviously expansionary migration brought the migrants into very diverse environments. As the Castilians moved into the central Meseta they found a countryside where they could develop cereal agriculture, viticulture and sheep-farming, if only they could bring in enough settlers and defend the land against Muslim raids. The Ebro valley and the valley of the Guadalquivir enjoyed a flourishing irrigative agriculture. East of the Elbe, in Silesia, Mecklenburg and Pomerania, there were thick woodlands which could be cleared to establish grain-growing farms – indeed, by the later Middle Ages the east Elbian lands formed the most important corn-exporting region in Europe. The area of German settlement extended northwards along the Baltic as far as the Gulf of Finland and eastwards into Transylvania – where by the late twelfth century Germans were planting vines, pasturing their pigs in the woods and receiving a privileged status from the king of Hungary – and into eastern Poland, eating into, but by no means completely removing, the thick natural covering of forest. The climatic variations in the zone of high medieval colonization were great. The average July temperature that western settlers found in the kingdom of Jerusalem was over 77°F, in the lordship of Ireland under 59°F. In some regions they had to drain the land, in others irrigate it. So the colonists found a wide range of natural and man-made ecologies into which they had to fit: subarctic forest, wet bog, fertile temperate soils, high plateaux, irrigated horticulture, semi-desert.

However, the social and institutional arrangements that the immigrants erected to provide a human framework in their new homelands were not as dissimilar as their geographical and agricultural diversity would suggest. Certain parallels immediately spring to our notice, for example, when we set side by side documents dealing with settlement in eastern Europe and in Spain. We may take a concrete instance. In 1127 Alfonso I of Aragon granted Sancho Garciez of Navascués the *castro* or *villa* of Término in the neighbourhood of Huesca 'so that you should settle that castle and village' (*ut popules illo castello et illa villa*). It was granted as a fief. The king was to have three *iubatas* (standard holdings) for his own demesne and three for the castle, while Sancho also received three as a hereditary estate. The future settlers were to receive two *iubatas* if they were of knightly rank and one if not, and were granted the *fuero* or law of Ejea. 'This I give you,' concluded the king, 'however many you settle there and however you divide it, Sancho Garciez.'

We may compare this with a document issued by Thomas, bishop of Wrocław (Breslau), in the middle of the thirteenth century. The bishop granted to his knight Godislaus, 'in consideration of his services', the village of Proschau (Proszów) 'to be settled according to German law in the same way that our adjoining villages, formerly owned by the crusading order, are settled'. The village was estimated to be able to maintain about fifty *mansi*, of which Godislaus was to receive ten. He, in his turn, conceded four of these ten to the bishop's proctor. Godislaus also had the right to construct a mill and a tavern in Proschau and received a third of the profits of justice as *scultetus* or *Schulze*, that is, local magistrate. The settlers were to have eight years free of tithe, in order to establish themselves, and were then to pay an eighth of a mark of silver per *mansus* as rent and tithes, which were to be collected in the field.

The important common points between the Spanish and the Polish cases are: the grant of land specifically 'to be settled'; the intermediary and entrepreneurial role of the feoffee; specified uniform plots offered to future settlers; the endowment of the feoffee with a multiple of these plots; and the application of a legal model already employed in nearby settlements. Such similarities show that in both areas the process of establishing new settlements had been thought about and regularized. Delegation and uniformity were the preferred organizing principles. The reason for this rough similarity of organizational form in two quite different areas of new settlement was that in both the Iberian peninsula and eastern Europe, as, indeed, in Ireland and Palestine, lords and colonists of a common cultural tradition – 'Frankish' or 'post-Carolingian' – were facing similar problems. They had an inherited repertoire of social resources – attitudes to land measurement, authority and liberty, the shape of rural communities, the documentary grant – and they faced the same pressing need: to recruit labour. Let us look first at the dilemma, then in more detail at the mechanics of the solution.

For most of the Middle Ages and in most parts of Europe it was more common for lords to have land and lack men to work it than the reverse. In a relatively scarcely populated continent, with plenty of forest, scrub and marsh, labour was a scarce commodity. Responses to this problem varied. One tactic that lords adopted was to impose restrictions on the mobility of labour by creating legal hindrances: peasant tenants were 'tied to the land', marriage outside the estate was forbidden, sons of tenants were not permitted to enter the priesthood. This was a minimalist response, since, although it did indeed aim at securing the labour supply that a given lord already controlled, it did so only by attempting to freeze the pattern of labour distribution. There was no dynamism in this policy of enserfment. Poaching one's neighbour's serfs was indeed a permanent temptation, and one that lords often sought to outlaw by mutual agreement, but theoretically a serf society would have no mechanisms and no incentives for labour mobility.

The reality was obviously different, partly because there actually was competition between lords for serfs, and partly because early medieval societies did have a more dynamic option for the appropriation of labour, in the form of slave-raiding and the forcible resettlement of population. For example, when Bretislaw I of Bohemia invaded Poland in 1038 and came to the fortification of Giecz, the inhabitants were unable to offer resistance and it was eventually agreed that they, with all their livestock and movable property, should be relocated in Bohemia. Bretislaw granted them a swath of woodland, which they were presumably to clear, and allowed them to live under their own headman and according to their own customs. Two generations later they were still identifiable among the Czech population as the *Gedcane*, the men of Giecz. A few decades later, in a different part of Europe, Robert Guiscard, leader of the Normans in southern Italy, was restoring and founding settlements in Calabria by placing in them the inhabitants of Sicilian towns he had raided and depopulated. In 1165 the Welsh prince Dafydd ab Owain Gwynedd 'ravaged Tegeingl and he removed the people and their cattle with him into Dyffryn Clwyd'. In all these cases the capture of a settlement was only important because of the capture of its inhabitants. The men, women, animals and chattels were the prize, not bare territory. Forcible transfers of population were one way of bringing fresh blood into a bond society.

Already in the eleventh century, however, at a time when enserfment and the capture of populations were certainly the most direct methods of securing labour, a new method of recruiting settlers for one's lands was being developed. Norman Sicily provides a nice intermediate case. In 1090 Guiscard's brother, Count Roger, secured the release of the Christian captives from Malta:

He called together all the captives whom he had freed from captivity and brought away with him and made them free. For those who wished to remain with him in Sicily he offered to construct a village at his own expense and to provide them with all things necessary to win a livelihood. The village would be called *Franca*, that is, free village, because it would be forever free of any impositions or servile dues. For those who wished to return to their own fields and kin, he granted free licence to go where they would.

The captives had been brought away from Malta after Count Roger had raided the island. He did not simply forcibly resettle them, as his brother had been doing some decades before, but offered them a choice between returning to their homes and taking up residence in a new village, which he would establish, which would be a 'free village' – *franca, libera* – free, that is, from 'servile dues'. Instead of the coercive direction of labour, we see the attempt to lure labour by the creation of favourable and attractive economic and legal conditions.

The vast movement of new settlement, migration and colonization that took place in the High Middle Ages was based on this model of labour recruitment, not on enserfment or capture. The free village, consciously designed to draw new settlers, could be found everywhere, most notably in the parts of Europe, such as the Iberian peninsula and the lands east of the Elbe, which were opened up to large-scale immigration in this period. The basic reciprocal transaction is put simply in the thirteenth-century German lawbook, the *Sachsenspiegel*: 'When peasants establish a new village through clearance, the lord of the village can give them hereditary tenure as rent-payers, even though they were not born to that estate.' The peasants change their birth status and become hereditary leaseholders. The lord grants them this new and favourable status in return for the peasants' activity as farmers and settlers. The lord augments his income, the peasants their income and status (such a reciprocal transaction is depicted in Plate 6).

Calculated seigneurial enterprise of this kind was clearly a very important element in the opening up of new land. For example, the documents that inform us of the gradual expansion of agricultural land and the arrival of peasant migrants east of the Elbe also describe, albeit in stereotyped rhetoric, the motives of the lords who directed and encouraged this process. Key words recur: 'usefulness' or 'profitability' (*utilitas*), 'improvement' (*melioratio*), 'reform' (*reformatio*). This is the language of active amelioration and it is given further force by a rhetoric of desire and prudence. The lord almost invariably 'desires' the improvement; he 'considers' the 'state' or 'condition' of his church or lordship. When Duke Boleslaw of Poland established a new settlement in his domain in 1266, he did so 'desiring to attain the improvement and reformation of our land, as is proper'. The overall impression this rhetoric evokes is that of the careful but enthusiastic pursuit of economic development.

The lords of the High Middle Ages, both lay and ecclesiastical, were keenly aware of the importance of revenues. The period 1050–1300 saw the development of new forms of book-keeping and accounting for both seigneurial and princely estates. Budgets and surveys proliferated.

Domesday Book was one of the earliest and most astonishing of these surveys, and one of its many purposes was to ask the land 'if more can be got out of it than is obtained now'. By the twelfth century the kings of England had annual audits whose results were stored in central archives, and the monarchs of France and Aragon were not far behind. Seigneurial surveys and accounts survive from the twelfth and thirteenth centuries, and the end of the period saw the growth of a technical literature dedicated to estate management. These documents are the product of the same mentality revealed, in a more homely way, by a thirteenth-century Austrian poem which depicts rural knights discussing how to get a cow to give more milk. It may be that feudal lords and great prelates always considered their monetary income a means rather than an end, a means to victory, glory or salvation, but they were increasingly hard-headed about the means. 'We have given a marsh to settlers to be cultivated, judging it better and more profitable to settle colonists there and to receive produce from their labours than for it to remain uncultivated and virtually useless,' proclaims one twelfth-century potentate. The same lords who had cast a freshly discerning eye on the woods, wastes and hills in search of sites for new castles, as described in Chapter 3 above, turned their attention to the marshes and forests that had previously yielded fish, firewood and game, beginning to imagine them as cornfields full of rent-paying tenants.

An example of the active and innovative lords who sponsored colonization in the twelfth century is Wichmann, archbishop of Magdeburg (1152–92). He came from a noble Saxon family, was related to the Wettin margraves through his mother and owed his promotion to the German emperor Frederick Barbarossa. He used the power and authority to which he had been born and which he acquired to develop the economic resources of the diocese. Even before he attained the see of Magdeburg, while he was bishop of Naumburg, he had dealings with settlers from the Low Countries ('a certain people from the land which is called Holland'), whom his predecessor had invited in. The settlers (who gave their name to Flemmingen near Naumburg) had economic and judicial privileges, including that of choosing their own local magistrate, or *Schulze*, and in return paid a money rent to the bishop. As archbishop, Wichmann developed a conscious policy of planned settlement, using *locatores*. The *locator* was an important figure in the colonization of eastern Europe. He was an entrepreneur who acted as a middleman between the lord eager to develop his land and the new settlers. The *locator* was responsible for the mechanics of settlement, such as the recruitment of the colonists and the division of the land, and received in return a substantial landed estate in the new settlement with hereditary privileges. For example, when Wichmann granted the *locator* Herbert the village of Pechau, south-east of Magdeburg, in 1159 'to settle and make fruitful', it was agreed that the *locator*'s reward was to be six holdings (*mansi*) of his own, the right to act as *Schulze* and a one-third share in the profits of justice, such as fines and confiscations. All these privileges were hereditary. In order to encourage settlers, the inhabitants of Pechau were granted the favourable terms of the law of Burg, near Magdeburg, and were to be free of the duty of working on castles for the first ten years they were settled there.

Such new villages were not founded in a complete legal void. Before Wichmann could hand over the village of Poppendorf, east of Magdeburg, to the *locatores* Werner of Paderborn and Gottfried, he had to buy out all those who had a feudal claim to the land. He clearly judged this a worthwhile investment and foresaw the time when

they will settle new colonists there, who will drain the marshy grasslands, which are presently good for nothing but grass and hay, and plough them and sow them and make them fruitful and then pay from that farmland an annual rent at fixed times for the use of the archbishop.

The rent was to consist of two shillings per *mansus*, plus two bushels of rye and two of barley, in addition to the full ecclesiastical tithe. The temporary drain on Wichmann's cash reserves occasioned by the full acquisition of the site was to be amply restored by an indefinite future of assured income in silver and grain.

Wichmann not only fostered settlement and rent-paying agriculture within the existing boundaries of his diocese, but also engaged in that expansionary movement eastwards against the remaining West Slav pagans that characterized the middle decades of the twelfth century. He was allied with Albert the Bear for the final campaign against Brandenburg in 1157. In 1159 when he exempted the Flemish settlers of Grosswusteritz on the Havel from work on castles, he added 'unless they are commanded to raise a rampart to protect themselves against the pagans nearby'. At some point, possibly during the Wendish Crusade of 1147, he acquired the land of Jüterbog beyond the Elbe. Here he envisaged a complex of urban and rural development. In 1174 he granted the inhabitants the same liberties as the city of Magdeburg itself enjoyed. He did this 'so that the diligence and good will which we have for building up the province of Jüterbog (*ad edificandam provinciam Iutterbogk*) may proceed more fruitfully and freely'. He decreed freedom of trade between the new province and the old archiepiscopal centres and intended the city of Jüterbog to be 'the beginning and head of the province'. Economic development and Christianity went together:

> With the help of God's grace and through our efforts, it has come about that in the province of Jüterbog, where pagan rites used to be celebrated and whence frequent attacks on Christians used to be made, now the Christian religion flourishes and the defence and protection of Christianity is firm and safe, and in many places in that region due service is shown to God. Hence, out of love of Christianity, we strive for the safety and advantage of all those who have entered this province or may wish to come with no less zeal than for income for our own advantage.

The phrase 'in the name of God and profit' is traditionally associated with the canny and pious merchants of Renaissance Italy, but it would certainly not be out of place when speaking of some of the feudal lords of the twelfth century.

Wichmann of Magdeburg fused various elements from previous experience of settlement and colonization into a new and fruitful whole. He was well aware of the value of dealing with rural communities and knew what legal privileges could mean: he drew up the first written version of Magdeburg Law, later to be enormously influential in central and eastern Europe, and sanctioned the first guilds in Magdeburg. He used *locatores* regularly and made detailed written agreements with them. He encouraged immigration from the Low Countries. In Jüterbog he had the vision of development upon a regional scale. It was the involvement of such high-born prelates that made new peasant settlement so swift and successful, and one of their principal means was the free village, 'free of any impositions or servile dues'.

THE MEANING OF FREEDOM

The settlers who came to newly established villages had to be given special conditions and privileges, both to encourage them to come and to enable them to establish themselves. There had to be compensations for the long journey, the severance of family and local ties and, perhaps, the disposal of other property. The new conditions and status that were offered to them on the frontiers of settlement must be a magnet strong enough to break the bonds that held people in place. Then, when the migrants reached their new destination, the early years might be hard and precarious, especially if the settlements were indeed entirely new and the arable had to be created by clearing woodland or draining marsh. Lords had to be ready to surrender some rights and income in the early years in order to ensure that the settlement would become viable and profitable.

In the first years of settlement it was customary that rents and tithes should be lower than usual or even waived completely. The number of years that the settlers enjoyed such exemptions and the degree of exemption varied. When Hermann Balk, *Landmeister* of the Teutonic Knights in Prussia, arranged for the settlement of some of his order's lands in Silesia in 1233, he specified a rent of a quarter of silver from each holding of two small *mansi*, in addition to full tithes; he added the proviso, however, that 'I have exempted them from the payment of tithes and rent, as a special privilege, for the next ten years, except for the land which is already prepared for cultivation, which shall pay tithes the first year it is settled.' The function of these exempt years in enabling clearance to be undertaken is thus fairly explicit in this document. The point emerges even more sharply in a grant that was made to new settlers in an area west of the Elbe in the previous century. In this the bishop of Hildesheim declared:

They have agreed to the following terms about clearing the arable fields. When someone has felled trees, uprooted undergrowth and rendered the land cultivable, he shall pay neither rent nor tithes while he is tilling the soil with a mattock. As soon as the land is ploughed and becomes more productive, he shall have seven rent-free years. In that seventh year, however, he shall pay two pence, in the eighth four pence, in the ninth eight pence, in the tenth a shilling, and that shall be his rent henceforth.

There is, in this instance, a sliding scale, partly based on the actual state of the holding, partly merely on the passage of years. The distinction between cultivation by mattock and cultivation by plough is significant. The mattock was a necessary tool for newly cleared land where roots, stones or other obstructions could make ploughing impracticable.

The number of exempt years also varied according to the envisaged eventual size of the holding. Thus, when Duke Conrad of Silesia organized the settlement of the village of Siedlce (Zedlitz) in 1257, the arrangement was that land that was already open or had only a cover of scrub should be divided into Flemish *mansi*, while the thick woodlands were to be apportioned into Frankish *mansi*. This made good sense, since a Flemish *mansus* was composed of various blocks of land, while a Frankish *mansus* was one continuous strip. The woods could not all be cleared in one season and hence the gradual extension of a Frankish *mansus*, producing the so-called *Waldhufen* landscape, was a practical and appropriate way of eating into them systematically. Open land, on the other hand, could be allocated at once and with an overall plan, such as the dispersed Flemish *mansus* required. There was also, however, a difference in size. The Flemish *mansus* was about forty acres, the Frankish about half as big again. Hence the fact that the Flemish *mansi* in Siedlce enjoyed five exempt years and the Frankish ten reflected both the size of the holding and the difficulty of clearing it. Another Silesian example, from late in the thirteenth century, has a grant of three exempt years for land that was already cultivable, nine for scrub and sixteen for thick wood. In 1270 the bishop of Olomouc (Olmütz) in Moravia offered to the settlers at Fryčovice (Fritzendorf) twelve exempt years, but to those holding in the direction of Staric (Staritsch) sixteen years, 'since their fields are worse than the others'.

The number of exempt years in thirteenth-century Silesia varied from one to twenty and this range seems representative for other regions too. In 1160 Bishop Gerung of Meissen granted ten rent-free years to the settlers of Buchwitz. A century later, when the Teutonic Knights wished to induce emigrants from Lübeck and its hinterland to come to settle in Courland, they offered peasant farmers as much land as they could cultivate, exempt from payments for six years. In 1276 the inhabitants of a village in Polish Galicia were granted thirteen rent-free years 'so that within that time they may strive with all their might to clear the forest and increase the crop-bearing holdings'. The Hospitallers who undertook the settlement of perhaps 1,500 colonists in their villages in New Castile in the 1230s and 1240s usually granted three rent-free years. When the Council of Toledo established the village community of Yébenes about twenty miles south of the city in 1258, its inhabitants were to enjoy exemption from payments for ten years. Exemptions might cover other obligations as well as that of paying rent and tithes. As mentioned above, Wichmann of Magdeburg granted ten years' freedom from the duty to do building work on castles, and in Silesia the exempt years sometimes brought freedom from most kinds of military service. Raymond Berengar IV of Barcelona granted the settlers (*populatores*) of San Esteban de Luesia seven years' exemption from *hoste*, military duty.

These early years of special privilege were not without corresponding duties. In particular, settlers were sometimes explicitly bound to build or to cultivate and might even be dispossessed if they did not. In 1185 Alfonso II of Aragon sponsored the settlement of Valmadrid in the Ebro valley by San Salvador of Saragossa and its procurator, Dominic, under such conditions:

I command that all those who come to settle there or who have a holding should build houses there by Christmas and if they do not build houses there by that date . . . Dominic . . . shall have the power of seizing the holding and giving it to others who will settle there and build houses.

The peasants of Yébenes were obliged to plant a certain area of vines in the first two years. It was sometimes also specified that, even if the settlers enjoyed the right to dispose of their land freely, they might not alienate it in the first year or years.

The terms and conditions of the early years were adapted to particular and temporary circumstances. They were enabling conditions. There were, of course, more substantial mutual benefits for colonist and magnate. Let us look in more detail at what expectation brought the migrants to their new homes. The most obvious thing that lords were offering and migrants seeking was land. In the crowded parts of the Rhineland, Flanders or England population increase was gradually but relentlessly diminishing the size of the peasant holding, or the prospect of obtaining one at all; in Europe east of the Elbe and Reconquest Spain there was land for the asking. In New Castile, for example, the usual amount of land granted was a *yugada*. The word is linked to 'yoke' and refers, in principle, to the amount of land which could be cultivated by a yoke of oxen. Anyone familiar with medieval systems of measurement will see that the exact dimensions of such a unit could vary enormously, but modern Spanish historians assume a *yugada* was about 80 acres of arable, and this does not seem implausible. East of the Elbe a peasant farm of 80 acres was also very widespread; for, although the usual unit of land here was the *mansus*, either the Flemish of 40 acres or the Frankish of around 60, holdings of two *mansi*, especially of two Flemish *mansi*, were common in Brandenburg, Prussia and Pomerania and could be found elsewhere, too. If we remember that in thirteenth-century England holders of a full virgate (25–30 acres) formed a tiny minority (perhaps 1 per cent in some areas) amidst a sea of smallholders, or that around 1300 over a third of the peasants of Picardy had less than half an acre, the vast opportunity that the lands of new settlement offered becomes clear.

However, it was not simply land that was offered to the colonists of the High Middle Ages, but land on favourable terms. East of the Elbe the land that was offered was normally held on low fixed rents. Thus, when the knight Gerbord of Köthen granted a woodland enclosure north of Szczecin (Stettin) to be settled, he specified that 'all the residents who settle this enclosure and cultivate its fields shall give one shilling from each manse and, in addition, tithes'. The rent on the *mansi* in 'Lamprechtsdorf' (Kamjontken/Liebe) in Prussia that Dietrich Stange granted to be settled in 1299 was half a mark. In Silesia, similarly, the usual burden of rent and tithes on the Flemish *mansus* was half a mark. These rent levels were favourable for the peasant tenants compared to those found in non-colonial areas of Europe. In Brandenburg, for example, the average burden of all dues owed to the lord, which by the late thirteenth century included consolidated tithes and taxes, amounted to about 26 bushels of grain per *mansus* per annum. A *mansus* of 40 acres could easily produce 120 bushels per annum if two-thirds of it was sown at one and a half bushels per acre with a yield of 1:3. Around 1300 Brandenburg peasants thus paid approximately 20 per cent of their grain output to their lords. The situation in Silesia was very similar, with the total burden on the *mansus* equivalent to 20–25 per cent of its product. In thirteenth-century England, in contrast, it has been calculated that the manorial dues as a proportion of a middling villein's gross output were 'near or above the 50 per cent mark' – and this excludes tithes and royal taxes. In contemporary Picardy the peasant's situation was little better.

Another very rough yardstick for comparison is provided by the total amount of silver that tenants owed per acre. In the late thirteenth and early fourteenth centuries English peasant farmers were paying fourpence to a shilling per acre, that is, between a fifth of an ounce and half an ounce of silver at the then current fineness of the English penny. An average Silesian tenant of the same period paid half a mark per *mansus* for rent and tithe. Using the Cologne mark of about 8 ounces and the Flemish *mansus* of approximately 40 acres, this comes to about one-tenth of an ounce per acre. However rough these calculations – and they are rough – the relative lightness of the burdens on the peasant settlers of the *Ostsiedlung* compared with those cultivating the 'old country' of England is clear.

In general, new settlers were not subjected to labour services (the duty to work on the lord's land) but paid rent in cash or produce, the former in fixed amounts, the latter either in fixed amounts or as a proportion of the produce. In the 1150s and 1160s the archbishop of Toledo was granting village settlers land in return for rents such as one-tenth of the grain, one-sixth of the grapes and the very slight burden of three labour-works per year, or in return for a fixed quantity of grain per *yugada*. References to labour services weighing on the new settlers of the *Ostsiedlung* are very rare. In Ireland the free tenants, who were predominantly English settlers, paid only fixed money rents, and even when demesnes were big, labour services were not an important part of the manorial economy. At Clonkeen in 1344 the customary tenants provided only 16 per cent of the total labour required for reaping. It seems as if lords were prepared to sacrifice direct claims on their tenants' labour in order to encourage settlement and increase their rent revenues.

It was not only the settlers' immediate lord who was willing to concede privileges in the hope of long-term benefits. The rulers, princes and 'lords of the land' (*domini terrae*), also engaged in this calculating self-curtailment, for they recognized that 'the glory of the prince is in the number of the people'. When James the Conqueror of Aragon wished to encourage 'those coming to settle Vilanova', he exempted them from a long array of renders: '*exercitus . . . cavalcata . . . peyta* or *questia . . . cena . . .* and any other royal exaction'. Exemption from *peito* or *pactum*, the standard royal exaction, or its fixing at a low level, was a common feature of Spanish charters of settlement. The colonists who came to Artasona, near Barbastro, in the reign of Alfonso I of Aragon (1104–34) were allowed complete freedom from *peito*, along with other privileges. Similarly, one of the essential parts of the *ius Teutonicum* that the settlers east of the Elbe enjoyed was freedom from a whole range of princely exactions:

I, Henry, by God's grace duke of Silesia, at the request of Vitoslas, abbot of St Mary's, Wrocław, and his brothers, grant German law to their settlers residing in Baudiss and the two villages called Kreidel, so that they be free of the services which are laid upon the Poles according to the custom of the land, which are called in the vernacular *povoz*, *prevod* and *zlad*, and from the payments which are exacted, such as *stroza*, *podvorove*, *swetopetro* and the like.

At the end of the thirteenth century Duke Przemysl of Cracow confirmed an exemption from 'all the services and burdens of Polish law, namely *naraz*, *povoz*, *prevod*, *podvorove*, *stroza*, *opole*, *ova*, *vacca*, "castle citation" or whatever name they may be called'. 'Polish law', as it was conceptualized in distinction to 'German law', thus comprised a variety of payments and burdens, some doubtless commuted or fixed, others unpredictable and exacted in kind or labour. From these claims new settlers were freed. This was a liberty that a prince alone could grant, and we see here the co-operation of princes and other lords in the creation of a homogeneous settlers' law. The end result was yet a further reduction of the colonists' compulsory outgoings.

Settlers thus had the prospect both of obtaining substantial farms and of retaining more of their produce. Additionally they were tempted by secure and generously defined heritability. Gerbord of Köthen, who, as described above, settled Pomeranian woodland with peasants paying one shilling per *mansus*, also promised that 'everything we grant to the residents of the enclosure we grant according to feudal law, so that, by that law, it shall pass down to their wives and children and their other relatives and kinsfolk'. Silesian settlers enjoyed 'hereditary right' or 'feudal and hereditary right'. Indeed, *ius hereditarium*, 'hereditary right', was sometimes used as an equivalent to *ius Teutonicum*, the 'German law' that the new settlers enjoyed. When Alfonso I of Aragon brought Mozarabs (Arabic-speaking Christians) from Muslim Spain to settle in Aragon, he promised that they should be free – 'you and your sons and every succeeding generation and descendant, so also any other man who may come to settle with you, with all that you can settle and cultivate in the villages and lands I will give you'. The same king promised the *populatores* of Artasona their rights and privileges freely and securely – 'you and your sons and every succeeding generation and your posterity'.

Beyond heritability lay alienability: 'if any man lacks the solace of an heir, that is, a son or daughter, the lord viscount shall have no rights to his chattels or property, but he may freely give or dispose of it to whomsoever he wishes', in the words of a charter of Bela IV of Hungary for settlers in the distant east of his huge kingdom. When the Hospitallers granted their settlers in Sena and Sijena in Aragon the Sierra de los Monegros they affirmed that 'they shall have this grant free and freely and in peace and security hereditarily, they and their sons and all their posterity, as their own to do with as they will, to sell or to mortgage, for ever'.

The only significant limitation on alienability arose from the lords' desire to ensure that the purpose of the new plantation, namely the creation of an active and flourishing, but subordinate and rent-paying peasantry, would not be subverted. There was no advantage to them in land speculation, absenteeism or the encroachment of outside grandees. Provisos were thus sometimes made explicit that the new colonists could only alienate their property to someone who would be an acceptable replacement. The settlers of Yébenes in New Castile were bound by such a condition:

Every resident or settler of the place can do with his property what he will, in selling, buying, mortgaging and exchanging, with any peasant like himself (*omme llano labrador tal commo el*) who will do and fulfil what is required, and may not sell or alienate any of his property to knight, lady or squire, nor to cleric or monk, nor to Jew or Moor, but to a peasant like himself who will live in the place and do and fulfil that which is required.

The same concern about residence is shown by the canons of Vyšehrad outside Prague, who organized the settlement of their prebends in 1252 with the proviso that 'the cultivators there may not transfer their rights to other persons who will not reside on the property'. In one German colony in Silesia, part of the estate of St Vincent's, Wrocław, it was ruled that 'none of them may leave unless they substitute another who will pay to the abbot what they themselves have to pay'. The nervousness about property slipping into knightly hands echoes in eastern Saxony – 'None of the settlers may give or sell his *mansus* or arable land to a knight or anyone who will become a knight' – in the Ebro valley, where free alienation was granted *exceptis cavalariis*, 'except to knights', and even in Palestine, where the same reservation applied to the otherwise free right of alienability bestowed on the colonists whom the Hospitallers settled at Beth Gibelin. Apart from this occasional proviso, however, the new settlers had relatively free disposability of property.

It is clear that the privileges new settlers enjoyed were not just economic. Their exemption from certain princely impositions had, of course, a juridical as well as a fiscal side. In addition, the *ius Teutonicum* of eastern Europe endowed colonists not only with a relatively low rent and tax burden, but also with a special status, seen most clearly in the rules of judicial procedure that applied to them. The grant made by dukes Bolesław and Henry III of Silesia in 1247 to the tenants of three villages owned by the Augustinians of Wrocław not only established a render to the dukes of two measures of corn per *mansus* per annum but specified other conditions. The tenants were freed from obligations to the dukes, such as carting services, and from the duty of going on military expeditions. 'We add also,' continues the charter, 'that they shall not be summoned or troubled by the chamberlain without letter and seal from us; we ordain that they shall be summoned and heard before our presence.' After granting exemption from *prevod*, *zlad* and the other range of Polish exactions, the dukes conclude by saying:

we decree that none of our advocates shall have any power of judging, regulating or administrating in these villages, but we shall have two-thirds of the proceeds from the more important and difficult cases, namely capital charges or serious assaults, which are part of high justice, and the canons shall have a third.

The judicial regime of these villages was thus characterized by 'access to the top'. The ducal chamberlain and advocates, potentially unwelcome intermediaries, were excluded and the tenants subjected only to direct ducal jurisdiction. Such regulations formed a standard part of the *ius Teutonicum* in Silesia. When Henry III granted the village of Psie Pole (Hundsfeld) to St Vincent's, Wrocław, 'according to German law', he exempted the village from all levies and exactions and from the other burdens of Polish law and from the jurisdiction of our castellan and of other Polish judges and officials. We reserve jurisdiction for ourself only over the most important cases and we shall take two-thirds of the profits from them and the abbot one-third. They shall not be subject to anyone's judgement unless they are summoned before us by our sealed written instruction, to answer in accordance with the provisions of German law.

Lower justice was often left to be determined locally, as when Casimir of Opole (Oppeln) ruled for the new settlers of the abbey of Lubiąż: 'our advocate or judge shall have no competence in matters of strife, blows and simple wounding when no one is killed, but they shall have justice among themselves (*iudicium inter se habeant*). We abolish the power of our judges to judge in the village, except in capital cases, which pertain to us.' Sometimes even capital cases might be delegated, as in the case of Domaniów (Thomaskirch) in 1234, where it was ruled that 'if anyone merits death, he shall be judged in that village with the *Schulze* of [neighbouring] Oława [Ohlau] and the *Schulze* of the village presiding'. The text then goes on to reveal something of the difficulties that such local delegation might encounter in practice:

If a man of some castellan or other noble has a suit with one of the Germans of the village and is unwilling to be subject to the *Schulze*, in order to be just to both parties, we wish that the case should be determined before the duke if he is nearby or before one of the castellans whom both parties are willing to accept.

Here access to the top was a remedy when the tangled web of aristocratic patronage made local delegation unworkable.

This set of judicial privileges probably had its origins in the rights of the Dutch and Flemish settlers on the lower Weser and middle Elbe in the twelfth century, who had been granted local arrangements for lower justice, a limitation on the level of fines and the abolition of unwelcome procedural rules. By the second half of the thirteenth century they were being granted to settlers in Great Poland, such as the villagers of Jerzyń (Jerzen), who, 'even if they have committed an offence in the [neighbouring] town of Pobiedziska (Pudewitz), are to be judged in the village by their elders . . . A man, of whatever status and tongue, who commits an offence in the lands of the village shall be judged and punished there.' In 1294 the cottagers of Kalisz were granted the privilege 'that they shall enjoy German law freely, and in their judgements and lawsuits shall not be held to answer to take their suits before any man except our official, when they are properly summoned to judgement as is the German custom'. In

Silesia certain courts were designated as chief courts for all who lived according to colonists' law. In 1286 Racibórz (Ratibor) was established in this way for all 'who settled according to Flemish law in our domains' by the dukes of Opole-Racibórz, and in 1290 the bishop of Wrocław made Nysa (Neisse) the chief court for all doubtful lay cases 'in our German cities and villages'. The settlers according to German law thus had not only special rights but also a distinctive path through the judicial system.

The exclusion of intermediary officials was also a fundamental theme of the charters of privileges (*fueros*) granted to Spanish communities in the period of the Reconquest. The right to be judged locally was highly valued, as is clear from Alfonso I's charters for the Mozarabs, who were assured 'you shall have all your judgements at your gate, with all other peoples of other lands', or for the settlers of Artasona, who 'shall answer to no man and no court except at your gate of Artasona and according to your law'. The settlers at Tudela in the 1120s and subsequently were 'to have your judgements among yourselves, directly and as among neighbours (*vicinalimente et diractamente*), before my justice who will be there to represent me'.

The word that summed up all these rights and privileges was simple but pregnant – freedom. The settlers whom the Hospitallers were allowed to establish on their Moravian lands in the early thirteenth century were 'to have in all things secure liberty, a firm and unchanging law' (*securam libertatem, ius stabile et firmum*). Christian immigrants to the reconquered Ebro were to be 'free and free-born' (*francos et ingenuos*) and to have their lands *francum et liberum et ingenuum et securum*. It was a freedom that transcended differences of race or condition. 'Let the men gathered there,' decreed Bela IV for the new settlers of Beregowo, 'of whatever status or language, live under one and the same liberty.' The laws of Santa María de Cortes in 1182 stated categorically that 'nobles and knights and Jews and Muslims who come to settle shall be liable to the same fines and the same judicial regime (*talem calumpniam et tale forum*) as the other settlers'. The simple terms of freedom encapsulated a programme, the same that Count Roger of Sicily had proposed with equally eloquent conciseness: 'the village would be called *Franca*, that is, free village'. The new lands of settlement were, like all of medieval Europe, lands of lords, but they were also, and not necessarily paradoxically, lands of freedom.

6. The New Landscape

===

You shall make your permanent residence there, building new houses and improving those already built . . . you shall work and till all those lands and vineyards, both cultivated and uncultivated, well and faithfully for our profit and for yours, you shall carefully clear all the oak woods on the land that are profitable and suitable for producing bread and bring them into permanent cultivation . . . and you shall improve everything.

In 1237 Bishop Thomas of Wrocław granted to Peter, the *Schulze* or local magistrate of Nysa (Neisse), the second city of his bishopric, 200 Flemish *mansi* in 'a black oak wood', to be cleared and settled. The lands granted formed a solid block running westwards from the left bank of the river Nysa, an important tributary of the Oder. Two hundred Flemish *mansi* represent about 8,000 acres, so this was clearly an ambitious undertaking. A century after this grant was made a survey of the lands of the bishopric enables us to see how successful the planned development had been. In the place of the 'black oak wood' stood four villages of various sizes (61, 20, 80 and 43 Flemish *mansi*) but with a total area of almost exactly 200 *mansi*. They bore German names, one, Petersheide ('Peter's heath'), probably enshrining the name of the original *locator*, Peter of Nysa; while two, Schönheide ('beautiful heath') and Friedewalde ('peaceful forest'), have the ring of promotional literature. Petersheide, Friedewalde and Gross Briesen each had a church, endowed with two *mansi*, and the inhabitants of the much smaller Schönheide (20 *mansi*) presumably attended one of them. The *Schulze* possessed substantial holdings (14, 4, 18 and 7 *mansi*) in each village. Gross Briesen had a tavern, Petersheide and Schönheide a tavern and a watermill, while Friedewalde, with its 80 *mansi* or 3,200 acres of arable, its two taverns and two watermills, was clearly a centre of local significance. Within a century a swath of natural woodland had been transformed into a human landscape with all the complex apparatus of food processing, sociability and cult that the high medieval community disposed of. What were the mechanics of such a revolution?

LEAVING HOME

New peasant settlement took many forms. It could be piecemeal, advancing on the edge of old settlements, or wholesale, as in the new planned villages carved out of the woodland in eastern Europe. Sometimes it was stimulated by the building of new fortifications or new ecclesiastical institutions, which acted like grit in an oyster, working on their environment and eventually surrounding themselves with a swath of new settlement. In 1101, for example, the monastery of Pegau, east of the Saale (the approximate boundary between German and Slav settlement at that time), was reformed and received a new abbot, Windolf, who immediately began reconstruction of the abbey buildings, working 'like a highly skilled maker of seals':

he considered the site and had the rough or marshy places levelled and cleared of thorns and brushwood. He widened and enlarged everything and he skilfully shaped the church which had been committed to him, just like a seal, into an image of perfect beauty . . . he began cultivation of the place which is now called *Abbatisdorf* ['Abbot's village'] after him, clearing the trees and undergrowth, uprooting the thick woods and expanding new fields; when a church had been built there and a manor house for the utility of the inhabitants, he granted it to the monks in perpetuity.

There is a recent tendency among historians to minimize the agricultural importance of the monasteries, especially the new foundations of the twelfth century, but in this case the older heroic picture seems more appropriate. New abbeys could lead to new villages.

Similarly, a new castle might generate settlement in its shadow. Fortifications were often located in wild places, either to gain the defensive advantage of inaccessibility or because they were on dangerous frontiers, like the military works planned by the monks of St Cugat in Catalonia in 1017 'in barren marches and in solitary places, against the ambushes of the pagans'. Once built and manned, however, defensive structures required labour and foodstuffs that could be supplied most conveniently by a nearby population of cultivators, while, of course, they simultaneously offered protection to such a population. A multiplication of settlements was indeed the outcome of the military construction on the Catalan frontier: 'there is scarcely one modern village in the region that does not owe its origin to a tenth-century fortress'.

William, archbishop of Tyre, describes the effects of another programme of castle-building, this one undertaken by the crusaders in the region between Jerusalem and Ascalon in the 1130s and 1140s:

Those who held property in the adjacent area had confidence in the protection of these neighbouring castles and built many settlements in their shadow (*suburbana loca*). These contained many households and tillers of the soil and, on account of their settlement there, the whole region became more secure and a great supply of food could be produced for the surrounding localities.

One of these new settlements was Beth Gibelin, where the Hospitallers granted the colonists favourable rights 'so that the land may be better populated'. The inhabitants each had a large holding of two carucates (perhaps 150 acres or so) and held it heritably in return for rent. A list of settlers dating to 1168 shows that many of them had come from western Europe: Sancho the Gascon, Stephen the Lombard, Peter the Catalan, Bruno of Burgundy, Gerard Fleming, Gilbert of Carcasonne, etc. The fortresses of the 1130s had spawned colonial settlements of European farmers and artisans.

While the evidence for the juridical structure of the new villages discussed in the previous chapter is reasonably extensive, the mechanics of migration can be reconstructed imaginatively but hardly documented to any extent. Migrants must have made arrangements about the disposal of their property, transport to the new site and acquisition of property there; they must have needed information and capital and help in their early years; but only the most general outline of these vital processes can be recovered from the evidence. We know, for instance, that in 1210 the brothers Peter and Fortunius García sold their land to the monastery of Santo Domingo de la Calzada for 166 *morabetinos* since 'they wished to go to join the new settlers in Moya' (*volentes ire ad populationem Mohie*). We do not know exactly how much land they sold, on what terms they acquired property in Moya or whether they made a profit – long-term or short-term – on the exchange. Even for the modern period it is difficult to trace individual migrants at both their starting point and their eventual goal, and for the Middle Ages it is usually impossible. References to migrants leaving their homes, such as that to the García brothers, are extremely rare. Our picture of the actual process of migration in the High Middle Ages will, then, have to remain general and somewhat speculative. We must do the best we can.

We can start with a peasant who wished to migrate and a colonial lord who wished to recruit tenants. The former might be a younger son, a criminal or simply someone driven by hunger, like 'the many who left their fields on account of a great famine in Germany and sought refuge in

Poland' in 1264. Naturally, there had to be some line of communication between the lord and this potential pool of migrants. This could be provided informally, by travellers' gossip and the like, but a surer way was organized advertisement. East German lords who wished to colonize the holdings they had in thinly settled border regions or newly acquired conquests often launched recruiting campaigns in the more densely settled parts of Germany to the west. An early example is Wiprecht of Groitzsch, 'the ruler of those parts inhabited by the [Slavic] Sorbs', who, around 1104, 'caused new land to be cleared in the diocese of Merseburg'. He then went to Franconia, where his mother was living with her second husband, and 'brought back many Franconian peasants and instructed them to cultivate the region, when they had cleared the forest, and to possess it by hereditary right'.

A particularly vivid series of recruiting drives is portrayed in the *Chronicle of the Slavs* of Helmold of Bosau, who wrote in the 1170s. He describes the settlement of newly conquered Wagria (eastern Holstein) by Count Adolf II in the 1140s:

Because the land was uninhabited, he sent messengers into all the regions, namely Flanders, Holland, Utrecht, Westphalia and Frisia, saying that whoever was oppressed by shortage of land to farm should come with their families and occupy this good and spacious land, which is fruitful, full of fish and meat, good for pasture ... At this appeal there arose an innumerable multitude from various nations, who took their families and chattels and came to Wagria to Count Adolf to take possession of the land he had promised to them.

In the following decades other German lords pursued the same policy. Albert the Bear of Brandenburg

sent to Utrecht and the places near the Rhine, especially to those who live near the Ocean and suffer the force of the sea, namely the men of Holland, Zeeland and Flanders, and brought a large number of these people whom he settled in the fortresses and towns of the Slavs.

Something of the flavour of these recruiting drives is provided by a document of 1108, an appeal to the leading men of Westphalia, Lotharingia and Flanders to help conquer the territory of the Wends. It is addressed to lords rather than peasants, of course, but perhaps these two classes had some common dreams regarding land:

These pagans are the worst of men but their land is the best, with meat, honey and flour. If it is cultivated the produce of the land will be such that none other can compare with it. That is what they say who know about it. So, O Saxons,

Franconians, Lotharingians and Flemings, here you will be able both to save your souls and, if you will, to acquire very good land to settle.

Westerners often remarked upon both the emptiness and the potential fertility of eastern Europe. Hungary, wrote Otto of Freising, uncle of the German emperor Frederick Barbarossa, 'is known to be rich both from the natural pleasantness of its appearance and from the fertility of its fields'. But, he lamented, 'its fields have scarcely felt the plough and mattock' and he puzzled over what had 'exposed a land as delectable as this to such, not men, but human monsters'. The French monk, Odo of Deuil, passing through the borderlands of Hungary and Bulgaria, commented that they 'abound in those good things which nature herself brings forth and could support the rest, if there were settlers'.

A fascinating, though flickering, light is cast upon the rudimentary mechanics of emigration by another passage in Helmold's *Chronicle*. Describing a pagan Slav attack on a colony of Frisians in Süsel in Wagria, not far from the Baltic Sea, he writes that, although the immigrant population numbered 400 men or more, 'when the Slavs arrived scarcely one hundred were to be found in the fortress, for the others had returned home to make arrangements about the property they had left behind' (*ceteris in patriam reversis propter ordinandum peculium illic relictum*). The distances involved here are not great, since it is less than a week's journey from Frisia to the Baltic, but we do see, perhaps uniquely, the toing and froing of emigrants, coming to see their new homes, returning to settle their affairs, making the eastward journey once again. In some cases, especially for those with substantial landed property, the links between old home and new might be regular. The twelfth-century *fuero* of Toledo, for example, makes provision for the citizen who might wish to go to France, Castile or Galicia, or visit 'his lands beyond the mountains' during the winter months.

Modern studies of migration lay considerable emphasis on two factors that one can scarcely document for the twelfth and thirteenth centuries. One is the issue of remittances home. In the twentieth century there has been a considerable flow of capital from 'guest workers' back to their families in their place of origin. However, in a time of silver coinage, such transfers were perhaps hardly possible for those outside the trading network. While Italian merchants could use letters of credit and the kings of England guard their barrels of pennies with soldiers, it was much more difficult for the prosperous or careful son in Andalusia or Prussia to send home money to his mother in Old Castile or Saxony. This aspect of migration was probably unimportant. Remigrants, the immigrants who came home, are another factor much evident in modern migration, and may also have been of some significance in the medieval period. The explanation for such a trajectory could be great wealth acquired away from home, which the emigrant now wished to flaunt on the only stage which was real for him, his birthplace; but, alternatively, return home could indicate the complete failure of the emigrant's plans, a sad homecoming to lick his wounds. In the case of the high medieval peasant colonization under discussion here, settlers went with the hope of taking up a farm in the colonial lands. Return and failure were thus synonyms. One document from the thirteenth century gives a little information on the subject of returning emigrants.

In 1236 the bishop of Hildesheim made an agreement with the count of Lauenrode. The county was divided into two parts, the 'small county' which went to the bishop and the 'large county' which was retained by the count's relatives. The inhabitants of each of the two parts were to remain in their respective county and anyone who fled from one county to another was to be returned. 'But anyone living either beyond the Elbe or elsewhere outside the land,' the agreement runs, 'will be free to return as he wishes to either the small or the large county.' This document is enlightening. It shows how normal a situation emigration beyond the Elbe was by the 1230s, so that it could be specified as a likely contingency. It also shows that the possibility of return from beyond the Elbe could also be readily envisaged. Perhaps not every emigrant found the favourable circumstances he had expected. Remigrants may have been a larger category than we imagine.

Some of the references already cited show emigrants leaving their fields or disposing of their property, and it is clear that many colonists were not landless men, but already peasant farmers in their homelands. Even those who were driven to emigrate by desperate circumstances sometimes had land to sell, like the bondsmen of Heiningen in Saxony who, 'devastated by rapine and arson and on account of their great poverty', surrendered five *mansi* to their lord and left the region, or the 'poor country-dwellers' in the Rhineland in the 1170s who were forced 'to sell their patrimonies and migrate to foreign lands'. In these cases the income from the disposal of property could have been used to support the emigrants in the transitional period before they obtained new land and in the difficult early years. Emigration requires resources as well as will, and it has been noticed in some modern migratory movements that the typical migrant is in the middle of the socio-economic range, neither rich nor destitute, and hence with both the incentive and the ability to move and make a new start. Experienced farmers will also have been more attractive than the landless or destitute to lords and others recruiting labour.

LAYING FOUNDATIONS

One of the first tasks in establishing new agricultural settlements was the demarcation of sites for houses, courtyards and fields. In heavily wooded country this was sometimes difficult. The delimitation of the lands of the Cistercian monastery of Henryków (Heinrichau) in Silesia involved observations from hilltop to hilltop and the use of smoke-signals as guides in the tree-covered valleys. Boundary marks were then cut on trees. In more open country a furrow drawn by a plough might be adequate. In the lands east of the Elbe the job was a complicated one, since not only demarcation but measurement was involved. The building block of the *Ostsiedlung* was the *mansus*, a holding of determined area, 40 acres in the case of the Flemish *mansus*, approximately 60 in the case of the Frankish. When a new village was laid out, the number of prospective *mansi* had to be specified and then measured out on the ground. Villages were sometimes even named after the number of *mansi* they contained, such as the 'village *septem mansi*' (Siebenhufen, now Siemisławice) in Silesia. Attempts were made at uniformity. For example, a size of sixty-four *mansi* was customary for new villages in some areas, such as the Neumark of Brandenburg, where over half the villages were of this size.

Sometimes the number of *mansi* in large grants must have been only an estimate, for it is hard to believe that when Wladislaw Odonicz of Great Poland endowed the Teutonic Knights with 500 *mansi* in 1224 or the Cistercians with stretches of land assessed at 2,000 and 3,000 *mansi* in 1233 the exact dimensions had been carefully measured – 3,000 *mansi* represents an area of about 200 square miles. Even in the case of smaller grants there was an element of approximation. One thirteenth-century ducal grant from Silesia, conceding that two villages may be settled according to German law, observes: 'Since the number of *mansi* to be established there is still uncertain, we cannot say what our total revenue will be.' The very earliest surviving settlement agreement from Silesia, issued by Duke Henry the Bearded in 1221, concerns a village of fifty *mansi*, but adds the proviso: 'if there is woodland there over and above the fifty *mansi*, we annex that to the village on the same terms'. Indeed, the possibility that later princely or seigneurial investigation might find the capacity for more *mansi* than originally estimated, and the fear that lords might increase the assessment in *mansi* and hence the economic burdens on the village, prompted some settlers of the *Ostsiedlung* to purchase immunity from disadvantageous remeasurement. The prince of Rügen received twenty-six marks in 1255 from some settlers 'so that their village with its *mansi* shall remain for ever in its old boundaries without remeasurement'. An examination of lands in Bohemia in the mid-fourteenth century revealed that there were at least sixty-four *mansi* on land estimated at sixty-one, and the inhabitants paid heavily that the upward reassessment should be limited to these three *mansi* – thus a 5 per cent increase in their burdens – and that the *mansi* 'should never be remeasured'. One Cistercian house with lands in Mecklenburg was quite blunt: 'if the lords of the land [i.e. the dukes of Mecklenburg] ask what is the number of *mansi*, care should be taken to dissimulate as much as possible'.

However, in most cases the measurement of *mansi* was not guesswork. The ducal village of Pogel in Silesia, established according to Flemish law in 1259, had been measured and delimited and estimated at twenty-one and a half *mansi* plus one *mansus* which was inundated and was to be regarded as common land. Measuring rods and measuring lines were used. The Polish and Czech words for the latter, *sznur* and *snura* respectively, are borrowed from the German *Schnur*, indicating the direction of influence. Measurement 'by line' (*per funiculi distinctionem* or *in funiculo distribucionis*), mentioned by the chronicler Helmold of Bosau and in charters, does indeed carry a whiff of the Psalmist – 'He cast out the heathen also before them and divided them an inheritance by line' (*divisit eis terram in funiculo distribucionis*) – but there were also physical rods and lines at work in the woods. The Silesian dukes had *mensuratores* or surveyors, and when Adolf, count of Holstein, tried to cheat the bishop of Oldenburg 'he had the land measured by a short line, unfamiliar to us' and included marsh and woodland in the assessment. In Henryków 'the cultivators were summoned once the measurement of the *mansi* was completed'. A Prussian document of 1254 refers to '135 standard lines, with which holdings in Prussia are measured'. Most convincingly of all, the rectilinear plan and approximate uniformity of the villages and holdings of the *Ostsiedlung*, as revealed in maps and surveys of the eighteenth and nineteenth centuries, is hard to explain except by planned layout in the period of colonization: these places were carved out with the measuring rod.

The process of measuring out land can be pictured from the grant made by the Teutonic Knights in Prussia to the Saxon aristocrat Dietrich of Tiefenau in 1236. They gave him a castle 'and 300 Flemish *mansi* at present uncultivated but cultivable, whose number he will measure'. The Flemish *mansus* was the standard holding in Prussia, as laid down in the Chełmno (Culm) charter of 1233. Dietrich's lands were described by rough boundaries: beginning from the estates appurtenant to Marienwerder

(Kwidzyn), going in one direction downstream along the river Nogat as far as the pine forest, and in the other in a straight line to the cultivated fields around Riesenburg (Prabuty). If the area so bounded did not contain 300 *mansi*, the Knights promised to make it up with cultivable land around Riesenburg. Pinewoods of *mansus* proportions within the delimited area were not to be counted towards the eventual total (as Count Adolf of Holstein *had* done). Practical trigonometry of the kind suggested here reached a point of formal elaboration in Prussia in the *Geometria Culmensis* of *c.* 1400, 'a book of practical geometry' supposedly written in response to the concern of the Grand Master of the Teutonic Knights 'about the measuring of fields'.

Of course, not every new village was carved out of the virgin forest. In eastern Europe there were often already settlements and, at the least, a named landscape into which or around which newcomers fitted. In Sicily the Norman conquerors retained 'the ancient divisions of the Saracens', and in the Iberian peninsula the prior human geography was even more strongly etched, for Muslim Spain had been fairly thickly settled, even if warfare and conquest had depopulated some areas, such as the village and lands of Aragosa, granted to the bishop of Sigüenza in 1143, whose 'limits were not known because of the long period of time in which it had been abandoned'. The distinction between appropriation of settled land and colonization of new land appears clearly from two virtually contemporary grants in Aragon, one of the houses of a named Muslim former proprietor 'as they were best held in the time of the Moors', another of unoccupied land with the right 'to build houses in that empty land (*eremo*) as best you can do it'. The phrase 'as they were best held in the time of the Moors' implies a continuity of legal geography, the words 'as best you can do it' a pioneer's *carte blanche*. Both situations existed in the newly colonized lands.

Once the new holdings had been marked out, they had to be allocated. The *mansi* of the *Ostsiedlung* seem to have been assigned by lot, since a Silesian document of 1223 refers to 'the allocation of *mansi* by lot in the German way', suggesting that the practice was a familiar part of the process of colonization. Naturally, attempts were made at fairness. When the monks of St Clement's, Toledo, settled Argance in 1340 each settler received a *yugada* of arable in three parts, one of good, one of medium and one of poor quality. The allocation of newly conquered property in Spain stimulated procedural rules and specialists. *Partitores* were active in twelfth-century Saragossa and houses were granted 'by the king's distributor according to the rule of distribution' (*a regis distributore distributionis iure*). This tendency culminated in the great *libros del repartimiento* of the thirteenth and fourteenth centuries, huge registers allocating property to the conquerors and immigrants.

The very greatest lords and landowners, kings, dukes, great bishops, like those of Toledo and Wrocław (Breslau), the military orders and the monasteries, were interested in developing their estates, but they had to have local men to organize and supervise at the village level. This was the role of the *locator*. Such a man must already have been a fairly wealthy and respected person before he undertook to establish a new settlement, for both capital and connections were prerequisites for the task, though the lord might well help him out, as in the case of the *locator* Peter of Nysa, who was granted twelve marks and 300 bushels of rye by the bishop of Wrocław 'as a help to the new settlement' (*in adiutorium locacionis*). Some *locatores* obviously acquired a reputation. The Bohemian king Przemysl Ottokar II granted Conrad of Löwendorf a new settlement since 'we have heard that he is the right man for such things and is experienced'. In Silesia *locatores* were sometimes of knightly origin, vassals of the dukes or bishops; from the mid-thirteenth century a few burgesses might also be active in this field; one or two cases suggest mere peasants. In Bohemia a moneyer and a royal servitor are fairly typical examples. Similar entrepreneurs of settlement in Spain are termed *populatores*, though the term is ambiguous, since it also meant the settlers themselves. When Alfonso VII of Castile granted land to build a castle to 'his *populator* and servant' in 1139, however, the sense is clear. Such men were rewarded, like their eastern European counterparts, with holdings in the villages they founded or peopled. Alfonso I granted one of his local officials 'two *iugatae* of land because you have organized that settlement'. If successful, the process of *locatio* reinforced the *locator*'s position. Even though they were not the landlords, the entrepreneurs of the *Ostsiedlung*, as farmers of 100 or 200 acres, as recognized intermediaries between lord and settler and as local magistrates (*Schulzen*), can easily be imagined as dominating village society.

Not every planned settlement was a success, as the thirteenth-century Polish Count Bronisz discovered. He had invited 'a certain German named Franco' to lease a corner of his estate and see 'if he could settle some Germans on that property for me'; and, at about the same time, Bronisz's German miller, William, who leased a mill that the count had built, suggested that 'if I agreed he would summon Germans and build and settle a German village'. Neither Franco nor William, however, came up to expectations: the former 'was not able to develop and settle the property because of poverty'; the latter, despite his promise to build a German village, 'was not able to do it and had no men to settle the village'. Bronisz eventually decided that the spiritual – and possible material – rewards of founding a religious house were preferable to these abortive projects and built a Cistercian monastery on the lands in question.

One urban *locatio* failed because 'dissension arose among the *locatores*, some died, some were oppressed by poverty and sold their share in the *locatio* for cash'. This possibility of failed *locatio* explains why lords might write penalty clauses into their agreements with *locatores*. When the canons of Vyšehrad by Prague granted their prebends to the *locator* Henry of Humpoletz, it was 'on condition that he settle cultivators in those properties within the year' and with the proviso that 'if he has not settled tenants within the year he shall lose all right to those properties and his guarantors . . . shall pay us thirty marks of silver'. As some of these citations reveal, one of the crucial factors determining success or failure was the amount of wealth the *locator* could apply to the project. New settlement required capital as well as labour.

One of the largest capital outlays involved in establishing new villages was the construction of a mill, the biggest machine of the medieval world. The use of water power for grinding grain was a normal part of European cereal agriculture in the High Middle Ages, despite the rational preference that some peasants showed for their own hand-mills. Mills were expensive but profitable, especially if they were built or owned by a lord who could force his tenants to bring their corn to be ground at his mill and pay for the privilege. Indeed, the seigneurial mill, whose construction was financed by lordly revenues from rents, courts, demesne farming, office or booty, was the most common type in this period. Less frequently found was the communal or jointly owned mill, such as the one that twenty-one small free proprietors sold to the abbot of Cardeña in 1012. The individual peasant could not normally expect to finance such a costly enterprise and there are cases of failed attempts by peasants to erect mills at their own expense. In the newly settled regions mills were sometimes seigneurial, but on occasion the colonists were granted the right to build their own. For example, in return for constructing a fortification, the settlers of Marcilla were allowed 'to construct free mills' (*molinos facere ingenuos*) by Peter I of Aragon. In the villages of the *Ostsiedlung* the right to build mills was very frequently one of the privileges enjoyed by the *locator*. Bishop Bruno of Olomouc (Olmütz) (1245–81), for example, who developed a virtually standard form of agreement for *locatio* in his diocese, usually granted *locatores* the right to construct a one-wheeled mill, which would be 'free'. Similarly, when Bishop Henry of Ermland entrusted his brother, John

Fleming, with an extensive project of settlement in Prussia in 1289, he granted the land 'with the mills that may be freely constructed there'.

QUESTIONS OF SCALE

Given what was said in the previous chapter about the deficiencies of medieval evidence for population history, it is not surprising that it is very difficult to give a statistical picture of the migratory movements. There are no passenger lists, no censuses which record place of birth (though toponymic surnames offer some help), and even casual explicit references to emigration are rare, though a few do exist. Siegfried Epperlein collected examples for his book on the causes of the east Elbian migration and some of these are enlightening. In 1238 serfs of the abbey of Iburg, south of Osnabrück, were in trouble for having sold a property that they held, it was claimed, as tenants and bailiffs, not as proprietors: 'knowing that they had committed a great offence against justice and against their lord, they set out for the lands beyond the Elbe, intending never to return'. In the following decade the provost of the church of the Holy Cross in Hildesheim, 'hearing that Alward, our bondsman, proposed to go to the lands beyond the Elbe', summoned the prospective emigrant and required from him an oath that he would do nothing in his new home to the prejudice of the house. Sometimes the evidence is more general. The chronicler of the monastery of Rastede, a house located in the flat lands where the Weser flows into the North Sea, complained of local aristocrats 'preying on the monastery's property so much that virtually all the tenants emigrated beyond the Elbe with their chattels'.

These references simply tell us that some German peasants went from the old-settled parts of Germany to the new lands beyond the Elbe. There is still no hint of the scale of migration. Attempts have been made to calculate this. One of the most exacting scholars to deal with the subject, Walter Kuhn, estimated the number of German rural colonists settling east of the Elbe–Saale line in the twelfth century at 200,000. He based this calculation on the number of *mansi* or peasant farms which can be demonstrated or reasonably assumed to have been created in this first wave of German settlement. The areas settled at this time, eastern Holstein, western Brandenburg and the Saxon marks, themselves then provided migrants for the regions further east, such as Mecklenburg, Pomerania, Silesia, the Sudetenland and Prussia, that were settled in the thirteenth century – pioneer parents producing pioneer children. Kuhn also pointed out, using modern parallels, the way immigrant populations in new lands can multiply quickly, doubling within a generation.

Even if it is difficult to attain an accurate figure for the number of German immigrants east of the Elbe, there is still at least good documentary evidence for the existence of such large-scale immigration. Hundreds of documents establishing the terms of new settlement (*Lokationsurkunden*) survive. When we turn to the question of immigration from England into the Celtic countries, such documentation is lacking. This is curious. Some writers have speculated that there were indeed *locator*-type figures at work in Ireland but, if so, they have left no trace, and this absence of explicit record means that it is possible for quite a wide difference of opinion to exist on the importance of immigration in colonial Ireland. Jocelyn Otway-Ruthven argued that 'the Norman settlement of Ireland was no mere military occupation but a part of that great movement of peasant colonization which dominates so much of the economic development of Europe from the eleventh to the fourteenth centuries', and she sought to demonstrate the existence in south-eastern Ireland by 1300 of 'an occupying, cultivating population of small free tenants of English, or occasionally Welsh, origin, who in some districts probably considerably outnumbered the native Irish'. Such a situation, she concluded, 'could only have been produced by a substantial immigration in the first couple of generations of the conquest'.

While Otway-Ruthven's position is not directly challenged, a quite different emphasis is advanced by the historical geographer R. E. Glasscock, who has written in the *New History of Ireland*: 'while this new colonial element may have been locally important, it cannot have been very large numerically in the context of Ireland as a whole'. Some aspects of the movement of people from England and Wales (not to mention Scotland) to Ireland in the late twelfth and thirteenth centuries can be quantified. For example, we know that the English and Welsh soldiers who went across the Irish Sea must have numbered in the thousands, starting with the 30 knights, 60 men-at-arms and 300 archers who landed with Robert fitz Stephen in 1169. Strongbow supposedly brought an army of 1,200 with him in the following year. Of course, not all of these men stayed in Ireland or even stayed alive, but many must have settled down. The Crown created over 400 knights' fees in the country, and even if there was no simple correspondence of one fee to one immigrant aristocrat, here again is a straw in the wind. Perhaps more significantly, over 200 boroughs were created. Many were clearly not 'urban' in the economic sense, but all presuppose at least a few burgesses, and the evidence tends to support the idea that these would be immigrants. This is certainly and dramatically the case for Dublin (see next chapter). We know also that the clerical establishment in the south-east of the country was anglicized, often to quite a lowly level in the hierarchy.

All this evidence, however, could point to no more than a 'Livonian' situation: an élite of feudal lords, burgesses and clerics ethnically and culturally distinct from the vast mass of the native rural population. Direct indications of peasant immigration scarcely exist. When Hamo de Valognes, former justiciar of Ireland, was granted 'licence to bring his men from wherever they may be to settle his land', or when, in 1251, there is reference to 'waste lands' which the justiciar of Ireland 'will cause to be settled', we have only the most general picture of landlords actively engaged in colonization and settlement – the new settlers could just as well be Irish as immigrant. Much more explicit, but also unique, is a royal mandate of 1219 commanding the custodian of County Waterford not to impede the bishop of Waterford from 'leasing out his land and receiving Englishmen to settle it'.

No one would, of course, deny that some settlers went to Ireland from England in the thirteenth century. The case for large-scale immigration rests upon two foundations. First, lists of peasant tenants do survive from the early fourteenth century for various parts of Ireland and a large number of the names are English and Welsh. Second, there is quite a lot of evidence for the implantation of the English language in Ireland at a local, rural level, and this would be improbable in the absence of substantial peasant settlement.

The early fourteenth century lists, on which Otway-Ruthven based her argument, are a little late to be ideal evidence. It is known, and Otway-Ruthven herself provided several examples, that some Irishmen adopted both English forenames and surnames. By the early fourteenth century, 150 years after the first coming of the Anglo-Normans, such a process might have gone far. We know, for example, that 150 years after the Norman Conquest of England the English peasantry had adopted the names of the Norman aristocracy even though there had been no substantial immigration from northern France (see Chapter 11). This involved forenames, however, and surnames are a slightly different issue. They are often ordinary language, such as 'Swift', 'Archer' or 'Mason', may give some hint of geographical origin (e.g. 'Devenish', 'Walsh') and, even when simple patronymics, at least push the evidence a generation or two further back.

One rich collection of early-fourteenth-century rentals and surveys is the so-called *Red Book of Ormond*, compiled for the Butlers and relating mainly to their property. Some twenty-eight individual surveys are recorded for the period 1300–1314. Various local situations emerge from these records. One category is exemplified by Corduff in County Dublin. This was a small manor but quite heavily populated. In 1311 it had a dilapidated manor house and dovecote, a garden used for pasture, a courtyard and barn. The demesne belonging to the manor amounted to 218 acres of arable, 20 of meadow and 15 of pasture. The tenants of the manor fell into two distinct groups. On the one hand, there were the free tenants and farmers, numbering seventeen, who rented arable holdings at eightpence or a shilling per acre. Then there were twenty-seven cottagers, who paid about sixpence each for their cottages and an additional fourpence as a monetary substitute for the labour services they had previously owed. There is no record of their having any arable land. Since their names are not given, it is impossible to use this clue to their nationality; but in those manors described in the *Red Book* where the names of cottagers are recorded, they are overwhelmingly Irish. The other group, of freeholders and farmers, possessed holdings that ranged in size from 1 acre to 45 acres, the average being 9 acres. Most of them bore names that suggest English descent, such as Lawrence Godsweyn, Robert of Newton, Stephen of England. Five, however, are clearly Irish, with names like Donald Mouenath, Gilmartin O Duffgan, etc. These five were among the least well-endowed, two having holdings of a single acre, the others holding respectively $1\frac{1}{2}$, 2 and $3\frac{1}{2}$ acres. Only two of those with English names had such small holdings. Hence the free tenants and farmers of probable English origin, comprising slightly less than a third of the total population, formed a local peasant aristocracy of wealth and status.

Elsewhere English settlement seems to have been more substantial. Of the sixty or so burgesses of Moyaliff in County Tipperary only two or three have Irish names. Many belonged to a few dominant families (White, Beech, Stonebreak), and Moyaliff seems to represent a tightly knit and reasonably populous settler community. At Gowran in County Kilkenny there were also burgesses, though their names are not recorded, and, in addition, about ninety free tenants holding land in the surrounding countryside in plots ranging from 20 acres to a whole fee (theoretically 1,200 acres). Moreover there were another 200 free tenants with smallholdings of land. Virtually every free tenant in Gowran had an English name. Indeed, this pattern is true of all the Butler estates described in the *Red Book*. When named, military tenants, free tenants and burgesses almost all have English names; farmers and gablars, next in the hierarchy, usually do so too; cottagers have Irish names; *betaghs*, members of the Irish servile class, though hardly ever named, are presumed to be of Irish origin.

The evidence of the *Red Book* and other comparable surveys supports the idea that Anglo-Welsh immigration into southern and eastern Ireland was significant. By 1300 it is even possible to talk of a partial anglicization of parts of Ireland, for this deeply rooted English-speaking landholding class had begun to leave a cultural imprint, particularly in language. Field names are one sign of this. In 1306 a marriage contract was drawn up by David Gerard of Gowran and William de Preston, regarding the marriage of David's son, Robert, and William's daughter, Alice. Alice was to receive an endowment from both her father and her prospective husband. William was to give her 8 acres in Gowran 'in the Schortebottes and the Botherfeld', while Robert was to grant her 60 acres, split between 'the field of Balycardyssan', 'the Brodfelde' and 'the Crosfelde', which last lay along the Gowran–Kilkenny road. By the early fourteenth century the fields of south-east Ireland had thus been given English names.

English settlement was not uniformly distributed in Ireland, being concentrated in town rather than country and in the south and east of the island rather than the north and west. Even as late as the seventeenth century, this south-eastern zone was the region most marked by anglicized land units like the ploughland, and to the present day its place names have a distinctive anglicized pattern. A regional distribution of this type is fairly easy to explain. First, the colony had a bridgehead character: the settlers came from, and often kept in touch with, English and Welsh ports that were nearer to the south and east coasts of Ireland. Second, the best soils are found in the south and east. The distribution of desirable farmland thus reinforced the immigrants' natural orientation. In these heavily colonized areas there was an immigrant peasantry.

NEW TOOLS

The new settlers represented a fresh influx of manpower in the regions they settled and their economic and legal privileges established a framework favourable to economic production. In some cases, but only some, they may also have introduced a superior agricultural technology. In the Iberian peninsula, of course, the settlers had as much to learn as to teach, and in many areas the problem they faced was the maintenance of a functioning system of irrigative farming, not its replacement by something more productive. When James I of Aragon confirmed the rights to use the water of the Valencian irrigation system, he stressed that this should continue to be done 'as it was of old and according to the manner it was established and accustomed to be done in the time of the Saracens'.

In eastern Europe the question is more hotly debated whether the new settlers generally brought with them an agricultural technology superior to the one they found or whether their main contribution was simply manpower. It is true that the colonial villages east of the Elbe possessed a remarkable regularity in plan and uniformity in structure that distinguished them, but it is hard to establish a direct link between right angles and productivity. While it may be the case, as the traditional German historiography has it, that the most important implement the immigrants brought with them was the heavy plough, the evidence on such vital issues as tools and farming practices is slight and ambiguous.

The plough, the chief agricultural implement of the medieval economy, is a complex instrument, which can be manufactured and used in a variety of ways. An important distinction is between the symmetrical action of the ard or scratch-plough (French *araire*, German *Haken*), which carves a groove, pushing the earth to either side, and the so-called 'heavy' plough (French *charrue*, German *Pflug*), which turns the soil over to right or left. To do this the latter must have an asymmetrical share and a mould-board (these are, in fact, its defining features rather than 'heaviness' – ards can be heavier than 'heavy' ploughs).

This fundamental distinction in action and effect is not the only significant variation in plough construction and function. Ploughs can be pulled by horses or by oxen; by many beasts or few (or by people or machines, of course); have wheels or not; employ the coulter – a vertical blade making an incision in the soil ahead of the share – or not; and so on. For the medieval period the intrinsic complexity of the issue is compounded by the scarcity and ambiguity of the sources. A credible agricultural story has to be teased out of passing references in clerical chronicles, cryptic entries in accounts and illustrations to psalters and calendars.

The earliest relevant written evidence on the question of German and Slavic ploughs comes in Helmold's *Chronicle of the Slavs*, dating to the 1170s. In three separate places he refers to a 'Slavic plough' (*Slavicum aratrum*) as a unit upon which tithes were assessed. On each occasion he explains the term: 'a pair of oxen or one horse makes up a Slavic plough', it is a plough 'which consists of two oxen or one horse', 'a Slavic plough is made up of two oxen or the same number of horses'. These references are not absolutely clear. Apart from the puzzling uncertainty about the number of horses in a Slavic plough – an uncertainty which may be a mere slip – there is the question of what it means to 'make up' a plough. If the reality behind the phrase is purely fiscal, that is, if the 'Slavic plough' is simply a unit of tithe assessment, then we may have learned nothing about the agricultural implement involved. Yet what, in Helmold's eyes, makes this plough 'Slavic' (it is surely not an appellation employed by the Slavs themselves)? It is possible that there was no physical difference between the plough used by Germans and Slavs, but that the Slavs only used two oxen or a horse (or two horses) for traction, while the Germans used more. It is possible that there was no difference at all between the two ploughs and their teams, but that the Slavs used the team as a unit of tithe assessment and the Germans did not – hence a 'Slavic plough' was 'a normal plough team upon which tithes were assessed'. Clearly Helmold provides us with a problem rather than an answer. His evidence must be supplemented with other material before we can form a more solid picture.

Documentary evidence of the later twelfth and thirteenth centuries provides both a range of apparent synonyms for the 'Slavic plough' and a variety of terms that are contrasted with or opposed to it. One of the most common equivalent terms is *uncus*, a Latin word originally meaning 'hook'. For example, the bishopric of Ratzeburg, re-established by Henry the Lion in the mid-twelfth century, was funded by imposts raised on the *uncus*. Princely taxes on the island of Rügen were also assessed on the *uncus*. In Silesia, too, the *uncus* was a unit of territorial measurement. The equivalence of *uncus* and 'Slavic plough' is fairly clear: in 1230 the Teutonic Knights promised to pay the bishop of Prussia a bushel of wheat as tithe from each 'Slavic plough' (*aratrum Slavicum*) in the territory of Chełmno, while about thirty years later an agreement about tithes in Ermland specified that they 'shall pay tithes in the same way as they are paid in the territory of Chełmno', now associating this with a payment per *uncus*. The king of Denmark's fiscal register of 1231 assesses settlements in *mansi* or other units, with the one exception of nine 'Slav villages' on the island of Fehmarn, which are assessed in *unci*. The *uncus* was also called the *Haken*, the German vernacular equivalent – '*unci*, called *Haken*', as a Pomeranian document of 1318 puts it. The circle is completed by the Chełmno charter of 1233, again specifying tithe payments, which prescribes a payment of a bushel of wheat from 'each Polish plough (*Polonicale aratrum*), which is called a *hake*'. The equivalence of 'Slavic plough', *uncus*, *Haken* and 'Polish plough' is thus demonstrated.

This unit, with its various names, was customarily contrasted with another. In the document of 1230 recording the agreement between the Teutonic Knights and the bishop of Prussia, for example, the 'Slavic plough' is contrasted with the 'German plough' (*aratrum Theutonicale*). This was a common unit of assessment, sometimes referred to simply as 'the plough' (*aratrum*) in contrast to *uncus* or *Haken*. One Prussian document of

1293 specifies a tithe payment of a bushel of wheat and a bushel of rye from each *aratrum* and a bushel of wheat alone from each *uncus*. In 1258 the 'German plough' was contrasted with the 'Prussian *uncus*'. In Poland, the terms of contrast were further elaborated. The Gniezno Synod of 1262 regulated tithe payments from 'each small plough, which is called *radlo*' and from 'the big plough, which is called *plug*'. Elsewhere the *Pflug* is contrasted with the *Haken*, which makes the equivalence of 'small plough' and *Haken*, and hence *uncus* and 'Slavic (or Polish) plough', on the one hand, and 'big plough' with 'German plough', fairly obvious.

The cumulative effect of this evidence is to suggest a perceived dichotomy between German and native 'ploughs'. It is yet to be established, however, whether such 'ploughs' were real agricultural implements rather than mere units of assessment, and, if so, what the differences between them were. The evidence for real physical difference between German or big ploughs and Slavic or small ploughs, also called *unci* or *Haken*, is slight but convincing. One thirteenth-century document refers to a levy of six shillings on 'each house from which a plough goes out' and three shillings on 'each house from which a *Haken* goes out'. Slightly later a Prussian charter mentions payments from tenants 'from their ploughs or *unci* with which they cultivate their fields'; and, even more explicitly, we read of '*unci* with which the Prussians and Poles are accustomed to cultivate their land'. There thus seems little doubt that the distinction we have discussed relates to the instruments of cultivation as well as to the abstractions of fiscal calculation.

The remaining crucial dimension of this distinction is quantitative: German or big ploughs were systematically assessed at twice the rate of Slav or small ploughs. For instance, the document of 1230 already cited several times specifies renders of two bushels of grain from each German plough and one from each Slav plough. The burdens laid on the German plough and the 'Polish plough, which is called a *hake*' in the Chełmno charter differ in the same way. One *scot* (1/24 of a mark) and a bundle of flax were levied from each *hoken*, two *scot* and two bundles of flax from each *pfluge*, according to another thirteenth-century document. The six-shilling/three-shilling distinction between ploughs and *Haken* has just been mentioned. Altogether there is strong evidence that the German or big plough was considered to be able to bear a heavier burden of tax, tithe or levy than the Slavic or small plough.

If there was a distinction in terminology, physical form and tax-yielding capacity, we have to ask in what it lay. The plough was big and German, the *uncus* or *Haken* small and Slav (or Prussian). The step that has been taken by many authors is to equate the former with the heavy plough, the latter with the ard or scratch plough. The justification for this consists in the following: the reasonable assumption that a major perceived difference between two types of plough would correspond to the major difference perceived between plough types by modern farmers and scholars; the fact that the term *Haken*, in modern German usage, applies to the ard or scratch plough; the association of long fields (best suited to the heavy plough) with German settlement; the idea that the 'heavy' plough is more productive than the ard and can hence support a heavier tax burden; lastly, in this array of modern and comparative factors, something based on medieval texts, the reference in a fourteenth-century Polish document to 'twenty big ploughs and twenty small, meaning by "big" share and coulter and by "small" the *radlicza*'. The *radlicza* is the 'small plough which is called *radlo*'. The big plough has coulter and share. Whether it has an asymmetrical share, or a mould-board – of wood, hence cheap and unimportant – is not specified. The weight of the evidence, however, despite the German triumphalism of it all, is that the Germans introduced a heavy, asymmetrical plough to a Slavic and Prussian world that had previously known only the ard.

CEREALIZATION

The new settlers, new ploughs and new mills meant 'improvement' (*melioratio terrae*), and 'improvement' meant the expansion of cereal cultivation. What was involved was thus not simply a shift from wild to tamed, but a move to a highly particular form of land use. In many parts of Europe the changes of the High Middle Ages involved a step away from a human ecology that could support only a sparse population but exploited a large variety of natural resources, such as fish, honey and game, as well as livestock and cultivated crops, towards a more densely populated monoculture. Symptomatic is the substitution of renders in corn for an earlier render of squirrel skins by Henry the Bearded of Silesia in the early thirteenth century. If results from elsewhere in the world are any guide, the outcome may have been a larger but less healthy population.

From the point of view of prince, prelate or enterprising *locator*, of course, the health of the settled population was not central. What was important about planned colonization was that it turned non-revenue-producing resources into a fountain of corn and silver. Richer lords and more peasants – that seems an undeniable outcome of the new settlements of the High Middle Ages. Despite the occasional failed settlement, the general atmosphere on the frontiers was optimistic and expansionist. Expansion of the arable landscape and the settlement of new farmers on the land were part of the vision of the future. Prospective grants covered revenues from the soil as well as new lordships. As early as 1175, when Duke Boleslaw of Silesia and Bishop Zyroslaw of Wrocław endowed the Cistercians of Lubiąż (Leubus), who had come from Germany and were expected to bring German settlers with them, they granted 'all the tithes from the new villages which are at present in the region of Legnica [Liegnitz] and from those which later may be founded there at any subsequent time'. Arrangements regarding future tithe income 'from new fields recently cultivated or which will in future be cultivated' or 'from all lands newly brought under cultivation' can be found throughout eastern Europe in the era of the *Ostsiedlung*. Sometimes more than future cultivation was envisaged. One also finds reference to the income from villages 'which are now inhabited by Slavs, if in future they should be possessed by Germans'. A future world of arable expansion and Germanization lurked at the back of the minds of the lords and prelates of eastern Europe.

Cerealization was a natural image for the prelates of the High Middle Ages as they contemplated the expansion of Latin Christendom in that period. They could draw on their own experience of arable agriculture as well as the resources of biblical rhetoric to pen such lines as the following, from a letter of Pope Honorius III in 1220 on the conversion of the Baltic pagans:

The hardness of the hearts of the Livonian pagans, like a vast desert land, has been watered by the showers of divine grace and cultivated by the ploughshare of holy preaching, the seed of the Lord is blessedly shooting up into a crop, nay, the lands are already white for the harvest.

The spread of cult and the spread of cultivation went hand in hand.

In the newly colonized parts of Europe it was natural for settlers to paint the past as a barbarous or primitive period, which could serve as a foil to the current order. The motif of a pre-agricultural or scarcely agricultural past, a time of wild and wooded emptiness, is particularly important, for, by exaggerating the emptiness of colonized territories in the period before the new arrivals, it produced a dramatic aesthetic effect, highlighting the story of a 'new plantation' in a 'place of horror and desolate solitude', as well as justifying the possessory claims of the newcomers. The *Henryków Chronicle*, produced in a Cistercian house in Silesia, describes how 'the first abbot of this monastery and his helpers . . . came to this place, then wild enough and covered with many woods; they furrowed the land with mattock and ploughshare, eating bread in the sweat of their face to sustain nature'. Plate 7 shows a thirteenth-century presentation of just such a heroic image of the Cistercians entering the wild wood armed with axe and mattock. In the case of Henryków, however, there is a complication, for evidence exists, some of it in other parts of the *Chronicle* itself, suggesting that there was already settlement in the area of the new monastery. The monks progressively obliterated the memory of these earlier settlers in favour of a founding myth of pioneers in an empty land.

Equally insistent on the primitiveness of the pre-settler past were the Cistercians of Lubiąż, the first house of the order in Silesia, who had brought German settlers into Poland in the late twelfth century. When they looked back to the days of their founding, they emphasized the underdevelopment and poverty of the Polish scene before their own transformative activities. Writing in verse in the early fourteenth century, a Lubiąż monk painted the landscape of the pre-Cistercian period in the following words:

> The land lacked cultivators and lay under woods
> And the Polish people were poor and idle,
> Using wooden ploughs without iron to furrow the sandy soil,
> Knowing only how to use two cows or oxen to plough.
> There was no city or town in the whole land,
> Only rural markets, an uncultivated field and a chapel near the castle.
> Neither salt, nor iron, nor coinage, nor metal,
> Nor good clothes, nor even shoes
> Did that people have, they just grazed their flocks.
> These were the delights that the first monks found.

The monk's characterization of the primitive state is negative. He describes what the Poles of those distant bygone years *lacked*. They had none of the benefits of towns, trade or metallurgy. Their arable agriculture was particularly inadequate. The overall impression is of a backward and poverty-stricken world. The passage rings with the same tone as that of a much later colonist, Bishop Diego de Landa of Yucatán, listing the benefits the Spaniards had brought to the New World. These include horses, domestic animals, iron, mechanical arts and money. The Indians, he concluded, now 'live more like men'. As in this sixteenth-century version of the civilizing mission of the newcomer, the Lubiąż 'before' and the Henryków 'before' serve to emphasize a very different 'after'. According to the Lubiąż writer it is the Cistercians' 'sweat' and 'labour' that performed the magic: 'this land was completely transformed (*tota referta*) by them'. It is not only modern historians who have created (and attacked) the image of the Cistercians as frontiersmen and colonizers. In the High Middle Ages it was already part of their self-presentation.

Writers like these thus saw themselves as bringing productive labour and arable technology to an idle people and an undercultivated land. It is certainly the case that arable cultivation was extended spectacularly in the High Middle Ages, but another result of cerealization was the creation of a new and vulnerable ecology, for 'waste' land and woodland were resources. Non-arable land was not barren land: fish, game, eggs, honey, nuts, berries, rushes, thatch, firewood, turf, timber and rough pasture were some of the riches that uncultivated land could offer. Woodlands were not simply untapped arable. As the king of Bohemia observed in the mid-fourteenth century: 'the density and wonderful height of the trees of our forests of the kingdom of Bohemia are not among the least of the glories of the kingdom'. A balance had to be struck between arable and non-arable resources, for damage could result if it were not. When the archbishop of Hamburg–Bremen arranged to have a marsh in his diocese cleared and settled, in 1149, he had to compensate the canons of Bremen, who had previously obtained their firewood from the site. They were not giving up a valueless resource. Even more telling is an event that occurred forty years later in the English Fenland. The men of Holland in Lincolnshire invaded neighbouring Crowland, desiring 'to have common of the marsh of Crowland. For since their own marshes have dried up, they have converted them into good and fertile ploughland. Whence it is that they lack common pasture more than most people.' The general lack of manure that cereal monoculture caused has, indeed, been blamed for a crisis in arable farming itself. Postan hypothesized that 'the continuous reduction of pasture could threaten the viability of arable cultivation itself' and was even willing to talk of 'the breakdown of the metabolic system' in the later Middle Ages, as overdependence on grainland reduced the supply of manure to such an extent that cereal yields began to fall. The evidence on yields is not so clear-cut that one is forced to adopt Postan's position; but of a shift towards cereal monoculture, a 'cerealization' of high medieval society, there is no doubt. It has also been suggested that a noticeable decrease in the average height of the population of about 2 inches between the early and late Middle Ages was one of the consequences of a change in diet stemming from a shift towards arable agriculture. Arable agriculture produces more calories per acre than pastoral farming or hunting and gathering, and can thus support a denser population, but that population is often not so healthy or physically well developed and may be dangerously dependent on one source of nourishment.

NON-WRITTEN EVIDENCE

The picture of peasant migration and settlement that we have built up so far is based largely on the written evidence that has survived, in one form or another, from the High Middle Ages. Such evidence has its limits. The clearance of land for cultivation and the establishment of new villages were a gradual process, largely undertaken by peasants, and it is not surprising that the monastic and clerical chroniclers of the High Middle Ages only rarely mention such activities. They focus rather on the highlights of political and ecclesiastical life: war, ceremony, squabbles over office, the building and adornment of churches. Documentary evidence offers a rather richer source of information than the narratives of the historians and, as we have seen, agreements between lords and *locatores* or negotiations about the proper allocation of tithes from newly settled land were sometimes written down and the resulting documents sometimes survive. Even so, the twelfth and thirteenth centuries form a period when a great deal of practical innovation and organization could be accomplished without leaving written record, and this fact, combined with the haphazard survival of written evidence, means that the documentary record is fragmentary and random.

In these circumstances it is natural to turn to the help of non-written evidence. This is relatively abundant and seems to hold out the prospect of more systematic knowledge. It also has its own peculiar dangers. There are, roughly speaking, three major kinds of non-written evidence: (1) the results of archaeological excavation and survey; (2) village and field morphology; (3) place names.

Archaeology

Archaeology is a method of historical research with enormous future potential, especially for periods as yet relatively unexamined by archaeologists, such as the High Middle Ages. In a hundred years' time, if archaeological research continues at its present pace, the picture of medieval rural settlement will be infinitely richer and more precise than it is today. The present yield, however, is rather limited. The number of excavations or intensive field studies of medieval sites, though always increasing, is still small. This is especially true of rural settlements, which tend to have less publicity value, and are thus difficult to fund as well as to find. Even the very active school of early medieval archaeologists in the former East Germany had, by 1983, fully excavated only two Wendish villages. A recent study of the Havelland district east of the Elbe states: 'Of the 149 late Slav settlement sites not one has been investigated systematically.' A survey of Irish medieval archaeology published in 1987 reported 'only portions of four possible medieval rural nucleated settlements have been excavated up to the present'. The sum total of medieval rural settlements which had been the subject of large-scale excavation in central Europe by 1973 was estimated at about seventy (and this for the whole medieval millennium).

An unusual example of the excavation of a high medieval colonial village, and one that shows the potential yield of such work, is that undertaken by the Czechoslovak archaeologist Vladimir Nekuda, who worked on the deserted site of Pfaffenschlag in south-western Moravia throughout the 1960s. He uncovered a village of sixteen houses in a linear pattern on either side of a stream. A typical house measured about 60 feet by 30 feet, had stone foundations and was divided internally into three separate spaces or rooms, one with a hearth. The settlement belongs to the period of intensive colonization and clearance that peaked in the thirteenth century, and among the finds from the site was an asymmetrical ploughshare. Here we have a precisely investigated instance of the new planned village of high medieval colonization. It must stand for the thousands of other unexplored examples.

Excavation is the most thorough and informative type of archaeological exploration, but it is also expensive and time-consuming. Many less exhaustive techniques are also able to yield useful information. Some are extremely simple, such as field-walking, which involves the systematic inspection of an area of land with an eye open for traces of earthworks, fossilized field or furrow patterns, pottery fragments and other visible clues to settlement history. The potential yield of even this relatively simple technique is demonstrated by the investigations of vanished rural settlement in England by Peter Wade-Martins, who walked for days around East Anglia, picking up pottery sherds. He was able to show that the Anglo-Saxon settlements had been grouped around the (now isolated) churches, and that the modern dispersed scatter of houses must be a later development. Such studies are, of course, highly dependent on the survival of pottery, the most durable of human debris, and general interpretation of such material demands as a prerequisite the establishment of a credible chronology for pottery. The intellectual foundation of most such chronologies is typological, that is, it is reached on the basis of shape (including size, thickness, curvature, etc.) and the superficial characteristics of the material. Although the future will bring more sophisticated chemical and physical techniques for dealing with pottery, the future is not yet here and many interpretations of the archaeological record have as their bedrock ceramic typologies. What is clear from reading the work of archaeologists is that some have their doubts about the exact reliability of such chronologies. Disquiet among the experts obviously awakens disquiet among the non-experts.

Village and field morphology

The study of village and field morphology – that is, the size, shape and layout of houses, farm buildings, roads and cultivated land – is a complicated business even when directed to the existing landscapes of the present day. It is far more difficult to analyse the human landscape of the distant past. Hardly any maps survive from the medieval period and those that do are either too large-scale or too schematic (or both) to be of much use in the investigation of villages and fields. Settlement historians are driven by necessity to use plans of a far later date, the eighteenth and nineteenth centuries, and project their data back into the Middle Ages. Such a technique is obviously risky. Common sense suggests that the five centuries between 1250 and 1750 would see many changes, and this belief is borne out by the recorded cases of change of house site, village layout, village site and field arrangement.

Some scholars have stressed the possibilities of the method, others the dangers. The divergence of national scholarly traditions is very clear. In Germany the history of such study is now a century old, but English scholarship has been particularly cautious. A twelve-month period in 1977–8, for example, saw the publication of both a textbook in Stuttgart dedicated to the settlement forms of central Europe, illustrated by a diagram showing the eight different possible stages of development of nine different settlement types, and a survey of medieval English economic history containing the cavalier statement: 'The classification of villages into types is apt to be an exercise in oversimplification. It is perhaps best to leave them in their infinite variety and their natural lack of order.' English scholars pursuing morphological studies are rather rare and the very eccentricity of their terminology – the inelegant 'green village' as a literal translation of the German *Angerdorf*, for example – shows how English morphological studies are attempting to do by precept what is almost second nature to German historical geographers. The scepticism is not merely instinctual, for elaborate morphological schemes only work if one presupposes basic continuities from the medieval to the modern period, and these continuities cannot always be safely assumed. One English writer mentions the 'constant changes in plan evidenced from the excavations of medieval villages', citing the case of Hangleton in Sussex, where four thirteenth-century houses were replaced in the fourteenth century by a single farmstead of three buildings, 'the boundaries of which went right through one of the earlier houses'.

Despite such reservations, the attempt to recreate the rural landscape of the Middle Ages need not be abandoned. There is a sense in which field arrangements, in particular, are very resistant to change. Once established, they require will-power and consensus to be altered, and the apparent benefit of the change must be very clear before major transformations are undertaken. Moreover, even though good local maps of the period 1200–1700 are rare, there is a mountain of estate records, rentals, surveys, court rolls, tax records and the like, which cast light on the earlier history of the villages and holdings first presented cartographically in the eighteenth and nineteenth centuries. For instance, Wolfgang Prange was able to reconstruct the probable medieval pattern of the village of Klinkrade in Lauenburg – two rows of four full *mansus*-holdings along a short street – by taking a map of 1770 as his basis and then stripping away holdings that could be proved from estate records to have come into existence only in the sixteenth or the seventeenth century. The relationship between modern patterns of village and field morphology and those of the High Middle Ages is analogous to that between modern and medieval distribution of the manuscripts of a medieval work. The modern situation, the pattern of libraries in which the work is found, does not replicate the medieval, but neither does it stand in a random, meaningless or inverse relationship to it, and it can help us reconstruct the medieval pattern.

One particularly vexed issue has been whether any relationship exists between settlement form and pattern of cultivation, on the one hand, and national origin, on the other. German historians traditionally took it as axiomatic that some village types were German and some Slavic, while historical geographers of the British Isles have often posited distinctive Celtic and Anglo-Saxon patterns of settlement. More recent scholarship has preferred to avoid such schemata. 'The size and type of settlements,' write the authors of one recent survey of the rural history of medieval England, 'were determined by topography rather than the racial origins of their inhabitants.' As long ago as 1915 the Russian historian Jegorov, who had, indeed, an axe to grind, since he was attempting to minimize the extent of the *Ostsiedlung*, asserted that 'the local conditions, the state of the soil, changes in water courses or the layout of new roads have influenced village and field form no less than national and racial peculiarities'. He then went on to show that the supposedly Slavic village form, the *Rundling*, a group of houses laid out in a horseshoe-shaped pattern, could be found frequently in Germanic Denmark and, on the other hand, was not very common in Slavic Pomerania and Mecklenburg.

It is, of course, the case that earlier nationalistic explanations of village and field types are lodged in a general ideology of national characterization. Celtic or Slavic settlements are supposedly small, irregular and scattered, English or German ones large, regular and nucleated. Images of order and power are closely tied to the more neutral issue of shape and size. In the nineteenth and early twentieth centuries these images served the purposes of a purely political nationalism. The apparent inability of medieval Celts or Slavs to build big villages and farm rectilinear fields buttressed the belief that they were equally incapable of organizing modern states of their own and required the tutelage of their better-organized Germanic neighbours.

It is useful, however, in discussing settlement and national origin, to make a distinction between the British Isles and Europe east of the Elbe. In the former case, the suggested distinction along national lines between nucleated and scattered settlement coincides with such a pronounced natural division between the east and the west, in terms of rainfall, temperature, relief and soil types, that it is redundant to hypothesize yet another explanation for the general difference between the two zones. In east Elbian Europe, on the other hand, the division between purportedly German and Slav settlement does not coincide very closely with any such natural distinction. The regular and rectilinear *Waldhufendörfer* are interspersed with other, less regular forms, like the *Sackdorf*, or 'cul-de-sac village', and the *Rundling*. A compelling ecological explanation does not therefore present itself. Moreover, the association of certain forms of village and field layout with German settlement does not, in itself, require the postulation of fixed national characteristics, for the German colonization of the east Elbian lands in the twelfth and thirteenth centuries was not only German, but also the result of planned immigration. The association of certain regular village and field forms with planned colonization does not seem at all implausible. The fact that most of the colonists were German-speaking is something to be pondered, but their 'Germanness' is not then an explanation of the landscape morphology. The planned landscape happened to be a German landscape, but what was formative was that it was planned.

Thus there is a real correspondence between German settlement and particular village and field forms in the lands east of the Elbe. This has been repeatedly demonstrated. Particularly striking is the distribution of *Waldhufendörfer*, villages in which the peasant farmsteads are set at regular intervals along a street and their holdings, in the form of a broad strip of land, stretch away behind them. The *Waldhufendorf* was first developed in the woodlands of western Germany and then became a characteristic feature of the *Ostsiedlung*. It was a form ideally suited to newly colonized localities, since the settlers could work their way gradually back from their homestead, clearing more land every season. Many *Waldhufendorf* farms do indeed end in patches of uncleared woodland at the extremities furthest from the street. The peasant holding, the *mansus*, in the *Waldhufendorf* was often of standard size, somewhat over 300 feet wide and over a mile in length, and the width of these holdings, and hence the distance between houses, meant that the villages were often extremely long, sometimes continuing in an unbroken row into adjoining villages.

Place names

The study of place names is an inviting occupation, something like a medievalist's equivalent to stamp-collecting, but apart from being fun, it also yields historical information. For example, place names give a reasonable indication of the language spoken by the people who gave the name, since they almost all comprise or contain elements of ordinary, i.e. non-naming, language. Thus, even if there were no other evidence, it would be clear from its place names that Cumberland in north-west England was once inhabited by speakers of a Britannic tongue, for it would otherwise be hard to explain the presence of places called Blencarn (from the British *blaen*, 'top', and *carn*, 'cairn') or Cumdivock (from *cwm*, 'valley', and *dyfoc*, 'black'). Hence debates over the relative importance of, say, Frankish settlement in Gaul or Viking settlement in the British Isles and Normandy have relied heavily, indeed often hinged, on place-name evidence.

On the other hand, even such a simple deduction from place name to language of speaker may be treacherous. It is clear that place names can become acclimatized to speakers of new languages, who take over old names and spread them further – 'London' is a Celtic name, but London, Ontario, was not settled by Celtic-speakers; or the cultural or symbolic prestige attached to some names may lead to a diffusion independent of language groups – there are few Greeks in Athens, Georgia. But even apart from this rather particular case of adoption by speakers of one language of names formed in another, there is the even more fundamental problem of dating names. Even if the toponomy of Cumberland tells us that British speakers once lived there, it does not tell us when.

The dating of place names is a rarified procedure. It has some fixed points, for instance, the first mention of a name in a document, which provides a clear *terminus ante quem*, but then rapidly diffuses into conjecture. Sometimes the attempt is made to date place names linguistically, by setting the name in the known or reconstructed history of the language concerned. For instance, the word *mar*, meaning 'marsh', occurs in German place names west of the Elbe, such as Weimar, but not in those east of the Elbe. One reasonable explanation is that the word was no longer current at the time the Germans settled east of the Elbe, that is, from the twelfth century onwards. Hence one can conclude that names like Weimar must be pre-twelfth century. The personal names included within place names (like Zulis von Wedel's Zühlsdorf, mentioned in Chapter 2) can be analysed in a similar fashion. Another major direction of research has been to take classes or groups of place names – for example, those containing the element *-ing* or the element *-rode* – and try to establish their relative chronology. If *-ing* names occur frequently as the names of settlements on fertile, easily worked soil, with early archaeological evidence, ancient church dedications and documentary record, it is reasonable to assume they are earlier than classes of names which do not. Adolf Bach's analysis of the Taunus region, east of the middle Rhine, showed that the settlements with names containing the element *-heim* were usually on fertile loess or clay soils under 650 feet high, those containing *-hausen* were beyond the fertile loess–clay belt and usually between 1,000 and 1,300 feet high, while those containing *-rod*, *-hain* or *-scheid* were mentioned late (after 1100) and located above 1,300 feet. There is nothing absolutely demonstrative about all this, but the evidence does tend to support Bach's belief that 'All in all, names have specific periods when they blossom into fashion.'

Place names change. If they did not, they would lose most of their value as historic evidence, but because they do, they require careful handling. In areas of new settlement and colonization, new place names were formed in a variety of ways: new names had to be created for new settlements, but old settlements might be renamed or have their names altered. In regions where more than one language was customarily spoken, places might have two or more names. On occasion these might be literal equivalents, as in the case of Oldenburg in Holstein: '*Aldenburg*, which is called in the Slav language *Starigard*, that is, "old city"'. An extensive process of renaming is revealed in the document Henry IV of Silesia granted to the Hospitallers in

1283. He was renewing their old privileges and listing their properties individually, he said,

because we know that some estates have been alienated by the Hospitallers and others exchanged for them, which are not contained in the old privilege, also because these estates, which had Polish names, were afterwards granted German law and deserved to have German names, also because some of these estates, which had many adjacent woods, could not be included in a single-village settlement on account of their great size, but many villages and manors were founded there and received various names.

The charter then goes on to list 'Chozenowiz now called Crucerdorf, Leucowiz now called Ditmarsdorf, Coiacowiz, later divided into two villages called Upper and Lower Concendorf'. Here there seems to be both a process of purely linguistic change in which German names replace Slav, and real relocation or reorganization of settlement. The submergence of villages is recorded in another Silesian source, the *Henryków Chronicle*, which mentions how the Polish lord Albert Lyka acquired two villages of thirty *mansi* and added them to his own, 'whence the names of these villages have completely disappeared'. It is hard to say whether the 'adding' of the villages involved actual destruction and relocation of houses and people, though archaeological evidence shows that such a process was not unknown.

The new settlements of the newly colonized areas needed new names. Sometimes one can catch a settlement in the moment of naming. The Ratzeburg Tithe Register of 1229–30, for example, which lists the holders of sub-enfeoffed tithes in various villages in the bishopric of Ratzeburg, often includes entries such as the following: 'Thankmar's village: Thankmar 1 [i.e. the tithe of one *mansus*]. John's village: John 1.' Clearly the Thankmar and John who gave their names to these settlements were still in evidence – this must be the first generation of the name. Similarly, Sturmieston in Glamorgan must take its name from the mid-twelfth-century Geoffrey Sturmy, who 'built his township in the wilderness which no one had previously ploughed'. When Wiprecht of Groitzsch brought new settlers to clear his forests east of the Elbe he had them 'name with their own name the village or property they had cultivated with their own labour'.

The settlement named after its first cultivator is perhaps the clearest kind of new naming. There were, however, other forms of onomastic innovation and invention that reveal something of the processes of settlement in the new lands. The territories east of the Elbe reveal the rich variety. In some places double settlements appear – 'German Harkensee' and 'Slav

Harkensee' are mentioned in the Ratzeburg Tithe Register, suggesting adjacent villages of native and immigrant farmers. Elsewhere one can find villages named after immigrant groups. Flemsdorf and Flemingsthal point to Flemish settlement, Frankendorf or Frankenberg to Franconian. Sometimes names were simply transplanted from the old territories to the new, with or without the prefix 'New': an urban example is provided by Brandenburg, which spread its name to New Brandenburg, founded in 1248 on the disputed northern frontier of the margraves' territories, and to Brandenburg in Prussia.

The place-name map of any area always reveals a deep stratification, with names ranging in time from the prehistoric period to yesterday. The areas of new settlement of the High Middle Ages show this feature particularly sharply. New Castile had a triple layer of place names. Some settlements had kept very ancient names, either pre-Roman, though usually in Romanized form, or Roman (e.g. Sigüenza, Oreja); then the Arabs had made their own toponymic contribution, most obviously recognizable in place names beginning with the Arabic article *al-* (e.g. Alcalá, 'the fortress') or prefixes such as *ben-*, 'descent group', *dar-*, 'house'; finally the Castilian settlers had named or renamed many places in their own medieval Romance, often forming names from natural features, such as Fuentelviejo ('old spring'), Valdeflores ('valley of flowers'), etc. Alfonso X of Castile (1252–84) had a conscious policy of giving new Castilian names to settlements in the recently reconquered lands. Of one of his grants it was said: 'He gave him the hamlet which was called Corcobina in the time of the Moors and to which King Alfonso gave the name Molina.' Such name-giving and renaming by new settlers on the peripheries of Latin Europe have left a linguistic deposit to this day.

Clearly if one considers the relative merits of documentary or archaeological evidence, morphological or place-name study, the best method to apply to understanding the history of rural settlement is all of the above. What is important is the cumulative effect of evidence of many different kinds. A good example of the light that can be shed by a thorough and imaginative methodological pluralism is the study by Herbert Helbig of settlement patterns in the region occupied by the Slavic Sorbs. He approached the problem by combining the results of place-name study, archaeology, documentary evidence and the analysis of field and village type. A simplified map of the results of his efforts in one region, Kreis Pirna on the Elbe above Dresden, makes clear the imperfect but very striking correlation of place names and field and village types (see

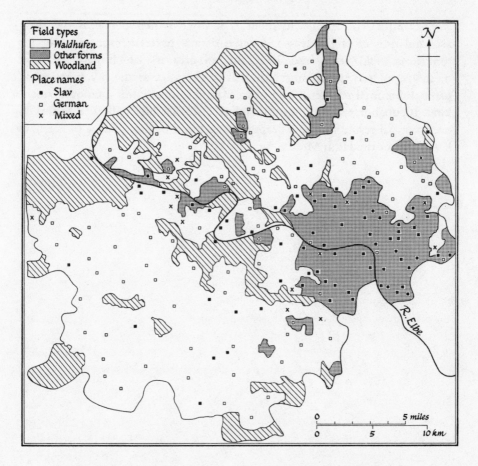

Legend:

Field types
- ☐ Waldhufen
- ▦ Other forms
- ▨ Woodland

Place names
- ■ Slav
- ☐ German
- × Mixed

R. Elbe

0   5 miles
0   5   10 km

Map 6. Place names and field types in Kreis Pirna (after Helbig, 1960)

Map 6). The less regular village forms, with their arable in blocks of furlongs, correspond with the areas in which Slavic place names predominate, the *Waldhufendörfer* (and some other regular forms) with those of mainly German nomenclature. The natural interpretation is that most of the early Slav settlements were grouped along the Elbe, where the place names and field forms are still influenced by this early medieval pattern, while the Germans cleared the areas beyond the old settlements, working their way into the forests, laying out *Waldhufendörfer*. A planned immigration of German settlers, which we can date to the twelfth century from the written evidence, is thus dramatically etched on the map.

The history of rural settlement is a topic which demands the slow accumulation of laboriously recovered data – pottery fragments, charter references, field maps, etc. It is also an area in which new scientific methods, such as the chemical analysis of ceramics or the investigation of plant and animal remains, promise ever richer information of a quite novel kind. If collaborative and multidisciplinary scholarship is allowed to thrive, one eventual result will be a deeper, sharper and livelier picture of the new landscapes of the High Middle Ages.

7. Colonial Towns and Colonial Traders

═══

A free and secure city, which can attract many men because of its freedom . . .

The twelfth and thirteenth centuries were a period of dramatic urbanization in virtually every part of Europe. The older cities grew in population and expanded beyond their Roman or early medieval limits, while hundreds of new towns were established, often as part of a highly self-conscious policy of development. Barnim of Pomerania, for instance, declared in 1234 that 'wishing to provide for our needs and requirements and strengthen ourselves with the customs of other regions, we have decided to inaugurate free towns in our land'. The story of these urban developments is an integral part of an account of the expansionary movement of the High Middle Ages.

A complication that arises immediately in dealing with the urban history of the Middle Ages is that two perfectly useful but distinct definitions of a town may be employed. One is economic. The town is a settlement of more than average population where exchange and the division of labour are relatively highly developed. Clearly, by this economic definition the town is a town in relation to its environment. A population level and economic complexity which would qualify a settlement as a town in the thirteenth century might not qualify it in the nineteenth. The towns are high points on a graph and, if the whole scale of the graph changes, certain absolute values find themselves in a new relative position. Places of the size and structure of many medieval towns would today be regarded as villages. The same observation is true if we consider geographical rather than chronological variation. Perhaps a Welsh town of the thirteenth century, transplanted (willingly or unwillingly) to Lombardy, might cease to merit the appellation in the minds of its new neighbours.

With this economic definition, we are dealing with a spectrum, with continuous criteria. The isolated farmstead is less populous, less specialized and usually less deeply involved in exchange than the village, which is, in turn, less populous and specialized than the small town. Where we draw the dividing line, where we choose to start talking about urban functions, is a matter of judgement, always with an admixture of the arbitrary. No one can demonstrate to another that a given place was or was not a town, in this economic sense, unless the two have already agreed on the dividing line between urban and non-urban. Medieval towns are thus settlements which historians identify and isolate from a gamut or range because they score high on certain selected scales (population, commercialization, specialization) – or, to speak more truthfully, because they give the impression that they would score highly on certain scales if we had the information to measure them.

The legal definition, the other way of approaching urbanism, is quite different in character. While the economic categorization is retrospective and relative, the legal definition is contemporary and absolute. Towns in the legal sense had a different status from other settlements and this status had to be known and observed by contemporaries. Indeed, it usually had to be conferred at a particular moment, which is the date often referred to as the 'foundation' of the town. In the legal sense a lordly *fiat* could turn a non-urban settlement into a town overnight. Clearly, towns as defined economically could not be created in the same way. Jural privilege, which defines the town legally, can spring from an act of individual will in a way that a new economic pattern cannot.

Given these two distinctions, the possibility, indeed probability, arises of an imperfect fit between the class of towns defined economically and those defined legally. Some places might be large, commercial and complex, but not enfranchised, others small and rural but legally urban. It is a situation very familiar to anyone who has studied the parliamentary system of *ancient régime* England, where minute 'rotten boroughs' enjoyed legal privileges denied to some of the new manufacturing metropolises, but the incongruity long predates industrialization. If we set side by side two maps representing the assessed wealth of England in 1334 (a date when fiscal records allow a fairly full picture) and the assessed wealth of the fiscal boroughs at the same period, we will be struck both by the overall lack of positive correlation between the wealth of a region and the frequency of boroughs in that region and also by the large number of poor boroughs. The 'Wessex' region (Devon, Somerset, Dorset, Wiltshire and Hampshire) had a very large number of boroughs, the wealthy counties of East Anglia and the Midlands relatively few. Indeed, the prosperous eastern coastal counties, from Norfolk to Kent, had one borough for every five in the south-west peninsula (Somerset, Devon and Cornwall). Clearly legal urbanization is not a simple epiphenomenon of economic development.

It is also clear that the lack of fit between towns defined legally and towns defined economically is not symmetrically askew, that is, there are many more places with urban status but no real urban function than vice versa. This must be largely explained by the fact that thriving communities could usually purchase urban rights, while settlements which had been granted such rights but had never developed economically had no incentive to abandon them. Hence the real discrepancy between jural and economic urbanism lay in the existence of a large number of places with chartered status but village functions.

A consequence of this duality in the sense of the word 'town' is the requirement, when sketching in the role of urbanization in the process of high medieval expansion, to tell two stories, not one. The growth of populous, complex and commercial centres is one theme; the diffusion of urban liberty, albeit closely connected with the first, is another. For example, if one discusses the urbanization of eastern Europe with only legal criteria in mind, it is true to say that eastern Europe was urbanized in the period 1150–1350 and on the basis of German models. The urban charters and laws surviving from this period are ample evidence for the restructuring of communities east of the Elbe according to blueprints from the great German cities like Lübeck and Magdeburg. These charters and laws are also plainly similar, in overall form, to those of France or England or the *fueros* of Spain, and there is therefore a strong case for seeing here the diffusion of western European forms into eastern Europe. Viewed from the economic standpoint, however, the picture is different. Towns, in the sense of populous, complex settlements involved in exchange, existed in eastern Europe long before the arrival of urban charters. The work of archaeologists, especially in the post-war period, has revealed trade routes and thriving mercantile centres, along the Baltic coast and up the great rivers, in the tenth century. There can be little doubt that granting urban law meant only recasting the organization of an existing town, not the foundation or establishment of the town. In such cases as Szczecin (Stettin) or Danzig the town already existed in an economic sense long before it was born in a legal sense. On the other hand, the granting of an urban charter was not a mere technicality. Even in cases where settlements already had an urban life, urban law restructured the patterns of that life and could reinforce or change its directions. There were, in addition, many cases where the grant of urban law did indeed constitute the foundation of a town and involved the transformation of a rural settlement or even the birth of an entirely new place. The foundation of Lübeck itself, the great mother city of the Baltic, which is discussed below, shows how the privileges enshrined in an urban charter could exercise an attraction strong enough to generate new settlement.

Hence the rhythms and patterns of urbanization in a legal or constitutional sense and urbanization in an economic sense differ. In Bohemia and Moravia, for example, the forms, institutions and terms of the chartered town were introduced from outside, in a relatively short period of time (the early thirteenth century) and under princely initiative. Important and relatively populous trading centres, however, had existed in the country for centuries. Prague, described even in the tenth century as 'the greatest trading centre in the land', and other important centres such as Brno (Brünn) and Olomouc (Olmütz), were not among the earliest towns in the legal sense; many insignificant places were. The story of urbanization in Bohemia is contrapuntal not monodic. An exactly comparable situation existed in Ireland, where towns in the economic sense had been established by the Vikings or had begun to form around monastic centres in the tenth and eleventh centuries, but towns in the legal sense were a consequence of the coming of the Anglo-Normans in the late twelfth century. Dublin, whose vigorous pre-Norman trading and artisanal life has been illuminated by the excavations of the 1970s, was clearly 'urban' long before the first Anglo-Normans set foot in the island. What the outsiders brought, and what does not appear to have existed previously, was a legal blueprint and a documentary framework. When the new lords of Ireland, Henry II and his son John, granted charters to Dublin in the late twelfth century, they were 'founding' the town only in a rather unusual sense. The most elaborate of these documents is John's grant of 1192, and a glimpse at its provisions will reveal the mixture of jural privilege and economic consideration that characterized the urban law of high medieval Europe.

By the terms of the charter of 1192 Dublin was constituted as a determined territorial unit, the boundaries of which are described in detail, and as a jural entity, a town or city that was also a 'hundred' with its own weekly hundred-court to deal with local judicial and administrative matters. Strongly emphasized in John's charter are a series of special privileges which the citizens of Dublin are to enjoy and which relate to legal procedure. They cannot be sued outside the city, are exempt from the judicial duel and the *murdrum* fine (levied on a community when an unidentified body was found within its bounds). They cannot be penalized for 'miskenning', verbal slips in their legal pleadings. No judicial inquests are to take place within the town. Limits are placed on the amounts of judicial fines. All these regulations give the citizens of Dublin special privileges in the law court. In addition they are to enjoy certain liberties of person and property. Their lands within Dublin are held 'in free burgage', they may build as they wish and have collective control of all space within the city bounds. No lord can control the marriage of their children or widows. They have the right to form guilds, 'just as the burgesses of Bristol have', Bristol being Dublin's mother town.

In addition to these legal rights there are a series of privileges of an economic nature. The most important was probably the exemption from toll (internal customs duties) throughout John's lands. In addition there are safeguards regarding debt. On the one hand, the citizens of Dublin are allowed to distrain for debt, that is, seize the property of those who have failed to pay their obligations to them. On the other hand, they themselves may only be distrained if they are personally the debtor or the guarantor of the debt – they are immune from the collective liability for other citizens' debts which was a common feature of the medieval urban regime. They also enjoy various economic monopolies within the city. Foreign merchants may not buy grain, hides or wool there except from the citizens, nor may they sell cloth at retail, run a tavern or spend more than forty days trading in the city. Clearly these economic provisions assume a citizen body already deeply involved in buying and selling. The legal privileges, on the other hand, would be attractive to any group seeking freedom from the cramped coerciveness of traditional legal procedure or some relaxation of seigneurial rights. Town law has this dual aspect – urban freedom always meant more than just freedom to trade.

Ireland also provides a good case study of a colonial land where widespread urban privileges were granted to utterly rural sites as incentives for settlement. These 'rural boroughs', as they have been termed, were extremely numerous. Around 240 Irish boroughs are known, which works out roughly at a chartered settlement every thirteen miles. This is a less dense network than contemporary England, where boroughs could be found at an average distance of ten miles apart, but England was a much more populous region (perhaps ten times as populous) with a far greater area under the plough. The Irish figure is exactly comparable with the density of chartered urban settlements in the colonial regions between the Elbe and the Oder; the towns of Mecklenburg, Pomerania and Silesia, for example, were also thirteen miles apart on average. Clearly, not all the 240 chartered settlements of Ireland were fulfilling urban functions in the economic sense. It has indeed been suggested that fewer than a quarter of them (fifty-six) were towns in this sense. Many were privileged rural settlements, part of that magnet of liberty that has been discussed in the previous chapter. For, at certain moments, the language of peasant enfranchisement spilled over in this way into the vocabulary of the town – 'borough', 'burgess', 'burgage', and their counterparts. In Sicily, similarly, the Latin colonists were termed 'burgesses' and enjoyed 'civic customs' even when they were simply privileged villagers.

Town freedom – the particular constellation of privileges and liberties associated with urban status – was thus an incentive for settlement even apart from any considerations of commercialization. Immigrants would settle in towns because they sought liberty, not simply because they wished to trade. The bishop of Riga declared that 'the city of Riga draws the faithful to settle there more because of its freedom than because of the fertility of its surroundings'. The numerous tiny towns to be found in many parts of the European frontier were intended to be stimuli to settlement as much as foci for commerce. Sometimes too, as in the Iberian peninsula, military requirements stimulated jural urbanization. After Alfonso VII of Castile captured Oreja from the Muslims in 1139, he granted the inhabitants freedom from tolls, a free right of alienation and other legal immunities and safeguards. 'I have judged it fitting,' he proclaimed, 'to give boundaries and rights to all those who come to settle in Oreja, lest the Moors, who used to possess it . . . should manage to recover it, through Christian weakness or lack of care.' The rights attracted the settlers, the settlers secured the conquest; of economic functions there is no mention.

Although they are summary and normative in form, the surviving urban charters and laws offer insights into the interests and constraints which shaped the new towns of Europe in the High Middle Ages. To analyse them is to explore the ambitions, fears and intentions of the men who created and expanded these towns. It is possible to see, in their wording and provisions, the end product of negotiations, clashes and concessions between all the parties involved in the formation of new towns – the lord, the urban entrepreneurs, the church and the new colonists. The town charter was a document of great symbolic value representing a new start.

FAMILIES OF URBAN LAW

The western European urban model, which was devised in the twelfth and thirteenth centuries, involved the privileging of a space and its inhabitants. Such a privileging required, by definition, an author, a lord. But the actual content of the privileges was not usually worked out afresh between each lord and his burgesses. Standardized sets of legal provisions were available by the twelfth century. At the most general level there were some basic principles of urban liberty, such as free status, exemption from tolls and the grant of limited monopolies, which were intrinsic to the very concept of a chartered town. On a more specific level, whole bodies of positive law regarding town administration, civil and criminal procedure and the regulation of economic activity could be borrowed by one town from another. The result was the creation of families of town law, groups of urban settlements whose legal arrangements were, at least initially, modelled on a 'mother town'.

One example is the family of towns possessing the law code of Cuenca–Teruel. This is an elaborate affair containing almost a thousand clauses, regulating matters as varied as inheritance rights, homicide, military obligations, Jewish–Christian relations, irrigation and pasturage, the public baths and even the penalties for taking roses and lilies from another's vineyard. The code was granted by Alfonso VIII of Castile soon after he conquered Cuenca from the Muslims in 1177. At about the same time, across the border in Aragon, Alfonso II granted a virtually identical code to the town of Teruel. From Cuenca and Teruel this family of law spread south with the Reconquest, reaching Andalusia by the 1220s. This particular urban model was thus not limited by political boundaries. It suited both Castile and Aragon and it could be implanted in lands newly won from Muslim rule. Other examples of families of town law transcending the frontiers of kingdom or lordships can easily be found. The law of Breteuil in Normandy, a town which was enfranchised by its lord, William fitz Osbern, around 1060, was granted by fitz Osbern to his new acquisition, Hereford, after the Norman Conquest of England. By 1086 the borough of Rhuddlan in north Wales enjoyed 'the laws and customs which are in Hereford and Breteuil'. The Anglo-Normans who came to Ireland in the decades after 1169 included many men, like the de Lacys, from the Welsh borders, and when they founded boroughs, like the de Lacy foundation of Drogheda, they too granted the laws of Breteuil. In this way, by a series of feudal conquests, this relatively unimportant Norman town became the explicit model for many new boroughs in Wales and Ireland. Most dramatically, the great urban constitutions of the *Ostsiedlung*, such as Lübeck law or Magdeburg law, provided the fundamental legal and institutional structure for hundreds of settlements as far east as Narva on the Gulf of Finland and Kiev in the Ukraine.

The degree of dependence between mother and daughter towns varied. Sometimes the new town was simply granted the customs of an existing town and there was no further connection. In other cases the affiliated town might turn to the mother town for a ruling when some point in the customs needed clarification. An even closer bond existed in town families such as Lübeck, whose mother town heard judicial appeals from the courts of the daughter towns. The starting point was the transmission of the customs and this certainly sometimes involved sending a book from mother to daughter town. The Göttingen codex of Lübeck law, for example, contains the text of the law as sent to Danzig in response to the request of the local prince and the burgesses of Danzig. 'In the year of the lord 1263,' it begins,

for the honour and love and at the request of the illustrious lord Sambor, duke of Pomerelia, and for the love and at the request of the citizens of Danzig, the consuls of the city of Lübeck have caused to be written down the law which was granted to them by the glorious lord Henry, duke of . . . Saxony . . . and confirmed by his charter. Here begins the fixed law of the city of Danzig, duly transmitted to it by the consuls of Lübeck.

In 1282 the burgesses of Litoměřice (Leitmeritz) in Bohemia sent to Magdeburg for a copy of the Magdeburg law code; the burgesses of Magdeburg dispatched one, mentioning in their accompanying letter that Litoměřice 'is said to have been founded with our laws'. The dissemination of the enormous code of Cuenca–Teruel could not have taken place without the circulation of books. Translation of law codes from Latin into the vernacular, which happened in both the Baltic and Iberian regions, also points to transmission through written texts.

Once a particular law was transmitted to a new region, daughter towns themselves became mother towns of new families or sub-families. In the early thirteenth century, for example, the law of Halle, itself a daughter of Magdeburg, became the model for new settlements in Silesia. The intermediary was the ducal town of Środa (Neumarkt), a community of burgesses about 180 miles – nine days' journey – east of Halle. A document survives in which the magistrates of Halle spell out in detail to the burgesses of Środa exactly what was involved in the 'urban law observed by our fathers'. The provisions concern the details of criminal and inheritance law, the frequency of court sessions, the applicable forms of proof and the structure of the chief guilds. It is a little encapsulated written outline of a German town, made available for dissemination in the lands to the east. Środa, the dutiful daughter, soon became a prolific mother. When, in 1223, Bishop Lawrence of Wrocław allowed his local representative, Walter, to settle Germans in a market town and villages on the upper Oder, he specified that they should enjoy 'the same law which Duke Henry's Neumarkt, alias Środa, applies'. One recent study lists 132 sites, the majority of them between the Oder and the Vistula, that had the town law of Środa/Neumarkt in the later Middle Ages.

Clearly certain centres became well known for the quality of their privileges. The Aragonese town of Jaca was an example, and in 1187 Alfonso II of Aragon proudly proclaimed: 'I know that in Castile and in Navarre and in other lands, they are accustomed to come to Jaca to learn good customs and liberties and take them to their own places.' Such admiration was not always uncritical, however, and one can also find modification and amplification of existing codes. When the Silesian dukes endowed Wrocław with Magdeburg law in 1261 they made a series of modifications, including halving the level of judicial fines. Such modifications created new species within the larger genus. The elucidation of these relationships has become almost an academic sub-discipline. German historical scholarship, in particular, has approached the subject of town law families in a vigorous spirit of Linnaean classificatory science.

Some towns were not simply models for others, but maintained a permanent judicial oversight of their daughters. The magistrates (*Schöffen, scabini*) of Magdeburg, for example, issued rulings for many of the members of their vast family of daughter towns, which stretched far to the east and south. In 1324 they sent letters to their daughter town of Litoměřice in Bohemia, replying to the questions which the judge, jurors and burgesses of the latter town had raised and giving rulings on such diverse subjects as the terms of the peace between Litoměřice and its nearby rival, Ustí (Aussig), the details of judicial procedure and the limits of jurisdiction, the consequences of outlawry, rules about inheritance and even the cut of the cloth in the textile trade. A superior or supervisory jurisdiction was thus being exercised, just as Litoměřice itself applied Magdeburg law to a large number of daughter towns in its own area. Lübeck had a similar role for the German trading cities of the Baltic. Over 3,000 appellate and clarificatory decisions of the Lübeck consuls have been printed, and this is only a small proportion of the original material. Similar judicial patterns could be found in Spain, where, for instance, in 1322 Alfonso XI of Castile reaffirmed the appellate jurisdiction of Logroño over 'all the places which have the law of Logroño'.

This transregional network of urban judicial authorities was not always favoured by princes, who could see in the existence of an alternative and external locus of jurisdiction a threat to their own position, and some rulers attempted to curtail such connections. In 1286 the dukes of Opole (Oppeln) ruled that

all and singular who are settled in our lordship under Flemish law, when there is doubt about that law, shall never seek to be informed about it outside our land or even within our land except in Racibórz [Ratibor], notwithstanding any privileges of cities or villages which seem contrary to this ordinance. Nor shall this city of Racibórz henceforth concern itself with other external places, on behalf of its own rights or others', but must determine all cases which arise there or, as is the custom, are brought there by appeal, with the fear of God before their eyes, as befits their faith, with no appeal allowed to us or to other places.

By this ruling the dukes wished to draw the jurisdiction strands that connected the settlers according to Flemish law into a single thread and to sever that thread at the level of Racibórz, one of their chief cities. Thus there would be one hierarchy within their lordship and no ties linking it to authorities beyond. It is a classic example of that enclosed jural homogeneity to which the sovereign state aspires. In the thirteenth century and later, however, that aspiration faced the powerful alternative of an international urban network that drew the lines more widely and fluidly from mother city to daughter city along the trade routes and the migratory paths rather than within the tight boundaries of the monarchical domain.

Princes wanted towns, because they were profitable, but they also harboured fears of them, because they might be unmanageable. Its stress on urban independence made some rulers suspicious of Lübeck law, and the Teutonic Knights, for example, discouraged it in their domains, preferring their own, less autonomous code, that of Chełmno (Culm). Danzig and Memel (Klaipeda), which originally had Lübeck law, were forced to abandon it under pressure from the Knights. It was not until the late Middle Ages, however, that the princely assault on urban autonomy became widespread or effective. Between the late fifteenth and the mid-seventeenth centuries the appellate jurisdiction of Lübeck collapsed as the towns were jurally integrated into the territories of neighbouring rulers or reduced to submission by their nominal overlords. In the High Middle Ages, however, princes were more interested in developing towns, even if they relied on models outside their domains, than they were in restricting them.

Urban networks – of trading contacts and family ties as well as legal bonds – had their places of origin in the core areas of central western Europe and extended outwards geographically. The very earliest sets of urban privileges arose in the lands around the Rhine, with those of Huy on the Meuse being one of the most explicit and well known. Towns elsewhere then began to borrow from Lotharingia and the Rhineland. The lines of influence radiate outwards, from Normandy to England to Wales to Ireland, or from Westphalia to Holstein to Estonia, or from New Castile to Andalusia. Scottish urban law originally derived from that of Newcastle upon Tyne, and the first constitutions in Bohemia draw on the Saxon models.

It is the same if we consider the terminology of town life. The very word 'burgess' (Latin *burgensis*), which seems to be a coinage of the period designed to denominate the person enjoying the new jural status of full member of a chartered urban community, originated in the central part of western Europe and spread outwards. First occurrences of the term are in eleventh-century Lotharingia, northern France and Flanders. *Burgenses* are mentioned in the Huy charter of 1066. In the British Isles, the word is recorded in 1086 in Domesday Book for England and Rhuddlan in Wales, in the first half of the twelfth century in Scotland and in the 1170s, in Henry II's charter for Dublin, in Ireland. The word also spread eastwards into Slavic Europe, the first instance of the term in Bohemia being in 1233. Originating as a Germano-Latin coinage, 'burgess', with its cognates, emerges as a loan word in every expansionary theatre: the Greek text of the *Chronicle of Morea* mentions *bourgeses*; Romanian has *burgar* or *pîrgar*, from *Bürger*; and the Welsh described the new urban settler as a *bwrdais*. The Latinized Germanic vocabulary of urban jural status was absorbed by the speakers of Celtic, Slavic and other languages because the formal models of the town – defined legally – were imported from the Romance–German lands into the world around.

BURGESS IMMIGRATION

Forms and terms that were born in experiments in Lotharingia or Flanders or Westphalia or northern Spain in the eleventh century were thus exported or borrowed as models by the urban settlements of northern and eastern Europe and by Reconquest Spain in the following centuries. It should be clear, however, that this dissemination of legal forms was not disembodied. In order to be towns in the economic sense as well as the legal, the new and expanding urban settlements of the High Middle Ages obviously required a flow of immigration to establish and maintain their populations. In the central areas of western Europe this immigration was often quite local, routing the surplus sons and daughters of the peasantry to nearby urban centres. Of the 47 burgesses of Stratford–upon–Avon identifiable by toponymic surname in 1252, for example, 42 (89 per cent) came from villages within 16 miles of the town. By contrast, in the frontier regions of Latin Christendom, like eastern Europe, Reconquest Spain and the Celtic lands, town populations, though equally immigrant, were usually of far more distant origin.

Already by the second half of the eleventh century the small towns that fringed the Pyrenees or stood on the Santiago pilgrim route had large numbers of burgesses from beyond the Pyrenees, especially from France, as is clear from the grants of privileges made to 'Franks', like that of Alfonso VI for the settlers in Longroño issued in 1095. The *Chronicle of Sahagún*, composed probably in the early twelfth century, tells how the same king

decreed that a town should be established there, assembling from all parts of the world burgesses of many different trades . . . Gascons, Bretons, Germans, English, Burgundians, Normans, Toulousains, Provençals and Lombards, and many other traders of various nations and foreign tongues; and thus he populated and established a town of no mean size.

In the Aragonese town of Huesca, which was conquered from the Muslims in 1096, settlers from northern France arrived within a generation or so: in 1135 there is mention of a property owner called Humphrey of Falaise, whose wife and children bore the distinctively Gallic names Odeline, William, John, Hué, Odette and Arremborge.

In those parts of the peninsula conquered from Muslims in the twelfth and thirteenth centuries urban development took place in a landscape that was already heavily imprinted with the mark of the city. In the tenth and eleventh centuries Muslim Spain was unquestionably the most highly urbanized region in western Europe. Hence one does not find that spate of new foundations of the High Middle Ages that characterizes, say, eastern Europe or the British Isles. There were, of course, some consciously planned new foundations or plantations, located where there had previously been no settlement of any kind or on the basis of purely rural precursors. An example is Ciudad Real, which Alfonso X founded in 1255:

he commanded people to come from his land and ordained how a town should be settled there and ordered that it should be called *Villa Real* and set out the streets and signalled the places where the enclosure should be made and he had a gate of stone made, where the road from Toledo enters.

The king proceeded to grant the new foundation the law of Cuenca. The city plan of Ciudad Real, with its simple symmetrical layout, in which roads lead from six gates ('puerta de Toledo', 'puerta de Calatrava', etc.) to the central market, flanked by the church of St Mary, shows its planned rather than adventitious origin. But such places were the exception in Spain.

On the other hand, many cities needed to be revived and resettled after long periods of frontier warfare and campaigns of conquest. When Tarragona was taken by the Christians in the early twelfth century, the count of Barcelona granted it to the diocese of Tarragona, describing it as 'the city of Tarragona which has remained destroyed and abandoned for many long years, without cultivator or inhabitant. I give it to you . . . to restore it . . . I give you the freedom . . . to gather men from wherever you can, of whatever rank, to settle that land.' After Ferdinand III took Jaén 'he sent for settlers into all regions, promising great liberties to whoever came to settle there'.

On other occasions the conquering Christian forces found cities with substantial populations already in place, like the great southern metropolises of Valencia, Cordoba and Seville. Seville fell to the king of Castile in 1248. Most of the Muslim population was expelled. In the following decade royal commissioners allocated the property in and around the city: 43 princes, magnates, bishops and military orders received very large estates, 200 knights were granted small estates, and even smaller ones were awarded to the footsoldiers. The king, the newly appointed archbishop and the city council also got their share. The new lords recruited a new population. Immigration into Reconquest Seville touched virtually every part of the Iberian peninsula and areas as distant as Galicia and Old Catalonia supplied many new settlers. The majority of immigrants came from Old Castile, with large numbers also originating in León and New Castile. These three regions formed a massive block of land in north-central Spain, from the Tagus to the northern mountains, that acted as a vast human reservoir, supplying a new Christian population for the city.

In these ways a major transplantation of people took place, bringing French settlers into northern Spain in the eleventh and twelfth centuries and taking Spaniards from the north to the centre and south of the peninsula into the newly founded, desolate or recaptured cities of the Reconquest. At this same time urban immigration was also transforming eastern Europe. Here urbanization was often accompanied by German settlement. When Queen Konstanze of Bohemia gave urban privileges to Hodonín (Göding) in south Moravia in 1228, she announced in her charter: 'we have summoned worthy Germans and settled them in our city'. Cracow provides a good example of a Polish site reshaped by both German immigration and borrowed German municipal law. The ancient Polish fortress was reorganized in 1257, when Duke Boleslaw, the local Piast ruler, established a town there according to Magdeburg law: 'the city of Cracow was converted to German law and the site of the market, the houses and the courtyards was changed by the duke's officials'. He intended 'to gather men there from many regions', but specifically excluded the Polish rural population from admittance as burgesses of the new town. His motive in imposing this restriction was fear of depopulation of his or other seigneurial estates rather than any national bias, but it added to the already very German nature of Cracow. The burgesses were German in name, language, culture and descent, and their legal model was an old German city. Many of the bigger trading cities of eastern Europe were either partially Germanized in this way, or (like Riga, discussed below), were entirely new foundations of German settlers.

Cities like Cracow and Riga specialized in long-distance trade. There was also, however, another kind of German-inspired urbanization in the eastern European hinterland in this period, the creation of a network of small local markets and centres. The towns of Mecklenburg present a good example. Apart from the two Baltic ports of Rostock and Wismar, the towns of Mecklenburg were essentially geared to the needs of the immediate vicinity and have to be explored on this local scale. The great long-distance trade routes, which are important in explaining the growth of the coastal and estuary commercial cities of the Baltic, do not explain the process of urbanization that produced the numerous small towns of inland Mecklenburg.

The earliest chartered towns in this general area were founded in the middle decades of the twelfth century by German conquerors, Lübeck by Count Adolf of Holstein, Schwerin by Henry the Lion of Saxony; but the development of towns by the native dynasty did not begin until 1218. In that year Henry Borwin of Mecklenburg granted Lübeck law to the city of Rostock. The grant lists ten *consules* of Rostock, all with German names, suggesting an immigrant oligarchy enjoying the favour of the dynasty. Rostock's charter was like a starting gun: in the following sixty years a network of small towns was created throughout Mecklenburg, at an average rate of one every two years or so. The most active initiators of this wave of jural urbanization were the rulers of Mecklenburg, who issued charter after charter in favour of their new foundations. Nicholas of Mecklenburg-Werle (1227–77), for example, Henry Borwin's grandson, endowed eight settlements with the town law of Schwerin as transmitted through the Mecklenburg town of Gadebusch. This was one of three dominant families of town law in the area, the others being Lübeck law, as transmitted through local settlements like Rostock and Wismar, and Parchim law. This latter town had been enfranchised in 1225–6 by Henry Borwin:

we have committed the land of Parchim – an inhospitable, empty and trackless land – to Christian colonists, inviting them from far and near. We have also built in that land a city, giving it rights and jurisdiction that are appropriate, beneficial and useful for the inhabitants of the land and the city.

First, we have granted that free city with all rights to all its inhabitants.

The specific content of the town laws of Mecklenburg was not, in outline, any different from that we have already encountered in such documents as the Dublin charter of 1192: freedom from toll, limitations on judicial fines, liberal inheritance law, and so on. A model was being applied, and part of its appeal was its easy reproducibility.

In this way the geography of Mecklenburg, a principality of about 4,500 square miles, was transformed. In the year 1300, unlike the year 1200, there would be everywhere little towns, with parish churches, markets and toll-booths, perhaps rudimentary defences. In the late thirteenth and fourteenth centuries some of these centres acquired religious houses, like the Dominican convent and the house of penitent prostitutes established at Röbel (urbanization brought new kinds of specialization). The urban culture was predominantly German, even if many of the towns had Slav villages as their core and Slav names. A nice example is Kröpelin, a town with a name of Slavic origin, whose councillors placed on their seal a cripple (*Krüppel*), punning on the German homonym. Whatever the roots of the town names, their inhabitants saw themselves as German burgesses. The German colonial settlement in eastern Europe was fundamentally different from the other great new trading network of the High Middle Ages, that of the Italians in the eastern Mediterranean, because of the existence of towns like Gadebusch, Parchim and Kröpelin, small market centres deeply involved with the surrounding countryside, whose burgesses were German-speaking traders and artisans of strictly limited horizons. It was the small market town that was the vehicle of ineradicable cultural transformation in the great land spaces of Europe.

Just as urbanization and Germanization went together in eastern Europe, so urbanization and anglicization accompanied one another in the Celtic lands. The new chartered towns that arose in Scotland, Ireland and Wales in the twelfth and thirteenth centuries were marked out by their immigrant, mainly English population. A piece of documentary evidence that throws light on the Dublin burgesses of the period around 1200 is the guild merchant roll preserved in the archives of the Corporation of Dublin, which lists the guildsmen of the Anglo-Norman town. The earliest part of this list (*c.* 1175–1205) contains approximately 2,800 names, of which around 40 per cent have a toponymic surname mentioning a specific place of origin, besides those of more general nature (Richard the Cornishman, Piers the Frenchman, etc.). Map 7 plots all specific places of origin (within the British Isles) of three or more Dublin guildsmen (a few places cannot be certainly identified). It is immediately apparent that the Dublin–Bristol connection had funnelled into the city large numbers of burgesses from the Severn basin, Bristol's natural hinterland. The majority of the immigrants came from south Wales, the border counties and the West Country, with a fair proportion from the midland towns. London and Winchester, ancient urban centres of the south-east, also provided a large contingent. Less important, but noticeable, are recruits from the north-west, especially Carlisle, and Scotland and the other Anglo-Norman towns of Ireland. Also striking is the fact that most of these citizens bore the names of settlements that were themselves urban. They were townsmen moving to a new town, not rural emigrants.

TRADING NETWORKS

The export of western European urban forms and the dissemination of a burgess population intertwined with that commercial expansion which began in the eleventh century and exploded throughout the Old World in the twelfth and thirteenth. Colonial towns were one of the offspring of colonial traders. Indeed, one of the clearest instances of an expansionary movement in the High Middle Ages is the spread of western seaborne commerce from the limited sphere within which it was constricted in the tenth century to the far-flung trading network of the Italian and German Hanseatic merchants that existed in the fourteenth century. The transformation took place gradually, but with a discernible quickening of pace in the eleventh century.

Italian trade

Commercial contact across the waters of the Mediterranean was nothing new in the High Middle Ages. Merchants from Amalfi and Venice sailed to the maritime cities of Byzantium and the Islamic world in the tenth century and earlier. In 996, for example, over a hundred Italian traders were killed and plundered in riots in Cairo. In the eleventh century, however, evidence for this trade increases, while some new cities entered the game, notably Pisa and Genoa. By the latter half of the century

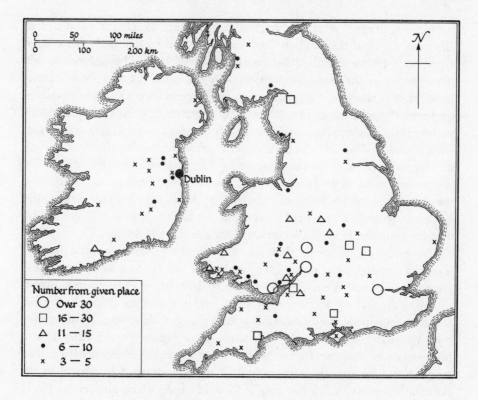

Map 7. Dublin citizens, c. 1200: origin by toponym

aggressive merchants-cum-pirates-cum-crusaders from these cities were landing the whole length of the Mediterranean coast, trading in the big ports
like Constantinople and Alexandria, plundering, as at al-Mahdiyyah in
north Africa in 1087, or trying to help establish crusading principalities, as
at Antioch in 1097–8 and Lattakieh in 1099. The Italians had seized the
initiative in the trading world of the Mediterranean, and for the rest of the
Middle Ages the acquisitive – and sometimes dangerous – Italian trader was
a ubiquitous figure in the region.

The creation of the Crusader States in the last decade of the eleventh
century and the first quarter of the twelfth gave a new opportunity to these
Italian overseas traders. The new states were bridgehead societies, 'Outremers', and heavily dependent on maritime supply, but they had no fleets of
their own and faced the powerful naval forces of their neighbours in Egypt
and Byzantium. In these circumstances the Crusader States very quickly
became dependent on the Italians, for the galleys of the western cities

provided a lifeline. A classic piece of bargaining, which shows in a very clear light what the Italians had to offer and what they wanted, is represented by the so-called *Pactum Warmundi* of 1123. This agreement was made between the doge of Venice, who had just led a very successful expedition against the Egyptian navy, and representatives of the kingdom of Jerusalem (the king himself was in captivity). It was an immediate preliminary to the crusaders' assault on Tyre, a coastal city still under Muslim rule. What the Venetians were offered was, in effect, a trading quarter in every city of the kingdom, judicial autonomy for all suits in which they were defendants and limitations on tolls and taxes. In addition they would receive a third of the cities of Ascalon and Tyre, when these were conquered, 'to be held freely and royally . . . for ever'. Within six months, with the help of a Venetian blockade, Tyre had fallen.

The trading settlement that the *Pactum Warmundi* envisaged for the Venetians in Palestine was a little section of the town where they could create a miniature Venice. They were to have their own church, street, square, bath and oven; they could buy and sell among themselves using Venetian measures; they possessed a 'court of the Venetians' to determine their internal lawsuits. Such settlements were typical of the cultural and jural enclaves that the Italian traders tried to establish everywhere they went. Acre, for example, the capital of the kingdom of Jerusalem in the thirteenth century, had a Genoese, a Venetian and a Pisan quarter, of 16, 11 and 7 acres respectively. The Venetian quarter had a church dedicated to the Venetian patron St Mark; a *fondaco* – that is, a complex of buildings including warehousing, shops and the seat of the Venetian officials in charge of the quarter; houses and stores which were rented out, sometimes annually, sometimes only for the *passagium*, the period when the Venetian convoys were in port; a harbour front; and a surrounding wall. In addition to the itinerant merchants there was a permanent population of immigrants, like the Nicholas Morosini mentioned in a document of 1203, whose father had lived along the coast in Tripoli and whose grandfather, Peter Morosini, had emigrated from Venice to the Holy Land in the twelfth century.

The Venetians, Pisans and Genoese negotiated trading rights throughout the Mediterranean, regardless of whether local powers were Latin, Greek or Muslim. The Venetians established a special quarter in Constantinople in 1082 and their rivals followed their example in the following century. In 1173 the Pisans set up a *fondaco* in Alexandria by treaty with the Egyptians. The establishment of these Italian trading outposts in the Mediterranean culminated eventually in the creation of genuine colonies. These were not privileged enclaves in maritime cities under the lordship of crusading kings,

Greek emperors or Muslim sultans, but autonomous territories, large and small, strung along the main trading routes. They had every cultural symptom of colonialism – small immigrant élites with close ties to the metropolis and large discontented populations of a different language and religious affiliation. Each of the major western commercial cities engaged in these enterprises, usually in bloody rivalry with each other.

Venice's great opportunity for territorial expansion came in 1204, though the city had been nibbling at the Dalmatian coast for some time before then. In that year bankrupt Frankish crusading knights were finally prevailed upon to do something that had been hinted at and discussed in the crusading camps for over a hundred years – to storm Constantinople and take it for themselves. Dependent as they were on Venetian shipping, they had to make generous concessions to that city. The agreement drawn up before the final assault envisaged that the Venetians would receive three-quarters of the booty, the right to appoint half of the members of the commission to choose the new Latin emperor and three-eighths of the conquests. Thereafter the doge of Venice bore the title 'lord of one quarter and a half of the whole empire of Romania'. Military and political reality ensured that Venice's possessions never attained such an improbable geometrical precision, but the Venetians did acquire territories in the Aegean, partly as direct dominions, partly as fiefs held by Venetian vassals.

Crete was the largest of Venice's territorial possessions, acquired by purchase in the confused aftermath of the fall of Constantinople, a time when the balance of Latin and Greek power was being determined by negotiation and warfare. It took several years of fighting against the Genoese interest before the Venetians could establish themselves on the island, but by 1212 they had defeated the Latin opposition and were beginning to organize a limited Venetian colonization of the island. They divided it into 'sixths', each bearing the name of one of the 'sixths' into which the city of Venice itself was divided (Cannaregio, San Marco, Santa Croce, etc.), a spectacular imprint of metropolitan geography on the conquered land. Knights and footsoldiers were recruited to settle in Crete, the earliest contingent being the 132 knights and 48 footsoldiers who settled there in 1211; other groups followed in 1222, 1233 and 1252. A Latin ecclesiastical hierarchy was set up, with an archiepiscopal seat at Candia and ten suffragan bishoprics, occupied by Venetians and other Italians, many of them friars. In 1264 Crete could be described as 'the strength and bulwark of the empire which the Latins have at present', and there is some justification for this view: the Venetians lost it, after fierce struggles, only in 1669.

Venice's most deadly rival was the Ligurian city of Genoa, which

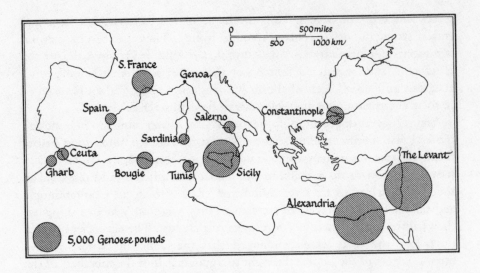

Map 8. Genoese investment in the Mediterranean region, 1155–64 (after Balard, 1978)

already in the tenth century had begun launching naval expeditions in the western Mediterranean and, in 958, had received what has been called 'one of the oldest urban privileges of Europe'. Like the Venetians, the Genoese profited from their involvement in the crusading movement. Bohemond of Antioch granted them a church, market, fountain and thirty houses in Antioch as early as 1098. The pattern of Genoese trade, as revealed in notarial documents of 1155–64, shows Alexandria, the Levantine coast and Sicily as the most important trading areas, followed by southern France, north Africa and Constantinople (see Map 8). Genoese ships were involved in the capture of the Spanish cities of Almería and Tortosa from the Muslims in 1147–9, and by the late twelfth century they were exporting Flemish cloth to Sicily.

The expansion of Genoese trade in the eastern Mediterranean led immediately to conflict with Venice. In 1170, for example, the Genoese trading quarter in Constantinople was plundered by the Venetians. Thereafter it seemed as if the Venetian triumph in the Fourth Crusade would eventually exclude the Genoese from the Aegean and the Black Sea altogether. In crusader Syria the hostilities known as the War of St Sabas, which began in 1256 in a dispute over territory in Acre, ended in defeat for the Genoese. The turning point in their fortunes came in 1261, when the commune allied with the Byzantine emperor, who, in the same year, recaptured his capital of Constantinople from the Latins. Now began a period when the Genoese 'not only excluded the Greeks from maritime transport and business but also surpassed the Venetians in wealth and resources'. In the following half-century they acquired a major settlement at Pera, opposite Constantinople, and the island of Chios, as well as commercial monopolies and access to the Black Sea trade.

Around the Black Sea, on the fringes of the Mongol world, as entrepôts on trade routes leading directly to China, the Genoese founded trading posts and colonies. Everywhere around these coasts one would encounter men from Genoa and its hinterlands. When Edward I of England sent his envoy, Geoffrey de Langley, to the court of the Ilkhan of Persia, in one of those improbable diplomatic exchanges that marked the second half of the thirteenth century, the loyal knight made his way via Genoa and Constantinople to Trebizond, before launching inland. At Trebizond the English envoys purchased a horse from 'Benedict, merchant of Genoa', while the ambassador stored his baggage in the house of Nicholas Doria, a member of a high Genoese family then acting as moneyer to the Comnenian ruler of Trebizond.

There were other Genoese settlements on the northern shore of the Black Sea, like that at Tana on the Sea of Azov, where, around 1360, one could find churches of St Mark, St Mary (Franciscan), St Dominic (Dominican) and St James, confraternities of St Anthony and St Mary and cemeteries of the mendicants and of other Catholics. It was to this last that 'Andalo Basso desired that his body should be carried by four camels'. The preservation of religious and cultural traditions in an alien ecological environment could hardly be more vividly encapsulated than in this vignette of a Genoese merchant going to his last Catholic rites borne by four desert animals.

Not far from Tana, on the southern coast of the Crimea, lay Caffa (modern Feodosiya), Genoa's most important Black Sea colony. The Genoese acquired it as a consequence of their alliance with the resurgent Byzantines and had installed a Genoese consul there by 1281. From that time until 1475, with one short interruption, it was the centre of their Black Sea trade, 'another Genoa', a market for silk, spices and slaves linking the furthest extremes of the Old World. The notarial records of Lamberto di Sambuceto of 1289–90 allow a fairly detailed picture of this thirteenth-century colony to be drawn. At this time the town probably had no walls, but an enclosure of some kind, outside of which lay the slaughterhouse. There were 'quarters' (*contrade*) within the town, as in Genoa itself, but no clear evidence of ethnic segregation – Italians, Greek, Armenians and

Syrians lived in close proximity. There were many *fondacos*, a Franciscan church, a hospital dedicated to St John and a large consular building on the main square, where the consul gave judgement and notaries drew up business documents. Of the 1,600 names that occur in Lamberto's records, almost 600 have been identifiable toponymic surnames. Of this group three-quarters came from the towns and villages of Liguria, especially those along the coast, with another 16 per cent from the Po basin. Most appear to be young unmarried males, intent, eventually, on returning home. An example would be Buonsignore Caffaraino, who can be traced in the 1270s and 1280s buying and selling in Majorca and Corsica as well as at Constantinople and around the Black Sea. He was involved in business with the powerful Doria family and with many men from San Remo, a dependency of Genoa and probably his home town. He bought and sold ships, like the *St Francis*, which we find him chartering out to carry fish from Tana to Constantinople, and had property and a temporary home in Caffa. The trade routes centred on Caffa criss-crossed the Black Sea, especially its eastern section, and led outwards to Constantinople and Genoa (see Map 9).

After a ruinous siege by the Tartars in 1307–8 the Genoese evacuated Caffa, but soon negotiated their return. The magistracy of the city of Genoa responsible for overseas affairs initiated a plan of reconstruction in 1316 and soon the settlement was again flourishing. Walls were built and extended, to form a towered defence line of over 2,000 feet by 1352 and over 16,000 feet in the late fourteenth century. A citadel, complete with clock tower, was erected. There were twenty-seven Latin churches, plus thirteen Greek and Armenian, as well as mosques and a synagogue. In 1322 Caffa became a bishopric and had a series of Franciscan and Dominican bishops, like Conrad of Bregenz (1358–76) and Jerome of Genoa (*c.* 1404), down to the time of its submission to the Ottomans. In 1386 a list names over a thousand Latin residents of Caffa. Its biggest trading commodity was slaves, at the rate of 1,500 a year, exported to the cities of Italy and Spain or to Mameluke Egypt, though perhaps its most spectacular export was the Black Death, which entered western Europe from Caffa on a Genoese ship in 1347. This, then, was 'Caffa, a Genoese city in the far parts of Europe'.

The pattern of the Italian colonial empires has some similarities to that of the British Empire of the year 1900 – a series of islands and headlands dotted along the main commercial pathways, linking the metropolis to distant markets. It has, indeed, been pointed out that the travelling times involved for these saltwater powers were closely comparable: 'one month

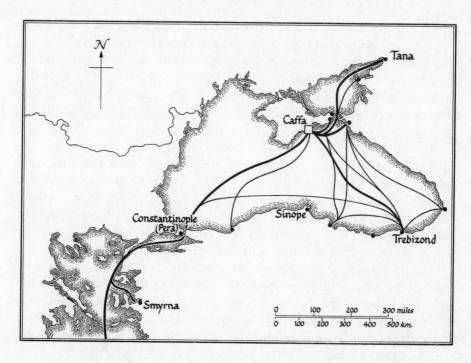

Map 9. Genoese commerce in the Black Sea, 1290 (after Balard, 1978)

from Venice to Canea [in Crete], just as a month was needed for the voyage from London to Bombay; seven to eight weeks from Venice to Constantinople, as from London to Hong Kong; nearly three months to link Venice and Trebizond or Tana, as London and New Zealand'. The scale of the age of the steamship was vaster than that of the age of galleys but the peculiar elongated cape-and-island geography or a maritime empire was still the same. The length of time the Italian voyages to the East took resulted from their coast-hugging navigation and their frequent calls in port. This meant that a round trip to the Black Sea, especially given the tendency to suspend sailing altogether in the winter, might well take nine months. It was only after the development of the great galley in the fourteenth century that it was possible to make two round trips to the eastern coasts per year.

The Italian vessels that dominated the Mediterranean and Black Sea in the High Middle Ages were of two basic types. One was the so-called round ship, whose shallow keel and curved stem- and stern-post gave it an almost semicircular profile. The round ship was powered by a triangular lateen sail and steered by steering oars at the stern. Some were very large, with two or three decks and two or three masts not uncommon by the thirteenth century. The second main type of ship was the galley, which relied upon oars as an auxiliary source of power and thus rode much lower in the water than the round ship. Oars were particularly useful for negotiating passage in and out of harbour or around islands and headlands but were not a long-term alternative to sail.

The preponderant position of Italian shipping in the Mediterranean in the High Middle Ages is shown not only by its monopoly of trans-Mediterranean routes linking the Latin West with the eastern and southern shores but also by its intrusion into such traffic as the trade carrying Muslim pilgrims between north-west Africa and Egypt. Without western naval superiority the establishment of colonial bridgeheads and bastions in the eleventh, twelfth and thirteenth centuries would have been impossible. Time and again the crusading enterprise was saved or secured by maritime power. As Saladin himself supposedly put it: 'As long as the seas bring reinforcements to the enemy ... our country will continue to suffer at their hands.' The inhabitants of the attenuated coastal strip which constituted the thirteenth-century kingdom of Jerusalem were equally aware of their lifeline:

The city which is now called Acre ... is the refuge of the Christians in the Holy Land because of the sea which adjoins it to the west, across which come the ships full of men, food and arms. Those who live there have great consolation from the islands which are in the sea.

Even in the last desperate days of the Crusader States in the Levant a Christian maritime fort could impede the Muslims' progress because they 'had no fleet strong enough to cut the supply-lines and prevent traffic reaching the fort', while a few Christians were able to escape by boat from the sack of Acre in 1291, sea power providing, like the helicopters of the late twentieth century, a door out when everything was lost.

The densest network of Italian trading, piracy and settlement was in the eastern Mediterranean, where the products of Eurasia debouched into the European system, but the western part of that sea was not neglected. The Italians sailed to and settled in the great islands, the cities of north Africa and the Iberian coastal towns. Eventually they went beyond the Mediterranean altogether. The first recorded Genoese vessels to sail via the Atlantic to northern European ports made their journey in 1277–8. The Venetians did not follow until early in the fourteenth century, but from around 1325 sent annual convoys through the straits of Gibraltar. It is unlikely that this route represented anything very substantial in bulk or value, but it serves to indicate the expansionary projects of the Italian traders and the way their activities integrated very disparate regions. The Genoese merchant Antonio di Negro, who was complaining in 1317 about how his shipment of salt had been seized by pirates between Southampton and Newcastle, belonged to a wealthy trading family whose members could also be found in the maritime cities of the eastern Mediterranean and the Black Sea. Back home in Liguria these men could compare notes on the trading conditions, political structures and natural resources of England, Greece and the Crimea. The Italians formed a circulatory system for information as well as goods and capital. The dramatic expansion of their horizons between the eleventh and fourteenth centuries had turned Latin Christendom into an integrated network in a way that it had never previously been.

German trade

In the eleventh century, as Italian merchants and sailors began to extend their routes outwards into the Mediterranean, the northern seas saw the beginning of commercial activity on the part of German merchants. Germans were visiting London to trade around the year 1000, and their westward commerce continued to flourish in later centuries, with permanent depots established at London and Bruges. It was eastward, however, via the Baltic, that the most innovative and exploratory trading world was created. The crucial step in this expansion was the definitive foundation of Lübeck, the German gateway to the Baltic, in 1159. Old Lübeck, a fortified centre of the Slavic kings of the Abodrites, with church, artisan quarters and 'a substantial colony of merchants', had flourished in the early twelfth century but was sacked by rival Slavs in 1138. A few years later, in 1143, as part of the German occupation of eastern Holstein, Count Adolf

came to the place which is called Bucu and found there the rampart of an abandoned fortress . . . and a very large island, encircled by two rivers. The Trave flows by on one side, the Wakenitz on the other, each having swampy and pathless banks. On that side where the land road runs, however, there is a little hill surmounted by the rampart of the fort. When, therefore, the prudent man saw the advantages of the site and the noble harbour, he began to build a city there and called it Lübeck, because it was not far from the old port and city which Prince Henry had at one time constructed.

Archaeology has revealed various early kernels of settlement on the virtual island that forms the heart of Lübeck: one around the old Slav fortification to the north, another around the harbour area on the river Trave and a third at the southern tip of the 'island', where the cathedral was later to be built. Count Adolf's new town incorporated these sites and began to flourish almost at once: 'there was peace in the land of the Wagrians and by the grace of God the new plantation gradually made progress. The market at Lübeck also developed day by day and the ships of its merchants multiplied.' However, despite this swift commercial development, there continued to be threats to Lübeck's security – Slav raids, like those that took place during the Wendish Crusade of 1147, devastating fire and, even more destructive than fire, the jealous hostility of Henry the Lion, duke of Saxony, who desired the promising new city for himself and, when he could not have it, placed it under an embargo and founded a rival market upstream. Eventually Count Adolf was forced to give way, and Henry the Lion took possession of the city:

At his bidding the merchants at once returned with joy and . . . started to rebuild the churches and the walls of the city. The duke sent messengers to the cities and kingdoms of the north – Denmark, Sweden, Norway, Russia – offering them peace so that they should have free access to his city of Lübeck. He also ordained there a mint and tolls and most honourable civic rights (*iura civitatis honestissima*). From that time on, the business of the city prospered and the number of its inhabitants multiplied.

This was in 1159. The following year the town became the site of a bishopric, when the see was moved there from the old Slavic centre of Oldenburg. The episcopal church was dedicated in 1163 and a twin-towered Romanesque cathedral begun in 1173. At the same time the 'most honourable civic rights', probably based on those of Soest in Westphalia, were being elaborated into what was to become the dominant law code of the Baltic.

Commercial activity radiated outwards from this new town. Germans were in Gotland, the great Baltic entrepôt, in 1161, and four years later there is mention of Westphalian merchants trading in Denmark and Russia. They began to visit the eastern Baltic littoral regularly, dealing in salt and cloth at the mouth of the Dvina, and making their way to Novgorod. By 1300 the Russia trade was routine (see Map 10). The German merchants who came to dominate the Baltic in the twelfth and thirteenth centuries sailed a ship known as the cog. This was ideally suited to carry bulk goods, though not as elegant or elastic as the Viking-style longship. The cog was a large vessel – indeed, it has been suggested that the big cog of the High Middle Ages was developed by building one ship on

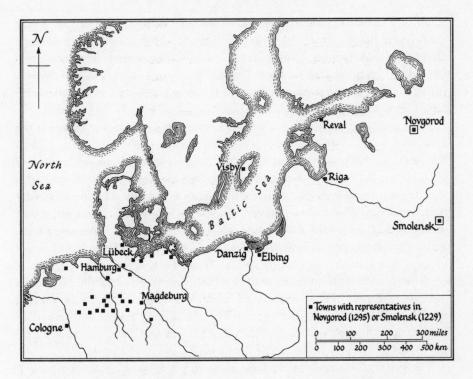

Map 10. German trade with the Baltic and Russia in the thirteenth century

top of another. An example from the fourteenth century was found
waterlogged in the Weser, not far from Bremen, in the 1960s, and it has
been recovered and reconstructed (see Plate 8). It was 76 feet long and 25
feet wide at its broadest and rose almost 14 feet above the keel. It was
constructed of oak planks 2 feet wide and 2 inches thick, had a flat bottom
and straight stem- and stern-post and carried a square sail. The planks were
nailed together with 3,000 nails and caulked with moss, which was held in
place by 8,000 iron clamps. Such a ship could carry a cargo of 80 tons. In
1368 almost 700 ships a year sailed into and out of the harbour of Lübeck,
often making multiple trips. Many of them would be the big trading cogs
of the type represented by the Bremen ship. This was the tool of German
merchant expansion.

   While the Italian traders in the Mediterranean sailed to shores that
already had obviously urban settlements, with, in some cases, a history as
cities going back a thousand years or more, and they only sought quarters

in already urbanized areas, when the Germans came to the eastern Baltic they found lands which had only a limited urban development. Here, along the trade routes, they planted cities whose topography and legal structure were modelled on those familiar to them from Lübeck or Soest – colonial cities, in the medieval sense of the word 'colony', new settlements rather than political dependencies.

Riga is a good example. The arrival of the first German merchants at the mouth of the Dvina is depicted in the *Livländische Reimchronik* of *c.* 1290, a late and lively but not totally misleading source (discussed above in Chapter 4). 'Merchants, rich and outstanding in honour and wealth, who had decided to seek profit, as many do' arrived and outfaced the originally hostile reaction of the native pagan Livonians. 'They had a large supply of goods which they sold there somewhat more profitably than elsewhere, and they were happy at heart. The pagans proposed that they should make a peace and that the merchants should come back again.' The peace was confirmed with oath-swearing and drinking ceremonies and the merchants did indeed return and were received 'as welcome guests'. They penetrated inland, 'where many pagans lived, with whom they traded and stayed so long that, with their permission, they built a fortified dwelling on a hill by the Dvina'. This was Üxküll, first site of the Livonian bishopric.

The site was, however, very vulnerable to pagan attack and, in addition, not the best port for the big German cogs. Albert, third bishop of Livonia and a former canon of the commercial city of Bremen, decided to found a new town that would be both an episcopal seat and a natural goal for merchants from Lübeck and Gotland. The site was reconnoitred in 1200, and the next summer 'the city of Riga was built in a wide field, alongside of which was a suitable site for a harbour'. Very soon the city was walled, had ecclesiastical buildings, including the headquarters of a new crusading military order, the Swordbrothers, and, presumably, merchant buildings. In 1209 a second church, St Peter's, is mentioned alongside the cathedral. Outside the walls a native community lived in its own village. In 1211 the merchants who traded in and from Riga, but who perhaps at first lived there only seasonally, received special privileges from Bishop Albert: freedom from toll and from trial by ordeal, exemption from the right of wreck, guarantees on the bishop's monetary policy and on wergild payments. Notably, offences committed by the merchants were to be judged according to their city of origin and they were forbidden to form a 'common guild'. These rules were later summarily described as 'Gotland law', i.e. the law of the German merchants in Visby, chief city of Gotland. In 1225 the citizens were able to expand them to include the right to appoint their own judge.

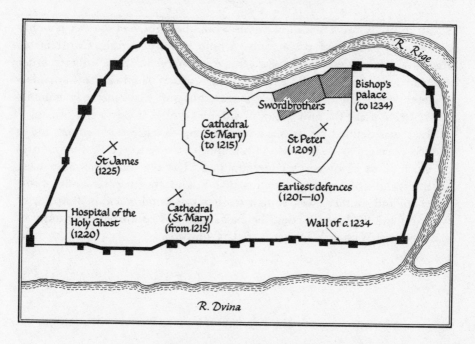

Map 11. Early Riga (after Benninghoven, 1961)

In the same year we find a town seal, with the legend 'The seal of the burgesses dwelling in Riga' and the symbols of a town wall, a cross and two keys (presumably St Peter's). Early the following year comes the earliest mention of the city council, the *consules Rigenses*. The citadel of the bishop and monastic knights was also a self-regulating trading community. In these same decades, especially after a destructive fire in 1215, Riga was rebuilt and extended to fill the whole space between the Dvina and the Rige (see Map 11). Immigrants from Westphalia and other parts of Saxony, coming via Lübeck and Visby, swelled the population to something between two and three thousand by the 1230s. The toponymic surnames of the fourteenth and fifteenth centuries show the burgesses of Riga being drawn from north Germany, especially Westphalia, which provided almost one in five of such names.

By the 1230s, then, a generation after its first founding in a field, Riga, with its turreted walls, the jutting profiles of St Mary's cathedral and the churches of St Peter and St James, its heavy cogs loading and unloading at the water's edge, the chatter of Low German in the streets, might have given a first impression indistinguishable from any north German trading town. In many ways first impressions would be right. Yet the city lay only a few days' ride from pagans who would happily sacrifice Christians to their gods. It was the centre of a great missionary see and a military order dedicated to holy war. Virtually every season shiploads of crusaders disembarked from the cogs. Riga was thus still a distinctively colonial town, or, to make the same point in different words, it was 'a city of God'.

Riga was defined by its place on the long-distance trade routes and it looked overseas to Visby and Lübeck and upstream to the Russian centres as much as to its own rural surroundings. The big maritime cities were wealthy and cosmopolitan centres that bound together far ends of the northern and southern seas, so that the news of London and of Riga, or of Valencia and Trebizond, could be exchanged and compared. The unity of the medieval West was, in part, a traders' unity.

8. Race Relations on the Frontiers of Latin Europe (1): Language and Law

========

> They are to be judged, according to the custom of their people,
> by an official chosen from among them.

Conquest and colonization created on the frontiers of Latin Christendom societies in which different ethnic groups lived side by side, and everywhere in the frontier zone of Latin Europe race relations were thus a central issue. It is worth stressing at the outset that, while the language of race – *gens, natio*, 'blood', 'stock', etc. – is biological, its medieval reality was almost entirely cultural. If we take a classic medieval formulation of the criteria of ethnicity, that of the canonist Regino of Prüm, writing around the year 900, we find that he offers four categories for classifying ethnic variation. 'The various nations,' he writes, 'differ in descent, customs, language and law' (*diversae nationes populorum inter se discrepant genere, moribus, lingua, legibus*). His first criterion, 'descent', is basic to modern forms of racism. The most notorious twentieth-century variants either, like colour racism in the USA, seize on clear biological markers or, like Nazi anti-Semitism, insist on invisible biological differences in the absence of such markers. In the Middle Ages racism of this kind was relatively insignificant. In these circumstances Regino's other criteria – customs, language and law – emerge as the primary badges of ethnicity. In contrast to descent, they share a common characteristic: all three are malleable. They can, indeed, with varying degrees of effect, be transformed not only from one generation to the next, but even within an individual lifetime. New languages can be mastered, new legal regimes adopted, new customs learned. To a point, therefore, medieval ethnicity was a social construct rather than a biological datum. If we define, say, 'German' and 'Slav' by customs, language and law rather than by descent, the grandchildren of Slavs could be Germans, the grandchildren of Germans Slavs. When we study race relations in medieval Europe we are analysing the contact between various linguistic and cultural groups, not between breeding stocks.

The term 'customs' (*mores*) referred to dress, domestic rituals, dietary habits, hair-styles and a host of other habitual practices that distinguished different populations. They were often critically important as differentiae of such groups. In Ireland, the English government legislated against the adoption of Irish hair-styles by loyal subjects: 'the degenerate English of modern times who wear Irish clothes, have their heads half shaved and grow their hair long at the back . . . making themselves like the Irish in clothing and appearance'. The Irish responded by a comparable assertion of identity through hair-style, and one sixteenth-century Irish poem attacks 'You who follow English ways, who cut short your curling hair'. It is indicative that one way to disguise oneself as a member of another race was to adopt their hair-styles. Pagan Slavs of the early twelfth century supposedly scalped German victims and 'after scalping them, they disguise themselves with their scalps and burst into Christian territories, passing themselves off as Christians'. Similarly, in 1190, Muslims trying to slip through the blockade of Acre shaved their beards (as well as putting on Frankish clothes and placing pigs on deck).

LANGUAGE

Language had a particularly important role in defining nationality. Medieval ecclesiastics and scholars, with their biblically based belief in the common descent of mankind and their theory of an original community of language, found it natural to see the post-Babel differentiation of language as the first step in the formation of races or peoples. 'Races arose from different languages, not languages from different races,' as Isidore of Seville, the schoolmaster of the Middle Ages, put it. The same point is expressed even more pithily by another Latin author: 'language makes race' (*gentem lingua facit*). The power of the linguistic bond was recognized. As a fourteenth-century chronicler reported: 'those who speak the same language are entwined in tighter bonds of love'. These tighter bonds of love often manifested themselves, as we shall see, in a sharper hatred of those of a different language, for, as is apparent to the present day, 'wars and various tribulations have arisen from the diversity of tongues'.

As the vernaculars emerge into literary and documentary record in the High Middle Ages, they reveal large tracts of Europe possessing a relatively high degree of linguistic and cultural homogeneity and dominated by more or less standard languages: examples are English in England, Languedoil north of the Loire, Languedoc south of it, Low German in north Germany, High German in south Germany. There were, naturally, variations in dialect and some areas of linguistic overlap, but one can still see a clear contrast between these core areas and the conquered and colonized peripheries, which were characterized by a ubiquitous mixture and intermingling of language and culture. In the central zone the languages of different areas adjoined, of course, but the fringe zone saw a pluralism of language within the same territorial limits, differentiated by race and class. Although there were enormous linguistic variations within the area in which, say, High German or Languedoc were spoken, they normally took the form of dialectical variation over space. As one travelled from Trier to Vienna or from Béarn to Provence, one would notice the shift from one local variant to another. In complete contrast, the conquered and colonized peripheries of Europe were familiar with languages of completely different language families being spoken in the same settlement or street. The interplay of languages was thus a common and sharply recognizable feature of the frontiers of Latin Europe. Here it was not at all surprising to observe that 'many of our people now speak various languages in the streets', as the Bohemian chronicler Peter of Zittau remarked. When Pope John XXII excommunicated the Franciscan minister-general, Michael of Cesena, in 1329, the letters notifying this action to Cracow were first read out there in Latin and then 'expounded to the people in the vernacular, both in Polish and in German, so that they might be understood better and more clearly by everyone'. The streams, hills and settlements of the frontier zones began to show signs of a double identity: 'the place is called *woyces* in Slavic and *enge water* in German', explains one east Pomeranian document. Names of human settlements underwent similar linguistic transformation. The Irish Ellach in Meath, for example, came to be named Scurlockstown after its new holders, the immigrant Scurlag family – the English suffix 'town' being an indelible mark of the regions of colonization and partial anglicization in eastern and southern Ireland. In New Castile a village known in Arabic as Algariva was rebaptized with the assertive Romance named Villafranca.

Bilingualism was not unusual at many social levels. Even in the tenth century Otto I of Germany had command of both German and Slav. In the Frankish Morea successful leaders would know French, Greek and perhaps even Turkish, and it is typical that there is still unresolved debate whether the primary chronicle source for the history of Frankish Greece was composed in French and then translated into Greek or vice versa. By the fourteenth century the descendants of the Anglo-Norman invaders of Ireland were composing poetry in Irish. Such bilingualism could sometimes be of highly practical relevance. In 1085 Count Roger, leading the Norman reconnaissance of Syracuse in Sicily, sent Philip, the son of a Greek dignitary, to spy out the Muslim fleet: 'he sailed through the Saracen fleet as if he were one of them, for he, and all the sailors with him, were as conversant in their language as in Greek'. The south Italian brigands who joined up with the Normans made the effort to acquire French.

In these linguistically mixed societies translators and interpreters naturally played an essential role. Sometimes they held official positions. In Valencia, for example, there were official translators, with the title *torcimana*, from the Arabic *tarjuman*. Along the Welsh border men held land explicitly 'in return for service as interpreter between the Welsh and the English'. As we shall see later, the law court was one place where interpreters were particularly important. Sometimes these regions where the coexistence of different languages stimulated bilingualism and facility in translation made a permanent cultural impact on Europe. It was from Spain and Sicily, for example, that the stream of translations of Greek and Arabic scientific and philosophical works spread to the universities of Latin Christendom. What eventually hatched into the Latin Aristotelianism of Thomas Aquinas had been incubated in the ethnically diverse societies of Reconquest Castile and southern Italy.

These bilingual or multilingual regions also provided the channels for linguistic borrowing from one language into another. It was in the maritime world of the Baltic, for example, that Poles picked up from Hanseatic traders and artisans some of the Low German vocabulary of commerce and urban life. Terms relating to units of measurement (Polish *laszt* and *punt*, from German *Last*, 'load', and *Pfund*, 'pound'), seafaring life (*balast* and *koga*, from *Ballast*, 'ballast', and *Kogge*, 'large merchant ship') or the tools of urban discipline (*praga*, from *Pranger*, 'pillory') passed from German into Polish in this way. Similarly, in late-medieval Wales, English and French terms of feudal and urban life, like 'baron', 'parliament' and 'burgess', were absorbed into Welsh (*barwn, parlmant, bwrdais*). New colonists not only imprinted their terms on native languages; they were also quite willing to borrow words from those they encountered, especially in areas of native expertise. In the Iberian peninsula the advancing Christian speakers of Romance languages adopted the Arab words for 'rice', 'barley' and 'tax collector', as well as terms for cosmetics, water conduits, cushions, caravans and poisons.

The variegated linguistic patterns of the frontier regions were reflected in their naming practices. A process of mutual influence meant that by the fourteenth century Slav farmers might be called Bernard and Richard, English settlers in Ireland might have Irish names, and a descendant of

Welsh upland princes might be quite unrecognizable as Sir Thomas de Avene. Simultaneous binomialism is an even sharper symptom of the linguistic and cultural pluralism of the frontier zones. In the tenth century Otto II was accompanied after the rout of Cap Colonne by 'one of his knights, Henry, who was called Zolunta in Slavic'. Several Slav princes of the twelfth and thirteenth centuries, such as the Bohemian rulers Przemysl Ottokar I and II and Henry Wladislaw of Moravia, also bore both German and Slav names. Przemysl Ottokar II even had two seals, one for his Czech-speaking lands, inscribed with the name Przemysl, one for his German-speaking lands, bearing the name Ottokar. Among the Mozarabs of Toledo, Romance–Arabic binomialism was widespread. 'In the name of God,' begins one document of 1115, 'I, Dominico Petriz, as I am called in Romance (*in latinitate*) and in Arabic (*in algariva*) Avelfaçam Avenbaço; also I, Dominiquiz, as I am called in Romance, and in Arabic Avelfacam Avencelema . . .'

It would be naïve to describe the cultural situation on the frontiers simply in terms of pluralism, diversity or mingling. Languages were not all equal. Some had higher prestige because of the political or economic power of those who spoke them. It is clear, for instance, that it was speakers of Romance and Germanic languages who were spreading through expansionary migration and conquest, while Celtic, Slavic, Baltic and Arabic were losing ground. These developments of the medieval period had a permanent effect on the linguistic map of Europe. There was a strong colonial flavour to this linguistic expansion: German in Livonia and French in Syria were languages of conquest, which might offer privileges to those who mastered them. But the patterns were not simple. Native vernaculars were resistant and could revive. Linguistic change was not all one-way and linguistic conflict could have more than one outcome.

A growing strand of linguistic nationalism or politicized linguistic consciousness emerges in the later Middle Ages. A symptom of the identification of language and people is the use of the word for language in contexts where it almost certainly means 'people'. The West Slav word *jazyk* denoted both 'language' and 'people', and when the fourteenth-century Czech nationalist writer known as Dalimil employs the term *jazyk cesky*, it is impossible to say in every instance whether the linguistic or the ethnic connotation is greater. The German translation of Dalimil uses *zung*, i.e. 'tongue', and this has a similar semantic complexity. *Iaith*, the Welsh word for 'language', was likewise 'charged in contemporary parlance with a far greater range of attributes than the purely linguistic one'. It is characteristic that the Welsh word for 'those who do not speak Welsh' could be equated

with that for 'aliens'. In Latin documents *lingua* enshrines the same ambiguity. Thus when the citizens of Cork refer to the *Hybernica lingua* as the
king's enemies, it is only possible to translate this as 'the Irish race'. The
Hospitallers in the Levant were grouped into 'tongues' according to their
place of origin in western Europe. In all these instances a semantic ambiguity
points to a conceptual one – ethnic and linguistic identity tended to blur
into one another.

The sense of belonging to a language community could become the
basis, not simply for a feeling of belonging or fellowship, but also for
political claims. When Przemysl Ottokar II of Bohemia appealed for Polish
support in his year of crisis, 1278, he (or, rather, his Italian notary) invoked
the closeness of Czechs and Poles based upon physical proximity, ties of
blood and the fact that 'the Polish nation . . . is united with us in harmony
of language'. The same linguistic affinity again served political purposes in
1300, when Ottokar's successor, Wenceslas II, was offered the Polish
throne. The Polish envoys reportedly said: 'there will be one king for us
and the Bohemians and we will live together amicably under a common
law. For it is fitting that those who do not differ much in speaking the
Slavic language enjoy the rule of a single prince.' The Polish claim to
Pomerelia, raised in opposition to the Teutonic Knights, was supported by
the argument 'that there is one and the same language in Poland and
Pomerelia and that all the people who customarily reside there speak
Polish'. At about the same time, but almost a thousand miles to the west,
the Bruce incursion into Ireland of 1315–18 also enlisted the rhetoric of
linguistic kinship. In 1315, while planning the expedition, King Robert
wrote a letter to the Irish which begins: 'Since we and you, our people and
your people, free since ancient times, have sprung from one national stock,
and a common language and common custom stir us to come together
eagerly and joyfully in friendship . . .' Donal O'Neill's justification of his
recognition of Edward Bruce as king, contained in the Remonstrance of
1317–18 addressed to John XXII, informed the pope that 'the kings of
lesser Scotia [Scotland] all trace their blood to our greater Scotia [Ireland]
and retain to some degree our language and customs'.

The counterpart to these aggressive claims that used linguistic community
as an argument were defensive protestations, such as the accusations, raised
especially in the later Middle Ages, that an enemy wished to destroy the
native language. Such charges were not limited to the frontiers of Latin
Europe. In 1295, when Edward I of England was trying to muster support
in his struggle with Philip IV of France, he charged that the French king
intended to invade England and 'wipe out the English language completely

from the land'. It was clearly, however, the kind of rumour or accusation that would arise naturally in the ethnically divided societies of the frontiers. According to one Polish chronicler, the Teutonic Knights intended 'to exterminate the Polish language' (*ydyoma Polonicum*). Accusations of this type were not mere paranoid fantasies, for some examples of attempts at forcible language change can be found. In addition to the rules governing the language of the law court (to be discussed below), there were some other general attempts at linguistic prescription and proscription. In 1495, for example, Bishop John IV of Wrocław (Breslau) ordered the inhabitants of his village of Woitz (Wójcice) to learn German within five years or be expelled. More systematic and persistent were the rules that the colonial government and the English settlers in Ireland applied to the use of the native Irish language. On the one hand, they repeatedly legislated that settlers should not use the native tongue. 'We have ordained,' runs an ordinance of Edward III of 1359–60, 'that no one of English descent shall speak in the Irish tongue with other Englishmen . . . but every Englishman should study the English language.' Conversely, there was an effort to spread English among the native population. In the 1380s English envoys were trying to get the pope to command the prelates of Ireland that 'they should get their subjects to learn the English language'. Attempts were made to enforce these regulations. In Waterford a certain William Power was imprisoned in 1371 'because he could not speak English' and released only when he found pledges to undertake that he would learn the language; and in the fifteenth century the same city admitted apprentices to the freedom of the city only if they were of 'Inglish aray, habite and speche'. But such precepts were unusual and, one may surmise, rarely effective. Cultural legislation, even in the modern state, always faces an uphill struggle. In medieval circumstances it cannot have been enforceable. Language change there certainly was, but it was the result of migration and cultural adaptation, not of administrative prescription.

Language death is the most dramatic example of language change. Languages which were spoken by rural and lower-class rather than by urban and upper-class speakers and which were not written down for documentary and literary purposes might shrivel and die. There are several instances from the fringes of Latin Europe. Prussian, for example, a Baltic language akin to Lithuanian and Latvian, which was spoken by the native population of Prussia, had died out by the seventeenth century, swamped by the German of immigrants and rulers. A simple catechetical literature was produced in Prussian after the Reformation, but this was too little too late. A note on the cover of one of the surviving Prussian texts records that

'This Old Prussian language has completely disappeared. In 1677 a single old man, who lived on the Courland Spit and who still knew the language, died.' The language was entered on the list of written tongues only to be inscribed almost at once on that of dead ones. Wendish, the Slavic spoken west of the Oder, also disappeared in the later Middle Ages. Only in Lausitz do Slav speakers, the Sorbs, survive to this day (now with their own protected status and institutes for Sorb studies). Elsewhere the various branches of Wendish slowly died. One Polabian innkeeper and farmer, Johannes Parum Schultze, who lived in the so-called 'Hanoverian Wendland' around Lüchow and Dannenberg, wrote in 1725: 'I am a man of forty-seven years of age. When I and three other people in our village have gone, then no one will rightly know what a dog is called in Wendish.'

In Spain it was Arabic which gradually retreated before the triumphant Romance languages. A graphic presentation of the documentation surviving from Toledo in the 140 years after the Christian conquest of 1085 (see Figure 3) shows that in the first hundred years of Christian rule Arabic was used more frequently than Latin or Romance for purposes of record and that in the late twelfth century, possibly due to immigration of Mozarabs from a Muslim Spain polarized by the fanatical Almohads, Arabic was actually increasingly frequent as a language of documentary literacy. The early thirteenth century, however, saw a quite discernible shift, as, for the first time, Latin and Romance documents became more common than Arabic (131:111 for the period 1201–25). The trend developed dramatically. By the 1290s there are only one or two Arabic documents per year, at a time when total output of records is ever increasing. In the fourteenth century the trickle of Arabic dries up. A fundamental linguistic transformation had taken place.

LAW

Ethnicity was constituted not only by custom and language, but also by law. The principle of 'personality of the law', according to which individuals had their own ethnic law – Gothic or Frankish or Roman – regardless of the territory they inhabited or the lord they served, was found not only in the early Middle Ages but throughout the High Middle Ages, especially, of course, in areas of ethnic mingling. Distinctive legal status was one way of recognizing or constituting separate ethnicity. When Sobieslaw II of

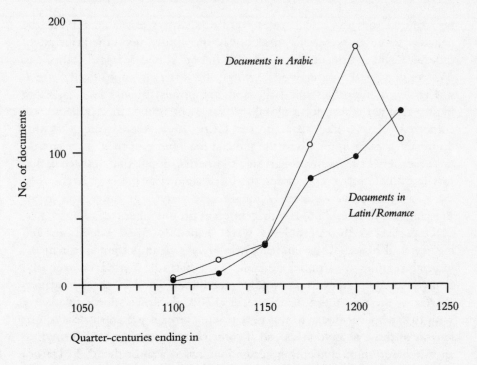

Figure 3. Arabic and Latin/Romance documents in Toledo (data from González, 1976, p. 89)

Bohemia defined the particular rights of the Germans resident in Prague in the 1170s, his charter based their distinctiveness on the principle that 'just as the Germans are different from the Bohemians [Czechs] by nation, so they should be distinct from the Bohemians in their law and custom'. On the frontiers of Prussia, Poland and Pomerania it was ruled that 'men who come there or traverse the land shall be judged on account of any crime or contract engaged in there according to Polish custom if they are Poles and according to German custom if they are Germans, following the practice of the land of Prussia'.

In regions where different ethnic groups lived side by side, the administration of justice was a sensitive issue. In the High Middle Ages most parts of Latin Europe included at least one minority, the Jews, marked out by their own legal regime. Special provisions were made regarding the rights of Jews to bring suit or bear witness, the exact nature of the testimony needed to prove their charges or to convict them and the form of oath they would be required to swear. Such rules were not always discriminatory in the negative sense but were, of course, always predicated upon the principle of different legal treatment for those of different ethnic–religious status. On the frontiers of the Latin world, where the different populations formed not enclosed minorities but large and ubiquitous groups, an even more highly charged ethnic–legal pluralism was to be found. In conquered and colonized regions, like Spain or the Celtic lands, there were fears that dominant groups might twist the judicial machinery in their own favour; in the eastern European monarchies the native population suspected that privileged colonists might escape the usual rigours of the law. Even when the balance of power was fairly equal, there were large differences in the substantive and procedural law that different groups inherited.

Responses to these problems were shaped by local conditions and history, and hence, while ethnicity was always an important factor in the judicial regimes of frontier Europe, its exact role varied enormously. Sometimes the law was avowedly race-blind. Thus in the foundation charter of the new town of Salzwedel (1247), the town's lords ruled: 'we wish that whoever flocks to this new town, German peasants or Slavs, our tenants or those of anyone else, shall come before the judge of that town to answer before him concerning accusations raised against them'. In Daroca in Aragon the local municipal regime required that 'Christians, Jews and Muslims shall have one and the same law regarding blows and accusations'. More frequently, however, the legal systems of the colonized fringes of Europe recognized a distinction between persons on the grounds of race, and hence legal systems were structured to deal with the problem of populations of mixed ethnicity. Sometimes a single system of courts and a single body of substantive law incorporated procedures and legal capacities which varied according to race. Thus, for example, a unitary judicial system applying a uniform concept of what constituted testimony might still debar certain individuals from serving as witnesses in certain cases on the grounds of their race. An example would be those versions of Lübeck law that did not allow Slavs to act as witnesses in cases of assault or breach of the peace, or the rule in the Frankish Morea that 'a Greek serf cannot be a witness against a liegeman in a criminal case involving life or limb', here mingling ethnic and social discrimination. On the other hand, there might be a more wide-reaching dualism, in which different and parallel systems of courts and substantive law existed for each of the races.

This latter type is found in the city of Toledo, captured from the Muslims in 1085. Thereafter Toledo had separate judicial regimes for the three main Christian ethnic groups now inhabiting the city. The Mozarabs,

Arabic-speaking Christians who had either lived in Toledo under Muslim rule or come there from other Muslim states in the Iberian peninsula, were granted a charter of rights in 1101 by Alfonso VI of Castile. This is addressed to 'all the Mozarabs of Toledo'. The same king also granted rights to the Castilian settlers and to the Franks, i.e. the immigrants from beyond the Pyrenees, though these are known only from later confirmations, the former addressed to 'all the Castilians in the city of Toledo', the latter to 'you, all the Franks of Toledo'. The judicial life of this great Reconquest city was thus clearly characterized by the existence of three ethnically designed groupings, each with its own law.

The occasion of Alfonso VI's charter of 1101 to the Mozarabs was a wave of property disputes in the city, which, the king ruled, were to be settled definitively by a judicial commission containing both Mozarab and Castilian members, but the document goes on to make more permanent and fundamental provisions. The property of the Mozarabs was to be secure and virtually freely alienable; their *pedites*, the less-wealthy who served as footsoldiers, were guaranteed the right to social mobility and protected against non-royal exactions. The judicial regime is regulated by two provisions regarding lawsuits and pleading. The first is important and unequivocal in tone: 'if there are judicial proceedings between them, the issue shall be decided according to the rules of the ancient *Book of Judges*'. This *Book of Judges* is the *Liber iudiciorum* or *Fuero Iuzgo*, a law code dating back to the days of the independent Visigothic kingdom in Spain and which contained an amalgam of Roman and Germanic law. It is rather unusual that the distinction between ethnic laws should be specified in this way by reference to a written code. At the same time as Alfonso VI recognized that Mozarab law meant the law of the *Liber iudiciorum*, he also specified that the scale of financial penalties for Mozarabs should be just the same 'as is proclaimed in the Castilians' charter . . . just like the Castilians who live in Toledo'. The point seems to be that favourable rules regarding fines and dues were to be extended to the Arabic-speaking as well as to the Romance-speaking population, even though the former had a separate, ethnically specific code of substantial and procedural law.

The three Christian ethnic groups of twelfth-century Toledo also had their own judges. 'You shall have a Mozarab and a Castilian *alcalde* (judge),' states the *fuero*, or charter, of Santa Olalla, which was based on that of Toledo. Toledan documents of the 1170s refer to 'the *alcalde* of the Castilians' and the '*alcalde* of the Mozarabs'. The first clause of Alfonso VII's confirmation of the rights of the Franks of Toledo in 1136 reads: 'You shall have your own *merino* and your own *saion* (magistrates).' The separate ethnic laws were thus applied by separate ethnic judiciaries. As late as the fourteenth century rules were being laid down about the proper demarcation of jurisdiction between the *alcaldes* who applied the *Fuero Iuzgo* and the Castilian *alcaldes*.

None of these ethnic groups, Mozarabs, Castilians and Franks, was a conquered people and all were Christian, even if the immigrant clergy and the papacy might grumble about the aberrant ecclesiastical practices of the Mozarabs. Though there is no doubt that there were social and economic inequalities between the three groups and that an irreversible cultural Castilianization took place in the thirteenth century, the legal ideal behind the judicial triplication of Reconquest Toledo was that of separate but equal ethnic and jural communities. Judicial dualism or pluralism can also be found, however, in the very different situation when ethnic communities confronted one another as conqueror and subject. Recognizing their jural autonomy was one way of trying to reconcile the conquered to their lot. The judicial regime of the Mudejars, the Muslim subjects of the Christian kings of the Iberian peninsula, was originally characterized by such guarantees. Many Muslim communities in the peninsula submitted by agreement with Christian rulers, and their terms of submission usually included provisions safeguarding jurisdiction and legal procedure. An early example is the charter which Alfonso I of Aragon granted to the Muslims of Tudela in 1115. The relevant clause reads: 'They shall be and remain in lawsuits and in pleas under their *qadi* and their *alguaciles* (judge and deputies), as it was in the time of the Moors.' It was repeatedly specified that their disputes should be regulated by Islamic law (*sunna*), not by any other custom. In general Muslims were expected to live among Christians, in the words of Alfonso X of Castile, 'preserving their own law and not reviling ours'. In Wales, too, separate courts and judges administered Welsh law in several of the marcher lordships. In 1356 the duke of Lancaster confirmed that the Welsh of Kidwelly should be tried and fined according to the law of Hywel Dda – that is, native Welsh law – and even recognized the inheritance rights of illegitimate children, an aspect of native law that English kings and prelates had deplored and rejected for two centuries. Kidwelly, along with other lordships, maintained 'a parallel system of English and Welsh courts'; in Denbigh and Dyffryn Clwyd, Welsh judges received annual payments from the lord. Such parallelism also characterized the situation of the immigrant minorities in eastern Europe. The Germans of Prague in the twelfth century and those of Hungary in the thirteenth were guaranteed their own judge. In 1244, for example, Bela IV of Hungary ruled that the Germans who settled in

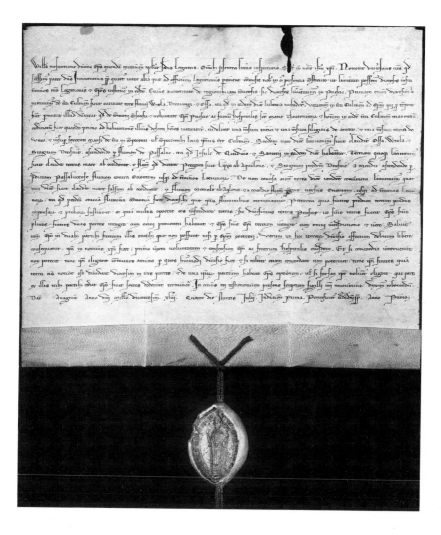

1 Document of William of Sabina establishing bishoprics in Prussia.

2 Carrickfergus Castle

3 Albert the Bear (right, with spear and shield) as depicted on one of his coins

4 Heavy cavalryman of the thirteenth century.

5 A trebuchet of the late twelfth century.

6 Peasants enfranchised in return for clearing land.

7 Cistercians clearing land.

8 The Bremen cog (*above*, reconstruction; *opposite, top*, side view)

9 Wends and Saxons could not judge or bear witness against each other.

10 First Wendish coins: *top*, Henry Pribislav of Brandenburg
(obverse and reverse); *above*, Jacza of Köpenik

Karpfen (modern Krupina in Slovakia) 'are not bound to stand to judgement before any judge . . . except their own particular judge'.

A procedural problem that immediately arose when two or more separate judiciaries and court systems existed was the proper jurisdiction in cases between parties of different races. The preferred solution in the early years of Reconquest Spain, to judge by the charters of privileges granted to the Muslims, was that the Christian party should be judged by a Christian judge and the Muslim party by a Muslim judge. 'If a Moor brings a lawsuit against a Christian or a Christian against a Moor,' decreed Alfonso I in his charter for Tudela, 'the *qadi* of the Moors shall render judgement on the Moor according to Islamic law (*zuna*) and the *qadi* of the Christians shall render judgement on the Christian according to his law.' Such rights were commonly granted by the Iberian kings and other Christian lords to Muslim communities. 'If a case arises between a Christian and a Saracen, the *amin* shall be the judge of the Saracen and a Christian shall be the judge of the Christian,' reads a charter granted by the master of the Hospitallers of Aragon in 1258, repeating exactly the provisions of Alfonso I's charter 150 years earlier. How such an arrangement actually worked in detail is quite unclear, and it is easy to imagine, in the words of the historian Fernández y González, 'the great practical difficulties' that it must have created. In Prussia, where the territorial lords, such as the Teutonic Knights and the bishops, often reserved jurisdiction over the native population, mixed cases were sometimes included in the same reserved category, though it was not unknown for them to be surrendered to local urban courts.

Another possibility was to privilege the defendant. For example, even more favourable to the Muslims than the simple concession of jural autonomy within their community is the right granted by James I of Aragon to the Muslims of Játiva: 'If a Christian brings a suit against a Saracen, he shall receive full justice from your *çalmedina* (*sahib al-madina* or magistrate) according to the law of the Saracens.' One of the privileges of the Germans settled in Prague was that all cases in which the German was the defendant should be heard before the 'judge of the Germans'. The equitable simplicity of the Romano-canonical maxim to this effect was invoked in the charter for the new town of Cracow, established in 1257 for German burgesses:

Since it is right that the plaintiff should plead in the court of the accused (*actor forum rei sequi debeat*), we ordain and will that when it happens that a citizen of the said city brings a case against a Pole of the diocese of Cracow, he should pursue his right before a Polish judge; conversely, if a Pole brings a case against a citizen, the advocates [of the town] should give judgement and determine the issue.

Whether the judicial regime countenanced parallel laws and jurisdictions or merely made special provision for those of a particular ethnic group, it was an especially acute question who constituted acceptable witnesses. Ethnic groups often lived together in a state of chronic mutual suspicion. A very telling provision of Duke Sobieslaw's privilege for the German settlers in Prague is the ruling that, though the Germans should be answerable for false money found in their chests, they are immune from prosecution on account of false money found elsewhere in their house or courtyard, 'because of the wicked and malicious people who are accustomed to throw such things into their houses or courtyards'. Such a fear of being framed would focus most intensely on the law courts, and it is in the context of such fears that we should see the reassurances that lords sometimes granted or custom allowed that one could not be judged by, or convicted solely on the testimony of, members of another ethnic group. The following is an example from the *Sachsenspiegel*, the compendium of Saxon law written in the 1220s:

When a court is held by the authority of the king's *Bann*, the lawfinders and judges ... should give judgement, fasting, on any man, be he German or Wendish, serf or free ... Where a court is not held by the authority of the king's *Bann*, then any man may give judgement on and be a witness against another, as long as he cannot be reproached as unlawworthy, except the Wend on the Saxon and the Saxon on the Wend. However, if the Wend or the Saxon is caught red-handed in a wrongful act and brought before the court with the hue and cry, the Saxon may bear witness against the Wend and the Wend against the Saxon and each of them must submit to the judgment of the other, if he has been caught in this way.

The distinction mentioned here, between courts held by the authority of the king's *Bann* (power of command) and those not held by such an authority, is probably that between the counties of the old-settled parts of Germany and the courts of the eastern marks. The implication is that the latter practised a racially divided jurisdiction: Saxons could not judge nor bear witness against Slavs, nor vice versa, except in the case of red-handed crime (the scene is shown in Plate 9). The Muslims of Castile and Aragon were also guaranteed witnesses of their own group: 'if a Moor is suspected of theft or fornication or anything for which justice must be done, the only witnesses that will be admitted against him will be trustworthy Moors; Christians will not be admitted'. It is reasonable to see these provisions as guarantees, within a single system of law courts, against false and ethnically motivated accusations.

Such rules must be placed in context. They existed alongside a great array of disabilities that were applied to native populations in the newly colonized areas. For, if a powerful local group might win its jural autonomy, weaker groups were subject to institutionalized discrimination. Procedural issues, such as the problem of appropriate jurisdiction in mixed cases, the appropriate form of oath or proof, the question of acceptable testimony or of language of pleading, were not decided on grounds of equity, but by the balance of ethnic power.

Wergild scales are a classic locus for such ethnic inequality. A wergild was a payment made in compensation by the killer or by his family to the family of a victim of homicide. It varied in value according to status and, on the frontiers of Europe, race. For example, according to the *Iura Prutenorum*, a law code for the native Prussian population of Pomesania, the required compensatory payments when 'a Prussian kills a free German' ran on a sliding scale from 8 marks for a propertyless German, through 12 marks for a smallholder to 30 marks for a fully endowed settler. Native Prussian wergilds ranged as high as 60 marks for the kings (*reges*), but were only 30 marks for the nobles (*nobiles*) and 16 for the common people (*communis populus*). German colonists with a farm or urban property were thus equated with the native nobility. In Reval (Tallinn) in Estonia the fine for wounding an Estonian was roughly a third of that for wounding a German settler. An even more extreme inequality, which goes beyond the bounds of a compensatory system altogether, is found in the *fuero* of Sepúlveda, which specifies a fine of 100 *maravedís* and exile for a Christian who kills a Muslim, but confiscation of property and death for a Muslim who kills a Christian. Racial disabilities were sometimes obliterated by considerations of wealth and status, as in the city of Wismar on the Baltic, where the local council insisted that men 'of whatever tongue' who had been received as burgesses could testify 'according to the quality of their goods', an explicit appeal to criteria of local standing and property in the face of discriminatory rules regarding testimoniary capacity often applied to Wends. Social discrimination and ethnic discrimination danced a complex minuet. Nevertheless, one thing that the mirror of ethnic law reflects is the balance of power between ethnic groups.

LANGUAGES OF LAW

Ethnic groups were linguistic groups and thus the law courts of frontier Europe would expect to hear more than one language spoken. Interpreters played an important role here. The aptly named Richard le Latimer (i.e. 'interpreter') held land near Dublin 'in return for service as a translator in the county court of Dublin', and the Prussian law code of the fourteenth century refers to the *Tolcken*, or interpreter, in the law courts. When mixed cases came to the law courts, one of the first issues that needed to be decided was the language of pleading. If Slav faced German or Welshman Englishman, rules were required to determine what the court would deem linguistically acceptable. Preservation of the right to plead in one's own language was obviously a crucial right, which both reflected and produced more general power and prestige for that community of language-speakers. When Ferdinand III of Castile granted the Basques of his kingdom the right to plead in Basque before the local royal judge, he honoured and recognized a constituent ethnic group. Conversely, it was an assault on the standing of the Irish language when, in the fifteenth century, the city magistrates of Waterford commanded that no inhabitant of the city 'shall implead nor defend in Irish tongue against any man in the court, but that all they that any matter shall have in court to be ministered shall have a man that can speak English to declare his matter'.

The interplay of languages in the courts is also revealed in the *Sachsenspiegel*. This contains a short section on dealings between Saxons and Slavs, discussing, as mentioned above, the capacity of a member of one people to give judgement on or testimony against a member of the other and – in a later, but still thirteenth-century, addition to the text – the rules governing the children of mixed marriages. These topics point to a world in which Saxon–Slav interaction was to be expected and required rules for regulation. The problem of the language of pleading is dealt with in the following words: 'Anyone against whom an accusation is made may refuse to answer if he is not accused in his mother tongue.' The provision is a clear statement of the principle that one need not answer a charge unless it is made in one's own vernacular. In the second recension of the *Sachsenspiegel*, however, this passage was elaborated:

Anyone against whom an accusation is made may refuse to answer if he is not accused in his mother tongue, if he does not know German and swears to that fact. If he is then accused in his own language, he must answer, or his representative must answer for him, in such a way that the accuser and the judge may understand. If he has made an accusation or answered one or given judgement before the court in German, and this can be proven, he must answer in German; except before the king, for there everyone has right according to his birth.

Here the simple vernacular egalitarianism of the first recension has been replaced by a series of requirements systematically slanted in favour of German. It is incumbent upon the accused to prove that he does not know German, and any earlier legal transactions in German can be used against him to ensure that he respond in German. Even if he demonstrates Slav monolingualism, he has to provide a German-speaking representative (it can hardly be doubted that 'in such a way that the accuser and the judge may understand' means 'in German'). The picture is still one of courts where one may expect to encounter both Slavs and Saxons, but courts where the Saxons are a dominating group and the Slavs experience pronounced linguistic discrimination.

A concrete and explicit instance of the replacement of Slav by German as a language of the law court, but one that is rather hard to assess, occurred on the lands of the east Saxon abbey of Nienburg in 1293. It is worth citing the relevant document, granted by the counts of Anhalt, at length:

Whereas it is well known that in the beginning the whole world was of one tongue and diversity of language arose from the presumptuous building of a tower and that those who had presumptuously attempted this were dispersed by the Lord into lands and regions throughout the length and breadth of the earth, so that in one and the same region one man can understand another's tongue only with difficulty or through an interpreter, we grant those men of the Slav tongue who are subject to the monastery of Nienburg and under our jurisdiction, some of whom have suffered many *varas* [see below] on account of inexperience and ignorance of their language in our courts, so that many fields have even been abandoned for this reason, that henceforth the Slav language be completely abandoned in our court and those of our advocates and that they be content with the German language.

This passage is enigmatic, but what is clear is that the Slav tenantry are depicted as suffering for their ignorance of the *Slavic* language. *Vara* is the equivalent of what was known in English law as 'miskenning', verbal slips or errors in pleading. The charter seems to suggest that certain, unnamed parties are taking advantage of the lack of linguistic fluency of these (Germanized?) Slavs to deprive them of their lands in the courts. It was certainly not unknown for calculating litigants or judges to squeeze every advantage out of the demanding formalism of many native legal systems. At the very same time that the counts of Anhalt were dealing with this problem, a royal justice in south Wales was insisting on proceedings taking place by Welsh law: 'The reason was financial: defendants were easily faulted on the technicalities of procedure in Welsh law even by a mere slip (*gwallgair*).' What is clear in the Anhalt case is that Slav ceased to be a language of law in that area.

Their status as languages of law had important consequences for the eventual fortunes of the various vernaculars of eastern Europe. To take two contrasting moments: in 1327 Duke Henry VI of Silesia exempted his burgesses of Wrocław from being impleaded in the Polish language; about twenty years later Charles IV ruled that all judges in Bohemia should be conversant in Czech. The former ruling is part of the gradual Germanization of Silesia that transformed it from a Polish duchy to, eventually, an integral component of the monarchy of Frederick the Great and Bismarck; the context of the latter provision is the late medieval efflorescence of Czech cultural nationalism that ensured that Bohemia would have a Slavic as well as a German future. Ethnic identities could be shaped in part by the balance of the languages of law.

THE CASE OF IRELAND

The most extreme form of legal discrimination in the colonized peripheries of Europe was to be found in Ireland. Here a very unusual kind of judicial dualism existed. After its submission to the English Crown in 1171, the English kings envisaged that their lordship of Ireland would be governed by the same laws as their kingdom of England. From the 1190s the institutions and forms of the common law are evidenced in Ireland, and in 1210 King John 'caused English laws and customs to be established there'. Subsequently there were persistent efforts to preserve uniformity, as in the letter of 1246 which stated that the king 'wishes that all common law writs which are current in England should likewise be current in Ireland'. This was monitored at a very detailed level. In 1223, for example, the royal government wrote to the justiciar of Ireland complaining that 'we are given to understand that pleas initiated in Ireland by the writ *de divisis faciendis* are conducted otherwise than in our realm of England'. After specifying the two different procedures, the letter orders that 'you must have pleas *de divisis* held and conducted in Ireland just as they are customarily held and conducted in our realm of England, as you well know that the laws of our land of Ireland and of England are and should be identical'. A court structure modelled on that of England, with county courts, itinerant justices, a common bench, exchequer and chancery, not to mention a parliament, was created in the thirteenth century. There seems solid ground for the characterization of this process as 'a conscious, efficient and uniform introduction to Ireland of English law'.

English law was not, however, available for all. It was primarily a settlers' law and the native Irish had very little access to its processes and protection. The main legal disabilities that the Irish suffered under the common law are listed in the Remonstrance, the long letter that some of the Irish princes sent to the pope in 1317 or 1318, justifying their alliance with the Bruces against the king of England. The discriminatory system of law was one of their complaints. 'Any non-Irishman,' they wrote, 'is allowed to bring any legal action against any Irishman, but an Irishman, cleric or lay, except only a prelate, is barred from every action by that fact alone.' This grievance, the inability of the ordinary Irishman to sue in the common law courts, is attested by judicial records of the later thirteenth and fourteenth centuries. There is some possibility that the situation was different earlier in the thirteenth century, but, be that as it may, there is clear evidence from mid-century onwards for the 'exception of Irishry', the refusal to answer a case on the grounds that the plaintiff was Irish. The defendant would claim 'that he is not held to answer in this matter since he [the plaintiff] is Irish and not of free blood', exemplifying in this form of words the way Irish blood was seen as equivalent to unfree blood.

The importance of this ethnic distinction can be illustrated by a case that found its way to the justiciar of Ireland in 1297. Gilbert le Paumer, a royal sergeant, was accused of having kept for himself the landed property of the recently deceased Philip Benet, the king's Irishman, who had lived near Castle Dermot in County Kildare, whereas by rights the land should have reverted to the king on Philip's death; since Philip was an Irishman and deemed to be unfree, his son had no legal right to inherit. Gilbert pleaded in his defence that while Philip was still alive a jury had found that he was not, in fact, an Irishman. The occasion for this was that he had been dispossessed of the estate in question by Richard de Geyton and, when he tried to recover it through the courts, Richard objected that Philip 'was an Irishman'. After the jury had found that he was English, Philip recovered his land. Hence, because of this prior finding, Philip's son and heir, Adam, did have the right to inherit and had vindicated this in court. It just so happened that Adam, the successful claimant to the inheritance, had then enfeoffed Gilbert, the royal sergeant, with the land. So, Gilbert argued, although he had indeed originally seized the land on the king's behalf and did now enjoy it as tenant in his own right, he had not usurped any of the king's rights. Gilbert's case was answered by John of Drogheda, who prosecuted on the king's behalf. He claimed that 'notwithstanding the assertion that Philip had proved himself an Englishman, he was Irish, of the surname of M'Kenabbyth, and born in the mountains of the O'Tooles'. A temporary agreement was made, returning the land to the king while further investigations were undertaken. The king sent a writ ordering the justiciar to make inquiries:

it appears that Richard de Geyton . . . imposed on Philip that he was Irish and used Irish laws and customs . . . [and] maliciously ejected him . . . and Philip impleaded Richard in the king's court . . . and by inquisition then taken it appeared that Philip was English and used English laws and customs . . . You . . . now asserting Philip to have been Irish, and that Adam ought not to succeed as his son and heir . . . the rolls . . . are to be searched and the record of the suit examined.

The result of the search indeed found a record that Philip had pleaded that he was 'of free condition and English and begotten of an Englishman' and that a jury had confirmed this. As a consequence Gilbert eventually recovered the land. The centrality of ascribed ethnic identity in these proceedings hardly needs emphasis.

The exception of Irishry thus constituted a claim that a defendant need not answer a plaintiff, on the simple grounds that the plaintiff was Irish, since Irishmen could not 'take writs and . . . be answered'. It placed a block in the way of dispossessed property-holders seeking recovery of their lands. Other civil disabilities also applied. Irish widows were denied the usual dower rights, i.e. the enjoyment of one-third of the estate during their lives. Irishmen were debarred from making wills and testaments. In the 1350s the archbishop of Armagh preached against 'those who obstruct the rights of Irishmen . . . to make their wills freely'.

Even more striking than these civil disabilities was the difference in the way that homicide was regarded depending on whether the victim were an Englishman or an Irishman. As the Irish Parliament of 1297 pithily expressed it: 'the killing of Englishmen and of Irishmen requires different modes of punishment'. This also was one of the complaints of the Remonstrance of 1317–18: 'when an Englishman treacherously and deceitfully kills an Irish-man, however noble or innocent, a cleric or layman, a monk or not, even if an Irish prelate is killed, then there is no punishment or remedy in the said [i.e. royal] court for such a nefarious killer'. This assertion seems to be more or less accurate. Court records show men accused of homicide who 'came and did not deny the killing, but say that [the dead man] was Irish and not of free blood'. The killer did not, however, have complete immunity. Although the killing of an Irishman was not a felony in common law, it was possible for the dead man's lord to sue for compensation. Such compensation became standardized at 70 shillings. An example is the case between Peter le Petit and Richard son of Maurice de Creus in 1297. Peter charged Richard with killing two of his Irishmen, and Richard's defence, that the two were public robbers, was rebutted by jurors, who said 'that said Irishmen, when Richard slew them, were at the king's peace'. Peter was awarded $10\frac{1}{2}$ marks (i.e. twice 70 shillings) as damages.

It is not too misleading to see these proceedings, when a lord sued for damages for the homicide of his Irishmen, as a kind of wergild system. Such systems of law, according to which homicides and assaults were not public offences but wrongs perpetrated by one individual upon another, have been very widespread. All early Germanic and Celtic law codes are based upon the principle. The native Irish law, that still practised in the parts of Ireland not controlled by the English, recognized a compensatory payment, *éraic*, for homicide. It is possible, then, to see the law that the royal courts in Ireland applied to the killing of Irishmen as a reflection of or parallel to native Irish law itself. What occasionally disturbed the English settlers was the tendency to extend this principle to the killing of Englishmen. The baronial courts of the Anglo-Norman magnates were certainly accepting 'redemption for an Englishman's death' in the first half of the thirteenth century, and in 1316 a complaint was raised that 'fines and ransoms were being taken for all felonies, even the death of Englishmen'. The settlers thus feared the erosion of their own criminal system of homicide by an alien compensatory system.

DIVERSITY AND UNIFORMITY OF LAW

It was natural that the coexistence of two or more bodies of law in the same region would lead to mutual influence and borrowing. This was sometimes informal and partial, as, apparently, in the adoption of the word and institution of warrantor (*baránta*) into native Irish law, but there are also cases of explicit acts of policy designed to reshape one body of law along the lines of another. For example, in both Wales and Prussia the new colonial overlords of the thirteenth century introduced female inheritance into systems of native law that had previously allowed inheritance only in the male line. Edward I's Statute of Wales of 1284 reads:

If henceforth an inheritance, for lack of a male heir, descend to the legitimate female heirs of the predecessor last seised of it, we wish of our special grace that those women may legitimately have their shares in it assigned in our court, although this is contrary to Welsh custom as previously practised.

There is no mention here of who was pressing for the change. In Prussia, however, the documentation makes it clear that the liberalization of inheritance laws was welcome to the native landholders. The Treaty of Christburg of 1249, which was made between the Teutonic Knights and their newly converted Prussian subjects, allowed inheritance successively by sons, unmarried daughters, surviving parents, brothers and fraternal nephews. 'The new converts have accepted this gratefully,' the text of the treaty reads, 'since in the days of paganism they had only, as they said, sons as heirs.' This case is clearly, and the Welsh instance possibly, an example of the way colonized peoples might take advantage of the intrusion of a different legal system to modify some of the more constricting features of their own inherited native law. Native women had greater property rights after the arrival of the colonizing power than they had before.

Apart from the modification of one ethnic law by another, it was possible for men living under a particular ethnic law to acquire another by grant or purchase. The acquisition of the law of another race was common in many frontier regions. It could take place piecemeal, by individual arrangement. The Prussian law code of Pomesania, for example, has a general ruling for such cases: 'If a man has Prussian law and wounds another and later obtains German law and is accused of the same deed in German law and confesses and the case is settled in that law, then he may not be further accused or troubled in Prussian law.' The individual purchase of German law is also envisaged in the mid-fourteenth-century Bohemian law code, the *Majestas Carolina*: 'if an inhabitant buys emphyteutic or German law . . .' The mention of parties who 'are both of Wendish stock but are yet not Wends' in various east German law codes shows how legal ethnicity and biological ethnicity could diverge in this way. In these cases the rule was that 'pleas according to Wendish custom' should not be allowed and that proceedings should be in German. Precisely similar provisions can be found applied to parties who 'are of Prussian stock but are yet not Prussians'. We must imagine the parties referred to in these codes as individuals of native descent who had acquired both the German language and German law.

Ethnic law could also be abolished, acquired or transferred on a group basis to whole communities or populations. The extension of German law to the native populations of eastern European villages in this way was one of the motors of cultural Germanization in that part of the world. In 1220 the count of Schwerin granted to the Slavs living in the village of Brüsewitz 'German law', *ius Teutonicale*, emphasizing that henceforth judicial fines for offences were to be 'according to what German laws demand'. Sometimes the universal application of German law was a condition of new urban foundation, as at Brzeg (Brieg) in Silesia in 1250, when the town lord commanded that 'a Pole or a free man of any language with a house there shall be subject to German law'.

Attempts were also made to extend English law to the Irish. The initiative sometimes came from the Irish themselves who sought to negotiate the purchase of English rights, either individually or collectively, as in the late 1270s, when 'all the Irish' offered the king 10,000 marks 'in order to have the common law which the English have and use in Ireland and to be treated as such Englishmen are treated'. Nothing came of these general attempts to enfranchise the Irish, even though in the early fourteenth century English settlers and administrators themselves came to be convinced that pernicious consequences flowed from 'the diversity of law'. In 1328 John Darcy, considering appointment as justiciar of Ireland, drew up a list of proposals that included the recommendation of extending English law to the Irish. In fact, legislation to this effect was issued in 1330–31, but it appears to have been a dead letter. Until Tudor times Irishmen could only enjoy the rights and protection of English law by individual grant.

It is clear that the idea of personality of law, that is, law specific to ethnic, racial or religious groups, was central in the frontier societies of the High Middle Ages. Pollock and Maitland wrote of England in 1066: 'it was too late for a system of "personal", that is of racial, law'. From the centralist viewpoint of the major monarchies, like France and England, this view may be defensible. On the continental peripheries and in eastern Europe, however, it is the opposite of truth. The racial laws of these regions were largely a creation of the colonization that was only beginning in the mid-eleventh century. In this sense Europe in 1050 had the great age of personal law ahead of it, not behind it.

This judicial pluralism was enshrined in legal institutions and procedures in three basic forms. There were, first, guarantees, in terms of jurisdiction or procedure, for vulnerable ethnic groups, either conquered colonial groups (e.g. the Mudejars) or minority immigrant groups under princely protection (e.g. urban Germans in eastern European monarchies). The usual pattern was that of jural enclaves, islands of ethnic–legal particularism within a wider, different and often hostile world. A different kind of pluralism appears in the legal disabilities applied to subject peoples (e.g. the Mudejars again, the Slavs in the German East); the harshest form of legal inequality, which took the form of an absolute denial of law, was found, remarkably, not in areas of conversion or clash of religion like Spain or the Baltic, but in Ireland. Third, one might find the coexistence of different bodies of substantial law, such as the inheritance rules for Welsh and English in Wales.

It is also clear that there was a gradual movement away from the judicial pluralism that characterized the period of initial conquest and colonization towards a new jural homogeneity. Sometimes this was largely a matter of ironing out anomalies and cannot have been strongly resented by the people affected. We have already examined, for example, the triple jural regime found in Reconquest Toledo. The same parallel systems as in Toledo originally existed in nearby Talavera too, but were modified by the general trend in New Castile towards judicial uniformity. In 1290 King Sancho IV decried the 'many disadvantages which the Mozarabs and the Castilians have on account of justice' and ruled that henceforth 'there shall be no distinction between them on the grounds that some say they are Mozarabs and others say they are Castilians, but they should all be one (*que sean todos unos*), called "of Talavera", without distinction, and all should be governed by the law code of León'. More often, however, the shift away from pluralism was towards the dominance of intrusive systems. In Wales, for instance, native Welsh law was gradually modified over the course of the later Middle Ages, adopting an ever-wider role for the jury and abandoning compensatory justice for the harsher 'law of London', i.e. capital punishment and individual liability. The climax came in 1536 when the English Parliament decreed that 'the laws, ordinances and statutes of this realm of England . . . shall be had, used, practised and executed in the said country or dominion of Wales' and announced its intention 'to extirp all and singular the sinister usages and customs differing from the same'; all legal proceedings were to be 'in the English tongue', command of English was made a condition for office-holding in Wales and Welsh dismissed as 'a speech nothing like nor consonant to the natural mother tongue used within this realm'. Similarly, Spanish Christian law replaced Muslim law in the Iberian peninsula and German law came to dominate the lands immediately east of the Elbe. The long-term trend between the twelfth and the sixteenth centuries was away from personality to territoriality of the law, away from pluralism to uniformity. The road to *un roi, une loi, une foi* is a long one, but this is certainly a paved section of it.

9. Race Relations on the Frontiers of Latin Europe (2): Power and Blood

———

Human nature is such that each man, whatever his land, loves his own people more than strangers.

In any ethnically diverse society political competitors seek to manipulate or harness racial feelings of hostility and solidarity and their success in doing so is shaped not only by the relative numbers and wealth of the different ethnic groups but also by the overall shape of social and political life in the society. Arenas of conflict vary with time and place. In the high medieval peripheries arenas of especial importance were the Church, the princely court and the burgess community.

THE CHURCH

The mingling of peoples that resulted from high medieval colonial migration did not always juxtapose Christian and non-Christian; it often gave rise to societies in which different Christian ethnic groups lived in contact. The lands of the *Ostsiedlung*, where Germans migrated into Slav lands, and the Celtic zones of the British Isles, settled by English and other western European migrants, are two regions where ethnic fissures existed without a difference in religion. Here racial antagonisms can be seen uncomplicated by divergences of rite and belief.

In these regions where Christian peoples of different law and language intermingled, the Church itself became an arena of ethnic competition. It was indeed one of the most highly charged fields of conflict and there are clear reasons for this. Ecclesiastical offices were profitable and brought power and so were obvious and visible targets for ambition, but more: since the clergy were the carriers of ritual authority, morality and learning, they defined and spoke for a community or group. To see one's prelates and pastors become strangers in speech and nationality was a loss of voice and a destabilization of identity. Moreover, the peculiar nature of ecclesiastical recruitment created a special vulnerability to such clerical colonization. Since clerics were, in theory, recruited meritocratically not dynastically, the ecclesiastical hierarchy was recurrently open to new types of applicant. While insertion of newcomers into an existing lay aristocracy was possible, through processes of purchase, intermarriage or appropriation, it usually took time; the personnel of a constantly recruiting bureaucracy, like the Church, could, in certain circumstances, be transformed in ethnic composition much more quickly.

The Church was an organization which had to recruit officials and make judgements on the suitability of potential candidates to office. Every year thousands of decisions were made about who was to be appointed to a particular bishopric, prebend, abbacy or parish. The conflicting demands of local religious communities and aristocratic families, of orders and prelates, of kings and popes, had to be managed. A set of rules about eligibility to Church office, covering such issues as unfreedom, illegitimacy, physical wholeness and age, was elaborated. In the areas under discussion here, the colonized edges of Latin Christendom, racial origin was another ingredient thrown into the bubbling broth of ecclesiastical preferment.

The Church was not simply an institution, but an institution with an avowed mission. Hence no struggle over ecclesiastical office took place without reference, if only tactical, to the duties of clerics, especially those entrusted with the cure of souls. Since pastoral care involved preaching, hearing confession, comforting, advising and condemning, it could only be effectively undertaken by a priest who could communicate with his flock in their vernacular. This was generally acknowledged. The chronicler Gerlach of Mühlhausen complained about the imposition of a German, 'completely ignorant of the Czech language', on the see of Prague in 1170 and attributed it to the candidate's family ties with the Bohemian queen, 'for of their own accord they [the electors] would not have chosen a foreigner ignorant of their tongue'. Conversely, Cosmas of Prague made a special point of recording that the Germans chosen as bishops of Prague in the tenth century 'knew the Slav tongue perfectly' or were 'perfectly trained in the Slav tongue'. When Gerald of Wales was campaigning for the see of St David's in the years around 1200 he claimed 'the chapter of St David's will not consent to [a candidate] ignorant of the language of our people, who cannot preach or receive confessions except through an interpreter'. The famous astrologer Michael Scot, who was nominated by the pope to the Irish archbishopric of Cashel, found an acceptable excuse for declining the offer in 'that he says he does not know the language of that land'.

In regions where speakers of two or more languages lived intermingled, the ideal solution was bilingual priests and preachers, like 'Brother Peter, called Narr, a preacher in each of our vernaculars', who was active in Bohemia in the fourteenth century. On occasion, clerical bilingualism was even prescribed. In 1293, for example, when arrangements were drawn up for the church of St Mary in the suburbs of Bautzen in Upper Lausitz, it was specified that the priest 'will take care at night-time of those who are sick and at death's door outside the town and in the surrounding villages. Therefore the parish priest should know both German and Slavic. If he does not know Slavic, he should keep with him a Slav colleague.' The document goes on to regulate the division of the offerings.

A different solution to the problem of mixed-language communities was attempted in early-thirteenth-century Szczecin, where German merchants and artisans had settled among the native Pomeranian population. It was ruled that 'all the Germans living within the fortification and wall . . . shall belong to the church of St James . . . but the Slavs within the fortification shall seek the sacraments at St Peter's church'. The division was not absolute, since the rural population was assigned to both parishes, nor did the arrangement endure, but it shows an attempt at ethnic rather than territorial allocation to parishes, which, at least in the case of the 'Slav' church of St Peter, would have produced monoglot congregations. A similar case of parallel provision existed in the Bohemian town of Ceský Krumlov (Krumau), which in the fourteenth century supported both 'John, the preacher of the Germans' and 'Nicholas, the preacher of the Bohemians [Czechs]'.

Bilingual priests were an ideal solution, ethnically defined parishes a possibility. The usual cases, however, were more contentious. In the pluralistic societies on the frontiers of Latin Europe it was competition between ethnic groups that characterized recruitment to Church office. Conquerors could impose members of their own group and powerful immigrant groups lobby for their own pastors. The partial anglicization of the episcopate in Wales and Ireland is a clear example of the former, the right of German settlers in Transylvania to choose their own priests an instance of the latter. Native inhabitants might resent the imposition of alien prelates or the gradual infiltration of the settlers' foreign-tongued clerics. In the frontier zones the Church itself became an arena of ethnic conflict.

The Polish church had come into existence in the late tenth century, and Poland's western neighbours, including, prominently, Germany, had served as models, transmitters of culture and providers of men. This was not itself a matter of concern or controversy. In the thirteenth century, however, the wave of German peasant and urban settlement that reached Poland transformed the context of ecclesiastical recruitment. There were now two distinct linguistic and cultural populations within the historical boundaries of Poland and a contest over control of church appointments followed. A particularly explicit and strident champion in this contest is the figure of Jakub Swinka, archbishop of Gniezno 1283–1314. He ruled his province at a time when parts of it, such as Silesia, were being rapidly Germanized, other parts, like Danzig, were being conquered by Germans and the whole region was experiencing German settlement and cultural influence. In these circumstances, Swinka took a robustly xenophobic stance. 'He was such a sharp enemy of the Germans,' reports the contemporary chronicler Peter of Zittau,

that he only ever referred to them as 'dog heads'. Once, when John, bishop of Brixen, had preached in church in the king's presence most eloquently in Latin, the archbishop said to the king, 'he would have preached very well if he were not a dog head and a German'.

The same attitude, expressed somewhat more circumspectly, is to be found in Swinka's provincial statutes of 1285. These were partly animated by an explicit desire 'to protect and promote the Polish language' (*ad conservacionem et promocionem lingue Polonice*). Priests were to expound the Creed, Lord's Prayer and Ave Maria to their parishioners every Sunday in Polish; general confession was presumed to be in the same language; schoolmasters were not to be employed 'unless they know the Polish language accurately and can expound the authors to the children in the Polish language'. A final and wide-ranging provision ruled 'that no one shall be invested with any benefice involving the cure of souls, unless he is born in the land and commands its language'. These uncompromising regulations, which were reiterated by Swinka's successor in the provincial synod of 1326, envisaged Polish as the exclusive vernacular of parochial religious life and of education. Potential priests and schoolmasters would have to pass a linguistic test.

Racial animosities surfaced in a clear-cut form in the dispute between Archbishop Swinka and Bishop John of Cracow, which culminated in the bishop's suspension in 1308. The charges brought against the bishop, by members of his own chapter among others, include the accusation that 'he is attempting to expel the lord Wladyslaw, duke of Cracow, the true heir, from his land, and to expel the Polish people and to introduce aliens into their works and possessions'. He supposedly affirmed: 'If I cannot complete what I have begun and expel the Polish people, I would rather die than live!' A recurrent charge, raised by no less than ten of the witnesses in the commission of inquiry, was his failure to appoint Poles to ecclesiastical office: 'he does not promote the Polish people but foreigners and Germans'; 'he does not promote worthy Poles, saying that they are unfit for benefices'; 'he does not promote Poles born in the land but foreign Germans'. Perhaps most significant of all is the testimony that 'he committed perjury . . . for he swore to the prelates before his consecration that he would never re- ceive or invest any German with a benefice of the church of Cracow, but going against his own oath, he has placed virtually none but Germans in the church of Cracow'. If the account of the dealings before the conse- cration is truthful, it shows an attempt to implement in practice the exclusionary provisions of the synod of 1285. It seems probable that the actual ethnic composition of the clergy was shaped most fundamentally by the ethnic composition of the population as a whole, and that German immigration into the lands of the Polish Crown made it inevitable that increasing numbers of benefices would be held by German-speaking priests. But this does not mean that the process was a smooth one, guided by an invisible demographic hand; and in the 1285 synod and in the pre- consecration oath and subsequent suspension of the bishop of Cracow we see a political campaign aimed at halting the Germanization of the Polish church.

In Poland and Bohemia, German immigrants settled in dominions which had as their lords, at least until the fourteenth century, native West Slav dynasts. In the Celtic lands, by contrast, the arrival of English and other foreign settlers accompanied and followed the displacement of native rule by alien conquest. Such displacement was, however, partial, and the political situation in Wales until the final conquest of 1282, and in Ireland permanently, was one in which competing native and settler powers sought to exercise their authority in the Church.

The appointment of bishops was the most crucial aspect of this struggle. It appears that from the early thirteenth century the English Crown and its subjects in Ireland sought to implement a policy of deliberate racial exclusion. In 1217 a letter from the English royal government to the justiciar of Ireland advised:

Since the election of Irishmen in our land of Ireland has often disturbed the peace of that land, we command you by the fealty that binds you to us, that henceforth you allow no Irishman to be elected in our land of Ireland or preferred in any cathedral. But by the counsel of our venerable father, the lord Henry, archbishop of Dublin, and by your own counsel, you should seek by all means to procure the election and promotion to vacant bishoprics and dignities of our clerks and other honest Englishmen, so indispensable for us and our kingdom.

Henry, archbishop of Dublin, was a singularly appropriate choice as executor of this policy. He was the son of a London alderman, and no less than three of his brothers held the position of sheriff of London. He himself had been educated for a clerical career, acquired the archdeaconry of Stafford by 1192 and served as royal judge, administrator and diplomat during John's reign. After his appointment as archbishop of Dublin he reshaped his see, both architecturally and institutionally, along Anglo-French lines, installing a cathedral chapter modelled on that of Salisbury, with one of his London nephews as first dean. The archbishop also served in a secular capacity in Ireland, acting as royal justiciar and rebuilding Dublin Castle. He was a true colonialist and it is no surprise to find him the recipient of a grant of an advowson in Staffordshire made 'to the archbishop and his successors who are not Irish'.

The policy of excluding the native Irish from episcopal office in Ireland drew the criticism of the papacy; nor was it strictly enforceable. But it recurs in the plans of English administrators in the following centuries. In the 1220s licence to elect was given to cathedral chapters with the proviso 'that they elect someone English', and a commission established by Edward I recommended that 'it is expedient to the king that no Irishman ever be archbishop ... because they always preach against the king and make provisions in their churches of Irishmen ... so that Irishmen may be elected bishops, to maintain their race'. In the following century rules were drawn up specifying that 'no one can be appointed to any benefice with cure of souls unless he can speak and understand the English language competently'. As in Poland, the vernacular language of the working parish priest was seen as critical in the maintenance of ethnic–political identity and power.

When we turn to the monastic Church, we find that ethnic conflict was of a rather different type. On the one hand, the issue of cure of souls was less prominent – though, of course, not irrelevant; on the other hand, the existence, by the twelfth century, of international monastic orders meant that disputes in the cloister reverberated far beyond it. Innocent III believed that 'it is no novelty or absurdity that convents of various nationalities should serve one Lord in monastic habit', but within such convents there was a natural inclination towards the formation of ethnic factions. In the circumstances of the twelfth, thirteenth and fourteenth centuries, when most regular communities were not independent local bodies, but parts of complex and far-flung jural congregations, these factions fought also to control, shape or resist the wider entities, the orders, of which they formed part.

The very territorial structure of the new orders was not without a national and political significance. Their jurisdictional centres were in France and in Italy; they had powerful secondary centres in England and Germany. The abbey of Cîteaux and her four 'oldest daughters', the earliest Cistercian foundations, were all situated in the kingdom of France. Meetings of the Dominican chapters-general in the thirteenth century took place 40 per cent of the time in Italy (never south of Rome); 35 per cent of the time in the kingdom of France; 10 per cent of the time in the Rhineland – needless to say, never in Celtic or Slavic countries. The new orders of the twelfth and thirteenth centuries came to the Celtic lands and the Slavic world via England and Germany and their naturalization in their new locales was never complete. There was clearly a mutual interplay of the political and the pastoral in their ecclesiastical geography. The autonomy of the Scottish Franciscans, for example, ebbed and flowed with the victories and defeats of the Scottish Wars of Independence: in 1329 they 'were wholly separated from the friars of England' in the aftermath of Robert the Bruce's successes, but they were subordinated once more later in the fourteenth century, when Edward III of England turned the tables. In eastern Europe, the margrave of Brandenburg was unwilling to allow a Dominican convent he planned for his domains to be part of the Polish province, since 'it is possible on this pretext that there may arise a dispute between our heirs and the lords of Poland concerning that territory'. As John Freed comments: 'the provincial assignment of a mendicant convent had become the potential basis for a territorial or feudal claim to the region in which it was situated'. One consequence of the German settlement and colonization of Silesia, Prussia and other trans-Oderine lands was the transfer of these territories to the Franciscan province of Saxony.

In the late thirteenth century the German mendicants were viewed by some Slav prelates and rulers as instruments of cultural colonization. 'Brothers of the German tongue,' reads one complaint from Bohemia,

more numerous than is needed, are sent to the individual Franciscan houses in our kingdom and in the Polish duchies, but the brothers of Slavic tongue are dispersed among foreign nations, where they can do no good. The result is that the souls of the Slavic people are greatly imperilled.

Jakub Swinka, unsurprisingly, took a firm stand on this infiltration and the spread of convents of German brothers. 'Certain religious,' he complained, 'scorn to receive our native-born Poles into their order and love foreigners instead.' He commanded that the bishops should deprive such religious of any benefices they held. The monasteries had, after all, he asserts, been founded 'for the salvation of the local people'. Sometimes racial exclusivity was even written into the foundation charters of religious houses and charitable institutions. In 1313, for example, Wladyslaw Lokietek of Poland founded a hospital in Brześć (Brest) in Cujavia with the stipulation that 'the brothers shall keep and maintain no German, cleric or lay, in that house and church'. Twenty years later, when the nationalistic bishop of Prague, John of Drazic, founded an Augustinian house at Roudnice (Raudnitz), he specified: 'we shall admit no one to this convent or monastery of any nation except a Bohemian [or Czech], born from two Czech-speaking parents'.

The Cistercian order, 'the first effective international organization in Europe', as it has been called, flourished in Ireland long before the Anglo-Normans came to conquer and settle. St Malachy, St Bernard's friend, had brought the first white monks to the country, and Mellifont, the first Irish Cistercian house, was founded in 1142. Mellifont was a prolific mother and most of the Irish houses were of her affiliation. After the English colonization of Ireland began in the late twelfth century, the native Irish kings and chieftains continued to patronize the order. By 1228 there were thirty-four Cistercian houses in Ireland, of which only ten were Anglo-Norman foundations.

Relations between the international order and the Irish houses were, however, strained, and in the first quarter of the thirteenth century culminated in the violence and scandal of the so-called 'conspiracy of Mellifont'. Cistercian visitors from overseas sent to correct abuses in the Irish Cistercian houses were ignored, mistreated and attacked. Fortifications were erected in the monasteries. Complaints were made that conventual life had completely disappeared among the daughters of Mellifont. Eventually, the chapter-general authorized Stephen of Lexington, abbot of the English Cistercian house of Stanley, to undertake a high-powered visitation, which would quell the opposition, insist on the observance of the regular life, exact obedience and not shun the aid of the secular power if required. In 1228 Stephen implemented this policy. Disciplinary measures were drastic. In the aftermath of his visitation (and that of its precursor of 1227), two houses were suppressed, a half-dozen abbots dismissed, monks from Irish houses distributed among Cistercian monasteries overseas and the pattern of affiliation completely redrawn, with English houses often assuming the place of previous mother houses, especially of Mellifont itself.

Looked at from one point of view, the suppression of the 'conspiracy of Mellifont' represents the successful reassertion of control by the central authorities of an international order over local and deviant members. From another perspective, however, we see that there was an ethnic aspect to the conflict. Stephen of Lexington himself, describing his work in Ireland, wrote: 'we have created there many abbots of a different tongue and nation'. He commended the new appointees to the chief English official of Leinster, the fief of the earl marshal: 'take good care of our new abbots of a different tongue newly created throughout Leinster, for the sake of the honour of the lord earl, your own honour and the peace of the land'. As we have just seen, one way he disciplined the Irish Cistercian houses was to transfer their affiliation from Irish to English or French mother houses. Moreover, as a punishment for the conspiracy, he forbade any Irishman to be appointed abbot in a Cistercian house in Ireland for a three-year period. Finally, he imposed his own brand of linguistic restrictions on conventual life. In his report to the abbot of Clairvaux, he writes:

we have ordained unconditionally that henceforth no one shall be admitted as a monk unless he can confess in French or Latin. The Rule is now expounded and will henceforth be expounded at Mellifont . . . and many other Irish houses only in French, so that when you come personally or send visitors on your behalf, they will understand those they are visiting and will be understood by them, nor, when the cover of an unknown language is taken away, will the ill-disciplined enjoy a hiding place. For how can anyone love cloister or book who knows only Irish?

This somewhat strident Gallocentrism is reinforced by a patronizing piece of advice:

We have enjoined the Irish that if they wish to receive anyone of their people in the order in future, they should ensure that they send them to Paris or Oxford or some other renowned city, where they can learn letters and eloquence and decent behaviour. We have stressed to them that the order does not intend to exclude any nation, but only the unsuitable, the unfit and those at variance with proper human behaviour.

This equation of nationally defined norms of conduct and culture with the rules of an international order is characteristic of the situation in the colonial peripheries of Europe. When a radical adaptation to local circumstances looked imminent, as in the Irish case, where the white monks in that island looked as if they were setting up an independent confederation of abbeys, something like an early Irish monastic *paruchia*, the Cistercian chapter-general sent out the Paris-trained Englishman, Stephen of Lexington, to forestall it. His goal, in his own words, was 'that there should be uniformity in the order'; his methods were the imposition of English abbots, the subordination of Irish houses to English houses and an assault upon the native language.

THE PRINCELY COURT

Another focal point for ethnic antagonisms was the court of the ruler, and the structural reasons why this was so are not hard to identify. Princely courts were, in the best of circumstances, culturally distinct from the surrounding society, centres of patronage, conspicuous consumption, cosmopolitanism and fashion, and their style might easily inflame clerical, puritanical or backwoods critics. If, in addition, a dominant faction at court, or even the ruler himself, were of alien birth or culture, these potential antagonisms would be given a sharper, ethnically phrased tone. By their very nature, princely courts tended to harbour foreign elements. They were the epicentre of political dynasticism, and dynasticism meant that political power was transmitted according to family not national priorities. Hence the recurrent unpredictable trauma of the wooing of foreign brides and the arrival of alien heirs. The structure of medieval and early modern court politics meant that time and again the Scots awaited their Margaret of Norway, the Spaniards their unknown Charles V.

The official policy of the Church, which encouraged exogamy, and the political prudence of avoiding polarizing alliances with the native aristocracy combined to lead many dynasties to seek wives from outside. If the new bride, with her ladies-in-waiting, chaplains, servants and, possibly, brothers, nephews, cousins or even parents, were from a different language group, the result was an immediate and highly visible cultural reorientation of the court. The courtiers of Edward I of England, for example, would, in the wake of his Castilian marriage, find the king's costume of relaxation the Spanish gown and biretta and his eldest son named Alfonso. In the frontier regions of Latin Christendom, the coexistence of an alien group at court and immigrant members of that language group already settled in the area created a volatile political situation.

The objections of a native aristocracy to a foreign queen are vividly expressed in the *Dalimil Chronicle*, a rhyming chronicle in Czech written in the early decades of the fourteenth century. The literary incident which provides the pretext for the expression of these opinions is the marriage of the eleventh-century Duke Udalrich with a Czech peasant girl. The duke explains to his retainers why he would rather marry her than 'a foreign king's daughter'. As becomes clear, this means a German princess:

Such a woman is wedded to her own language;
That is why a foreigner will never please me;
She would not be loyal to my people.
A foreigner would have foreign kin.
She would teach my children German
And change their customs.
So, in the language
There would be a parting of the ways,
And for the land
Absolute ruin.
Lords . . .
Who wishes to take an interpreter
When he stands before my German wife?

The foreign queen thus brought the danger of cultural alienation, of a fissure between the young half-blood princes and the indigenous aristocracy. This was a perennial feature of dynastic politics. In the eleventh century, for example, the Byzantines had supposedly objected to their emperor taking a Norman bride for his son because the half-Norman princes in the palace might provide 'a better opportunity of access' for Norman expansionism. The concerns of the *Dalimil Chronicle* were those of the Czech nobility as a group. It was at their insistence that the French and Luxembourgeois household of young Blanche of Valois, who came to Bohemia in 1334 to marry their heir to the throne, was sent home and replaced by a household of Bohemians. Even so, the fears expressed in the *Dalimil* passage seem to have been realized. Blanche and her mother-in-law, Queen Beatrice, do not seem to have made great progress in their language lessons: it was remarked that 'he who is unable to speak French will not be able to talk with them easily'.

Foreign kings were less common than foreign queens, but might be even more of a difficulty for local dominant classes. In the later medieval period the foreign ruler was a particularly important figure in the history of eastern Europe because of the disappearance of local ruling families. In the fourteenth century the native royal dynasties of Bohemia, Poland and Hungary died out. These families, the Przemyslids, Piasts and Arpads, who had brought their territories into the Christian world in the tenth and eleventh centuries and ensured their political survival thereafter, finally ran out of genealogical luck. The last Arpad, Andrew II, died in 1301, the last Przemyslid, Wenceslas III, in 1306, and the Piasts, after reviving the united kingdom of Poland in 1320, left no male heirs in the royal line in 1370. As a consequence of this series of extinctions, the crowns of eastern Europe were available for contenders from both within and beyond the region. During the later Middle Ages, Bohemia and Hungary were ruled by a succession of French dynasts, German nobles and local strongmen, before, in the sixteenth century, they came under Habsburg control. Poland experienced two shorter but similar periods of uncertainty in the fourteenth century, first before the revival of the kingdom in 1320 and then between 1370 and 1386, in which year the pagan Jagellons of Lithuania accepted both the baptism and the Polish crown.

The arrival of foreign rulers was a time for the local aristocracies to state their terms. When John, count of Luxemburg, became king of Bohemia in 1310 he had to promise not to appoint anyone 'foreign born' (*alienigena*) to position in the kingdom. Even the acquisition of real property was theoretically barred to them. The king does not seem to have kept his promise to the letter, however, for, within a few years, it was reported that 'he had around him many counts and nobles from Germany who were distinguished by their wisdom rather than their power, by whose counsel virtually every piece of business in his realm was settled and to whom he gave royal fiefs and offices'. In 1315 the Czech barons complained: 'All peoples are accustomed not to bear it well when immigrants from another land are so enriched and lord it over them', and John had to send his Germans away. Several years later the foreign king was still having to promise 'not to appoint any foreign born to command over any royal fortress or any castle as an official or in any way or to make them burgraves there, but to appoint only Bohemians'.

Sometimes ethnic tension resulted not from foreign queens or kings but from native-born rulers who favoured foreigners and fostered an ethnically distinct body of soldiers, administrators and courtiers. There are many examples among the Piast dukes of Poland, although such xenophile princes often encountered a dangerous nativist backlash. Boleslaw II of Silesia (1242–78), although, according to one account, speaking only pidgin German, 'began to act harshly to the Poles and insolently preferred Germans to Poles and gave them many estates. On this account the Poles refused him homage and renounced his lordship.' The chronicler who wrote this account attributes Boleslaw's later seizure of the bishop of Wrocław to 'diabolic madness and the persuasion of the Germans by whose counsel he was ruled'. Xenophobic disaffection also occurred among the Polish aristocracy of Cujavia, who transferred their allegiance from their duke because of his close involvement with the Teutonic Knights. The Poznań annalist complained of the young Silesian dukes who succeeded in 1309 that 'the Germans held and bound them with their counsels, so that they could do nothing except what pleased the Germans'.

THE BURGESS COMMUNITY

The medieval urban population was an immigrant population. This was true everywhere, but was especially significant in frontier regions where townsmen, or a large proportion of them, were often ethnically distinct from the rural population. Long-distance immigration often had a town as its goal, and in regions like eastern Europe and the Celtic lands the town–country dichotomy came to be paralleled and reinforced by ethnic opposi-tions, for many urban settlements were inhabited predominantly or exclusively by immigrants. A story that illuminates the cultural equation of German and town and Czech and country is the account of a miracle in 1338, set in Prague. Various artisans were discussing how to celebrate St Wenceslas's day, when one of their number, a German, asserted that 'he was not willing to celebrate the feast of that peasant'. After he was struck with paralysis and cured by Wenceslas's relics, 'the Germans began to hold our patron in greater reverence'. The racial tension is here encased in town–country contempt.

In eastern Europe, German was especially a language of the towns and of princely courts. The lists of new burgesses admitted to the old city of Prague in the fourteenth century shows that, of those with nationally identifiable names, between 63 per cent and 80 per cent bore German names, and the same is overwhelmingly true of the city council members. The monoglot Frenchwoman Queen Blanche of Bohemia sought to establish a better rapport with her subjects by learning not Czech but German, 'for in almost all the cities of the kingdom and in the king's presence the employment of the German tongue was more usual than that of Czech'. A similar situation existed in Poland. When the future archbishop of Lvov (Lemberg) came to Cracow from the Polish countryside in the middle of the fifteenth century, 'he found that all public and private business was transacted in German', and he eventually went to Germany proper to improve his language skills. Especially as one went further east, into the areas where German peasant settlement was thin, the towns had the character of German islands in Slav, Baltic, Estonian or Magyar seas.

The towns of the British Isles had a similarly distinctive linguistic character. French was spoken in them much more than in the surrounding countryside. French settlers had established themselves in many urban centres in the period after the Norman Conquest – Domesday Book mentions forty-three French burgesses in Shrewsbury – and the cultural developments of the following centuries encouraged this Gallic cultural orientation. In the early fourteenth century town-dwellers were five times as likely to be able to speak in French as countryfolk. In the Celtic lands French was also a language of towns and colonizers. One of the chief monuments of Old French literature from Ireland is the poem about the building of the walls of New Ross, a new town of the thirteenth century which quickly became the busiest port of the Lordship. It is characteristic that this piece of urban, colonizing and trading triumphalism should be in French. In Wales and Ireland, however, French was joined by English as a tongue of privilege and prestige. The language of lower prestige in its own homeland became a language of higher prestige in the colonized territories to the west. In the twelfth century immigrants into the new towns of Wales and Ireland were drawn from a wide area, one early-twelfth-century writ referring to 'all the burgesses, French, English and Flemish' of Kidwelly; but over the course of the thirteenth and later centuries the urban population of the colonized Celtic regions became ever more assertively English in its self-presentation. One fourteenth-century petition was in the name of 'the English burgesses of the English borough towns in north Wales' (it is written, characteristically, in French), and another claimed that 'no Welshman ought to live in an enfranchised town in Wales'. The towns of Wales and Ireland were often, like those of Polish Galicia or Livonia, linguistic islands.

Although towns often had this character of ethnic islands, they rarely attained complete racial homogeneity. Native populations lived within the walls, sometimes in the humble position of manual labourers, sometimes as artisans or even merchants. The expanding urban economy of the twelfth and thirteenth centuries seems to have allowed both immigrant and native to prosper. The picture darkens as the recession of the later Middle Ages begins. As the meal shrank, the diners began to eye each other more suspiciously.

One consequence of the dynastic uncertainties in eastern Europe during the later Middle Ages was that the German burgess population had a far more complicated and demanding political course to steer. In the twelfth and thirteenth centuries they had enjoyed fairly consistent patronage from native rulers whose own position was usually relatively secure. In the new world of the fourteenth and fifteenth centuries they often had to make difficult choices and sometimes chose wrong. Sometimes local princes suspected the Germans of being a fifth column, as in Pomerelia in 1290, when the native Slav ruler accused 'the Germans inhabiting Pomerelia' of siding with his German enemy, the margrave of Brandenburg. Sometimes the German population seems to have attempted to get German kings. In the early fourteenth century, during the dynastic manoeuvring that culminated in the revival of the Polish kingdom under Wladyslaw Lokietek, the German burgesses of Cracow made a serious miscalculation. They backed first the Luxemburg, then a Silesian aspirant, rather than Lokietek, were abandoned by their allies, and suffered savage reprisals, which took the form of a racial persecution. The highly hostile *Annales capituli Cracoviensis* record how

in the year of the incarnation of our lord Jesus Christ 1312 the burgesses of Cracow, inflamed by the madness of German rage, being friends of fraud and cloaked and secret enemies of peace, offered the security of an oath, just as Judas gave a kiss to Jesus, but then laid aside fear of God and defied Wladyslaw, duke of Cracow and Sandomierz and lord of the whole Polish realm.

After Wladyslaw regained control of the city he had some of the burgesses dragged through the streets by horses before they were hanged on a gallows outside the city 'until the tendons rotted and the framework of bones dissolved'. The *Krasiński Annals* add the detail that 'anyone who could not pronounce *soczewic* (lentil), *koło* (wheel), *miele* (grinds) and *młyn* (mill) was executed'. The application of this shibboleth gave events a starkly ethnic–linguistic imprint. This linguistic chauvinism manifested itself in another development of the same year. On 18 November 1312 the official records of the city of Cracow, which until that time had been kept in German, began to be written in Latin. 'Here begin the acts and property transfers of the city of Cracow compiled in Latin,' reads the text at this point. The exclusion of the German language clearly reflects the anti-German pogrom of that year. Its replacement by Latin rather than Polish reminds us how undeveloped this vernacular was as a written idiom. (Similarly, when Old English disappeared from documents such as wills and writs after the conquest of England by a French-speaking aristocracy in 1066, it was Latin that replaced it. Eleventh-century French, like fourteenth-century Polish, had not yet won the esteem of a language of official record.) In the century following the rising of 1311–12, Cracow was gradually Polonized. Wladyslaw Lokietek himself apparently insisted that Poles should be allowed to occupy the prestigious properties facing the market square and thus become *Ringbürger* (from *Ring*, 'market'), and during the years 1390–1470 new burgesses of Polish origin increased from 25 per cent to 60 per cent of the total. Cracow had become a Polish city with a German minority rather than a German city in Poland.

THE GROWTH OF RACISM IN THE LATER MIDDLE AGES

Many scholars see in the later Middle Ages a tendency for racial discrimination to become sharper and racial boundaries to be more shrilly asserted. The hardening of anti-Jewish feeling between the eleventh and the fifteenth centuries is recognized by all who work on the subject and they disagree only on their dating of the crucial change for the worse: the pogroms associated with the First Crusade, the Talmud trials of the mid-thirteenth century, the expulsions and persecutions of the 1290s, the ominous massacres in cosmopolitan Spain in 1391. There is, at any rate, no doubt that the Christian Europe of 1492, the year of the expulsion of the Jews from Spain, had a starker and grimmer attitude to its minorities than had been the case 400 years earlier.

The same trend can be seen on the peripheries of Latin Europe. The change in atmosphere in the German colonial towns of the Baltic has been characterized as 'the gradual transition from an initially tolerant to an ever more negative attitude towards non-Germans'. Among the Teutonic Knights it was only in the fifteenth century that German birth became a rigidly inescapable qualification for membership. The change in the pattern of relations between Welsh and English has been analysed as 'a sharpening of the dichotomy between Welsh and English in unmistakably racial terms ... a hardening and a heightening of the distinctions', in which the thirteenth century formed a critical divide.

Such harshness was not a monopoly of immigrant or colonial groups. Native populations could express their own racial savagery. The *Dalimil Chronicle* is animated throughout by hostility to and suspicion of German settlers in Bohemia. Its survey of Bohemian history, organized mainly around the reigns of the successive princes, springs into vivid life whenever the subject of German–Czech hostility arises. One anti-German prince is reported to have paid 100 marks of silver 'to anyone who brought him a hundred noses cut off from the Germans'.

The sharp anti-German feeling in *Dalimil* is expressed even more violently in another work from fourteenth-century Bohemia, the short Latin tract *De Theutonicis bonum dictamen*, probably written by an educated Czech-speaking townsman, possibly a notary or other official. When the races were spread throughout the world after the building of the Tower of Babel, writes the author, the Germans were singled out as a slave race, without a home of their own, but destined to serve other races. This explains why 'there is no region which is not full of Germans'. Gradually, however, the Germans usurped land and the privileges of freedom. They could do this because their pre-eminence as traders enabled them to accumulate capital and thus 'acquire many free and noble properties'. Nowadays, the author complains, the Germans have a finger in every pie:

The wise man should observe and the prudent man consider how this crafty and deceitful race has intruded itself into the most fertile prebends, the best fiefs, the richest possessions, even into the prince's council ... the sons of this race enter into the lands of others ... Then they are chosen councillor, plunder public property by subtle exactions and secretly send back gold, silver ... and other property from the lands in which they are settlers to their own land; thus they plunder and devastate all lands; thus enriched they begin to oppress their neighbours and rebel against the princes and their other proper lords. Thus did Judas and Pilate behave. No one with any experience doubts that the Germans are wolves in the flock, flies in the food, serpents in the lap, whores in the house.

The treatise goes on to specify charges that the Germans dominate the town councils and form artisan 'conspiracies', i.e. guilds, to keep prices high. The author apostrophizes the prince and powers of the land, asking them why they tolerate the Germans. His own ideal solution to the problem, embodied in his account of a supposed early event, was a final one:

Oh God! The foreigner is preferred, the native crushed underfoot. It would be profitable, just and customary if the bear stayed in the wood, the fox in his den, the fish in water and the German in Germany. The world was healthy when the Germans were placed as a target for the arrow – in one place eyes were torn out, in another they were hung up by the foot, in one place they were thrown outside the walls, in another they gave their nose as a toll payment, in one place they were killed peremptorily in the sight of the princes, in another they were forced to eat their own ears, in one place they were punished one way and in another in a different way.

Under the loose cover of a pseudo-historical allusion, this passage is an appeal for a pogrom.

The intensification of racial feeling in the later Middle Ages also involved the growth of a new biological racism. This emerges, for example, in the clearest surviving written evidence for ethnic competition in the towns of colonized Europe, the explicitly discriminatory urban legislation of the later Middle Ages. From the beginning of the fourteenth century town councils and guild authorities began to issue statutes or decrees that imposed racial bars to membership in certain privileged groups or eligibility to certain offices. One of the most widespread examples of such a provision was the so-called *Deutschtumsparagraph* in eastern Europe, the requirement that applicants for guild membership be of, and sometimes prove, German descent. The earliest case seems to be that of the Brunswick tailors in 1323, and the *Deutschtumsparagraph* became a fairly common provision of guild statutes. In Brandenburg it occurs in 28 of the 120 surviving series of statutes from between the mid-thirteenth and mid-seventeenth centuries (i.e. 23 per cent). Two examples from fourteenth-century Beeskow, a town close to the large Slav populations of Lausitz and less than twenty miles from the Oder, illustrate the specific form of the ruling:

An apprentice who comes to learn his craft among the cobblers should be brought before the master and guild members. If he is of such folk and birth that he is allowed to work after his apprenticeship, he shall learn the craft, otherwise not. For we forbid the sons of barbers, linen-weavers, shepherds, Slavs, the children of priests and all illegitimate children to practise a craft in our town.

The Beeskow bakers were equally exclusionary: 'Whoever wishes to be a member must bring proof to the councillors and the guildsmen that he is born of legitimate, upright German folk ... No one of Wendish stock may be in the guild.' Applicants for guild membership seeking to prove that they were 'right and proper German and not Wendish' (*echte und rechte dudesch und nicht wendish*) often had to produce a *Geburtsbrief*, naming their parents and grandparents and testifying that the bearer was 'of good German stock' or 'of German blood and tongue'; some of these letters survive in eastern European archives.

A corollary of this exclusionary legislation was the enactment of rules forbidding intermarriage. In 1392, for example, the Riga bakers guild ordained: 'Whoever wishes to have the privilege of membership in our company shall not take as wife any woman who is ill-famed, illegitimate or non-German (*unteutsch*); if he does marry such a woman, he must leave the company and office.' Town office was sometimes subject to similarly exclusionary rules. In the early fifteenth century it was a requirement of the town judge of Ofen (Pest), a German burgess settlement in Hungary, that he have four German grandparents. Biological descent replaced cultural identity as the first criterion of race.

In late medieval Ireland the burgesses were equally anxious. Urban statutes barred the native Irish from town citizenship or guild membership in several Anglo-Irish cities. In the mid-fourteenth century the archbishop of Armagh denounced in his sermons to the Anglo-Norman burgesses of Drogheda their practice of excluding Irishmen from their guilds. 'No one of Irish blood or birth' was to be admitted to civic office or to apprentice-ship in fifteenth-century Limerick. Similarly Dublin artisans were com-manded to take 'noo prentice but that he be of Englis berthe'. Examples could be multiplied from other Irish and Welsh towns. The use of the term 'blood' in fifteenth-century Irish discriminatory rules shows the new concept of race at work. As in eastern Europe a colonial and ethnically distinct urban population was attempting to surround itself with barriers in the face of economic recession and native assertion.

At the same time there was an attempt to protect the cultural purity of the colonists. Starting very soon after the initial incursion of the Anglo-Normans into Ireland, and climaxing in the fourteenth century, the new alien government attempted not only to discriminate against the native population, but also to ensure that the colonists did not go native. The most elaborate precautions of this kind were embodied in the Statutes of Kilkenny of 1366, which summarized and extended earlier legislation. The statutes ruled that there were to be no marriages between those of im-migrant and native stock; that the English inhabitants of Ireland must employ the English language and bear English names; that they must ride in the English way, i.e. with saddles, and have English apparel; that no Irishmen were to be granted ecclesiastical benefices or admitted to monaster-ies in the English parts of Ireland; and that the Irish game of hurling and the maintenance of Irish minstrels were forbidden to English settlers. Here, on the edges of Europe, conquest and colonization had run out of steam. There was, indeed, a recognition of the danger that the colonizers would themselves be assimilated by the native population. A colonial population was adopting, in the words of the Statutes of Kilkenny, 'the manners, fashion and language of the Irish enemies'. Far from culminating in a smooth incorporation into a majority culture, the English enterprise in Ireland produced a small colony within the Pale, living according to English norms, encompassed by Gaelicized settlers as well as hostile Gaels. One result was an aggressively defensive racism within the Pale.

The ethnically mixed societies of the European peripheries existed in a wider European culture that seems to have been moving, over the course of the medieval period, towards an ever-higher estimation of uniformity. In the eleventh or twelfth century a Hungarian cleric had observed: 'As immigrants come from various lands, so they bring with them various languages and customs, various skills and forms of armament, which adorn and glorify the royal household and quell the pride of external powers. A kingdom of one race and custom is weak and fragile.' A few centuries later the racist legislation of some of the colonial polities shows how this confident pluralism had disappeared. On all the newly settled, conquered or converted peripheries, one can find the subjection of native populations to legal disabilities, the attempt to enforce residential segregation, with natives expelled into suburbs, such as the 'Irishtowns' of colonial Ireland, and the attempt to proscribe certain cultural forms of native society. Ghettoization and racial discrimination marked the later centuries of the Middle Ages.

Eventually images of natural or immemorial hostility came to dominate race relations in the frontier regions. A French Dominican referred easily to the 'natural hatred' between Poles and Germans, while a fourteenth-century commentator on the *Sachsenspiegel* explained its rules that Saxons and Wends could not bear witness against each other or judge each other by the fact that 'they have been mutual enemies from of old'. A similar perspective took root in Ireland. 'Implacable enmities and perpetual wars' is the phrase used to characterize the relations of English and Irish in the Remonstrance of the native Irish princes of 1317; and a generation later Richard fitz Ralph, archbishop of Armagh, explained to the pope that 'the two nations are always opposed to one another from a traditional hatred, the Irish and Scots being always at variance with the English'.

The case of the Mudejars, the Spanish Muslims under Christian rule, exemplifies this trend. It is clear that their position gradually worsened over the course of the later Middle Ages. According to the terms of their original capitulations in the twelfth and thirteenth centuries, Iberian Muslims usually preserved their own property, judges and law, together with the right to worship in mosques. 'I have many Saracens in my country,' wrote James I of Aragon. 'All retain their law just as well as if they were in the country of the Saracens.' However, although James's successors, and other Christian kings, might stridently reassert their general privileges, erosion of the Muslims' judicial autonomy was clear and irreversible. The principle that they could only be convicted by witnesses of their own ethnic group was breached in Valencia in 1301, when James II ordained that 'two Christian witnesses of good reputation can testify and their testimony be credited against Jews and Saracens, notwithstanding the privileges which we or our ancestors granted to the Jews and the Saracens'. The same monarch later ruled that in all his realms crimes of Muslims against Christians should be heard only by Christian judges according to Christian law, though cases between Muslims or civil suits brought by Christians against Muslims were still to be heard by Muslim judges according to Muslim law. The fourteenth and fifteenth centuries saw sustained assaults on Muslim jural autonomy. A Castilian ruling of 1412 proclaimed:

'from henceforth the communities of Muslims in my kingdom shall not have their own judges . . . cases, both civil and criminal, between Muslims shall henceforth be heard before the city judge'.

At the same time as they were losing their separate law, the Mudejars experienced the gradual disappearance of Arabic. A striking monument to the erosion of the ancestral tongue is the Castilian-language *Compendium of the Chief Commands and Prohibitions of the Law and Sunna (Abbreviation of the Sunna)* made by Iça Jeddih, imam of Segovia, in 1462. His prologue explains that experts have a duty to expound the law 'to all creatures in the world in a language that they understand'. He writes in Castilian 'since the Moors of Castile, with great oppression and great constraint and many tributes, hardships and labours, have lost their wealth and their schools of Arabic'. Only in Valencia and Granada did large groups of Arabic-speakers survive.

Eventually, in the wake of the conquest of Granada, the last Muslim state in the Iberian peninsula, in 1492, the completely uniformitarian religious polity seemed within the grasp of the conquerors. The expulsion of the Jews in that same year was soon followed by the forcible conversion of the Muslims: this took place in Granada, despite the terms of the treaty of 1492, in the years after 1499; in Castile in 1502; in Aragon in 1526. Spanish Christians found, however, that the destruction of their enemies' law and faith was not enough to satisfy them. The Moriscos, as the new Christians of Muslim background are termed, retained certain unassimilated features. As in the case of the *conversos*, reluctantly converted Jews, outward or superficial conformity to the dominant religion no longer satisfied the authorities. The proscription of the Muslim religion was thus followed by an assault on the daily habits and practices of the Morisco population. Moorish costume was forbidden, women were ordered to give up the veil in the street, Arabic was prohibited in those areas where it was still employed, Spanish names made compulsory. The response to this policy of cultural genocide was the Morisco rebellion of 1568. Even after the suppression of the rising, the new exclusive mentality of the conqueror could not be satisfied. In 1609–14 the Moriscos themselves were physically expelled. Possibly as many as one-third of a million left the peninsula for ever.

As mentioned in the previous chapter, Regino of Prüm had, around the year 900, identified peoples by their descent, customs, language and law. In the later Middle Ages the Muslims of Spain were robbed of their law and gradually lost their language. The culmination of this assault came when they lost their 'law' in the deepest sense, their religion, in the forcible conversions of the years around 1500. In the sixteenth century it was their customs that proved unacceptable to the Christian majority. By the opening years of the seventeenth century it had been decided that their very stock, their *genus*, could no longer be tolerated. In early modern Spain a crucial criterion for promotion and power was 'purity of blood', a descent untainted by Jewish or Moorish ancestry. A blood racism of the modern kind had been born.

10. The Roman Church and the Christian People

===

Those who are about to go and fight for Christendom should
mark their clothes with the sign of the cross.

THE ROLE OF THE PAPACY

The definition of Latin Christendom advanced in the opening chapter of
this book was twofold: Latin Christendom was a rite and an obedience.
The two aspects were closely related. Over the course of the High Middle
Ages they became more so. Other religions and other types of Christianity
have often tolerated greater liturgical diversity within their organizational
framework, while some have valued liturgical uniformity but have not
linked it closely to any particular jurisdictional authority; but Latin
Christendom was characterized by both an emphasis on uniformity of
public worship and a virtual (though not absolute) equation of liturgical
practice and institutional loyalty – rite and obedience.

The obedience in question, and the liturgical standard, was, of course,
Roman. One bishop, the bishop of Rome, was superior to all others. One
order of service was model. 'Rome is . . . the head of the world', and it is
'the Roman Church which holds the superior power of correcting the
whole of Christendom'. Latin Christendom was constituted by the lands
and peoples admitting these claims. One of the things that marks a
distinction between the early Middle Ages and the High Middle Ages was
the significance attached to such claims and the degree of success in
enforcing them. For, while the papacy had enjoyed a position of prestige
and centrality in western Europe since the very birth of official Christianity
under Constantine, the means and mechanics supporting that position
underwent a transformation during and after the eleventh century. Starting
with the reform movement of the middle and later years of that century,
papal power became greater, papal decisions more enforceable, ritual
uniformity more real. One consequence was that Latin Christians identified
themselves more often and more deeply as such. Reverence to St Peter,

obedience to the pope and commitment to certain forms of worship and church government mingled and intensified. The self-definition of the men and women of the High Middle Ages cannot be disentangled from the claims and structures of the Roman Church. He who steered the course of 'the Holy Roman Church' (*sancta Romana ecclesia*) could legitimately demand the obedience of 'the Christian people' (*populus christianus*), and the *populus christianus* increasingly thought of itself as such. One of the most delicate issues in this analysis of 'expansion' is the relationship between this self-appellation and other characterizations – social, economic, military – that are available when discussing the inhabitants of Europe in the Middle Ages.

John Mundy has acutely remarked that 'From the days of the Gregorians until the turmoil of the fourteenth and fifteenth centuries, what led Europe was an inadvertent, rarely conscious, but very real alliance between Europe's aristocracies and the see of Peter', and while this is not the whole truth, it is a truth. Any reader of the *Register* of Pope Gregory VII (1073–85), the founding father of the high medieval papal monarchy, will see how well formulated Mundy's concept is. Here, preserved in a document from the very heart of the reformed papacy, are the letters that witness the establishment and nurturing of links between the pope and the Italian and transalpine nobility. Between the triumphant opening words of the *Register* – 'Regnante domino nostro Iesu Christo . . .' – and its disintegration, over 200 folios later, in a confusion and neglect that mirror Gregory's own chaotic final years, one can find a recurrent series of commands, exhortations and negotiations directed at actual or potential aristocratic allies.

Some of these connections antedated Gregory's pontificate. From his letter to 'the princes who wish to undertake an expedition to Spain', for example, it is clear that formal agreements had already been drawn up in the pontificate of his predecessor between the pope and members of the northern French aristocracy, detailing the terms and conditions of conquests from the Iberian Muslims. The alliance between the papacy and the great Italian noblewomen Beatrice and Matilda of Tuscany, 'beloved daughters of St Peter', and the bond of fealty that tied the Norman prince Richard of Capua to the Roman see were also a political inheritance from earlier popes. But, in this as in other things, Gregory took an existing feature of the reformed papacy and energized and transformed it.

The initiatives for contact between Rome and the aristocratic rulers of the Christian world were not one-sided. An alliance requires some mutual interests. For example, Gregory's letter of September 1073 to Rudolf, duke of Swabia, after praising Rudolf's 'love for the honour of the holy Roman

Church', goes on to mention Rudolf's letters to Gregory on the topic of the proper relationship between priestly and imperial authority. Rudolf had thus already been in contact with the pope and obviously thought he had something to gain from direct lines of communication with the papacy. The nature of that common interest between German duke and reforming pope is hinted at in the second part of Gregory's letter. Here the pope informs Rudolf not only that he has no ill will towards the German king, Henry IV, but that he wishes to have no ill will towards anyone. After this sinister expression of goodwill, he concludes by saying that he intends to discuss this issue of the harmony of priestly and imperial power with Rudolf, Beatrice of Tuscany and 'other God-fearers': 'So we ask Your Prudence that you should always strive to grow in loyalty to St Peter and should not delay coming to his shrine both to pray and to consider this matter of such great importance.' Within four years Rudolf had been elected king in opposition to Henry IV and, while Gregory studiously maintained that he 'helped neither party, unless that which justice favoured', his eventual decision was that justice favoured Rudolf's party. In March 1080 he acknowledged Rudolf as king and granted his adherents absolution from all their sins. The vaguely formulated friendship of the earlier years had borne fruit in king-making and holy war.

The ties between the anti-imperialist magnates north and south of the Alps, the reformed papacy and the advocates of holy war both within and beyond the boundaries of Christendom were sometimes close and familiar. One example is provided by the family tree in Figure 4. Here, within the confines of a few generations and some significant marriage alliances, we find the leader of the dissident nobility of Lotharingia; an innovative occupant of the papal throne; Gregory VII's chief Italian supporters; and the man whom the first crusading army chose as ruler after its triumph in Jerusalem. Not every figure in this genealogy was a friend or ally of every other − far from it − but the ties symbolize a world of connections. It was in this milieu that expeditions against the Muslims, the proper relationship of priestly and imperial power and the demands of St Peter were common subjects of discussion and rumination; this was the milieu that fostered the reformed papacy, defied the Salian monarchy and led Christians in arms to the Holy Land. Here is Mundy's 'alliance between Europe's aristocracies and the see of Peter'.

The correspondence of Gregory VII can also be used to give us a picture of the geographical vistas of the reformed papacy. Over 400 of his letters survive, and Table 3 shows the distribution of their recipients. The vast majority, about 65 per cent, went to the bishops and other prelates of

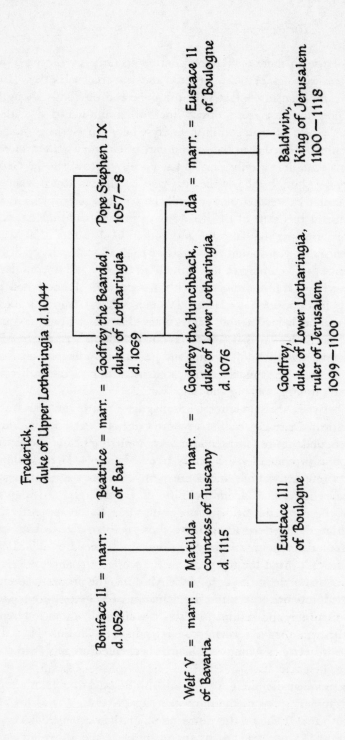

Figure 4. *The house of Lotharingia and its connections*

Table 3. *Recipients of Gregory VII's letters*

Region	Ecclesiastics	Rulers	Other lay	Totals
France★	138	2	22	162
Italy	68	0	33	101
Germany	62	8	8	78
Bohemia	4	10	0	14
England	5	9	0	14
Spain	3	9	0	12
Hungary	1	7	0	8
Denmark	0	6	0	6
Other	5	9	2	16
Totals	*286*	*60*	*65*	*411*

★Including the kingdom of Burgundy.

France, Italy and Germany; this is not surprising. But a fairly large number were addressed to those secular magnates we have already discussed, the dukes and counts of the post-Carolingian world. Gregory wrote far more often to these magnates than to the kings of France or Germany. Beyond the boundaries of the old Carolingian empire, papal correspondence shrank dramatically: fewer than a fifth of Gregory's letters to localized recipients went to this zone. Some areas, such as Bohemia and England, were nevertheless clearly not unfamiliar with Gregory's particular style. What is striking is the fact that in this 'outer zone' papal letters were directed most often to kings and their families. Although fewer letters were sent, they were directed towards the top: the ruling princes of Ireland, England, Denmark, Norway, Sweden, Poland, Bohemia, Russia, Hungary, Byzantium, Serbia, Aragon, Navarre, León and even Muslim north Africa all received advice, encouragement or chastisement from Gregory. In France, Germany and Italy, letters to members of regal families represent only three in every hundred; outside this area they form almost three-quarters of the total surviving epistolary activity.

There were two reasons for this pattern of distribution. The first was the obvious one that Gregory and the members of his court were far more familiar with France, Italy and Germany than they were with the regions beyond. Their own local origins were Italian or Lotharingian; the experience of the reformed papacy since 1046 had forged close ties with the great French and Italian monasteries of Cluny and Monte Cassino; the vigorous itineration of Leo IX had brought northern France clearly within the papal orbit; and Gregory's own diplomatic and legatine experience made the lands between the Alps and the North Sea familiar to him. But the dominance of kings and princes among the recipients of his letters outside this area is not explicable solely as a function of his lack of detailed local knowledge, an inability to establish direct contact with local aristocracies or ecclesiastical establishments. It is also the case that, although the military aristocracy of Italy, France or Germany offered natural allies to the reformed papacy, outside that region kings were a better bet. Sometimes this was because the programme of Christianization (as in Sweden) or struggle against the Muslim (as in Spain) was deemed to require strong royal direction. In some countries, such as Poland or Hungary, these considerations were reinforced by the fact of the prince's dominant monarchical position. While the more decentralized polities of Italy or France made it natural for the pope to seek allies among the great feudal magnates, in the new Christian monarchies of northern and eastern Europe a direct link with the monarch was of more value. All this was compounded, of course, by the fact that these more distant rulers made no claims to overlordship in Italy.

Gregory's letters to these rulers blended pastoral advice with a concern for the proprietary rights of St Peter; for one aspect of his programme was the assertion that large parts of the Christian world were actually the property of the saint and his earthly representative, the pope. The kingdom of Hungary, he claimed, 'was long ago handed over to the holy Roman Church as its property'. He transferred the government of the Russian kingdom to Iaropolk son of Isjaslaw 'acting as representative of St Peter' (*ex parte beati Petri*). In 1079 he wrote to the Slav noble Wezelinus expressing his surprise 'that you, who recently promised fealty to St Peter and to us, have rebelled against the man whom the apostolic authority has made king of Dalmatia'. The pope informed the kings of the Iberian peninsula that 'the realm of Spain . . . was handed over to Saint Peter and the holy Roman Church as its rightful property'. Petrine proprietary rights were not, in the event, to play a major part in the elaborated theory of papal monarchy, but they provided, one might say, the initial jolt that got the vehicle moving.

One sign of loyalty to the authority of Rome was cultic and ritual uniformity, and Gregory was a vigorous campaigner for this cause. He insisted, for example, that the clergy of Sardinia should 'follow the custom of the holy Roman Church' and shave their beards. This, he asserted, had been 'the practice of the whole Western Church from the very beginning', and any Sardinian ecclesiastic who refused to conform should have his property confiscated. Gregory's energy was also addressed to more general issues, especially the question of liturgical conformity. He refused permission for a vernacular liturgy in Bohemia and won a particularly striking victory in Spain, where his campaign of Romanization culminated in the abandonment of the Mozarabic liturgy and the introduction of the Roman rite. Alfonso VI of León–Castile, with his French wives and close ties with Cluny, the most prestigious abbey in France, was a ruler predisposed to adopt trans-Pyrenean norms, but, even so, it was only with some difficulty that 'the Roman law entered into Spain'. In 1074 Pope Gregory was busy with a campaign of encouragement, writing to Alfonso and his fellow monarch, Sancho IV of Navarre: 'I exhort you to acknowledge the Roman Church as your mother in very truth . . . to receive the order and office of the Roman Church . . . as you are bound, like the other kingdoms of the west and the north.' Seven years later he was in celebratory mood: 'Your excellency, most dearly beloved, know that one thing pleases us greatly – or, rather, pleases God's clemency – namely, that in the churches of your realm you have caused the order of the mother of all, the holy Roman Church, to be received and celebrated in the ancient way.'

Gregory's correspondence, which reached to Russia, Africa, Armenia, Poland and Ireland, shows the widening range of the papacy as it redefined its nature and expanded its horizons. Indeed, the impact of the new, interventionist papacy has often been traced by looking at the growth in frequency and scope of such channels of communication and authority as papal legates, letters and councils. The earliest papal legate to visit the Iberian peninsula was cardinal Hugh Candidus in 1065, sent there by a pope convinced that 'in Spain the unity of the Catholic faith has dwindled from its fullness and almost everyone has strayed from ecclesiastical discipline and the cult of the divine mysteries'. As we have seen, Gregory VII wrote twelve letters to Spanish recipients. His successors continued to maintain regular contact with the region, but it is only with the next surviving papal register, that of Innocent III (1198–1216), that we see how familiar the missives of the reformed papacy had become there: Innocent issued over 400 letters relating to Spain in his sixteen years as pope.

In both the Celtic countries and eastern Europe the late eleventh and early twelfth centuries marked a new start in regular contact with Rome.

Gregory VII's letter to Turlough O'Brien, 'king of Ireland', was the first extant since the seventh century. The first papal legate to visit Wales and Scotland was John of Crema, who came to Britain in 1125. In 1073 Gregory VII wrote to the duke of Bohemia, thanking him for the respect he had shown to the papal legates, but also threatening those who, like the bishop of Prague, opposed the pope's envoys. 'Because, through the negligence of our predecessors,' he wrote, 'and the remissness of your ancestors . . . messengers of the apostolic see have seldom been sent to your country, some among you regard this as a novelty.' Whatever may have been the pre-Gregorian history, the presence of papal legates was to be no 'novelty' in the High Middle Ages. By the first quarter of the thirteenth century, when papal letters were issued in their hundreds each year, when over 400 bishops came to Rome for the Lateran Council of 1215 and papal legates ruled as regents in England, sought to establish a church state in Livonia and led armies of mercenaries in warfare against the Holy Roman Emperor, then it might indeed be thought that the papacy had realized Gregory's boast – 'how great is the authority of this see'.

THE CONCEPT OF CHRISTENDOM

From around 1050 Rome thus created a new institutional and cultural uniformity in the western Church. Alongside the development of this machinery of authority and communication, however, one sees the strengthening of something less easily defined or dated, namely an identity. Ever since the age of conversion, of course, self-definition as Christian had been important for the peoples of the Mediterranean region and western Europe, but in the High Middle Ages this definition strengthened and took particular forms.

Christianity is many things; one of them is a name. Indeed, it was the very name of Christian that had been the grounds for persecution under the Roman empire – 'the legal issue is the name' (*nomen in causa est*), as Tertullian had written. In the High Middle Ages the phrase 'the Christian name' was in frequent use. Thus, the chronicler Malaterra, after describing a Muslim victory over the Christians in Sicily, tells how the victors 'were overjoyed at such a disgrace to the Christian name'. In a letter written from Antioch, the leaders of the First Crusade described it as 'the chief and capital city of the Christian name' (with reference to the fact that it was the place where Christians were first so called). When Tyre was taken by a joint army of Venetians and men from the kingdom of Jerusalem in 1124, the chronicler William of Tyre describes it as being 'restored to the Christian name'. Non-Christians could be characterized by their hostility to the name. Thus the First Crusade was directed against 'enemies of the Christian name', and the same label could be bestowed on Jews. Given enemies, the name needed defenders. Count Roger of Sicily, famous for his victories over the Muslims, was hailed as 'a bold destroyer of enemies of the Christian name', and the purpose of the Spanish military order of St James was 'to fight for the defence of the Christian name'.

In cases such as these the 'name' clearly has a greater meaning than that of mere appellation. Yet the power of the phrase 'the Christian name' is a power of labelling. By identifying and differentiating, it gave the prelates, princes and chroniclers of Christendom a means of referring to themselves. When the great imperialist popes of the High Middle Ages wished to express the extent of their claims they could specify that 'all realms in which the Christian name is revered regard the Roman Church as a mother'. The circumlocution 'all realms in which the Christian name is revered' gave a conceptual exactitude to the sphere of papal claims. It also, of course, constituted a swath of peoples and lands.

The Latin term *nomen* ('name') can also be translated 'family' or 'stock', and there is a sense in which the label 'Christian' came to have a quasi-ethnic meaning. It is true that Christians are made – by baptism – not born, but the vast majority of those born in Christian Europe in the High Middle Ages underwent baptism as a matter of course. They could easily think of themselves, not as voluntary recruits to a particular community of believers, but as members of a Christian race or people. As Montaigne says: 'we are Christians by the same title that we are either Perigordins or Germans'. This ethnic sense of 'Christian' can be found repeatedly and perhaps increasingly in the High Middle Ages. The term 'the Christian people' (*populus christianus*), which was common, implies no more than 'the community of Christians'; but when the Saxons were forcibly converted to Christianity by Frankish arms in the decades around the year 800, adoption of the new religion made them 'one *race*, as it were (*quasi una gens*), with the Franks'. The expansion of the new millennium brought Christians 'where Christians had never come before', and the circumstances of these new juxtapositions reinforced the sense that Christians were a people or tribe or race. They encountered populations of quite different traditions, speech, law and language and often established themselves as a privileged minority. Credal difference and ethnic identity became inextricably entwined.

In 1098, for example, during the First Crusade, after the crusaders had taken Antioch, Jesus appeared in a vision to a priest in the army, asked: 'Man, what race is this (*quaenam est hec gens*) that has entered the city?' and received the answer: 'Christians.' Gregory VII referred to 'the Christian race' (*christiana gens*), and the phrase 'the holy race of Christians' (*gens sancta, videlicet Christianorum*) can be found in the German chronicler Arnold of Lübeck. French *chansons* and rhymed chronicles talk of *la gent cristiane*, and in one of them, the crusading epic *La chanson d'Antioche*, Jesus is pictured hanging on the cross, explaining to the good thief alongside him that 'from across the sea a new people (*novele gent*) will come, who will take revenge for the death of their father'. Particularly explicit on the 'ethnicization' of Christianity is the French prelate Baudry de Bourgueil, writing in the early twelfth century. He explains in the preface to his history of the First Crusade that he has attempted to be fair to both Christians and pagans, even though 'I am a Christian and have descended from Christian ancestors and now, so to speak, possess God's sanctuary as an inheritance, and have claimed for myself the hereditary title of the Christian profession.' He goes on to say that belittling the military abilities of the pagans would not do justice to the fortitude of the Christians, since it would be portraying 'our race' (*genus nostrum*) fighting 'an unwarlike race' (*gens imbellis*).

These examples show Latin Christians, as they encountered alien peoples in the course of their high medieval expansion, adopting the terms of race and blood to describe their group identity. Some of those they encountered made the same equation. 'The name of Christendom,' wrote the Franciscan missionary William of Rubruck, 'seems to them [the Mongols] the name of a particular race.' Parallel to this 'racializing' trend was another, which stressed not descent but territory. Christians were a people or a race; they also had their own lands or regions, which could be described geographically. The most usual term for this land of the Christians was Christendom, and it is striking both that there is an enormous increase in the use of the term in the later eleventh century and that its semantic range moves increasingly towards a territorial, rather than an abstract, sense.

Christianitas had a long history. Its usual meaning in the early Middle Ages was 'the Christian faith', 'that which makes one Christian', but gradually the concept was territorialized. When Gregory VII wrote to the German bishops of the dangers that would be done 'not only to your people and the kingdom of the Germans but as far as the bounds of Christendom (*fines Christianitatis*) reach', his 'Christendom' is clearly characterized by geographical extent. Similarly, Louis VII's generosity to clerics drew them to Paris 'from all the ends of Christendom'; the wave of enthusiasm for the Third Crusade moved 'in Normandy and in France and through the whole of Christendom'; and the Council of Lyons in 1245 assembled prelates 'from the breadth of virtually the whole of Christendom'. Examples such as these show the way that Christendom could be envisaged as a specific part of the globe, a region characterized by its religion – 'all realms in which the Christian name is revered'.

The term attained its sharpest territorial sense when it was seen as describing an area whose boundaries were expanding at the expense of other alien territories. Of course, the great growth of Latin Christendom that occurred in the High Middle Ages could be conceptualized in many different ways, for instance as 'the growth in number and merit of the Christian people', but it was images of physical extension and enlargement (*dilatio*) that came to predominate. On every front – the implication of grand strategy is entirely appropriate – the same nouns and verbs came easily to the pens of the writers of letters, charters and chronicles. In Sicily, Count Roger 'expanded (*dilatavit*) the Church of God greatly in the lands of the Saracens'; on the Christian–Muslim frontier in the centre of the Iberian peninsula a pious Castilian noble worked for 'the expansion (*dilatio*) of the bounds of the Christian faith'; in Prussia the Teutonic Knights set out on campaign 'to expand (*ad dilatandum*) the frontiers of the Christians'. Naturally the crusades were the focus *par excellence* of such terminology; the great crusading encyclicals talked of the crusaders who had zealously striven 'to spread (*dilatare*) the Christian name in those parts', and papal legates prayed before battle that God might 'extend (*dilataret*) the kingdom of Christ and the Church from sea to sea'.

What made expansion such an identity-heightening experience was the fact that one quasi-ethnic territorial entity encountered others. Men who thought of themselves as living in Christendom were conscious that the rest of the world was not Christendom. This emerges in the dualistic pendant vocabulary in which Christians and Christendom are contrasted and set against their defining opposites. The young warriors of Norman Sicily, stirred by the prospect of the crusading expedition to Jerusalem in 1096, 'vowed that they would attack the lands of the Christian name (*fines christiani nominis*) no longer, until they had penetrated the lands of the pagans (*paganorum fines*)'. Here is a simple example of a comprehensive territorial dichotomy that shaped mental geography in the eleventh, twelfth and thirteenth centuries. The abstract 'Christendom' also summoned into being its mirror image: 'heathendom'. Unconquered Haifa in the Holy Land was 'the head and pride of all heathendom' (*paganismus*); the evasive Byzantine emperor, Manuel Comnenus, was blamed for 'strengthening heathendom' (*paganismus*); the Norman minstrel Ambroise, on the Third Crusade, writes of 'the best Turks one could find in heathendom' (*paenie*). The world was seen as the arena of the clash of great religio-territorial spheres. The fall of Jerusalem in 1099, for example, was not primarily a moment of triumph for the western leaders involved or exclusively a vindication of the Franks as a chosen race, but essentially 'a day when paganism was diminished and Christianity strengthened'. The capture of the city was an event that drew its significance from a wide backdrop in which empires of good and evil clashed in the world. Thus the inhabitants of Christian Europe came increasingly to think of themselves as inhabiting a part of the world called Christendom, to picture an opposing and surrounding 'heathendom' and to regard as a praiseworthy and thinkable goal the expansion or extension of Christendom. Jesus was not only the 'author of the Christian name' but also the 'propagator of the extension of Christendom'.

The Christendom that became newly aware of itself in the eleventh, twelfth and thirteenth centuries was not the Christendom of Constantine, but an assertively western or Latin Christendom. The Greek and Latin churches of the High Middle Ages had, of course, a common ancestry in the Church of apostolic and early medieval times. In the Mediterranean region there was originally no sharp barrier between them, and, although a jurisdictional boundary existed between the eastern patriarchates and Rome, this did not always coincide with the geography of rite, and nor was it immutable. Especially in the Balkans and southern Italy there was a highly complex and changing pattern of authority and cult, where the world of Latin liturgy and papal primacy shaded into the varied rites and hierarchical ambiguities of the eastern Mediterranean. However, between the time of the last ecumenical councils (680, 787, 869) and the mutual excommunications of 1054, a date traditionally (but no longer generally) given to the definitive schism between the two churches, problems between the eastern and the western parts of the Church became increasingly sharp. One arena where issues of authority and cult were fought out was the Mediterranean, where popes, patriarchs and emperors held councils, exchanged letters and ultimately uttered condemnations. Another arena was the new missionary world of northern and eastern Europe. Choices which were sometimes disguised in the Mediterranean basin, where centuries of contact and common tradition counterbalanced emerging hostilities and differences, were starker in the zone of evangelization. Here new Christian communities had to subscribe to the practices and the guidance either of the Greek or of the Latin world. Issues which could be left unresolved or ambiguous in the old Graeco-Roman cities were presented starkly to barbarian kings.

From the ninth century Latin and Greek missionaries came into contact and often into conflict in the Balkans and eastern Europe. Cases such as that of Constantine and Methodius (mentioned in Chapter 1) revolved around the twin issues of liturgical uniformity and ecclesiastical authority. The future cultural shape of Europe was determined as one king or people chose Rome, another the Greek Church. The Russians chose east, the Poles and Magyars west. A fissure slowly opened up within European Christendom. The final stages of this development took place around the shores of the Baltic in the thirteenth and fourteenth centuries. Here, as German and Scandinavian Christians gradually established themselves in the eastern Baltic, they there came into contact with Russians, who supposedly 'followed the Greek rite, condemned Latin baptism as hateful, failed to observe the solemn days and statutory fasts and dissolved the marriages that had been contracted among new converts'. There was to be no compromise with such 'insolence' and 'schism'. 'We command,' wrote Pope Honorius III in 1222, 'that these Russians should be forced to observe the rites of the Latins where they have followed those of the Greeks, in separation from the head, that is, the Roman Church.' The clash of Greek and Latin in the Mediterranean basin went back centuries; now, as a consequence of the expansion of Latin Christendom in the High Middle Ages, there was a new Greek–Latin frontier. Gradually the two observances came into contact along their whole north–south extent. By the middle decades of the thirteenth century adherents of the Roman and Greek churches were engaged in military combat from Constantinople, where 'the men of the law of Rome' had established their own Latin empire, to icy Lake Peipus on the Novgorod road. With the official conversion of Lithuania in 1386, contact was joined along the whole line: the antagonists stood hand to hand and belly to belly. New levels of contiguity and a new intensity of hatred and suspicion had made Latins more Latin and Greeks more Greek.

THE RELIGIOUS ORDERS

The institutional skeleton that supported this intense Latin Christian identity was provided not only by the rejuvenated papacy but also by an entirely novel kind of organization, the international religious order, born in the twelfth century and elaborated in the thirteenth. In the period under discussion here (950–1350) one can distinguish four stages in the development of the monastic orders, which roughly correspond with the four centuries between the tenth and the thirteenth. In the first stage, in the tenth century, the majority of monasteries followed a common basic rule, the Benedictine, which prescribed details about the running of the house and also embodied a philosophy of, or approach to, the monastic life. Each house was independent of the others, its abbot was the supreme internal authority, and monks were expected to remain in the monastery in which they had made their formal profession. Benedictine monks were supported by substantial landed endowments, composed of villages and farms providing produce and rents to feed and clothe the monks and pay for their spectacular buildings, vestments, books and ornaments. The larger Benedictine monasteries were the richest corporations in Europe.

The next stage in the organization of western monasticism is marked by a major innovation that began in the tenth century but did not reach a zenith until the late eleventh. This was associated with the abbey of Cluny in Burgundy. The Cluniac system did involve ties between different houses, ties of two kinds. The tighter bond was between the abbey of Cluny and its dependent priories. The heads of these priories were appointed by the abbot of Cluny and could be dismissed by him. The monks in their priories were, in theory, monks of Cluny and made their profession in the mother house. A much looser connection existed between Cluny and those abbeys that followed her particular variant of the monastic life, her customs, without being subject to her. Many were united in *societas*, a form of confraternity which involved the obligation of mutual prayer. So, although Cluniac monasteries were bound together, the ties involved, in the case of the priories, a simple personal dependence on the abbot of Cluny, without delegation, representation or internal articulation, and, in the cases of the abbeys bound by confraternity, a liturgical and ritual bond without juridical subordination. Like the independent Benedictine houses, Cluniac houses required a fairly substantial landed endowment for their support.

If we turn from the Cluniac monasticism that flowered in the eleventh century to the Cistercian order which blossomed in the twelfth, we find a set of contrasts. Cluny was geographically limited, there being scarcely any dependencies of Cluny in Germany, for example; but the Cistercians spread from their Burgundian mother house of Cîteaux and her first four dependencies (La Ferté, Pontigny, Clairvaux and Morimond) to countries as distant as Ireland, Norway and north-west Spain within fifty years of their foundation: 'From these four branches, springing from the root of Cîteaux, the whole order has grown, which the Lord has multiplied both in number of abbeys and in extent of virtue, to the four corners of the world.'

Institutionally the Cluniacs were relatively unsophisticated, relying on the simple subordination to the abbot of Cluny; the Cistercians developed an elaborate system of affiliation, delegation and representation, which ensured a flow of information and command through the order. The central principle was affiliation. Each Cistercian house was founded from and subject to another, in a chain of dependence that led back, eventually, to Cîteaux itself. In contrast to the independent Benedictine houses, there was a structure of authority; in contrast to the Cluniac system, this structure worked through delegation and the head did not have to do all, since the mother houses supervised daughter houses. There were also central institutions: annual chapters of, in theory, all abbots were held, and general legislation was passed. If Cluny tended towards a prayer union, the Cistercians fashioned something more like an administrative network. So the order was geographically widespread and institutionally sophisticated, and it offered a clear constitutional template for those interested in founding new houses; its growth was remarkable. On the other hand, the Cistercians still embraced claustration, the monk's duty to remain in one house, and needed substantial, usually landed endowment. Hence they still required heavy investment and upheld the principle of immobility of personnel.

In the fourth phase of monastic development, which occurred in the thirteenth century, the complex organization of the Cistercians was maintained and developed, but the principle of immobility and the need for heavy investment were abandoned. The new orders of friars that spread dramatically across Europe and beyond in this period had a complex, articulated, international organization, with elective and legislative elements; coupled to this the doctrine of mendicancy and their concentration in towns meant that they could survive initially without endowment. They did, of course, eventually build up wealth, but often in the form of rents or other urban incomes rather than landed estates that they exploited directly. The lack of claustration meant that promising friars could be moved to wherever the order thought they might do most good. By the mid-thirteenth century they were bidding to take over the university of Paris, where some of their major intellectual figures, like the Dominican Thomas Aquinas, had been concentrated. One Dominican author tells a story of how the Cistercians, astonished at the personal mobility of the early mendicants, spied on the young friars to find fault with them. Dominic supposedly rebuked them: 'Why do you spy on my disciples? . . . I know for certain that my young men will go out and come back . . . but your young men will be kept locked up and will still go out.' This juxtaposition of resentful cloistered monks seeking illicit nocturnal pleasures and mobile but responsible young Dominicans, despite its patently partisan origin, enshrines a truth about the thirteenth-century shift in the ideal of the religious life.

The four stages of western monasticism represent a movement towards greater administrative complexity and personal mobility, away from the localism of the earlier monastery and towards the ever-wider horizons of the international orders. The independent houses of the early period, deeply involved with their surrounding areas, had been supplemented by systems that tied the houses together across long distances. The new orders of the twelfth century, such as the Cistercians and the Templars, or of the thirteenth, such as the Franciscans and Dominicans, had formal, institutional features which enabled them to spread rapidly but also, in the process, to maintain their distinctive character. They combined the reproductive rate of the rabbit with the self-containment of the crustacean. New foundations could be made with confidence that they would transform their environment as much as adapt to it. In the first century of their existence the Cistercians established over 500 religious houses, and in the first century of theirs, the Franciscans notched up over 1,400.

Map 12 shows the dissemination of the Cistercian order in north-eastern Europe, where it eventually established communities as distant as Tuterø, within 200 miles of the Arctic Circle, and Falkenau, on the frontiers of Russia. The direction of expansion is clearly from south and west to north and east, and an important role was played by colonies of monks from neighbouring lands, such as the English in Norway and the Germans in parts of Poland. A chain of subordination and communication linked these houses to the great mother abbeys of France, especially Morimond, which was the superior of the vast majority of the Cistercian monasteries founded in north-eastern Europe. Mogiła near Cracow, for example, which was founded in 1222, was a daughter of Lubiąż in Silesia, which was in turn a daughter of Pforta in Thuringia, itself a daughter of Walkenried in the Harz; Walkenried was a daughter of Altenkamp in the Lower Rhineland, which had been founded in 1123 from Morimond. Over the course of the century a chain of six monasteries had been created, extending over 500 miles eastwards from the cradle of the order in eastern France. Foundations such as those in Portugal, Greece or Syria provide even more striking examples of the wide geographical horizons of the new orders.

Such rapid and organized growth was made possible by a new level of legal articulation and international organization, based on written constitutions. One of the keys to this was the development of reproducible models, often spelled out in documents. The reproducibility involved

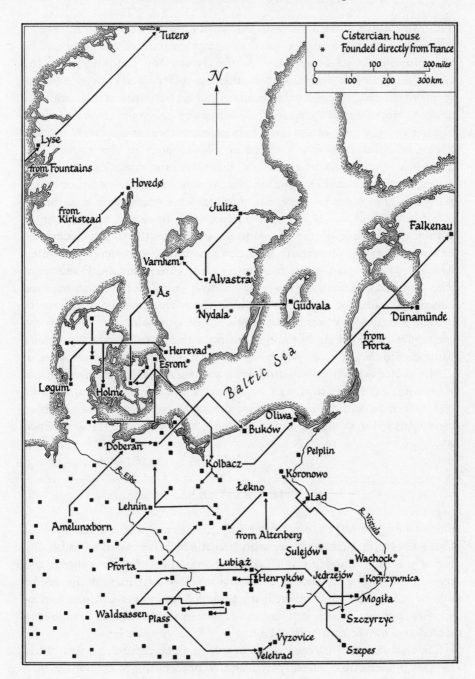

Map 12. Cistercian houses in north-east Europe (showing selected affiliations)

transplantability, in the Cistercian case of the model house, in the case of the friars a transplantability of the very personnel of the order. The objectification of structure found in the statutes and constitutions of the international orders was linked to their mobility. They were effective agents of the dissemination of a common culture by virtue of this combination of structure and movement. The newer religious orders, like the Cistercians, military orders and mendicants, were well placed to take advantage of the expansion of Latin Christendom in the twelfth and thirteenth centuries. Indeed, some of them, like the crusading orders and the missionary-minded Franciscans, were founded in order to promote that expansion. The older monastic communities were relatively less important in the new frontier lands. Thus the Benedictine houses of northern Spain did not get much from the Reconquest, and it was the secular cathedrals, military orders and mendicants who dominated the reconquered territories. Along the Baltic coast it was crusading orders, Cistercians and Dominicans who acquired ecclesiastical power and wealth. In 1236, for example, Pope Gregory IX devised a plan to establish three Dominicans as bishops in Prussia. The new features of the religious orders enabled them to become extraordinarily far-flung but also to maintain their aspect as the bearer of a common culture. It is not surprising that it was a Franciscan friar who, in 1254, debated with Muslims, Buddhists and pagans before the Great Khan at his court in Mongolia; it was also natural that, far from home though he was, he carried with him the standard theological textbook by the Parisian theologian Peter Lombard and a carving of the Madonna 'in the French style'.

THE CRUSADES

One of Gregory VII's favourite biblical quotations was from the book of Jeremiah (48:10): 'Cursed be he who keepeth back his sword from blood', and it was under his aegis and that of his successors that the concept and practice of holy war became a familiar and essential part of the life of western Christians. Just as the papacy provided leadership, Christendom an identity and the orders an institutional network, the crusades offered a shared goal for the men of the West.

The crusade was 'the common enterprise of all Christians', a political and military undertaking virtually universally praised and very widely supported by the aristocrats, clerics and people of western Europe. This is what the thirteenth-century chronicler Matthew Paris has to say, when he explains why he has included so much discussion of the crusades in his *History of the English*: 'It does not seem to me irrelevant in chronicles and histories of English affairs . . . to describe briefly this glorious war, especially because on this depended at that time the whole state and condition of the entire Church, or indeed of the Catholic faith itself.' A similar universalism can be found in the words of the leaders of the First Crusade, writing in triumph from Jerusalem, who invited the exultation of 'the whole Latin race' (*gens latina*). This supra-national quality of the crusade struck its participants. 'Who has ever heard,' asked the crusader Fulcher of Chartres,

of speakers of so many languages in one army? . . . If a Breton or German wished to ask me something, I was completely unable to reply. But although we were divided by language, we seemed to be like brothers in the love of God and like near neighbours of one mind.

The avowed internationalism of the crusade was constituted by its divine authorization. Participants bore the common symbol of Christians, the cross, not a dynastic or national badge. A crusading army, in Palestine or in Spain, was 'the army of God' (*exercitus Dei*). In the French epics of the twelfth century the army of the First Crusade was 'the host of God', 'the host of Jesus', 'the company of God', 'the holy company', 'the retinue of Jesus' and 'the chivalry of God'. The kingdom of Jerusalem was not simply yet another dynastic lordship, but 'a new colony of Holy Christendom'. Despite the realities of ethnic and political squabbling that characterized the crusades from their very beginning, the language, symbolism and, to a great extent, reality of crusading were the common heritage of Latin Christians.

Those who witnessed the events of the 1090s recognized their remarkable nature. 'In our time,' wrote Guibert of Nogent, 'God has instituted holy war'; while Orderic Vitalis referred to the crusade as 'that unanticipated transformation that took place in our times'. But, once the remarkable events of 1095–9 had occurred, they could be familiarized and adapted to serve as a model in new situations. Urban II, who initiated the First Crusade, had not known exactly what was going to happen. Men of the twelfth century, however, knew what had happened – and could hope for a repetition. The leaders of the Second Crusade of 1147–9 were constantly looking over their shoulders at the First Crusade. Even after his army had suffered terribly in Anatolia, Louis VII of France was extremely reluctant to seek the easy option of concluding the journey by sea: 'let us follow the route of our forefathers, whose incomparable prowess won them fame on earth and glory in heaven'. During the Fourth Crusade, as the crusaders

debated who should be the new Latin ruler of Constantinople, Baldwin of
Flanders or Boniface of Montferrat, they reflected: 'If we elect one of these
two great men the other will be so jealous that he will lead off all his
people. Thus this land could be lost, just as Jerusalem was nearly lost when
they elected Godfrey de Bouillon after that land was conquered.' The
French knights who conquered Constantinople in 1204 thus felt that they
stood in a clear tradition as heirs of the French knights who had waded
through blood in the city of Jerusalem in the summer of 1099. Crusading
could, indeed, become part of a proud family or ethnic tradition. Nicholas
of St Omer, the ruler of Thebes in Frankish Greece, and formerly husband
of Mary of Antioch, built a castle in Thebes and 'inside he covered its walls
with murals depicting how the Franks conquered Syria'. Similarly, Eleanor,
queen of England from 1236, had an Antioch chamber in Westminster
Palace, decorated with depictions of the siege of Antioch in the First
Crusade. Her husband, Henry III, commissioned paintings of his uncle,
Richard the Lionheart, in combat with Saladin, for his chambers and
castles. Every time they moved through these chambers courtiers and
servants would encounter a visual reminder of the centrality of the crusade
and the glory of the crusader.

Even in the unpromising soil of eastern Europe the crusade could
become a powerful organizing principle. In the year 1108 a document was
drawn up which purported to be an appeal by the bishops of the province
of Magdeburg and other east Saxon leaders to the chief men of the rest of
Saxony, Lotharingia and Flanders, inviting them to join in a campaign
against the pagan Slavs. The true authorship of the letter is doubtful but its
tenor is not. After reciting the atrocities perpetrated on Christians by the
pagans, the writer incites the clerics and monks of Saxony, Franconia,
Lotharingia and Flanders to 'imitate the men of Gaul (*Gallorum imitatores
. . . estote*) . . . proclaim this in your churches: "Sanctify war, arouse the
mighty men!"' He urges the Christian warriors:

Assemble yourselves and come, all you lovers of Christ and the Church, and
prepare yourselves like the men of Gaul to free Jerusalem! Our Jerusalem . . . has
been made a bondmaid . . . may He, who with his strong arm, gave triumph over
his enemies to the men of Gaul, who came from the furthermost west to the
distant east, give you will and power to subdue these inhuman pagans who are our
neighbours.

This is a direct appeal to the memory of the First Crusade and an attempt
to harness that memory to a quite new purpose, war against the pagan
Slavs east of the Elbe. The province of Magdeburg becomes 'our Jerusalem';

the warriors of western Germany and Flanders are urged to emulate 'the men of Gaul' (*Galli*) who had won victory in 'the distant east'. A whole rhetoric, imagery and historical memory were being invoked in order to be redirected.

The appeal of 1108 did not bear immediate fruit. It makes clear, however, that within a decade of the fall of Jerusalem to the crusaders the events and images of the First Crusade were providing material for a reformulation of the nature and meaning of warfare in a very different part of Christendom. The full consequence of this emerged in 1147, the year when the Second Crusade was preached. In 1147 Christian holy war was generalized. 'Each province of Catholics,' wrote the Danish chronicler Saxo Grammaticus, 'was commanded to attack that part of the barbarian world nearest to them.' Campaigns took place in the eastern Mediterranean, in the Iberian peninsula and in eastern Europe, where the so-called Wendish Crusade brought the terminology, institutions and practices of crusading warfare into the region for the first time. The results were meagre in military terms, but a precedent had been established. 'An army of those with the sign [of the cross]' had campaigned east of the Elbe.

The next attempt to use the ever more sophisticated institutions and ideology of crusade in the Baltic region occurred in 1171, in connection with efforts to establish a bishopric in Estonia under Danish tutelage. In that year Pope Alexander III issued a bull addressed to the Christian rulers and people of Scandinavia, in which he skilfully combined praise for their religious loyalty, an assertion of papal authority and an exhortation to support the local church along with the crusading appeal. He indeed lamented 'the savagery of the [pagan] Estonians . . . towards God's faithful people', but also gave thanks to God 'that you have steadfastly and firmly persisted in the Catholic faith and in loyalty to the holy Roman Church, which is the head of all churches, a mistress appointed by the Lord and ruler by divine authority of all other churches'. The pope urged the Scandinavians to persevere in their loyalty and obedience, to refrain from plundering raids, to obey and honour the prelates of the Church and to pay them the tithes and other revenue they were owed. Finally came the crusading promise:

Relying on God's mercy and the merits of the apostles Peter and Paul, we grant to those who fight with force and sincerity against these pagans remission of one year of the sins which they have confessed and for which they have received penance, just as we grant it to those who visit the Lord's sepulchre; to those who fall in battle, we grant remission of all their sins, if they have received penance.

Remission of sins for those who fight to defend Christendom against pagans and plenary remission for those who die – the formula is explicitly that of the Holy Land crusade. Yet the application of this new tool of the reformed papacy, developed mainly in Mediterranean contexts over the previous century, to a theatre of war 1,250 miles from Rome was not simply a mechanical transferral. The opportunity was taken, as the crusade was implanted in the Baltic, to tighten the links with Rome, to insist upon papal supremacy and to buttress the local churches materially and psychologically. The sanctification of war carried with it detailed obligations as a Christian people.

Nothing seems to have come of Pope Alexander's appeal, and Estonia remained pagan and unconquered until the next century, but the apparatus of crusade, once introduced into the Baltic region, was to have a glittering and bloody future. The establishment of a missionary bishopric in Livonia in the 1180s and the conversion of some of the native population meant that there was now, in the very heart of the Baltic littoral, a new and vulnerable church, which would very likely need the defence and protection of Christian arms. In 1199 Innocent III, the crusading pope *par excellence*, who played that particular instrument with variety and novelty, called upon the Saxons 'in remission of your sins . . . to rise up powerfully and manfully in the name of the God of hosts and defend the Christians in those parts [i.e. Livonia]'. A crusading army did indeed go to Livonia, but encountered complete military disaster. The bishop of Livonia was himself killed. It was his successor, Albert of Buxtehude, who was to establish Christian Livonia on a firm foundation and he chose as one of his essential tools the most distinctive institution to arise from the crusading movement – the military order.

Crusading military orders, such as the Templars, Hospitallers and Teutonic Knights, were, in part, successful because they were improbable. Their animating idea involved a fusion of opposites. The eleventh-century knight was violent, acquisitive, unruly and lascivious. The eleventh-century monk was dedicated to peace, poverty, obedience and chastity. From these contradictory sources sprang the crusading orders of the twelfth century: knights who were poor, chaste and obedient, monks who were fighters. This combination of aggression and self-abnegation had enormous appeal, and soon these orders became among the wealthiest and most prestigious corporations in Christendom. They were the most powerful and enduring institutional results of the militarization of Christianity that characterized the eleventh and twelfth centuries.

The model order, on which the others were based, was that of the

Templars, founded around 1118 by a knight from Champagne, Hugh de Payns, who had undertaken the task of protecting pilgrims on their way to Jerusalem from the Mediterranean port of Jaffa. They were granted a residence in Jerusalem by King Baldwin II, which was situated within the Temple enclosure and gave them their name, 'the poor fellow knights of Christ and the Temple of Solomon', as their rule terms them. Looking back from the middle of the twelfth century, one western chronicler describes them in the following words: 'around this time there arose in Jerusalem a new kind of knighthood . . . they lived like monks, preserved chastity, kept discipline at home and on campaign, ate in silence, had everything in common, but took arms against the pagans and expanded greatly'. One of the reasons this 'new kind of knighthood . . . expanded greatly' is that it was taken under the wing of the religious genius of the day, Bernard of Clairvaux. Soon after the Templar rule was confirmed at the Council of Troyes in 1128, Bernard composed a treatise eulogizing this 'new knighthood':

The word has gone round that a new kind of knighthood has arisen . . . It is a new kind of knighthood, I say, unknown to the ages, for it fights an endless double battle, against flesh and blood and against spiritual wickedness in high places . . .

The knights of Christ fight the battles of their Lord with untroubled minds, fearing neither sin from killing the enemy nor danger in their own death, since there is no guilt and much deserved glory in either bearing death or inflicting it for Christ . . . The knight of Christ, I say, kills with an untroubled mind, dies with an even less troubled one . . . a Christian glories in the death of a pagan, since Christ is glorified.

The Templars were extremely successful, not only in terms of their own growth in numbers and wealth, but also as a model for other crusading orders. The Hospitallers (or Knights of St John), for example, who had their origins in a group dedicated to the care of the sick from the time of the First Crusade and hence were older than the Templars, were militarized during the course of the twelfth century under Templar influence. The Teutonic Knights, founded in the 1190s, explicitly adopted the Templar rule. The birth of the first of the Spanish orders, that of Calatrava, shows the influence of the Templars even in the spawning of distinct new corporations. In 1147 Alfonso VII of Castile conquered Calatrava from the Muslims and entrusted it to the Templars; when it was threatened and they judged it indefensible, they returned it to the monarchy. At this point Raymond, the Cistercian abbot of Fitero, and an ex-knight monk of his, Diego Velázquez, asked for it to defend; the archbishop of Toledo preached remission of sins for the defence of Calatrava and a confraternity formed following the Cistercian rule. In 1164 the new association won papal approval:

we take into our protection and that of St Peter the place of Calatrava ... We confirm the arrangements made by our beloved sons, the abbot and Cistercian brothers in that place, that you should serve their order firmly and, girded with knightly arms, fight manfully to defend the place against the Saracens.

The Cistercian former knight, inspired by the Templar model, which had itself been fostered by his own order, created a local and initially miniature replica.

By 1200 the military orders were extremely wealthy and had acquired property throughout Latin Christendom: the place names Teach Temple in Connacht, Tempelhof in eastern Germany and Templo de Huesca in the Iberian peninsula are reminders of how widely convents of Templars could be found. The Temples of London and Paris became important financial centres. In the Holy Land, the burden of defence fell largely on the shoulders of the orders. A grim mark of respect was shown to the Templars and Hospitallers by Saladin after the crushing Christian defeat at Hattin in 1187. They were rounded up and decapitated. 'He had these particular men killed,' explained Ibn al-Athīr, 'because they were the fiercest of all the Frankish warriors.'

When Bishop Albert chose to create a crusading order in Livonia, he was therefore drawing on a tradition almost a century long. His originality was that he was midwife to the first successful 'Order State', a political lordship under the dominion of a crusading order. There had been some hints earlier of such a development. In 1131 the king of Aragon left his kingdom in his will to the Templars, but this was never effected. Later in the century Cyprus was in the Templars' hands briefly in the early 1190s. Livonia was, however, the first enduring Order State. The Swordbrothers, instituted by Bishop Albert in 1202, were endowed with one-third of the new colony in 1207 – 'so arose the first Order State in history'. The Swordbrothers, with their Templar-inspired rule and symbols of cross and sword, were the epitome of the professional holy warrior. Now they became also lords of the land. In 1210 the territorial relations of the bishop of Riga and the Swordbrothers were the subject of an agreement. The knights were to hold a third of Livonia and Lettia from the bishop, owing no temporal service, though with their perpetual function as defenders of the region against pagan attack understood. They and their priests paid no tithes to the bishop, though their peasant tenants owed tithes to the local churches and a quarter of this sum went to the bishop. The order also had the right of presentation to these churches.

The principle of condominium was one that was to govern relations between episcopate and order in the Baltic conquest states throughout their existence, but the balance shifted heavily in favour of the order after the Teutonic Knights arrived on the scene. They were offered a base in Poland to fight the pagan Prussians and from 1230, from their centres at Toruń (Thorn) and Chełmno (Culm), they slowly established a new territory, Christian Prussia. In 1237 they absorbed the Swordbrothers. The whole eastern Baltic littoral was now in the hands of a major crusading order. A vast military and political establishment premised on holy war was an entirely appropriate child of the aggressive Christianity of the high medieval period. It is also characteristic that this establishment took a non-dynastic form. Like the other international orders, the crusading orders had elective officials and bureaucratic routines. Joinville reports that the Muslim extremist group, the Assassins, whose special political ploy was exactly what their name suggests, would not bother to kill the Masters of the Templars or the Hospitallers, since they could be immediately replaced. Unlike the murder of a king or prince, which could fling an army or a kingdom into complete disarray, the death of a high official of the crusading orders was followed by a rational, institutionalized process, whereby one competent adult male warrior replaced another.

The crusade integrated Christendom, and the orders are perhaps its most solidly international creation. Despite some national coloration (especially strong in the Spanish orders), the monastic knights had wide horizons. The order of Calatrava obtained an estate at Thymau (Tymawa) on the lower Vistula; the Teutonic Knights held land at Higares on the Tagus. A quickening and widening flow of capital throughout Christendom was one result. Grants like that made by Duke Henry Borwin II of Mecklenburg of sixty *mansi* (holdings) around Lake Mirow to the Hospitallers meant that income from Mecklenburg estates was now being channelled into such 'pan-Latin-Christian' institutions as the crusading orders and could be applied, eventually, to such purposes as the defence of the Holy Land. Another Mecklenburg document reveals this incorporation of the region into an international Latin network yet more sharply. At the Franciscan convent in Erfurt in 1289 the lord of Mecklenburg acknowledged receipt from the Grand Master of the Teutonic Knights of 296 marks, which his father, Henry of Mecklenburg, had deposited with the knights in Acre before his capture by the Saracens. The crusading orders here appear in their guise as international bankers, guiding the streams of cash through

Christendom. The transaction gains in significance when we remember that this Henry of Mecklenburg was the descendant of pagan Slav princes, who in the mid-twelfth century had been, not crusaders, but the targets of crusade. His forebear would perhaps have found something odd in the prediction that his descendant would fall into the hands of Saracens while wearing the cross. These examples show how a massive redeployment of men and resources had taken place in this period, drawing the people and the wealth of remote pagan parts into the central programmes of Latin Christendom. By 1219, for example, the clergy of Riga, a province of the Latin Church which had not existed a generation previously, were making contributions to the campaign against Damietta. The international stage on which the papacy and the Latin Church moved was continually expanding in the eleventh, twelfth and thirteenth centuries, and previously quite unconnected regions were being brought together in unexpected ways: the funding of an offensive against Egypt from the profits of Livonian trade and agriculture was one such connection.

11. The Europeanization of Europe

We avoid many great inconveniences when we make the doings
of our own time perpetual through the power of writing.

The phrase 'the Europeanization of Europe' may initially sound paradoxical. A moment's reflection, however, makes it clear that such terms serve as
a shorthand to point to a variety of complex processes. If one considers the
parallel term 'Americanization', as applied to post-war Europe, the range
of these interrelated trends becomes apparent: from the clear-cut but
limited impact of military occupation, through the more diffuse but also
more widespread process of cultural and social imitation to the global issue
of convergent development. From this it follows, and this too emerges
from the analogy, that terms such as 'Americanization' and 'Europeanization' do not always imply a strictly localizable 'Europe' or 'America'
behind the process. The 'America' in the term 'Americanization' is not
geographically exact; it is a construct. Similarly, 'Europe' is a construct, an
image of a set of societies that can be seen as sharing something. The phrase
'the Europeanization of Europe' is intended to convey the point that there
was a dramatic change in what was shared and how widely over the course
of the High Middle Ages.

By saying Europe is a construct we are not saying that it is a purely
metaphorical creation. The Europeanization of Europe, in so far as it was
indeed the spread of one particular culture through conquest and influence,
had its core areas in one part of the continent, namely in France, Germany
west of the Elbe and north Italy, regions which had a common history as
part of Charlemagne's Frankish empire. In part the cultural homogenization
of Europe was thus a function of the Frankish military hegemony described
in earlier chapters of this book. It was from this part of western Europe
that expansionary expeditions were launched in all directions, and by 1300
these wars had created a ring of conquest states on the peripheries of Latin
Christendom. It would be easy to concentrate a strictly military eye on this
expansionary movement, but as important is the process of cultural change
which interwove with the more simply military tale and was not merely a
function of it.

It is indeed notable that historians of the Middle Ages have used the term 'Europeanization' especially when referring to those regions which underwent cultural and social transformation in the High Middle Ages without the pressure of foreign invasion or conquest. The Hungarian historian Fügedi writes: 'We maintain that Hungary was Europeanized (*europäisiert*) in the course of the twelfth and thirteenth centuries.' Alfonso VI of León–Castile, a ruler active on another flank of post-Carolingian Europe, the Iberian peninsula, has been characterized as 'anxious to Europeanize his realms', pursuing a programme part of which was the 'Europeanizing of the liturgy'. The term crops up too in discussion of the 'modernizing' kings of twelfth-century Ireland. The usage is, of course, incorrect, if not meaningless, in a strictly geographical sense, since Ireland, Spain and Hungary all form part of the continent of Europe as defined geographically. Its significance rests rather on the assumption that there was a culture or society (perhaps at this level of generality the distinction between these two concepts does not matter much) that had its centres in the old Frankish lands, was Latin and Christian but was not synonymous with Latin Christendom, was marked by certain social and cultural features and was expanding into the surrounding regions during the High Middle Ages, changing as it did so. Some of those social and cultural features form the subject of this chapter.

SAINTS AND NAMES

Saints and names are closely related subjects. Parents or others responsible for the choice of a child's name often gave preference to the names of those saints who particularly mattered to them. Among the medieval Bohemians it was apparently the custom 'that they gave to their children the names of saints on whose days they were born into this world'. Geographical and chronological variations in the popularity of saints and the popularity of names thus often coincided.

In the early Middle Ages most regions of Europe had highly localized repertoires of names. It is easy, given a few personal names, to tell which region or ethnic group is being talked about. Among aristocratic Germans it is even possible to make a good guess at the family, so distinct and particular are the naming patterns. Those who moved permanently from one linguistic or cultural world to another would feel the pressure to adopt a new name, as a tactic designed to avoid outlandishness. On his arrival in Normandy in 1085, for example, the child oblate Orderic was renamed:

'the name of Vitalis was given me in place of my English name, which sounded harsh to the Normans'. When noble ladies married into foreign royal families who spoke a different language, it was not uncommon for them to adopt a new name. The Bohemian princesses Swatawa and Markéta became, respectively, the German countess Liutgard and Dagmar, queen of Denmark. Henry I of England's wife was 'Matilda, who had previously been called Edith'. The tight bonding of name and ethnic or local group explains the pressure for such diplomatic renaming.

The same intense regionalism is true of saints. Their cults usually had one or two main centres, where the chief relics were situated, surrounded by a limited zone of relative cultic density where one might expect to encounter churches dedicated to the saint, perhaps subsidiary relics and men named after the saint, a zone which shaded off into the zones of other adjoining local saints. If we find a town whose churches are dedicated to Saints Chad, Mary and Alcmund, we know we are in the English Midlands (the example is Shrewsbury). This regional concentration is characteristic even of the more successful cults. For example, though there were over 700 churches dedicated to St Remi, 80 per cent of them were located within 200 miles of his chief centre at Rheims. The historian Charles Higounet mapped the places named after the saints of Merovingian Aquitaine and found that they stopped abruptly at the Loire, the Rhône and the Gironde.

In the eleventh and twelfth centuries this highly compartmentalized world began to change. A circulation of names and saints through the system began. Sometimes this occurred as a result of conquest. England provides a neat example of such a change. In 1066 the country was conquered by an army of French-speakers from northern France. Within a few years that army had transformed itself into a landed aristocracy – a French-speaking aristocracy ruling an English-speaking peasantry. Not only did the two groups speak different languages, they bore different names. Although Norman and Anglo-Saxon nomenclatures were both, in origin, Germanic, the two countries had developed quite different repertories of names. English Ethelreds, Alfreds and Edwards faced Norman Williams, Henrys and Roberts. In the eleventh century the distinction is fairly watertight: a name is a virtually certain indicator of ethnic origin. In the twelfth century this situation changed. Names are, of course, among the most malleable elements of linguistic culture, offering, as they do, the repeated chance of choice; and soon, it seems, the English population of England chose to adopt the names of their conquerors. The kinds of pressure at work are shown by the story of one young boy, born in the area of Whitby around 1110, whose parents initially christened him Tostig but, 'when his youthful companions mocked the name', changed it to the respectably Norman William. This process began among the higher clergy and townsmen. The canons of St Paul's, London, for example, around thirty in number, include only one or two with English names after the start of the twelfth century. Eventually the peasantry took up the fashion. A list of the peasant tenants of the bishop of Lincoln in 1225, a century and a half after the Norman Conquest, shows how the rural lower class had adopted the names of their lords. Over 600 men are listed; three-quarters of them bore a fairly limited number of names – there were fifteen names that were clearly most popular. Of this group three-quarters again bore names of Norman origin. There were 86 Williams, 59 Roberts, and so on. Less than 6 per cent bore names of Anglo-Saxon or Anglo-Scandinavian origin.

England's saints proved more resilient than England's names, and their story in the post-conquest period offers a nice counterpoint to the history of nomenclature. Immediately after 1066 the Normans seem to have viewed the local saints with suspicion and derision. The conquest had brought them from the sphere of one set of saints, familiar to them, to the sphere of another set, alien and unsettling saints with strange names. Lanfranc, the first Norman archbishop of Canterbury, wrote: 'These Englishmen among whom we are living have set up for themselves certain saints whom they revere. But sometimes when I turn over in my mind their own accounts of who they were, I cannot help having doubts about the quality of their sanctity.' He acted on his doubts by dropping St Elphege and St Dunstan from the Canterbury liturgy. At the abbey of St Albans there was a wholesale destruction of the shrines of pre-conquest saints by the first Norman abbot, who regarded his Anglo-Saxon predecessors as *rudes et idiotas* – 'uncouth and illiterate'. The kind of competition between cults that resulted and the tensions this brought to local society are vividly revealed in the following story, taken from an account of the life and miracles of the Anglo-Saxon saint Ethelbert:

There was living in the neighbourhood of the place where the church of the martyr [Ethelbert] was built a man called Vitalis, who was of Norman origin. Because of the great inborn hatred between English and Normans he deemed our martyr unworthy of honour and reverence. On the day of his wife's churching he made her go to another church and perform the solemn rites of purification there. She completed the service and returned. Vitalis happened to enter the house of a certain knight of great righteousness called Godiscalc, and the lady of the house, Lecelma, criticized him for daring to treat St Ethelbert's church with such contempt. He, however, torn by an insanity of spirit and half mad, said, 'I would rather have my wife worship the mangers of my cows than him whom you call

Ethelbert.' As he said it the wretched man fell immediately to the ground and died miserably before them all.

But the conquerors were not always so limited in their cultic sympathies. The great churches, with much invested in their saints, survived. A newly planted aristocracy gradually became a local aristocracy. By the later twelfth century worshippers of both English and Norman stock could be found at the shrines of the old saints. A symbolic climax came in the reign of Henry III. Himself the descendant of French aristocrats, a man who specified that his heart should be buried in Fontevrault in the Loire valley, he was, nevertheless, an ardent adherent of St Edward the Confessor, the last of the Wessex line of kings who had died in 1066. Henry invested thousands of pounds in giving this Anglo-Saxon saint a suitable home in Westminster abbey, now rebuilt according to the latest French style, and in 1239 he had his first-born son christened Edward. He was the first king since the Norman Conquest to give his children Anglo-Saxon names, and his case shows how the Normanization of English nomenclature was modified by a contrary movement as the immigrant French dynasts and aristocrats adopted the cults of the native saints.

Clearly, in this English case, conquest spread one element of the conquerors' linguistic culture, nomenclature, while simultaneously exposing them to the influence of unfamiliar cults. The migrations and new conquests of the High Middle Ages made such situations familiar. When the English and Welsh settled in Ireland they brought their saints with them, so that in thirteenth-century Dublin the feast of St Edward the Confessor was celebrated with 800 lighted candles, while St David's Day became a perfectly natural term for leases in early-fourteenth-century Munster. The crusades stimulated transplantations of this kind particularly intensely. On the one hand, itinerant crusaders picked up relics on their travels. Count Robert of Flanders, passing through Apulia on his way to participate in the First Crusade, obtained 'some of the hair of the blessed mother of God . . . and relics of St Matthew the Apostle and Nicholas, the confessor of Christ, whose bodies, there is no doubt, rest in Apulia'; these he sent back to his wife in Flanders. Over three years later, returning from Jerusalem, 'he brought with him the arm of St George the martyr, which he sent to the church of Anchin'. The sack of Constantinople in 1204 set off a massive explosion of relics, with fragments falling over every part of Europe in the years following. On the other hand, crusaders brought occidental saints to the East. In the 1190s the Frankish and Armenian populations of Antioch came to blows over whether a chapel should be dedicated to the Armenian

St Sarquis or to St Hilary of Poitiers, obviously an imported Gallic saint. A generation later, to honour the role of the English in the capture of Damietta in 1219, two mosques in the town were converted into churches and dedicated to their national saints, Edmund the Martyr and Thomas Becket. The erection of the shrine of a Suffolk saint in a great Egyptian port city vividly illustrates the new internationalism of the saints.

Our picture must, however, be complicated by one more factor. For the spread of some names or some saints from one part of Europe to another, by conquest or otherwise, was not the most important development of the twelfth and thirteenth centuries. Simultaneously changes were taking place in the very pattern of naming and worship of the saints throughout Latin Christendom. Everywhere the universal saints and the dominical cult were increasing in importance. The apostolic saints, especially Peter and John, the Mother of God, and God himself, as Trinity, Holy Saviour or Corpus Christi, were eclipsing the local shrines and cults of earlier medieval Europe. In the twelfth century, for example, the churches of Wales adopted universal saints, like Mary and Peter, as additional patrons, to reinforce their obscure local saints. In the thirteenth century, after the arrival of the friars, 'the cults of universal saints and their relics began to take strong hold in Brittany'. And, following in the wake of their rise to prominence, European naming patterns began to homogenize as parents, kin and priests began to choose names for children from these universal saints. The highly localized name repertoires of the early Middle Ages were replaced by a more standard pattern in which the universal saints were increasingly common.

Transformation and convergence – these are the two terms which describe the naming patterns of Europe in the medieval period. Two examples from specific families may be taken to illustrate these processes (see the genealogical charts, Figures 5 and 6). The first is the dynasty of the Scottish kings, the second that of the rulers of Mecklenburg (who had earlier been kings of the pagan Slav Abodrites). For the former we have a detailed genealogy going back deep into the early medieval period; for the latter we must rest content with a progenitor who lived around the middle of the twelfth century (his connection with earlier Abodrite kings is plausible but not provable). The absolute chronology of the two genealogies is thus different, but the relative chronology is strikingly similar. The early generations exhibit indisputably regional names. Duncan, Malcolm and Donald, for example, are names that would be found nowhere in Europe in the eleventh century except in Scotland. Similarly, Niklot, Pribislaw and Wartislaw mark out their bearers unequivocally as Slavs. However, within

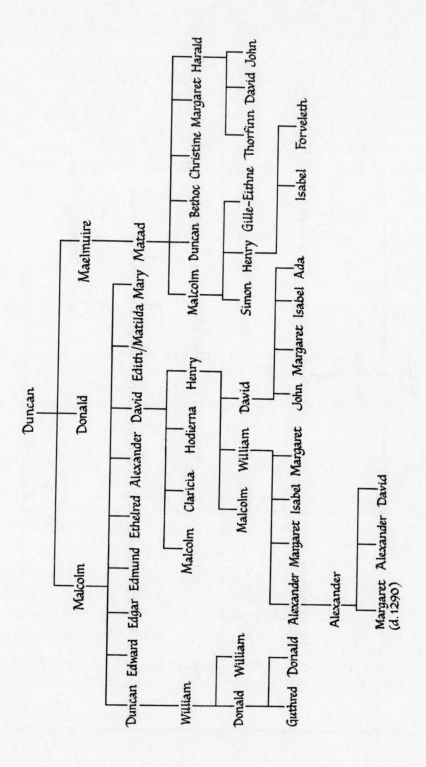

Figure 5. Descendants of Duncan I of Scotland (1034–40)

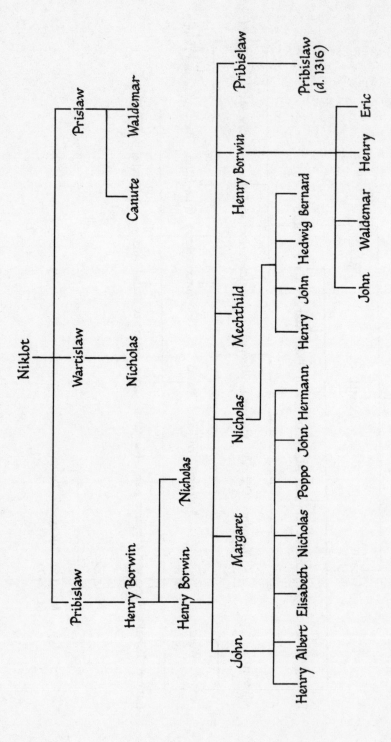

Figure 6. Descendants of Niklot, ruler of the Abodrites (Mecklenburg) (d. 1160)

both these dynasties a point is reached, in the late eleventh century in the Scottish case, a hundred years later in that of Mecklenburg, when a major transformation occurs in nomenclature. The Scots go through a brief Anglo-Saxon paroxysm and then settle down to a very syncretistic pattern, in which Gaelic names are unusual. In the fifth generation after Duncan I only two of a total of twelve names are Gaelic (and the only male example is in a dissident and excluded branch). For the rulers of Mecklenburg the change is equally marked. After 1200 their name choices are strongly influenced by new German imports. The generation of the late thirteenth century has only one Slavic name out of a total of sixteen.

Part of the change, both in Scotland and in Mecklenburg, is simple cultural emulation of a powerful neighbour. Scots called themselves William and Henry, the names of the Norman kings of England; the Slavs adopted Henry and Hedwig, the names of important German rulers and saints. Since these Norman and German traditions of the name Henry had themselves a common origin in the naming habits of the late Carolingian aristocracy, one can again see, in this small example, the impact of the Carolingian cultural sphere on lands and families on its fringes, slowly drawing them, even in their names, into its orbit of influence. Also important in the Scottish and Mecklenburg genealogies are the rising universal saints. The names John and Margaret, unknown in earlier generations, begin to appear in both dynasties from *c.* 1200. The first member of the Scottish royal line to be christened Margaret was the daughter of King William the Lion born between 1186 and 1195 (although the junior line of Matad of Atholl used the name somewhat earlier). She was clearly named after her royal ancestress, the wife of Malcolm Canmore, but that Margaret's name was itself a breach with prior family naming patterns in favour of the universal saints. The first John in the house of Mecklenburg was born around 1211. Saints' names were being adopted among the English and German populations in this very same period and hence here is another path towards convergence with their neighbours. The final result is a shift from the completely distinct Scottish and Mecklenburg name repertoires of the earlier period to a pool of names that overlaps both with neighbouring peoples and with each other. Up to the late twelfth century the rulers of Scotland and the Slav dynasty of Mecklenburg have no names in common; thereafter one finds certain names, sometimes Germanic, like Henry, but also saints' names, like John and Margaret, occurring in both families.

By the later Middle Ages the process of homogenization in naming patterns had gone far. Of the fourteenth-century town councillors of

Dresden, for example, over 30 per cent bore the name John, almost 24 per cent the name Nicholas, over 15 per cent the name Peter. The fact that almost 70 per cent of the councillors bore these three names is clear indication of a contraction in the name hoard; the fact that they bore, not Germanic names, but the names of apostolic or universally popular saints, shows the increasing cultural uniformity at work in this period. Everywhere the naming history of individual families is marked by a fissure, when the new, imported or self-consciously Christian names intrude on local practice. In Reconquest Toledo there are men called Dominic and John who are grandsons of a Suleiman; in twelfth-century Wales there is reference to 'Cadwgan ap Bleddyn's son, who had been born of the Frenchwoman and was called Henry'; in Mecklenburg many a Germanic-sounding Henry was the son of a Pribislaw or Plochimir. Sometimes the two strands of nomenclature delicately balanced for a while, as in the case of the two sons of the counts of Bar named Henry-James and Theobald-John: 'they thus had their names as nobles on the one hand and their names as Christians on the other'.

The evidence is not always unambiguous. Names in religion are a particular example. When the Czechs Radim and Milic took the names of Gaudentius and Daniel respectively, upon their elevation to the bishoprics of Gniezno (1000) and Prague (1197), the adoption of a Christian or biblical name upon consecration seems quite straightforward. More difficult to construe is the case of the bishop of Olomouc (Olmütz), consecrated in 1126: 'Zdik was ordained and, as he was ordained, put off his barbarous name and was called Henry.' Here the new name is not biblical, though it might be argued that it is a saint's name; what is apparent, however, is that a 'barbarous name' was exchanged for a German one. The expansion of the names of particular dominant groups and the simultaneous rise of certain saints' names cannot always be easily disentangled.

Names like Mary, Catherine, John and Nicholas, which we find in the later generations of the dynasties of Scotland and Mecklenburg, had a part to play in the process of ethnic integration. The adoption of common biblical or saints' names rather than ethnically distinct ones was one way that immigrants could diminish their cultural distinctiveness without completely aping the host population. For example, the Styrian aristocrats who entered the service of the king of Hungary in the twelfth century and eventually became known as the Hahót dynasty originally, of course, bore German names. Over the generations this changed (see Table 4). All three male members of the first two Hahót generations bore German names; about half of the members of the third generation did so; a quarter of the

Table 4. *Naming patterns of the Hahót family*

Generation	1	2	3	4	5
No. of males	1	2	12	20	11
No. of German names	1	2	7	5	1
No. of Magyar names	0	0	2	2	1

members of the fourth generation likewise; while by the fifth generation only one of the 11 male members of the family had a German name. But the level of Magyarization in this name hoard was slight: in the younger generations only 5 males of a total of 43 (11.6 per cent) bore Hungarian names. It was the common Christian names like John and Nicholas that predominated. The choice of such a name was a way of being neither assertively foreign nor assertively native.

The contraction of name repertoires and the efflorescence of pan-Christian names and saints can be seen in an extreme form in those parts of Europe which were conquered from Muslims or pagans in this period. In such areas, where a prior root-system of local saints was absent or tenuous, the universal saints came into their own. As pagan Prussia and Livonia were slowly conquered by Christians, it was that least localizable of all the saints, the Virgin Mary, who was adopted by the crusaders as patron of their newly Christian lands. An analysis of the dedications of churches and chapels in Prussia prior to 1350 shows that over 56 per cent of the total were Marian, dominical or apostolic. The remaining 44 per cent were to such popular and geographically widespread saints as Nicholas, George, Catherine and Lawrence. Very few of the dedications have a local character. It is true that the relatively large number of dedications to St Nicholas (8 of the total 83) is a characteristic feature of the Baltic littoral, and a few saints did have particular ties to Prussia, such as Adalbert, who was martyred there in the tenth century, and Barbara, whose head had come into the possession of the Teutonic Knights in the thirteenth century. But, on the whole, the titular saints of ecclesiastical establishments in Prussia do not display regional peculiarities. The very place names of Prussia – Marienwerder, Marienburg, Christburg – enshrined the new, less particularist Christianity that was absorbing the pagan world at its edges.

Reconquest Spain was another region where the reign of the Virgin Mary was particularly uncontested. Not only the cathedrals of the great

Reconquest cities, but dozens of churches in the newly settled villages bore her name. The military orders and Cistercians were active champions in this 'complete triumph of the cult of St Mary'. Similarly the apostles and other universal saints flourished in the Iberian peninsula, pushing the Visigothic martyr saints into the shadow. In Valencia, which fell to the Christians in 1238, the first ten churches to be established had the following dedications: the Holy Saviour, St Stephen, St Thomas, St Andrew, St Martin, St Catherine, St Nicholas, St Bartholomew, St Lawrence, St Peter. There is nothing distinctively Spanish about this. Nor, for that matter, if we look at the names of the first rectors of those ten churches, do we find much that would be surprising in other parts of Europe: three Peters, two Johns, two Williams, a Thomas, a Dominic and a (slightly more tell-tale) Raymond.

The cultural homogenization of naming patterns and saints' cults that took place in the High Middle Ages was not absolute. In the fourteenth century it is still possible to identify distinctive patterns in the names and preferred saints of different regions. In a German town of the Baltic we would find many men called John, Henry, Hermann and Nicholas, in a southern French town men called Peter, John, William and Raymond. The names Hermann and Nicholas suggest north Germany; the name Raymond suggests southern France. Yet none of these names is absolutely unique to a particular area and most of them could be found throughout Europe. The transformation of cult and nomenclature between the tenth and thirteenth centuries was thus not simply a matter of the spread of certain names and saints in the wake of conquest and colonization. This certainly did happen, but it was paralleled and encompassed by the other trend, a shift towards a universalist nomenclature and cult which was more than just a successful localism writ large. Just as the English peasants of the twelfth and thirteenth centuries adopted the names of their lords, so the European populace, when choosing their children's names, came to favour Mary and the apostles, those aristocrats among the saints.

COINS AND CHARTERS

A more obviously diffusionist picture, but one in which military conquest was even less important, emerges if we turn from saints and names to coins and charters, two other distinctive features of the cultural ensemble that came to constitute Europe. They are, of course, things that were made, not things that were said, and hence could not spread so freely as names or prayers. There are techniques for their manufacture and these had to be learned. But they can be learned, and the centuries between 950 and 1350 saw ever-increasing numbers of those who could make them and, as a consequence, ever-increasing numbers familiar with pennies and parchment.

The minting of silver coins was a technology that spread slowly across Europe. It was not discovered independently in several places, but had an identifiable point of origin and a recoverable history of diffusion. The production of silver pennies, the standard coin of around 1.7 grams issued by Charlemagne and immediately imitated by the Anglo-Saxon kings, was taken up at different times by different peoples. For example, before 900 there were no mints east of the Rhine; soon thereafter, however, minting of pennies on a large scale began in Saxony. From at least the middle of the tenth century the Bohemian dukes minted silver pennies (by now of around 1.2 grams) that drew directly on English models. Slightly later, perhaps from 980 or so, the Polish dukes did likewise. It appears to be a pattern that the minting of coins followed shortly after conversion to Christianity. The establishment of the first Christian hierarchy in Hungary and the beginnings of a Hungarian coinage both date to 1000–1001. In Denmark, although there had been a light coinage minted in the trading centre of Hedeby in the ninth and tenth centuries, the first apparently royal Scandinavian currency was that issued by Harald Bluetooth (d. *c.* 985), the king who, in his own words, 'won for himself all Denmark and Norway and made the Danes Christians', and the first heavy penny coinage in Denmark was that of his son Sweyn Forkbeard (*c.* 985–1014). Contemporary with Sweyn Forkbeard's native silver coinage is that of Olaf Tryggvason of Norway and Olaf Sköttkonung of Sweden. The millennium thus sees a burst of new mints from the middle Danube to the Baltic and North Sea coasts.

Not all these new princely Christian currencies lasted. In Poland there is a hiatus of half a century (1020–70) before Boleslaw II reinstated native mints, and in Sweden minting was eclipsed for an even longer period as a native coinage ceased for over a century after *c.* 1030. In other regions, however, the tenth-century revolution was definitive. Canute the Great minted large numbers of pennies, at five Danish sites, especially Lund, some of which carry Christian texts. Even in the case of Poland, with its long eleventh-century gap, minting was eventually resumed with vigour. Boleslaw II issued around 2 million silver pennies (of about 0.8 grams) in the 1070s.

A comparably erratic entry into the world of the mint took place in

Ireland around the millennium. In 997 the Norse kings of Dublin initiated a silver coinage imitating English models and even using some stolen English die stamps. The rulers of Man followed their example in the 1030s. This tradition was not major or enduring, however, and the effective introduction of the mint into the Celtic world was a consequence of the Anglo-Norman expansion of the later eleventh and twelfth centuries. In Wales, Norman conquerors had established mints at Rhuddlan, Cardiff and possibly St David's by 1087, and others followed later. In Ireland the year 1185 marks the definitive establishment of minting in the country, when silver halfpennies were issued at Dublin in the name of John, lord of Ireland, the son of King Henry II. It is possible that the kings of Connacht or Leinster issued some bracteates (thin, single-sided coins) around the middle of the twelfth century, but in general it is true to say that the native rulers of Wales and Ireland never developed their own mints, and their vassals and subjects relied for minted coin on the silver currency produced by Anglo-Norman settlers or by the kingdom of England.

A quite different story is found in Scotland, although its situation in the early twelfth century was comparable to that of Ireland or Wales, since at that time there was no native currency and all monetary transactions involved the use of imported English coin. In 1140 or thereabouts, however, David I of Scotland began minting his own silver pennies. This was a period when several feudal lords were eroding the English royal monopoly of issuing coin, but only the kings of Scots maintained their own currency after the authority of the English Crown was re-established in the 1150s. Although English coins were everyday objects north of the border and the Scottish penny was clearly an imitation of the English, there was now a silver coinage that bore the name of the king of Scots.

In this respect, as in several others, developments in Scotland were not like those in other lands of Celtic or partly Celtic tradition. They are closer, in fact, to those in the West Slav regions between the Elbe and the Oder, whose rulers also consciously strengthened their polities in the twelfth and thirteenth centuries by encouraging foreign immigrants, enfeoffing foreign knights and drastically remodelling their institutions (which, in the West Slav case, involved the adoption of Christianity too). Around the middle of the twelfth century these West Slav tribes, the Wends as they are generically known, had no native coinage. The chronicler Helmold observed that the Rani, who lived on the island of Rügen, 'have no money and do not customarily employ coins in their buying and selling, but whatever you want to purchase in the market, you pay for with a linen cloth'. This use of cloths of standard size as a medium of exchange among the West Slavs had been remarked upon by the Jewish merchant Ibrahim ibn Jacub as early as the tenth century. In the second quarter of the twelfth century, just like the Scots, the Slavs east of the Elbe began silver minting. West Slav princes in Old Lübeck, Brandenburg and Köpenick issued coins modelled on those of Germany or Bohemia (see the coins of Henry Pribislav of Brandenburg and Jacza of Köpenick illustrated in Plate 10). From *c.* 1170 the princes of Pomerania, Mecklenburg and Rügen began striking their own coins at towns along the south Baltic coast. Finally, in the thirteenth century, the establishment of German colonial centres in the south-east and eastern Baltic brought the technology and ideology of minting to the whole Baltic littoral.

Once monetization began, it could develop very rapidly. Scotland had no mints in 1100; by 1300 the Scottish coinage amounted to 40 million silver pennies. As in the case of naming patterns, transformation also involved convergence, for the coinages of northern and eastern Europe were modelled on those of England and Germany, which were both themselves of ultimately Carolingian ancestry, and the silver coinages of non–Mediterranean Europe thus formed an identifiable family. As physical artefacts the pennies of, say, early–twelfth–century Scotland, Scandinavia and eastern Europe were recognizably akin. Even in the Crusader States a Frankish-style silver coinage was struck from the 1140s, consisting of coins that 'were quite exceptional in that part of the world' and can only be understood in the context of western colonial expansion.

At the same time as this wave of silver pennies spread through Europe, another artefact was following the same route. This was the charter, the formal written grant, usually on parchment and sealed. It had various antecedents, but the most important were again Carolingian. The charter, like the penny, diffused gradually into eastern and northern Europe.

The sequence of charters in a newly documented region follows a fairly regular pattern:

(1) The earliest documentary material concerning the area in question usually consists of grants of land or rights within the area by authorities outside it. Papal bulls are a common example.
(2) Later there are grants of lands or rights within the area made by local ecclesiastics.
(3) At a yet later stage grants are made in the name of local secular rulers, but the documents themselves are prepared by the recipients, invariably churches or religious houses or orders.
(4) Finally we see the birth of native secular chancelleries, undertaking the routine issue of documents from the ruler's or magnate's household.

The sequence is well exemplified in the Slav principality of Pomerania. In this case, stage (1) was reached in the 1130s, when popes and emperors began to claim to make dispositions regarding Pomerania or parts of it. A more crucial moment was the establishment of an independent Pomeranian bishopric in 1140, which was a necessary preliminary to the second stage, the issue of a document by a native ecclesiastic. It was Bishop Adalbert, the first incumbent of the see, who caused such a document to be drawn up some time between 1155 and 1164. This was the written confirmation of the endowment of the Benedictine monastery of Stolpe on the Peene, founded by monks from Berg near Magdeburg. 'In nomine sancte et individue Trinitatis. Adelbertus dei gratia primus Pomeranorum episcopus' ('In the name of the holy and undivided Trinity, Adalbert, by grace of God first bishop of the Pomeranians'), it begins, proclaiming, in form, language and content, the opening of a new age in Pomeranian history as well as the birth of a new form of evidence for that history. The German monks who witnessed the document would be familiar with such proceedings, but the scratch of the quill, the curl of the parchment and the smell of hot wax may have been a less routine experience for the 'noble laymen Panteyen and Domazlau', who also witnessed it.

The 1150s and 1160s saw the continued issue of papal and imperial documents pertaining to Pomerania, and a few more by the bishops of Pomerania. The charter of 1159 issued by Bishop Adalbert, which survived in the original in Szczecin at least until World War II, is, if still extant, the oldest surviving charter issued in Pomerania. Some years later, in 1174, we reach stage (3), with the charter of Duke Casimir I for the Cistercian monastery of Dargun. Here a Pomeranian prince speaks for the first time in his own person, though, of course, in borrowed accents: 'Ego Kazimarus Diminensium et Pomeranorum princeps' ('I, Casimir, prince of the men of Demmin and the Pomeranians'). Attached to this charter is the oldest surviving seal of a Pomeranian duke. From the 1170s on, the production of charters in the name of the dukes of Pomerania, as well as the continued issue of documents by popes, emperors and Pomeranian bishops, is regular. Charters of Bogislaw II (d. 1220), for example, survive from 1187, between 1191–4 (both during his minority), between 1200–1208 (two), 1208, 1212–13 (two), 1214 (two), 1216, 1218 (two) and 1219 (two). This makes a total of twelve charters over the twenty years or so of his adult rule. The likelihood is that these documents were produced by the recipient, as we know explicitly in the case of a charter of his uncle Casimir, which is in favour of the monastery of Kolbacz and includes the clause 'These were made by the hand of the lord abbot Eberhard' (*Per manum domini Everardi abbatis facta sunt hec).* A ducal chancery (stage (4)) seems to have come into existence during the reign of Wartislaw III (d. 1264).

Between the early twelfth century and the latter part of the thirteenth Pomerania thus made the transition from a non-literate and undocumented region to the world of the chancery. Its official practices had been reshaped according to the models of Latin literacy, documentary thinking and bureaucratic organization prevalent among its powerful western neighbours. The Pomeranian experience was, in this respect, not unusual. In Silesia, although the region had been Christianized much earlier than Pomerania, the first indigenous document dates to only 1139, the first secular charter to 1175 and a chancery to the years after 1240. An early medieval tradition of written record existed in the Celtic countries, but the late eleventh and twelfth centuries saw both the introduction of new Carolingian models and an increase in charter production. Around 1100 the Scottish kings began the issue of 'the sealed writ, a Latin document of Anglo-Saxon origin, adapted and developed in Norman England and now transferred to Scotland', with its appended image of the king in majesty. It has been commented of the charters issued by Earl David of Huntingdon (1152–1219), the brother of King William the Lion, that 'it is impossible to tell from physical characteristics whether an act was issued in Scotland or England'. In Ireland the first charters of continental type were issued by the native kings in the middle decades of the twelfth century. The earliest surviving original charter is a grant made by Dermot Mac-Murrough, king of Leinster, in the early 1160s. This is the same ruler who was responsible for the introduction of Anglo-Norman arms into Ireland, and it has been argued that the adoption by such princes of the continental Latin charter tradition was but part of a process of 'modernization and Europeanization'.

The spread of documentation into the continental peripheries coincided with a vast increase in the quantity of written record in the central, post-Carolingian parts of Europe, that movement that has been characterized as the 'shift from sacral script to practical literacy'. In Picardy the documentation of the twelfth century dwarfs that of all previous centuries, and that of the thirteenth century is four times as great as that of the twelfth. Over this same period formal chanceries were being organized throughout Europe, chanceries of common type, for it was 'the Carolingian chancery [that] fathered all the chanceries of medieval Europe'. More and more, in the duchies of Poland as in the valleys of the Seine or Rhine, men were deciding 'it is necessary that a matter worthy of memory should be confirmed in writing, so that hoary deeds of long ago may be repeatedly renewed'.

The silver penny and the post-Carolingian charter can be used as trace elements or indicators, whose paths of diffusion alert us to wider and less visible currents of change. The drawing up of the first charters and the minting of the first pennies by the kings of Scots in the late eleventh and twelfth centuries, or by the Slav dynasties between the Elbe and the Oder in the mid- to late twelfth century, reflect the fuller and deeper incorporation of Scotland and the trans-Elbian lands into the Latin and Frankish world. It is not only as indicators, however, that the penny and the formal charter have importance. They are not simply artefacts, like pots of a certain style or tools of a certain shape, whose spread can be taken as evidence of migration, trade or influence. For while coins and charters are, of course, artefacts, they are artefacts of a very special type and it is this that made their adoption of particular significance. Their power does not reside in a purely material efficacy. A small disc of metal and a piece of sheepskin have little intrinsic utility – unlike the pot or tool. Their power lies, instead, in the way they objectify human relationships.

Money can be conventional in many different ways. If one chooses to allow the term 'money' to apply to the cattle by which power or obligation were measured in some early medieval societies, then here was a medium of exchange that could be eaten. And, in some circumstances, whether it could be eaten might be the only relevant question to ask of wealth. At the other extreme, modern paper money not only cannot be eaten, but cannot be employed for any other useful purpose – not even for writing on, since the state has already pre-empted us here. The silver coinage of the period after cows and before banknotes was intermediate: it had no intrinsic utility, but the material of which it was made, silver, did have high exchange value apart from the particular form which the authorities stamped upon it.

Nevertheless, the stamping by the authorities made a difference. Coins were not simply bullion (though they could sometimes be treated as such). Rather they were, or were intended to be, tokens of a universal medium of exchange whose predictable worth was authenticated by the powers above. As such, they had both a utility for the peasant at market and an attraction for the lord and his moneyer. Economic transactions and accounting were facilitated at the same time as kings were gratified by sending out their image and their name in millions of copies to every part of their realm and beyond; for, as Ptolemy of Lucca put it: 'nothing which pertains to a king or lord is handled by men so much as the coin . . . coinage makes a lord's majesty shine out'. Between the tenth and the thirteenth centuries authorities over an ever-widening area sought the regalian gratification of their own minted coinage.

The formal charter shared some, but not all, of the characteristics of the minted coin. Unlike silver pennies, charters had no material value distinct from the form whose conventions they followed. Take away the round shape and the king's name from a penny, and one would have a valuable lump of alloyed silver. Remove the words from the charter, however, and its social meaning would disappear. Nevertheless, the charter and the coin were alike in being conventional objectifications of social meanings. The charter at first recorded and later actually effected a transfer of wealth or authority and the creation of new sets of relationships. Its possession, like the possession of a coin, gave power that was removed from either physical strength or the immediate possession of usable material goods. Charters and coins gave incarnation to the most abstract aspect of social relations: rights and claims, much less tangible than grass and beef, were hereby given tangible form.

This tangibility made money and charters manipulable; their conventional form, small, durable objects, meant that this manipulation could be extremely elastic and convenient. They were portable; they could be stored. Power could be focused in treasuries and archives, whose diverse contents – pennies or grants – represented equally promises to pay. The loss of a royal baggage train, like Philip Augustus's at the rout of Fréteval in 1194, was a state disaster not only because of the chests full of pennies that were lost but also because of the disappearance of the king's seal, financial records and other documents. When Edward I of England wished to underline his destruction of the regality of the Welsh princes of Gwynedd in the late thirteenth century, he not only dispossessed them and hunted them down, but had the metal matrices of their seals melted to make into a chalice for his favourite abbey. Everywhere in the twelfth and thirteenth centuries prudent powers began to assemble boxes of charters as well as barrels of pennies. Both were nuggets of social power; or, more appropriately, both were a currency.

The minting of coins and the issue of written dispositions changed the political culture of the societies in which these new practices appeared. The spread of these forms into new parts of north-western, northern and eastern Europe in the period between the tenth and the thirteenth centuries thus not only marks the outward dynamic of Frankish aristocracies and traders; it also measures the adaptability of the non-Frankish regimes to novel sources of power. Many Celtic or Slavic lords were willing to seize these new objectifying conventions to raise themselves yet higher in the saddle, even if they ended up riding a horse of a different colour.

THE UNIVERSITY

Europeanization meant not only the spread of certain elements of linguistic and religious culture or the dissemination of new artefacts of power, but also the development of new institutional agencies of cultural change. The chartered town and the international religious order are two examples that have been discussed earlier. Another important agency of integration was the university.

The university was one of the most powerful instruments of cultural homogeneity to arise in the High Middle Ages. Growing gradually from the schools of logic, law and theology of the eleventh and twelfth centuries, these international centres of learning and education had, by the thirteenth century, acquired something like their modern form: corporate, degree-granting institutions run by teachers who lectured to, disciplined and examined students. Their geographical distribution was very uneven. France and Italy were easily predominant both in numbers of universities and in the fact that each possessed one of the outstanding academic centres of the Middle Ages – Paris, for arts and theology; Bologna, for law. The Iberian kingdoms and England also had universities in the thirteenth century, but these were far less important than those of France or Italy. Beyond this area – which would be roughly included in a triangle with its angles at Cambridge, Seville and Salerno – there were no universities before 1350. In the thirteenth and early fourteenth centuries, therefore, anyone outside this academic triangle, that is, anyone from Germany, Scandinavia, eastern Europe or the Celtic countries, who wished for a formal higher education, had to travel, to go from Dublin to Oxford, from Norway to Paris, from Bavaria to Bologna. As described in Chapter 9, Stephen of Lexington, who conducted a visitation of the Cistercian monasteries in Ireland in 1228, lamented the preponderance of monoglot Irish among the monks and 'enjoined that, if henceforth they wish an Irishman to be received into the order, they make sure to send him to Paris or Oxford or some other renowned city to learn letters and eloquence'. A kind of metropolitan cultural dominance had been established.

Most of these itinerant students eventually returned home, and the more successful of them attained high ecclesiastical and political positions in their native societies. Thus, by 1300, the non-military élite of the Latin West was being shaped by a standard educational experience. There was a uniformity to their technical language, intellectual habits, pedagogic expectations and teenage memories. By the thirteenth century the great prelates who helped run Europe had a common collegiate background in the lecture rooms of Paris and Bologna.

The example of Denmark shows how this process operated in detail. In the Viking Age, the ninth, tenth and eleventh centuries, the Danes had been pagan, non-literate raiders and traders, whose periodic attacks inspired terror in the Christian lands of the West. During the late tenth and eleventh centuries a very gradual process of conversion, supported by Danish kings, began to incorporate the Danes into the Christian Church. By 1100 there were eight bishoprics in Denmark, and in 1104 one of them, Lund, was raised to archiepiscopal status, thus completing the development of the standard ecclesiastical hierarchy in this part of Scandinavia. The introduction of Christian ritual and the establishment of the institutions of the Church were preconditions for the deeper cultural incorporation of Denmark which took place from the twelfth century onwards. One perceptive observer, the German chronicler Arnold of Lübeck, writing around 1200, noticed the ways that the Danes had 'adjusted themselves to other nations'. Among other things, such as their adoption of German costume and of the mounted warfare characteristic of feudal Europe, he pointed to their intellectual pilgrimages:

They are also distinguished in their knowledge of letters since the nobles send their sons to Paris, not only to secure promotion in the Church, but also to instruct them in secular affairs. There they become proficient both in letters and the local vernacular and excel in the liberal arts and theology. Indeed, because of their natural facility of tongue, they are not only subtle logicians but also excellent canon and civil lawyers when dealing with ecclesiastical business.

One aristocratic Dane who acquired such familiarity with the learning of the Latin West was Anders Sunesen, who was archbishop of Lund from 1201 to 1224. A Dane of high birth destined for the Church, he took a period of study abroad for granted; before the twelfth century such a plan would have been unusual. Sunesen studied at the very best academic centres, visiting France, Italy and England, and acquired a respectable body of theological and legal learning. The training he received, in combination with his aristocratic birth, obviously made him an attractive prospect for potential employers and patrons in both the lay and the ecclesiastical establishment in his native country and, upon his return to Denmark, he was soon appointed chancellor to the king and provost of Roskilde cathedral. The prior expansion of royal administration and the creation of an endowed church had provided a niche for such educated men.

Sunesen had gone abroad to seek contemporary learning that was not available in his own country, and after his return to Denmark he tried to make sure that such learning became more accessible at home. He produced two extant works in Latin. The first is his *Hexaemeron*, a verse compendium of Christian doctrine heavily dependent upon the Paris theologians of the twelfth century and best described as a work of *haute vulgarization*, presenting the latest Paris ideas in a simplified way. His other surviving work represents a rather more complex interplay between the native and the imported. It is a Latin version of the customary laws of Scania, at that time a part of Denmark. Now these laws also survive in the vernacular and hence it is possible to compare them with Sunesen's Latin version. The comparison shows that his translation of the native laws is very free and that many traces of his training in Roman law intrude themselves. Rules of inheritance which are simply stated in the vernacular text are 'ordained by natural equity' in Sunesen's. Thus Sunesen's version shared characteristics of two cultures. It was based on the traditional native laws, customary in origin, oral in transmission, but as it rendered them into the universal language of learning, Latin, it classicized and Romanized them in tone.

Sunesen's activities were not limited to the purely literary or cultural. He was also, for a full generation, the head of the Danish church, and was an active and innovative head. He campaigned against clerical marriage, held reforming councils and, in 1223, founded the first Dominican house in Denmark. In addition, he was deeply involved in the establishment of the new missionary church in the eastern Baltic, the lands of the pagan Estonians and Livonians. In 1206–7 he preached and participated in a crusade against the Estonians, spent the winter giving theological instruction to the missionaries and, in the spring, 'after taking the children of the Livonian aristocracy as hostages, had priests sent out to preach'. Later, in 1219–20, he was left in charge of the fortress of Reval (Tallinn) after the Danes had conquered it, weathered a siege by the pagans and continued evangelization. He concentrated on the symbolic essentials: wooden crosses were set up in the pagan villages and teams organized to distribute holy water.

Anders Sunesen was both an agent and a beneficiary or recipient of the Europeanization process. In Paris he could learn from men with generations of scholastic discourse behind them and participated in the cultural life of a pre-eminent academic centre, where new translations from Greek and Arabic were beginning to circulate and where the formal structures of the university were taking shape. In his dealings with the Estonians he confronted a non-literate, polytheistic Finno-Ugric people whose cultural and social distance from Latin Christendom was enormous. Denmark acted as a middle point. On the one hand, its ecclesiastical establishment was comparatively young and its Latin culture still thin. It needed Sunesen's simplified textbooks. On the other, it was a centre for the Christianization and cultural transformation of the Estonians. Denmark was a transmitter of religious and cultural forms and patterns even before it had fully assimilated them itself.

In contrast to the early Middle Ages, the pace of cultural change in the twelfth and thirteenth centuries was much hotter. For example, while the Benedictine monasticism of the earlier period had taken over five centuries to spread from its Italian homeland to Scandinavia, Sunesen founded a Dominican house in Lund only seven years after the official foundation of the Dominican Order and, indeed, while St Dominic himself was still alive. This is partly explained by organizational characteristics of the Dominicans, such as their ability to survive without the massive endowments of earlier monasticism, but that itself is an important fact about the High Middle Ages as compared with earlier centuries – the mechanisms of communication and transmission were that much faster and better oiled. One of the results of this was the starker juxtaposition of contrasting worlds – the evangelization of the pagans of Estonia was organized by a man who had studied in the schoolrooms of France and Italy.

By 1300 Europe existed as an identifiable cultural entity. It could be described in more than one way, but some common features of its cultural face are the saints, names, coins, charters and educational practices touched upon in this chapter. By the late medieval period Europe's names and cults were more uniform than they had ever been; Europe's rulers everywhere minted coins and depended upon chanceries; Europe's bureaucrats shared a common experience of higher education. This is the Europeanization of Europe.

12. The Political Sociology of Europe after the Expansion

This land was completely transformed by them.

THE CHANGING SHAPE OF EUROPEAN CHRISTENDOM

One aspect of the expansion of Latin Christendom in the High Middle Ages was geopolitical. Between 950 and 1350 Latin Christendom roughly doubled in area, and, while this religious expansion did not always involve either conquest or immigration, it often did. In the Iberian peninsula, in the Crusader States of the eastern Mediterranean and in many parts of eastern Europe, the incorporation of new territories into the framework of the Roman Church was accompanied by the establishment of new military and clerical élites and the settlement of urban and rural colonists. As a consequence the geography of power changed. Places which had been the victimized sufferers of pagan or Muslim attack became the attackers in their turn. Hamburg, whose fields were plundered by pagan Slavs as late as 1110, was, in the fourteenth century, one of the leading cities of the Hanseatic league, whose merchants had planted Christian German trading cities the length of the Baltic coast. The lower Elbe was no longer a precarious frontier, but the fulcrum of a vast trading system linking London and Novgorod. Similarly, in the tenth century Saracen raiders had roamed the Tyrrhenian coast freely; in 1004 they sailed up the Arno and burnt Pisa. Soon, however, the Pisans were taking the fighting to the Muslim cities of Sicily and Africa. In 1087 a big expedition of Pisans, Amalfitans and Genoese sacked the north African port of al-Mahdiyyah and massacred its inhabitants. The plunder was used in part to adorn the cathedral of the Virgin Mary at Pisa and build the church of San Sisto in Cortevecchia. Yesterday's prey were today's predators. Or, again, Barcelona was sacked by al-Mansur, the great Cordoban general, in 985, but by 1350 the Catalans were running a Mediterranean empire. All along the borders of Latin Christendom there was thus a dramatic reversal of the pattern of victimization. Places like Hamburg, Pisa and Barcelona lost their frontier status and became instead prosperous centres of colonizing and mercantile activity.

From the eleventh century the mariners of western Europe showed a power they had not previously possessed, the ability to land armies at almost any point in their known world. From the time of the Pisan–Genoese conquest of Sardinia that began in 1016 the Italians were increasingly in control of the Mediterranean sea routes. Almeria, al-Mahdiyyah, Damietta, Constantinople: armies of western knights could be set down at any point in the Mediterranean basin, even if what happened to them thereafter was not always fortunate – the military superiority of western armies was not perhaps as clear-cut as the naval superiority of their ship-borne counterparts. From the twelfth century the Germans were making the Baltic a Catholic lake, with Lübeck as its focal point. From the mouth of the Trave, German expeditionary forces sailed almost yearly to establish the Germanized and Christianized rim of the Baltic, which eventually stretched from Lübeck to Finland. Danish and Swedish fleets shared in this process. The day of the pagan forces who had criss-crossed the Baltic on plundering raids was over. Just like Muslim sea power in the Mediterranean, pagan sea power in the north was checked and rolled back. The dominance of Christian navies was a distinctive feature of the High Middle Ages.

Gradually western merchants reached out to all the transit points where their own society had contact with the rest of the Old World. Penetrating the Baltic the Germans established trading posts in Novgorod and Smolensk. A little to the south, in Kiev, one could meet Italian merchants coming from Constantinople. The maritime trading networks of the Venetians and Genoese extended from the Black Sea, throughout the entire length of the Mediterranean and, eventually, via the Atlantic to Bruges and Southampton. Here the Italians and Hanseatic merchants rubbed shoulders. The commercial expansion of the High Middle Ages took the form of a gigantic double pincer movement, hinged on Hamburg and Lübeck in the north and Genoa and Venice in the south, whereby Italians stretched eastwards to Egypt and Russia and westwards to north Africa and the Atlantic, while Germans entered Eurasia via the Baltic rivers as well as trading west to the cloth towns of Flanders and the wool markets of England. The trading cities of Germany and Italy simultaneously expanded and integrated the economy and culture of the West.

Another important geopolitical change that resulted from high medieval expansion stemmed from a curious feature of Latin Christendom in the early and High Middle Ages, that its symbolic centres, those places that generated its religious coherence and provided its mental identity, were far removed from its political and (to a lesser degree) economic centres. This is clear in the case of Rome. At the beginning of the tenth century the city was located on the edge of Latin Christendom, within a hundred miles of Saracen bases and Greek churches, its port prey to Muslim pirates. Connections with Rome's more distant ecclesiastical subjects, in Asturias, Ireland or Scotland, were tenuous. Over the course of the eleventh and twelfth centuries, as Latin rule was established in southern Italy and the islands of the central Mediterranean, this precariousness diminished. Yet Rome itself, and its hinterland, never occupied that central position attained politically and culturally by the north of France, or economically by Lombardy, Flanders or the Rhineland. Pilgrims visiting Rome from Paris, Milan or even London went to a city immeasurably rich in its ancient imperial traditions, its holy bones and its churches, but they did not move from political, economic or cultural peripheries towards the centre. Rome was metropolitan only in the formal legal sense. Indeed, one of the arguments advanced in favour of siting the papacy in Avignon in the fourteenth century was that 'it is more equidistant from the modern boundaries of the Catholic Church'.

Especially in the early Middle Ages, the correlation between the physically peripheral and the religiously central was quite high. Pilgrimage centres were supposed to be at the ends of the earth. Not only did this make them suitable as sites for liminal experiences, but it meant that they really did serve one of the common purposes of pilgrimage, the penitential function. Places like Santiago in north-west Spain or, in a more minor key, St David's on the west coast of Wales were located at the very edge of the dry land. The situation of the Holy Land was even more eccentric. Jerusalem, the birthplace and symbolic heart of Christianity, the heavenly city which represented and consummated every local city of the West, the goal of Christian pilgrimage and martial endeavour for centuries, was at the extreme eastern limit of Latin power, 2,000 miles from the valleys of the Rhine, Seine or Thames, and in Christian hands for a total of only ninety-nine years in the entire medieval period. Yet its physical and verbal representations could be found everywhere in the West, where churches were dedicated to, and supposedly modelled on, the Holy Sepulchre, and the Templars took the name of Solomon's Temple to their settlements in every part of western Europe.

The changes of the High Middle Ages meant that these sites of great cultural significance became much less geographically peripheral. Jerusalem was actually under Christian rule for a century. Rome could now look south to the Latin churches of the kingdom of Sicily or eastwards to Frankish Greece. Santiago, which had lost its great bells to the Muslim expedition of al-Mansur in 997, saw them restored from the mosque at Cordoba when that city fell to Ferdinand III in 1236: the vulnerable shrine-city of the tenth century was now buffered by miles of Christian territory. Thus, by the thirteenth century the symbolic centre of gravity of Latin Christendom had come much closer to its socio-economic centre of gravity. Its holy places and its most populous cities, its shrines and its productive centres were more closely tied together than in the early Middle Ages.

The long frontier of Catholic Europe, which extended from Spain to Finland, consisted of two very distinct zones. In the Mediterranean, Catholics confronted Muslim (and Greek) societies which were at least as wealthy, as urbanized and as literate as their own. While those they faced were abhorrent to them on grounds of religious belief, they were adherents of monotheistic, scriptural, revealed and – whatever the less informed might claim – non-idolatrous religions. The situation in eastern and northern Europe was entirely different. Here Catholics encountered less populous, less urbanized and non-literate societies, whose religions were local, polytheistic and idolatrous. This fundamental distinction between the Mediterranean Muslim and the European pagan had important consequences for both the actual process of conquest and conversion and the intellectual and doctrinal position of the Church.

The first major consequence is the fact that in northern and eastern Europe conversion to Christianity could be seen as one aspect of a wider reorientation or, more precisely, 'occidentation', a shift towards the ways and norms of Romano-Germanic civilization as it had developed in the territories of the former Carolingian empire. The incorporation of the pagan West Slavs into Catholic Christendom in the twelfth century coincided with the beginnings of documentary literacy, the creation of chartered towns and the introduction of minting. The arrival of writing, towns and money was part of a large social and cultural transformation in which Christianization had a vital but not an exclusive role. The pagan aristocracies were themselves aware of the prestige and power of the Christian world and they characteristically converted earlier than the mass of the population. In one debate which took place during a missionary campaign in 1128, the group among the pagan Pomeranians who favoured conversion argued 'that it was incredibly stupid to separate themselves like miscarried children from the lap of Holy Mother Church, when all the provinces of the surrounding nations and the whole Roman world had submitted to the yoke of the Christian faith'. We may note, in passing, that this tendentious piece of pleading is recorded by a Christian author, but need not doubt that the allure of 'the whole Roman world' was an important force for conversion. As early as the eighth century Christian missionaries had been advised to remind pagans of 'the dignity of the Christian world, in comparison with which they are very few indeed who still keep to their ancient superstition'.

In the Mediterranean the situation was not at all comparable. Here, it seems, the submission of Muslims to Christians was almost invariably the consequence of military defeat, and the rate of conversion from Islam to Christianity was very low. Muslims had a far more articulated and universalist religion than the pagans of eastern and northern Europe and could rely on written scripture, their own law and the prospect of help from, or refuge among, coreligionists in neighbouring Islamic countries. They were part of a wider world which easily matched the West in power, wealth and culture.

The difference in the colonial situation on these two sectors of the Catholic frontier was intensified by the different attitudes of Christian authorities regarding the rights of unbelievers to practise their religion. In the case of polytheistic idolatrous paganism no official sanction was ever granted. Sometimes the sheer expediencies of power meant that popular syncretism did exist, but no Christian ruler or ecclesiastical establishment ever conceded approval to pagan cult. Indeed, sometimes major disruptions of the native class structure were engineered simply to protect the neophyte and repress the apostate. In Prussia the Teutonic Knights, who were faced with major rebellions like the 'Great Apostasy' of 1260, dealt with the situation by making loyalty, as expressed in persistence in the Christian faith, the major test applied to the local population. Loyal natives were granted personal liberty and favourable inheritance rights whatever their earlier status had been in Prussian law. Political loyalty was equated with the abandonment of non-Christian religion.

In the Mediterranean, however, Muslim communities were often conceded rights like those of the Jews, that is, the guarantee that they could continue communal worship undisturbed within certain limits. In Spain, while the chief mosques in the cities conquered from Muslims were indeed converted into churches, the Mudejars, Muslim subjects of Christian kings, continued to practise the Islamic religion down to the early sixteenth century. As the historian Robert I. Burns, writing of Valencia, puts it: 'In this Christian land far more muezzins could be heard calling from minarets than bells clanging in steeples.'

One apparently paradoxical result of this difference in Christian policy regarding paganism and Islam was the fact that the native inhabitants in the Mediterranean area were much more clearly recognizable as a subordinate and colonial population than many of those in the north and east. In pagan eastern Europe the choice was a sharp one between resistance and conversion, and many shrewd native dynasties and élites chose the latter. In the Mediterranean there was a third possibility, that of continued existence as a defeated but tolerated community. Hence in regions like Scandinavia and the West Slav principalities there was no political hiatus at conversion, and native dynasties remained in power. The grand dukes of Mecklenburg, for example, who ruled until 1918, were direct descendants of the twelfth-century pagan prince Niklot. In the Mediterranean native rulers exercised authority only within the protected but separated community of unbelievers, the *dhimmi* to use the equivalent Muslim term.

It is clearly the case that many of the institutions and experiences of new settlement in the peripheral parts of Europe were identical to those in the core. When land was cleared and settled in western Germany, France or England, favourable conditions, such as low rents and free status, were often granted to the colonists; their early years might be just as hard as for those involved in the *Ostsiedlung*. The establishment of new towns took very similar forms within the core and on the external frontiers. Princes like Henry the Liberal, count of Champagne in the late twelfth century, clearing scrub and building mills, or his contemporary Philip of Alsace, count of Flanders, minting increasing amounts of coin, draining land and founding towns, were entrepreneurs of settlement and economic development in the same sense as their contemporaries active on the frontiers of Christendom, such as Wichmann of Magdeburg.

Two things, however, distinguished the external frontier from the internal: one was the scale of settlement. In the Iberian peninsula and in eastern Europe new settlement often involved planning on a vast scale. Thousands of acres might be involved, and immigrants might number in the tens of thousands. In the Toledo region the 100 or so settlements that existed at the time of the Christian Reconquest of 1085 were augmented by 80 new settlements established in the succeeding centuries by the Christians. It has been estimated that almost 100 towns and 1,000 villages were established under the auspices of the Teutonic Knights in Prussia and that the course of the thirteenth and early fourteenth centuries saw the creation of 120 towns and 1,200 villages in Silesia. Only a very few parts of the central area of western Europe could show anything like this in the Middle Ages. Domesday Book England had scarcely any spaces of this kind. In Picardy it has been calculated that about 75,000 acres were cleared systematically in the High Middle Ages, an area which represents only 1.2 per cent of the total territory of Picardy. Even if gradual peasant nibbling at forest and waste, which went largely unrecorded, is included at the generous estimate of 300,000 to 375,000 acres, total clearance would still only represent 7 per cent of the surface.

The second major hallmark of the external frontier was that it brought into contact people of different races, languages or religions. In the case of new settlement in the central regions the newcomers might at first be resented or mistrusted, but within a generation social contacts, intermarriage, property transfers and familiarity would make the host population and the migrants completely indistinguishable. Such a process could occur on the external frontier, but the cultural barriers between migrant and native were much more enduring. The peripheries of Europe were charged with racial, religious and linguistic tension. A new town in Wales or Silesia meant something different from a new town in Bedfordshire or Westphalia simply because the new form was carried by newcomers.

As just remarked, the Spanish Reconquest and, to a lesser extent and less permanently, the Christian conquest of Sicily and Syria produced subject populations separated by religion from the rulers and new settlers. But this was not the only form that colonial subjection took in medieval Europe. Alongside an intense sense of self-identity as Christian, as the *populus christianus*, whose members, in the immortal words of *The Song of Roland*, were 'right', just as pagans were 'wrong', medieval colonialism also generated institutional and attitudinal racism. In a few regions, of course, the prior population was so sparse and immigration so dense that the immigrants' chief enemies would be tree stumps and bogs, but this was unusual. In general, as the expansionary colonial movements of the period took ethnic and linguistic groups, as conquerors or colonists, to new areas, medieval Catholic Europe acquired a fringe of linguistically and ethnically divided societies. In the eastern Baltic or in Ireland, for example, new settlers formed a prosperous and governing élite, while the majority of the country folk retained their native language, culture and social organization.

Clearly, the local pattern of race relations was shaped by the extent and nature of foreign immigration. It made a great deal of difference whether the immigrants were conquerors or peaceful colonists, an overwhelming majority or a thin trickle, landowners or labourers, capitalists or ecclesiastics. One large zone of ethnic intermingling was eastern Europe, as it was transformed in the High Middle Ages by the eastward migration of Germans, the so-called *Ostsiedlung*. Although a common feature of the *Ostsiedlung* was the settlement of Germans in parts of eastern Europe where they had never lived before, the ethnic situations which resulted were extremely diverse. In some places Germanization was absolute. In the Mittelmark of Brandenburg, for example, a conquering German dynasty from the old kingdom of Germany, the Ascanians, established a new lordship within the framework of which German peasants settled and German burgesses founded new towns. By the close of the Middle Ages the Slavic language had virtually disappeared from the Mittelmark. Since that time the area has been continuously part of Brandenburg, or its successor-states, Prussia, the German Democratic Republic and the German Federal Republic. Elsewhere, Germanization took different forms. In Silesia, which was a Polish duchy ruled by a branch of the Piast dynasty, the traditional rulers of Poland, a process of cultural Germanization occurred in the thirteenth century as German immigrants were encouraged to settle by the local dukes and prelates. The dynasty itself began to adopt German names and learned to speak German. By the sixteenth century, when Silesia came under Habsburg rule, parts of the duchy were as thoroughly Germanized as Brandenburg. Wrocław (Breslau), the site of the first German *Reichstag* east of the Elbe (1420), was undeniably a German city. In other parts of Silesia, however, German settlers, or, rather, the descendants of German settlers, were being Slavicized. The story of Pomerania was, in essentials, the same as that of Silesia. In all these cases, extensive peasant settlement by Germans was important.

Further east, in parts of Poland, Hungary and Bohemia, German immigration was more limited and concentrated especially in the towns. In these kingdoms the majority of the rural population, substantial minorities in the towns and the aristocratic and royal dynasties remained Slavic or Magyar. German burgesses formed a scattered, privileged class, often relying on the support and patronage of native kings: the German settlers in Transylvania were brought there by the Hungarian Arpad dynasty and received extensive special privileges from them, such as those specified in the *Andreanum*, which Andrew II issued to his 'loyal guests, the Germans of Transylvania' in 1224. Clearly, the pattern of ethnic relations in the towns of eastern Europe which were set in a countryside of indigenous peasants and nobles was very different from that in the Germanized lands around Brandenburg and Wrocław. Yet another distinct scenario occurred in the eastern Baltic littoral, from Memel northwards, where political power was in the hands of an exclusively German institution, the order of the Teutonic Knights, and the local towns were all German foundations, but the native populations of Baltic or Finno-Ugric origin remained in an overwhelming majority, especially in the countryside. Here the relation of German town and non-German countryside was similar to that in Poland, Hungary and Bohemia, while the German monopoly of political power resembled rather the conquest principality of Brandenburg.

Such variables as the extent of German immigration, the distribution of political power between native and immigrant groups and, one can add, the history of conversion to Christianity all made a difference. This last factor was important. The duchies and kingdoms of Poland, Bohemia and Hungary had all become officially Christian and established ecclesiastical hierarchies before the wave of German immigration began. The Wends, those West Slavs living between the Germans, the Bohemians, the Poles and the Baltic, remained pagan, however, well into the twelfth century. As late as the thirteenth century the princes and prelates of German colonial territories like Brandenburg were prepared to squeeze every benefit from their posture as champions of Christendom, even though official West Slav paganism had ended with the sack of the temple of Arkona on the island of Rügen in 1168. Shortly thereafter, as the mission to Livonia and the settlement of Germans in the eastern Baltic began, a quite new form of political structure took shape, a state run by a crusading order, whose *raison d'être* was armed struggle against pagans and schismatics. Prussia and Livonia formed a German theocracy, locked in endless war with local pagan populations. Clearly, ethnic relations differed if they could be identified with or overlapped with religious oppositions. The dichotomy Christian–pagan could reinforce, transcend or simply be irrelevant to the distinction German–non-German. Colonization and conversion were sometimes synonyms and sometimes not.

The direct historical consequences of high medieval migration and ethnic mingling are with us to the present day. As German-speakers from eastern Europe still trickle back into Germany or men still die fighting for or against the rights of the British Crown to Irish soil, we can see how fundamental political problems of the twentieth century have their origins in the dynamic period of conquest and colonization that occurred six or seven centuries ago. The cultural identity and political fortunes of the inhabitants of the Celtic lands or eastern Europe have been irrevocably shaped by that expansionary movement.

TRANSFORMATION ON THE PERIPHERY

The implantation of new aristocracies, encastellation, urbanization, new peasant settlement, the development of documentary literacy, all effected a fundamental transformation in those lands along the periphery of Latin Europe where they were experienced. The political outcome was varied. The conquest states of Brandenburg and Ulster have been discussed in Chapter 2. They were not the only examples. All around the fringes of Europe garrison societies could be found. A particularly remarkable example is the *Ordensstaat* of the Teutonic Knights, a state ruled by an alien military élite which would never integrate with local society, since it was composed of celibates recruited from overseas (only Rhodes provides a limited parallel). Elsewhere one could find other bridgehead lordships and 'Outremers' – in the Levant, in Greece and in the Celtic lands. Often the best description of such places is 'half-conquered countries'. Ireland is a notorious instance; Wales before 1282 provides another; the Crusader States may possibly be categorized in the same way. A dominant, newly arrived population, led by knights and clerics, stiffened by burgesses and some farmers, but still, overall, a minority, confronted a large native majority, alien in language, culture, social structure and, often, religion. The minority had to take care of its own security, ensure its profits and control, suppress or transform the native population. Beyond the sometimes precariously held colonial towns and fiefs lay native polities that were not subjected: Gaelic or Lithuanian kings, Greek or Islamic states, that nurtured long-term plans of revanchism and revival. In polities like these warfare and competition between newcomer and native, settler and indigenous population, were taken for granted as a permanent feature of life.

Not all native leaders were hostile. In many cases outsiders were invited in and encouraged by local aristocrats eager to gain an edge in their own competitive arena. An alliance with powerful outsiders was an alluring ploy for chiefs who were losing in the political struggle or who wished to be raised above their peers. Dermot MacMurrough of Leinster, who brought in Anglo-Norman mercenaries to restore him to his kingdom, is an obvious example. Likewise, the Normans obtained their first foothold in Sicily with the help of the dissident Muslim emir Ibn at Timnah. 'The Christians are nearby,' advised a Livonian under attack from the Lithuanians. 'Let us ride to the Master [of the Teutonic Knights] . . . Let us willingly ally ourselves with the Christians and thus avenge our sorrows.' A link with powerful outside forces could be the crucial advantage in internal kin conflicts. Henry I of England, for example, could entice a favoured Welsh prince by promising to exalt him 'higher than anyone of your kin . . . so that all your kin shall feel envy towards you'.

The changes we are discussing did not come only in the wake of conquest. The eleventh, twelfth and thirteenth centuries are marked by a series of energetic rulers who consciously embraced the transformation. Alfonso VI of León–Castile (1065–1109) married into the French princely aristocracy, encouraged the immigration of French knights, ecclesiastics and burgesses, established close links with the papacy and the Cluniac order, Romanized the liturgy, may have minted the first Castilian coinage and established new urban communities based on communal liberties. David I of Scotland (1124–53) minted the first Scots coinage, introduced the new monastic orders into his country, fostered an immigrant Anglo-French knightly class and developed trading towns. In Silesia, German rural settlement with grants of German law and the creation of towns with constitutions modelled on those of the commercial centres of Saxony took place under the aegis of Duke Henry the Bearded (1201–38), whose mother and wife were both noble German ladies.

Rulers who took this stance usually ensured the survival of their dynasty, even if the society they ruled underwent a cultural and social transformation. In Scotland, Silesia, Pomerania and Mecklenburg alien aristocracies were invited in by native dynasties, and in all these cases the dynasty survived. These princes rode the tide of change. Other political units, like the Welsh principality of Gwynedd, were moving in the same direction, but with less favourable circumstances, too late and too slowly. The thirteenth-century princes of Gwynedd built stone castles, fostered fledgling boroughs and issued charters, so that, by the time of its final conquest in the 1280s, Gwynedd was more like the England it was facing, in terms of the political structure, than ever before. It is not too fanciful to imagine an alternative political development in Wales, in which the path of Mecklenburg, Pomerania or Silesia could have been followed: as if the Llywelyns had called themselves Edward, spoken English and invited English knights and burgesses in – though perhaps the presence of a unified political entity in the expansive metropolitan area (the kingdom of England) as distinct from a fragmented one (the kingdom of Germany) made this alternative unlikely. A real, rather than counter-factual, contrast is provided by Scotland, another political unit of Celtic origin which had tried to transform itself in the twelfth and thirteenth centuries. Scotland, however, had started earlier, under less direct threat and with the guiding hand of a powerful dynasty. Thus, in the reign of Edward I, while the gradually developing state of the Llywelyns went under to concentrated attack, the Scottish kingdom was strong enough to survive. It survived because it was more like England and it survived under the leadership of one of the families of Anglo-Norman origin implanted into Scotland in the twelfth century. David I had known what he was doing.

An immigrant aristocracy can establish itself in the land to which it comes in a variety of ways: by expropriation, by assimilation or by finding a new ecological niche. In the first case the native aristocracy is killed, exiled or pushed down the social scale and the newcomers take its position. England after 1066 is a classic example, and similar situations occurred in parts of Ireland and Wales and some of the German marks. In the second case the immigrants are first settled on land made available by the native prince or by a great church or are married to local heiresses; they establish a powerful position by drawing on existing resources, but do not enter into mortal competition with native aristocrats. The initial establishment of alien aristocracies in Scotland or Pomerania provides a good example. Finally, there is the possibility that such an aristocracy can be supported by the exploitation of new resources, by the establishment of 'clearance lordships', large or small, composed of newly cleared or newly drained land, pioneer farms and villages, or by drawing on the new cash flows generated by urbanization and commercialization. The actual history of the High Middle Ages shows various admixtures of these three forms of aristocratic immigration, but it is particularly the last – the creation of new niches for lordship – that had the most profound implications.

The introduction of an alien castle-building cavalry élite into the Celtic lands and eastern Europe was followed by peasant immigration, a rise in the importance of cereal farming, the establishment or tighter organization of the Church and urbanization. The foundation of chartered towns and the encouragement of peasant settlement, monetization and documentary culture in the societies of the periphery meant that the very social and economic basis of life changed. In many of these societies direct predation had been an important structural feature. It was not the occasional excess of the lawless but the prime activity of the free adult male population; not a sideline, but an essential method of obtaining goods and labour; not a cause for shame but, if successful, a source of pride. The primary purpose of such predation was the kidnapping of people and livestock from neighbours. The killing of enemy males was largely a means to this end or a precautionary measure to prevent retaliation, though, of course, there was pleasure in it too. But the main purpose of the warfare practised by the Irish kings or the Lithuanian chiefs was to obtain cattle, horses and slaves. Obviously non-animate wealth, such as furs or precious metals, was extremely acceptable but, overall, less important.

In these societies successful predatory activity won status. The pagan Prussians, for example, had a special class of priest whose task (in the words of a hostile Christian source) was to officiate at burials, 'praising the dead for their thefts and predations, the filthiness, robbery and other vices and sins they perpetrated while alive'. It was also essential to release the wealth accumulated by such raiding back into social circulation. In Ulster this was done by potlatches; as an English commentator put it: 'over the course of the year they accumulated through theft and robbery what was consumed the next Easter in extravagant feasts ... There was great competition among them lest anyone should be outdone by another in the lavish preparation and serving of courses of food.' After the new peasant farms and trading towns of the twelfth and thirteenth centuries had been established, rents, tithes and tolls were now available to support the military and ecclesiastical ruling class. As a consequence the relative significance of direct predation diminished. The new rulers could thus exercise a somewhat complacent hostility to native practice in this respect. The Prussians were forced to give up their specialist funeral orations. In Ulster, as our English source describes it, 'when they were conquered this most superstitious custom came to an end, along with their freedom'.

Just as the immigrant knights came to seek fiefs rather than plunder, so the Church saw the possibility of tithes – guaranteed extraction from a new sedentary Christian population. All around the peripheries the High Middle Ages saw the new enforcement of tithes. Although their compulsory payment had been a feature of the legislation of the Carolingians and the Wessex kings of England, it seems that they were enforced in the regions beyond this Anglo-Frankish area only in the course of the twelfth and thirteenth centuries. In Scotland an assize ascribed to David I made them compulsory. The obituary of Cathal Crovderg O'Connor of Connacht, who died in 1224, records that 'it is in the time of this king that tithes were first levied for God in Ireland'. The enforcement of tithes in Moravia was attributed to the efforts of Bishop Bruno of Olomouc (1245–81), whom we have already encountered promoting the colonization of his estates. In these Celtic and Slav lands the regular and obligatory payment of tithes was introduced into already Christian societies, as part of the process whereby they transformed themselves in the twelfth and thirteenth centuries to become more like their neighbours of direct Carolingian tradition. At the same time Latin Christendom was itself expanding and, as it did so, tithes were extracted from lands and peoples who had never recognized such an obligation. When the Germans settled in pagan Wagria 'tithes were increased in the land of the Slavs'. In some areas east of the Elbe the creation of tithe income and replacement of Slavs by Germans were seen as equivalents: 'after the Slavs have been ejected and the land made tithable', reads one document for the diocese of Ratzeburg.

Linked with the declining importance of direct predation and its replacement by extraction of rent and tithe was a shift from an economy in which
slavery was important to one in which it was peripheral. This seems to
have some connection with military developments. On the one hand, the
encastellation of the regions that had been traditional hunting grounds for
slaving made slave-raiding more difficult. The castles offered protection to
the prey. This is what happened when the missionary Meinhard built a
stone castle for the Livonians or when Northumberland was covered with
castles in the late eleventh century. In addition, castles required a more
intense exploitation of local labour and offered a more secure position in
the countryside to the lords who built them. As in Hungary, 'the new type
of castle is ... connected to a lord's dominion over his tenants ... The
castle ceased to serve merely as a defence of its area, but became the seat of
the landowner.' The castle-builders were thus able to acquire a dominance
over surrounding rural populations that made the maintenance of slave
labour less pressing. The slaving raids of the tenth-century Germans, the
eleventh-century Poles, the twelfth-century Scots or the thirteenth-century
Lithuanians serviced economies in which slave labour, domestic, artisanal
and agricultural, was significant – as late as 1170 there were 700 Danes for
sale at the Mecklenburg slave market. As the importance of slavery
decreased, the control of a settled, non-slave peasant population mattered
more. Castles were ideal instruments for controlling and milking such a
population.

Changes in weapons and armament and in methods of waging war were
thus closely tied to changes in the goals and purposes of war – 'war aims' as
they might anachronistically be called. Some wars, like those of Malcolm
III's Scottish raiders of the eleventh century, involved not conquest or
permanent appropriation, but rather the constitution of 'hunting grounds',
from which slaves, booty and tribute could be raised. Sometimes there
might be a more enduring dominance of the region, based on the exaction
of tribute and hostages and, possibly, the levying of contingents for
military service. Conquest, however, in the sense of a permanent suppression of one set of rulers by another, was a high medieval rather than an
early medieval phenomenon. In one privileged moment, we can see the
shift from one to the other before our eyes. The Saxons plundered, raided
and enslaved the Slavs for centuries. Sometimes they came off worse. From
the beginning of the twelfth century, they tended to come off better. In
1147, in the so-called Wendish Crusade, a large body of Saxons invaded
the Slav lands east of the Elbe and began, as was customary, to kill, burn
and enslave. Finally they began to wonder what they were doing. 'Is it

not,' they asked, 'our own land that we are destroying?' They were right. Such fine lands could serve them better as the seats of a permanent conquest than as the occasional scenes of satisfying carnage and lucrative freebooting.

MEDIEVAL AND MODERN COLONIALISM

The 'expansion of Europe' in the High Middle Ages clearly shared many characteristics with the overseas expansion of post-medieval times. It showed, also, however, certain distinctive structural features. One characteristic in particular distinguishes it sharply from, say, European imperialism of the nineteenth and twentieth centuries, at least as that phenomenon is classically described. Modern imperialism, it is usually held, intensified the large-scale regional differentiation of the globe: industrialized areas, greedy for raw materials and markets, became enmeshed in a pattern of systematic interdependence with regions which supplied the raw materials and helped to purchase the products of the industrial zones. There is, doubtless, an element of caricature in this picture, but even a rudimentary acquaintance with the history of rubber or copper in modern times shows that there is some truth in this image.

The colonialism of the Middle Ages was quite different. When Anglo-Normans settled in Ireland or Germans in Pomerania or Castilians in Andalusia, they were not engaged in the creation of a pattern of regional subordination. What they were doing was reproducing units similar to those in their homelands. The towns, churches and estates they established simply replicated the social framework they knew from back home. The net result of this colonialism was not the creation of 'colonies', in the sense of dependencies, but the spread, by a kind of cellular multiplication, of the cultural and social forms found in the Latin Christian core. The new lands were closely integrated with the old. Travellers in the later Middle Ages going from Magdeburg to Berlin and on to Wrocław, or from Burgos to Toledo and on to Seville, would not be aware of crossing any decisive social or cultural frontier.

This is indeed one reason why the formulation 'core–periphery' is not entirely fortunate (though hard to avoid) as a tool to describe the expansionism of the High Middle Ages. On the one hand, of course, there is a sense in which the centre-outwards perspective is perfectly justifiable: by 1300 the descendants of men from France ruled in Ireland and Greece, those of men from Germany in Prussia and Brandenburg, those of men from

England in Ireland and Wales, those of men from Italy in Crete, those of men from Castile in Andalusia. There is clearly an outward movement of people and power not balanced by movement in the other direction. But 'core–periphery' is still perhaps misleading, for the concept is often taken to imply a permanent or long-term functional subordination of the periphery to the core. This is exactly what high medieval colonialism was not – it was a process of replication, not differentiation.

This expansion through replication had, as its characteristic agents, not the powerful monarchies – we might be tempted to say, not the state – but consortia, entrepreneurial associations of Frankish knights, Latin priests, merchants, townsmen and, as non-voting members, peasants. The freelance nature of such expansionary enterprises as the Anglo-Norman penetration of the Celtic world or the spread of Germans into eastern Europe has often been remarked. One consequence was the creation of many independent or virtually independent lordships on the fringes of Europe – the Villehardouin principality of the Morea, the early Norman lordships in southern Italy, autonomous Valencia under the Cid, Strongbow's Leinster and de Courcy's Ulster, Brandenburg under its margraves. Only in a few cases did the expansion take the form of a growth of kingdoms, with the Iberian peninsula providing the main example. Even here, although monarchical direction was crucially important in the Spanish Reconquest, there was a significant place for autonomous urban communities, with their own *fueros*, militias and regime of local border warfare.

The situation along the eastern frontiers of the kingdom of Germany shows clearly how a lack of central direction need be no hindrance to successful expansionary movement. In the twelfth and thirteenth centuries conquest and colonization virtually doubled the sphere of German settlement and political control. The involvement of the German kings in this process was minimal. In the tenth century, by contrast, full-blooded German royal involvement under the Ottonian dynasty had been a prerequisite for territorial expansion on the eastern frontier. In that earlier period the concentration of resources under monarchical leadership had been the only thing that made even a precarious conquest possible; in the High Middle Ages there was a spontaneous many-headed movement that took German lords and settlers deep into eastern Europe.

Indeed, it may be that the strengthening of some of the major kingdoms of western Europe that is noticeable around the year 1300 actually provided some kind of brake on the expansion of Latin Europe. The amorphous petty warfare of the eleventh and twelfth centuries had left plenty of energy, i.e. manpower, resources and political will, for enterprises external to the Frankish world; but by the thirteenth century the larger princely states were seeking to monopolize aggression and, though more powerful than the smaller powers of the earlier period, would often concentrate their resources upon each other to the neglect of expansionary enterprises further afield. Charles of Anjou, whose far-flung claims to overlordship embraced such classic products of the expansionary period as Sicily, the Morea and the kingdom of Jerusalem, was actually far too busily engaged in fighting his western rivals to be a prop to the Latin states of the eastern Mediterranean. As Outremer finally fell to the Muslims in 1291, the two great powers of France and Aragon were at each other's throats. Philip the Fair of France was the most powerful ruler in Christendom, but none of his efforts were directed towards the expansion of Christendom. The example of his contemporary, Edward I of England, whose incorporation of Wales may be seen as the final consummation of Anglo-Norman expansion in that part of the Celtic world, shows that when the great unitary polities of the thirteenth and fourteenth centuries did concentrate upon expansion, they could be devastatingly effective; but more characteristic of this period was the endless struggle between the western European powers dubbed the Hundred Years War.

It was thus the knightly–clerical–mercantile consortium, not the apparatus of kingly power, that orchestrated the most characteristic expansionary movements of the eleventh and twelfth centuries. The classic case of an enterprise launched by such a consortium was the eastern Mediterranean crusade. The political map of the Levant was transformed in the twelfth and thirteenth centuries not by royal or imperial statecraft but by a curious assemblage of western magnates and knights, ecclesiastics of both a papalist and an independent bent and Italian merchants, impelled by motives as diverse as their status and origins. Contemporaries remarked how the armies of the First Crusade were 'without lord, without prince' or how they 'fought without king, without emperor'; but the establishment of Outremer was only the most striking example of the way the warrior-aristocrats, clerical élite and urban merchants of the Latin West could combine forces, often in the complete absence of monarchical orchestration, to produce new polities and new settlements. The colonization of the eastern Baltic shows how an entirely new social and political form, the Ordensstaat, the 'Order State', could emerge from the activities of German merchants and missionaries, land-hungry nobles and peasants, all under the general direction and authority of one of the international military orders.

The interests of the knights, merchants, peasants and clerics who were members of these consortia did not, of course, always harmonize. In pagan eastern Europe the missionary priest raised his voice against the avarice and brutality of the secular conquerors, whose greed and violence provided the native population no incentive to peaceful conversion. The Teutonic Knights might blithely tell the German merchants that 'we have been fighting to expand the faith and your trade', but in virtually every theatre of crusade commercial interests were intertwined with the crusading movement in a way that was as often mutually destructive as it was symbiotic. The repeated and futile papal prohibitions on Italian merchants trading war materials with Muslim powers are an unambiguous example. The merchants' position is comprehensible. Alexandria, to take an instance, was not only a great Islamic centre, but also one of the biggest commercial cities of the Mediterranean. It was not at all clear that the Venetian, Genoese or Pisan trader would prefer to sack it in alliance with Frankish nobles rather than buy and sell there under the protection of a Muslim ruler. The Frankish aristocrats of the eastern Mediterranean often had no autonomy or authority in regard to the Italian traders who controlled their maritime lifelines. In 1298 the king of Cyprus told a Venetian merchant who complained of being robbed by some Genoese that 'the king did not interfere between Genoese and Venetians'. It was prudent for this Frankish crusader king to keep out of Italian mercantile disputes altogether.

The absence of political masterminding in the colonial ventures of the Middle Ages is illustrated not only by the prominent role of these eclectic consortia, that is, by the agents of expansion, but also by the distinctive nature of the forms of expansion. With the exception of Ireland – which can perhaps be termed a colony in the modern sense – the eventual result of the outward movements of the Middle Ages was never the permanent political subordination of one area to another. The kingdom of Valencia, the kingdom of Jerusalem and the dominions of the Teutonic Knights in Prussia and Livonia were autonomous replicas, not dependencies, of western and central European polities. And the ease with which these 'new colonies of Holy Christendom' could become replicas without political subordination is best explained by the existence, in the Latin West, of international legal forms or blueprints, which could generate new structures quite independently of an encompassing political matrix.

The expansionary power and deepening cultural uniformity of the Latin West between the tenth and thirteenth centuries is partly explained by the development in western Europe of these legal and institutional blueprints or models which were easily exportable and adaptable but also resistant. In new circumstances these forms could be modified and survive, but they also transformed their surroundings. Codifiable blueprints such as the

chartered town, the university and the international religious order crystal-
lized in the West between 1050 and 1200. As the image of crystallization
suggests, many of the elements that composed them were already in
existence but not yet in the exact arrangement or relationship that they
were to assume. From a fusion of the monastic rule and the knightly ethos
came the military orders; from the immunity and the market, the chartered
town; from the priesthood and the guild, the university. What was
characteristic of these forms was their uniformity and reproducibility. They
were vectors of expansion because they could be set down anywhere and
still thrive. They all show how a legal blueprint, codifiable and transmissible, was able to diffuse new forms of social organization throughout
Europe quite independently of centralized political direction. Such forms
were perfect instruments for the lay-ecclesiastical consortia we have just
described.

These forms were distinguished by two vital features: they were legal
and they were international. The two features were linked. Because social
forms were defined legally, they were codifiable and transmissible. They
gained a certain independence from local circumstances and were able to be
transplanted into alien environments and survive. The town, as envisaged
in innumerable borough charters, *Stadtrechte* and *fueros*, was a picture, a set
of norms that could be adapted to, rather than swamped by, local situations.
Hence, as discussed in Chapter 7, German urban law formed the model for
towns far into eastern Europe, Norman customs could be transplanted to
Wales, and the *fueros* of Christian Spain could be introduced into the towns
of the Reconquest. Like the towns, the new monastic orders of the twelfth
century had a normative and self-defining quality. Compared with their
Cluniac predecessors, the Cistercians achieved new levels of legal articulation and international organization. Cistercian affiliation tied together
hundreds of religious communities from Ireland to Palestine. As in the case
of the chartered town, new members of such orders could be created with
the confidence that they would change their environment as much as adapt
to it. Here was a formula for successful expansion.

The success of these blueprints is a little like that of the alphabet. Of the
various forms of writing that have arisen, the alphabet is the most colourless.
Unlike pictograms, alphabetic symbols carry no obvious reference beyond
the alphabetic code itself. They do not even symbolize sounds as the letters
of a syllabary do. The alphabet is the absolutely minimal system of coding
possible for the representation of sounds. But that is its great strength.
Because the components of the system have few intrinsic associations or
connotations, they can be combined for an infinite variety of purposes. A

Chinese character is full of cultural meaning; it has associated sounds and concepts; writing it and reflecting on it can be a religious exercise. And there are thousands of these potent symbols. In contrast there are less than thirty letters of the alphabet, none of which have intrinsic cultural connotations. But this bleaching out of the colour and resonance of the symbols is the precondition for the creation of enormous operational efficacy. It is the alphabetic system that dominates in the world and is making inroads even in the heart of the Orient.

This is, in a sense, what happened in medieval Europe. The world of the early Middle Ages was one of a diversity of rich local cultures and societies. The story of the eleventh, twelfth and thirteenth centuries is of how that diversity was, in many ways, superseded by a uniformity. The cultural and political forms that spread in this period were marked, like the alphabet, by a lack of local association and resonance: the western town and the new religious orders were blueprints, and that means they were neither coloured nor constricted by powerful local ties. The Benedictines and local dynasties of the early Middle Ages had deep roots, but the new organisms of the High Middle Ages could seed aerially. Like the alphabet, these supra-local, legal forms carried the minimum intrinsic information and had the maximum operational efficacy. On the other hand, these bare models which spread so far, transmuting local universes, did themselves have an origin in a specific place and time, in a local world. The alphabet was hatched in the commercial cities of the Levant, the chartered town and the orders in the fertile confusion of post-Carolingian Europe. The story of the spread of powerful new blueprints in the twelfth and thirteenth centuries is also the story of how one of the many local cultures and societies of the Middle Ages attained a position of hegemony over the others.

The process of cultural diffusion and assimilation so far described was not effortlessly smooth. It encountered opposition and generated tensions. For, as Frankish knights and Latin ecclesiastics carried their cultural and social dreams and habits into diverse parts of the world, native responses were not lacking. There was cultural resistance as well as cultural assimilation. For many, the conquests and expansionary movements of the High Middle Ages were a loss, a pain and a tragedy. 'What? Have they not, marked it with ignominy?' grieved the Muslim poet Ibn Hamdīs of Sicily. 'Have they not, Christian hands, changed its mosques into churches . . .? I see my homeland abused by the Latins, which was so glorious and proud under my people.' The Welsh cleric Rhigyfarch, witness to the Norman conquest of south Wales in the late eleventh century, sounded a similar note:

The people and the priest are despised
By the word, heart and deeds of the Frenchmen.
They burden us with tribute and consume our possessions.
One of them, however lowly, shakes a hundred natives
With his command and terrifies them with his look.
Alas, our fall, alas the deep grief.

Native peoples subject to the violence of the military aristocracy of the Latin world did not only grieve. Sometimes reaction on the part of native societies was strong enough to produce enduring states, hammered out in the very process of resistance. The Lithuanian state was born in response to the German threat and went on to outlast the *Ordensstaat* and, by the late Middle Ages, to dominate eastern Europe. Faced with the challenge of German crusaders in the Baltic, the pagan Lithuanians reacted not only by engaging in stubborn military resistance but also by creating a more centralized state structure with unitary dynastic leadership. The birth of this dynamic and expansionary political structure was linked to a vigorous reavowal of their traditional religion. It is sometimes overlooked that by the mid-fourteenth century this state, ruled by pagans, was the largest in Europe. There was nothing atavistic about it: its deployment of artillery was as sophisticated as anyone's. Its gods were old, but its guns were new.

Native reactions elsewhere, if less dramatic, were equally dogged. In areas such as Ireland, where the invaders were unable to establish undisputed authority, one can find complex situations in which a partial conquest produced a strong reaction from native rulers, who were, nevertheless, unable to oust the conquerors completely. The native rulers of the north and west of the island preserved their autonomy during the high tide of Anglo-Norman colonialism, then, from the late thirteenth century, began to roll back English control. In the fourteenth and fifteenth centuries it was the local English population that began to Gaelicize, much to the dismay of the colonial authorities. The 'half-conquered' state of Ireland involved a mutual borrowing in the military as well as the cultural field. By the fifteenth century the Irish were building stone castles, but many of the Anglo-Normans, strangely enough, had abandoned the stirrup.

In Spain the conquered Muslims, the Mudejars, usually submitted only on condition that they were granted free exercise of their religion and judicial autonomy. There were some mass expulsions from certain cities, and the chief mosques were rededicated as cathedrals; but down to the time of Columbus there were large Muslim minorities – Muslim even if, as was increasingly the case, they spoke Spanish and bore Christian names –

practising the Islamic religion in the Christian kingdoms of the West. They were largely debarred from political power and suffered some social and legal disabilities, but they showed no signs of disappearing.

Lithuania, Ireland, the Mudejars: the extremities of Europe experienced the process of homogenization as a process of polarization. The very same forces that drew the English, the Pomeranians or the Danes into a more uniform cultural world could, in these outlying areas, actually erect starker cultural boundaries. By the fourteenth century a large part of Europe, including England, France, Germany, Scandinavia and northern Italy and Spain, had come to possess a relatively high degree of cultural homogeneity. The whole fringe around this area, however, was characterized by a mixture of, and often conflict between, languages, cultures and, sometimes, religions. Everywhere in this fringe zone race relations mattered in a way they scarcely did in the more homogeneous central zone – and these relations were not between equals: they involved domination and subordination, control and resistance.

This book then tells both how a more uniform cultural pattern was created and extended on the continent of Europe and also how that same process produced a surrounding ring of linguistically and ethnically divided societies. This tale of increasing cultural homogeneity coupled with stark cultural divisions should have a familiar ring for those who study later periods of history, including our own. There is a connecting thread. It has been shown, reasonably conclusively, how the mental habits and institutions of European racism and colonialism were born in the medieval world: the conquerors of Mexico knew the problem of the Mudejars; the planters of Virginia had already been planters of Ireland.

There is no doubt that the Catholic societies of Europe had deep experience of colonialist enterprises prior to 1492. They were familiar with the problems and the promise involved in new territorial settlement and had confronted the issues raised by contact with peoples of very different culture. Of course there was nothing in their experience as dramatically 'out of the blue' as the contact established in 1492. Both ecologically and historically the medieval Latin world was contiguous and often continuous with the neighbouring cultures and societies. Nevertheless, from the Iberian peninsula in a wide arc east across the Mediterranean and north to the Arctic Circle, Catholic Europe did have a frontier and, from the tenth century, a frontier that was moving outwards.

Conquest, colonization, Christianization: the techniques of settling in a new land, the ability to maintain cultural identity through legal forms and nurtured attitudes, the institutions and outlook required to confront the strange or abhorrent, to repress it and live with it, the law and religion as well as the guns and ships. The European Christians who sailed to the coasts of the Americas, Asia and Africa in the fifteenth and sixteenth centuries came from a society that was already a colonizing society. Europe, the initiator of one of the world's major processes of conquest, colonization and cultural transformation, was also the product of one.

Abbreviations Used in Notes and Bibliography

AQ	*Ausgewählte Quellen zur deutschen Geschichte des Mittelalters*
Helbig & Weinrich	Herbert Helbig and Lorenz Weinrich (eds.), *Urkunden und erzählende Quellen zur deutschen Ostsiedlung im Mittelalter* (*AQ* 26, 2 vols., Darmstadt, 1968–70)
J.–L.	*Regesta pontificum Romanorum . . . ad annum . . . 1198*, ed. P. Jaffé, rev. S. Loewenfeld *et al.* (2 vols., Leipzig, 1885–8)
Lacarra	José María Lacarra (ed.), 'Documentos para el estudio de la reconquista y repoblación del Valle del Ebro', *Estudios de Edad Media de la Corona de Aragon* 2 (1946), pp. 469–574 (docs. 1–93), 3 (1947–8), pp. 499–727 (docs. 94–286), 5 (1952), pp. 511–668 (docs. 287–400); repr. in 2 vols., *Textos medievales* 62–3 (Saragossa, 1982–3)
MF	*Mitteldeutsche Forschungen*
MGH	*Monumenta Germaniae historica*
MPH	*Monumenta Poloniae historica*
n.s.	new series
PL	*Patrologia cursus completus, series latina*, ed. J.-P. Migne (221 vols., Paris, 1844–64)
Po.	*Regesta pontificum Romanorum inde ab annum . . . 1198 ad a. 1304*, ed. A. Potthast (2 vols., Berlin, 1874–5)
RHC.Occ.	*Recueil des historiens des croisades, Historiens occidentaux* (5 vols., Paris, 1844–95)
RS	*Rerum Britannicarum Medii Aevi Scriptores* ('Rolls Series') (251 vols., London, 1858–96)
SRG	*Scriptores rerum Germanicarum in usum scholarum separatim editi* (*MGH*)
SS	*Scriptores* (*MGH*)
UB	*Urkundenbuch*

Notes

Notes are keyed to significant phrases in text. At the first mention of a work in each chapter full bibliographical information is given, thereafter short title. Full bibliographical information is also, of course, available in the Bibliography.

1. The Expansion of Latin Christendom

'*He brought masons from far and wide . . .*': Geoffrey Malaterra, *De rebus gestis Rogerii Calabriae et Siciliae comitis et Roberti Guiscardi ducis fratris eius* 3.19, ed. Ernesto Pontieri (*Rerum italicarum scriptores*, n.s., 5/1, Bologna, 1928), pp. 68–9 (the bishopric of Troina was soon transferred to Messina).

'*We are not in any bishopric*': Orderic Vitalis, *Historia ecclesiastica* 3, ed. and tr. Marjorie Chibnall (6 vols., Oxford, 1968–80), 2, p. 26.

This analysis of *the bishoprics of medieval Christendom* takes as its starting point the lists in Pius Bonifatius Gams, *Series episcoporum ecclesiae catholicae* (Regensburg, 1873) (presently being revised) and Conrad Eubel, *Hierarchia catholica medii aevi 1 (1198–1431)* (2nd ed., Münster, 1913), augmented and corrected by individual entries in the *Dictionnaire d'histoire et de géographie ecclésiastiques* (21 vols. to date, Paris, 1912–) and the *Lexicon für Theologie und Kirche*, ed. Josef Höfer and Karl Rahner (2nd ed., 11 vols., Freiburg im Breisgau, 1957–67), the maps and bibliographies in *Atlas zur Kirchengeschichte*, ed. Hubert Jedin *et al.* (2nd ed., Freiburg im Breisgau, 1987), and various national or regional studies, some of which are listed below.

Magdeburg: *Diplomata Conradi I, Heinrici I et Ottonis I*, ed. Theodor Sickel (*MGH*, *Diplomata regum et imperatorum Germaniae* 1, Hanover, 1879–84), no. 366, pp. 502–3.

General studies of *the establishment of an episcopacy in eastern Europe* include A. P. Vlasto, *The Entry of the Slavs into Christendom* (Cambridge, 1970), chapter 3; Francis Dvornik, *The Making of Central and Eastern Europe* (London, 1949); for the lands between Elbe and Oder see Jürgen Petersohn, *Der südliche Ostseeraum im kirchlich-politischen Kräftespiel des Reichs, Polens und Dänemarks vom 10. bis 13. Jahrhundert* (Cologne and Vienna, 1979), part I, and the various diocesan histories, e.g. Dietrich Claude, *Geschichte des Erzbistums Magdeburg bis in das 12. Jahrhundert* (2 vols., MF 67, Cologne, 1972–5); Fritz Curschmann, *Die Diözese*

Brandenburg (*Veröffentlichungen des Vereins für Geschichte der Mark Brandenburg*, Leipzig, 1906).

'The cohorts of Latins': *Vita Constantini* 15, tr. Marvin Kantor and Richard S. White, *The Vita of Constantine and the Vita of Methodius* (*Michigan Slavic Materials* 13, Ann Arbor, 1976), p. 47.

Adam of Bremen: *Gesta Hammaburgensis ecclesiae pontificum* 3.77, ed. Werner Trillmich, in *Quellen des 9. und 11. Jahrhunderts zur Geschichte der Hamburgischen Kirche und des Reiches* (*AQ* 11, Darmstadt, 1961), pp. 135–503, at pp. 428–30.

Pagan Uppsala: ibid. 4.26–7, ed. Trillmich, pp. 470–72.

Ansgar: Malaterra, *De rebus gestis Rogerii* 4.7, ed. Pontieri, pp. 88–90; see, in general, Dieter Girgensohn, 'Dall'episcopato greco all'episcopato latino nell'Italia meridionale', in *La chiesa greca in Italia dall'VIII al XVI secolo* (3 vols., *Italia sacra* 20–22, Padua, 1973) 1, pp. 25–43.

Richard Palmer and Walter Offamil: Charles Homer Haskins, 'England and Sicily in the Twelfth Century', *English Historical Review* 26 (1911), pp. 433–47, 641–65, at p. 437.

Vic: Paul Freedman, *The Diocese of Vic* (New Brunswick, 1983), pp. 14–15.

For general *accounts of the Reconquest*: Derek W. Lomax, *The Reconquest of Spain* (London, 1978); Charles J. Bishko, 'The Spanish and Portuguese Reconquest, 1095–1492', in Kenneth M. Setton (ed.), *A History of the Crusades* (Philadelphia and Madison, 6 vols., 1955–89) 3: *The Fourteenth and Fifteenth Centuries*, ed. Harry W. Hazard, pp. 396–456; Angus MacKay, *Spain in the Middle Ages: From Frontier to Empire, 1000–1500* (London, 1977), pp. 1–78; details of individual dioceses can be found in *Diccionario de historia eclesiástica de España*, ed. Quintín Aldea Vaquero *et al.* (4 vols., Madrid, 1972–5).

Toledo charter of 1086: *Privilegios reales y viejos documentos de Toledo*, ed. Juan Francisco Rivera Recio *et al.* (limited ed., Madrid, 1963), no. 1.

Conquest of Lisbon: *De expugnatione Lyxbonensi: The Conquest of Lisbon*, ed. and tr. Charles W. David (New York, 1936), pp. 178–80 and n. 5.

'When the noble king Don Ferdinand': *Primera crónica general de España* 1129, ed. Ramón Menéndez Pidal (2 vols., Madrid, 1955), 2, p. 769.

The Latin Church in the eastern Mediterranean: Bernard Hamilton, *The Latin Church in the Crusader States: The Secular Church* (London, 1980); Hans Eberhard Mayer, *Bistümer, Klöster und Stifte im Königreich Jerusalem* (*MGH, Schriften* 26, Stuttgart, 1977), part 1; Jean Richard, 'The Political and Ecclesiastical Organization of the Crusader States', in Kenneth M. Setton (ed.), *A History of the Crusades* (Philadelphia and Madison, 6 vols., 1955–89) 5: *The Impact of the Crusades on the Near East*, ed. Norman P. Zacour and Harry W. Hazard, pp. 193–250; Giorgio Fedalto, *La Chiesa Latina in Oriente* (2nd ed., 3 vols., Verona, 1981); R. L. Wolff, 'The Organization of the Latin Patriarchate of Constantinople, 1204–1261', *Traditio* 6 (1948), pp. 33–60.

Church of Athens: Innocent III, 14 July 1208, *Sacrosancta Romana ecclesia*, Po. 3456; *Registrum sive epistolae* 11.113, *PL* 214–16, at 215, col. 1433; see Jean

Longnon, 'L'organisation de l'église d'Athènes par Innocent III', in *Mémorial Louis Petit: Mélanges d'histoire et d'archéologie byzantines (Archives de l'Orient chrétien* 1, Bucharest, 1948), pp. 336–46; for the *composition of the chapter* Leo Santifaller, *Beiträge zur Geschichte des Lateinischen Patriarchats von Konstantinopel (1204–1261) und der venezianischen Urkunden* (Weimar, 1938), pp. 130–40; for the *oath* G. L. F. Tafel and G. M. Thomas (eds.), *Urkunden zur älteren Handels- und Staatsgeschichte der Republik Venedig* (3 vols., *Fontes rerum Austriacarum* II, 12–14, Vienna, 1856–7) 2, p. 101, no. 209.

Bishoprics in the Baltic region: Petersohn, *Der südliche Ostseeraum*; the present writer's 'The Conversion of a Pagan Society in the Middle Ages', *History* 70 (1985), pp. 185–201; Karl Jordan, *Die Bistumsgründungen Heinrichs des Löwen* (*MGH, Schriften* 3, Leipzig, 1939); Eric Christiansen, *The Northern Crusades* (London, 1980).

The Swordbrothers: Friedrich Benninghoven, *Der Order der Schwertbrüder* (Cologne and Graz, 1965). There is an enormous secondary literature on the *Teutonic Knights*: a good recent survey is Hartmut Boockmann, *Der Deutsche Orden* (Munich, 1981).

Notker: Gesta Karoli 1.10, ed. Reinhold Rau, *Quellen zur karolingischen Reichsgeschichte* 3 (*AQ* 7, Darmstadt, 1960), pp. 321–427, at pp. 334–6.

On the *suppression of other rites* see Chapter 10.

'*Tota latinitas*': Orderic Vitalis, *Historia ecclesiastica* 12.43, ed. Chibnall, 6, p. 364.

On the history of *Ireland in the twelfth and thirteenth centuries* see Robin Frame, *Colonial Ireland 1169–1369* (Dublin, 1981); *idem, The Political Development of the British Isles 1100–1400* (Oxford, 1990); A. J. Otway-Ruthven, *A History of Medieval Ireland* (2nd ed., London, 1980); for a comparison of colonial settlement in Ireland and eastern Europe see the present writer's 'Colonial Aristocracies of the High Middle Ages', in Robert Bartlett and Angus MacKay (eds.), *Medieval Frontier Societies* (Oxford, 1989), pp. 23–47.

St Bernard's criticisms: Vita sancti Malachiae 8.16, in J. Leclerq and H. M. Rochais (eds.), *Opera* 3 (Rome, 1963), pp. 295–378, at p. 325.

'*Barbarous laws*': ibid. 8.17, ed. Leclerq and Rochais, p. 326; the biblical citation is Hosea 2:23.

'*Land or pence . . .*': *Song of Dermot and the Earl*, lines 431–5, ed. and tr. Goddard H. Orpen (Oxford, 1892), p. 34.

'*Some show of religion*': Walter Bower, *Scotichronicon* 12.27, ed. D. E. R. Watt, 6 (Aberdeen, 1991), p. 388 (Remonstrance of 1317–18).

'*Christians only in name . . .*': Bernard, *Vita sancti Malachiae* 8.16, ed. Leclerq and Rochais, p. 325.

Song of Roland: Chanson de Roland, laisse 72, line 899, ed. F. Whitehead (Oxford, 1942), p. 27.

Welsh: John of Salisbury, *Letters, 1: The Early Letters (1153–61)*, ed. W. J. Millor, H. E. Butler and C. N. L. Brooke (London, etc., 1955), no. 87, p. 135.

Ruthenians: *Schlesisches UB*, ed. Heinrich Appelt and Winfried Irgang (4 vols. to date, Graz, Cologne and Vienna, 1963–), 1, no. 11, pp. 8–9 (1143–5).

2. The Aristocratic Diaspora

'A good knight by the fame of his valour . . .': Philip of Novara (Philippe de Navarre), *Les quatres âges de l'homme* 1.16, ed. Marcel de Fréville (Paris, 1888), p. 11.

Joinvilles: The standard account of the family is Henri-François Delaborde, *Jean de Joinville et les seigneurs de Joinville* (Paris, 1894), which gives full references to the narrative sources and includes (pp. 239–487) a catalogue of Joinville *acta*.

Debate in Damietta: Jean de Joinville, *Histoire de Saint Louis* XXXVI (167), ed. Natalis de Wailly (Paris, 1874), p. 92.

'A judgement concerning prey taken in the marches': *Calendar of the Gormanston Register*, ed. James Mills and M. J. McEnery (Dublin, 1916), p. 182.

Joinville's epitaph on his ancestors: Joinville, *Histoire*, ed. de Wailly, p. 545.

On *the Grandmesnil family* see Orderic Vitalis, *Historia ecclesiastica*, ed. and tr. Marjorie Chibnall (6 vols., Oxford, 1968–80), indices, *s.v.* 'Grandmesnil'; family tree ibid. 2, opposite p. 370, and in Marjorie Chibnall, *The World of Orderic Vitalis* (Oxford, 1984), p. 227; Leon-Robert Ménager, 'Inventaire des familles normandes et franques emigrées en Italie méridionale et en Sicile (XIe–XIIe siècles)', in *Roberto il Guiscard e il suo tempo* (*Fonti e studi del Corpus membranarum italicarum*, Centro di studi normanno-suevi, Università degli studi di Bari, Rome, 1975), pp. 259–387, at pp. 316–18.

Abbot of St Évroul threatened to be hanged: Orderic Vitalis, *Historia ecclesiastica* 3, ed. Chibnall, 2, p. 94.

'Funambuli': *Gesta Francorum* 9.23, ed. and tr. Rosalind Hill (London, 1962), p. 56; Baudri de Bourgueil, *Historia Jerosolimitana, RHC, Occ.* 4, pp. 1–111, at pp. 64–5.

'This warlike marcher often fought': Orderic Vitalis, *Historia ecclesiastica* 8.3, ed. Chibnall, 4, pp. 138–40.

Robert of Rhuddlan in Wales: *Domesday Book*, ed. Abraham Farley (2 vols., London, 1783), 1, fol. 269; map in H. C. Darby, *Domesday England* (Cambridge, 1977), p. 332, fig. 111; Rees Davies, *Conquest, Coexistence and Change: Wales 1063–1415* (Oxford, 1987), pp. 30–31, 82–3; John Le Patourel, *The Norman Empire* (Oxford, 1976), pp. 62–3, 312–14.

Sourdevals: *Domesday Book* 1, fols. 298, 305–8, 373; Lewis C. Loyd, *The Origins of Some Anglo-Norman Families*, ed. C. T. Clay and D. C. Douglas (*Harleian Society Publications* 103, 1951), p. 99; Ménager, 'Inventaire des familles normandes', p. 346; *Red Book of the Exchequer*, ed. Hubert Hall (3 vols., RS, 1896), 2, p. 602;

Register of the Abbey of St Thomas Dublin, ed. John T. Gilbert (RS, 1889), nos. 106, 349–50, pp. 92, 302–4.

Gaston V of Béarn, etc.: Derek W. Lomax, *The Reconquest of Spain* (London, 1978), p. 62.

Sibyl, the daughter of William Capra: Orderic Vitalis, *Historia ecclesiastica*, 13.5, ed. Chibnall, 6, p. 404.

Röhricht on Germans in Outremer: Reinhold Röhricht, *Beiträge zur Geschichte der Kreuzzüge 2: Deutsche Pilger- und Kreuzfahrten nach dem heiligen Lande (700–1300)* (Berlin, 1878), pp. 297–359.

Charters of Barnim I: Pommersches UB 1: 786–1253, ed. Klaus Conrad (2nd ed., Cologne and Vienna, 1970), nos. 213, 485, pp. 261–3, 579–80.

German knights recruited to Pomerania: For a general survey see O. Eggert, *Geschichte Pommerns* 1 (Hamburg, 1974), pp. 150–60, and also the bibliography cited there, pp. 263–4.

'In those parts any duke or prince . . .': *Schlesisches UB*, ed. Heinrich Appelt and Winfried Irgang (4 vols. to date, Graz, Cologne and Vienna, 1963–), 2, no. 346, p. 208 (1248).

On *John de Courcy and the creation of the lordship of Ulster* see T. E. McNeill, *Anglo-Norman Ulster: The History and Archaeology of an Irish Barony 1177–1400* (Edinburgh, 1980), esp. chapter 1; Goddard H. Orpen, *Ireland under the Normans, 1169–1333* (4 vols., Oxford, 1911–20) 2, pp. 5–23, 114–18, 134–44; *New History of Ireland 2: Medieval Ireland, 1169–1534*, ed. Art Cosgrove (Oxford, 1987), pp. 114–16, 135.

For a similar process of *the construction of castles and the implantation of a body of vassals* in contemporary Meath see the present writer's 'Colonial Aristocracies of the High Middle Ages', in Robert Bartlett and Angus MacKay (eds.), *Medieval Frontier Societies* (Oxford, 1989), pp. 23–47, at pp. 31–41.

De Courcy's campaign of 1201: *Annals of Ulster (Annála Uladh)*, ed. and tr. William M. Hennessy and Bartholomew MacCarthy (4 vols., Dublin, 1887–1901), 2, pp. 235–7; his *raid of 1197* ibid. 2, p. 229.

De Courcy's grant to St Patrick's, Down: William Dugdale, *Monasticon Anglicanum*, ed. John Caley *et al.* (6 vols. in 8, London, 1846), 6/2, p. 1125 (with incomplete witness lists); Gearóid MacNiocaill, 'Cartae Dunenses XII–XIII Céad', *Seanchus Ard Mhaca* 5/2 (1970), pp. 418–28, at p. 420, nos. 4–5.

On *John de Courcy's coinage* see William O'Sullivan, *The Earliest Anglo-Irish Coinage* (Dublin, 1964), pp. 1–5, 20–21 and plate 1.

De Courcy as 'dominus de Ulvestire' and 'princeps regni de Ulvestir': Roger of Howden, *Chronica*, ed. William Stubbs (4 vols., RS, 1868–71), 4, pp. 176 and 25; cf. Jocelyn of Furness, *Vita sancti Patricii*, *Acta sanctorum Martii 2* (Antwerp, 1668), pp. 540–80, at p. 540, who refers to de Courcy as *Ulidiae princeps*.

For *general orientation on Brandenburg* see Eberhard Schmidt, *Die Mark Brandenburg unter den Askaniern (1134–1320)* (*MF* 71, Cologne and Vienna, 1973); Johannes Schultze, *Die Mark Brandenburg 1: Entstehung und Entwicklung unter den askanischen Markgrafen (bis 1319)* (Berlin, 1961); Hermann Krabbo and Georg Winter, *Regesten der Markgrafen von Brandenburg aus Askanischem Hause* (Leipzig, Munich and Berlin, 1910–55).

'*The birthdate of the Mark of Brandenburg*': Schultze, *Die Mark Brandenburg 1*, p. 74.

'*So, in the year of the incarnation of the Lord 1157 . . .*': Henry of Antwerp, *Tractatus de captione urbis Brandenburg*, ed. Oswald Holder-Egger, *MGH, SS* 25 (Hanover, 1880), pp. 482–4, at p. 484.

'*After they had grown to be young men they lived together harmoniously . . .*': *Cronica principum Saxonie*, ed. Oswald Holder-Egger, *MGH, SS* 25 (Hanover, 1880), pp. 472–80, at p. 478.

For *the von Wedel family* see Helga Cramer, 'Die Herren von Wedel im Lande über der Oder: Besitz und Herrschaftsbildung bis 1402', *Jahrbuch für die Geschichte Mittel- und Ostdeutschlands* 18 (1969), pp. 63–129; the document of 1212 is in *Hamburgisches UB* (4 vols. in 7, Hamburg, 1907–67) 1, no. 387, pp. 342–3. Many documents concerned with the family are to be found in the relatively rare *UB zur Geschichte des schlossgesessenen Geschlechts der Grafen und Herren von Wedel*, ed. Heinrich Friedrich Paul von Wedel (4 vols. in 2, Leipzig, 1885–91); for instance, an extract from the document of 1212 is printed in 1, no. 1, p. 1; because of its inaccessibility, however, it will be cited only for documents not in print elsewhere.

Ludwig von Wedel excommunicated by Albertus Magnus: Pommersches UB 2 (Stettin, 1881–5, repr. Cologne and Graz, 1970), no. 891, pp. 218–19.

Current Polish names of places marked on Map 4: Cremzow (Krępcowo), Driesen (Drezdenko), Falkenburg (Złocieniec), Freienwalde (Chociwel), Kürtow (Korytowo), Märkische-Friedland (Mirosławiec), Neuwedel (Drawno), Schivelbein (Świdwin), Uchtenhagen (Krzywnica); rivers Ihna (Ina), Netze (Noteć), Drage (Drawa).

Ludwig von Wedel and his brothers vassals of the margrave of Brandenburg: UB . . . von Wedel 2/1, no. 3, p. 3 (1272), nos. 7–8, p. 6 (1281).

Ludolf von Wedel's charter to Dietrich and Otto von Elbe: ibid. no. 113, pp. 65–6.

Von Wedel promise to serve 'with a hundred well armed knights, etc.': *Codex diplomaticus Brandenburgensis*, ed. Adolph Friedrich Riedel (41 vols., Berlin, 1838–69), A XVIII, pp. 151–3, no. 87 (1388); *document of 1314 for Märkisch-Friedland*: ibid., pp. 102–3, no. 5; *grant of 1338 to Freienwalde*: ibid., pp. 111–12, no. 22; *purchase of the Land Schivelbein*: ibid., pp. 218–19, no. 9.

'*Quasi-princely position*': Cramer, 'Die Herren von Wedel', p. 119: 'nahezu landesherrliche Stellung'.

There is a convenient compendium of information on *the family of Montferrat* in Leopoldo Usseglio, *I marchesi di Monferrato in Italia ed in oriente durante i secoli*

XII e XIII, ed. Carlo Patrucco (2 vols., *Bibliotheca della società storica subalpina* 100–101, Turin, 1926).

For the *characterization of William the Old's eldest son*: William of Tyre, *Chronicle* 21.12(13), ed. R. B. C. Huygens (2 vols., *Corpus Christianorum, Continuatio mediaevalis* 63–63A, Turnhout, 1986), 2, p. 978.

'*A devil incarnate in his ability* . . .': Francesco Gabrieli (ed.), *Arab Historians of the Crusades* (Eng. tr., Berkeley and London, 1969), p. 177 (Ibn al-Athīr).

Peire Vidal: Poesie, ed. D'Arco Silvio Avalle (2 vols., Milan and Naples, 1960), 2, pp. 159–61, no. 19 ('Per mielhs sofrir'), lines 49–50, at p. 161.

The *fifteen royal monarchs* are the kings or queens of Portugal, León–Castile, Aragon, Navarre, France, England, Scotland, Norway/Sweden, Denmark, Poland, Hungary, the Holy Roman Empire (and Bohemia), Naples, Sicily and Cyprus; other rulers (e.g. some Irish dynasts) used the regal title in certain contexts but were not generally conceded it by neighbours or the great international institutions. Jerusalem and Armenia have been excluded.

Raymond 'of the stock of the Franks': Marcelin Defourneaux, *Les Français en Espagne aux XIe et XIIe siècles* (Paris, 1949), p. 197, n. 1; Bernard F. Reilly, *The Kingdom of León–Castilla under King Alfonso VI, 1065–1109* (Princeton, 1988), pp. 194 and n., 254–5.

Cyprus: Richard I had previously given it to the Templars, who had to be bought out.

'*Lord, we wonder greatly at your good chivalry* . . .': Robert of Clari, *La conquête de Constantinople* 106, ed. Philippe Lauer (Paris, 1924), p. 102.

'*A vast crowd of kinsmen, fellow countrymen* . . .': Geoffrey Malaterra, *De rebus gestis Rogerii Calabriae et Siciliae comitis et Roberti Guiscardi ducis fratris eius* 1.11, ed. Ernesto Pontieri (*Rerum italicarum scriptores*, n.s., 5/1, Bologna, 1928), p. 14. The biblical citation is Luke 6:38.

'*What he could carry off he gave and did not keep* . . .': Amatus of Montecassino, *Storia de' Normanni* 2.45, ed. Vincenzo de Bartholomaeis (*Fonti per la storia d'Italia* 76, Rome, 1935), p. 112.

'*These settlers were of modest origin* . . .': Joshua Prawer, *Crusader Institutions* (Oxford, 1980), p. 21.

'*Who was poor over there, God makes rich here* . . .': Fulcher of Chartres, *Historia Hierosolymitana* 3.37, ed. Heinrich Hagenmeyer (Heidelberg, 1913), p. 749.

First German nobles in Livonia: *Livländische Reimchronik*, lines 612–18, ed. Leo Meyer (Paderborn, 1876), p. 15.

'*Whoever shall wish for land or pence* . . .': *Song of Dermot and the Earl*, lines 431–6, ed. and tr. Goddard H. Orpen (Oxford, 1892), p. 34.

'*Those who had been on foot became horsemen*': *Cantar de Mío Cid*, line 1213, ed. Ramón Menéndez Pidal (rev. ed., 3 vols., Madrid, 1944–6), 3, p. 945.

'*Having seized the spoils of victory* . . .': Malaterra, *De rebus gestis Rogerii* 1.16, ed. Pontieri, p. 17.

'The heavy traffic in necessary generosity': Georges Duby, *The Early Growth of the European Economy* (Eng. tr., London, 1974), p. 51.

Tacitus: Germania 13–14.

'So it was given to me to repay in battle . . .': *Beowulf*, lines 2490–93, ed. F. Klaeber (3rd ed., Boston, 1950), p. 94.

'There is a general lack of places . . .': Bede, *Epistola ad Ecgbertum episcopum*, in Charles Plummer (ed.), *Opera historica* (2 vols., Oxford, 1896) 1, pp. 405–23, at pp. 414–17.

'O lord king, we have served you unceasingly . . .': Dudo of Saint-Quentin, *De moribus et actis primorum Normanniae ducum* 4.83, ed. Jules Lair, *Mémoires de la Société des Antiquaires de Normandie*, 3rd ser., 3 (Caen, 1858–65), p. 238.

Sachsenspiegel, Lehnrecht, ed. Karl August Eckhardt (*Germanenrechte*, n.s., Göttingen, 1956), *passim*.

'I have my fief . . .': Walther von der Vogelweide, *Die Lieder*, ed. Friedrich Maurer (Munich, 1972), no. 74/11, p. 232 ('Ich han min lehen').

'It may not be necessary to look further . . .': Le Patourel, *The Norman Empire*, p. 303; *'one source, perhaps the main source . . .'*: ibid., p. 290.

Extinction rate of European aristocracies: Osnabrück – Werner Hillebrand, *Besitz- und Standesverhältnisse des Osnabrücker Adels bis 1300* (Göttingen, 1962), p. 211; *Eichstätt* – Benjamin Arnold, *German Knighthood 1050–1300* (Oxford, 1985), p. 180; *Namurois* – Léopold Génicot, *L'économie rurale namuroise au Bas Moyen Age 2: Les hommes – la noblesse* (Louvain, 1960), p. 140; *Forez* – Edouard Perroy, 'Social Mobility among the French *Noblesse* in the Later Middle Ages', *Past and Present* 21 (1962), pp. 25–38.

'They saw that as their neighbours grew old . . .': Malaterra, *De rebus gestis Rogerii* 1.5, ed. Pontieri, p. 9.

Tancred to his sons: Orderic Vitalis, *Historia ecclesiastica* 3, ed. Chibnall, 2, p. 98.

'This land you inhabit is everywhere shut in by the sea . . .': Robert the Monk, *Historia Iherosolimitana*, *RHC*, *Occ.* 3, pp. 717–882, at p. 728.

Likelihood of a married couple producing sons: Jack Goody, *The Development of the Family and Marriage in Europe* (Cambridge, 1983), p. 44.

On the *structure of the aristocratic family*: Karl Schmid, 'Zur Problematik von Familie, Sippe und Geschlecht, Haus und Dynastie beim mittelalterlichen Adel', *Zeitschrift für die Geschichte des Oberrheins* 105 (1957), pp. 1–62; *idem*, 'The Structure of the Nobility in the Earlier Middle Ages', in Timothy Reuter (ed.), *The Medieval Nobility* (Amsterdam, etc., 1978), pp. 37–59; Georges Duby, 'Lineage, Nobility and Knighthood', in his *The Chivalrous Society* (Eng. tr., London and Berkeley, 1977), pp. 59–80, at pp. 68–75; for an attempt to extend the model to England see James C. Holt, 'Feudal Society and the Family in Early Medieval England', *Transactions of the Royal Historical Society*, 5th ser., 32 (1982), pp. 193–212; 33 (1983), pp. 193–220; 34 (1984), pp. 1–25; 35 (1985), pp. 1–28, esp. 32 (1982), pp. 199–200; critics of varying degrees of intensity include Karl Leyser, 'The German Aristocracy from the Ninth to the Early Twelfth Century: A Historical and Cultural Sketch', *Past and Present* 41 (1968), pp. 25–53, esp. pp. 32–6, repr. in his *Medieval Germany and its Neighbours* (London, 1982), pp. 161–89, at pp. 168–72; Constance B. Bouchard, 'Family Structure and Family Consciousness among the Aristocracy in the Ninth to the Eleventh Centuries', *Francia* 14 (1987), pp. 639–58.

Scotland 'a land for younger sons': Geoffrey Barrow, *The Anglo-Norman Era in Scottish History* (Oxford, 1980), title of chapter 1.

Knightly immigration to Outremer: Prawer, *Crusader Institutions*, p. 24.

'According to the law of the realm of England . . .': Glanvill, *The Treatise on the Laws and Customs of England commonly called Glanvill*, ed. and tr. G. D. H. Hall (London, 1965), p. 75.

1185 Breton decree: *Assise au comte Geffroy* 1, ed. Marcel Planiol, *La très ancienne coutume de Bretagne* (Rennes, 1896, repr. Paris and Geneva, 1984), pp. 319–25, at pp. 321–2.

'Who made brothers unequal . . .?': London, British Library, Add. MS 11283, fols. 21v–22. Wendy Davies was kind enough to check this reference.

'Narrowing and tightening of the family . . .': Duby, 'Lineage, Nobility and Knighthood', p. 75; *'did not the appearance of new structures of kinship . . .'*: idem, 'The Structure of Kinship and Nobility', in his *The Chivalrous Society* (Eng. tr., London and Berkeley, 1977), pp. 134–48, at p. 148; *a military class 'more firmly rooted . . .'*: idem, *Early Growth of the European Economy*, p. 171.

'The reorganization of the Norman knightly class . . .': Lucien Musset, 'L'aristocratie normande au XIe siècle', in Philippe Contamine (ed.), *La noblesse au Moyen Age* (Paris, 1976), pp. 71–96, at p. 95.

Transmission of resources intact: Holt, 'Feudal Society and the Family', *Transactions of the Royal Historical Society* 32 (1982), p. 201.

Limburg document of 1035: Lorenz Weinrich (ed.), *Quellen zur deutsche Verfassungs-, Wirtschafts- und Sozialgeschichte bis 1250* (AQ 32, Darmstadt, 1977), no. 25, pp. 106–8.

'Homage and the fief came in the wake of conquest': Graham Loud, 'How "Norman" was the Norman Conquest of Southern Italy?', *Nottingham Medieval Studies* 25 (1981), pp. 13–34, at p. 26.

Subinfeudation of the Morea: *Chronicle of Morea*, tr. Harold E. Lurier, *Crusaders as Conquerors* (New York, 1964), pp. 125–8; Lurier translates *sirgentes* as 'squires'.

Brandenburg 'ministeriales': Hans K. Schulze, *Adelsherrschaft und Landesherrschaft: Studien zur Verfassungs- und Besitzgeschichte der Altmark, des ostsächsischen Raumes und des hannoverschen Wendlandes im hohen Mittelalter* (MF 29, Cologne and Graz, 1963).

Feudal structure of Ireland: A. J. Otway-Ruthven, *A History of Medieval Ireland* (2nd ed., London, 1980), pp. 102–3; *eadem*, 'Knight Service in Ireland', *Journal of the Royal Society of Antiquaries of Ireland* 89 (1959), pp. 1–15.

'Thus well rooted . . .': *Song of Dermot*, lines 3206–7, ed. Orpen, p. 232.

Size of knights' fees in Ireland: Otway-Ruthven, *History of Medieval Ireland*, p. 105.

Money fiefs in the Crusader States: Joshua Prawer, 'Social Classes in the Latin Kingdom: The Franks', in Kenneth Setton (ed.), *A History of the Crusades* (Philadelphia and Madison, 6 vols., 1955–89) 5: *The Impact of the Crusades on the Near East*, ed. Norman Zacour and Harry Hazard, pp. 117–92, at p. 135.

Fiefs 'varied in value [and] . . . extent . . .': Frank Stenton, *The First Century of English Feudalism 1066–1166* (2nd ed., Oxford, 1961), p. 166.

Number of fiefs owing knight service: England and Normandy – Thomas K. Keefe, *Feudal Assessments and the Political Community under Henry II and His Sons* (Berkeley, etc., 1983), pp. 42, 141; *Champagne* – Theodore Evergates, 'The Aristocracy of Champagne in the Mid-Thirteenth Century: A Quantitative Description', *Journal of Interdisciplinary History* 5 (1974–5), pp. 1–18; *Jerusalem* – Alan V. Murray, 'The Origins of the Frankish Nobility in the Kingdom of Jerusalem, 1100–1118', *Mediterranean Historical Review* 4/2 (1989), pp. 281–300, at pp. 281–2; for detailed discussion of the evidence for the kingdom of Jerusalem see Jean Richard, 'Les listes des seigneuries dans le livre de Jean d'Ibelin', *Revue historique de droit français et étranger* 32 (1954), pp. 565–77.

Leinster fees: A. J. Otway-Ruthven, 'Knights' Fees in Kildare, Leix and Offaly', *Journal of the Royal Society of Antiquaries of Ireland* 91 (1961), pp. 163–81, at p. 164, n. 10.

Sicilian survey: *Catalogus baronum*, ed. Evelyn Jamison (*Fonti per la storia d'Italia* 101, Rome, 1972); see, in general, Claude Cahen, *Le régime féodale d'Italie normande* (Paris, 1940).

'Now I will tell you what King Guy did . . .': *L'estoire d'Eracles empereur et la conqueste de la terre d'Outremer*, *RHC*, *Occ.* 2, pp. 1–481, at pp. 188–90 (note); also as *La continuation de Guillaume de Tyr (1184–1197)* 136, ed. Margaret R. Morgan (*Documents relatifs à l'histoire des croisades* 14, Paris, 1982), p. 139 (cf. also p. 138); see Peter Edbury, *The Kingdom of Cyprus and the Crusades 1191–1374* (Cambridge, 1991), chapter 3, 'Settlement'.

'Early Scottish feudalism . . .', etc.: Barrow, *Anglo-Norman Era*, pp. 132, 44 and n. 59, 40, 62, 127.

Grant to Alexander de Saint Martin: *Early Scottish Charters prior to 1153*, ed. Archibald C. Lawrie (Glasgow, 1905), no. 186, p. 150.

Scottish kings 'had expelled the Scots, men of vile habits . . .': Gervase of Tilbury, *Otia imperialia* 2.10, ed. G. W. Leibnitz, *Scriptores rerum brunsvicensium illustrationi inservientes* (3 vols., Hanover, 1707–11) 1, pp. 881–1004; 2, pp. 751–84; at 1, p. 917, with better readings at 2, p. 772.

Hungarian loan words for 'helmet', etc.: K. Schunemann, *Die Deutsche in Ungarn bis zum 12. Jahrhundert* (Berlin, 1923), p. 130.

Irish 'ritire': (Contributions to a) Dictionary of the Irish Language (Royal Irish Academy, Dublin, 1913–76), s.v.

Polish and Czech loan words: Perry Anderson, Passages from Antiquity to Feudalism (London, 1974), p. 231.

Normans generalize word 'fief' in southern Italy: Cahen, Régime féodale, p. 47.

Clusters of Normans in Shropshire: J. F. A. Mason, 'Roger de Montgomery and his Sons (1067–1102)', Transactions of the Royal Historical Society, 5th ser., 13 (1963), pp. 1–28, at pp. 6–12.

Noble settlers in the kingdom of Jerusalem: Murray, 'Origins of the Frankish Nobility', p. 293.

Immigrant magnates in Hungary: Erik Fügedi, 'Das mittelalterliche Königreich Ungarn als Gastland', in Walter Schlesinger (ed.), Die deutsche Ostsiedlung als Problem der europäischen Geschichte (Vorträge und Forschungen 18, Sigmaringen, 1975), pp. 471–507, at pp. 495–6.

Muslim aristocracy in Valencia: Robert I. Burns, Islam under the Crusaders: Colonial Survival in the Thirteenth-Century Kingdom of Valencia (Princeton, 1973), esp. chapter 13.

Scottish earldoms in 1286: Barrow, Anglo-Norman Era, pp. 157–8.

Magnates in late medieval Hungary: Fügedi, 'Das mittelalterliche Königreich Ungarn', pp. 495–6.

Welsh and Lombard fees: William Rees, South Wales and the March 1284–1415 (Oxford, 1924), pp. 145–7; Cahen, Régime féodale, pp. 38–9, 82–9; the comparison is made by Otway-Ruthven, 'Knight Service', pp. 14–15.

'He [Pandulf] gave him his sister as wife': Amatus of Montecassino, Storia de' Normanni 1.42, ed. de Bartholomaeis, pp. 53–4.

Wives of the first margraves of Brandenburg: Bernhard Guttmann, 'Die Germanisierung der Slawen in der Mark', Forschungen zur brandenburgischen und preussischen Geschichte 9 (1897), pp. 39 (395)–158 (514), at p. 70 (426).

'He who was "of Rheims" or "of Chartres" . . .': Fulcher of Chartres, Historia Hierosolymitana 3.37, ed. Hagenmeyer, p. 748.

Knights settled in Sicily: Henri Bresc, 'Féodalité coloniale en terre d'Islam: La Sicile (1070–1240)', in Structures féodales et féodalisme dans l'Occident mediterranéen (Xe-XIIIe s.) (Paris, 1980), pp. 631–47, at p. 640.

'The bannerets of Morea . . .': Chronicle of Morea, tr. Lurier, p. 165.

On the de Lacy family: W. E. Wightman, The Lacy Family in England and Normandy 1066–1194 (Oxford, 1966).

Benedictine houses in Wales: Davies, Conquest, Coexistence and Change, p. 181.

Followers of the de Lacys in Meath: Bartlett, 'Colonial Aristocracies', pp. 38–40.

Properties of houses of Béarn and Bigorre: Lacarra, nos. 354, 366.

'A big crowd of knights from beyond the mountains . . .': Julio González, El reino de Castilla en la epoca de Alfonso VIII (3 vols., Madrid, 1960) 3, no. 897, pp. 567–8.

Dietrich of Tiefenau: Helbig & Weinrich 1, no. 121, pp. 448–50; Queden (Klein Queden) is the German Tiefenau and modern Polish Tychnowy.

3. Military Technology and Political Power

'*For who denies that castles are necessary things?*': *Codex iuris Bohemici*, ed. Hermenegild Jiriček (5 vols. in 12, Prague, 1867–98), 2/2, p. 114 (*Majestas Carolina* 7).

The *Leiden Book of Maccabees* is Leiden, University Library, MS Perizoni 17; it was produced in St Gallen; reproductions can be found in A. Merton, *Die Buchmalerei in St Gallen* (Leipzig, 1912), plates LV–LVII.

The *Bayeux Tapestry* is reproduced in Frank Stenton *et al.*, *The Bayeux Tapestry* (London, 1957); see also the contribution of Sir James Mann in the same volume, 'Arms and Armour', pp. 56–69.

Force 'all of iron': Thietmar of Merseburg, *Chronicon* 4.12, ed. Werner Trillmich (*AQ* 9, Darmstadt, 1957), p. 126, describing Saxon forces in 990.

Pawned mail coats: Lacarra, no. 238 (*c.* 1145); Gerald of Wales (Giraldus Cambrensis), *De principis instructione* 2.13, in J. S. Brewer, J. F. Dimock and G. F. Warner (eds.), *Opera* (8 vols., RS, 1861–91) 8, pp. 183–4.

The total *weight of a knight's gear* is based upon the following assumed weights: mail coat 30 lb; sword 4 lb; helmet 3 lb; lance-head 2 lb; horseshoes, bit, bridle, stirrups and spurs 11 lb. These weights are deduced partly from archaeological finds, partly from general metallurgical considerations and partly from projection back from later medieval armaments. For some such indications see J. F. Finó, 'Notes sur la production du fer et la fabrication des armes en France au Moyen Age', *Gladius* 3 (1964), pp. 47–66; R. F. Tylecote, *Metallurgy in Archaeology* (London, 1962), p. 276; H. Nickel *et al.*, *The Art of Chivalry: European Arms and Armour from the Metropolitan Museum of Art* (New York, 1982); James Mann, *Wallace Collection Catalogues: European Arms and Armour* (2 vols., London, 1962).

The figure of 5,000 for *Otto II's army* is deduced from an incomplete muster list for 981, the *Indiculus loricatorum*, in *Constitutiones et acta publica imperatorum et regum* 1, ed. Ludwig Weiland (*MGH*, Hanover, 1893), no. 436, pp. 632–3; see Karl Ferdinand Werner, 'Heeresorganisation und Kriegführung im Deutschen Königreich des 10. und 11. Jahrhunderts', in *Ordinamenti militari in Occidente nell'alto medioevo* (*Settimane di studio del Centro italiano di studi sull'alto medioevo* 15, 2 vols., Spoleto, 1968) 2, pp. 791–843.

Forge production: Finó, 'Notes sur la production du fer'.

'*Before the Black Death, wheat was being sold . . .*': William Beveridge, *Prices and Wages in England* 1 (London, 1939), pp. xxv–xxvi.

'*Noble horses*': e.g. William of Poitiers, *Gesta Guillelmi ducis Normannorum* 1.13, 40, ed. Raymonde Foreville (Paris, 1952), pp. 26, 98; Matthew Paris, *Chronica majora*, ed. Henry R. Luard (7 vols., RS, 1872–84), 4, pp. 135–6; see in general R. H. C. Davis, *The Medieval Warhorse* (London, 1989).

The most recent edition of the *agreement between Henry I of England and the count of Flanders in 1101* is Pierre Chaplais (ed.), *Diplomatic Documents preserved in the Public Record Office 1:1101–1272* (Oxford, 1964), pp. 1–4.

See Philippe Contamine, *War in the Middle Ages* (Eng. tr., Oxford, 1984), p. 67, for *thirteenth-century horsemen* with five mounts.

There is a very large body of secondary literature on *the semantics of knighthood*. The best starting point is P. Guilhiermoz, *Essai sur l'origine de la noblesse en France au Moyen Age* (Paris, 1902). More recent discussions include George Duby, 'The Origins of Knighthood', in his *The Chivalrous Society* (Eng. tr., London and Berkeley, 1977), pp. 158–70; *idem*, 'La diffusion du titre chevaleresque', in Philippe Contamine (ed.), *La noblesse au Moyen Age* (Paris, 1976), pp. 39–70; the articles collected in Arno Borst (ed.), *Das Rittertum im Mittelalter* (*Wege der Forschung* 349, Darmstadt, 1976); the collected essays of Léopold Genicot, *La noblesse dans l'Occident médiéval* (London, 1982); and the works of Jean Flori, *L'essor de la chevalerie* (Geneva, 1986), and *L'idéologie du glaive: Préhistoire de la chevalerie* (Geneva, 1983).

'Never or hardly ever have "milites" been summoned . . .': William of Poitiers, *Gesta Guillelmi* 2.29, ed. Foreville, p. 218.

Davis, *The Medieval Warhorse*, argues for 'the rapid development of the *size of the warhorse*' (p. 69) between the mid-eleventh and late thirteenth centuries but on very slight evidence such as the size of horses depicted on seals (pp. 21–2); such evidence would also support the claim that medieval merchant ships were no bigger than rowing boats.

'In the war against the Welsh . . .': Gerald of Wales (Giraldus Cambrensis), *Itinerarium Kambriae* 1.4, in J. S. Brewer, J. F. Dimock and G. F. Warner (eds.), *Opera* (8 vols., RS, 1861–91) 6, pp. 1–152, at p. 54.

There are several references to crossbows (*acrobalistae*) in the tenth-century chronicle by Richer, *Historiae* 2.92; 3.98, 104, ed. R. Latouche, *Histoire de France* (2 vols., Paris, 1930–37) 1, p. 282; 2, pp. 126, 134. It has been remarked that these references 'pourraient n'être que de simples réminiscences littéraires, sans aucun rapport avec la réalité', but that the existence of a drawing of a crossbow in a manuscript of around the year 1000 makes its use in the tenth century probable, J. F. Finó, *Forteresses de la France médiévale* (3rd ed., Paris, 1977), p. 89. The manuscript is Paris BN lat. 12,302, Haimo of Auxerre's *Commentary on Ezekiel*.

'Barbarian bow . . .': Anna Comnena, *Alexiad* 10.8.5, ed. B. Leib (3 vols., Paris, 1937–45), 2, pp. 217–18.

Prohibition of 1139: *Conciliorum oecumenicorum decreta*, ed. J. Alberigo *et al.* (3rd ed., Bologna, 1973), p. 203 (canon 29).

'Let them have crossbowmen': *Constitutiones et acta publica imperatorum et regum* 2, ed. Ludwig Weiland (*MGH*, Hanover, 1896), no. 335, p. 445.

On the *skulls from Visby* see B. Thordemann, *Armour from the Battle of Wisby 1361* (2 vols., Stockholm, 1939) 1, pp. 186–7.

Incidents and quotations of the *English civil war of 1215–17* from Roger of Wendover, *Flores historiarum*, ed. H. G. Hewlett (3 vols., RS, 1886–9), 2, pp. 116, 151, 194, 212, 215–16; this material was incorporated into Matthew Paris, *Chronica majora*, ed. Luard, 2, pp. 586–7, 626, 666; 3, pp. 18, 21.

Crossbowmen's pay in France: E. Audouin, *Essai sur l'armée royale au temps de Philippe Auguste* (Paris, 1913), pp. 113–14.

Land held 'per arbalisteriam': e.g. *Red Book of the Exchequer*, ed. Hubert Hall (3 vols., RS, 1896), 2, pp. 458–9, 467; see also J. H. Round, *The King's Serjeants and Officers of State* (London, 1911), pp. 13–14, for crossbow service in Domesday Book.

Silesian crossbowman: *Liber fundationis episcopatus Vratislaviensis*, ed. H. Markgraf and J. W. Schulte (*Codex diplomaticus Silesiae* 14, Breslau, 1889), pp. 14–15.

Expenditure on crossbows, etc.: in 1215 King John ordered 10,000 bolts for his castle of Marlborough, *Close Roll 16 John* (Pipe Roll Society, n.s., 31, 1955), p. 130. For Philip Augustus's armories see Audouin, *Essai*, pp. 187–97. See also Contamine, *War in the Middle Ages*, pp. 71–2.

'Because they were not all lords of castles . . .': Hariulf, *Gesta ecclesiae Centulensis* 4.21, ed. F. Lot, *Chronique de l'abbaye de Saint-Riquier* (Paris, 1894), p. 230.

Frederick of Swabia: Otto of Freising, *Gesta Friderici I imperatoris* 1.12, ed. Georg Waitz and Bernhard von Simson (*SRG*, Hanover and Leipzig, 1912), p. 28.

Plan of *Old Sarum* in J. P. Bushe-Fox, *Old Sarum* (London, etc., 1930).

Castles of the Auvergne: G. Fournier, *Le peuplement rural en Basse Auvergne durant le haut Moyen Age* (Paris, 1962), pp. 329–99.

Skidrioburg: *Atlas vorgeschichtlicher Befestigungen in Niedersachsen*, ed. A. von Oppermann and C. Schuchhardt (Hanover, 1888–1916), pp. 67–8, fig. 53. The modern name is Herlingsburg.

Nezenna: Karl Wilhelm Struve, 'Die slawischen Burgen in Wagrien', *Offa* 17–18 (1959–61), pp. 57–108, at pp. 61, 99–100.

Notes to Figure 2: burhs – C. A. Ralegh Radford, 'Later Pre-Conquest Boroughs and their Defences', *Medieval Archaeology* 14 (1970), pp. 83–103; *Aggersborg* – David M. Wilson, 'Danish Kings and England in the Late 10th and Early 11th Centuries – Economic Implications', in *Proceedings of the Battle Conference on Anglo-Norman Studies* 3 (1980), ed. R. Allen Brown, pp. 188–96, at pp. 192–3; *Slav forts in Wagria* – Struve, 'Die slawischen Burgen', p. 60; *Austrian castles* – W. Götting and G. Grüll, *Burgen in Oberösterreich* (Wels, 1967), p. 317 (figures for *Hauptburg*); *motte* – Contamine, *War in the Middle Ages*, p. 44.

English castles in 1100: Sidney Painter, 'English Castles in the Early Middle Ages: Their Numbers, Location, and Legal Position, *Speculum* 10 (1935), pp. 321–32, at p. 322; C. Warren Hollister, *The Military Organization of Norman England* (Oxford, 1965), p. 138 and notes. For *France* see Contamine, *War in the Middle Ages*, p. 46.

'*The keep is a queen* . . .': Lawrence of Durham, *Dialogi* 1, lines 367–8, ed. James Raine (Surtees Society 70, 1880 for 1878), p. 11.

For the *average size of mottes* Contamine, *War in the Middle Ages*, p. 44. Some, of course, were considerably larger; see, for example, A. Herrnbrodt, 'Stand der frühmittelalterlichen Mottenforschung im Rheinland', *Château Gaillard* 1 (1964 for 1962), pp. 77–100, at p. 81; H. W. Heine, 'Ergebnisse und Probleme einer systematischen Aufnahme und Bearbeitung mittelalterlicher Wehranlagen zwischen junger Donau und westlichen Bodensee', ibid. 8 (1976), pp. 121–34, at p. 126.

Suger's *Life of Louis the Fat*: *Vita Ludovici Grossi regis* 24 (Crécy), 19 (Le Puiset), 18 (Mantes), 3 ('arming' of a castle – *turrim sibi armis et armatis satagit munire*), ed. H. Waquet (Paris, 1929), pp. 176, 140, 124, 20.

Alpert of Metz, *De diversitate temporum* 2.2, ed. Hans van Rij and Anna Sapir Abulafia (Amsterdam, 1980), pp. 42–4. The phrase *novae res* is Sallustian in origin: *Jugurtha* 19.1, *Catiline* 28.4 and elsewhere. It was used frequently by medieval chroniclers. Alpert may well have drawn it from Caesar's *Gallic War* 1.9 (see van Rij and Abulafia's edition, p. 125).

Henry IV's castle-building: Bruno, *De bello Saxonico liber* 16, 27, ed. H. E. Lohmann (*MGH, Deutsches Mittelalter* 2, Leipzig, 1937), pp. 22, 31.

Okehampton: Maurice Beresford, *New Towns of the Middle Ages* (London, 1967), pp. 172 (fig. 40), 425.

Landgraves of Thuringia: Cronica Reinhardsbrunnensis, ed. Oswald Holder-Egger, *MGH, SS* 30/1 (Hanover, 1896), pp. 490–656, at pp. 518–21; Hans Patze and Walter Schlesinger, *Geschichte Thüringens* 2/1 (*MF* 48, Cologne and Vienna, 1974), pp. 10–13.

Expenditure on English royal castles: R. A. Brown, H. M. Colvin and A. J. Taylor, *The History of the King's Works: The Middle Ages* (2 vols., London, 1963) 1, pp. 64–5, 113; 2, pp. 630, 1023, 1029.

Knight's pay under Edward I: Michael Prestwich, *War, Politics and Finance under Edward I* (London, 1972), p. 160.

Trebuchets: T. F. Tout, 'The Fair of Lincoln and the "Histoire de Guillaume le Maréchal"', in his *Collected Papers* (3 vols., Manchester, 1932–4) 2, pp. 191–220, at pp. 218–20; Lynn White, *Medieval Technology and Social Change* (Oxford, 1962), p. 102; J. F. Finó, 'Machines de jet médiévales', *Gladius* 10 (1972), pp. 25–43; D. R. Hill, 'Trebuchets', *Viator* 4 (1973), pp. 99–114.

There are several facsimiles of *Villard de Honcourt's 'Sketchbook'*, e.g. Hans R. Hahnloser, *Villard de Honnecourt: Kritische Gesamtausgabe des Bauhüttenbuches ms. fr. 19093 der Pariser Nationalbibliothek* (2nd ed., Graz, 1972), trebuchet at plate 59, text and commentary pp. 159–62, or *The Sketchbook of Villard de Honnecourt*, ed. Theodore Bowie (Bloomington, 1959), plate 61.

Siege of Haldersleben: Annales Pegavienses, ed. George Heinrich Pertz, *MGH, SS* 16 (Hanover, 1859), pp. 232–70, at p. 264.

Welsh levies of 1247: *Littere Wallie*, ed. John Goronwy Edwards (Cardiff, 1940), no. 3, pp. 7–8 (Treaty of Woodstock).

Irish horsemen: Katharine Simms, 'Warfare in the Medieval Gaelic Lordships', *The Irish Sword* 12 (1975–6), pp. 98–108; Peter Harbison, 'Native Irish Arms and Armour in Medieval Gaelic Literature, 1170–1600', ibid., pp. 173–99, 270–84. Gerald of Wales, writing of the Irish in 1188, commented: 'they do not use the saddle or spurs when riding', Gerald of Wales (Giraldus Cambrensis), *Topographia Hibernica* 3.10, in J. S. Brewer, J. F. Dimock and G. F. Warner (eds.), *Opera* (8 vols., RS, 1861–91) 5, pp. 1–204, at p. 150.

Pomeranian horsemen: Herbord, *Dialogus de vita sancti Ottonis episcopi Babenbergensis* 2.23, ed. Jan Wikarjak and Kazimierz Liman, *MPH*, n.s., 7/3 (Warsaw, 1974), pp. 101–2.

Latin siege warfare in the Mediterranean is the subject of a forthcoming book by Randall Rogers.

'The infidel cavalry waited . . .': Francesco Gabrieli (ed.), *Arab Historians of the Crusades* (Eng. tr., Berkeley and London, 1969), p. 58 (Ibn al-Qalānisi).

Christian knights in Spain: Elena Lourie, 'A Society Organized for War: Medieval Spain', *Past and Present* 35 (1966), pp. 54–76, at p. 69.

'Nothing can withstand them . . .': Ambroise, *L'estoire de la guerre sainte*, lines 6816–18, ed. Gaston Paris (Paris, 1897), col. 182.

Crossbowmen in Spain: e.g. Julio González, *El reino de Castilla en la epoca de Alfonso VIII* (3 vols., Madrid, 1960) 3, no. 705, pp. 247–9 (1201); Emilio Sáez (ed.), 'Fueros de Puebla de Alcocer y Yébenes', *Anuario de historia del derecho español* 18 (1947), pp. 432–41, at p. 435; Julio González, *Repoblación de Castilla la Nueva* (2 vols., Madrid, 1975–6) 2, p. 350, n. 169.

Bows 'fitted together with glue': Fulcher of Chartres, *Historia Hierosolymitana* 1.34, ed. Heinrich Hagenmeyer (Heidelberg, 1913), p. 342.

Henry of Livonia: *Chronicon Livoniae* 1.5–9 (Meinhard), 9.3 (the knight Conrad), 15.3 (knights 'charged through . . . the enemy'), 10.8 ('the unarmoured enemy were wounded everywhere . . .'), 15.3 ('[the Estonians] were unarmoured . . .'), 10.12 (attack on Üxküll), 23.8 ('some of them built a tower'), 14.11 ('the Germans built a machine'), 10.12 ('the Russians also made a little machine . . .'), 26.3 (the Oeselians), 27.3 (*ars Theutonicorum*), 28.3 (*ars Osiliarum*), 11.8 (king of Kukenois), 12.1 (mailcoats from corpses), 27.3 (capture of armour, etc.), 28.3 (strengthened fortifications recaptured), ed. Leonid Arbusow and Albert Bauer (*AQ* 24, Darmstadt, 1959), pp. 4–6, 38, 134, 54, 132, 58, 242, 126, 60, 282, 298, 304, 80, 84, 296, 304. Üxküll and Mesoten are modern Latvian Ikškile and Mežotne, Fellin, Oesel and Warbole modern Estonian Viljandi, Saaremaa and Varbola.

'After the Normans had conquered the English . . .': *Gesta Stephani*, ed. K. R. Potter and R. H. C. Davis (Oxford, 1976), p. 14.

'The king sent to Gilbert fitz Richard . . .': *Brut y Tywysogyon or The Chronicle of the*

Princes: Red Book of Hergest Version, ed. and tr. Thomas Jones (Cardiff, 1955), pp. 71–3 (translation slightly modernized).

'*The Foreigners and the Irish of Teamhair . . .*': Giolla Brighde Mac Con Midhe, *Poems*, ed. and tr. N. J. A. Williams (Irish Texts Society 51, Dublin, 1980) XIII, 20, p. 141 (a poem on the defeat of Brian O Neill at Downpatrick, 1260).

O'Connors' attack on Athenry: Annals of Loch Cé, ed. and tr. William M. Hennessy (2 vols., RS, 1871), 1, p. 389.

'*After the manner of the French*': *History of Gruffydd ap Cynan*, ed. and tr. Arthur Jones (Manchester, 1910), p. 133.

Welsh princes' castles and siege machinery: Brut y Tywysogyon, ed. Jones, pp. 175, 177; Gerald of Wales, *Itinerarium Kambriae*, 2.6, ed. Brewer *et al.*, p. 123; Richard Avent, *Cestyll Tywysogion Gwynedd/Castles of the Princes of Gwynedd* (Cardiff, 1983), p. 7.

'*Lords barons all . . .*': *Song of Dermot and the Earl*, lines 666–70, ed. and tr. Goddard H. Orpen (Oxford, 1892), p. 50.

For *difficulties of terrain* in *Wales and Ireland* see Gerald of Wales (Giraldus Cambrensis), *Descriptio Kambriae* 2.8, in J. S. Brewer, J. F. Dimock and G. F. Warner (eds.), *Opera* (8 vols., RS, 1861–91) 6, pp. 153–227, at pp. 220–21; *idem*, *Expugnatio Hibernica* 2.38, ed. A. B. Scott and F. X. Martin (Dublin, 1978), pp. 246–8; John of Salisbury, *Policraticus* 6.6, 16, ed. C. C. J. Webb (2 vols., Oxford, 1909), 2, pp. 18, 42–4. For *eastern European examples* see Gallus Anonymus, *Chronicon* 1.25; 3.23, ed. K. Maleczynski, *MPH*, n.s., 2 (Cracow, 1952), pp. 50, 152.

Death of William of Holland: Matthew Paris, *Chronica majora*, ed. Luard, 5, p. 550.

'*The young men and the young women . . .*': Symeon of Durham, *Historia regum*, in *Symeonis monachi opera omnia*, ed. Thomas Arnold (2 vols., RS, 1882–5), 2, pp. 3–283, at pp. 191–2.

Queen Margaret ransoming slaves: Turgot, *Vita sancti Margaretae reginae*, ed. James Raine in *Symeonis Dunelmensis opera et collectanea* 1, ed. J. Hodgson Hinde (Surtees Society 51, 1868), pp. 234–54, at p. 247.

Raid of 1091: Symeon of Durham (attrib.), *De miraculis et translationibus sancti Cuthberti* 10, in *Symeonis monachi opera omnia*, ed. Thomas Arnold (2 vols., RS, 1882–5), 1, pp. 229–61; 2, pp. 333–62, at 2, p. 339.

Scots' ruse in 1070: Symeon of Durham, *Historia regum*, ed. Arnold, 2, p. 190.

'*The men of Hexham were aware of the king's anger . . .*': Aelred of Rievaulx, *De sanctis ecclesiae Haugustaldensis*, ed. James Raine in *The Priory of Hexham* (2 vols., Surtees Society 44, 46, 1864–5) 1, pp. 172–203, at p. 178; cf. Symeon of Durham, *Historia regum*, ed. Arnold, 2, pp. 36–7.

'*Trust in the protection of that peace . . .*': Symeon of Durham, *De miraculis . . . sancti Cuthberti* 10, ed. Arnold, 2, p. 339.

Vindictive saints: Gerald of Wales, *Topographia Hibernica* 2.54, ed. Brewer *et al.*,

p. 137. There was, of course, good sense in relying upon both castles and saints. In some areas saints had a particular role as guardians of the gate of the castle, C. L. Salch, 'La protection symbolique de la porte au Moyen Age dans les châteaux-forts alsaciens', in *Hommage à Geneviève Chevrier et Alain Geslan: Études médiévales* (Strasbourg, 1975), pp. 39–44.

New castles: Durham – Symeon of Durham, *Historia regum*, ed. Arnold, 2, pp. 199–200; *Newcastle* – ibid., p. 211; *Carlisle* – *Anglo-Saxon Chronicle, s.a.* 1092, ed. C. Plummer and J. Earle, *Two of the Saxon Chronicles Parallel* (2 vols., Oxford, 1892–9) 1, p. 227; *Norham* – Symeon of Durham's continuator, *Historia Dunelmensis ecclesiae*, in *Symeonis monachi opera omnia*, ed. Thomas Arnold (2 vols., RS, 1882–5), 1, pp. 135–60, at 1, p. 140.

On the *Anglo-French immigrant aristocracy in Scotland* see Geoffrey Barrow, *The Anglo-Norman Era in Scottish History* (Oxford, 1980); *idem, Kingship and Unity: Scotland 1000–1306* (London, 1981), chapter 3; A. A. M. Duncan, *Scotland: The Making of the Kingdom* (Edinburgh, 1975), chapters 6–8; R. L. G. Ritchie, *The Normans in Scotland* (Edinburgh, 1954).

Annandale charter of 1124: Early Scottish Charters prior to 1153, ed. Archibald C. Lawrie (Glasgow, 1905), no. 54, pp. 48–9.

Enslaving in 1138: John of Hexham, *Historia*, in *Symeonis monachi opera omnia*, ed. Thomas Arnold (2 vols., RS, 1882–5), 2, pp. 284–332, at p. 290.

Picts' brutality: e.g. Richard of Hexham, *Historia*, ed. Richard Howlett in *Chronicles of the Reigns of Stephen, Henry II and Richard I* (4 vols., RS, 1884–9) 3, pp. 137–78, at pp. 156–7.

Men of Galloway braining babies: Aelred of Rievaulx, *Relatio de Standardo*, ed. Howlett, ibid., pp. 179–99, at pp. 187–8.

Sallies from castles: e.g. Richard of Hexham, *Historia*, ed. Howlett, p. 157; John of Hexham, *Historia*, ed. Arnold, p. 291.

David's siege of Wark: John of Hexham, *Historia*, ed. Arnold, p. 289.

'With a great army he occupied . . .': Richard of Hexham, *Historia*, ed. Arnold, p. 145.

For the *quarrel before the battle of the Standard* see Aelred of Rievaulx, *Relatio*, ed. Howlett, pp. 189–98. The phrase 'unarmoured and naked' is from Henry of Huntingdon, *Historia Anglorum*, ed. Thomas Arnold (RS, 1879), p. 263.

William the Lion's invasion of 1173–4: Jordan Fantosme, *Chronicle*, lines 640–41 ('He cherished, loved and held dear . . .'), 266 ('lordship in castle . . .'), 1242–9 (misfire of siege machine), 1766 (William *pruz* and *hardi*), 1828 (*mult bons vassaus*), 1858–67 (Mortimer vs Balliol), ed. and tr. R. C. Johnston (Oxford, 1981), pp. 48, 20, 92–4, 132, 136, 138.

William mistakes the English for his own men: William of Newburgh, *Historia rerum Anglicarum* 2.33, ed. Richard Howlett in *Chronicles of the Reigns of Stephen, Henry II and Richard I* (4 vols., RS, 1884–9) 1–2, at 1, p. 184.

Galloway rising: Gesta regis Henrici secundi Benedicti abbatis, ed. William Stubbs (2 vols., RS, 1867), 1, pp. 67–8.

'*Unarmoured and naked*' *Manxmen*: *Annals of Furness*, ed. Richard Howlett in *Chronicles of the Reigns of Stephen, Henry II and Richard I* (4 vols., RS, 1884–9) 2, pp. 503–83, at pp. 570–71.

Danish civil wars of the 1130s: Saxo Grammaticus, *Gesta Danorum* 13.9.6, ed. J. Olrik and H. Raeder (2 vols., Copenhagen, 1931–57), 1, pp. 361–2; see also the comments of Eric Christiansen in his version of Saxo, *Danorum regum heroumque historia, Books X–XVI* (3 vols., *British Archaeological Reports, International Series* 84, 118/1–2, Oxford, 1980–81) 1, pp. 322–3, n. 84 (Christiansen must be wrong, however, in seeing this as a counterweighted rather than a torsion-based machine); *Annales Erphesfurdenses Lothariani*, ed. Oswald Holder-Egger, *Monumenta Erphesfurtensia* (*SRG*, Hanover and Leipzig, 1899), pp. 34–44, at p. 40. See also Lucien Musset, 'Problèmes militaires du monde scandinave (VIIe–XIIe s.)', in *Ordinamenti militari in Occidente nell'alto medioevo* (*Settimane di studio del Centro italiano di studi sull'alto medioevo* 15, 2 vols., Spoleto, 1968) 1, pp. 229–91, at pp. 288–90.

On the struggle between *innovators and traditionalists in Scandinavia* S. U. Palme, 'Les impôts, le Statut d'Alsno et la formation des ordres en Suède (1250–1350)', in R. Mousnier (ed.), *Problèmes de stratification sociale* (Paris, 1968), pp. 55–66.

German warrior immigrants in eastern Europe: Karl Bartels, *Deutsche Krieger in polnischen Diensten von Misika I. bis Kasimir dem Grossen, c. 963–1370* (Berlin, 1922); K. Schunemann, *Die Deutsche in Ungarn bis zum 12. Jahrhundert* (Berlin, 1923); Benedykt Zientara, 'Die deutschen Einwanderer in Polen vom 12. bis zum 14. Jahrhundert', in Walter Schlesinger (ed.), *Die deutsche Ostsiedlung des Mittelalters als Problem der europäischen Geschichte* (*Vorträge und Forschungen* 18, Sigmaringen, 1975), pp. 333–48. Not all such *hospites* were German; see H. Gockenjan, *Hilfsvölker und Grenzwächter in mittelalterlichen Ungarn* (Wiesbaden, 1972).

'*As immigrants come from various lands* . . .': *Libellus de institutione morum*, ed. J. Balogh, *Scriptores rerum Hungaricarum* 2 (Budapest, 1938), pp. 611–27, at p. 625. The *Libellus* is an eleventh- or twelfth-century *Fürstenspiegel*, formerly attributed to St Stephen, the first Christian ruler of Hungary.

4. The Image of the Conqueror

'*The charter of the sword* . . .': Eleanor Knott, *Irish Classical Poetry* (*Irish Life and Culture* 6, Dublin, 1957), p. 59, citing Maol Seachluinn O Huiginn.

Early chroniclers of the Norman conquest in southern Italy: Geoffrey Malaterra, *De rebus gestis Rogerii Calabriae et Siciliae comitis et Roberti Guiscardi ducis fratris eius*, ed. Ernesto Pontieri (*Rerum italicarum scriptores*, n.s., 5/1, Bologna, 1928); William of Apulia, *La geste de Robert Guiscard*, ed. Marguerite Mathieu (Palermo, 1961); Amatus of Montecassino, *Storia de' Normanni*, ed. Vincenzo de Bartholomaeis (*Fonti per la storia d'Italia* 76, Rome, 1935).

Malaterra on energy: De rebus gestis Rogerii 1.3, 7, 12, 38; 2.35; 3.13, 24, ed. Pontieri, pp. 9, 11, 14, 24, 46, 64, 71; see Ovidio Capitani, 'Specific Motivations and Continuing Themes in the Norman Chronicles of Southern Italy in the Eleventh and Twelfth Centuries', in *The Normans in Sicily and Southern Italy (Lincei Lectures 1974)* (Oxford, 1977), pp. 1–46, at pp. 7, 30–33, n. 15.

Malaterra on Norman courage: e.g. De rebus gestis Rogerii 1.9, ed. Pontieri, p. 13.

Amatus, Storia de' Normanni 1.23 ('knights of great prowess'); 2.17 ('the city of Aversa'); 1.43 ('the honour of the Normans grew'); 2.8 ('To tell the truth'); 2.21 (*corage* and *hardiesce*); 2.22 (*hardiesce* and *vaillantize*), ed. de Bartholomaeis, pp. 30, 75, 54–5, 67, 80, 83.

'The people of Gaul . . .': William of Apulia, *La geste* 3, lines 101–2, ed. Mathieu, p. 168.

'Then it was the turn of our men . . .': Malaterra, *De rebus gestis Rogerii* 1.7, ed. Pontieri, p. 11.

'Ferocious Normans': William of Apulia, *La geste* 3, line 217, ed. Mathieu, p. 176; cf. 1, line 320, p. 116.

'A savage, barbarous and horrible race . . .': ibid. 2, lines 427–8, ed. Mathieu, p. 154.

Killing of envoy's horse: Malaterra, *De rebus gestis Rogerii* 1.9, ed. Pontieri, p. 12.

Defeat of men of Palermo: ibid. 2.42, ed. Pontieri, p. 50.

'Everywhere the Norman race . . .': William of Apulia, *La geste* 2, lines 323–9, ed. Mathieu, p. 150.

Cariati: ibid. 2, line 383, ed. Mathieu, p. 152.

'Innate military ferocity': Malaterra, *De rebus gestis Rogerii* 3.24, ed. Pontieri, p. 71.

'They spread here and there . . .': Amatus, *Storia de' Normanni* 1.2, ed. de Bartholomaeis, pp. 10–11.

'The Normans are a crafty race . . .': Malaterra, *De rebus gestis Rogerii* 1.3, ed. Pontieri, p. 8.

'Greedy for lordship': ibid. 2.38; 3.7, ed. Pontieri, pp. 48, 60.

Orderic and 'strenuus': Orderic Vitalis, *Historia ecclesiastica*, ed. and tr. Marjorie Chibnall (6 vols., Oxford, 1968–80), 1, index verborum, pp. 372–3.

'We know well and have learned by experience . . .': De expugnatione Lyxbonensi: The Conquest of Lisbon, ed. and tr. Charles W. David (New York, 1936), p. 98; *Hervey de Glanville's speech*: ibid., pp. 106–7; *'it is not poverty that is driving you . . .'*: ibid., p. 120.

'No hereditary right drew us . . .': Orderic Vitalis, *Historia ecclesiastica* 11.24, ed. Chibnall 6, p. 102.

Femaleness of Greeks: Amatus, *Storia de' Normanni* 1.21; 2.17, ed. de Bartholomaeis, pp. 27, 75.

Anna Comnena, Alexiad 10.5.4 ('he was alarmed at their approach . . .'); 10.5.10 ('the Celtic race is . . . extremely reckless . . .'); 10.6.4 ('the Latin race is . . . avaricious . . .'); 11.6.3 ('the Celtic race is independent . . .') ed. B. Leib (3 vols., Paris, 1937–45), 2, pp. 206–7, 210, 211; 3, p. 28.

'Among the Franks . . .': Francesco Gabrieli (ed.), *Arab Historians of the Crusades* (Eng. tr., Berkeley and London, 1969), p. 73.

Anna Comnena, Alexiad 10.5.10 ('Each of the Celts . . .'); 4.8.2 (Guiscard's 'heart full of passion'); 13.10.5 (Bohemond 'harsh and savage'); 14.2.4 (Tancred 'acting like his race'), ed. Leib, 2, p. 209; 1, p. 167; 3, pp. 123, 147.

'In everything he was the boldest . . .': Malaterra, *De rebus gestis Rogerii* 1.17, ed. Pontieri, p. 17.

'Bloodthirsty and warlike men . . .': Michael Attaleiates, *Historia*, ed. Immanuel Bekker (*Corpus scriptorum historiae Byzantinae* 50, Bonn, 1853), p. 107.

'The Franks . . . animals . . .': Usamah Ibn-Munqidh, *An Arab-Syrian Gentleman and Warrior . . . Memoirs of Usamah Ibn-Munqidh*, tr. Philip K. Hitti (New York, 1929), p. 161.

'Victory as a fief': Aelred of Rievaulx, *Relatio de Standardo*, ed. Richard Howlett in *Chronicles of the Reigns of Stephen, Henry II and Richard I* (4 vols., RS, 1884–9) 3, pp. 179–99, at p. 185 (Walter Espec on the Normans, before the battle of the Standard, 1138).

'Future duke of Sicily': Deusdedit, *Collectio canonum* 3.284–5 (156–7), ed. Victor Wolf von Glanvell, *Die Kanonessammlung des Kardinals Deusdedit* (Paderborn, 1905), p. 393; *Le liber censuum de l'église romaine*, ed. Paul Fabre *et al.* (3 vols., Paris, 1889–1910), 1, pp. 421–2, nos. 162–3.

Castile–Barcelona agreement: *Colección de documentos inéditos del archivo general de la Corona de Aragón* 4, ed. Próspero de Bofarull y Mascaró (Barcelona, 1849), no. 62, pp. 168–74.

Raymond III of Tripoli's grant of Homs: Jonathan Riley-Smith, *The Knights of St John in Jerusalem and Cyprus c. 1050–1310* (London, 1967), pp. 66–7 (with other examples of such grants).

Raymond Berengar IV's grants to the Templars: *Colección de documentos . . . de la Corona de Aragón* 4, ed. de Bofarull y Mascaró, no. 43, pp. 93–9; also in *Cartulaire général de l'ordre du Temple*, ed. Marquis d'Albon (Paris, 1913), no. 314, pp. 204–5.

Sancho Ramírez re Ejea: Lacarra, no. 94 (1086–94).

Swordbrothers and bishop of Riga: Henry of Livonia, *Chronicon Livoniae* 11.3, ed. Leonid Arbusow and Albert Bauer (*AQ* 24, Darmstadt, 1959), pp. 68–70.

'That man will certainly conquer the enemy . . .': William of Poitiers, *Gesta Guillelmi ducis Normannorum* 2.5, ed. Raymonde Foreville (Paris, 1952), p. 158.

Prospective grants in Wales: *Rotuli chartarum in turri Londinensi asservati (1199–1216)*, ed. T. D. Hardy (London, 1837), p. 66 (1200); *Calendar of the Patent Rolls (1258–66)* (London, 1910), p. 674 (1266); see Rees Davies, *Domination and Conquest: The Experience of Ireland, Scotland and Wales 1100–1300* (Cambridge, 1990), p. 36.

Grant of Connacht: *Rotuli chartarum . . . (1199–1216)*, pp. 218–19 (1215).

Nicholas de Verdon's grant: *Register of the Abbey of St Thomas Dublin*, ed. John T. Gilbert (RS, 1889), no. 44, pp. 42–3 (1203–17).

Roelinus's grant: *Irish Cartularies of Llanthony Prima and Secunda*, ed. Eric St John Brooks (Irish Manuscripts Commission, Dublin, 1953), no. 75, pp. 87–8 (*c.* 1181–91).

William Iron Arm's offer: Amatus, *Storia de' Normanni* 2.29, ed. de Bartholomaeis, p. 94.

Robert Guiscard and Roger: Malaterra, *De rebus gestis Rogerii* 1.29, ed. Pontieri, p. 22.

Monk of Benevento's dream: Amatus, *Storia de' Normanni* 5.1–2, ed. de Bartholomaeis, p. 223.

'As a poet of modern times . . .': William of Apulia, *La geste*, prologue, lines 2–5, ed. Mathieu, p. 98.

'Oh, time so longed for! . . .': Fulcher of Chartres, *Historia Hierosolymitana* 1.29, ed. Heinrich Hagenmeyer (Heidelberg, 1913), p. 305.

Dating from 'the liberation of the city': William of Tyre, *Chronicle* 20.14, ed. R. B. C. Huygens (2 vols., *Corpus Christianorum, Continuatio mediaevalis* 63–63A, Turnhout, 1986), 2, p. 927.

Capture of Brandenburg: Henry of Antwerp, *Tractatus de captione urbis Brandenburg*, ed. Oswald Holder-Egger, *MGH, SS* 25 (Hanover, 1880), pp. 482–4, at p. 484.

'It was the day of the translation of St Isidore . . .': *Primera crónica general de España* 1125, ed. Ramón Menéndez Pidal (2 vols., Madrid, 1955), 2, p. 767.

'Roger Pipard, a conqueror . . .': *Calendar of the Justiciary Rolls . . . of Ireland (1295–1303)*, ed. James Mills (Dublin, 1905), pp. 281–2.

'Hearing and understanding the charters . . .': *Chartularies of St Mary's Abbey Dublin*, ed. John T. Gilbert (2 vols., RS, 1884), 1, no. 254, pp. 275–7.

Tenure 'as of conquest' in the Morea: *Chronicle of Morea*, tr. Harold E. Lurier, *Crusaders as Conquerors* (New York, 1964), p. 171 and n. 40; *Chronique de Morée* 241, ed. Jean Longnon (Paris, 1911), p. 87; *Les assises de Romanie* 71, 90, 95, 98, ed. Georges Recoura (Paris, 1930), pp. 210, 220, 222–3, 224.

'The law of the Morea . . .': *Les assises*, ed. Recoura, editorial comment at p. 40.

'Now this land of Morea, my lord . . .': *Chronicle of Morea*, tr. Lurier, p. 196.

'My ancestors came with William the Bastard . . .': Walter of Guisborough, *Chronicle*, ed. Harry Rothwell (Camden 3rd ser., 89, 1957), p. 216.

Earl of Gloucester re Glamorgan: *Placitorum abbreviatio* (Record Commission, London, 1811), p. 201.

'After the great massacre . . .': Fulcher of Chartres, *Historia Hierosolymitana*, 1.29, ed. Hagenmeyer, p. 304.

Christian capture of a city: Usamah, tr. Hitti, *An Arab-Syrian Gentleman*, p. 178; cf. Joshua Prawer, *Crusader Institutions* (Oxford, 1980), pp. 253–4, n. 11.

'In the time of the Irish': Examples in Richard Butler, *Some Notices of the Castle and of the Ecclesiastical Buildings of Trim* (Trim, 1835), pp. 252–3 ('from Sir William Betham's collections'); *'in the time of the Moors, etc.'*: Lacarra, nos. 5, 123, 134; *'in the time of the Greeks'*: Giorgio Fedalto, *La Chiesa Latina in Oriente* (2nd ed., 3 vols., Verona, 1981) 1, pp. 388–9.

Prospective grant of Denia: *Colección de documentos . . . de la Corona de Aragón* 4, ed. de Bofarull y Mascaró, no. 62, p. 169.

'The coming of the English': Eric St J. Brooks, 'A Charter of John de Courcy to the Abbey of Navan', *Journal of the Royal Society of Antiquaries of Ireland* 63 (1933),

pp. 38–45, at p. 39; *'the conquest of Ireland by the English'*: *Dignitas decani*, ed. Newport B. White (Dublin, 1957), no. 111, pp. 112–13 (= *Crede mihi*, ed. John T. Gilbert (Dublin, 1897), no. 74, p. 67); *'the coming of the Franks into Ireland'*: *Calendar of the Charter Rolls, 1226–1516* (6 vols., London, 1903–27) 1, pp. 230–31; *'the arrival of the English and the Welsh in Ireland'*: *Reports of the Deputy Keeper of the Public Records of Ireland 1–55* (Dublin, 1869–1923), 20, no. 130, pp. 57–8; *'the first arrival of earl Richard [Strongbow] in Ireland'*: William Dugdale, *Monasticon Anglicanum*, ed. John Caley *et al.* (6 vols. in 8, London, 1846), 6/2, p. 1131, calendared in *Calendar of the Patent Rolls (1358–61)* (London, 1911), p. 488.

Tuam complaint of 1256: *Close Rolls of the Reign of Henry III (1254–56)* (London, 1931), p. 413.

Limit of legal memory in Ireland: e.g. Geoffrey Hand, 'English Law in Ireland, 1172–1351', *Northern Ireland Legal Quarterly* 23 (1972), pp. 393–422, p. 401, citing PRO S.C. 1/23, no. 85; *Calendar of Documents relating to Ireland (1171–1307)*, ed. H. S. Sweetman (5 vols., London, 1875–86), 2, pp. 281–2, no. 1482 (1278).

'Wales is a land of conquest . . .': *Registrum vulgariter nuncupatum 'The Record of Caernarvon'*, ed. Henry Ellis (Record Commission, London, 1838), p. 149.

'Novella plantacio': *Mecklenburgisches UB* (25 vols. in 26, Schwerin and Leipzig, 1863–1977) 3, no. 1781, p. 164.

'Here begins the history of those who conquered Constantinople . . .': Robert of Clari, *La conquête de Constantinople* 1, ed. Philippe Lauer (Paris, 1924), p. 1.

Geoffrey de *Villehardouin*, *La conquête de Constantinople*, ed. Edmond Faral (2nd ed., 2 vols., Paris, 1961).

'Livre dou conqueste': *Les gestes des Chiprois*, ed. Gaston Raynaud (*Publications de la Société de l'Orient latin, Série historique* 5, Geneva, 1887), pp. 5, 9, 17, 52; *RHC, Occ.* 2, p. xiii; on this complex material see M. R. Morgan, *The Chronicle of Ernoul and the Continuations of William of Tyre* (Oxford, 1973).

'Stormed the ramparts of Ireland': Gerald of Wales (Giraldus Cambrensis), *Itinerarium Kambriae* 1.12, in J. S. Brewer, J. F. Dimock and G. F. Warner (eds.), *Opera* (8 vols., RS, 1861–91) 6, pp. 1–152, at p. 91.

'Noble deeds could promise each of them . . .': Gerald of Wales, *Expugnatio Hibernica* 2.10, ed. A. B. Scott and F. X. Martin (Dublin, 1978), p. 156.

Song of Dermot and the Earl, lines 644–5 ('Lord barons . . . know that . . .'), 485 ('sanz mentir'), 1763 ('de verite'), 407 ('solum le dist de mun cuntur'), 456 ('Cum nus recunte le chanson'), 820–23 ('They sent everywhere for physicians . . .'), ed. and tr. Goddard H. Orpen (Oxford, 1892), pp. 48, 36, 130, 32, 34, 62.

For discussion of the *composition and date of the 'Song'* see J. Long, 'Dermot and the Earl: Who Wrote the Song?', *Proceedings of the Royal Irish Academy* 75C (1975), pp. 263–72.

Criticism of German judges: Henry of Livonia, *Chronicon Livoniae* 10.15, ed. Arbusow and Bauer, p. 66.

William of Sabina: ibid. 29.3 ed. Arbusow and Bauer, p. 318; compare the entire account of the legate's visit, 29.2–8, pp. 316–26.

Livländische Reimchronik, ed. Leo Meyer (Paderborn, 1876); on the poet's sources and attitudes see Lutz Mackensen, 'Zur livländischen Reimchronik', in his *Zur deutschen Literatur Altlivlands* (Würzburg, 1961), pp. 21–58, and the perceptive brief remarks of Eric Christiansen, *The Northern Crusades* (London, 1980), pp. 91–3.

Song of Dermot, lines 125 ('To avenge his shame'), 136–41 ('Traisun', 'felun', 'traitur'), 282–3 ('Wrongfully my own people . . .'), 201 and 1409 (Dermot 'curteis'), 3086–99 ('Earl Richard then gave . . .'), ed. Orpen, pp. 10, 12, 22, 16 and 104, 224–5.

'*A sort of original Domesday Book* . . .': ibid., p. 303 (editorial note).

'*Praise of his family*': Expugnatio Hibernica 2.10, ed. Scott and Martin, p. 156.

On the *manuscript tradition of the 'Expugnatio'* see the present writer's *Gerald of Wales 1146–1223* (Oxford, 1982), pp. 214–16, 178, n. 3.

Livländische Reimchronik, lines 103–4 ('God's wisdom made Christendom wide'), 93 ('Where no aspostle ever came'), 120–22, ('How Christianity came to Livonia'), 669–76 ('They came to Jersika . . .'), 1466–8 ('Slew many a powerful man . . .'), 8397–402 ('So you could see many an undismayed hero . . .'), ed. Meyer, pp. 3, 16, 34, 192.

De expugnatione Lyxbonensi, ed. David, pp. 54–6 ('Peoples of various races . . .'), 104 (Bretons and Scots), 134 (fierce Flemings), 106 (barbarian Scots), 128 ('Our men, that is, the Normans and the English'), 106 ('Who does not know . . .' – from Hervey de Glanville's speech). There is no certain evidence in the account that any men from Normandy participated in the expedition; the 'Normans' may well all have been 'Anglo-Normans'.

Ibid., pp. 132 ('Two churches were constructed . . .'), 56 (rules about the women accompanying the fleet), 68 ('the ships of the Franks'), 110–12 ('the agreement between me and the Franks').

On the *term 'Frank' in the First Crusade* see Peter Knoch, *Studien zu Albert von Aachen* (Stuttgart, 1966), chapter 4, pp. 91–107, 'Die "Franken" des ersten Kreuzzugs in den Augenzeugenberichten'; Bernd Schneidmüller, *Nomen patriae: Die Entstehung Frankreichs in der politisch-geographischen Terminologie (10.–13. Jahrhundert)* (Sigmaringen, 1987), chapter 5(a), pp. 106–24, 'Franci: Kreuzfahrer oder Nordfranzosen in der Kreuzzugshistoriographie?'

See Reinhard Wenskus, *Stammesbildung und Verfassung: Das Werden der frühmittelalterlichen gentes* (Cologne and Graz, 1961), pp. 512–41, for the *origin, possible meaning and spread of the name Frank*.

Muslim 'Faranǧa': André Miquel, *La géographie humaine du monde musulman jusqu'au milieu du 11e siècle 2: Géographie arabe et représentation du monde: La terre et l'étranger* (Paris, 1975), chapter 7, pp. 343–80, 'L'Europe de l'Ouest', esp. pp. 354–9 (Remie Constable kindly provided this reference); see also Bernard Lewis, *The Muslim Discovery of Europe* (New York and London, 1982), pp. 137–46.

Cerularius and Humbert: Humbert of Silva Candida, *Adversus Graecorum calumnias*,

PL 143, cols. 929–74, at cols. 929, 934; for general context see Anton Michel, *Humbert und Kerullarios* (2 vols., Paderborn, 1924–30).

Eleventh-century Byzantine writers: e.g. Michael Attaleiates, *Historia*, ed. Bekker, index, *s.v.* 'Franci'; George Cedrenus, *Historiarum compendium*, ed. Immanuel Bekker (2 vols., *Corpus scriptorum historiae Byzantinae* 34–5, Bonn, 1838–9), 2, pp. 545, 617.

Sigurd I 'a Frankish king': Gabrieli, *Arab Historians*, p. 27 (Ibn al-Qalānisi).

'The barbarians are accustomed to call all westerners Franks': Ekkehard of Aura, *Hierosolymita* 16.2, *RHC*, *Occ.* 5, pp. 1–40, at p. 25; *Raymond of Aguilers: Liber (Historia Francorum qui ceperunt Iherusalem)* 6, ed. John H. Hill and Laurita L. Hill (Paris, 1969), p. 52.

'All the people who live beyond the sea . . .': Simon of Saint Quentin, *Historia Tartarorum*, ed. Jean Richard (Paris, 1965), p. 52.

'Pilgrim knights of Christ': *Gesta Francorum* 10.30, ed. and tr. Rosalind Hill (London, 1962), p. 73.

'The honour of the Roman Church and the Frankish people', 'pilgrim church of the Franks': Raymond of Aguilers, *Liber* 10, ed. Hill and Hill, pp. 79, 83.

'First king of the Franks': William of Tyre, *Chronicle* 11.12, ed. Huygens, 1, p. 513.

'When Syria was recovered . . .': Ambroise, *L'estoire de la guerre sainte*, lines 8494–505, 8509–10, ed. Gaston Paris (Paris, 1897), cols. 227–8.

'Men living in Constantinople . . .': Walter Map, *De nugis curialium* 2.18, ed. and tr. M. R. James, rev. C. N. L. Brooke and R. A. B. Mynors (Oxford, 1983), p. 178.

'The village of the immigrant Franks': Albert of Aachen, *Historia Hierosolymitana* 1.8, *RHC*, *Occ.* 4, pp. 265–713, at p. 277 (cf. 2.6, p. 303); see György Székely, 'Wallons et Italiens en Europe centrale aux XIe–XVIe siècles', *Annales Universitatis Scientiarum Budapestinensis de Rolando Eötuös Nominatae*, sectio historica 6 (1964), pp. 3–71, at pp. 16–17.

Welsh chroniclers: e.g. *Brut y Tywysogyon or The Chronicle of the Princes: Red Book of Hergest Version*, ed. and tr. Thomas Jones (Cardiff, 1955), index, *s.v.* 'French'.

'The Franks of Ireland': Donnchá O Corráin, 'Nationality and Kingship in Pre-Norman Ireland', in T. W. Moody (ed.), *Nationality and the Pursuit of National Independence* (*Historical Studies* 11, Belfast, 1978), pp. 1–35, at p. 35.

'The more recent kings of the Scots . . .': Walter of Coventry, *Memoriale*, ed. William Stubbs (2 vols., RS, 1872–3), 2, p. 206 (the 'Barnwell Chronicle').

'Forum Francorum', etc.: *Documentos de Don Sancho I (1174–1211)* 1, ed. Rui de Azevado *et al.* (Coimbra, 1979), no. 86, pp. 138–9; *Fuero de Logroño*, ed. T. Moreno Garbaya, *Apuntes históricos de Logroño* (Logroño, 1943), pp. 42–9.

'New Francia': Honorius III, 20 May 1224, *Novit regia celsitudo*, Po. 7258; *Opera omnia*, ed. César Auguste Horoy (5 vols., Paris, 1879–82), 4, no. 227, col. 653; also in *Recueil des historiens des Gaules et de la France*, ed. Martin Bouquet *et al.* (new ed., 24 vols., Paris, 1869–1904), 19, p. 754.

'Privileged Franks': *Chronicle of Morea*, tr. Lurier, p. 157.

'Frankish law' in eastern Europe: e.g. Helbig & Weinrich 2, nos. 29, 30, 36, 80, 81, 111, 114, pp. 162–3, 180, 306, 310, 418, 430.

'Fo-lang-ki': Louis Dermigny, *La Chine et l'Occident: Le commerce à Canton au XVIIIe siècle 1719–1833* 1 (Paris, 1964), p. 292.

5. The Free Village

'It profits the commonwealth greatly . . .': José María Font Rius (ed.), *Cartas de población y franquicia de Cataluña* (2 vols., Madrid and Barcelona, 1969) 1, no. 223, pp. 308–9 (Peter I of Aragon, 1207).

New towns in England: Maurice Beresford, *New Towns of the Middle Ages* (London, 1967), pp. 637–41.

Walls of Florence: Daniel Waley, *The Italian City Republics* (London, 1969), p. 35.

'Strong inflationary pressures': Peter Spufford, *Money and its Use in Medieval Europe* (Cambridge, 1988), p. 243.

'The lure of aggregates': *Cambridge Economic History of Europe 1: The Agrarian Life of the Middle Ages*, ed. M. M. Postan (2nd ed., Cambridge, 1966), p. 561; for the scholar who has yielded to the lure most whole-heartedly see Josiah Cox Russell, *British Medieval Population* (Albuquerque, 1948); cf. J. Z. Titow, *English Rural Society 1200–1350* (London, 1969), pp. 66–73.

Domesday population: H. C. Darby, *Domesday England* (Cambridge, 1977), pp. 87–91, 'Total Population'.

Landless in Domesday: *Cambridge Economic History* 1, ed. Postan, p. 562; M. M. Postan, *The Medieval Economy and Society* (London, 1972), p. 31.

Growth rates for England after 1541 are from E. A. Wrigley and R. S. Schofield, *The Population History of England 1541–1871* (Cambridge, Mass., 1981).

Taunton evidence: J. Z. Titow, 'Some Evidence of the Thirteenth-Century Population Increase', *Economic History Review*, 2nd ser., 14 (1961), pp. 218–24.

Nice evidence: Georges Duby, *Rural Economy and Country Life in the Medieval West* (Eng. tr., London, 1968), p. 119.

'The power of the Franks . . .': Francesco Gabrieli (ed.), *Arab Historians of the Crusades* (Eng. tr., Berkeley and London, 1969), p. 3 (Ibn al-Athīr).

Templar estates: Charles Higounet, 'Mouvements de population dans le Midi de la France du XIe siècle d'après les noms de personne et de lieu', in his *Paysages et villages neufs du Moyen Age* (Bordeaux, 1975), pp. 417–37, at p. 421.

Lubiąż: Helbig & Weinrich 2, no. 1, p. 70.

Raymond the Fleming: Orderic Vitalis, *Historia ecclesiastica* 7.5, ed. and tr. Marjorie Chibnall (6 vols., Oxford 1968–80), 4, p. 12.

Writ of William I: *Regesta Regum Anglo-Normannorum* 1, ed. H. W. C. Davis (Oxford, 1913), appendix, 2 *bis*, p. 118 (= calendar no. 33).

Flemings in 1173–4: Jordan Fantosme, *Chronicle*, lines 788–9, 417–18, 994–8, ed. R. C. Johnston (Oxford, 1981), pp. 58–9, 30–31, 72–3.

Flemings in Scotland: Geoffrey Barrow, *The Anglo-Norman Era in Scottish History* (Oxford, 1980), pp. 44–6 and 57 (map 7); *Acts of Malcolm IV, King of Scots, 1153–65*, ed. Geoffrey Barrow (*Regesta Regum Scottorum* 1, Edinburgh, 1960), no. 175, pp. 219–20; K. J. Stringer, *Earl David of Huntingdon, 1152–1219: A Study in Anglo-Scottish History* (Edinburgh, 1985), app., no. 55, pp. 254–5 (1172–99); A. A. M. Duncan, *Scotland: The Making of the Kingdom* (Edinburgh, 1975), pp. 137, 138, 189.

Flemings in burghs and Berwick: Duncan, *Scotland*, p. 476; Walter of Guisborough, *Chronicle*, ed. Harry Rothwell (Camden 3rd ser., 89, 1957), p. 275.

Flemings in Vienna: Helbig & Weinrich 2, no. 125, p. 474.

Flemings in cities of 'Ostsiedlung': e.g. Liselotte Feyerabend, *Die Rigauer und Revaler Familiennamen im 14. und 15. Jahrhundert* (Cologne and Vienna, 1985), p. 74.

Praise of Baldwin V: Gervase of Rheims, *Epistola de vita sancti Donatiani*, ed. Oswald Holder-Egger, *MGH, SS* 15/2 (Hanover, 1888), pp. 854–6, at p. 855.

Charter of Gerung of Meissen: Helbig & Weinrich 1, no. 6, p. 58; this case is discussed at length in Walter Schlesinger, 'Flemmingen und Kühren: Zur Siedlungsform niederländischer Siedlungen des 12. Jahrhunderts im mittel-deutschen Osten', in *idem* (ed.), *Die deutsche Ostsiedlung als Problem der europäischen Geschichte* (*Vorträge und Forschungen* 18, Sigmaringen, 1975), pp. 263–309; he thinks only fifteen *mansi* were occupied (p. 284).

Charter of Arnold of Ballenstedt: Helbig & Weinrich 1, no. 8, pp. 62–4.

On the *Flemish 'mansus'*: Walter Kuhn, 'Flämische und fränkische Hufe als Leit-formen der mittelalterlichen Ostsiedlung', in his *Vergleichende Untersuchungen zur mittelalterlichen Ostsiedlung* (Cologne and Vienna, 1973), pp. 1–51.

Netherlandish dialect east of Elbe: Hermann Teuchert, *Die Sprachreste der niederländischen Siedlungen des 12. Jahrhunderts* (2nd ed., *MF* 70, Cologne and Vienna, 1972); Karl Bischoff, *Sprache und Geschichte an der mittleren Elbe und der unteren Saale* (*MF* 52, Cologne and Graz, 1967), chapter 4.

Transylvanian documents: *UB zur Geschichte der Deutschen in Siebenbürgen* 1, ed. Franz Zimmermann and Carl Werner (Hermannstadt, 1892), nos. 2, 4–5, pp. 2–5; on interpretation of the term 'Fleming' here Karl Reinerth, 'Siebenbürger and Magdeburger Flandrenses-Urkunden aus dem 12. Jahrhundert', *Südostdeutsches Archiv* 8 (1965), pp. 26–56.

'A certain folk of strange origin and custom . . .': *Brut y Tywysogyon or The Chronicle of the Princes: Red Book of Hergest Version*, ed. Thomas Jones (Cardiff, 1955), p. 53.

Wizo 'chief of the Flemings': *Cartulary of Worcester Cathedral Priory*, ed. R. R. Darlington (Pipe Roll Society, n.s., 37, 1968 for 1962–3), no. 252, pp. 134–5; *Freskin son of Ollec*: *Pipe Roll 31 Henry I*, ed. J. Hunter (Record Commission, London, 1833), p. 136; *divinatory practices*: Gerald of Wales (Giraldus Cambrensis), *Itinerarium Kambriae* 1.2, in J. S. Brewer, J. F. Dimock and G. F. Warner (eds.), *Opera* (8 vols., RS, 1861–91) 6, pp. 1–152, at pp. 87–9; *Flemish language in Pembrokeshire*: *idem*, *Speculum Duorum*, ed. Yves Lefèvre and R. B. C. Huygens, general ed. Michael Richter (Cardiff, 1974), p. 36.

Llywelyn ap Iorwerth: *Brut y Tywysogyon*, ed. Jones, p. 221.

'They are a brave and sturdy people . . .': *Itinerarium Kambriae* 1.13, ed. Brewer *et al.*, p. 83.

'Fleet of the Flemings': *Annals of the Kingdom of Ireland by the Four Masters*, ed. and tr. John O'Donovan (4 vols., Dublin, 1851), 2, p. 1173, *s.a.* 1169.

Gerard Fleming: *Recueil des historiens des croisades, Lois* 2 (Paris, 1843), pp. 528–9, no. 44; *Michael Fleming*: *Liber cartarum Sancte Crucis*, ed. Cosmo Innes (Bannatyne Club, Edinburgh, 1840), app. 2, no. 7, p. 213 (cf. *Acts of William I, King of Scots, 1165–1214*, ed. Geoffrey Barrow (*Regesta Regum Scottorum* 2, Edinburgh, 1971), no. 560, p. 477); *Henry Fleming*: Helbig & Weinrich 1, no. 130, pp. 480–82.

Alfonso I for Sancho Garciez: Lacarra, no. 132; a charter of Alfonso for Ejea dating to 1118 is printed in *Colección de fueros municipales y cartas pueblas de los reinos de Castilla, León, Corona de Aragón y Navarra*, ed. Tomás Muñoz y Romero (Madrid, 1847), pp. 299–300.

Thomas of Wrocław for Godislaus: *Schlesisches UB*, ed. Heinrich Appelt and Winfried Irgang (4 vols. to date, Graz, Cologne and Vienna, 1963–), 3, no. 2, pp. 15–16.

'Gedcane': Cosmas of Prague, *Chronica Boemorum* 2.1, ed. Berthold Bretholz (*SRG*, n.s., Berlin, 1923), p. 83.

Robert Guiscard in Calabria: Geoffrey Malaterra, *De rebus gestis Rogerii Calabriae et Siciliae comitis et Roberti Guiscardi ducis fratris eius* 2.36–7, ed. Ernesto Pontieri (*Rerum italicarum scriptores*, n.s., 5/1, Bologna, 1928), p. 47.

Dafydd ab Owain Gwynedd: *Brut y Tywysogyon*, ed. Jones, p. 145; cf. ibid., p. 109, and the comments of Rees Davies, *Conquest, Coexistence and Change: Wales 1063–1415* (Oxford, 1987), pp. 119–20.

'He called together all the captives . . .': Malaterra, *De rebus gestis Rogerii* 4.16, ed. Pontieri, pp. 95–6.

'When peasants establish a new village . . .': *Sachsenspiegel, Landrecht* 3.79.1, ed. Karl August Eckhardt (*Germanenrechte*, n.s., Göttingen, 1955), p. 262.

'Desiring to attain the improvement . . .': Helbig & Weinrich 2, no. 67, p. 256; for an anthology of such phrases from Silesian documents see Josef Joachim Menzel, *Die schlesischen Lokationsurkunden des 13. Jahrhunderts* (Würzburg, 1977), p. 184.

'If more can be got out of it . . .': *Inquisitio Eliensis*, ed. N. E. S. A. Hamilton, *Inquisitio comitatus Cantabrigiensis, subjicitur Inquisitio Eliensis* (London, 1876), pp. 97–183, at p. 97.

Thirteenth-century Austrian poem: Alfred Haverkamp, *Medieval Germany 1056–1273* (Eng. tr., Oxford, 1988), p. 301, referring to a scene in the *Kleiner Lucidiarius* of Seifried Helblinc.

'We have given a marsh to settlers . . .': Helbig & Weinrich 1, no. 24, p. 114.

On *Wichmann* in general see Dietrich Claude, *Geschichte des Erzbistums Magdeburg bis in das 12. Jahrhundert* (2 vols., MF 67, Cologne, 1972–5) 2, pp. 71–175.

Charters of Wichmann: Helbig & Weinrich 1, no. 5, pp. 54–6 (as bishop of Naumburg); no. 10, pp. 68–70 (Pechau); no. 11, pp. 72–4 (Poppendorf); no. 12, p. 74 (Grosswusteritz); no. 13, pp. 78–80 (Jüterbog).

Magdeburg law and guilds: *UB des Erzstifts Magdeburg* 1, ed. Friedrich Israël and Walter Möllenberg (Magdeburg, 1937), no. 421, pp. 554–6; *Gesta archiepiscoporum Magdeburgensium*, ed. Wilhelm Schum, *MGH, SS* 14 (Hanover, 1883), pp. 361–486, at p. 416.

Charter of Hermann Balk: Helbig & Weinrich 2, no. 17, p. 134.

'They have agreed to the following terms . . .': ibid. 1, no. 23, p. 108.

Conrad of Silesia for Siedlce: ibid. 2, no. 30, pp. 164–6.

Nine free years for scrub, sixteen for thick wood: Menzel, *Die schlesischen Lokationsurkunden*, p. 250; *Regesten zur schlesischen Geschichte* 3 (*Codex diplomaticus Silesiae* 7/3, Breslau, 1886), no. 2251, p. 179 (Zator, 1292).

Fryčovice: Helbig & Weinrich 2, no. 109, p. 412.

Exempt years in Silesia: Menzel, *Die schlesischen Lokationsurkunden*, p. 250.

Charter of Gerung of Meissen: Helbig & Weinrich 1, no. 7, p. 62.

Teutonic Knights settling Courland: ibid. 1, no. 150, p. 546.

Polish Galicia: ibid. 2, no. 84, p. 320.

Hospitallers in New Castile: Julio González, *Repoblación de Castilla la Nueva* (2 vols., Madrid, 1975–6) 1, p. 333; cf. p. 153 and n. 402.

Yébenes: Emilio Sáez (ed.), 'Fueros de Puebla de Alcocer y Yébenes', *Anuario de historia del derecho español* 18 (1947), pp. 432–41, at p. 438.

Exemption from military service in Silesia: Menzel, *Die schlesischen Lokationsurkunden*, p. 247.

Raymond Berengar for San Esteban: Lacarra, no. 374 (1154).

Alfonso II for Valmadrid: ibid., no. 275.

Vines in Yébenes: González, *Repoblación* 2, p. 50; Sáez, 'Fueros de Puebla de Alcocer y Yébenes', p. 438; cf. González, *Repoblación* 2, p. 191, n. 120.

Limits on early alienation: González, *Repoblación* 2, p. 191, n. 120.

'Yugada' in New Castile: ibid. 2, p. 188; *Diccionario de la lengua española*, ed. Real Academia de España (19th ed., Madrid, 1970), p. 1360, s.v.

Size of holdings east of Elbe: Walter Kuhn, 'Bauernhofgrossen in der mittelalterlichen Nordostsiedlung', in his *Vergleichende Untersuchungen zur mittelalterlichen Ostsiedlung* (Cologne and Vienna, 1973), pp. 53–111.

Virgate holders in England: E. A. Kosminsky, *Studies in the Agrarian History of England in the Thirteenth Century* (Eng. tr., Oxford, 1956), p. 216.

Size of holdings in Picardy: Robert Fossier, *La terre et les hommes en Picardie jusqu'à la fin de XIIIe siècle* (2 vols., Paris and Louvain, 1968) 2, p. 647.

Charter of Gerbord of Köthen: Helbig & Weinrich 1, no. 95, pp. 356–8.

Charter of Dietrich Stange: ibid. 1, no. 129, p. 478.

Rent and tithes in Silesia: Menzel, *Die schlesischen Lokationsurkunden*, pp. 234–8.

Dues in Brandenburg: William W. Hagen, 'How Mighty the Junkers? Peasant Rents and Seigneurial Profits in Sixteenth-Century Brandenburg', *Past and Present* 108 (1985), pp. 80–116, at p. 85.

Calculations of yield of 'mansus': ibid., p. 86; J. Z. Titow, *Winchester Yields: A Study in Medieval Agricultural Productivity* (Cambridge, 1972), p. 4; Walter of Henley,

Husbandry 59–60, ed. Dorothea Oschinsky, *Walter of Henley and other Treatises on Estate Management and Accounting* (Oxford, 1971), pp. 307–43, at p. 324. These are low assumptions.

Level of dues in Silesia: Menzel, *Die schlesischen Lokationsurkunden*, p. 236.

Level of dues in England: Postan, *Medieval Economy and Society*, p. 125: a 'middling villein' held 10 to 15 acres.

Level of dues in Picardy: Fossier, *La terre et les hommes en Picardie* 2, pp. 637–40.

English rent per acre: H. E. Hallam (ed.), *The Agrarian History of England and Wales 2: 1042–1350* (Cambridge, 1988), pp. 665–6, 694–5.

For total *peasant outlay in silver equivalent* see also the figures in Richard Hoffmann, *Land, Liberties and Lordship in a Late Medieval Countryside: Agrarian Structures and Change in the Duchy of Wrocław* (Philadelphia, 1989), p. 127.

The phrase *'old country'* is from Reginald Lennard, *Rural England, 1086–1135: A Study of Social and Agrarian Conditions* (Oxford, 1959), p. 1.

Archbishop of Toledo's tenants: González, *Repoblación* 2, pp. 48–9.

An example of light *labour services owed by settlers 'iure Teutonico'* in Helbig & Weinrich 2, no. 45, p. 202 (Silesia, 1319).

Labour services at Clonkeen: Kevin Down, 'The Agricultural Economy of Colonial Ireland', in *New History of Ireland 2: Medieval Ireland, 1169–1534*, ed. Art Cosgrove (Oxford, 1987), pp. 450–81, at p. 465.

'The glory of the prince . . .': Helbig & Weinrich 2, no. 96, p. 364 (Przemysl Ottokar II of Bohemia, 1265).

James of Aragon for Vilanova: Font Rius, *Cartas de población* 1/i, no. 327 (1274).

Artasona: *Colección de fueros . . .*, ed. Muñoz y Romero, pp. 512–13 (1134).

'I, Henry, by God's grace duke of Silesia . . .': Helbig & Weinrich 2, no. 10, p. 88 (1221); Stanisław Trawkowski, 'Die Rolle der deutschen Dorfkolonisation und des deutschen Rechtes in Polen im 13. Jahrhundert', in Walter Schlesinger (ed.), *Die deutsche Ostsiedlung als Problem der europäischen Geschichte* (*Vorträge und Forschungen* 18, Sigmaringen, 1975), pp. 349–68, at p. 362, n. 38, believes this document is interpolated. Baudiss is now Budziszów, Gross Kreidel Krzydlina Wielka and Klein Kreidel Krzydlina Mała.

Charter of Przemysl of Cracow: Helbig & Weinrich 2, no. 80, p. 306 (1290).

An excellent recent general discussion of *'German law'* can be found in Hoffmann, *Land, Liberties and Lordship in a Late Medieval Countryside*, chapter 4, '*Locare iure Theutonico*: Instrument and Structure for a New Institutional Order', pp. 61–92; see also Menzel, *Die schlesischen Lokationsurkunden*, pp. 229–81.

Charter of Gerbord of Köthen: Helbig & Weinrich 1, no. 95, pp. 356–8.

'Hereditary right' in Silesia: Menzel, *Die schlesischen Lokationsurkunden*, p. 233, n. 351.

'Ius Teutonicum' as 'ius hereditarium': *Quellenbuch zur Geschichte der Sudetenländer* 1, ed. Wilhelm Weizsäcker (Munich, 1960), no. 19, p. 47 (1254 for Police [Politz]).

Alfonso I for Mozarabs: Lacarra, no. 51 (1126).

Artasona: *Colección de fueros . . .*, ed. Muñoz y Romero, pp. 512–13 (1134).

Charter of Bela IV of Hungary: Helbig & Weinrich 2, no. 139, p. 524 (1247).

Hospitallers for Sena and Sijena: Lacarra, no. 391 (1174).

Yébenes: Sáez (ed.), 'Fueros de Puebla de Alcocer y Yébenes', p. 439.

Charter of canons of Vyšehrad: Helbig & Weinrich 2, no. 95, p. 364.

'None of them may leave . . .': ibid. 2, no. 3, p. 76.

'None of the settlers may give . . .': ibid. 1, no. 50, pp. 212–14 (bishop of Meissen, 1185).

Alienation 'except to knights': Lacarra, no. 17 (1120) – urban property in this case.

Colonists at Beth Gibelin: Recueil des historiens des croisades, Lois 2, pp. 528–9, no. 4.

Charter of Boleslaw and Henry III of Silesia: Helbig & Weinrich 2, no. 28, pp. 160–62.

Charter for Psie Pole: Schlesisches UB 3, no. 43, pp. 39–40; *for Lubiąż settlers*: ibid. 1, no. 254, pp. 185–6; *for Domaniów*: ibid. 2, no. 86, pp. 56–7.

Rights of Flemish and Dutch settlers: Helbig & Weinrich 1, nos. 1–12, 14, 18, 24–6, pp. 42–76, 80–82, 92–4, 114–24; *charter for Jerzyń*: ibid. 2, no. 67, p. 258 (1266); *for Kalisz*: ibid. 2, no. 75, p. 286; *Racibórz and Nysa as chief courts*: ibid. 2, nos. 41–2, pp. 192–6.

Alfonso I for Mozarabs: Lacarra, no. 51.

Charter for Artasona: Colección de fueros . . ., ed. Muñoz y Romero, pp. 512–13; *for Tudela*: ibid., p. 421 (1127).

'Secure liberty, a firm and unchanging law': Helbig & Weinrich 2, no. 102, p. 388.

'Francos et ingenuos', etc.: Colección de fueros . . ., ed. Muñoz y Romero, pp. 512–13 (Alfonso I for Artasona, 1134).

Bela IV for Beregowo: Helbig & Weinrich 2, no. 139, p. 524 (1247).

Laws of Santa María de Cortes: González, Repoblación 2, pp. 141–2, n. 359.

6. The New Landscape

'You shall make your permanent residence there . . .': José María Font Rius (ed.), Cartas de población y franquicia de Cataluña (2 vols., Madrid and Barcelona, 1969) 1, no. 287, pp. 416–19 (abbot of Poblet for the settlers of Granja de Codoç, 1246).

Thomas of Wrocław for Peter of Nysa: Schlesisches UB, ed. Heinrich Appelt and Winfried Irgang (4 vols. to date, Graz, Cologne and Vienna, 1963–), 2, no. 128, pp. 83–4; Helbig & Weinrich 2, no. 20, p. 140; *subsequent survey*: Liber fundationis episcopatus Vratislaviensis, ed. H. Markgraf and J. W. Schulte (Codex diplomaticus Silesiae 14, Breslau, 1889), p. 6. Modern Polish names are Friedewalde – Kopań; Gross Briesen – Brzeziny; Petersheide – Czarnolas; Schönheide – Wielochów.

Abbot Windolf: Annales Pegavienses, ed. Georg Heinrich Pertz, MGH, SS 16 (Hanover, 1859), pp. 232–70, at pp. 246–7.

St Cugat: Cartulario de Sant Cugat del Vallés, ed. José Rius Serra (3 vols., Barcelona, 1945–7), 2, p. 112, no. 464; Font Rius (ed.), Cartas de población 1/2, pp. 681–2.

'*There is scarcely one modern village . . .*': Pierre Bonnassie, *La Catalogne de milieu du Xe à la fin du XIe siècle* (2 vols., Toulouse, 1975) 1, p. 123 and map on p. 124.

William of Tyre: *Chronicle* 15.25, ed. R. B. C. Huygens (2 vols., *Corpus Christianorum, Continuatio mediaevalis* 63–63A, Turnhout, 1986), 2, p. 708.

Beth Gibelin: *Recueil des historiens des croisades, Lois* 2 (Paris, 1843), pp. 528–9, no. 44, discussed by Joshua Prawer, *Crusader Institutions* (Oxford, 1980), pp. 119–26, and Jonathan Riley-Smith, *The Knights of St John in Jerusalem and Cyprus c. 1050–1310* (London, 1967), pp. 435–7.

Peter and Fortunius García: *Cartularios de Santo Domingo de la Calzada*, ed. Agustín Ubieto Arteta (Saragossa, 1978), no. 99, p. 82.

Famine of 1264: *Annales Wratislavienses antiqui* and *Annales magistratus Wratislaviensis*, ed. Wilhelm Arndt, *MGH, SS* 19 (Hanover, 1866), pp. 526–31, at p. 528.

Wiprecht of Groitzsch: *Frutolfi et Ekkehardi Chronica necnon Anonymi Chronica imperatorum*, ed. Franz-Josef Schmale and Irene Schmale-Ott (*AQ* 15, Darmstadt, 1972), p. 198 ('ruler of those parts . . .'); *Annales Pegavienses, MGH, SS* 16, p. 247 ('caused new land to be cleared . . .', etc.).

'*Because the land was uninhabited . . .*': Helmond of Bosau, *Chronica Slavorum* 1.57, ed. Heinz Stoob (*AQ* 19, Darmstadt, rev. ed., 1973), p. 210.

Albert the Bear: ibid. 1.89, ed. Stoob, p. 312.

Appeal of 1108: Helbig & Weinrich 1, no. 19, pp. 96–102.

Otto of Freising: *Gesta Friderici I imperatoris* 1.32, ed. Georg Waitz and Bernhard von Simson (*SRG*, Hanover and Leipzig, 1912), pp. 49–50.

Odo of Deuil: *De profectione Ludovici VII in Orientem* 2, ed. and tr. Virginia G. Berry (New York, 1948), p. 32.

Frisians in Süsel: Helmold, *Chronica Slavorum* 1.64, ed. Stoob, pp. 224–6.

'*Fuero' of Toledo*: Alfonso García-Gallo, 'Los Fueros de Toledo', *Anuario de historia del derecho español* 45 (1975), pp. 341–488, at p. 475.

Lauenrode: *UB des Hochstifts Hildesheim und seiner Bischöfe* 2, ed. H. Hoogeweg (Hanover and Leipzig, 1901), no. 445, pp. 208–10; *Heiningen*: ibid., no. 932, pp. 467–8 (1253).

'*Poor country-dwellers*': *Miracula sancti Annonis* 2.43, ed. Mauritius Mittler (Siegburg, 1966–8), p. 114.

Henryków: *Liber fundationis claustri sanctae Mariae virginis in Heinrichow* 1.9, ed. Roman Grodecki, *Księga Henrykowska* (Poznań and Wrocław, 1949), pp. 235–370, at p. 298; Helbig & Weinrich 2, no. 13, p. 120.

Furrow drawn by a plough: *Codex diplomaticus Brandenburgensis*, ed. Adolph Friedrich Riedel (41 vols., Berlin, 1838–69), A 18, sect. 7, no. 3, pp. 442–3 (Neumark, 1298).

On the *mansus*: Walter Kuhn, 'Flämische und fränkische Hufe als Leitformen der mittelalterlichen Ostsiedlung', in his *Vergleichende Untersuchungen zur mittelalterlichen Ostsiedlung* (Cologne and Vienna, 1973), pp. 1–51.

Siebenhufen: Fritz Curschmann, *Die deutschen Ortsnamen im Norddeutschen Kolonialgebiet* (Stuttgart, 1910), p. 41, n. 4.

New villages of Neumark: Hans K. Schulze, 'Die Besiedlung der Mark Brandenburg im hohen und späten Mittelalter', *Jahrbuch für die Geschichte Mittel- und Ostdeutschlands* 28 (1979), pp. 42–178, at p. 127.

Wladislaw Odonicz's grants: Helbig & Weinrich 2, nos. 49–52, pp. 214–24.

'Since the number of "mansi" . . .': ibid. 2, no. 31, p. 168.

Charter of Henry the Bearded: ibid. 2, no. 9, p. 88.

'So that their village with its "mansi" . . .': *Pommersches UB* 2 (Stettin, 1881–5, repr. Cologne and Graz, 1970), no. 616, p. 27.

'Mansi' 'should never be remeasured': Helbig & Weinrich 2, no. 100, pp. 378–84.

'If the lords of the land . . .': *Codex diplomaticus Brandenburgensis* A 1, sect. 7, no. 9, p. 458.

Pogel: Helbig & Weinrich 2, no. 32, p. 170.

'Sznur' and 'snura': Kuhn, 'Flämische und fränkische Hufe', p. 3.

'Per funiculi distinctionem', etc.: Helmold, *Chronica Slavorum* 1.92, ed. Stoob, p. 318; Helbig & Weinrich 1, no. 82, p. 316 (Rügen, 1221); 2, no. 98, p. 374 (Bohemia, 1291). The biblical echo is from Psalm 78:55 (Vulgate 77:54).

Silesian 'mensuratores': Kuhn, 'Flämische und fränkische Hufe', p. 4; *Schlesisches UB* 4, no. 278, p. 188 (1276).

'He had the land measured by a short line . . .': Helmold, *Chronica Slavorum* 1.84, ed. Stoob, p. 294.

'The cultivators were summoned . . .': *Liber fundationis . . . Heinrichow* 1.9, ed. Grodecki, p. 296; Helbig & Weinrich 2, no. 13, p. 118.

Prussian document of 1254: *Preussisches UB* (6 vols. to date, Königsberg and Marburg, 1882–) 1/i, no. 283, pp. 214–15.

Charter for Dietrich of Tiefenau: Helbig & Weinrich 1, no. 121, pp. 448–50, with note.

'Geometria Culmensis': ibid. 1, no. 143, pp. 524–30 (excerpts).

'Ancient divisions of the Saracens': Henri Bresc, 'Féodalité coloniale en terre d'Islam: La Sicile (1070–1240)', in *Structures féodales et féodalisme dans l'Occident mediterranéen (Xe–XIIIe s.)* (Paris, 1980), pp. 631–47, at p. 635.

Aragosa: Julio González, *Repoblación de Castilla la Nueva* (2 vols., Madrid, 1975–6) 1, p. 159.

Two grants from Aragon: Lacarra, nos. 5–6 (1103, 1105).

'Allocation of mansi by lot . . .': Helbig & Weinrich 2, no. 22, p. 144.

Argance: González, *Repoblación* 2, p. 184.

'The king's distributor . . .': Lacarra, nos. 91 (1138), 138 (1127).

Peter of Nysa: Helbig & Weinrich 2, no. 20, p. 140 (1237).

Conrad of Löwendorf: ibid. 2, no. 96, p. 366 (1265).

Silesian 'locatores': Josef Joachim Menzel, *Die schlesischen Lokationsurkunden des 13. Jahrhunderts* (Würzburg, 1977), pp. 215–17.

Bohemian 'locatores': Helbig & Weinrich 2, nos. 95 (1252), 98 (1291), pp. 360–64, 372–6.

Grant of Alfonso VII: González, *Repoblación* 2, p. 168; another unambiguous case is Lacarra, no. 216 (1140).

Grant of Alfonso I: Lacarra, no. 127 (1125).

Count Bronisz's plans: Helbig & Weinrich 2, nos. 47–8, pp. 210–14 (1236).

'Dissension arose among the "locatores" . . .': ibid. 2, no. 25, p. 154 (Silesia, 1250).

Henry of Humpoletz: ibid. 2, no. 95, pp. 362–4 (1252).

Communal mill at Cardeña: Jean Gautier-Dalché, 'Moulin à eau, seigneurie, communauté rurale dans le nord de l'Espagne (IXe–XIIe siècles)', in *Études de civilisation médiévale, IXe–XII siècles: Mélanges offerts à Edmond-René Labande* (Poitiers, 1974), pp. 337–49, at p. 340.

Failed peasant mills: Robert Fossier *La terre et les hommes en Picardie jusqu'à la fin de XIIIe siècle* (2 vols., Paris and Louvain, 1968) 2, p. 448.

Marcilla: Lacarra, no. 4 (1102).

Examples of *Bruno of Olomouc's settlements* in Helbig & Weinrich 2, nos. 106–9, pp. 402–12 (1256–70).

Henry of Ermland's charter: ibid. 1, no. 131, p. 484.

Siegfried Epperlein: *Bauernbedrückung und Bauernwiderstand im hohen Mittelalter: Zur Erforschung der Ursachen bäuerlichen Abwanderung nach Osten im 12. und 13. Jahrhundert* (Berlin, 1960).

Serfs of Iburg: *Osnabrücker UB* 2, ed. F. Philippi (Osnabrück, 1896), no. 380, pp. 298–9.

Bondsman Alward: *UB des Hochstifts Hildesheim* 2, no. 795, pp. 403–4 (1247).

Chronicler of Rastede: *Historia monasterii Rastedensis* 35, ed. Georg Waitz, *MGH, SS* 25 (Hanover, 1880), pp. 495–511, at p. 509.

Number of German settlers: Walter Kuhn, 'Die Siedlerzahlen der deutschen Ostsiedlung', in *Studium Sociale: Karl Valentin Müller dargebracht* (Cologne and Opladen, 1963), pp. 131–54; idem, 'Ostsiedlung und Bevölkerungsdichte', in his *Vergleichende Untersuchungen zur mittelalterlichen Ostsiedlung* (Cologne and Vienna, 1973), pp. 173–210.

Anglo-Norman settlement of Ireland: A. J. Otway-Ruthven, 'The Character of Norman Settlement in Ireland', in J. L. McCracken (ed.), *Historical Studies* 5 (London, 1965), pp. 75–84, at pp. 77, 83 (cf. her *A History of Medieval Ireland* (2nd ed., London, 1980), pp. 113–16); R. E. Glasscock, 'Land and People *c.* 1300', in *New History of Ireland 2: Medieval Ireland, 1169–1534*, ed. Art Cosgrove (Oxford, 1987), pp. 205–39, at p. 213.

Armies of 1169–70: Gerald of Wales, *Expugnatio Hibernica* 1.3, 16, ed. A. B. Scott and F. X. Martin (Dublin, 1978), pp. 30, 64.

Number of boroughs in Ireland: Geoffrey Martin, 'Plantation Boroughs in Medieval Ireland, with a Handlist of Boroughs to *c.* 1500', in David Harkness and Mary O'David (eds.), *The Town in Ireland* (*Historical Studies* 13, Belfast, 1981), pp. 25–53.

Anglicization of Irish hierarchy: J. A. Watt, *The Church and the Two Nations in Medieval Ireland* (Cambridge, 1970), esp. chapters 3 and 8; idem, *The Church in Medieval Ireland* (Dublin, 1972), pp. 87–109.

Hamo de Valognes: *Rotuli chartarum in turri Londinensi asservati (1199–1216)*, ed. T. D. Hardy (London, 1837), p. 96 (1200).

'*Waste lands . . . to be settled*': *Close Rolls of the Reign of Henry III (1247–51)* (London, 1922), p. 480.

Mandate of 1219 re Waterford: *Rotuli litterarum clausarum in turri Londinensi asservati (1204–27)*, ed. T. D. Hardy (2 vols., London, 1833–44), 1, p. 394.

Surveys from the *Red Book of Ormond*, ed. Newport B. White (Irish Manuscripts Commission, Dublin, 1932), pp. 1–17, 19–83, 127–35, 145–58.

Corduff: ibid., pp. 25–7.

Examples of named cottagers: ibid., pp. 33–4, 153; but note the situation at Lisronagh in 1326, where most of the fourteen cottagers bore English names, Edmund Curtis, 'Rental of the Manor of Lisronagh, 1333, and Notes on "Betagh" Tenure in Medieval Ireland', *Proceedings of the Royal Irish Academy* 43 (1935–7) C, pp. 41–76.

Moyaliff: *Red Book of Ormond*, ed. White, pp. 64–7.

Gowran: ibid., pp. 34–41, 41–5, 46–7, 74–83; the Gowran rental of 1303 has become disorganized and split into several parts; see C. A. Empey, 'Conquest and Settlement: Patterns of Anglo-Norman Settlement in North Munster and South Leinster', *Irish Social and Economic History Journal* 13 (1986), pp. 5–31, at pp. 26–7 and n. 67.

Gerard–Preston marriage contract: *Red Book of Ormond*, ed. White, pp. 108–11.

Ploughlands and place names in south-eastern Ireland: Thomas McErlean, 'The Irish Townland System of Landscape Organization', in Terence Reeves-Smyth and Fred Hamond (eds.), *Landscape Archaeology in Ireland* (*British Archaeological Reports, British Series* 116, Oxford, 1983), pp. 315–39, at p. 317, table 1; T. Jones Hughes, 'Town and *Baile* in Irish Place-Names', in Nicholas Stephens and Robin E. Glasscock (eds.), *Irish Geographical Studies in Honour of E. Estyn Evans* (Belfast, 1970), pp. 244–58.

Valencian irrigation system: *Els Furs de Valencia* 35, ed. Rafael Gayano-Lluch (Valencia, 1930), p. 206.

For general discussion on *the history of ploughs* see Ulrich Bentzien, *Haken und Pflug* (Berlin, 1969); Walter Kuhn, 'Der Pflug als Betriebseinheit in Altpreussen' and 'Der Haken in Altpreussen', in his *Vergleichende Untersuchungen zur mittelalterlichen Ostsiedlung* (Cologne and Vienna, 1973), pp. 113–40, 141–71; André G. Haudricourt and Mariel Jean-Brunhes Delamarre, *L'homme et la charrue à travers le monde* (4th ed., Paris, 1955).

'*Slavic plough*': Helmold, *Chronica Slavorum* 1.12, 14, 88, ed. Stoob, pp. 70, 74, 312.

Levies from 'uncus' in Ratzeburg: *Die Urkunden Heinrichs des Löwen*, ed. Karl Jordan, *MGH, Laienfürsten- und Dynastenurkunden der Kaiserzeit* (Leipzig and Weimar, 1941–9), no. 41, pp. 57–61; also in *Mecklenburgisches UB* (25 vols. in 26, Schwerin and Leipzig, 1863–1977) 1, no. 65, p. 58 (purportedly 1158, a thirteenth-century forgery with a genuine core); ibid., no. 375, p. 376 (*c*. 1230).

Taxes in Rügen: *Pommersches UB* 6 (Stettin, 1907, repr. Cologne and Graz, 1970), no. 3601, pp. 110–11 (1322).

'*Uncus*' *in Silesia*: *Schlesisches UB* 1, no. 82, p. 54 (1202).

Chełmno document of 1230: Preussisches *UB*, 1/i, no. 74, pp. 54–5.

Ermland tithes: Codex diplomaticus Warmiensis 1, ed. Carl Peter Woekly and Johann Martin Saage (Mainz, 1860), no. 42, pp. 79–80.

Fehmarn: Kong Valdemars Jordebog, ed. Svend Aakjaer (3 vols., Copenhagen, 1926–43), 2, pp. 50–52.

Pomeranian document of 1318: Pommersches *UB* 5 (Stettin, 1905, repr. Cologne and Graz, 1970), no. 3234, pp. 408–15.

Chełmno charter: Preussisches *UB* 1/i, no. 105, pp. 77–81, at p. 80; *document of 1230*: ibid. 1/i, no. 74, pp. 54–5; *of 1293*: ibid. 1/ii, no. 612, pp. 387–8; *of 1258*: ibid. 1/ii, no. 67, pp. 62–3.

Gniezno Synod: Codex diplomaticus Maioris Poloniae, ed. Ignacy Zakrzewski and Franciszek Piekosiński (5 vols., Poznań, 1877–1908), 1, no. 402, pp. 354–5.

'Pflug'/'Haken' contrast: e.g. Preussisches *UB* 1/ii, no. 366, pp. 247–51, at p. 248 (1278 translation of earlier document).

'Each house from which a plough goes out', etc.: *UB* zur Geschichte der Herzöge von Braunschweig und Lüneburg und ihrer Lande 1, ed. H. Sudendorf (Hanover, 1859), no. 122, pp. 75–6.

'From their ploughs or "unci" …': Codex diplomaticus Warmiensis 1, no. 214, pp. 366–8 (1323).

'"Unci" with which the Prussians and Poles …': Preussisches *UB* 1/i, no. 140, p. 105 (1242).

Differing assessments: ibid. 1/i, no. 74, pp. 54–5 (document of 1230); ibid. 1/i, no. 105, pp. 77–81, at p. 80 (Chełmno charter); ibid. 1/ii, no. 366, pp. 247–51, at p. 248 (*scot* and flax; 1278 translation of earlier document).

'Twenty big ploughs and twenty small …': Visitationes bonorum archiepiscopatus necnon capituli Gnesnensis saeculi XVI, ed. Boleslaw Ulanowski (Cracow, 1920), p. 365.

Squirrel skins: Schlesisches *UB* 1, no. 164, p. 117 (1217).

Legnica tithes: Helbig & Weinrich 2, no. 1, p. 72.

Citations regarding *new tithes* from Helbig & Weinrich 1, no. 40, p. 178 (bishopric of Zeitz-Naumburg, 1145): Preussisches *UB* 1/i, no. 74, pp. 52–4 (Prussia, 1230).

Villages 'which are now inhabited by Slavs …': Codex diplomaticus Brandenburgensis A 10, no. 9, p. 75 (1173).

'The hardness of the hearts …': Honorius III, 18 April 1220, *Etsi non sic*, Po. 6229; Liv-, esth- und curländisches *UB*, ed. F. G. von Bunge et al. (1st ser., 12 vols., Reval and Riga, 1853–1910), 1, no. 51, col. 54.

'New plantation' and *'place of horror …'* are phrases used virtually as clichés to describe the new settlements and the preceding wilderness: e.g. Mecklenburgisches *UB* 1, no. 255, p. 240 (1219); Helbig & Weinrich, 1, no. 82, p. 316 (1221); Helmold, *Chronica Slavorum* 1. 47, 55, 71, ed. Stoob, pp. 182, 204, 252. They have biblical antecedents: Pslam 143 (Vulgate 144):12 refers to *filii sicut novellae plantationes*, and, according to Deuteronomy 32:10, God found the children of Israel *in loco horroris et vaste solitudinis*. Use of the phrase was not limited to

eastern Europe: see *Liber feudorum major*, ed. Francisco Miquel Rosell (2 vols., Barcelona, 1945–7), 1, nos. 255, 259, pp. 275–6, 282–3 (1076), referring to the area north of Tarragona.

'*The first abbot of this monastery . . .*': *Liber fundationis . . . Heinrichow* 2, preface, ed. Grodecki, p. 309; cf. Genesis 3:19: *In sudore vultus tui vesceris pane.* See the perceptive comments on this text by Piotr Górecki, *Economy, Society and Lordship in Medieval Poland, 1100–1250* (New York and London, forthcoming).

Lubiąż verses: 'Rocznik lubiąski 1241–1281, oraz wiersz o pierwotnych zakonniach Lubiąża' [*Versus lubenses*], ed. August Bielowski, *MPH* 3 (Lwów, 1878, repr. Warsaw, 1961), pp. 707–10, at pp. 709–10; for the translation of *broca* as 'uncultivated field' see *Słownik Łaciny Średniowiecznej w Polsce* 1, ed. Mariana Plezi (Wrocław, etc., 1953–8), p. 1158.

Diego de Landa: John Elliott, 'The Discovery of America and the Discovery of Man', *Proceedings of the British Academy* 58 (1972), pp. 101–25, at p. 112.

'*This land was completely transformed . . .*': 'Rocznik lubiąski . . .' ed. Bielowski, p. 710; again, see the comments of Górecki, *Economy, Society and Lordship.*

King of Bohemia: *Codex iuris Bohemici*, ed. Hermenegild Jiriček (5 vols. in 12, Prague, 1867–98), 2/2, p. 145 (*Majestas Carolina* 49); cf. the rules protecting woods, ibid., pp. 145–50 (clauses 49–57).

Archbishop of Hamburg–Bremen: Helbig & Weinrich 1, no. 2, p. 46.

Holland and Crowland: cited in H. E. Hallam, *Settlement and Society: A Study of the Early Agrarian History of South Lincolnshire* (Cambridge, 1965), p. 166.

Postan theory: M. M. Postan, *The Medieval Economy and Society* (London, 1972), pp. 57, 66.

'*Cerealization*': Andrew M. Watson, 'Towards Denser and More Continuous Settlement: New Crops and Farming Techniques in the Early Middle Ages', in J. A. Raftis (ed.), *Pathways to Medieval Peasants* (Toronto, 1981), pp. 65–82, at p. 69.

Decrease in height: Helmut Wurm, 'Körpergrösse und Ernährung der Deutschen im Mittelalter' in Bernd Herrmann (ed.), *Mensch und Umwelt im Mittelalter* (Stuttgart, 1986), pp. 101–8, with further articles listed on p. 108.

Excavation of rural sites in former East Germany: Eike Gringmuth-Dallmer, *Die Entwicklung der frühgeschichtlichen Kulturlandschaft auf dem Territorium der DDR unter besonderer Berücksichtigung der Siedlungsgebiete* (Berlin, 1983), p. 68; *in the Havelland*: Wolfgang Ribbe (ed.), *Das Havelland im Mittelalter* (Berlin, 1987), p. 79; *in Ireland*: T. B. Barry, *The Archaeology of Medieval Ireland* (London, 1987), p. 72; *in central Europe*: Walter Janssen, 'Dorf und Dorfformen des 7. bis 12. Jahrhunderts im Lichte neuer Ausgrabungen in Mittel- und Nordeuropa', in Herbert Jankuhn *et al.* (eds.), *Das Dorf der Eisenzeit und des frühen Mittelalters* (*Abhandlungen der Akadamie der Wissenchaft in Göttingen, philosophisch-historische Klasse*, 3rd ser., 101, 1977), pp. 285–356, at p. 341.

Pfaffenschlag: Vladimir Nekuda, 'Zum Stand der Wüstungsforschung in Mähren (ČSSR)', *Zeitschrift für Archäologie des Mittelalters* 1 (1973), pp. 31–57, *passim* (with plans and photographs).

Peter *Wade-Martins*, 'The Origins of Rural Settlement in East Anglia', in P. J. Fowler (ed.), *Recent Work in Rural Archaeology* (Bradford-upon-Avon, 1975), pp. 137–57; also summarized *idem*, 'The Archaeology of Medieval Rural Settlement in East Anglia', in Michael Aston *et al.* (eds.), *The Rural Settlements of Medieval England* (Oxford, 1989), pp. 149–65, at pp. 159–60.

Textbook in Stuttgart: Martin Born, *Geographie der ländlichen Siedlungen 1: Die Genese der Siedlungsformen in Mitteleuropa* (Stuttgart, 1977), inserts after p. 156.

'The classification of villages into types . . .': Edward Miller and John Hatcher, *Medieval England: Rural Society and Economic Change 1086–1348* (London, 1978), p. 87.

'Green village': e.g. Brian K. Roberts, *The Green Villages of County Durham* (Durham, 1977).

Hangleton: J. G. Hurst, 'The Changing Medieval Village in England', in J. A. Raftis (ed.), *Pathways to Medieval Peasants* (Toronto, 1981), pp. 27–62, at pp. 51, 48 and plan 2. 8.

Klinkrade: Wolfgang Prange, *Siedlungsgeschichte des Landes Lauenburg im Mittelalter* (Neumünster, 1960), pp. 166–7 and map 45.

'The size and type of settlements . . .': Miller and Hatcher, *Medieval England*, p. 86.

Dmitrii *Jegorov*, *Die Kolonisation Mecklenburgs im 13. Jahrhundert* (German tr., 2 vols., Breslau, 1930; original Russian ed., 1915) 1, pp. 391–2.

For a collection of articles dealing with 'The Problem of the *Rundling*' see Hans-Jürgen Nitz (ed.), *Historisch-genetische Siedlungsforschung* (Darmstadt, 1974), part 3: 'Die Rundlingsfrage'.

On the origins of the *Waldhufendorf* see Hans-Jürgen Nitz, 'The Church as Colonist: The Benedictine Abbey of Lorsch and Planned *Waldhufen* Colonization in the Odenwald', *Journal of Historical Geography* 9 (1983), pp. 105–26.

Blencarn and Cumdivock: Eilert Ekwall, *The Concise Oxford Dictionary of Place Names* (4th ed., Oxford, 1960), pp. xxiii, 49 and 136.

Element 'mar': Adolph Bach, *Deutsche Namenkunde* (2nd ed., 3 vols., Heidelberg, 1952–6) 2/ii, p. 126.

Taunus region: ibid., pp. 129–36.

'Names have specific periods . . .': ibid., p. 125.

'Starigard': Helmold, *Chronica Slavorum* 1. 12, ed. Stoob, p. 68.

Document of Henry IV of Silesia: *Liber fundationis episcopatus Vratislaviensis*, p. 168; preamble in Helbig and Weinrich 2, no. 39, p. 188.

Albert Lyka: *Liber fundationis . . . Heinrichow* 1. 3, ed. Grodecki, p. 257; Helbig and Weinrich 2, no. 13, p. 104.

An example of *destruction and relocation* in Adriaan von Müller, 'Zum hochmittel-alterlichen Besiedlung des Teltow (Brandenburg): Stand eines mehrjährigen archäologisch-siedlungsgeschichtlichen Forschungsprogrammes', in Walter Schlesinger (ed.), *Die deutsche Ostsiedlung als Problem der europäischen Geschichte* (*Vorträge und Forschungen* 18, Sigmaringen, 1975), pp. 311–32.

The most recent edition of the *Ratzeburg Tithe Register* is by Hans Wurm in Hans-

Georg Kaack and Hans Wurm, *Slawen und Deutsche im Lande Lauenburg* (Ratzeburg, 1983), pp. 137–205; a facsimile is included in Jegorov, *Die Kolonisa-tion Mecklenburgs*; there are excerpts in Helbig & Weinrich 1, no. 63, pp. 260–66.

Sturmieston: Cartae et alia munimenta . . . de Glamorgan, ed. George T. Clark (6 vols., Cardiff, 1910), 1, no. 151, p. 152; Davies, *Conquest*, pp. 153, 188.

Wiprecht of Groitzsch: Annales Pegavienses, MGH, SS 16, p. 247.

Flemish and Franconian names: Charles Higounet, *Die deutsche Ostsiedlung im Mittelalter* (Berlin, 1986), p. 110; cf. p. 252.

Names in New Castile: González, *Repoblación* 1, p. 172; 2, pp. 271–99.

'He gave him the hamlet . . .': Repartimiento de Sevilla, ed. Julio González (2 vols., Madrid, 1951), 1, pp. 251–3; 2, pp. 14, 18–19.

Helbig's study: Herbert Helbig, 'Die slawische Siedlung im sorbischen Gebiet', in Herbert Ludat (ed.), *Siedlung und Verfassung der Slawen zwischen Elbe, Saale und Oder* (Giessen, 1960), pp. 27–64.

7. *Colonial Towns and Colonial Traders*

'A free and secure city . . .': Schlesisches UB, ed. Heinrich Appelt and Winfried Irgang (4 vols. to date, Graz, Cologne and Vienna, 1963–), 3, no. 103, p. 75 (Głogów [Glogau], 1253).

Barnim of Pomerania: Helbig & Weinrich 1, no. 87, pp. 328–33.

English wealth and boroughs 1334: R. E. Glasscock, 'England *circa* 1334', in H. C. Darby (ed.), *A New Historical Geography of England before 1600* (Cambridge, 1976), pp. 136–85, at pp. 139 (fig. 35) and 178 (fig. 40).

Prague 'greatest trading centre': G. Jacob (ed.), *Arabische Berichte von Gesandten an germanische Fürstenhöfe aus dem 9. und 10. Jahrhundert* (Berlin and Leipzig, 1927), p. 12 (Ibrahim ibn Jacub's account).

Chartered towns in Bohemia: Jiři Kejř, 'Die Anfänge der Stadtverfassung und des Stadtrechts in den Böhmischen Ländern', in Walter Schlesinger (ed.), *Die deutsche Ostsiedlung des Mittelalters als Problem der europäischen Geschichte* (*Vorträge und Forschungen* 18, Sigmaringen, 1975), pp. 439–70.

The *Dublin charter* is edited by Gearóid MacNiocaill, *Na Buirgéisí* (2 vols., Dublin, 1964) 1, pp. 78–81, and *Elenchus fontium historiae urbanae* 2/2, ed. Susan Reynolds *et al.* (Leiden, etc., 1988), pp. 162–5; earlier charters of Henry II and John are in *Na Buirgéisí*, pp. 75–7, *Elenchus fontium*, pp. 161–2.

Number of Irish boroughs: Geoffrey Martin, 'Plantation Boroughs in Medieval Ireland, with a Handlist of Boroughs to *c.* 1500', in David Harkness and Mary O'David (eds.), *The Town in Ireland* (*Historical Studies* 13, Belfast, 1981), pp. 25–53.

Density of towns in Mecklenburg, etc.: Karl Hoffmann, 'Die Stadtgründungen Mecklenburg-Schwerins in der Kolonisationszeit vom 12. bis zum 14. Jahrhundert', *Jahrbuch für mecklenburgische Geschichte* 94 (1930), pp. 1–200; Walter

Kuhn, 'German Town Foundations of the Thirteenth Century in Western Pomerania', in H. B. Clarke and Anngret Simms (eds.), *The Comparative History of Urban Origins in Non-Roman Europe* (*British Archaeological Reports, International Series* 255, 2 vols., Oxford, 1985) 2, pp. 547–80, at p. 569.

Irish boroughs with urban functions: John Bradley, 'Planned Anglo-Norman Towns in Ireland', in Clarke and Simms (eds.), *Comparative History* 2, pp. 411–67, at p. 420.

Sicilian 'burgesses': Henri Bresc, 'Féodalité coloniale en terre d'Islam: La Sicile (1070–1240)', in *Structures féodales et féodalisme dans l'Occident mediterranéen (Xe–XIIIe s.)* (Paris, 1980), pp. 631–47, at p. 644.

'The city of Riga draws the faithful . . .': *Liv-, esth- und curländisches UB*, ed. F. G. von Bunge *et al.* (1st ser., 12 vols., Reval and Riga, 1853–1910), 1, no. 53, col. 57 (1221).

Alfonso VII for Oreja: Alfonso García-Gallo, 'Los Fueros de Toledo', *Anuario de historia del derecho español* 45 (1975), pp. 341–488, doc. 8, at pp. 469–71.

Rhuddlan: *Domesday Book*, ed. Abraham Farley (2 vols., London, 1783), 1, fol. 269.

On the laws of Breteuil: Mary Bateson, 'The Laws of Breteuil', *English Historical Review* 15 (1900), pp. 73–8, 302–18, 496–523, 754–7; 16 (1901), pp. 92–110, 332–45.

Göttingen codex: *Das alte Lübische Recht*, ed. Johann Friedrich Hach (Lübeck, 1839), p. 185.

Litoměřice: *Codex iuris municipalis regni Bohemiae* 2, ed. Jaromír Čelakovský (Prague, 1895), p. 38.

Halle for Środa: Helbig & Weinrich 2, no. 15, pp. 124–31 (1235); *Lawrence of Wrocław for Walter*: ibid., 2, no. 22, pp. 144–7.

List of sites with Środa law: Zbigniew Zdrójkowski, 'Miasta na prawie Średzkim', *Śląski kwartalnik historyczny Sobótka* 41 (1986), pp. 243–51.

Alfonso II re Jaca: *Colección de fueros municipales y cartas pueblas de los reinos de Castilla, León, Corona de Aragón y Navarra*, ed. Tomás Muñoz y Romero (Madrid, 1847), p. 243; the 'customs and liberties' of Jaca can be found in the *Fuero de Jaca*, ed. Mauricio Molho (Saragossa, 1964).

Silesian dukes for Wrocław: *Schlesisches UB* 3, no. 373, pp. 241–2.

Magdeburg to Litoměřice: *Quellenbuch zur Geschichte der Sudetenländer* 1, ed. Wilhelm Weizsäcker (Munich, 1960), no. 23, pp. 52–4; on Litoměřice as a superior court itself see the bibliography listed in Helbig & Weinrich, 2, p. 361, n. 4.

Lübeck appellate decisions: Wilhelm Ebel (ed.), *Lübecker Ratsurteile* (4 vols., Göttingen, 1955–67).

Alfonso XI re Logroño: Narciso Hergueta, 'El Fuero de Logroño: su extensión a otras poblaciónes', *Boletín de la Real Academia de la Historia* 50 (1907), pp. 321–2.

'All and singular who are settled . . .': Helbig & Weinrich 2, no. 41, pp. 192–5.

Huy: André Joris, *Huy et sa charte de franchise, 1066* (Brussels, 1966).

Term 'burgess' in Bohemia: Kejř, 'Die Anfänge der Stadtverfassung', pp. 461–2.

Loan word 'burgess' in Greek, Romanian and Welsh: *Chronicle of Morea*, tr. Harold E.

Lurier, *Crusaders as Conquerors* (New York, 1964), p. 137; Raimund Friedrich Kaindl, *Geschichte der Deutschen in den Karpathenländern* (3 vols., Gotha, 1907–11) 2, p. 405; T. H. Parry-Williams, *The English Element in Welsh* (*Cymmrodorion Record Series* 10, London, 1923), p. 155.

Stratford-upon-Avon: E. M. Carus-Wilson, 'The First Half-Century of the Borough of Stratford-upon-Avon', *Economic History Review*, 2nd ser., 18 (1965), pp. 46–63.

Alfonso VI for Logroño: *Fuero de Logroño*, ed. T. Moreno Garbaya, *Apuntes históricos de Logroño* (Logroño, 1943), pp. 42–9.

Sahagún: *Crónicas anónimas de Sahagún* 15, ed. Antonio Ubieto Arteta (*Textos medievales* 75, Saragossa, 1987), pp. 19–21.

Humphrey of Falaise: Lacarra, no. 187.

'He commanded people to come . . .': *Crónica del rey don Alfonso X* 11, in *Crónicas de los reyes de Castilla* 1 (*Biblioteca de autores españoles* 66, Madrid, 1875), pp. 1–66, at p. 9.

The *foundation charter of Ciudad Real* is printed in Margarita Peñalosa Esteban-Infantes, *La fundación de Ciudad Real* (Ciudad Real, 1955), pp. 9–11; cf. Julio González, *Repoblación de Castilla la Nueva* (2 vols, Madrid, 1975–6) 1, pp. 349–50. For a *plan of the city* ibid. 2, p. 95.

Tarragona: José María Font Rius (ed.), *Cartas de población y franquicia de Cataluña* (2 vols., Madrid and Barcelona, 1969) 1, no. 49, pp. 82–4.

Jaén: *Primera crónica general de España* 1071, ed. Ramón Menéndez Pidal (2 vols., Madrid, 1955), 2, p. 747.

For the *pattern of immigration into Seville* see the map in *Repartamiento de Sevilla*, ed. Julio González (2 vols., Madrid, 1951), 1, opposite p. 314.

Hodonín: *Codex diplomaticus et epistolaris regni Bohemiae*, ed. Gustavus Friedrich *et al.* (5 vols. to date, Prague, 1904–), 2, no. 381, p. 429; the editors' doubts about the authenticity of the document seem groundless; see Kejř, 'Die Anfänge der Stadtverfassung', p. 458.

'The city of Cracow was converted . . .': *Annales capituli Cracoviensis (Rocznik Kapitulny Krakowski)*, ed. August Bielowski, *MPH* 2 (Lwów, 1872, repr. Warsaw, 1961), pp. 779–816, at p. 806.

Boleslaw's charter for Cracow: Helbig & Weinrich 2, no. 77, pp. 290–96.

Parchim: ibid. 1, no. 69, pp. 276–9.

Röbel: *Mecklenburgisches UB* (25 vols. in 26, Schwerin and Leipzig, 1863–1977) 3, no. 2100, pp. 402–4 (1291); 4, no. 2503, pp. 58–9 (1298).

Kröpelin seal: Hoffmann, 'Die Stadtgründungen Mecklenburg-Schwerins', p. 68.

Dublin citizen roll: *The Dublin Guild Merchant Roll c. 1190–1265*, ed. Philomena Connolly and Geoffrey Martin (Dublin, 1992), pp. 1–39.

Cairo riots: Claude Cahen, 'Un texte peu connu relatif au commerce oriental d'Amalfi au Xe siècle', *Archivio storico per le province napoletane*, n.s., 34 (1955 for 1953–4), pp. 61–6.

'Pactum Warmundi': G. L. F. Tafel and G. M. Thomas (eds.), *Urkunden zur älteren*

Handels- und Staatsgeschichte der Republik Venedig (3 vols., *Fontes rerum Austriacarum* II, 12–14, Vienna, 1856–7) 1, no. 40, pp. 79–89; William of Tyre, *Chronicle* 12.25, ed. R. B. C. Huygens (2 vols., *Corpus Christianorum, Continuatio mediaevalis* 63–63A, Turnhout, 1986), 1, pp. 577–81.

Italian quarters in Acre: Joshua Prawer, *Crusader Institutions* (Oxford, 1980), p. 232, n. 40; *Nicolas Morosini*: ibid., pp. 226–7.

Pisan 'fondaco' in Alexandria: Wilhelm Heyd, *Histoire du commerce du Levant au Moyen Age* (2 vols., Leipzig, 1885–6) 1, p. 397.

Venetian division of Crete: Tafel and Thomas, *Urkunden . . . der Republik Venedig* 2, no. 232, pp. 143–5, there dated 1212; Freddy Thiriet, *La Romanie vénitienne au Moyen Age: Le développement et l'exploitation du domaine colonial vénitien (XII–XIV s.)* (Paris, 1959), pp. 125–6, n. 3, prefers a date of 1209.

'The strength and bulwark of the empire . . . : Tafel and Thomas, *Urkunden . . . der Republik Venedig* 3, no. 350, pp. 56–9, at p. 57.

'One of the oldest urban privileges . . .': Edith Ennen, *Die europäische Stadt des Mittelalters* (4th ed., Göttingen, 1987), p. 132.

Bohemond of Antioch's grant: Heinrich Hagenmeyer (ed.), *Epistulae et chartae ad historiam primi belli sacri spectantes* (Innsbruck, 1901), no. 13, pp. 155–6.

Genoese exporting Flemish cloth: David Abulafia, *The Two Italies* (Cambridge, 1977), p. 255.

Genoese 'not only excluded the Greeks . . .': George Pachymeres, *De Michaele et Andronico Palaeologis*, ed. Immanuel Bekker (2 vols., *Corpus scriptorum historiae Byzantinae* 24–5, Bonn, 1835), 1, pp. 419–20.

Geoffrey de Langley's embassy: Cornelio Desimoni (ed.), 'I conti dell'ambasciata al chan di Persia nel 1292', *Atti della Società ligure di storia patria* 13/3 (1879), pp. 537–698, at pp. 608, 614; Michael Balard, *La Romanie génoise (XIIe–début du XVe siècle)* (2 vols., Rome, 1978) 1, pp. 134, 138.

Tana: Balard, *La Romanie génoise* 1, pp. 154–5.

'Another Genoa': ibid. 1, 'Trois autres gênes' (i.e. Caffa, Pera and Chios), title to chapter 4.

Caffaraino: ibid. 1, pp. 199–202, 235–48, 339–41; the documents are edited in Michel Balard (ed.), *Gênes et l'Outre-mer I: Les actes de Caffa du notaire Lamberto di Sambuceto 1289–90* (Paris, 1973).

Caffa in general: Balard, *La Romanie génoise* 1, pp. 202–14, 250, 289–302; Giorgio Fedalto, *La Chiesa Latina in Oriente* (2nd ed., 3 vols., Verona, 1981) 2, pp. 61–3.

Sailing times from Venice: Thiriet, *La Romanie vénitienne*, p. 187; *from Genoa*: Balard, *La Romanie génoise* 1, pp. 473–4; 2, pp. 576–85.

On *ships and sea routes in the Mediterranean* see the excellent recent work by John H. Pryor, *Geography, Technology and War: Studies in the Maritime History of the Mediterranean, 649–1571* (Cambridge, 1988).

'As long as the seas . . .': Francesco Gabrieli (ed.), *Arab Historians of the Crusades* (Eng. tr., Berkeley and London, 1969), p. 214 (Abu Shama).

'The city which is now called Acre . . .': Matthew Paris, caption to the depiction of

Acre in his map of the Holy Land, reproduced in Suzanne Lewis, *The Art of Matthew Paris in the 'Chronica Majora'* (Berkeley, etc., 1987), p. 350, fig. 214; text in *Itinéraires à Jerusalem,* ed. Henri Michelant and Gaston Raynaud (*Publications de la Société de l'Orient latin, Série géographique* 3, Geneva, 1882), pp. 136–7.

Muslims 'had no fleet strong enough . . .': Gabrieli, *Arab Historians,* p. 340 (Tashrīf).

Di Negro family: Robert S. Lopez and Irving W. Raymond (eds.), *Medieval Trade in the Mediterranean* (New York, 1955), doc. 158, p. 322; Balard, *La Romanie génoise,* index *s.v.* 'Negro (di)'.

A useful summary in English of the *origins of Lübeck* is Günther Fehring, 'The Archaeology of Early Lübeck: The Relation between the Slavic and the German Settlement Sites', in H. B. Clarke and Anngret Simms (eds.), *The Comparative History of Urban Origins in Non-Roman Europe* (*British Archaeological Reports, International Series* 255, 2 vols., Oxford, 1985) 1, pp. 267–87.

Lübeck and Count Adolf: Helmold of Bosau, *Chronica Slavorum* 1.48 (Old Lübeck), 1.57 (Count Adolf 'came to the place which is called Bucu . . .'), 1.71 ('There was peace in the land . . .'), 1.63, 76, 86 (vicissitudes of early Lübeck), 1.86 ('At his bidding . . .'), ed. Heinz Stoob (*AQ* 19, Darmstadt, rev. ed., 1973), pp. 186, 212, 252, 222–4, 264, 302–4.

On the *Soest model* Arnold of Lübeck, *Chronica Slavorum* 2.21, ed. Johann Martin Lappenberg (*SRG,* Hanover, 1868), p. 65; in general see Wilhelm Ebel, *Lübisches Recht* (Lübeck, 1971).

German traders in Gotland: Die Urkunden Heinrichs des Löwen, Herzogs von Sachsen und Bayern, ed. Karl Jordan, *MGH, Laienfürsten- und Dynastenurkunden der Kaiserzeit* (Leipzig and Weimar, 1941–9), no. 15, pp. 9–10; *in Denmark and Russia: Hansisches UB* 1, ed. Konstantin Höhlbaum (Halle, 1876), no. 17, p. 10.

Bremen cog: Detlev Ellmers, 'The Cog of Bremen and Related Boats', in Sean McGrail (ed.), *The Archaeology of Medieval Ships and Harbours in Northern Europe* (*British Archaeological Reports, International Series* 66, Oxford, 1979), pp. 1–15, at pp. 9–11; Siegfried Fliedner and Rosemarie Pohl-Weber, *The Cog of Bremen* (Eng. tr., 3rd ed., Bremen, 1972).

Lübeck traffic in 1368: Georg Lechner (ed.), *Die hansischen Pfundzollisten des Jahres 1368* (*Quellen und Darstellungen zur hansischen Geschichte,* n.s., 10, Lübeck, 1935), p. 66.

'Merchants, rich and outstanding . . .': Livländische Reimchronik, lines 127–228, ed. Leo Meyer (Paderborn, 1876), pp. 4–6.

'The city of Riga was built . . .': Henry of Livonia, *Chronicon Livoniae,* 4.5, 5.1, ed. Leonid Arbusow and Albert Bauer (*AQ* 24, Darmstadt, 1959), pp. 18–20.

Early development of Riga: Friedrich Benninghoven, *Rigas Entstehung und der Frühhansische Kaufmann* (Hamburg, 1961), pp. 41–7.

Privileges of 1211: Hansisches UB 1, no. 88, p. 38; *of 1225:* ibid. 1, no. 194, pp. 60–61.

Seal: Benninghoven, *Rigas Entstehung,* plates opposite pp. 80, 105.

'Consules Rigenses': Liv-, esth-, und curländisches UB 6, no. 2717, cols. 4–6.

Early population: Benninghoven, *Rigas Entstehung*, pp. 54–62, 98–100, 105–9.

Riga surnames: Liselotte Feyerabend, *Die Rigauer und Revaler Familiennamen im 14. und 15. Jahrhundert* (Cologne and Vienna, 1985), p. 149.

'City of God': Henry of Livonia, *Chronicon Livoniae*, 9.4, ed. Arbusow and Bauer, p. 38.

8. Race Relations on the Frontiers of Latin Europe (1): Language and Law

'They are to be judged . . .': *Rerum Hungaricarum monumenta Arpadiana*, ed. S. L. Endlicher (St Gallen, 1849), pp. 399–400 (King Emmerich of Hungary for *hospites* settled in Sárospatak, 1201).

'The various nations . . .': Regino of Prüm, *Epistula ad Hathonem archiepiscopum missa*, ed. Friedrich Kurze, *Reginonis . . . chronicon* (*SRG*, Hanover, 1890), pp. xix–xx.

Hair-style: *Statutes and Ordinances and Acts of the Parliament of Ireland: King John to Henry V*, ed. Henry F. Berry (Dublin, 1907), p. 210; Kenneth H. Jackson (ed.), *A Celtic Miscellany* (rev. ed., Harmondsworth, 1971), p. 218; Helbig & Weinrich 1, no. 19, p. 98; Francesco Gabrieli (ed.), *Arab Historians of the Crusades* (Eng. tr., Berkeley and London, 1969), pp. 200–201 (Bahā' ad-Din).

Isidore of Seville: *Etymologies* 9.1.1, ed. W. M. Lindsay (2 vols., Oxford, 1911, unpaginated).

'Language makes race': Claudius Marius Victor, *Alethia* 3, line 274, ed. Carl Schenkl, *Poetae Christiani minores* 1 (*Corpus scriptorum ecclesiasticorum latinorum* 16/1, Vienna, etc., 1888), pp. 359–436, at p. 416.

'Those who speak the same language . . .': Peter of Zittau, *Chronicon Aulae Regiae* 1.68, ed. J. Emler, *Fontes rerum Bohemicarum* 4 (Prague, 1884), pp. 1–337, at p. 83.

'Wars and various tribulations . . .': Edouard Perroy, *L'Angleterre et le Grand Schisme d'Occident* (Paris, 1933), pp. 394–5 (the English envoys at the Roman curia in 1381, referring to Ireland).

Peter of Zittau: *Chronicon Aulae Regiae* 2.23, ed. Emler, p. 301; the translation of the phrase *in constratis* as 'in the streets' is supported by the *Latinitatis Medii Aevi Lexicon Bohemiae: Slovník Středověké Latiny v Českých Zemích* (Prague, 1977–), pp. 910–11.

Cracow excommunication: *Monumenta Poloniae Vaticana 3: Analecta Vaticana*, ed. Jan Ptaśnik (Cracow, 1914), no. 247, p. 278.

'The place is called "woyces" . . .': *Pommerellisches UB*, ed. Max Perlbach (Danzig, 1881–2), no. 492, pp. 442–3 (1292).

Ellach: *Register of the Abbey of St Thomas Dublin*, ed. John T. Gilbert (RS, 1889), nos. 36, 269, 302, pp. 37, 224, 258; on the *suffix 'town'* see T. Jones Hughes, 'Town and Baile in Irish Place-Names', in Nicholas Stephens and Robin E.

Glasscock (eds.), *Irish Geographical Studies in Honour of E. Estyn Evans* (Belfast, 1970), pp. 244–58.

Algariva: Ramón Menéndez Pidal (ed.), *Documentos lingüísticos de España* 1 (Madrid, 1919, repr. 1966), p. 353.

Otto I bilingual: Widukind of Corvey, *Res gestae Saxonicae* 2.36, ed. Albert Bauer and Reinhold Rau, *Quellen zur Geschichte der sächsischen Kaiserzeit* (*AQ* 8, rev. ed., Darmstadt, 1977), pp. 1–183, at p. 118.

Frankish Morea: *Chronicle of Morea*, tr. Harold E. Lurier, *Crusaders as Conquerors* (New York, 1964), pp. 37–56, 192, 223–4.

The best-known example of an *Anglo-Norman composing Irish verse* is Gearóid Iarla (i.e. Gerald fitz Maurice fitzGerald, earl of Desmond) whose poems are edited by Gearóid MacNiocaill, 'Duanaire Ghearóid Iarla', *Studia Hibernica* 3 (1963), pp. 7–59.

Philip in Syracuse: Geoffrey Malaterra, *De rebus gestis Rogerii Calabriae et Siciliae comitis et Roberti Guiscardi ducis fratris eius* 4.2, ed. Ernesto Pontieri (*Rerum italicarum scriptores*, n.s., 5/1, Bologna, 1928), p. 86.

South Italian brigands: William of Apulia, *La geste de Robert Guiscard* 1, lines 165–8, ed. Marguerite Mathieu (Palermo, 1961), p. 108.

Translators in Valencia: John Boswell *The Royal Treasure: Muslim Communities under the Crown of Aragon in the Fourteenth Century* (New Haven, 1977), pp. 74, n. 41, 384; along *Welsh border*: *Book of Fees* (2 vols. in 3, London, 1920–31) 1, p. 146; *Red Book of the Exchequer*, ed. Hubert Hall (3 vols., RS, 1896), 2, p. 454 (Wrenoc ap Meurig, 1212); see in general Constance Bullock-Davies, *Professional Interpreters and the Matter of Britain* (Cardiff, 1966).

Loan words in Polish: Walter Kaestner, 'Mittelniederdeutsche Elemente in der polnischen und kaschubischen Lexik', in P. Sture Ureland (ed.), *Sprachkontakt in der Hanse . . . Akten des 7. Internationalen Symposions über Sprachkontakt in Europa, Lübeck 1986* (Tübingen, 1987), pp. 135–62; *in Welsh*: T. H. Parry-Williams, *The English Element in Welsh* (Cymmrodorion Record Series 10, London, 1923), pp. 68, 76–7, 155 (see the comments of Rees Davies, *Conquest, Coexistence and Change: Wales 1063–1415* (Oxford, 1987), p. 104); *from Arabic*: J. N. Hillgarth, *The Spanish Kingdoms 1250–1516* (2 vols., Oxford, 1976–8) 1, p. 185.

Name changes: *Codex diplomaticus Brandenburgensis*, ed. Adolph Friedrich Riedel (41 vols., Berlin, 1838–69), A 22, p. 114; *Statutes . . . of the Parliament of Ireland: King John to Henry V*, pp. 434–5 (clause 3); *Glamorgan County History 3: The Middle Ages*, ed. T. B. Pugh (Cardiff, 1971), p. 359. For a fuller discussion of changes in naming patterns see Chapter 11.

Henry Zolunta: Thietmar of Merseburg, *Chronicon* 3.21, ed. Werner Trillmich (*AQ* 9, Darmstadt, 1957), p. 108.

Bohemian binomialism: Heinz Zatschek, 'Namensänderungen und Doppelnamen in Böhmen und Mähren im hohen Mittelalter', *Zeitschrift für Sudetendeutsche Geschichte* 3 (1939), pp. 1–11, at p. 10.

Arabic binomialism: Angel González Palencia, *Los mozárabes toledanos en los siglos XII y XIII* ('volumen preliminar' and 3 vols., Madrid, 1926–30), vol. prel., p. 123.

Term 'jazyk': František Graus, *Die Nationenbildung der Westslawen im Mittelalter* (*Nationes* 3, Sigmaringen, 1980), pp. 21, 93. For Dalimil, see below.

Term 'iaith': Rees Davies, 'Race Relations in Post-Conquest Wales', *Transactions of the Honourable Society of Cymmrodorion* (1974–5), pp. 32–56, at p. 34.

'Those who do not speak Welsh: Davies, *Conquest*, p. 17.

'Hybernica lingua': Gearóid MacNiocaill, *Na Buirgéisí* (2 vols., Dublin, 1964) 2, no. 77, pp. 351–2 (1279–80).

Hospitaller 'tongues': Jonathan Riley-Smith, *The Knights of St John in Jerusalem and Cyprus c. 1050–1310* (London, 1967), pp. 283–4.

Przemysl Ottokar II's appeal: *Regesta diplomatica nec non epistolaria Bohemiae et Moraviae*, ed. K. J. Erben, J. Emler *et al.* (7 vols., to date, Prague, 1854–), 2, no. 1106, pp. 466–8.

'There will be one king . . .': Peter of Zittau, *Chronicon Aulae Regiae* 1.68, ed. Emler, p. 83.

Polish claim to Pomerelia: *Lites ac res gestae inter Polonos Ordinemque Cruciferorum* (2nd ser., 3 vols., Poznań and Warsaw, 1890–1935) 1, p. 163.

King Robert's letter: Ranald Nicholson, 'A Sequel to Edward Bruce's Invasion of Ireland', *Scottish Historical Review* 42 (1963), pp. 30–40, at pp. 38–9; see also Geoffrey Barrow, *Robert Bruce and the Community of the Realm of Scotland* (2nd ed., Edinburgh, 1982), p. 434.

Remonstrance of 1317–18: Walter Bower, *Scotichronicon* 12.32, ed. D. E. R. Watt, 6 (Aberdeen, 1991), p. 402.

Edward I's charge: 'linguam Anglicam . . . omnino de terra delere proponit', William Stubbs (ed.), *Select Charters* (9th ed., Oxford, 1913), p. 480; it is possible that *lingua* should here be translated as 'people'.

'To exterminate the Polish language': *Annales capituli Cracoviensis (Rocznik Kapitulny Krakowski)*, ed. August Bielowski, *MPH* 2 (Lwów, 1872, repr. Warsaw, 1961), pp. 779–816, at p. 815.

Woitz: Karl Gottfried Hugelmann, 'Die Rechtsstellung der Wenden im deutschen Mittelalter', *Zeitschrift der Savigny-Stiftung für Rechtsgeschichte, Germanistische Abteilung* 58 (1938), pp. 214–56, at p. 238.

Edward III's ordinance: Historical Manuscripts Commission, *10th Report, appendix 5* (London, 1885), pp. 260–61, no. 8; cf. the Statutes of Kilkenny of 1366, *Statutes . . . of the Parliament of Ireland: King John to Henry V*, pp. 434–5 (clause 3).

'They should get their subjects . . .': Perroy, *L'Angleterre et le Grand Schisme*, pp. 394–5 (cf. p. 403).

William Power: James Lydon, 'The Middle Nation', in *idem* (ed.), *The English in Medieval Ireland* (Dublin, 1984), pp. 1–26, at pp. 22–3.

Waterford apprentices: Historical Manuscripts Commission, *10th Report, app. 5*, p. 308.

Old Prussian: William R. Schmalstieg, *Studies in Old Prussian* (University Park, Pa.,

1976), esp. pp. 68–97, for surviving texts; *idem, An Old Prussian Grammar* (University Park, Pa., 1974), p. 3, for the quotation.

'I am a man of forty-seven years . . .': Reinhold Olesch (ed.), *Fontes linguae dravaeno-polabicae minores et Chronica Venedica J. P. Schultzii* (Cologne and Graz, 1967), p. 165.

Arabic documents in Toledo: Julio González, *Repoblación de Castilla la Nueva* (2 vols., Madrid, 1975–6) 2, pp. 87–90.

Sobieslaw of Bohemia's charter: Helbig & Weinrich 2, no. 93, p. 352; *'men who come there or traverse'*: *Pomerellisches UB*, no. 159, pp. 133–4.

A useful summary of the imperial provisions on *procedural law applying to Jews* can be found in Friedrich Lotter, 'The Scope and Effectiveness of Imperial Jewry Law in the High Middle Ages', *Jewish History* 4 (1989), pp. 31–58, at pp. 48–9.

Salzwedel: Helbig & Weinrich 1, no. 36, p. 158.

Daroca: Colección de fueros municipales y cartas pueblas de los reinos de Castilla, León, Corona de Aragón y Navarra, ed. Tomás Muñoz y Romero (Madrid, 1847), p. 537 (1142).

Slav witnesses in Lübeck law: Das alte Lübische Recht, ed. Johann Friedrich Hach (Lübeck, 1839), p. 302, no. 110 (contrast p. 206, no. 68); Gustav Korlén (ed.), *Norddeutsch Stadtrechte 2: Das mittelniederdeutsche Stadtrecht von Lübeck nach seinen ältesten Formen* (Lund and Copenhagen, 1951), p. 104 (clause 75); Wilhelm Ebel, *Lübisches Recht* (I) (Lübeck, 1971), pp. 275–6; Wolfgang Zorn, 'Deutsche und Undeutsche in der städtischen Rechtsordnung des Mittelalters in Ost-Mitteleuropa', *Zeitschrift für Ostforschung* 1 (1952), pp. 182–94, at p. 184.

Greek witnesses in the Morea: Les assises de Romanie 198, ed. Georges Recoura (Paris, 1930), p. 282.

All three *Toledo charters* are edited in Alfonso García-Gallo, 'Los Fueros de Toledo', *Anuario de historia del derecho español* 45 (1975), pp. 341–488.

'If there are judicial proceedings . . .', etc.: '. . . si inter eos fuerit ortum aliquod negotio de aliquo judicio, secundum sententiam in Libro iudicum antiquitus constitutam discutiatur', García-Gallo, 'Los Fueros de Toledo', app., doc. 1, p. 460.

Santa Olalla: ibid., doc. 3, p. 463.

'Alcaldes' of Castilians and Mozarabs: González, *Repoblación* 2, pp. 94–6; María Luz Alonso, 'La perduración del Fuero Juzgo y el Derecho de los castellanos de Toledo', *Anuario de historia del derecho español* 48 (1978), pp. 335–77, at p. 345 with n. 29.

'You shall have your own "merino" . . .': García-Gallo, 'Los Fueros de Toledo', doc. 6, p. 467. These officials may, however, have been executive rather than judicial; for reservations on this point see García-Gallo, pp. 429, n. 199, 437, and Luz Alonso, 'El Fuero Juzgo', p. 343, n. 24.

Fourteenth-century rules: Luz Alonso, 'El Fuero Juzgo', pp. 346–9, and doc. 1, pp. 374–5.

Tudela: Colección de fueros . . ., ed. Muñoz y Romero, pp. 415–17.

Right to 'sunna': e.g. Boswell, *Royal Treasure*, p. 131, n. 79 (1348).

'*Preserving their own law . . .*': *Las Siete Partidas* 7.24. 1, ed. Real Academia de la Historia (3 vols., Madrid, 1807), 3, p. 676.

Kidwelly: Rees Davies, 'The Law of the March', *Welsh History Review* 5 (1970–71), pp. 1–30, at p. 4; for earlier criticisms of Welsh acknowledgement of the rights of the illegitimate see the present writer's *Gerald of Wales 1146–1223* (Oxford, 1982), pp. 41–2; and the Statute of Wales, *Statutes of the Realm* (11 vols., Record Commission, 1810–28) 1, pp. 55–68 (12 Edward I), at p. 68.

English and Welsh courts: Davies, 'Law of the March', p. 16; for the general context see his *Lordship and Society in the March of Wales 1282–1400* (Oxford, 1978), pp. 149–75, 'Judicial Lordship', and pp. 310–12.

Karpfen: Helbig & Weinrich 2, no. 138, p. 520.

'*If a Moor brings a lawsuit . . .*': *Colección de fueros . . .*, ed. Muñoz y Romero, pp. 415–17.

'*If a case arises between a Christian and a Saracen . . .*': José María Font Rius (ed.), *Cartas de población y franquicia de Cataluña* (2 vols., Madrid and Barcelona, 1969) 1/i, no. 303, pp. 444–6.

'*Great practical difficulties*': Francisco Fernández y González, *Estado social y político de los mudéjares de Castilla* (Madrid, 1866), p. 119, n. 2.

Mixed cases in Prussia: e.g. Helbig & Weinrich 1, nos. 132 (1286), 141 (1351), pp. 488–90, 522.

Játiva: Fernández y González, *Estado . . . de los mudéjares*, doc. 24, p. 325.

Germans in Prague: Helbig & Weinrich 2, no. 93, p. 354.

Cracow: Helbig & Weinrich 2, no. 77, p. 294; *actor forum rei*, etc., is from the *Codex Iustinianus* 3.13.2 and 3.19.3, ed. Paul Krueger (*Corpus iuris civilis* 2, Berlin, 1895), pp. 128–9, and was incorporated into Gregory IX's *Decretals* 2.2.5, ed. Emil Friedberg (*Corpus iuris canonici* 2, Leipzig, 1881), col. 249 (from a letter of Alexander III): Richard Helmholz kindly identified this citation.

'*Because of the wicked and malicious people . . .*': Helbig & Weinrich 2, no. 93, p. 354.

'*When a court is held by the authority . . .*': *Sachsenspiegel, Landrecht* 3.69–70, ed. Karl August Eckhardt (*Germanenrechte*, n.s., Göttingen, 1955), pp. 254–6.

'*If a Moor is suspected of theft . . .*': *Colección de fueros . . .*, ed. Muñoz y Romero, pp. 415–17.

Wergilds in Prussia: *Iura Prutenorum* 18, ed. Józef Matuszewski (*Towarzystwo Naukowe w Toruniu: Fontes* 53, Toruń, 1963), p. 29; Reinhard Wenskus, *Ausgewählte Aufsätze zum frühen und preussischen Mittelalter*, ed. Hans Patze (Sigmaringen, 1986), p. 422.

Reval: *Liv-, esth- und curländisches UB*, ed. F. G. von Bunge *et al.* (1st ser., 12 vols., Riga and Reval, 1853–1910), 1, no. 435, cols. 549–50; no. 437, col. 551 (1273).

Fueros de Sepúlveda, ed. Emilio Sáez (Segovia, 1953), p. 74 ('Fuero romanceado' 41).

Wismar: *Mecklenburgisches UB* (25 vols. in 26, Schwerin and Leipzig, 1863–1977) 14, no. 8773, p. 616.

Court interpreters in Ireland: *Rotuli chartarum in turri Londinensi asservati (1199–1216)*, ed. T. D. Hardy (London, 1837), p. 172 (cf. Davies, 'Race Relations', p. 34); *in Prussia*: *Iura Prutenorum* 89, ed. Matuszewski, p. 49.

Basque: Thomas Glick, *Islamic and Christian Spain in the Early Middle Ages* (Princeton, 1979), p. 191.

Waterford pleas: Historical Manuscripts Commission, *10th Report, app. 5*, p. 323.

'Anyone against whom an accusation is made . . .': *Sachsenspiegel, Landrecht* 3. 71, ed. Eckhardt, pp. 256–7.

Nienburg document: Richard Siebert (ed.), 'Elf ungedruckte Urkunden aus einem im Herzoglichen Haus- und Staatsarchiv zu Zerbst befindlichen Nienburger Copiale', *Mitteilungen des Vereins für Anhaltinische Geschichte und Altertumskunde* 9 (1904), pp. 183–94, at pp. 190–91.

'Gwallgair' in Wales: Rees Davies, 'The Twilight of Welsh Law, 1284–1506', *History* 51 (1966), pp. 143–64, at p. 160.

Wrocław: *Breslauer UB* 1, ed. G. Korn (Breslau, 1870), no. 121, pp. 110–11.

Charles IV: *Codex iuris Bohemici*, ed. Hermenegild Jiriček (5 vols. in 12, Prague, 1867–98), 2/2, p. 125 (*Majestas Carolina* 19).

'Caused English laws and customs . . .': Roger of Wendover, *Flores historiarum*, ed. H. G. Hewlett (3 vols., RS, 1886–9), 2, p. 56; on the general subject see Geoffrey Hand, *English Law in Ireland 1290–1324* (Cambridge, 1967), chapter 1, and Paul Brand, 'Ireland and the Literature of the Early Common Law', *The Irish Jurist*, n.s., 16 (1981), pp. 95–113.

'Wishes that all common law writs . . .': *Foedera, conventiones, litterae et . . . acta publica . . .*, ed. Thomas Rymer (new ed., 4 vols. in 7 parts, Record Commission, 1816–69), 1.1, p. 266; cf. *Calendar of the Patent Rolls (1232–47)* (London, 1906), p. 488.

'We are given to understand . . .': *Rotuli litterarum clausarum in turri Londinensi asservati (1204–27)*, ed. T. D. Hardy (2 vols., London, 1833–44), 1, p. 497.

'A conscious, efficient and uniform . . .': Hand, *English Law*, p. 1.

Remonstrance of 1317–18: Bower, *Scotichronicon* 12.26–32, ed. Watt, 6, pp. 384–402; see the analysis in Hand, *English Law*, pp. 198–205.

Possibly better situation of Irish in early thirteenth century: Kenneth Nicholls, 'Anglo-French Ireland and After', *Peritia* 1 (1982), pp. 370–403, at pp. 374–6.

'That he is not held to answer . . .': Hand, *English Law*, p. 199, citing a case of 1301.

Paumer–Benet case: *Calendar of the Justiciary Rolls . . . of Ireland (1295–1303)*, ed. James Mills (Dublin, 1905), pp. 121–3.

'Take writs and . . . be answered': ibid., p. 14.

Archbishop of Armagh: Katherine Walsh, *A Fourteenth-Century Scholar and Primate: Richard FitzRalph in Oxford, Avignon and Armagh* (Oxford, 1981), p. 334.

'The killing of Englishmen . . .': *Statutes . . . of the Parliament of Ireland: King John to Henry V*, p. 210.

'When an Englishman treacherously . . .': Bower, *Scotichronicon* 12.28, ed. Watt, 6, p. 390.

'Came and did not deny . . .': Hand, *English Law*, p. 202, citing a case of 1301.

Petit–de Creus case: *Calendar of the Justiciary Rolls . . . of Ireland (1295–1303)*, p. 156.

'*Redemption for an Englishman's death*': *Calendar of Archbishop Alen's Register*, ed. Charles McNeill (Dublin, 1950), pp. 103, 115.

'*Fines and ransoms were being taken . . .*': Hand, *English Law*, p. 208; *Foedera* 2. 1, pp. 293–4.

'*Baránta*': Gearóid MacNiocaill, 'The Interaction of Laws', in James Lydon (ed.), *The English in Medieval Ireland* (Dublin, 1984), pp. 105–17, at pp. 106–7.

Statute of Wales: *Statutes of the Realm* 1, p. 68.

Treaty of Christburg: *Preussisches UB* (6 vols. to date, Königsberg and Marburg, 1882–) 1/i, no. 218, pp. 158–65, at p. 159.

'*If a man has Prussian law . . .*': *Iura Prutenorum* 25, ed. Matuszewski, p. 31.

'*If an inhabitant buys . . .*': *Codex iuris Bohemici* 2/2, p. 167 (*Majestas Carolina* 82).

'*Of Wendish stock . . .*', etc.: *Das Magdeburg-breslauer systematische Schöffenrecht* 3.1.4, ed. Paul Laband (Berlin, 1863), p. 55; *Das alte Kulmische Recht* 3. 4, ed. C. K. Leman (Berlin, 1838), p. 53.

Brüsewitz: Helbig & Weinrich 1, no. 66, p. 270; *Brzeg*: ibid. 2, no. 25, p. 154.

Purchase of English law by Irish: A. J. Otway-Ruthven, 'The Request of the Irish for English Law, 1277–80', *Irish Historical Studies* 6 (1948–9), pp. 261–70, at p. 269; see also Aubrey Gwynn, 'Edward I and the Proposed Purchase of English Law for the Irish', *Transactions of the Royal Historical Society*, 5th ser., 10 (1960), pp. 111–27.

'*Diversity of law*': MacNiocaill, *Na Buirgeísí* 2, p. 336, n. 21; a petition from the cities of Ireland, dated 'early Edward III' by Geoffrey Hand, 'English Law in Ireland, 1172–1351', *Northern Ireland Legal Quarterly* 23 (1972), pp. 393–422, at p. 413 and n. 3.

Darcy's proposals: Hand, *English Law*, p. 409.

Legislation of 1330–31: *Statutes . . . of the Parliament of Ireland: King John to Henry V*, p. 324 ('quod una et eadem lex fiat tam Hibernicis quam Anglicis').

'*It was too late . . .*': Frederick Pollock and Frederic William Maitland, *The History of English Law before the Time of Edward I* (2nd ed., 2 vols., Cambridge, 1898, reissued 1968) 1, p. 91.

Sancho IV's ruling: Mercedes Gaibrois de Ballesteros, *Historia del reinado de Sancho IV de Castilla* (3 vols., Madrid, 1922–8) 3, doc. 295, pp. 184–5.

Modifications of Welsh law: Davies, 'Twilight'; *idem*, *Conquest*, pp. 422–4; the phrase 'law of London' is from a fifteenth-century Welsh poem, *Oxford Book of Welsh Verse*, ed. T. Parry (Oxford, 1962), p. 139.

Incorporation of Wales, 1536: *Statutes of the Realm* 3, pp. 563–9 (27 Henry VIII c. 26), at pp. 563, 567.

9. Race Relations on the Frontiers of Latin Europe (2): Power and Blood

'*Human nature is such . . .*': Cosmas of Prague, *Chronica Boemorum* 2.23, ed. Bertold Bretholz (*SRG*, n.s., Berlin, 1923), p. 116.

Gerlach of Mühlhausen: *Chronicon*, ed. Wilhelm Wattenbach, *MGH, SS* 17 (Hanover, 1861), pp. 683–710, at p. 685.

'Perfectly trained in the Slav tongue': Cosmas of Prague, *Chronica Boemorum* 1. 23, 31, ed. Bretholz, pp. 44–5, 56.

Gerald of Wales (Giraldus Cambrensis): *Symbolum Electorum* 1.28, in J. S. Brewer, J. F. Dimock and G. F. Warner (eds.), *Opera* (8 vols., RS, 1861–91) 1, pp. 197–395, at p. 306.

Michael Scot: Honorius III, 20 June 1224, *Cum olim fuisses*, Po. 7272, and *Cum olim venerabilis* (not in Potthast); *Pontificia Hibernica: Medieval Papal Chancery Documents concerning Ireland 640–1261*, ed. Maurice P. Sheehy (2 vols., Dublin, 1962–5), 1, nos. 167–8, pp. 253–5.

Peter Narr: František Graus, *Die Nationenbildung der Westslawen im Mittelalter* (*Nationes* 3, Sigmaringen, 1980), p. 97, n. 78.

St Mary's, Bautzen: *Codex diplomaticus Lusatiae superioris* 1, ed. Gustav Köhler (2nd ed., Görlitz, 1856), no. 86, pp. 137–8.

Szczecin: Helbig & Weinrich 1, no. 85, pp. 324–6 (1237); see the comments of Jürgen Petersohn, *Der südliche Ostseeraum im kirchlich-politischen Kräftespiel des Reichs, Polens und Dänemarks vom 10. bis 13. Jahrhundert* (Cologne and Vienna, 1979), pp. 323–4.

Ceský Krumlov: *UB des ehemaligen Cistercienserstiftes Goldenkron in Böhmen*, ed. M. Pangerl (*Fontes rerum Austriacarum* II, 37, Vienna, 1872), no. 79, p. 146 and n. 3.

'He was such a sharp enemy . . .': Peter of Zittau, *Chronicon Aulae Regiae* 1.68, ed. J. Emler, *Fontes rerum Bohemicarum* 4 (Prague, 1884), pp. 1–337, at p. 84.

Statutes of 1285: *Codex diplomaticus Maioris Poloniae*, ed. Ignacy Zakrzewski and Franciszek Piekosiński (5 vols., Poznań, 1877–1908), 1, no. 551, pp. 510–15; *of 1326*: ibid. 2, no. 1061, p. 396.

Swinka–John of Cracow dispute: *Monumenta Poloniae Vaticana 3: Analecta Vaticana*, ed. Jan Ptaśnik (Cracow, 1914), pp. 82 ('he is attempting to expel . . .'), 90 ('if I cannot complete . . .'), 86, 88–9, 87, 90, 92, 93 ('he does not promote . . .'), 84–5 ('he committed perjury . . .').

'Since the election . . .': *Patent Rolls of the Reign of Henry III (1216–32)* (2 vols., London, 1901–3) 1, p. 23; cf. p. 22; on this whole subject see J. A. Watt, *The Church and the Two Nations in Medieval Ireland* (Cambridge, 1970), pp. 69–84; idem, *The Church in Medieval Ireland* (Dublin, 1972), pp. 100–109.

For a recent sketch of the career of *Henry of Dublin* see Ralph V. Turner, *Men Raised from the Dust: Administrative Service and Upward Mobility in Angevin England* (Philadelphia, 1988), pp. 91–106; the advowson grant is in *Rotuli chartarum in turri Londinensi asservati (1199–1216)*, ed. T. D. Hardy (London, 1837), p. 218.

Papal criticism of exclusion of Irish: Honorius III, 6 August 1220, *Pervenit ad audientiam nostram*, Po. 6323, and 26 April 1224, *Sicut ea que rite*, Po. 7227; *Pontificia Hibernica*, ed. Sheehy 1, nos. 140, 158, pp. 225, 245–6.

Licences to elect: *Patent Rolls of the Reign of Henry III* 2, p. 59 (1226); cf. *Rotuli litterarum clausarum in turri Londinensi asservati (1204–27)*, ed. T. D. Hardy (2 vols., London, 1833–44), 2, pp. 29, 31 (1225).

'It is expedient to the king . . .': J. A. Watt, 'English Law and the Irish Church: The Reign of Edward I', in J. A. Watt, J. B. Morrall and F. X. Martin (eds.), *Medieval Studies presented to A. Gwynn* (Dublin, 1961), pp. 133–67, at pp. 150–51, n. 71; cf. *Calendar of Documents relating to Ireland (1171–1307)*, ed. H. S. Sweetman (5 vols., London, 1875–86), no. 2, p. 10.

'No one can be appointed . . .': Edouard Perroy, *L'Angleterre et le Grand Schisme d'Occident* (Paris, 1933), pp. 394–5.

'It is no novelty . . .': Innocent III, 14 September 1204, *Venientes ad apostolicam*, Po. 2280; *Registrum sive epistolae* 7.128, *PL*, 214–16, at 215, cols. 417–19.

Figures for *Dominican chapters-general* calculated from *Acta capitulorum generalium ordinis praedicatorum 1 (1220–1303)*, ed., Benedictus Maria Reichert (*Monumenta ordinis fratrum praedicatorum historica* 3, Rome and Stuttgart, 1898).

Scottish Franciscans: W. Moir Bryce, *The Scottish Grey Friars* (2 vols., Edinburgh and London, 1909), 1, pp. 5–15; a rather suspect source records that, after the English conquered Scotland in 1296, the Franciscan vicariate-general of Scotland was subordinated to the English Franciscan province, André Callebaut, 'À propos du bienheureux Jean Duns Scot de Littledean', *Archivum Franciscanum Historicum* 24 (1931), pp. 305–29, at p. 325.

Brandenburg Dominicans: Heinrich Finke (ed.), *Ungedruckte Dominikanerbriefe des 13. Jahrhunderts* (Paderborn, 1891), no. 15, pp. 59–60.

John Freed: The Friars and German Society in the Thirteenth Century (Cambridge, Mass., 1977), p. 72.

Transfer of Franciscan houses: ibid., pp. 74–5.

'Brothers of the German tongue . . .': *Regesta diplomatica nec non epistolaria Bohemiae et Moraviae*, ed. K. J. Erben, J. Emler *et al.* (7 vols. to date, Prague, 1854–), 2, no. 2505, p. 1078. The text is from a formulary datable to *c.* 1272; see Graus, *Nationenbildung*, p. 97, n. 79.

Swinka: Codex diplomaticus Maioris Poloniae 1, no. 551, p. 513.

Brzésć: Graus, *Nationenbildung*, p. 122, n. 254.

Roudnice: Regesta diplomatica nec non epistolaria Bohemiae et Moraviae 3, no. 2008, p. 782 (1333).

'The first effective international organization . . .': R. W. Southern, *Western Society and the Church in the Middle Ages* (Harmondsworth, 1970), p. 255.

Figures for *Cistercian houses in Ireland* calculated from Aubrey Gwynn and R. Neville Hadcock, *Medieval Religious Houses: Ireland* (London, 1970), pp. 121–44.

On the '*conspiracy of Mellifont*' see Watt, *Church and Two Nations*, chapter 4, pp. 85–107, 'The Crisis of the Cistercian Order in Ireland'; *idem*, *The Church in Medieval Ireland*, pp. 53–9; Barry O'Dwyer, *The Conspiracy of Mellifont, 1216–1231* (Dublin, 1970).

'We have created there . . .': Stephen of Lexington, *Registrum epistolarum*, ed. P. Bruno Griesser, *Analecta sacri ordinis Cisterciensis* 2 (1946), pp. 1–118, at p. 51, no. 40. It should be noted that a reordering of the documents in the *Registrum* has been suggested by Barry O'Dwyer and followed in his translation, *Letters from Ireland 1228–1229* (Kalamazoo, Mich., 1982).

'Take good care . . .': *Registrum*, p. 81, no. 85; *prohibition on Irish appointments*: ibid., p. 93, no. 95; cf. p. 92, no. 94; *'we have ordained unconditionally . . .'*: ibid., p. 47, no. 37; cf. pp. 57–8, 93, 102, nos. 52, 95, 104 (clause 40); *'that there should be uniformity . . .'*: ibid., p. 102, no. 104 (clause 40).

I have used the Middle German versions of the *Dalimil Chronicle*, ed. J. Jiriček, *Fontes rerum Bohemicarum* 3 (Prague, 1882), pp. 5–224, *Di tutsch kronik von Behem lant* (verse), and pp. 257–97, *Die pehemische Cronica dewcz* (prose); the *Udalrich passage* is verse 41, lines 25–38, pp. 83–4 (verse) and corresponds to section 30, p. 273 (prose).

'A better opportunity of access': Geoffrey Malaterra, *De rebus gestis Rogerii Calabriae et Siciliae comitis et Roberti Guiscardi ducis fratris eius* 3.13, ed Ernesto Pontieri (*Rerum italicarum sciptores*, n.s., 5/1, Bologna, 1928), p. 64.

'He who is unable to speak French . . .': Peter of Zittau, *Chronicon Aulae Regiae* 3.2, 12, ed. Elmer, pp. 320, 331.

John of Luxemburg: *Regesta diplomatica nec non epistolaria Bohemiae et Moraviae* 2, no. 2245, pp. 973–5; 3, no. 893, pp. 351–2, no. 1046, pp. 403–4; Peter of Zittau, *Chronicon Aulae Regiae* 1.126, ed. Emler, p. 228.

Boleslaw II of Silesia: *Chronicon principum Polonie* 23, ed. Zygmunt Węclewski, *MPH* 3 (Lwów, 1878, repr. Warsaw, 1961), pp. 421–578, at p. 497; *Chronica Poloniae Maioris* 72, ed. Brygida Kürbis, *MPH*, n.s., 8 (Warsaw, 1970), p. 88; cf. 88, p. 94.

'Diabolic madness . . .': *Chronica Poloniae Maioris* 116, ed. Kürbis, p. 105.

Cujavia: ibid. 156, ed. Kürbis, p. 124; see Paul Knoll, 'Economic and Political Institutions on the Polish–German Frontier in the Middle Ages: Action, Reaction, Interaction', in Robert Bartlett and Angus MacKay (eds.), *Medieval Frontier Societies* (Oxford, 1989), pp. 151–74, at p. 169.

'The Germans held . . .': *Annales capituli Posnaniensis*, ed. Brygida Kürbis, *MPH*, n.s., 6 (Warsaw, 1962), pp. 21–78, at pp. 54–5.

Wenceslas miracle: Francis of Prague, *Cronicae Pragensis libri III* 3.12, ed. J. Emler, *Fontes rerum Bohemicarum* 4 (Prague, 1884), pp. 347–456, at pp. 426–7.

Prague burgesses: Ernst Schwarz, 'Die Volkstumsverhältnisse in den Städten Böhmens und Mährens vor den Hussitenkriegen', *Bohemia: Jahrbuch des Collegium Carolinum* 2 (1961), pp. 27–111, at fig. 1, p. 34.

'For in almost all the cities . . .': Peter of Zittau, *Chronicon Aulae Regiae* 3.2, ed. Emler, p. 320.

Archbishop of Lvov: Filippo Buonaccorsi, alias Callimachus, *Vita et mores Gregorii Sanocei*, ed. Ludwik Finkel, *MPH* 6 (Cracow, 1893, repr. Warsaw, 1961), pp. 163–216, at p. 179; Piotr Górecki kindly provided this reference.

French burgesses in Shrewsbury: *Domesday Book*, ed. Abraham Farley (2 vols., London, 1783), 1, fol. 252; see John Le Patourel, *The Norman Empire* (Oxford, 1976), pp. 38–40.

French in fourteenth-century towns: Michael Richter, *Sprache und Gessellschaft im Mittelalter* (Stuttgart, 1979), p. 190.

New Ross poem: H. E. Shields, 'The Walling of New Ross – a Thirteenth-Century Poem in French', *Long Room* 12–13 (1975–6), pp. 24–33.

Kidwelly burgesses: Rees Davies, *Conquest, Coexistence and Change: Wales 1063–1415* (Oxford, 1987), p. 166.

'*The English burgesses* . . .': *Calendar of Ancient Petitions relating to Wales*, ed. William Rees (Cardiff, 1975), p. 439, no. 13,029; *no Welshman ought* . . .': ibid., p. 172, no. 5,433.

Burgesses in Pomerelia: *Pommerellisches UB*, ed. Max Perlbach (Danzig, 1881–2), no. 465, p. 416.

German burgess support for German kings emerges in Ofen in the early fourteenth century, Raimund Friedrich Kaindl, *Geschichte der Deutschen in den Karpathenländern* (3 vols., Gotha, 1907–11) 2, pp. 37–8, and in Stockholm in the late fourteenth century, Manfred Hamann, *Mecklenburgische Geschichte* (*MF* 51, Cologne, 1968), p. 195.

Lokietek and Cracow burgesses: *Annales capituli Cracoviensis (Rocznik Kapitulny Krakowski)*, ed. August Bielowski, *MPH* 2 (Lwów, 1872, repr. Warsaw, 1961), pp. 779–816, at p. 815; the *shibboleth*: *Annales Krasinsciani (Rocznik Krasińskich)*, ed. August Bielowski, *MPH* 3 (Lwów, 1878, repr. Warsaw, 1961), pp. 127–33, at p. 133; *change in language of record*: *Liber actorum, resignationum nec non ordinationum civitatis Cracoviae*, ed. Franciszek Piekosiński (*Monumenta Medii Aevi historica res gestas Poloniae illustrantia* 4/1, Cracow, 1878), p. 28.

'*Ringbürger*': *Liber actorum* . . . *Cracoviae*, ed. Piekosiński, p. 39; *ethnic balance of burgesses*: Wolfgang Zorn, 'Deutsche und Undeutsche in der städtischen Rechtsordnung des Mittelalters in Ost-Mitteleuropa', *Zeitschrift für Ostforschung* 1 (1952), pp. 182–94, at p. 186.

Increase in racial feeling in Baltic towns: Paul Johansen and Heinz von zur Mühlen, *Deutsch und Undeutsch im mittelalterlichen und frühneuzeitlichen Reval* (Cologne and Vienna, 1973), p. 12; *among Teutonic Knights*: Reinhard Wenskus, 'Das Ordensland Preussen als Territorialstaat des 14. Jahrhunderts', in Hans Patze (ed.), *Der Deutsche Territorialstaat im 14. Jahrhundert* 1 (*Vorträge und Forschungen* 13, Sigmaringen, 1970), pp. 347–82, esp. p. 366, n. 81; *idem*, 'Der Deutsche Orden und die nichtdeutsche Bevölkerung des Preussenlandes mit besonderer Berücksichtigung der Siedlung', in Walter Schlesinger (ed.), *Die deutsche Ostsiedlung als Problem der europäischen Geschichte (Vorträge und Forschungen* 18, Sigmaringen, 1975), pp. 417–38, at pp. 422–3; *in Wales*: Rees Davies, 'Race Relations in Post-Conquest Wales', *Transactions of the Honourable Society of Cymmrodorion* (1974–5), pp. 32–56, at p. 45.

'*To anyone who brought him* . . .': *Dalimil Chronicle* (German version), prose 49, ed. Jiriček, pp. 283–4; cf. verse 67, lines 4–46, pp. 139–40.

De Theutonicis bonum dictamen: ed. Wilhelm Wostry, 'Ein deutschfeindliches Pamphlet aus Böhmen aus dem 14. Jahrhundert', *Mitteilungen des Vereins für Geschichte der*

Deutschen in Böhmen 53 (1914–15), pp. 193–238, at pp. 226–32. Wostry dates it to *c.* 1325–50, Graus (*Nationenbildung*, app. 14, pp. 221–3) to 1380–93.

On the *Deutschtumsparagraph* in Brandenburg see Werner Vogel, *Der Verbleib der wendischen Bevölkerung in der Mark Brandenburg* (Berlin, 1960), pp. 121–33.

Beeskow guilds: Codex diplomaticus Brandenburgensis, ed. Adolph Friedrich Riedel (41 vols., Berlin, 1838–69), A 20, pp. 350–51, no. 16 (1353), pp. 365–7, no. 38 (1387).

'*Echte und rechte dudesch*': ibid., A 14, pp. 241–2 (Neustadt Salzwedel, 1428).

On the *Geburtsbrief* see Vogel, *Verbleib*, pp. 127–8, n. 9; Dora Grete Hopp, *Die Zunft und die Nichtdeutschen im Osten, insbesondere in der Mark Brandenburg* (Marburg/Lahn, 1954), p. 98, n. 84.

Riga bakers: Liv-, esth- und curländisches UB, ed. F. G. von Bunge *et al.* (1st ser., 12 vols., Reval and Riga, 1853–1910), 3, no. 1305, col. 642 (art. 7).

Ofen: Das Ofner Stadtrecht 32, ed. Karl Mollay (Weimar, 1959), p. 70.

Drogheda: Katherine Walsh, *A Fourteenth-Century Scholar and Primate: Richard FitzRalph in Oxford, Avignon and Armagh* (Oxford, 1981), pp. 341–3.

Limerick: Gearóid MacNiocaill, *Na Buirgéisí* (2 vols., Dublin, 1964) 1, pp. 245–6.

Dublin: Calendar of Ancient Records of Dublin 1, ed. John T. Gilbert (Dublin, 1889), p. 331 (1469).

Statutes of Kilkenny of 1366: *Statutes and Ordinances and Acts of the Parliament of Ireland: King John to Henry V*, ed. Henry F. Berry (Dublin, 1907), pp. 430–69.

'*As immigrants come . . .*': *Libellus de institutione morum*, ed. J. Balogh, *Scriptores rerum Hungaricarum* 2 (Budapest, 1938), pp. 611–27, at p. 625.

'*Natural hatred*' of *Poles and Germans: Anonymi descriptio Europae orientalis*, ed. Olgierd Górka (Cracow, 1916), p. 56; *of Saxons and Wends*: Johannes von Buch's gloss on *Sachsenspiegel, Landrecht* 3.70, cited here from *Sachsenpiegel*, ed. Jacob Friedrich Ludovici (rev. ed., Halle, 1750), p. 555, note (b); *of English and Irish*: Walter Bower, *Scotichronicon* 12.27, ed. D. E. R. Watt, 6 (Aberdeen, 1991), p. 388; Aubrey Gwynn, 'The Black Death in Ireland', *Studies* 24 (1935), pp. 25–42, at p. 31.

'*I have many Saracens . . .*': James I, *Llibre dels feyts (Crónica)* 437, ed. Josep María de Casacuberta (9 vols. in 2, Barcelona, 1926–62), 8, p. 26.

James II in Valencia: Aureum opus regalium privilegiorum civitatis et regni Valentie (Valencia, 1515, facsimile ed., *Textos medievales* 33, 1972), fol. 42 (p. 143); *on crimes of Muslims against Christians*: John Boswell, *The Royal Treasure: Muslim Communities under the Crown of Aragon in the Fourteenth Century* (New Haven, 1977), pp. 133–4, n. 83 (1316).

Castilian ruling of 1412: Francisco Fernández y González, *Estado social y político de los mudéjares de Castilla* (Madrid, 1866), doc. 77, p. 401; on this ordinance and prior judicial restrictions see Juan Torres Fontes, 'Moros, judíos y conversos en la regencia de Don Fernando de Antequera', *Cuadernos de historia de España* 31–2 (1960), pp. 60–97. It was not fully implemented.

'*Abbreviation of the Sunna*': Içá Jeddih, *Suma de los principales mandamientos y devedamientos de la ley y çunna, Memorial histórico español* 5 (Real Academia de la Historia, Madrid, 1853), pp. 247–421, at p. 248; there is a recent discussion of the author and his work by L. P. Harvey, *Islamic Spain 1250–1500* (Chicago, 1990), pp. 78–97.

General *surveys of Morisco history* include Antonio Domínguez Ortiz and Bernard Vincent, *Historia de los moriscos* (Madrid, 1978); Henry Charles Lea, *The Moriscos of Spain* (London, 1901).

10. The Roman Church and the Christian People

'*Those who are about to go . . .*': William of Malmesbury, *Gesta regum* 4, ed. William Stubbs (2 vols., RS, 1887–9), 2, p. 396 (Urban II at Clermont).

'*Rome is . . . the head . . .*': Robert the Monk, *Historia Iherosolimitana* 2.20, *RHC, Occ.* 3, pp. 711–882, at p. 751; '*the Roman Church which holds . . .*': Fulcher of Chartres, *Historia Hierosolymitana* 1.5, ed. Heinrich Hagenmeyer (Heidelberg, 1913), p. 152.

'*Sancta Romana ecclesia*' and '*populus christianus*': Gregory VII, *Registrum* 3.6*, ed. Erich Caspar (*MGH, Epistolae selectae*, 2, Berlin, 1920–23), p. 253.

John Mundy: *Europe in the High Middle Ages* (London, 1973), p. 26; rephrased and modified in the second edition of 1991 (p. 16).

Gregory VII's correspondence: *Registrum* 1.7 (expedition to Spain); 1.11 ('beloved daughters'); 1.21a (Richard of Capua); 1.19 (to Rudolf of Swabia); 7.14a ('helped neither party . . .', acknowledgement of Rudolf); 2.13 (Hungary); 2.74 (Russia); 7.4 (Dalmatia); 4.28 (Petrine rights in Spain) (cf. 1.7); 8.10 (Sardinia); 7.11 (Bohemian liturgy), ed. Caspar, pp. 11–12, 18, 35–6, 31–2, 485–6, 145, 236, 463, 343–7 (cf. 11–12), 528–30, 473–5.

'*Roman law entered into Spain*': *Chronicon Burgense, s.a.* 1078, ed. Enrique Flórez, *España sagrada* 23 (Madrid, 1767), pp. 305–10, at p. 309.

'*I exhort you to acknowledge . . .*': Gregory VII, *Registrum* 1.64, ed. Caspar, pp. 92–4; cf. 1.63, pp. 91–2.

'*Your excellency, most dearly beloved . . .*': ibid. 9.2, ed. Caspar, pp. 569–72.

Analysis of legates, letter and councils notably in Richard W. Southern, *Western Society and the Church in the Middle Ages* (Harmondsworth, 1970), pp. 106–9.

'*In Spain the unity of the Catholic faith . . .*': Alexander II, 18 October 1071, *Apostolicae sedi*, J.–L. 4691; *Epistolae et decreta*, ep. 80, *PL* 146, cols. 1279–430, at col. 1362; *La documentación pontificia hasta Inocencio III*, ed. Demetrio Mansilla (Rome, 1955), no. 4, p. 8; see Bernard F. Reilly, *The Kingdom of León–Castilla under King Alfonso VI, 1065–1109* (Princeton, 1988), pp. 95–6; Ramón Gonzálvez, 'The Persistence of the Mozarabic Liturgy in Toledo after AD 1080', in Bernard F. Reilly (ed.), *Santiago, Saint-Denis and Saint Peter: The*

Reception of the Roman Liturgy in León–Castile in 1080 (New York, 1985), pp. 157–85, at p. 158, with refs. at p. 180, n. 3.

Figures for *papal letters to Spain* based on *La documentación pontificia*, ed. Mansilla.

Gregory VII to Turlough O'Brien: *Pontificia Hibernica: Medieval Papal Chancery Documents concerning Ireland 640–1261*, ed. Maurice P. Sheehy (2 vols., Dublin, 1962–5), 1, no. 2, pp. 7–8; *The Epistolae Vagantes of Pope Gregory VII*, ed. and tr. H. E. J. Cowdrey (Oxford, 1972), no. 57, pp. 138–40.

John of Crema: Rees Davies, *Conquest, Coexistence and Change: Wales 1063–1415* (Oxford, 1987), pp. 191–2; A. A. M. Duncan, *Scotland: The Making of the Kingdom* (Edinburgh, 1975), p. 259.

Gregory VII to duke of Bohemia: *Registrum* 1.17, ed. Caspar, p. 27.

'How great is the authority . . .'; ibid., ed. Caspar, p. 28.

Tertullian: *Ad nationes* 1.3.

'Disgrace to the Christian name . . .': Geoffrey Malaterra, *De rebus gestis Rogerii Calabriae et Siciliae comitis et Roberti Guiscardi ducis fratris eius* 3.30, ed. Ernesto Pontieri (*Rerum italicarum scriptores*, n.s., 5/1, Bologna, 1928), p. 75.

'Chief and capital city . . .': Heinrich Hagenmeyer (ed.), *Epistulae et chartae ad historiam primi belli sacri spectantes* (Innsbruck, 1901), no. 16, pp. 161–5, at p. 164; the biblical reference is *Acts* 11:26.

'Restored to the Christian name': William of Tyre, *Chronicle* 13.14, ed. R. B. C. Huygens (2 vols., *Corpus Christianorum, Continuatio mediaevalis* 63–63A, Turnhout, 1986), 1, p. 602.

'Enemies of the Christian name': e.g. Guibert de Nogent, *Historia quae dicitur Gesta Dei per Francos* 1.1, *RHC, Occ.* 4 (Paris, 1879), pp. 113–263, at p. 124 (First Crusade); Thomas of Monmouth, *The Life and Miracles of St William of Norwich* 1.16; 2.4, ed. and tr. Augustus Jessopp and Montague Rhodes James (Cambridge, 1896), pp. 44, 71 (Jews).

Roger of Sicily: Innocent II, 27 July 1139, *Quos dispensatio*, J.–L. 8043; *Epistolae et privilegia*, ep. 416, *PL* 179, cols. 53–658, at cols. 478–9.

Order of St James: Alexander III, 5 July 1175, *Benedictus Deus in donis suis*, J.–L. 12504; *Epistolae et privilegia*, ep. 1183, *PL* 200, col. 1026.

'All realms in which . . .': Innocent III, 3 May 1199, *Quanta debeat esse*, Po. 686; *Regestum Innocentii III papae super negotio Romani imperii*, ed. Friedrich Kempf (Rome, 1947), no. 2, p. 8.

Montaigne: *Essays* 2.12: 'Nous sommes Chrestiens à même titre que nous sommes ou Perigordins ou Alemans.'

Saxons and Franks 'one race': Widukind of Corvey, *Res gestae Saxonicae* 1.15, ed. Albert Bauer and Reinhold Rau, *Quellen zur Geschichte der sächsischen Kaiserzeit* (*AQ* 8, rev. ed., Darmstadt, 1977), pp. 16–182, at p. 44; cf. Einhard, *Vita Karoli Magni* 7, ed. Reinhold Rau, *Quellen zur karolingischen Reichsgeschichte* 1 (*AQ* 5, Darmstadt, 1955), pp. 163–211, at p. 176.

'Where Christians had never come before': *Livländische Reimchronik*, line 3349, ed. Leo Meyer (Paderborn, 1876), p. 77.

'Man, what race is this . . .': Raymond of Aguilers, *Liber (Historia Francorum qui ceperunt Iherusalem)* 10, ed. John H. Hill and Laurita L. Hill (Paris, 1969), pp. 72–3.

'Christian race': Gregory VII, *Epistolae Vagantes*, ed. Cowdrey, no. 65, p. 146; *'holy race . . .'*: Arnold of Lübeck, *Chronica Slavorum* 5.25–9, ed. Johann Martin Lappenberg (*SRG*, Hanover, 1868), p. 196.

'La gent cristiane': Ambroise, *L'estoire de la guerre sainte*, line 42, ed. Gaston Paris (Paris, 1897), col. 2; *Chanson de Roland*, line 3392, ed. F. Whitehead (Oxford, 1942), p. 99.

'From across the sea a new people . . .': *Chanson d'Antioche* laisse 9, lines 206–7, ed. Suzanne Duparc-Quioc (Paris, 1976), p. 27.

'I am a Christian . . .': Baudri de Bourgueil, *Historia Jerosolimitana*, prologue, *RHC, Occ.* 4, pp. 1–111, at p. 10.

'The name of Christendom . . .': William of Rubruck, *Itinerarium* 16.5, ed. Anastasius van den Wyngaert, *Sinica Franciscana 1: Itinera et relationes fratrum minorum saeculi XIII et XIV* (Quaracchi, 1929), pp. 164–332, at p. 205.

On the *concept of Christendom* see, in general, Jean Rupp, *L'idée de Chrétienté dans la pensée pontificale des origines à Innocent III* (Paris, 1939); Paul Rousset, 'La notion de Chrétienté aux XIe et XIIe siècles', *Le Moyen Age*, 4th ser., 18 (1963), pp. 191–203.

Gregory VII to German bishops: *Registrum* 5.7, ed. Caspar, p. 358.

Clerks drawn to Paris: Walter Map, *De nugis curialium* 5.5, ed. and tr. M. R. James, rev. C. N. L. Brooke and R. A. B. Mynors (Oxford, 1983), p. 226; *appeal of Third Crusade*: Ambroise, *L'estoire de la guerre sainte*, lines 18–19, ed. Paris, col. 1; *Council of Lyons*: Matthew Paris, *Chronica majora*, ed. Henry Richards Luard (4 vols., RS, 1872–7), 4, p. 430.

'The growth in number and merit . . .': Honorius III, 19 April 1220, *Personam tuam sincera*, Po. 6230; *Liv-, esth- und curländisches UB*, ed. F. G. von Bunge et al. (1st ser., 12 vols., Reval and Riga, 1853–1910), 1, no. 52, col. 55.

'Dilatio', etc.: *Count Roger*: Malaterra, *De rebus gestis Rogerii* 4.29, ed. Pontieri, p. 108 (Urban II, 1098); *Castilian noble*: Julio González, *El reino de Castilla en la epoca de Alfonso VIII* (3 vols., Madrid, 1960) 1, p. 108 (1222); *Prussia*: Peter of Dusburg, *Chronica terre Prussie* 3. 175, ed. Klaus Scholz and Dieter Wojtecki (*AQ* 25, Darmstadt, 1984), p. 294; *Crusades*: Eugenius III, 1 December 1145, *Quantum predecessores*, J.–L. 8796; *Epistolae et privilegia*, *ep.* 48, *PL* 180, cols. 1013–1606, at col. 1064; Hagenmeyer (ed.), *Epistulae*, no. 18, pp. 171–2.

Warriors of Norman Sicily: Malaterra, *De rebus gestis Rogerii* 4.24, ed. Pontieri, p. 102.

'Heathendom': *Historia de translatione sanctorum Nicolai, etc.* 40, *RHC, Occ.* 5, pp. 253–92, at p. 275 (*Haifa*); Odo of Deuil, *De profectione Ludovici VII in Orientem* 5, ed. and tr. Virginia G. Berry (New York, 1948), p. 90 (*Manuel Comnenus*); Ambroise, *L'estoire de la guerre sainte*, ed. Paris, lines 2146, 2326, 5810, 8968, cols. 58, 63, 155, 240 (*'paenie'*).

'*A day when paganism was diminished . . .*': Raymund of Aguilers, *Liber (Historia Francorum)* 18, ed. Hill and Hill, p. 151.

Jesus 'propagator': Baudri de Bourgueil, *Historia Jerosolimitana*, *RHC*, *Occ.* 4, p. 9: *amplitudinis christianae . . . propagator.*

'*We command that these Russians . . .*': Honorius III, 8 February 1222, *Ex parte venerabilis*, Po. 6783; *Liv-, esth- und curländisches UB* 1, no. 55, cols. 58–9.

'*The men of the law of Rome*': Robert of Clari, *La conquête de Constantinople* 18, ed. Philippe Lauer (Paris, 1924), p. 16 and *passim*.

'*From these four branches . . .*': Albert of Stade's reworking of Alexander of Bremen (Alexander Minorita), *Expositio in Apocalypsim*, ed. Alois Wachtel (*MGH*, *Quellen zur Geistesgeschichte des Mittelalters* 1, Weimar, 1955), p. 349; Cambridge, University Library, MS Mm 5 31, fol. 113r.

'*Why do you spy on my disciples? . . .*': Stephen de Salaniaco, *De quattuor in quibus Deus Praedicatorum Ordinem insignivit* 1.7, ed. T. Kaeppeli (*Monumenta ordinis fratrum praedicatorum historica* 22, Rome, 1949), p. 10.

Gregory IX's plan for Prussia: 30 May 1236, *Cum exaltatione spiritus*, Po. 10173; *Preussisches UB* (6 vols. to date, Königsberg and Marburg, 1882–) 1, no. 125, pp. 94–5.

Franciscan friar in Mongolia: William of Rubruck, *Itinerarium* 16.3 (*Sentences*), 30.13 (*Madonna*), ed. van den Wyngaert, pp. 204, 282.

'*The common enterprise of all Christians*': Honorius III, 2 January 1219, *Exercitus christianus rem*, Po. 5956; *Liv-, esth- und curländisches UB* 1, no. 42, col. 47.

'*It does not seem to me irrelevant . . .*': Matthew Paris, *Historia Anglorum*, ed. Frederic Madden (3 vols., R S, 1866–9), 1, p. 79.

'*The whole Latin race*': Hagenmeyer (ed.), *Epistulae*, no. 18, p. 173.

'*Who has ever heard . . .*': Fulcher of Chartres, *Historia Hierosolymitana* 1.13.4, ed. Hagenmeyer, pp. 202–3.

'*Exercitus Dei*': e.g. Hagenmeyer (ed.), *Epistulae*, no. 18, p. 168; González, *El reino de Castilla* 3, no. 897, pp. 566–72 (Las Navas, 1212).

French epics: Hermann Kleber, 'Pèlerinage – vengeance – conquête: la conception de la première croisade dans le cycle de Graindor de Douai', in *Au carrefour des routes d'Europe: La chanson de geste* (Xe Congrès international de la Société Rencesvals pour l'étude des épopées romanes, 2 vols., Aix-en-Provence, 1987) 2, pp. 757–75, at p. 762.

'*A new colony . . .*': Guibert de Nogent, *Historia quae dicitur Gesta Dei per Francos* 7.25, *RHC*, *Occ.* 4, p. 245.

'*In our time . . .*': ibid. 1.1, *RHC*, *Occ.* 4, p. 124.

'*That unanticipated transformation . . .*': Orderic Vitalis, *Historia ecclesiastica* 9.1, ed. and tr. Marjorie Chibnall (6 vols., Oxford, 1968–80), 5, p. 4.

'*Let us follow the route . . .*': Odo of Deuil, *De profectione Ludovici VII* 7, ed. Berry, p. 130.

'*If we elect . . .*': Geoffrey de Villehardouin, *La conquête de Constantinople* 8 (257), ed. Edmond Faral (2nd ed., 2 vols., Paris, 1961), 2, p. 62.

Nicholas of St Omer: *Chronicle of Morea*, tr. Harold E. Lurier, *Crusaders as Conquerors* (New York, 1964), p. 298.

Antioch chamber: Christopher Tyerman, *England and the Crusades, 1095–1588* (Chicago, 1988), p. 117.

Document of 1108: Helbig & Weinrich 1, no. 19, pp. 96–102.

'Each province of Catholics . . .': Saxo Grammaticus, *Gesta Danorum* 14.3, ed. J. Olrik and H. Raeder (2 vols., Copenhagen, 1931–57), 2, p. 376.

'An army of those with the sign': Helmold of Bosau, *Chronica Slavorum* 1.62, ed. Heinz Stoob (*AQ* 19, Darmstadt, rev. ed., 1973), p. 220.

Bull of Alexander III, 11 September 1171, *Non parum animus noster*, J.–L. 12118; *Epistolae et privilegia*, ep. 980, *PL* 200, cols. 860–61; *Liv-, esth- und curländisches UB* 1, no. 5, cols. 5–6.

Bull of Innocent III, 5 October 1199, *Sicut ecclesiasticae religionis (al. laesionsis)*, Po. 842; *Registrum sive epistolae* 2. 191, *PL* 214–16, at 214, cols. 739–40 (cf. *PL* 217, cols. 54–5, supplement, *ep.* 25); *Liv-, esth- und curländisches UB* 1, no. 12, cols. 13–15; *Die Register Innocenz' III* 2, ed. Othmar Hageneder *et al.* (Rome and Vienna, 1979), no. 182, pp. 348–9.

'The poor fellow knights . . .': *La règle du Temple*, ed. Henri de Curzon (Paris, 1886), p. 11.

'Around this time there arose . . .': Richard of Poitou, *Chronica* (excerpts, with continuations), ed. Georg Waitz, *MGH, SS* 26 (Hanover, 1882), pp. 74–86, at p. 80.

Bernard of Clairvaux, *De laude novae militiae* 1.3, in J. Leclerq and H. M. Rochais (eds.), *Opera* 3 (Rome, 1963), pp. 205–39, at pp. 214, 217.

'We take into our protection . . .': Alexander III, 25 September 1164, *Justis petentium desideriis*, J.–L. 11064; *Epistolae et privilegia*, ep. 273, *PL* 200, cols. 310–12.

Ibn al-Athīr: Francesco Gabrieli (ed.), *Arab Historians of the Crusades* (Eng. tr., Berkeley and London, 1969), p. 124.

Alfonso the Battler's will is printed in *Cartulaire général de l'ordre des Hospitaliers de St-Jean de Jérusalem*, ed. J. Delaville Le Roulx (4 vols., Paris, 1894–1906), 1, no. 95, pp. 85–6; for recent debate see Elena Lourie, 'The Will of Alfonso "El Batallador", King of Aragon and Navarre: A Reassessment', *Speculum* 50 (1975), pp. 635–51; A. J. Forey, 'The Will of Alfonso I of Aragon and Navarre', *Durham University Journal* 73 (1980), pp. 59–65; Lourie, 'The Will of Alfonso I of Aragon and Navarre: A Reply to Dr Forey', and Forey, 'A Rejoinder', ibid. 77 (1985), pp. 165–72 and p. 173.

'So arose the first Order State . . .': Friedrich Benninghoven, *Der Order der Schwertbrüder* (Cologne and Graz, 1965), p. 81.

Agreement of 1210: *Liv-, esth- und curländisches UB* 1, nos. 16–18, cols. 22–5; cf. nos. 23 and 25, cols. 30–33.

Thymau and Higares: *Pommerellisches UB*, ed. Max Perlbach (Danzig, 1881–2), no. 28, p. 24; Walter Kuhn, *Vergleichende Untersuchungen zur mittelalterlichen Ostsiedlung* (Cologne and Vienna, 1973), pp. 142, 350, 427; Benninghoven, *Der*

Order der Schwertbrüder, pp. 8–9, 263–4; Julio González, *Repoblación de Castilla la Nueva* (2 vols., Madrid, 1975–6) 2, p. 31, n. 120.

Lake Mirow: *Mecklenburgisches UB* (25 vols. in 26, Schwerin and Leipzig, 1863–1977) 1, no. 344, pp. 334–5 (a confirmation by his sons in 1227).

Document of 1289: ibid. 25A, no. 13,794, p. 33.

11. *The Europeanization of Europe*

'*We avoid many great inconveniences* . . .': Helbig & Weinrich 1, no. 68, p. 274 (Borwin of Mecklenburg for Gadebusch).

Erik *Fügedi*, 'Das mittelalterliche Königreich Ungarn als Gastland', in Walter Schlesinger (ed.), *Die deutsche Ostsiedlung als Problem der europäischen Geschichte (Vorträge und Forschungen* 18, Sigmaringen, 1975), pp. 471–507, at p. 494; cf. p. 480: 'die Europäisierung Ungarns'.

Alfonso VI as Europeanizer: Derek W. Lomax, *The Reconquest of Spain* (London, 1978), pp. 56, 63.

'*Modernizing' kings of Ireland*: Marie Therese Flanagan, 'Monastic Charters from Irish Kings of the Twelfth and Thirteenth Centuries' (Unpublished MA thesis, University College, Dublin, 1972), p. 213.

Bohemian naming: Peter of Zittau, *Chronicon Aulae Regiae* 6, ed. J. Emler, *Fontes rerum Bohemicarum* 4 (Prague, 1884), pp. 1–337, at p. 12.

Orderic Vitalis: *Historia Ecclesiastica* 13.45, ed. and tr. Marjorie Chibnall (6 vols., Oxford, 1968–80), 6, p. 554.

Swatawa and Markéta: Heinz Zatschek, 'Namensänderungen und Doppelnamen in Böhmen und Mähren im hohen Mittelalter', *Zeitschrift für Sudetendeutsche Geschichte* 3 (1939), pp. 1–11, at pp. 3–4.

Matilda/Edith: Orderic Vitalis, *Historia ecclesiastica* 8.22, ed. Chibnall, 4, p. 272.

Shrewsbury churches: *Victoria County History of Shropshire* 2 (London, 1973), p. 5.

An excellent graphic presentation of the *cult of St Remi* in *Grosser historischer Weltatlas 2: Mittelalter*, ed. Bayerisch Schulbuch-Verlag (rev. ed., Munich, 1979), map 68a: 'Die Verehrung des Hl. Remigius'.

Aquitaine: Charles Higounet, 'Les saints mérovingiens d'Aquitaine dans la toponymie', in his *Paysages et villages neufs du Moyen Age* (Bordeaux, 1975), pp. 67–75.

'*When his youthful companions* . . .': Geoffrey of Durham, *Vita Bartholomaei Farnensis* 1, in *Symeonis monachi opera omnia*, ed. Thomas Arnold (2 vols., RS, 1882–5), pp. 295–325, at p. 296.

Canons of St Pauls: Christopher Brooke, 'The Composition of the Chapter of St Paul's, 1086–1163', *Cambridge Historical Journal* 10 (1951), pp. 111–32.

Lincoln tenants: Gillian Fellows Jensen, 'The Names of the Lincolnshire Tenants of the Bishop of Lincoln *c.* 1225', in *Otium et negotium: Studies in Onomatology and*

Library Science presented to Olof von Feilitzen (*Acta Bibliothecae Regiae Stockholmiensis* 16, Stockholm, 1973), pp. 86–95.

'*These Englishmen among whom we are living . . .*': Eadmer, *Life of St Anselm*, ed. and tr. R. W. Southern (London, etc., 1962), p. 51; for a different viewpoint on Norman attitudes to Anglo-Saxon saints see Susan Ridyard '*Condigna veneratio*: Post-Conquest Attitudes to the Saints of the Anglo-Saxons', in *Anglo-Norman Studies* 9 (1986), ed. R. Allen Brown, pp. 179–206; David Rollason, *Saints and Relics in Anglo-Saxon England* (Oxford, 1989), pp. 217–38.

Canterbury liturgy: Margaret Gibson, *Lanfranc of Bec* (Oxford, 1978), pp. 170–72.

St Albans: *Gesta abbatum monasterii sancti Albani*, ed. Henry T. Riley (3 vols., RS, 1867–9), 1, p. 62.

Ethelbert: Gerald of Wales (Giraldus Cambrensis), *Vita Ethelberti*, ed. Montague R. James, 'Two Lives of St Ethelbert, King and Martyr', *English Historical Review* 32 (1917), pp. 222–36, at pp. 235–6.

Ireland: *Close Rolls of the Reign of Henry III (1237–42)* (London, 1911), p. 227 (1240) (*Edward*); *Red Book of Ormond*, ed. Newport B. White (Irish Manuscripts Commission, Dublin, 1932), p. 48 (*David*).

Robert of Flanders in Apulia: Edmond de Coussemaker (ed.), *Documents relatifs à la Flandre maritime* (Lille, 1860), pp. 65–6 (Clementia of Flanders for Watten, 1097); text also in Heinrich Hagenmeyer, *Chronologie de la première croisade 1094–1100* (reprint in one vol., Hildesheim and New York, 1973), p. 50, no. 103; *and St George*: *Continuatio Aquicinctina* of Sigebert of Gembloux, ed. Ludwig Bethmann, *MGH, SS* 6 (Hanover, 1844), pp. 268–474, at p. 395.

Sarquis–Hilary dispute: *L'estoire d'Eracles empereur et la conqueste de la terre d'Outremer, RHC, Occ.* 2, pp. 1–481, at p. 209, variant; also as *La continuation de Guillaume de Tyr (1184–1197)* 155, ed. Margaret R. Morgan (*Documents relatifs à l'histoire des croisades* 14, Paris, 1982), p. 169 (see also p. 168).

Damietta: Walter of Coventry, *Memoriale*, ed. William Stubbs (2 vols., RS, 1872–3), 2, p. 242 (the 'Barnwell Chronicle').

Welsh churches adopt universal saints: Rees Davies, *Conquest, Coexistence and Change: Wales 1063–1415* (Oxford, 1987), pp. 181–2, 207; Wendy Davies, *The Llandaff Charters* (Aberystwyth, 1979), p. 20.

Brittany: Julia Smith, 'Oral and Written: Saints, Miracles and Relics in Brittany, *c.* 850–1250', *Speculum* 65 (1990), pp. 309–43, at pp. 336–7.

The *Scottish royal genealogy* is based upon A. A. M. Duncan, *Scotland: The Making of the Kingdom* (Edinburgh, 1975), pp. 628–9, supplemented by *Handbook of British Chronology*, ed. E. B. Fryde *et al.* (3rd ed., London, 1986), pp. 56–8, 500–501, 503, and, for the descendants of Matad, earl of Atholl, *Liber vitae ecclesiae Dunelmensis*, ed. A. Hamilton Thompson (facsimile ed., Surtees Society 136, 1923), fol. 60; for the elucidation of the 'Kelehathoni' of the *Liber vitae* as 'Gille-Eithne' see Geoffrey Barrow, *The Anglo-Norman Era in Scottish History* (Oxford, 1980), p. 159, n. 80; *the Mecklenburg genealogy* is drawn from that in Manfred Hamann, *Mecklenburgische Geschichte* (*MF* 51, Cologne, 1968) (insert).

Dresden councillors: Wolfgang Fleischer, *Die deutschen Personennamen* (Berlin, 1964), p. 51; *idem*, 'Die Namen der Dresdener Ratsmitglieder bis 1500', *Beiträge zur Namenforschung* 12 (1961), pp. 44–87.

Intergenerational name changes: Julio González, *Repoblación de Castilla la Nueva* (2 vols., Madrid, 1975–6) 2, pp. 78–85 (*Toledo*); *Brut y Tywysogyon or The Chronicle of the Princes: Red Book of Hergest Version*, ed. Thomas Jones (Cardiff, 1955), p. 65 (*s.a.* 1110) (*Cadwgan ap Bleddyn*); Dmitrii Jegorov, *Die Kolonisation Mecklenburgs im 13. Jahrhundert* (German tr., 2 vols., Breslau, 1930) 1, p. 286, n. 16 (*Mecklenburg*).

Counts of Bar: Michel Parisse, 'La conscience chrétienne des nobles aux XIe et XIIe siècles', in *La cristianità dei secoli XI e XII in occidente: Coscienza e strutture di una società* (*Miscellanea del Centro di studi medioevali* 10, Milan, 1983), pp. 259–80, at p. 263.

Radim/Gaudentius: Cosmas of Prague, *Chronica Boemorum* 1.34, ed. Berthold Bretholz (*SRG*, n.s., Berlin, 1923), p. 60; *Milic/Daniel*: Gerlach of Mühlhausen, *Chronicon*, ed. Wilhelm Wattenbach, *MGH*, *SS* 17 (Hanover, 1861), pp. 683–710, at p. 708.

Zdik: *Canonici Wissegradensis continuatio* (to Cosmas of Prague), ed. Rudolf Köpke, *MGH*, *SS* 9 (Hanover, 1851), pp. 132–48, at p. 133.

Hahót family: Fügedi, 'Das mittelalterliche Königreich Ungarn', p. 497, n. 78.

Prussian church dedications: Erika Tidick, 'Beiträge zur Geschichte der Kirchenpatrozinien im Deutsch-Ordensland Preussen bis 1525', *Zeitschrift für die Geschichte und Altertumskunde Ermlands* 22 (1926), pp. 343–464 (figures extracted from the data on pp. 437–55, excluding Pomerelia).

'*Complete triumph of the cult of St Mary*': González, *Repoblación* 2, p. 253.

Valencia: Robert I. Burns, *The Crusader Kingdom of Valencia: Reconstruction on a Thirteenth-Century Frontier* (2 vols., Cambridge, Mass., 1967) 1, pp. 92–7.

Names in Baltic towns: Theodor Penners, *Untersuchungen über die Herkunft der Stadtbewohner im Deutsch-Ordensland Preussen bis in die Zeit um 1400* (Leipzig, 1942), p. 11; *in southern French towns*: Anna Rutkowska-Plachcinska, 'Les prénoms dans le sud de la France aux XIIIe et XIVe siècles', *Acta Poloniae Historica* 49 (1984), pp. 5–42, at p. 7.

On the *spread of mints in eastern Europe and the Baltic* region see Arthur Suhle, *Deutsche Münz- und Geldgeschichte von den Anfängen bis zum 15. Jahrhundert* (2nd ed., Berlin, 1964) (with a useful map insert); Stanisław Suchodolski, *Początki mennictwa w Europie środkowej, wschodniej i północnej* (Wrocław, 1971) (English summary, pp. 249–57); *idem*, *Mennictwo Polskie w XI i XII wieku* (Wrocław, etc., 1973) (English summary, pp. 144–52); Kirsten Bendixen, *Denmark's Money* (Copenhagen, 1967), pp. 7–22; Peter Spufford, *Money and its Use in Medieval Europe* (Cambridge, 1988), esp. chapters 4 and 8; Rolf Sprandel, *Das mittelalterliche Zahlungssystem nach Hansisch-Nordischen Quellen des 13.–15. Jahrhunderts* (Stuttgart, 1975), map 1 and pp. 163–93.

'*Won for himself all Denmark* . . .': Gwyn Jones, *A History of the Vikings* (Oxford, 1968), p. 117 (Jelling inscription).

John's halfpennies: William O'Sullivan, *The Earliest Anglo-Irish Coinage* (Dublin, 1964); Michael Dolley, *Medieval Anglo-Irish Coins* (London, 1972), pp. 1–5.

Coinage in Scotland: D. M. Metcalf (ed.), *Coinage in Medieval Scotland (1100–1600)* (*British Archaeological Reports* 45, Oxford, 1977).

Rani: Helmold of Bosau, *Chronica Slavorum* 1.38, ed. Heinz Stoob (*AQ* 19, Darmstadt, rev. ed., 1973), p. 158.

Ibrahim ibn Jacub: G. Jacob (ed.), *Arabische Berichte von Gesandten an germanische Fürstenhöfe aus dem 9. und 10. Jahrhundert* (Berlin and Leipzig, 1927), p. 13.

Slavs east of Elbe: Joachim Herrmann (ed.), *Die Slawen in Deutschland: Ein Handbuch* (new ed., Berlin, 1985), pp. 132–4 and plate 49.

Size of Scottish coinage: Ian Stewart, 'The Volume of the Early Scottish Coinage', in D. M. Metcalf (ed.), *Coinage in Medieval Scotland (1100–1600)* (*British Archaeological Reports* 45, Oxford, 1977), pp. 65–72.

Crusader silver coins 'quite exceptional': John Porteous, 'Crusader Coinage with Latin or Greek Inscriptions', in Kenneth M. Setton (ed.), *A History of the Crusades* (Philadelphia and Madison, 6 vols., 1955–89) 6: *The Impact of the Crusades on Europe*, ed. Harry W. Hazard, pp. 354–420, at p. 370.

Pomeranian documents: there was a false dawn in the mid-tenth century, when Otto I included parts of Pomerania west of the Oder in his newly founded bishoprics and granted some of the tribute from the Slavic peoples inhabiting that area to St Maurice Magdeburg: *Pommersches UB 1: 786–1253*, ed. Klaus Conrad (2nd ed., Cologne and Vienna, 1970), nos. 11–13, 15–16, pp. 12–15, 16–18. This was a very transitory phase, however, and Pomerania then slips out of documentary record again for over 150 years. For the *documents of the 1130s*, ibid., nos. 23, 27, pp. 23–5, 28–9; *of 1140*: no. 30, pp. 32–4; *Adalbert's first charter*: no. 43, pp. 47–8; *Adalbert's 1159 charter*: no. 48, pp. 51–3; *Casimir I for Dargun*; no. 62, pp. 77–81 – the charter survives in two originals in the Landeshauptarchiv Schwerin, 1. Kloster Dargun Nr. 2; there is a picture in M. Gumowski, 'Pieczęcie książąt pomorskich', *Zapiski Towarzystwo naukowe w Toruniu* 14 (1950), pp. 23–66 (and plates I–XXI), plate I; there is some dispute over the authenticity of the document; see the editor's notes in the *Pommersches UB*. An apparently genuine seal of Casimir I is also found attached to a forged document attributed to 1170, ibid., no. 54, pp. 63–7.

Charters of Bogislaw II: ibid., nos. 106, 126, 140–41, 146, 156–7, 162–3, 170, 181, 188, 195–6, pp. 136–8, 167–8, 179–80, 184–6, 195–7, 202–4, 211–12, 225–6, 232–3, 241–3; *Casimir for Kolbacz*: no. 68, pp. 87–8 (Helbig & Weinrich 1, no. 80, p. 312) (1176).

Silesian documents: Josef Joachim Menzel, *Die schlesischen Lokationsurkunden des 13. Jahrhunderts* (Würzburg, 1977), pp. 127–35.

Celtic documentary tradition: Wendy Davies, 'The Latin Charter Tradition in Western Britain, Brittany and Ireland in the Early Medieval Period', in Dorothy Whitelock *et al.* (eds.), *Ireland in Early Medieval Europe* (Cambridge, 1982), pp. 258–80.

Sealed writ in Scotland: Duncan, *Scotland*, p. 126.

David of Huntingdon: K. J. Stringer, 'The Charters of David, Earl of Huntingdon and Lord of Garioch: A Study in Anglo-Scottish Diplomatic', in *idem* (ed.), *Essays on the Nobility of Medieval Scotland* (Edinburgh, 1985), pp. 72–101, at p. 79.

Irish native charters: Flanagan, 'Monastic Charters from Irish Kings', p. 213; the MacMurrough charter is Dublin, National Library of Ireland, D 1, and is reproduced in *Facsimiles of National Manuscripts of Ireland*, ed. John T. Gilbert (4 parts in 5 vols., Dublin, 1874–84), 2, plate lxiii.

'Shift from sacral script . . .': Michael Clanchy, *From Memory to Written Record: England 1066–1307* (London and Cambridge, Mass., 1979), p. 263.

Documentation in Picardy: Robert Fossier, *La terre et les hommes en Picardie jusqu'à la fin de XIIIe siècle* (2 vols., Paris and Louvain, 1968) 1, p. 263; 2, p. 570, n. 1.

'The Carolingian chancery [that] fathered . . .': David Ganz and Walter Goffart, 'Charters Earlier than 800 from French Collections', *Speculum* 65 (1990), pp. 906–32, at p. 921 (Goffart).

'It is necessary that a matter . . .': *Codex diplomaticus Maioris Poloniae*, ed. Ignacy Zakrzewski and Franciszek Piekosiński (5 vols., Poznań, 1877–1908), 1, no. 381, pp. 337–8 (1259).

Ptolemy of Lucca: *De regimine principum* 2. 13, ed. Pierre Mandonnet, in Thomas Aquinas, *Opuscula omnia* 1 (Paris, 1927), pp. 312–487, at p. 370 (the work was begun by Thomas and completed by Ptolemy).

Rout of Fréteval: Roger of Howden, *Chronica*, ed. William Stubbs (4 vols., RS, 1868–71), 3, pp. 255–6; William the Breton, *Gesta Philippi Augusti*, ed. H.-F. Delaborde, *Oeuvres de Rigord et de Guillaume le Breton* (2 vols., Paris, 1882–5), 1, pp. 168–333, at pp. 196–7; *idem*, *Philippidos* 4, lines 530–48, ed. Delaborde, ibid. 2, pp. 118–19; comments by John Baldwin, *The Government of Philip Augustus* (Berkeley and Los Angeles, 1986), pp. 405–12.

Welsh seal matrices: Davies, *Conquest, Coexistence and Change*, pp. 355–6.

Stephen of Lexington: *Registrum epistolarum* 37, ed. P. Bruno Griesser, *Analecta sacri ordinis Cisterciensis* 2 (1946), pp. 1–118, at p. 47; cf. 'The problems caused by the lack of facilities for higher studies in Ireland were set out in considerable detail in a petition addressed to Pope Clement V when Archbishop John Lech of Dublin attended the Council of Vienne in 1311–12, and as a result that pontiff issued a bull on 13 July 1312 authorizing the establishment of a university in Dublin', Katherine Walsh, *A Fourteenth-Century Scholar and Primate: Richard FitzRalph in Oxford, Avignon and Armagh* (Oxford, 1981), p. 11, citing ASV, Reg. Vat. 59, fol. 196v, 'inaccurately printed' in W. H. Monck Mason, *The History and Antiquities of the Collegiate and Cathedral Church of St Patrick* (Dublin, 1820), app., pp. ix–x.

Arnold of Lübeck: *Chronica Slavorum* 3.5, ed. Johann Martin Lappenberg (*SRG*, Hanover, 1868), p. 77.

Sunesen: education: Saxo Grammaticus, *Gesta Danorum*, preface, 1.2, ed. J. Olrik and H. Raeder (2 vols., Copenhagen, 1931–57), 1, p. 3; *Hexaemeron*: ed. Sten Ebbesen and L. B. Mortensen (2 vols., Copenhagen, 1985–8); *Scanian law*: *Antique leges Scanie* 14, in *Danmarks gamle landskabslove* 1, ed. J. Brøndum-Nielsen (Copenhagen, 1920–33), pp. 467–667, 'ordained by natural equity' at p. 480; cf. *Skånske lov – Text III* 1. 33, ibid., pp. 265–466, at p. 288.

For *Sunesen as reformer* Innocent III, 17 December 1203, *Ad nostram noveritis*, Po. 2060, and 19 January 1206, *Benedictus Deus a*, Po. 2664; *Registrum sive epistolae* 6. 198 and 8. 196, *PL* 214–16, at 215, cols. 223, 774; for the *Dominicans in Lund*: *De Ordine Praedicatorum de Tolosa in Dacia*, ed. M. C. Gertz, *Scriptores minores historiae Danicae* (2 vols., Copenhagen, 1917–22) 2/1, pp. 369–74; Jarl Gallén, *La province de Dacie de l'ordre des frères prêcheurs* (Helsingfors, 1946), pp. 1–11; it should be noted that Dominic himself had visited Denmark in 1204–5 as member of a Castilian embassy, ibid., pp. 196–216; for *Sunesen's activities in Estonia*: Henry of Livonia, *Chronicon Livoniae* 10.13–14; 23.2; 24.2; 25.1, ed. Leonid Arbusow and Albert Bauer (*AQ* 24, Darmstadt, 1959), pp. 60–64, 230–32, 256–8, 268.

12. The Political Sociology of Europe after the Expansion

'This land was completely transformed . . .': 'Rocznik lubiąski 1241–1281, oraz wiersz o pierwotnych zakonniach Lubiąża' [*Versus lubenses*], ed. August Bielowski, *MPH* 3 (Lwów, 1878, repr. Warsaw, 1961), pp. 707–10, at p. 710.

Slav raid on Hamburg: Helmold of Bosau, *Chronica Slavorum* 1.35, ed. Heinz Stoob (*AQ* 19, Darmstadt, rev. ed., 1973), pp. 146–8.

Attack on al-Mahdiyyah: Bernardo Maragone, *Annales Pisani*, ed. Michele Lupo Gentile (*Rerum italicarum scriptores*, n.s., 6/2, Bologna, 1930), pp. 1–74, at pp. 6–7, *s.a.* 1088; *Carmen in victoriam Pisanorum*, lines 70–72, ed. H. E. J. Cowdrey, 'The Mahdia Campaign of 1087', *English Historical Review* 92 (1977), pp. 1–29, text at pp. 23–9, relevant stanza p. 28 (reprinted in his *Popes, Monks and Crusaders* (London, 1984), chapter 12 (with same pagination)).

'It is more equidistant . . .': cited in Denys Hay, *Europe: The Emergence of an Idea* (2nd ed., Edinburgh, 1968), p. 74.

Restoration of Santiago bells: Luke of Tuy, *Chronicon mundi*, ed. Andreas Schottus, *Hispaniae illustratae* (4 vols., Frankfurt/Main, 1603–8) 4, pp. 1–116, at p. 116.

'That it was incredibly stupid . . .': Ebo, *Vita sancti Ottonis episcopi Babenbergensis* 3.6, ed. Jan Wikarjak and Kazimierz Liman, *MPH*, n.s., 7/2 (Warsaw, 1969), p. 106.

'The dignity of the Christian world . . .': *Sancti Bonifatii et Lulli epistolae*, ed. Michael Tangl (*MGH, Epistolae selectae* 1, Berlin, 1916), no. 23, pp. 40–41 (Bishop Daniel of Winchester to Boniface, 723–4).

'*In this Christian land* . . .': Robert I. Burns, *Islam under the Crusaders: Colonial Survival in the Thirteenth-Century Kingdom of Valencia* (Princeton, 1973), p. 187.

Henry the Liberal and Philip of Alsace: Peter Spufford, *Money and its Use in Medieval Europe* (Cambridge, 1988), p. 245.

Settlements around Toledo: Julio González, *Repoblación de Castilla la Nueva* (2 vols., Madrid, 1975–6) 2, pp. 271, 277.

Settlements in Prussia and Silesia: Herbert Grundmann, *Wahlkönigtum, Territorialpolitik und Ostbewegung im 13. und 14. Jahrhundert* (*Gebhardts Handbuch der deutschen Geschichte* 5, Munich, 1973), pp. 269, 284.

Clearance in Picardy: Robert Fossier *La terre et les hommes en Picardie jusqu'à la fin de XIIIe siècle* (2 vols., Paris and Louvain, 1968) 1, p. 330.

'*Andreanum*': Helbig & Weinrich 2, no. 144, p. 536.

Ibn at Timnah: Ferdinand Chalandon, *Histoire de la domination normande en Italie et en Sicilie, 1009–1194* (2 vols., Paris, 1907) 1, pp. 191–8.

'*The Christians are nearby* . . .': *Livländische Reimchronik*, lines 2768–78, ed. Leo Meyer (Paderborn, 1876), p. 64.

'*Higher than anyone of your kin*': *Brut y Tywysogyon or The Chronicle of the Princes: Peniarth MS. 20 Version*, tr. Thomas Jones (Cardiff, 1952), p. 38 (slightly modernized).

The standard political narrative for *thirteenth-century Gwynedd* is J. E. Lloyd, *A History of Wales* (3rd ed., 2 vols., London, 1939) 2, chapters 16–20. See also David Stephenson, *The Governance of Gwynedd* (Cardiff, 1984).

'*Praising the dead for their thefts* . . .': *Preussisches UB* (6 vols. to date, Königsberg and Marburg, 1882–) 1, no. 218, p. 161 (Treaty of Christburg, 1249).

'*Over the course of the year* . . .': William of Newburgh, *Historia rerum Anglicarum* 3.9, ed. Richard Howlett, *Chronicles of the Reigns of Stephen, Henry II and Richard I* (4 vols., RS, 1884–9) 1–2, at 1, p. 239.

Assize of David I: A. A. M. Duncan, *Scotland: The Making of the Kingdom* (Edinburgh, 1975), pp. 298–9; *Acts of Malcolm IV, King of Scots, 1153–65*, ed. Geoffrey Barrow (*Regesta regum Scottorum* 1, Edinburgh, 1960), pp. 65–6.

Cathal Crovderg: *Annals of Connacht (Annála Connacht)*, ed. A. Martin Freeman (Dublin, 1944), p. 5.

Bruno of Olomouc: *Dictionnaire d'histoire et de géographie ecclésiastiques* (21 vols. to date, Paris, 1912–) 10, col. 963.

Wagria: Helmold, *Chronica Slavorum* 1. 88, ed. Stoob, p. 312.

'*After the Slavs have been ejected* . . .': *Die Urkunden Heinrichs des Löwen*, ed. Karl Jordan, *MGH, Laienfürsten- und Dynastenurkunden der Kaiserzeit* (Leipzig and Weimar, 1941–9), no. 41, pp. 57–61; also in *Mecklenburgisches UB* (25 vols. in 26, Schwerin and Leipzig, 1863–1977) 1, no. 65, p. 58 (purportedly 1158, a thirteenth-century forgery with a genuine core).

'*The new type of castle* . . .': Erik Fügedi, *Castle and Society in Medieval Hungary (1000–1437)* (*Studia historica Academiae Scientiarum Hungaricae* 187, Budapest, 1986), p. 62.

Mecklenburg slave market: Helmold, *Chronica Slavorum* 2. 109, ed. Stoob, p. 376.

'Is it not our own land . . .': ibid. 1. 65, ed. Stoob, p. 228.

Spanish urban militias: James F. Powers, *A Society Organized for War: The Iberian Municipal Militias in the Central Middle Ages, 1000–1284* (Berkeley and Los Angeles, 1988).

First Crusade: Guibert de Nogent, *Historia quae dicitur Gesta Dei per Francos* 1. 1, *RHC, Occ.* 4 (Paris, 1879), pp. 113–263, at p. 123 ('without lord, without prince'); Baudri de Bourgueil, *Historia Jerosolimitana*, prologue, *RHC, Occ.* 4, pp. 1–111, at p. 9 ('fought without king, without emperor').

'We have been fighting . . .': Paul Johansen, 'Eine Riga-Wisby-Urkunde des 13. Jahrhunderts', *Zeitschrift des Vereins für Lübeckische Geschichte und Altertumskunde* 38 (1958), pp. 93–108, at p. 97 (1268).

'The king did not interfere . . .': Robert S. Lopez and Irving W. Raymond (eds.), *Medieval Trade in the Mediterranean World* (New York, 1955), doc. 157, p. 319.

Ibn Hamdīs: Michele Amari (ed.), *Bibliotheca arabo-sicula* (Italian version, 2 vols., Turin and Rome, 1880–81) 2, pp. 234–5.

Rhigyfarch's lament: Michael Lapidge (ed.), 'The Welsh-Latin Poetry of Sulien's Family', *Studia Celtica* 8–9 (1973–4), pp. 68–106, at p. 90, lines 16–21.

Lithuania: Manfred Hellmann, *Grundzüge der Geschichte Litauens und des lituauischen Volkes* (Darmstadt, 1966), pp. 14–32, gives a brief summary of the *history of the Lithuanian principality* before the dynastic union with Poland; for penetrating comments see also Eric Christiansen, *The Northern Crusades* (London, 1980), chapter 6, 'The Interminable Crusade, 1283–1410'.

Castles and stirrups in Ireland: Katharine Simms, 'Warfare in the Medieval Gaelic Lordships', *The Irish Sword* 12 (1975–6), pp. 98–108, at p. 107; Kenneth Nicholls, *Gaelic and Gaelicized Ireland in the Middle Ages* (Dublin, 1972), pp. 84–7.

Bibliography of Works Cited

===

SOURCES

Acta capitulorum generalium ordinis praedicatorum 1 (1220–1303), ed. Benedictus Maria Reichert (*Monumenta ordinis fratrum praedicatorum historica* 3, Rome and Stuttgart, 1898).

Acts of Malcolm IV, King of Scots, 1153–65, ed. Geoffrey Barrow (*Regesta Regum Scottorum* 1, Edinburgh, 1960).

Acts of William I, King of Scots, 1165–1214, ed. Geoffrey Barrow (*Regesta Regum Scottorum* 2, Edinburgh, 1971).

Adam of Bremen, *Gesta Hammaburgensis ecclesiae pontificum*, ed. Werner Trillmich in *Quellen des 9. und 11. Jahrhunderts zur Geschichte der Hamburgischen Kirche und des Reiches* (*AQ* 11, Darmstadt, 1961), pp. 135–503.

Aelred of Rievaulx, *Relatio de Standardo*, ed. Richard Howlett in *Chronicles of the Reigns of Stephen, Henry II and Richard I* (4 vols., RS, 1884–9) 3, pp. 179–99.

idem, *De sanctis ecclesiae Haugustaldensis*, ed. James Raine in *The Priory of Hexham* (2 vols., Surtees Society 44, 46, 1864–5) 1, pp. 172–203.

Albert of Aachen, *Historia Hierosolymitana*, RHC, *Occ.* 4, pp. 265–713.

Alexander II, *Epistolae et decreta*, PL 146, cols. 1279–1430.

Alexander III, *Epistolae et privilegia*, PL 200.

Alexander of Bremen (Alexander Minorita), *Expositio in Apocalipsim*, ed. Alois Wachtel (*MGH, Quellen zur Geistesgeschichte des Mittelalters* 1, Weimar, 1955).

Alpert of Metz, *De diversitate temporum*, ed. Hans van Rij and Anna Sapir Abulafia (Amsterdam, 1980).

Das alte Kulmische Recht, ed. C. K. Leman (Berlin, 1838).

Das alte Lübische Recht, ed. Johann Friedrich Hach (Lübeck, 1839).

Amari, Michele (ed.), *Bibliotheca arabo-sicula* (Italian version, 2 vols., Turin and Rome, 1880–81).

Amatus of Montecassino, *Storia de' Normanni*, ed. Vincenzo de Bartholomaeis (*Fonti per la storia d'Italia* 76, Rome, 1935).

Ambroise, *L'estoire de la guerre sainte*, ed. Gaston Paris (Paris, 1897).

Anglo-Saxon Chronicle, ed. C. Plummer and J. Earle, *Two of the Saxon Chronicles Parallel* (2 vols., Oxford, 1892–9).

Annales capituli Cracoviensis (Rocznik Kapitulny Krakowski), ed. August Bielowski, *MPH* 2 (Lwów, 1872, repr. Warsaw, 1961), pp. 779–816.

Annales capituli Posnaniensis, ed. Brygida Kürbis, *MPH*, n.s., 6 (Warsaw, 1962), pp. 21–78.

Annales Erphesfurdenses Lothariani, ed. Oswald Holder-Egger, *Monumenta Erphesfurtensia* (*SRG*, Hanover and Leipzig, 1899), pp. 34–44.

Annales Krasinsciani (Rocznik Krasińskich), ed. August Bielowski, *MPH* 3 (Lwów, 1878, repr. Warsaw, 1961), pp. 127–33.

Annales Pegavienses, ed. Georg Heinrich Pertz, *MGH*, *SS* 16 (Hanover, 1859), pp. 232–70.

Annales Wratislavienses antiqui and *Annales magistratus Wratislaviensis*, ed. Wilhelm Arndt, *MGH*, *SS* 19 (Hanover, 1866), pp. 526–31.

Annals of Connacht (Annála Connacht), ed. A. Martin Freeman (Dublin, 1944).

Annals of Furness, ed. Richard Howlett in *Chronicles of the Reigns of Stephen, Henry II and Richard I* (4 vols., RS, 1884–9) 2, pp. 503–83.

Annals of Loch Cé, ed. and tr. William M. Hennessy (2 vols., RS, 1871).

Annals of the Kingdom of Ireland by the Four Masters, ed. and tr. John O'Donovan (7 vols., Dublin, 1848–51).

Annals of Ulster (Annála Uladh), ed. and tr. William M. Hennessy and Bartholomew MacCarthy (4 vols., Dublin, 1887–1901).

Anonymi descriptio Europae orientalis, ed. Olgierd Górka (Cracow, 1916).

Arnold of Lübeck, *Chronica Slavorum*, ed. Johann Martin Lappenberg (*SRG*, Hanover, 1868).

Assise au comte Geffroy, ed. Marcel Planiol, *La très ancienne coutume de Bretagne* (Rennes, 1896, repr. Paris and Geneva, 1984), pp. 319–25.

Les assises de Romanie, ed. Georges Recoura (Paris, 1930).

Attaleiates, Michael, *Historia*, ed. Immanuel Bekker (*Corpus scriptorum historiae Byzantinae* 50, Bonn, 1853).

Aureum opus regalium privilegiorum civitatis et regni Valentie (Valencia, 1515, facsimile ed., *Textos medievales* 33, 1972).

Balard, Michel (ed.), *Gênes et l'Outre-mer* 1: *Les actes de Caffa du notaire Lamberto di Sambuceto 1289–90* (Paris, 1973).

Baudri de Bourgueil, *Historia Jerosolimitana*, *RHC*, *Occ.* 4, pp. 1–111.

Bede, *Epistola ad Ecgbertum episcopum*, in Charles Plummer (ed.), *Opera historica* (2 vols., Oxford, 1896) 1, pp. 405–23.

Beowulf, ed. F. Klaeber (3rd ed., Boston, 1950).

Bernard of Clairvaux, *Vita sancti Malachiae*, in J. Leclerq and H. M. Rochais (eds.), *Opera* 3 (Rome, 1963), pp. 295–378.

idem, *De laude novae militiae*, ibid., pp. 205–39.

Bernardo Maragone, *Annales Pisani*, ed. Michele Lupo Gentile (*Rerum italicarum scriptores*, n.s., 6/2, Bologna, 1930), pp. 1–74.

Sancti Bonifatii et Lulli epistolae, ed. Michael Tangl (*MGH, Epistolae selectae* 1, Berlin, 1916).

Book of Fees (2 vols. in 3, London, 1920–31).

Bower, Walter, *Scotichronicon*, ed. D. E. R. Watt, 6 (Aberdeen, 1991).

Breslauer UB 1, ed. G. Korn (Breslau, 1870).

Brooks, Eric St J., 'A Charter of John de Courcy to the Abbey of Navan', *Journal of the Royal Society of Antiquaries of Ireland* 63 (1933), pp. 38–45.

Bruno, *De bello Saxonico liber*, ed. H. E. Lohmann (*MGH, Deutsches Mittelalter* 2, Leipzig, 1937).

Brut y Tywysogyon or The Chronicle of the Princes: Peniarth MS. 20 Version, tr. Thomas Jones (Cardiff, 1952).

Brut y Tywysogyon or The Chronicle of the Princes: Red Book of Hergest Version, ed. and tr. Thomas Jones (Cardiff, 1955).

Calendar of Ancient Petitions relating to Wales, ed. William Rees (Cardiff, 1975).

Calendar of Ancient Records of Dublin 1, ed. John T. Gilbert (Dublin, 1889).

Calendar of Archbishop Alen's Register, ed. Charles McNeill (Dublin, 1950).

Calendar of Documents relating to Ireland (1171–1307), ed. H. S. Sweetman (5 vols., London, 1875–86).

Calendar of the Charter Rolls, 1226–1516 (6 vols., London, 1903–27).

Calendar of the Gormanston Register, ed. James Mills and M. J. McEnery (Dublin, 1916).

Calendar of the Justiciary Rolls . . . of Ireland (1295–1303), ed. James Mills (Dublin, 1905).

Calendar of the Patent Rolls (1232–47), (1258–66), (1358–61) (London, 1906, 1910, 1911).

Callimachus (Filippo Buonaccorsi), *Vita et mores Gregorii Sanocei*, ed. Ludwik Finkel, *MPH* 6 (Cracow, 1893, repr. Warsaw, 1961), pp. 163–216.

Canonici Wissegradensis continuatio (to Cosmas of Prague), ed. Rudolf Köpke, *MGH, SS* 9 (Hanover, 1851), pp. 132–48.

Cantar de Mío Cid, ed. Ramón Menéndez Pidal (rev. ed., 3 vols., Madrid, 1944–6).

Carmen in victoriam Pisanorum, ed. H. E. J. Cowdrey, 'The Mahdia Campaign of 1087', *English Historical Review* 92 (1977), pp. 1–29, text at pp. 23–9.

Cartae et alia munimenta . . . de Glamorgan, ed. George T. Clark (6 vols., Cardiff, 1910).

Cartulaire général de l'ordre des Hospitaliers de St-Jean de Jérusalem, ed. J. Delaville Le Roulx (4 vols., Paris, 1894–1906).

Cartulaire général de l'ordre du Temple, ed. Marquis d'Albon (Paris, 1913).

Cartulario de Sant Cugat del Vallés, ed. José Rius Serra (3 vols., Barcelona, 1945–7).

Cartularios de Santo Domingo de la Calzada, ed. Agustín Ubieto Arteta (Saragossa, 1978).

Cartulary of Worcester Cathedral Priory, ed. R. R. Darlington (Pipe Roll Society, n.s., 37, 1968 for 1962–3).

Catalogus baronum, ed. Evelyn Jamison (*Fonti per la storia d'Italia* 101, Rome, 1972).

Chanson d'Antioche, ed. Suzanne Duparc-Quioc (Paris, 1976).

Chanson de Roland, ed. F. Whitehead (Oxford, 1942).

Chaplais, Pierre (ed.), *Diplomatic Documents preserved in the Public Record Office 1: 1101–1272* (Oxford, 1964).

Chartularies of St Mary's Abbey Dublin, ed. John T. Gilbert (2 vols., RS, 1884).

Chronica Poloniae Maioris, ed. Brygida Kürbis, *MPH*, n.s., 8 (Warsaw, 1970).

Chronicle of Morea, tr. Harold E. Lurier, *Crusaders as Conquerors* (New York, 1964).

Chronicon Aulae Regiae, see Peter of Zittau.

Chronicon Burgense, ed. Enrique Flórez, *España sagrada* 23 (Madrid, 1767), pp. 305–10.

Chronicon principum Polonie, ed. Zygmunt Węclewski, *MPH* 3 (Lwów, 1878, repr. Warsaw, 1961), pp. 421–578.

Chronique de Morée, ed. Jean Longnon (Paris, 1911).

Close Roll 16 John (Pipe Roll Society, n.s., 31, 1955).

Close Rolls of the Reign of Henry III (1237–42), (1247–51), (1254–56) (London, 1911, 1922, 1931).

Codex diplomaticus Brandenburgensis, ed. Adolph Friedrich Riedel (41 vols., Berlin, 1838–69).

Codex diplomaticus et epistolaris regni Bohemiae, ed. Gustavus Friedrich *et al.* (5 vols. to date, Prague, 1904–).

Codex diplomaticus Lusatiae superioris 1, ed. Gustav Köhler (2nd ed., Görlitz, 1856).

Codex diplomaticus Maioris Poloniae, ed. Ignacy Zakrzewski and Franciszek Piekosiński (5 vols., Poznań, 1877–1908).

Codex diplomaticus Warmiensis 1, ed. Carl Peter Woelky and Johann Martin Saage (Mainz, 1860).

Codex iuris Bohemici, ed. Hermenegild Jiriček (5 vols. in 12, Prague, 1867–98).

Codex iuris municipalis regni Bohemiae 2, ed. Jaromír Čelakovský (Prague, 1895).

Codex Iustinianus, ed. Paul Krueger (*Corpus iuris civilis* 2, Berlin, 1895).

Colección de documentos inéditos del archivo general de la Corona de Aragón 4, ed. Próspero de Bofarull y Mascaró (Barcelona, 1849).

Colección de fueros municipales y cartas pueblas de los reinos de Castilla, León, Corona de Aragón y Navarra, ed. Tomás Muñoz y Romero (Madrid, 1847).

Comnena, Anna, *Alexiad*, ed. B. Leib (3 vols., Paris, 1937–45).

Conciliorum oecumenicorum decreta, ed. J. Alberigo *et al.* (3rd ed., Bologna, 1973).

Constitutiones et acta publica imperatorum et regum 1–2, ed. Ludwig Weiland (*MGH*, Hanover, 1893–6).

Continuatio Aquicinctina of Sigebert of Gembloux, ed. Ludwig Bethmann, *MGH*, *SS* 6 (Hanover, 1844), pp. 268–474.

Cosmas of Prague, *Chronica Boemorum*, ed. Berthold Bretholz (*SRG*, n.s., Berlin, 1923).

Coussemaker, Edmond de (ed.), *Documents relatifs à la Flandre maritime* (Lille, 1860).

Crede mihi, ed. John T. Gilbert (Dublin, 1897).

Crónica del rey don Alfonso X, in *Crónicas de los reyes de Castilla* 1 (*Biblioteca de autores españoles* 66, Madrid, 1875), pp. 1–66.

Cronica principum Saxonie, ed. Oswald Holder-Egger, *MGH*, *SS* 25 (Hanover, 1880), pp. 472–80.

Cronica Reinhardsbrunnensis, ed. Oswald Holder-Egger, *MGH, SS* 30/1 (Hanover, 1896), pp. 490–656.

Crónicas anónimas de Sahagún, ed. Antonio Ubieto Arteta (*Textos medievales* 75, Saragossa, 1987).

Curtis, Edmund, 'Rental of the Manor of Lisronagh, 1333, and Notes on "Betagh" Tenure in Medieval Ireland', *Proceedings of the Royal Irish Academy* 43 (1935–7) C, pp. 41–76.

Dalimil Chronicle (Middle German versions), ed. J. Jiriček, *Fontes rerum Bohemicarum* 3 (Prague, 1882), pp. 5–224, *Di tutsch kronik von Behem lant* (verse), and pp. 257–97, *Die pehemische Cronica dewcz* (prose).

De expugnatione Lyxbonensi: The Conquest of Lisbon, ed. and tr. Charles W. David (New York, 1936).

De Ordine Praedicatorum de Tolosa in Dacia, ed. M. C. Gertz, *Scriptores minores historiae Danicae* (2 vols., Copenhagen, 1917–22) 2/1, pp. 369–74.

De Theutonicis bonum dictamen, ed. Wilhelm Wostry, 'Ein deutschfeindliches Pamphlet aus Böhmen aus dem 14. Jahrhundert', *Mitteilungen des Vereins für Geschichte der Deutschen in Böhmen* 53 (1914–15), pp. 193–238.

Desimoni, Cornelio (ed.), 'I conti dell'ambasciata al chan di Persia nel 1292', *Atti della Società ligure di storia patria* 13/3 (1879), pp. 537–698.

Deusdedit, *Collectio canonum*, ed. Victor Wolf von Glanvell, *Die Kanonessammlung des Kardinals Deusdedit* (Paderborn, 1905).

Dignitas decani, ed. Newport B. White (Dublin, 1957).

Diplomata Conradi I, Heinrici I et Ottonis I, ed. Theodor Sickel (*MGH, Diplomata regum et imperatorum Germaniae* I, Hanover, 1879–84).

La documentación pontificia hasta Inocencio III, ed. Demetrio Mansilla (Rome, 1955).

Documentos de Don Sancho I (1174–1211) 1, ed. Rui de Azevado *et al.* (Coimbra, 1979).

Domesday Book, ed. Abraham Farley (2 vols., London, 1783).

The Dublin Guild Merchant Roll c. 1190–1265, ed. Philomena Connolly and Geoffrey Martin (Dublin, 1992).

Dudo of Saint-Quentin, *De moribus et actis primorum Normanniae ducum*, ed. Jules Lair, *Mémoires de la Société des Antiquaires de Normandie*, 3rd ser., 3 (Caen, 1858–65).

Dugdale, William, *Monasticon Anglicanum*, ed. John Caley *et al.* (6 vols. in 8, London, 1846).

Eadmer, *Life of St Anselm*, ed. and tr. R. W. Southern (London, etc., 1962).

Early Scottish Charters prior to 1153, ed. Archibald C. Lawrie (Glasgow, 1905).

Ebel, Wilhelm (ed.), *Lübecker Ratsurteile* (4 vols., Göttingen, 1955–67).

Ebo, *Vita sancti Ottonis episcopi Babenbergensis*, ed. Jan Wikarjak and Kazimierz Liman, *MPH*, n.s., 7/2 (Warsaw, 1969).

Einhard, *Vita Karoli Magni*, ed. Reinhold Rau, *Quellen zur karolingischen Reichsgeschichte* 1 (*AQ* 5, Darmstadt, 1955), pp. 163–211.

Ekkehard of Aura, *Hierosolymita, RHC, Occ.* 5, pp. 1–40.

Elenchus fontium historiae urbanae 2/2, ed. Susan Reynolds *et al.* (Leiden, etc., 1988).

L'estoire d'Eracles empereur et la conqueste de la terre d'Outremer, RHC, Occ. 2, pp. 1–481; also as *La continuation de Guillaume de Tyr (1184–1197)*, ed. Margaret R. Morgan (*Documents relatifs à l'histoire des croisades* 14, Paris, 1982).

Eugenius III, *Epistolae et privilegia, PL* 180, cols. 1013–1606.

Facsimiles of National Manuscripts of Ireland, ed. John T. Gilbert (4 parts in 5 vols., Dublin, 1874–84).

Fantosme, Jordan, *Chronicle*, ed. and tr. R. C. Johnston (Oxford, 1981).

Finke, Heinrich (ed.), *Ungedruckte Dominikanerbriefe des 13. Jahrhunderts* (Paderborn, 1891).

Foedera, conventiones, litterae et . . . acta publica . . ., ed. Thomas Rymer (new ed., 4 vols. in 7 parts, Record Commission, 1816–69).

Font Rius, José María (ed.), *Cartas de población y franquicia de Cataluña* (2 vols., Madrid and Barcelona, 1969).

Francis of Prague, *Cronicae Pragensis libri III*, ed. J. Emler, *Fontes rerum Bohemicarum* 4 (Prague, 1884), pp. 347–456.

Frutolfi et Ekkehardi Chronica necnon Anonymi Chronica imperatorum, ed. Franz-Josef Schmale and Irene Schmale-Ott (*AQ* 15, Darmstadt, 1972).

Fuero de Jaca, ed. Mauricio Molho (Saragossa, 1964).

Fuero de Logroño, ed. T. Moreno Garbaya, *Apuntes históricos de Logroño* (Logroño, 1943), pp. 42–9.

Fueros de Sepúlveda, ed. Emilio Sáez (Segovia, 1953).

Fulcher of Chartres, *Historia Hierosolymitana*, ed. Heinrich Hagenmeyer (Heidelberg, 1913).

Els Furs de Valencia, ed. Rafael Gayano-Lluch (Valencia, 1930).

Gabrieli, Francesco (ed.), *Arab Historians of the Crusades* (Eng. tr., Berkeley and London, 1969).

Gallus Anonymus, *Chronicon*, ed. K. Maleczynski, *MPH*, n.s., 2 (Cracow, 1952).

Gearóid Iarla (i.e. Gerald fitz Maurice fitzGerald, earl of Desmond), 'Duanaire Ghearóid Iarla', ed. Gearóid MacNiocaill, *Studia Hibernica* 3 (1963), pp. 7–59.

Geoffrey of Durham, *Vita Bartholomaei Farnensis*, in *Symeonis monachi opera omnia*, ed. Thomas Arnold (2 vols., RS, 1882–5), 1, pp. 295–325.

George Cedrenus, *Historiarum compendium*, ed. Immanuel Bekker (2 vols., *Corpus scriptorum historiae Byzantinae* 34–5, Bonn, 1838–9).

George Pachymeres, *De Michaele et Andronico Palaeologis*, ed. Immanuel Bekker (2 vols., *Corpus scriptorum historiae Byzantinae* 24–5, Bonn, 1835).

Gerald of Wales (Giraldus Cambrensis), *Symbolum Electorum*, in J. S. Brewer, J. F. Dimock and G. F. Warner (eds.), *Opera* (8 vols., RS, 1861–91) 1, pp. 197–395.

idem, Topographia Hibernica, ibid. 5, pp. 1–204.

idem, Itinerarium Kambriae, ibid. 6, pp. 1–152.

idem, Descriptio Kambriae, ibid. 6, pp. 153–227.

idem, De principis instructione, ibid. 8.

idem, Expugnatio Hibernica, ed. A. B. Scott and F. X. Martin (Dublin, 1978).

idem, Speculum Duorum, ed. Yves Lefèvre and R. B. C. Huygens, general ed. Michael Richter (Cardiff, 1974).

idem, Vita Ethelberti, ed. Montague R. James, 'Two Lives of St Ethelbert, King and Martyr', *English Historical Review* 32 (1917), pp. 222–36.

Gerlach of Mühlhausen, *Chronicon*, ed. Wilhelm Wattenbach, *MGH, SS* 17 (Hanover, 1861), pp. 683–710.

Gervase of Rheims, *Epistola de vita sancti Donatiani*, ed. Oswald Holder-Egger, *MGH, SS* 15/2 (Hanover, 1888), pp. 854–6.

Gervase of Tilbury, *Otia imperialia*, ed. G. W. Leibnitz, *Scriptores rerum brunsvicensium illustrationi inservientes* (3 vols., Hanover, 1707–11) 1, pp. 881–1004; 2, pp. 751–84.

Gesta abbatum monasterii sancti Albani, ed. Henry T. Riley (3 vols., RS, 1867–9).

Gesta archiepiscoporum Magdeburgensium, ed. Wilhelm Schum, *MGH, SS* 14 (Hanover, 1883), pp. 361–486.

Gesta Francorum, ed. and tr. Rosalind Hill (London, 1962).

Gesta regis Henrici secundi Benedicti abbatis, ed. William Stubbs (2 vols., RS, 1867).

Gesta Stephani, ed. K. R. Potter and R. H. C. Davis (Oxford, 1976).

Les gestes des Chiprois, ed. Gaston Raynaud (*Publications de la Société de l'Orient latin, Série historique* 5, Geneva, 1887).

Glanvill, *The Treatise on the Laws and Customs of England commonly called Glanvill*, ed. and tr. G. D. H. Hall (London, 1965).

Gregory VII, *Registrum*, ed. Erich Caspar (*MGH, Epistolae selectae*, 2, Berlin, 1920–23).

idem, The Epistolae Vagantes of Pope Gregory VII, ed. and tr. H. E. J. Cowdrey (Oxford, 1972).

Gregory IX, *Decretals*, ed. Emil Friedberg (*Corpus iuris canonici* 2, Leipzig, 1881).

Guibert de Nogent, *Historia quae dicitur Gesta Dei per Francos, RHC, Occ.* 4, pp. 113–263.

Hagenmeyer, Heinrich (ed.), *Epistulae et chartae ad historiam primi belli sacri spectantes* (Innsbruck, 1901).

Hamburgisches UB (4 vols. in 7, Hamburg, 1907–67).

Hansisches UB 1, ed. Konstantin Höhlbaum (Halle, 1876).

Hariulf, *Gesta ecclesiae Centulensis*, ed. F. Lot, *Chronique de l'abbaye de Saint-Riquier* (Paris, 1894).

Helbig, Herbert, and Lorenz Weinrich (eds.), *Urkunden und erzählende Quellen zur deutschen Ostsiedlung im Mittelalter* (*AQ* 26, 2 vols., Darmstadt, 1968–70).

Helmold of Bosau, *Chronica Slavorum*, ed. Heinz Stoob (*AQ* 19, Darmstadt, rev. ed., 1973).

Henry of Antwerp, *Tractatus de captione urbis Brandenburg*, ed. Oswald Holder-Egger, *MGH, SS* 25 (Hanover, 1880), pp. 482–4.

Henry of Huntingdon, *Historia Anglorum*, ed. Thomas Arnold (RS, 1879).

Henry of Livonia, *Chronicon Livoniae*, ed. Leonid Arbusow and Albert Bauer (*AQ* 24, Darmstadt, 1959).

Herbord, *Dialogus de vita sancti Ottonis episcopi Babenbergensis*, ed. Jan Wikarjak and Kazimierz Liman, *MPH*, n.s. 7/3 (Warsaw, 1974).

Historia de translatione sanctorum Nicolai, etc., *RHC, Occ.* 5, pp. 253–92.

Historia monasterii Rastedensis, ed. Georg Waitz, *MGH, SS* 25 (Hanover, 1880), pp. 495–511.

Historical Manuscripts Commission, *10th Report, appendix 5* (London, 1885).

History of Gruffydd ap Cynan, ed. and tr. Arthur Jones (Manchester, 1910).

Honorius III, *Opera omnia*, ed. César Auguste Horoy (5 vols., Paris, 1879–82).

Humbert of Silva Candida, *Adversus Graecorum calumnias*, *PL* 143, cols. 929–74.

Iça Jeddih, *Suma de los principales mandamientos y devedamientos de la ley y çunna*, *Memorial histórico español* 5 (Real Academia de la Historia, Madrid, 1853), pp. 247–421.

Innocent II, *Epistolae et privilegia*, *PL* 179, cols. 53–658.

Innocent III, *Registrum sive epistolae*, *PL* 214–16.

idem, Die Register Innocenz' III 2, ed. Othmar Hageneder *et al.* (Rome and Vienna, 1979).

idem, Regestum Innocentii III papae super negotio Romani imperii, ed. Friedrich Kempf (Rome, 1947).

Inquisitio Eliensis, ed. N. E. S. A. Hamilton, *Inquisitio comitatus Cantabrigiensis, subjicitur Inquisitio Eliensis* (London, 1876), pp. 97–183.

Irish Cartularies of Llanthony Prima and Secunda, ed. Eric St John Brooks (Irish Manuscripts Commission, Dublin, 1953).

Isidore of Seville, *Etymologies*, ed. W. M. Lindsay (2 vols., Oxford, 1911, unpaginated).

Itinéraires à Jerusalem, ed. Henri Michelant and Gaston Raynaud (*Publications de la Société de l'Orient latin, Série géographique* 3, Geneva, 1882).

Iura Prutenorum, ed. Józef Matuszewski (*Towarzystwo Naukowe w Toruniu: Fontes* 53, Toruń, 1963).

Jackson, Kenneth H. (ed.), *A Celtic Miscellany* (rev. ed., Harmondsworth, 1971).

Jacob, G. (ed.), *Arabische Berichte von Gesandten an germanische Fürstenhöfe aus dem 9. und 10. Jahrhundert* (Berlin and Leipzig, 1927).

James I, *Llibre dels feyts (Crónica)*, ed. Josep María de Casacuberta (9 vols. in 2, Barcelona, 1926–62).

Jocelyn of Furness, *Vita sancti Patricii*, *Acta sanctorum Martii* 2 (Antwerp, 1668), pp. 540–80.

John of Hexham, *Historia*, in *Symeonis monachi opera omnia*, ed. Thomas Arnold (2 vols., RS, 1882–5), 2, pp. 284–332.

John of Salisbury, *Letters, 1: The Early Letters (1153–61)*, ed. W. J. Millor, H. E. Butler and C. N. L. Brooke (London, etc., 1955).

idem, Policraticus, ed. C. C. J. Webb (2 vols., Oxford, 1909).

Joinville, John de, *Histoire de Saint Louis*, ed. Natalis de Wailly (Paris, 1874).

Kong Valdemars Jordebog, ed. Svend Aakjaer (3 vols., Copenhagen, 1926–43).

Korlén, Gustav (ed.), *Norddeutsch Stadtrechte 2: Das mittelniederdeutsche Stadtrecht von Lübeck nach seinen ältesten Formen* (Lund and Copenhagen, 1951).

Lacarra, José María (ed.), 'Documentos para el estudio de la reconquista y repoblación del Valle del Ebro', *Estudios de Edad Media de la Corona de Aragon* 2 (1946), pp. 469–574 (docs. 1–93), 3 (1947–8), pp. 499–727 (docs. 94–286), 5 (1952), pp. 511–668 (docs. 287–400); repr. in 2 vols., *Textos medievales* 62–3 (Saragossa, 1982–3).

Lapidge, Michael (ed.), 'The Welsh-Latin Poetry of Sulien's Family', *Studia Celtica* 8–9 (1973–4), pp. 68–106.

Lawrence of Durham, *Dialogi*, ed. James Raine (Surtees Society 70, 1880 for 1878).

Lechner, Georg (ed.), *Die hansischen Pfundzollisten des Jahres 1368* (*Quellen und Darstellungen zur hansischen Geschichte*, n.s., 10, Lübeck, 1935).

Libellus de institutione morum, ed. J. Balogh, *Scriptores rerum Hungaricarum* 2 (Budapest, 1938), pp. 611–27.

Liber actorum, resignationum nec non ordinationum civitatis Cracoviae, ed. Franciszek Piekosiński (*Monumenta Medii Aevi historica res gestas Poloniae illustrantia* 4/1, Cracow, 1878).

Liber cartarum Sancte Crucis, ed. Cosmo Innes (Bannatyne Club, Edinburgh, 1840).

Le liber censuum de l'église romaine, ed. Paul Fabre *et al.* (3 vols., Paris, 1889–1910).

Liber feudorum major, ed. Francisco Miquel Rosell (2 vols., Barcelona, 1945–7).

Liber fundationis claustri sanctae Mariae virginis in Heinrichow, ed. Roman Grodecki, *Księga Henrykowska* (Poznań and Wrocław, 1949).

Liber fundationis episcopatus Vratislaviensis, ed. H. Markgraf and J. W. Schulte (*Codex diplomaticus Silesiae* 14, Breslau, 1889).

Liber vitae ecclesiae Dunelmensis, ed. A. Hamilton Thompson (facsimile ed., Surtees Society 136, 1923).

Lites ac res gestae inter Polonos Ordinemque Cruciferorum (2nd ser., 3 vols., Poznań and Warsaw, 1890–1935).

Littere Wallie, ed. John Goronwy Edwards (Cardiff, 1940).

Liv-, esth- und curländisches UB, ed. F. G. von Bunge *et al.* (1st ser., 12 vols., Reval and Riga, 1853–1910).

Livländische Reimchronik, ed. Leo Meyer (Paderborn, 1876).

Lopez, Robert S., and Irving W. Raymond (eds.), *Medieval Trade in the Mediterranean World* (New York, 1955).

Luke of Tuy, *Chronicon mundi*, ed. Andreas Schottus, *Hispaniae illustratae* (4 vols., Frankfurt/Main, 1603–8) 4, pp. 1–116.

Mac Con Midhe, Giolla Brighde, *Poems*, ed. and tr. N. J. A. Williams (Irish Texts Society 51, Dublin, 1980).

MacNiocaill, Gearóid, *Na Buirgéisí* (2 vols., Dublin, 1964).

idem, 'Cartae Duneneses XI–XII Céad', *Seanchus Ard Mhaca* 5/2 (1970), pp. 418–28.

Das Magdeburg-breslauer systematische Schöffenrecht, ed. Paul Laband (Berlin, 1863).

Malaterra, Geoffrey, *De rebus gestis Rogerii Calabriae et Siciliae comitis et Roberti Guiscardi ducis fratris eius*, ed. Ernesto Pontieri (*Rerum italicarum scriptores*, n.s., 5/1, Bologna, 1928).

Mecklenburgisches UB (25 vols. in 26, Schwerin and Leipzig, 1863–1977).

Menéndez Pidal, Ramón (ed.), *Documentos lingüísticos de España* 1 (Madrid, 1919, repr. 1966).

Miracula sancti Annonis, ed. Mauritius Mittler (Siegburg, 1966–8).

Monumenta Poloniae Vaticana 3: Analecta Vaticana, ed. Jan Ptaśnik (Cracow, 1914).

Notker, *Gesta Karoli*, ed. Reinhold Rau, *Quellen zur karolingischen Reichsgeschichte* 3 (*AQ* 7, Darmstadt, 1960), pp. 321–427.

Odo of Deuil, *De profectione Ludovici VII in Orientem*, ed. and tr. Virginia G. Berry (New York, 1948).

Das Ofner Stadtrecht, ed. Karl Mollay (Weimar, 1959).

Olesch, Reinhold (ed.), *Fontes linguae dravaeno-polabicae minores et Chronica Venedica J. P. Schultzii* (Cologne and Graz, 1967).

Orderic Vitalis, *Historia ecclesiastica*, ed. and tr. Marjorie Chibnall (6 vols., Oxford, 1968–80).

Osnabrücker UB 2, ed. F. Philippi (Osnabrück, 1896).

Otto of Freising, *Gesta Friderici I imperatoris*, ed. Georg Waitz and Bernhard von Simson (*SRG*, Hanover and Leipzig, 1912).

Oxford Book of Welsh Verse, ed. T. Parry (Oxford, 1962).

Paris, Matthew, *Chronica majora*, ed. Henry R. Luard (7 vols., R S, 1872–84).

idem, *Historia Anglorum*, ed. Frederic Madden (3 vols., R S, 1866–9).

Patent Rolls of the Reign of Henry III (1216–32) (2 vols., London, 1901–3).

Peire Vidal, *Poesie*, ed. D'Arco Silvio Avalle (2 vols., Milan and Naples, 1960).

Peter of Dusburg, *Chronica terre Prussie*, ed. Klaus Scholz and Dieter Wojtecki (*AQ* 25, Darmstadt, 1984).

Peter of Zittau, *Chronicon Aulae Regiae*, ed. J. Emler, *Fontes rerum Bohemicarum* 4 (Prague, 1884), pp. 1–337.

Philip of Novara (Philippe de Navarre), *Les quatre âges de l'homme*, ed. Marcel de Fréville (Paris, 1888).

Pipe Roll 31 Henry I, ed. J. Hunter (Record Commission, London, 1833).

Placitorum abbreviatio (Record Commission, London, 1811).

Pommerellisches UB, ed. Max Perlbach (Danzig, 1881–2).

Pommersches UB 1: 786–1253, ed. Klaus Conrad (2nd ed., Cologne and Vienna, 1970).

Pommersches UB 2, 5, 6 (Stettin, 1881–5, 1905, 1907, repr. Cologne and Graz, 1970).

Pontificia Hibernica: Medieval Papal Chancery Documents concerning Ireland 640–1261, ed. Maurice P. Sheehy (2 vols., Dublin, 1962–5).

Preussisches UB (6 vols. to date, Königsberg and Marburg, 1882–).

Primera crónica general de España, ed. Ramón Menéndez Pidal (2 vols., Madrid, 1955).

Privilegios reales y viejos documentos de Toledo, ed. Juan Francisco Rivera Recio *et al.* (limited ed., Madrid, 1963).

Ptolemy of Lucca (and Thomas Aquinas), *De regimine principum*, ed. Pierre Mandonnet, in Thomas Aquinas, *Opuscula omnia* 1 (Paris, 1927), pp. 312–487.

Quellenbuch zur Geschichte der Sudetenländer 1, ed. Wilhelm Weizsäcker (Munich, 1960).

Ratzeburg Tithe Register, ed. Hans Wurm, in Hans-Georg Kaack and Hans Wurm, *Slawen und Deutsche im Lande Lauenburg* (Ratzeburg, 1983), pp. 137–205.

Raymond of Aguilers, *Liber (Historia Francorum qui ceperunt Iherusalem)*, ed. John H. Hill and Laurita L. Hill (Paris, 1969).

Recueil des historiens des croisades, Lois 2 (Paris, 1843).

Recueil des historiens des Gaules et de la France, ed. Martin Bouquet *et al.* (new ed., 24 vols., Paris, 1869–1904).

Red Book of Ormond, ed. Newport B. White (Irish Manuscripts Commission, Dublin, 1932).

Red Book of the Exchequer, ed. Hubert Hall (3 vols., R S, 1896).

Regesta diplomatica nec non epistolaria Bohemiae et Moraviae, ed. K. J. Erben, J. Emler *et al.* (7 vols. to date, Prague, 1854–).

Regesta Regum Anglo-Normannorum 1, ed. H. W. C. Davis (Oxford, 1913).

Regesten zur schlesischen Geschichte 3 (*Codex diplomaticus Silesiae* 7/3, Breslau, 1886).

Regino of Prüm, *Epistula ad Hathonem archiepiscopum missa*, ed. Friedrich Kurze, *Reginonis . . . chronicon* (*SRG*, Hanover, 1890), pp. xix–xx.

Register of the Abbey of St Thomas Dublin, ed. John T. Gilbert (R S, 1889).

Registrum vulgariter nuncupatum 'The Record of Caernarvon', ed. Henry Ellis (Record Commission, London, 1838).

La règle du Temple, ed. Henri de Curzon (Paris, 1886).

Repartimiento de Sevilla, ed. Julio González (2 vols., Madrid, 1951).

Reports of the Deputy Keeper of the Public Records of Ireland 1–55 (Dublin, 1869–1923).

Rerum Hungaricarum monumenta Arpadiana, ed. S. L. Endlicher (St Gallen, 1849).

Richard of Hexham, *Historia*, ed. Richard Howlett in *Chronicles of the Reigns of Stephen, Henry II and Richard I* (4 vols., RS, 1884–9) 3, pp. 137–78.

Richard of Poitou, *Chronica* (excerpts, with continuations), ed. Georg Waitz, *MGH, SS* 26 (Hanover, 1882), pp. 74–86.

Richer, *Historiae*, ed. R. Latouche, *Histoire de France* (2 vols., Paris, 1930–37).

Robert of Clari, *La conquête de Constantinople*, ed. Philippe Lauer (Paris, 1924).

Robert the Monk, *Historia Iherosolimitana, RHC, Occ.* 3, pp. 717–882.

'Rocznik lubiąski 1241–1281, oraz wiersz o pierwotnych zakonniach Lubiąża' [*Versus lubenses*], ed. August Bielowski, *MPH* 3 (Lwów, 1878, repr. Warsaw, 1961), pp. 707–10.

Roger of Howden, *Chronica*, ed. William Stubbs (4 vols., RS, 1868–71).

Roger of Wendover, *Flores historiarum*, ed. H. G. Hewlett (3 vols., RS, 1886–9).

Rotuli chartarum in turri Londinensi asservati (1199–1216), ed. T. D. Hardy (London, 1837).

Rotuli litterarum clausarum in turri Londinensi asservati (1204–27), ed. T. D. Hardy (2 vols., London, 1833–44).

Sachsenspiegel (with the glosses of Johannes von Buch), ed. Jacob Friedrich Ludovici (rev. ed., Halle, 1750).

Sachsenspiegel: Landrecht and *Lehnrecht*, ed. Karl August Eckhardt (*Germanenrechte*, n.s., 2 vols., Göttingen, 1955–6).

Sáez, Emilio, 'Fueros de Puebla de Alcocer y Yébenes', *Anuario de historia del derecho español* 18 (1947), pp. 432–41.

Saxo Grammaticus, *Gesta Danorum*, ed. J. Olrik and H. Raeder (2 vols., Copenhagen, 1931–57).

idem, Danorum regum heroumque historia, Books X–XVI, tr. Eric Christiansen (3 vols., British Archaeological Reports, International Series 84, 118/1–2, Oxford, 1980–81).

Schlesisches UB, ed. Heinrich Appelt and Winfried Irgang (4 vols. to date, Graz, Cologne and Vienna, 1963–).

Siebert, Richard (ed.), 'Elf ungedruckte Urkunden aus einem im Herzoglichen Haus- und Staatsarchiv zu Zerbst befindlichen Nienburger Copiale', *Mitteilungen des Vereins für Anhaltische Geschichte und Altertumskunde* 9 (1904), pp. 183–94.

Las Siete Partidas, ed. Real Academia de la Historia (3 vols., Madrid, 1807).

Simon of Saint Quentin, *Historia Tartarorum*, ed. Jean Richard (Paris, 1965).

Skånske lov – Text III, in *Danmarks gamle landskabslove* 1, ed. J. Brøndum-Nielsen (Copenhagen, 1920–33), pp. 265–466.

Song of Dermot and the Earl, ed. and tr. Goddard H. Orpen (Oxford, 1892).

Statutes and Ordinances and Acts of the Parliament of Ireland: King John to Henry V, ed. Henry F. Berry (Dublin, 1907).

Statutes of the Realm (11 vols., Record Commission, 1810–28).

Stephen de Salaniaco, *De quattuor in quibus Deus Praedicatorum Ordinem insignivit*, ed. T. Kaeppeli (*Monumenta ordinis fratrum praedicatorum historica* 22, Rome, 1949).

Stephen of Lexington, *Registrum epistolarum*, ed. P. Bruno Griesser, *Analecta sacri ordinis Cisterciensis* 2 (1946), pp. 1–118.

idem, *Letters from Ireland 1228–1229*, tr. Barry O'Dwyer (Kalamazoo, Mich., 1982).

Stubbs, William (ed.), *Select Charters* (9th ed., Oxford, 1913).

Suger, *Vita Ludovici Grossi regis*, ed. H. Waquet (Paris, 1929).

Sunesen, Anders, *Antique leges Scanie*, in *Danmarks gamle landskabslove* 1, ed. J. Brøndum-Nielsen (Copenhagen, 1920–33), pp. 467–667.

idem, *Hexaemeron*, ed. Sten Ebbesen and L. B. Mortensen (2 vols., Copenhagen, 1985–8).

Symeon of Durham, *Historia regum*, in *Symeonis monachi opera omnia*, ed. Thomas Arnold (2 vols., RS, 1882–5), 2, pp. 3–283.

idem (attrib.), *De miraculis et translationibus sancti Cuthberti*, ibid. 1, pp. 229–61; 2, pp. 333–62.

Symeon of Durham's continuator, *Historia Dunelmensis ecclesiae*, ibid. 1, pp. 135–60.

Tafel, G. L. F., and G. M. Thomas (eds.), *Urkunden zur älteren Handels- und Staatsgeschichte der Republik Venedig* (3 vols., *Fontes rerum Austriacarum* II, 12–14, Vienna, 1856–7).

Thietmar of Merseburg, *Chronicon*, ed. Werner Trillmich (*AQ* 9, Darmstadt, 1957).

Thomas of Monmouth, *The Life and Miracles of St William of Norwich*, ed. and tr. Augustus Jessopp and Montague Rhodes James (Cambridge, 1896).

Turgot, *Vita sancti Margaretae reginae*, ed. James Raine in *Symeonis Dunelmensis opera et collectanea* 1, ed. J. Hodgson Hinde (Surtees Society 51, 1868), pp. 234–54.

UB des ehemaligen Cistercienserstiftes Goldenkron in Böhmen, ed. M. Pangerl (*Fontes rerum Austriacarum* II, 37, Vienna, 1872).

UB des Erzstifts Magdeburg 1, ed. Friedrich Israël and Walter Möllenberg (Magdeburg, 1937).

UB des Hochstifts Hildesheim und seiner Bischöfe 2, ed. H. Hoogeweg (Hanover and Leipzig, 1901).

UB zur Geschichte der Deutschen in Siebenbürgen 1, ed. Franz Zimmermann and Carl Werner (Hermannstadt, 1892).

UB zur Geschichte der Herzöge von Braunschweig und Lüneburg und ihrer Lande 1, ed. H. Sudendorf (Hanover, 1859).

UB zur Geschichte des schlossgesessenen Geschlechtes der Grafen und Herren von Wedel, ed. Heinrich Friedrich Paul von Wedel (4 vols. in 2, Leipzig, 1885–91).

Die Urkunden Heinrichs des Löwen, Herzogs von Sachsen und Bayern, ed. Karl Jordan, *MGH*, *Laienfürsten- und Dynastenurkunden der Kaiserzeit* (Leipzig and Weimar, 1941–9).

Usamah Ibn-Munqidh, *An Arab-Syrian Gentleman and Warrior . . . Memoirs of Usamah Ibn-Munqidh*, tr. Philip K. Hitti (New York, 1929).

Victor, Claudius Marius, *Alethia*, ed. Carl Schenkl, *Poetae Christiani minores* 1 (*Corpus scriptorum ecclesiasticorum latinorum* 16/1, Vienna, etc., 1888), pp. 359–436.

Villard de Honcourt, *Sketchbook*, ed. Hans R. Hahnloser, *Villard de Honnecourt: Kritische Gesamtausgabe des Bauhüttenbuches ms. fr. 19093 der Pariser Nationalbibliothek* (2nd ed., Graz, 1972); ed. Theodore Bowie, *The Sketchbook of Villard de Honnecourt* (Bloomington, 1959).

Villehardouin, Geoffrey de, *La conquête de Constantinople*, ed. Edmond Faral (2nd ed., 2 vols., Paris, 1961).

Visitationes bonorum archiepiscopatus necnon capituli Gnesnensis saeculi XVI, ed. Boleslaw Ulanowski (Cracow, 1920).

Vita Constantini, tr. Marvin Kantor and Richard S. White, *The Vita of Constantine and the Vita of Methodius* (*Michigan Slavic Materials* 13, Ann Arbor, 1976).

Walter Map, *De nugis curialium*, ed. and tr. M. R. James, rev. C. N. L. Brooke and R. A. B. Mynors (Oxford, 1983).

Walter of Coventry, *Memoriale*, ed. William Stubbs (2 vols., RS, 1872–3).

Walter of Guisborough, *Chronicle*, ed. Harry Rothwell (Camden 3rd ser., 89, 1957).

Walter of Henley, *Husbandry*, ed. Dorothea Oschinsky, *Walter of Henley and other Treatises on Estate Management and Accounting* (Oxford, 1971), pp. 307–43.

Walther von der Vogelweide, *Die Lieder*, ed. Friedrich Maurer (Munich, 1972).

Weinrich, Lorenz (ed.), *Quellen zur deutschen Verfassungs-, Wirtschafts- und Sozialgeschichte bis 1250* (*AQ* 32, Darmstadt, 1977).

Widukind of Corvey, *Res gestae Saxonicae*, ed. Albert Bauer and Reinhold Rau, *Quellen zur Geschichte der sächsischen Kaiserzeit* (*AQ* 8, rev. ed., Darmstadt, 1977), pp. 1–183.

William of Apulia, *La geste de Robert Guiscard*, ed. Marguerite Mathieu (Palermo, 1961).

William of Malmesbury, *Gesta regum*, ed. William Stubbs (2 vols., RS, 1887–9).

William of Newburgh, *Historia rerum Anglicarum*, ed. Richard Howlett in *Chronicles of the Reigns of Stephen, Henry II and Richard I* (4 vols., RS, 1884–9) 1–2.

William of Poitiers, *Gesta Guillelmi ducis Normannorum*, ed. Raymonde Foreville (Paris, 1952).

William of Rubruck, *Itinerarium*, ed. Anastasius van den Wyngaert, *Sinica Franciscana 1: Itinera et relationes fratrum minorum saec. XIII et XIV* (Quaracchi, 1929), pp. 164–332.

William of Tyre, *Chronicle*, ed. R. B. C. Huygens (2 vols., *Corpus Christianorum, Continuatio mediaevalis* 63–63A, Turnhout, 1986).

William the Breton, *Gesta Philippi Augusti*, ed. H.-F. Delaborde, *Oeuvres de Rigord et de Guillaume le Breton* (2 vols., Paris, 1882–5) 1, pp. 168–333.

idem, *Philippidos*, ed. H.-F. Delaborde, ibid. 2.

SECONDARY WORKS

Abulafia, David, *The Two Italies* (Cambridge, 1977).

Anderson, Perry, *Passages from Antiquity to Feudalism* (London, 1974).

Arnold, Benjamin, *German Knighthood 1050–1300* (Oxford, 1985).

Atlas vorgeschichtlicher Befestigungen in Niedersachsen, ed. A. von Opperman and C. Schuchhardt (Hanover, 1888–1916).

Atlas zur Kirchengeschichte, ed. Hubert Jedin *et al.* (2nd ed., Freiburg im Breisgau, 1987).

Audouin, E., *Essai sur l'armée royal au temps de Philippe Auguste* (Paris, 1913).

Avent, Richard, *Cestyll Tywysogion Gwynedd/Castles of the Princes of Gwynedd* (Cardiff, 1983).

Bach, Adolf, *Deutsche Namenkunde* (2nd ed., 3 vols., Heidelberg, 1952–6).

Balard, Michel, *La Romanie génoise (XIIe–début du XVe siècle)* (2 vols., Rome, 1978).

Baldwin, John, *The Government of Philip Augustus* (Berkeley and Los Angeles, 1986).

Barrow, Geoffrey, *The Anglo-Norman Era in Scottish History* (Oxford, 1980).

idem, *Kingship and Unity: Scotland 1000–1306* (London, 1981).

idem, *Robert Bruce and the Community of the Realm of Scotland* (2nd ed., Edinburgh, 1982).

Barry, T. B., *The Archaeology of Medieval Ireland* (London, 1987).

Bartels, Karl, *Deutsche Krieger in polnischen Diensten von Misika I. bis Kasimir dem Grossen, c. 963–1370* (Berlin, 1922).

Bartlett, Robert, *Gerald of Wales 1146–1223* (Oxford, 1982).

idem, 'The Conversion of a Pagan Society in the Middle Ages', *History* 70 (1985), pp. 185–201.

idem, 'Colonial Aristocracies of the High Middle Ages', in *idem* and Angus MacKay (eds.), *Medieval Frontier Societies* (Oxford, 1989), pp. 23–47.

Bateson, Mary, 'The Laws of Breteuil', *English Historical Review* 15 (1900), pp. 73–8, 302–18, 496–523, 754–7; 16 (1901), pp. 92–110, 332–45.

Bendixen, Kirsten, *Denmark's Money* (Copenhagen, 1967).

Benninghoven, Friedrich, *Rigas Entstehung und der Frühhansische Kaufmann* (Hamburg, 1961).

idem, *Der Order der Schwertbrüder* (Cologne and Graz, 1965).

Bentzien, Ulrich, *Haken und Pflug* (Berlin, 1969).

Beresford, Maurice, *New Towns of the Middle Ages* (London, 1967).

Beveridge, William, *Prices and Wages in England* 1 (London, 1939).

Bischoff, Karl, *Sprache und Geschichte an der mittleren Elbe und der unteren Saale* (*MF* 52, Cologne and Graz, 1967).

Bishko, Charles J., 'The Spanish and Portuguese Reconquest, 1095–1492', in

Kenneth M. Setton (ed.), *A History of the Crusades* (Philadelphia and Madison, 6 vols., 1955–89) 3: *The Fourteenth and Fifteenth Centuries*, ed. Harry W. Hazard, pp. 396–456.

Bonnassie, Pierre, *La Catalogne de milieu du Xe à la fin du XIe siècle* (2 vols., Toulouse, 1975).

Boockmann, Hartmut, *Der Deutsche Orden* (Munich, 1981).

Born, Martin, *Geographie der ländlichen Siedlungen 1: Die Genese der Siedlungsformen in Mitteleuropa* (Stuttgart, 1977).

Borst, Arno (ed.), *Das Rittertum im Mittelalter* (*Wege der Forschung* 349, Darmstadt, 1976).

Boswell, John, *The Royal Treasure: Muslim Communities under the Crown of Aragon in the Fourteenth Century* (New Haven, 1977).

Bouchard, Constance B., 'Family Structure and Family Consciousness among the Aristocracy in the Ninth to the Eleventh Centuries', *Francia* 14 (1987), pp. 639–58.

Bradley, John, 'Planned Anglo-Norman Towns in Ireland', in H. B. Clarke and Anngret Simms (eds.), *The Comparative History of Urban Origins in Non-Roman Europe* (*British Archaeological Reports, International Series* 255, 2 vols., Oxford, 1985) 2, pp. 411–67.

Brand, Paul, 'Ireland and the Literature of the Early Common Law', *The Irish Jurist*, n.s., 16 (1981), pp. 95–113.

Bresc, Henri, 'Féodalité coloniale en terre d'Islam: La Sicile (1070–1240)', in *Structures féodales et féodalisme dans l'Occident mediterranéen (Xe–XIIIe s.)* (Paris, 1980), pp. 631–47.

Brooke, Christopher, 'The Composition of the Chapter of St Paul's, 1086–1163', *Cambridge Historical Journal* 10 (1951), pp. 111–32.

Brown, R. A., H. M. Colvin and A. J. Taylor, *The History of the King's Works: The Middle Ages* (2 vols., London, 1963).

Bryce, W. Moir, *The Scottish Grey Friars* (2 vols., Edinburgh and London, 1909).

Bullock-Davies, Constance, *Professional Interpreters and the Matter of Britain* (Cardiff, 1966).

Burns, Robert I., *The Crusader Kingdom of Valencia: Reconstruction on a Thirteenth-Century Frontier* (2 vols., Cambridge, Mass., 1967).

idem, *Islam under the Crusaders: Colonial Survival in the Thirteenth-Century Kingdom of Valencia* (Princeton, 1973).

Bushe-Fox, J. P., *Old Sarum* (London, etc., 1930).

Butler, Richard, *Some Notices of the Castle and of the Ecclesiastical Buildings of Trim* (Trim, 1835).

Cahen, Claude, *Le régime féodale d'Italie normande* (Paris, 1940).

idem, 'Un texte peu connu relatif au commerce oriental d'Amalfi au Xe siècle', *Archivio storico per le province napoletane*, n.s., 34 (1955 for 1953–4), pp. 61–6.

Callebaut, André, 'À propos du bienheureux Jean Duns Scot de Littledean', *Archivum Franciscanum Historicum* 24 (1931), pp. 305–29.

Cambridge Economic History of Europe 1: The Agrarian Life of the Middle Ages, ed. M. M. Postan (2nd ed., Cambridge, 1966).

Capitani, Ovidio, 'Specific Motivations and Continuing Themes in the Norman Chronicles of Southern Italy in the Eleventh and Twelfth Centuries', in *The Normans in Sicily and Southern Italy (Lincei Lectures 1974)* (Oxford, 1977), pp. 1–46.

Carus-Wilson, E. M., 'The First Half-Century of the Borough of Stratford-upon-Avon', *Economic History Review*, 2nd ser., 18 (1965), pp. 46–63.

Chalandon, Ferdinand, *Histoire de la domination normande en Italie et en Sicilie, 1009–1194* (2 vols., Paris, 1907).

Chibnall, Marjorie, *The World of Orderic Vitalis* (Oxford, 1984).

Christiansen, Eric, *The Northern Crusades* (London, 1980).

Clanchy, Michael, *From Memory to Written Record: England 1066–1307* (London and Cambridge, Mass., 1979).

Claude, Dietrich, *Geschichte des Erzbistums Magdeburg bis in das 12. Jahrhundert* (2 vols., *MF* 67, Cologne, 1972–5).

Contamine, Philippe, *War in the Middle Ages* (Eng. tr., Oxford, 1984).

Cowdrey, H. E. J., *Popes, Monks and Crusaders* (London, 1984).

Cramer, Helga, 'Die Herren von Wedel im Lande über der Oder: Besitz und Herrschaftsbildung bis 1402', *Jahrbuch für die Geschichte Mittel- und Ostdeutschlands* 18 (1969), pp. 63–129.

Curschmann, Fritz, *Die Diözese Brandenburg (Veröffentlichungen des Vereins für Geschichte der Mark Brandenburg*, Leipzig, 1906).

idem, Die deutschen Ortsnamen im Norddeutschen Kolonialgebiet (Stuttgart, 1910).

Darby, H. C., *Domesday England* (Cambridge, 1977).

Davies, Rees, *Lordship and Society in the March of Wales 1282–1400* (Oxford, 1978).

idem, Conquest, Coexistence and Change: Wales 1063–1415 (Oxford, 1987).

idem, Domination and Conquest: The Experience of Ireland, Scotland and Wales 1100–1300 (Cambridge, 1990).

idem, 'The Twilight of Welsh Law, 1284–1506', *History* 51 (1966), pp. 143–64.

idem, 'The Law of the March', *Welsh History Review* 5 (1970–71), pp. 1–30.

idem, 'Race Relations in Post-Conquest Wales', *Transactions of the Honourable Society of Cymmrodorion* (1974–5), pp. 32–56.

Davies, Wendy, *The Llandaff Charters* (Aberystwyth, 1979).

eadem, 'The Latin Charter Tradition in Western Britain, Brittany and Ireland in the Early Medieval Period', in Dorothy Whitelock *et al.* (eds.), *Ireland in Early Medieval Europe* (Cambridge, 1982), pp. 258–80.

Davis, R. H. C., *The Medieval Warhorse* (London, 1989).

Defourneaux, Marcelin, *Les Français en Espagne aux XIe et XIIe siècles* (Paris, 1949).

Delaborde, Henri-François, *Jean de Joinville et les seigneurs de Joinville* (Paris, 1894).

Dermigny, Louis, *La Chine et l'Occident: Le commerce à Canton au XVIIIe siècle 1719–1833* 1 (Paris, 1964).

Diccionario de historia eclesiástica de España, ed. Quintín Aldea Vaquero *et al.* (4 vols., Madrid, 1972–5).

Diccionario de la lengua española, ed. Real Academia de España (19th ed., Madrid, 1970).

(Contributions to a) Dictionary of the Irish Language (Royal Irish Academy, Dublin, 1913–76).

Dictionnaire d'histoire et de géographie ecclésiastiques (21 vols. to date, Paris, 1912–).

Dolley, Michael, *Medieval Anglo-Irish Coins* (London, 1972).

Domínguez Ortiz, Antonio, and Bernard Vincent, *Historia de los moriscos* (Madrid, 1978).

Down, Kevin, 'The Agricultural Economy of Colonial Ireland', in *New History of Ireland 2: Medieval Ireland, 1169–1534*, ed. Art Cosgrove (Oxford, 1987), pp. 450–81.

Duby, Georges, *Rural Economy and Country Life in the Medieval West* (Eng. tr., London, 1968).

idem, *The Early Growth of the European Economy* (Eng. tr., London, 1974).

idem, 'La diffusion du titre chevaleresque', in Philippe Contamine (ed.), *La noblesse au Moyen Age* (Paris, 1976), pp. 39–70.

idem, 'Lineage, Nobility and Knighthood', in his *The Chivalrous Society* (Eng. tr., London and Berkeley, 1977), pp. 59–80.

idem, 'The Origins of Knighthood', ibid., pp. 158–70.

idem, 'The Structure of Kinship and Nobility', ibid., pp. 134–48.

Duncan, A. A. M., *Scotland: The Making of the Kingdom* (Edinburgh, 1975).

Dvornik, Francis, *The Making of Central and Eastern Europe* (London, 1949).

Ebel, Wilhelm, *Lübisches Recht* (Lübeck, 1971).

Edbury, Peter, *The Kingdom of Cyprus and the Crusades 1191–1374* (Cambridge, 1991).

Eggert, O., *Geschichte Pommerns* 1 (Hamburg, 1974).

Ekwall, Eilert, *The Concise Oxford Dictionary of Place Names* (4th ed., Oxford, 1960).

Elliott, John, 'The Discovery of America and the Discovery of Man', *Proceedings of the British Academy* 58 (1972), pp. 101–25.

Ellmers, Detlev, 'The Cog of Bremen and Related Boats', in Sean McGrail (ed.), *The Archaeology of Medieval Ships and Harbours in Northern Europe* (*British Archaeological Reports, International Series* 66, Oxford, 1966), pp. 1–15.

Empey, C. A., 'Conquest and Settlement: Patterns of Anglo-Norman Settlement in North Munster and South Leinster', *Irish Social and Economic History Journal* 13 (1986), pp. 5–31.

Ennen, Edith, *Die europäische Stadt des Mittelalters* (4th ed., Göttingen, 1987).

Epperlein, Siegfried, *Bauernbedrückung und Bauernwiderstand im hohen Mittelalter:*

Zur Erforschung der Ursachen bäuerlichen Abwanderung nach Osten im 12. und 13. Jahrhundert (Berlin, 1960).

Eubel, Conrad, *Hierarchia catholica medii aevi 1 (1198–1431)* (2nd ed., Münster, 1913).

Evergates, Theodore, 'The Aristocracy of Champagne in the Mid-Thirteenth Century: A Quantitative Description', *Journal of Interdisciplinary History* 5 (1974–5), pp. 1–18.

Fedalto, Giorgio, *La Chiesa Latina in Oriente* (2nd ed., 3 vols., Verona, 1981).

Fehring, Günther, 'The Archaeology of Early Lübeck: The Relation between the Slavic and the German Settlement Sites', in H. B. Clarke and Anngret Simms (eds.), *The Comparative History of Urban Origins in Non-Roman Europe* (*British Archaeological Reports, International Series* 255, 2 vols., Oxford, 1985) 1, pp. 267–87.

Fellows Jensen, Gillian, 'The Names of the Lincolnshire Tenants of the Bishop of Lincoln *c.* 1225', in *Otium et negotium: Studies in Onomatology and Library Science presented to Olof von Feilitzen* (*Acta Bibliothecae Regiae Stockholmiensis* 16, Stockholm, 1973), pp. 86–95.

Fernández y González, Francisco, *Estado social y político de los mudéjares de Castilla* (Madrid, 1866).

Feyerabend, Liselotte, *Die Rigauer und Revaler Familiennamen im 14. und 15. Jahrhundert* (Cologne and Vienna, 1985).

Finó, J. F., *Forteresses de la France médiévale* (3rd ed., Paris, 1977).

idem, 'Notes sur la production du fer et la fabrication des armes en France au Moyen Age', *Gladius* 3 (1964), pp. 47–66.

idem, 'Machines de jet médiévales', *Gladius* 10 (1972), pp. 25–43.

Flanagan, Marie Therese, 'Monastic Charters from Irish Kings of the Twelfth and Thirteenth Centuries' (Unpublished MA thesis, University College, Dublin, 1972).

Fleischer, Wolfgang, *Die deutschen Personennamen* (Berlin, 1964).

idem, 'Die Namen der Dresdener Ratsmitglieder bis 1500', *Beiträge zur Namenforschung* 12 (1961), pp. 44–87.

Fliedner, Siegfried, and Rosemarie Pohl-Weber, *The Cog of Bremen* (Eng. tr., 3rd ed., Bremen, 1972).

Flori, Jean, *L'idéologie du glaive: Préhistoire de la chevalerie* (Geneva, 1983).

idem, *L'essor de la chevalerie* (Geneva, 1986).

Forey, A. J., 'The Will of Alfonso I of Aragon and Navarre', *Durham University Journal* 73 (1980), pp. 59–65.

idem, 'A Rejoinder' (to Elena Lourie, q.v.), ibid. 77 (1985), p. 173.

Fossier, Robert, *La terre et les hommes en Picardie jusqu'à la fin de XIIIe siècle* (2 vols., Paris and Louvain, 1968).

Fournier, G., *Le peuplement rural en Basse Auvergne durant le haut Moyen Age* (Paris, 1962).

Frame, Robin, *Colonial Ireland 1169–1369* (Dublin, 1981).

idem, The Political Development of the British Isles 1100–1400 (Oxford, 1990).

Freed, John, *The Friars and German Society in the Thirteenth Century* (Cambridge, Mass., 1977).

Freedman, Paul, *The Diocese of Vic* (New Brunswick, 1983).

Fügedi, Erik, *Castle and Society in Medieval Hungary (1000–1437)* (*Studia historica Academiae Scientiarum Hungaricae* 187, Budapest, 1986).

idem, 'Das mittelalterliche Königreich Ungarn als Gastland', in Walter Schlesinger (ed.), *Die deutsche Ostsiedlung als Problem der europäischen Geschichte* (*Vorträge und Forschungen* 18, Sigmaringen, 1975), pp. 471–507.

Gaibrois de Ballesteros, Mercedes, *Historia del reinado de Sancho IV de Castilla* (3 vols., Madrid, 1922–8).

Gallén, Jarl, *La province de Dacie de l'ordre des frères prêcheurs* (Helsingfors, 1946).

Gams, Pius Bonifatius, *Series episcoporum ecclesiae catholicae* (Regensburg, 1873).

Ganz, David, and Walter Goffart, 'Charters Earlier than 800 from French Collections', *Speculum* 65 (1990), pp. 906–32.

García-Gallo, Alfonso, 'Los Fueros de Toledo', *Anuario de historia del derecho español* 45 (1975), pp. 341–488.

Gautier-Dalché, Jean, 'Moulin à eau, seigneurie, communauté rurale dans le nord de l'Espagne (IXe–XIIe siècles)', in *Études de civilisation médiévale, IXe–XII siècles: Mélanges offerts à Edmond-René Labande* (Poitiers, 1974), pp. 337–49.

Génicot, Léopold, *L'économie rurale namuroise au Bas Moyen Age 2: Les hommes – la noblesse* (Louvain, 1960).

idem, La noblesse dans l'Occident médiéval (London, 1982).

Gibson, Margaret, *Lanfranc of Bec* (Oxford, 1978).

Girgensohn, Dieter, 'Dall'episcopato greco all'episcopato latino nell'Italia meridionale', in *La chiesa greca in Italia dall'VIII al XVI secolo* (3 vols., *Italia sacra* 20–22, Padua, 1973) 1, pp. 25–43.

Glamorgan County History 3: The Middle Ages, ed. T. B. Pugh (Cardiff, 1971).

Glasscock, R. E., 'England *circa* 1334', in H. C. Darby (ed.), *A New Historical Geography of England before 1600* (Cambridge, 1976), pp. 136–85.

idem, 'Land and People *c.* 1300', in *New History of Ireland 2: Medieval Ireland, 1169–1534*, ed. Art Cosgrove (Oxford, 1987), pp. 205–39.

Glick, Thomas F., *Islamic and Christian Spain in the Early Middle Ages* (Princeton, 1979).

Göckenjan, H., *Hilfsvölker und Grenzwächter im mittelalterlichen Ungarn* (Wiesbaden, 1972).

González, Julio, *El reino de Castilla en la epoca de Alfonso VIII* (3 vols., Madrid, 1960).

idem, Repoblación de Castilla la Nueva (2 vols., Madrid, 1975–6).

González Palencia, Angel, *Los mozárabes toledanos en los siglos XII y XIII* ('volumen preliminar' and 3 vols., Madrid, 1926–30).

Gonzálvez, Ramón, 'The Persistence of the Mozarabic Liturgy in Toledo after

AD 1080', in Bernard F. Reilly (ed.), *Santiago, Saint-Denis and Saint Peter: The Reception of the Roman Liturgy in León–Castile in 1080* (New York, 1985), pp. 157–85.

Goody, Jack, *The Development of the Family and Marriage in Europe* (Cambridge, 1983).

Górecki, Piotr, *Economy, Society and Lordship in Medieval Poland, 1100–1250* (New York and London, forthcoming).

Götting, W., and G. Grüll, *Burgen in Oberösterreich* (Wels, 1967).

Graus, František, *Die Nationenbildung der Westslawen im Mittelalter* (*Nationes* 3, Sigmaringen, 1980).

Gringmuth-Dallmer, Eike, *Die Entwicklung der frühgeschichtlichen Kulturlandschaft auf dem Territorium der DDR unter besonderer Berücksichtigung der Siedlungsgebiete* (Berlin, 1983).

Grosser historicher Weltatlas 2: Mittelalter, ed. Bayerische Schulbuch-Verlag (rev. ed., Munich, 1979).

Grundmann, Herbert, *Wahlkönigtum, Territorialpolitik und Ostbewegung im 13. und 14. Jahrhundert* (*Gebhardts Handbuch der deutschen Geschichte* 5, Munich, 1973).

Guilhiermoz, P., *Essai sur l'origine de la noblesse en France au Moyen Age* (Paris, 1902).

Gumowski, M., 'Pieczęcie książąt pomorskich', *Zapiski Towarzystwo naukowe w Toruniu* 14 (1950), pp. 23–66 (and plates I–XXI).

Guttmann, Bernhard, 'Die Germanisierung der Slawen in der Mark', *Forschungen zur brandenburgischen und preussischen Geschichte* 9 (1897), pp. 39 (395)–158 (514).

Gwynn, Aubrey, 'The Black Death in Ireland', *Studies* 24 (1935), pp. 25–42.

idem, 'Edward I and the Proposed Purchase of English Law for the Irish', *Transactions of the Royal Historical Society*, 5th ser., 10 (1960), pp. 111–27.

idem, and R. Neville Hadcock, *Medieval Religious Houses: Ireland* (London, 1970).

Hagen, William W., 'How Mighty the Junkers? Peasant Rents and Seigneurial Profits in Sixteenth-Century Brandenburg', *Past and Present* 108 (1985), pp. 80–116.

Hagenmeyer, Heinrich, *Chronologie de la première croisade 1094–1100* (reprint in one vol., Hildesheim and New York, 1973).

Hallam, H. E., *Settlement and Society: A Study of the Early Agrarian History of South Lincolnshire* (Cambridge, 1965).

idem (ed.), *The Agrarian History of England and Wales 2: 1042–1350* (Cambridge, 1988).

Hamann, Manfred, *Mecklenburgische Geschichte* (*MF* 51, Cologne, 1968).

Hamilton, Bernard, *The Latin Church in the Crusader States: The Secular Church* (London, 1980).

Hand, Geoffrey, *English Law in Ireland 1290–1324* (Cambridge, 1967).

idem, 'English Law in Ireland, 1172–1351', *Northern Ireland Legal Quarterly* 23 (1972), pp. 393–422.

Handbook of British Chronology, ed. E. B. Fryde *et al.* (3rd ed., London, 1986).

Harbison, Peter, 'Native Irish Arms and Armour in Medieval Gaelic Literature, 1170–1600', *The Irish Sword* 12 (1975–6), pp. 173–99, 270–84.

Harvey, L. P., *Islamic Spain 1250–1500* (Chicago, 1990).

Haskins, Charles Homer, 'England and Sicily in the Twelfth Century', *English Historical Review* 26 (1911), pp. 433–47, 641–65.

Haudricourt, André G., and Mariel Jean-Brunhes Delamarre, *L'homme et la charrue à travers le monde* (4th ed., Paris, 1955).

Haverkamp, Alfred, *Medieval Germany 1056–1273* (Eng. tr., Oxford, 1988).

Hay, Denys, *Europe: The Emergence of an Idea* (2nd ed., Edinburgh, 1968).

Heine, H. W., 'Ergebnisse und Probleme einer systematischen Aufnahme und Bearbeitung mittelalterlicher Wehranlagen zwischen junger Donau und westlichen Bodensee', *Château Gaillard* 8 (1976), pp. 121–34.

Helbig, Herbert, 'Die slawische Siedlung im sorbischen Gebiet', in Herbert Ludat (ed.), *Siedlung und Verfassung der Slawen zwischen Elbe, Saale und Oder* (Giessen, 1960), pp. 27–64.

Hellmann, Manfred, *Grundzüge der Geschichte Litauens und des lituauischen Volkes* (Darmstadt, 1966).

Hergueta, Narciso, 'El Fuero de Logroño: su extensión a otras poblaciónes', *Boletín de la Real Academia de la Historia* 50 (1907), pp. 321–2.

Herrmann, Joachim (ed.), *Die Slawen in Deutschland: Ein Handbuch* (new ed., Berlin, 1985).

Herrnbrodt, A., 'Stand der frühmittelalterlichen Mottenforschung im Rheinland', *Château Gaillard* 1 (1964 for 1962), pp. 77–100.

Heyd, Wilhelm, *Histoire du commerce du Levant au Moyen Age* (2 vols., Leipzig, 1885–6).

Higounet, Charles, *Die deutsche Ostsiedlung im Mittelalter* (Berlin, 1986).

idem, 'Les saints mérovingiens d'Aquitaine dans la toponymie', in his *Paysages et villages neufs du Moyen Age* (Bordeaux, 1975), pp. 67–75.

idem, 'Mouvements de population dans le Midi de la France du XIe siècle d'après les noms de personne et de lieu', ibid., pp. 417–37.

Hill, D. R., 'Trebuchets', *Viator* 4 (1973), pp. 99–114.

Hillebrand, Werner, *Besitz- und Standesverhältnisse des Osnabrücker Adels bis 1300* (Göttingen, 1962).

Hillgarth, J. N., *The Spanish Kingdoms 1250–1516* (2 vols., Oxford, 1976–8).

Hoffmann, Karl, 'Die Stadtgründungen Mecklenburg-Schwerins in der Kolonisationszeit vom 12. bis zum 14. Jahrhundert', *Jahrbuch für mecklenburgische Geschichte* 94 (1930), pp. 1–200.

Hoffmann, Richard, *Land, Liberties and Lordship in a Late Medieval Countryside: Agrarian Structures and Change in the Duchy of Wrocław* (Philadelphia, 1989).

Hollister, C. Warren, *The Military Organization of Norman England* (Oxford, 1965).

Holt, James C., 'Feudal Society and the Family in Early Medieval England',

Transactions of the Royal Historical Society, 5th ser., 32 (1982), pp. 193–212; 33 (1983), pp. 193–220; 34 (1984), pp. 1–25; 35 (1985), pp. 1–28.

Hopp, Dora Grete, *Die Zunft und die Nichtdeutschen im Osten, insbesondere in der Mark Brandenburg* (Marburg/Lahn, 1954).

Hugelmann, Karl Gottfried, 'Die Rechtsstellung der Wenden im deutschen Mittelalter', *Zeitschrift der Savigny-Stiftung für Rechtsgeschichte, Germanistische Abteilung* 58 (1938), pp. 214–56.

Hurst, J. G., 'The Changing Medieval Village in England', in J. A. Raftis (ed.), *Pathways to Medieval Peasants* (Toronto, 1981), pp. 27–62.

Janssen, Walter, 'Dorf und Dorfformen des 7. bis 12. Jahrhunderts im Lichte neuer Ausgrabungen in Mittel- und Nordeuropa', in Herbert Jankuhn *et al.* (eds.), *Das Dorf der Eisenzeit und des frühen Mittelalters (Abhandlungen der Akadamie der Wissenschaft in Göttingen, philosopisch-historische Klasse*, 3rd ser., 101, 1977), pp. 285–356.

Jegorov, Dmitrii, *Die Kolonisation Mecklenburgs im 13. Jahrhundert* (German tr., 2 vols., Breslau, 1930; original Russian ed., 1915).

Johansen, Paul, 'Eine Riga-Wisby-Urkunde des 13. Jahrhunderts', *Zeitschrift des Vereins für Lübeckische Geschichte und Altertumskunde* 38 (1958), pp. 93–108.

idem, and Heinz von zur Mühlen, *Deutsch und Undeutsch im mittelalterlichen und frühneuzeitlichen Reval* (Cologne and Vienna, 1973).

Jones, Gwyn, *A History of the Vikings* (Oxford, 1968).

Jones Hughes, T., 'Town and *Baile* in Irish Place-Names', in Nicholas Stephens and Robin E. Glasscock (eds.), *Irish Geographical Studies in Honour of E. Estyn Evans* (Belfast, 1970), pp. 244–58.

Jordan, Karl, *Die Bistumsgründungen Heinrichs des Löwen* (*MGH, Schriften* 3, Leipzig, 1939).

Joris, André, *Huy et sa charte de franchise, 1066* (Brussels, 1966).

Kaestner, Walter, 'Mittelniederdeutsche Elemente in der polnischen und kaschubischen Lexik', in P. Sture Ureland (ed.), *Sprachkontakt in der Hanse . . . Akten des 7. Internationalen Symposions über Sprachkontakt in Europa, Lübeck 1986* (Tübingen, 1987), pp. 135–62.

Kaindl, Raimund Friedrich, *Geschichte der Deutschen in den Karpathenländern* (3 vols., Gotha, 1907–11).

Keefe, Thomas K., *Feudal Assessments and the Political Community under Henry II and His Sons* (Berkeley, etc., 1983).

Kejř, Jiři, 'Die Anfänge der Stadtverfassung und des Stadtrechts in den Böhmischen Ländern', in Walter Schlesinger (ed.), *Die deutsche Ostsiedlung des Mittelalters als Problem der europäischen Geschichte* (*Vorträge und Forschungen* 18, Sigmaringen, 1975), pp. 439–70.

Kleber, Hermann, 'Pèlerinage – vengeance – conquête: la conception de la première croisade dans le cycle de Graindor de Douai', in *Au carrefour des routes d'Europe:*

La chanson de geste (Xe Congrès international de la Société Rencesvals pour l'étude des épopées romanes, 2 vols., Aix-en-Provence, 1987) 2, pp. 757–75.

Knoch, Peter, *Studien zu Albert von Aachen* (Stuttgart, 1966).

Knoll, Paul, 'Economic and Political Institutions on the Polish–German Frontier in the Middle Ages: Action, Reaction, Interaction', in Robert Bartlett and Angus MacKay (eds.), *Medieval Frontier Societies* (Oxford, 1989), pp. 151–74.

Knott, Eleanor, *Irish Classical Poetry* (*Irish Life and Culture* 6, Dublin, 1957).

Kosminsky, E. A., *Studies in the Agrarian History of England in the Thirteenth Century* (Eng. tr., Oxford, 1956).

Krabbo, Hermann, and Georg Winter, *Regesten der Markgrafen von Brandenburg aus Askanischem Hause* (Leipzig, Munich and Berlin, 1910–55).

Kuhn, Walter, *Vergleichende Untersuchungen zur mittelalterlichen Ostsiedlung* (Cologne and Vienna, 1973).

idem, 'Flämische und fränkische Hufe als Leitformen der mittelalterlichen Ostsiedlung', ibid., pp. 1–51.

idem, 'Bauernhofgrossen in der mittelalterlichen Nordostsiedlung', ibid., pp. 53–111.

idem, 'Der Pflug als Betriebseinheit in Altpreussen', ibid., pp. 113–40.

idem, 'Der Haken in Altpreussen', ibid., pp. 141–71.

idem, 'Ostsiedlung und Bevölkerungsdichte', ibid., pp. 173–210.

idem, 'Die Siedlerzahlen der deutschen Ostsiedlung', in *Studium Sociale. Karl Valentin Müller dargebracht* (Cologne and Opladen, 1963), pp. 131–54.

idem, 'German Town Foundations of the Thirteenth Century in Western Pomerania', in H. B. Clarke and Anngret Simms (eds.), *The Comparative History of Urban Origins in Non-Roman Europe* (*British Archaeological Reports, International Series* 255, 2 vols., Oxford, 1985) 2, pp. 547–80.

Latinitatis Medii Aevi Lexicon Bohemiae: Slovník Středověké Latiny v Českých Zemích (Prague, 1977–).

Le Patourel, John, *The Norman Empire* (Oxford, 1976).

Lea, Henry Charles, *The Moriscos of Spain* (London, 1901).

Lennard, Reginald, *Rural England, 1086–1135: A Study of Social and Agrarian Conditions* (Oxford, 1959).

Lewis, Bernard, *The Muslim Discovery of Europe* (New York and London, 1982).

Lewis, Suzanne, *The Art of Matthew Paris in the 'Chronica Majora'* (Berkeley, etc., 1987).

Lexicon für Theologie und Kirche, ed. Josef Höfer and Karl Rahner (2nd ed., 11 vols., Freiburg im Breisgau, 1957–67).

Leyser, Karl, 'The German Aristocracy from the Ninth to the Early Twelfth Century: A Historical and Cultural Sketch', *Past and Present* 41 (1968), pp. 25–53, repr. in his *Medieval Germany and its Neighbours* (London, 1982), pp. 161–89.

Lloyd, J. E., *A History of Wales* (3rd ed., 2 vols., London, 1939).

Lomax, Derek W., *The Reconquest of Spain* (London, 1978).

Long, J., 'Dermot and the Earl: Who Wrote the Song?', *Proceedings of the Royal Irish Academy* 75C (1975), pp. 263–72.

Longnon, Jean, 'L'organisation de l'église d'Athènes par Innocent III', in *Mémorial Louis Petit: Mélanges d'histoire et d'archéologie byzantines* (*Archives de l'Orient chrétien* 1, Bucharest, 1948), pp. 336–46.

Lotter, Friedrich, 'The Scope and Effectiveness of Imperial Jewry Law in the High Middle Ages', *Jewish History* 4 (1989), pp. 31–58.

Loud, Graham, 'How "Norman" was the Norman Conquest of Southern Italy?', *Nottingham Medieval Studies* 25 (1981), pp. 13–34.

Lourie, Elena, 'A Society Organized for War: Medieval Spain', *Past and Present* 35 (1966), pp. 54–76.

eadem, 'The Will of Alfonso "El Batallador", King of Aragon and Navarre: A Reassessment', *Speculum* 50 (1975), pp. 635–51.

eadem, 'The Will of Alfonso I of Aragon and Navarre: A Reply to Dr Forey', *Durham University Journal* 77 (1985), pp. 165–72.

Loyd, Lewis C., *The Origins of Some Anglo-Norman Families*, ed. C. T. Clay and D. C. Douglas (*Harleian Society Publications* 103, 1951).

Luz Alonso, María, 'La perduración del Fuero Juzgo y el Derecho de los castellanos de Toledo', *Anuario de historia del derecho español* 48 (1978), pp. 335–77.

Lydon, James, 'The Middle Nation', in *idem* (ed.), *The English in Medieval Ireland* (Dublin, 1984), pp. 1–26.

McErlean, Thomas, 'The Irish Townland System of Landscape Organization', in Terence Reeves-Smyth and Fred Hamond (eds.), *Landscape Archaeology in Ireland* (*British Archaeological Reports*, *British Series* 116, Oxford, 1983), pp. 315–39.

MacKay, Angus, *Spain in the Middle Ages: From Frontier to Empire, 1000–1500* (London, 1977).

Mackensen, Lutz, 'Zur livländischen Reimchronik', in his *Zur deutschen Literatur Altlivlands* (Würzburg, 1961), pp. 21–58.

McNeill, T. E., *Anglo-Norman Ulster: The History and Archaeology of an Irish Barony 1177–1400* (Edinburgh, 1980).

MacNiocaill, Gearóid, 'The Interaction of Laws', in James Lydon (ed.), *The English in Medieval Ireland* (Dublin, 1984), pp. 105–17.

Mann, James, *Wallace Collection Catalogues: European Arms and Armour* (2 vols., London, 1962).

Martin, Geoffrey, 'Plantation Boroughs in Medieval Ireland, with a Handlist of Boroughs to *c.* 1500', in David Harkness and Mary O'David (eds.), *The Town in Ireland* (*Historical Studies* 13, Belfast, 1981), pp. 25–53.

Mason, J. F. A., 'Roger de Montgomery and his Sons (1067–1102)', *Transactions of the Royal Historical Society*, 5th ser., 13 (1963), pp. 1–28.

Mason, W. H. Monck, *The History and Antiquities of the Collegiate and Cathedral Church of St Patrick* (Dublin, 1820).

Mayer, Hans Eberhard, *Bistümer, Klöster und Stifte im Königreich Jerusalem* (*MGH, Schriften* 26, Stuttgart, 1977).

Ménager, Leon-Robert, 'Inventaire des familles normandes et franques emigrées en Italie méridionale et en Sicile (XIe–XIIe siècles)', in *Roberto il Guiscard e il suo tempo* (*Fonti e studi del Corpus membranarum italicarum*, Centro di studi normanno-suevi, Università degli studi di Bari, Rome, 1975), pp. 259–387.

Menzel, Josef Joachim, *Die schlesischen Lokationsurkunden des 13. Jahrhunderts* (Würzburg, 1977).

Merton, A., *Die Buchmalerei in St Gallen* (Leipzig, 1912).

Metcalf, D. M. (ed.), *Coinage in Medieval Scotland (1100–1600)* (*British Archaeological Reports* 45, Oxford, 1977).

Michel, Anton, *Humbert und Kerullarios* (2 vols., Paderborn, 1924–30).

Miller, Edward, and John Hatcher, *Medieval England: Rural Society and Economic Change 1086–1348* (London, 1978).

Miquel, André, *La géographie humaine du monde musulman jusqu'au milieu du 11e siècle 2: Géographie arabe et représentation du monde: La terre et l'étranger* (Paris, 1975).

Morgan, M. R., *The Chronicle of Ernoul and the Continuations of William of Tyre* (Oxford, 1973).

Mundy, John, *Europe in the High Middle Ages* (London, 1973, 2nd ed., 1991).

Murray, Alan V., 'The Origins of the Frankish Nobility in the Kingdom of Jerusalem, 1100–1118', *Mediterranean Historical Review* 4/2 (1989), pp. 281–300.

Musset, Lucien, 'Problèmes militaires du monde scandinave (VIIe–XIIe s.)', in *Ordinamenti militari in Occidente nell'alto medioevo* (*Settimane di studio del Centro italiano di studi sull'alto medioevo* 15, 2 vols., Spoleto, 1968) 1, pp. 229–91.

idem, 'L'aristocratie normande au XIe siècle', in Philippe Contamine (ed.), *La noblesse au Moyen Age* (Paris, 1976), pp. 71–96.

Nekuda, Vladimir, 'Zum Stand der Wüstungsforschung in Mähren (ČSSR)', *Zeitschrift für Archäologie des Mittelalters* 1 (1973), pp. 31–57.

New History of Ireland 2: Medieval Ireland, 1169–1534, ed. Art Cosgrove (Oxford, 1987).

Nicholls, Kenneth, *Gaelic and Gaelicized Ireland in the Middle Ages* (Dublin, 1972).

idem, 'Anglo-French Ireland and After', *Peritia* 1 (1982), pp. 370–403.

Nicholson, Ranald, 'A Sequel to Edward Bruce's Invasion of Ireland', *Scottish Historical Review* 42 (1963), pp. 30–40.

Nickel, H., *et al.*, *The Art of Chivalry: European Arms and Armour from the Metropolitan Museum of Art* (New York, 1982).

Nitz, Hans-Jürgen, 'The Church as Colonist: The Benedictine Abbey of Lorsch and Planned *Waldhufen* Colonization in the Odenwald', *Journal of Historical Geography* 9 (1983), pp. 105–26.

idem (ed.), *Historisch-genetische Siedlungsforschung* (Darmstadt, 1974).

O Corráin, Donnchá, 'Nationality and Kingship in Pre-Norman Ireland', in T. W. Moody (ed.), *Nationality and the Pursuit of National Independence* (*Historical Studies* 11, Belfast, 1978), pp. 1–35.

O'Dwyer, Barry, *The Conspiracy of Mellifont, 1216–1231* (Dublin, 1970).

O'Sullivan, William, *The Earliest Anglo-Irish Coinage* (Dublin, 1964).

Orpen, Goddard H., *Ireland under the Normans, 1169–1333* (4 vols., Oxford, 1911–20).

Otway-Ruthven, A. J., *A History of Medieval Ireland* (2nd ed., London, 1980).

eadem, 'The Request of the Irish for English Law, 1277–80', *Irish Historical Studies* 6 (1948–9), pp. 261–70.

eadem, 'Knight Service in Ireland', *Journal of the Royal Society of Antiquaries of Ireland* 89 (1959), pp. 1–15.

eadem, 'Knights' Fees in Kildare, Leix and Offaly', *Journal of the Royal Society of Antiquaries of Ireland* 91 (1961), pp. 163–81.

eadem, 'The Character of Norman Settlement in Ireland', in J. L. McCracken (ed.), *Historical Studies* 5 (London, 1965), pp. 75–84.

Painter, Sidney, 'English Castles in the Early Middle Ages: Their Numbers, Location, and Legal Position', *Speculum* 10 (1935), pp. 321–32.

Palme, S. U., 'Les impôts, le Statut d'Alsno et la formation des ordres en Suède (1250–1350)', in R. Mousnier (ed.), *Problèmes de stratification sociale* (Paris, 1968), pp. 55–66.

Parisse, Michel, 'La conscience chrétienne des nobles aux XIe et XIIe siècles', in *La cristianità dei secoli XI e XII in occidente: Coscienza e strutture di una società* (*Miscellanea del Centro di studi medioevali* 10, Milan, 1983), pp. 259–80.

Parry-Williams, T. H., *The English Element in Welsh* (*Cymmrodorion Record Series* 10, London, 1923).

Patze, Hans, and Walter Schlesinger, *Geschichte Thüringens* 2/1 (*MF* 48, Cologne and Vienna, 1974).

Peñalosa Esteban-Infantes, Margarita, *La fundación de Ciudad Real* (Ciudad Real, 1955).

Penners, Theodor, *Untersuchungen über die Herkunft der Stadtbewohner im Deutsch-Ordensland Preussen bis in die Zeit um 1400* (Leipzig, 1942).

Perroy, Edouard, *L'Angleterre et le Grand Schisme d'Occident* (Paris, 1933).

idem, 'Social Mobility among the French *noblesse* in the Later Middle Ages', *Past and Present* 21 (1962), pp. 25–38.

Petersohn, Jürgen, *Der südliche Ostseeraum im kirchlich-politischen Kräftespiel des Reichs, Polens und Dänemarks vom 10. bis 13. Jahrhundert* (Cologne and Vienna, 1979).

Pollock, Frederick, and Frederic William Maitland, *The History of English Law before the Time of Edward I* (2nd ed., 2 vols., Cambridge, 1898, reissued 1968).

Porteous, John, 'Crusader Coinage with Latin or Greek Inscriptions', in Kenneth M. Setton (ed.), *A History of the Crusades* (Philadelphia and Madison, 6 vols., 1955–89) 6: *The Impact of the Crusades on Europe*, ed. Harry W. Hazard, pp. 354–420.

Postan, M. M., *The Medieval Economy and Society* (London, 1972).

Powers, James F., *A Society Organized for War: The Iberian Municipal Militias in the Central Middle Ages, 1000–1284* (Berkeley and Los Angeles, 1988).

Prange, Wolfgang, *Siedlungsgeschichte des Landes Lauenburg im Mittelalter* (Neumünster, 1960).

Prawer, Joshua, *Crusader Institutions* (Oxford, 1980).

idem, 'Social Classes in the Latin Kingdom: The Franks', in Kenneth Setton (ed.), *A History of the Crusades* (Philadelphia and Madison, 6 vols., 1955–89) 5: *The Impact of the Crusades on the Near East*, ed. Norman Zacour and Harry Hazard, pp. 117–92.

Prestwich, Michael, *War, Politics and Finance under Edward I* (London, 1972).

Pryor, John H., *Geography, Technology and War: Studies in the Maritime History of the Mediterranean, 649–1571* (Cambridge, 1988).

Ralegh Radford, C. A., 'Later Pre-Conquest Boroughs and their Defences', *Medieval Archaeology* 14 (1970), pp. 83–103.

Rees, William, *South Wales and the March 1284–1415* (Oxford, 1924).

Reilly, Bernard F., *The Kingdom of León–Castilla under King Alfonso VI, 1065–1109* (Princeton, 1988).

Reinerth, Karl, 'Siebenbürger und Magdeburger Flandrenses-Urkunden aus dem 12. Jahrhundert', *Südostdeutsches Archiv* 8 (1965), pp. 26–56.

Ribbe, Wolfgang (ed.), *Das Havelland im Mittelalter* (Berlin, 1987).

Richard, Jean, 'Les listes des seigneuries dans le livre de Jean d'Ibelin', *Revue historique de droit français et étranger* 32 (1954), pp. 565–77.

idem, 'The Political and Ecclesiastical Organization of the Crusader States', in Kenneth M. Setton (ed.), *A History of the Crusades* (Philadelphia and Madison, 6 vols., 1955–89) 5: *The Impact of the Crusades on the Near East*, ed. Norman P. Zacour and Harry W. Hazard, pp. 193–250.

Richter, Michael, *Sprache und Gesellschaft im Mittelalter* (Stuttgart, 1979).

Ridyard, Susan, '*Condigna veneratio*: Post-Conquest Attitudes to the Saints of the Anglo-Saxons', in *Anglo-Norman Studies* 9 (1986), ed. R. Allen Brown, pp. 179–206.

Riley-Smith, Jonathan, *The Knights of St John in Jerusalem and Cyprus c. 1050–1310* (London, 1967).

Ritchie, R. L. G., *The Normans in Scotland* (Edinburgh, 1954).

Roberts, Brian K., *The Green Villages of County Durham* (Durham, 1977).

Röhricht, Reinhold, *Beiträge zur Geschichte der Kreuzzüge 2: Deutsche Pilger- und Kreuzfahrten nach dem heiligen Lande (700–1300)* (Berlin, 1878).

Rollason, David, *Saints and Relics in Anglo-Saxon England* (Oxford, 1989).

Round, J. H., *The King's Serjeants and Officers of State* (London, 1911).

Rousset, Paul, 'La notion de Chrétienté aux XIe et XIIe siècles', *Le Moyen Age* 4th ser., 18 (1963), pp. 191–203.

Rupp, Jean, *L'idée de Chrétienté dans la pensée pontificale des origines à Innocent III* (Paris, 1939).

Russell, Josiah Cox, *British Medieval Population* (Albuquerque, 1948).

Rutkowska-Plachcinska, Anna, 'Les prénoms dans le sud de la France aux XIIIe et XIVe siècles', *Acta Poloniae Historica* 49 (1984), pp. 5–42.

Salch, C. L., 'La protection symbolique de la porte au Moyen Age dans les châteaux-forts alsaciens', in *Hommage à Geneviève Chevrier et Alain Geslan: Études médiévales* (Strasbourg, 1975), pp. 39–44.

Santifaller, Leo, *Beiträge zur Geschichte des Lateinischen Patriarchats von Konstantinopel (1204–1261) und der venezianischen Urkunden* (Weimar, 1938).

Schlesinger, Walter (ed.), *Die deutsche Ostsiedlung als Problem der europäischen Geschichte* (*Vorträge und Forschungen* 18, Sigmaringen, 1975).

idem, 'Flemmingen und Kühren: Zur Siedlungsform niederländischer Siedlungen des 12. Jahrhunderts im mitteldeutschen Osten', ibid., pp. 263–309.

Schmalstieg, William R., *An Old Prussian Grammar* (University Park, Pa., 1974).

idem, *Studies in Old Prussian* (University Park, Pa., 1976).

Schmid, Karl, 'Zur Problematik von Familie, Sippe und Geschlecht, Haus und Dynastie beim mittelalterlichen Adel', *Zeitschrift für die Geschichte des Oberrheins* 105 (1957), pp. 1–62.

idem, 'The Structure of the Nobility in the Earlier Middle Ages', in Timothy Reuter (ed.), *The Medieval Nobility* (Amsterdam, etc., 1978), pp. 37–59.

Schmidt, Eberhard, *Die Mark Brandenburg unter den Askaniern (1134–1320)* (*MF* 71, Cologne and Vienna, 1973).

Schneidmüller, Bernd, *Nomen patriae: Die Entstehung Frankreichs in der politisch-geographischen Terminologie (10.–13. Jahrhundert)* (Sigmaringen, 1987).

Schultze, Johannes, *Die Mark Brandenburg 1: Entstehung und Entwicklung unter den askanischen Markgrafen (bis 1319)* (Berlin, 1961).

Schulze, Hans K., *Adelsherrschaft und Landesherrschaft: Studien zur Verfassungs- und Besitzgeschichte der Altmark, des ostsächsischen Raumes und des hannoverschen Wendlands im hohen Mittelalter* (*MF* 29, Cologne and Graz, 1963).

idem, 'Die Besiedlung der Mark Brandenburg im hohen und späten Mittelalter', *Jahrbuch für die Geschichte Mittel- und Ostdeutschlands* 28 (1979), pp. 42–178.

idem, '*Slavica lingua penitus intermissa*: Zur Verbot des Wendischen als Gerichtssprache', in *Europa slavica – Europa orientalis: Festschrift für H. Ludat* (Berlin, 1980), pp. 354–67.

Schunemann, K., *Die Deutsche in Ungarn bis zum 12. Jahrhundert* (Berlin, 1923).

Schwarz, Ernst, 'Die Volkstumsverhältnisse in den Städten Böhmens und Mährens vor den Hussitenkriegen', *Bohemia: Jahrbuch des Collegium Carolinum* 2 (1961), pp. 27–111.

Shields, H. E., 'The Walling of New Ross – a Thirteenth-Century Poem in French', *Long Room* 12–13 (1975–6), pp. 24–33.

Simms, Katharine, 'Warfare in the Medieval Gaelic Lordships', *The Irish Sword* 12 (1975–6), pp. 98–108.

Słownik Łaciny Średniowiecznej w Polsce 1, ed. Mariana Plezi (Wrocław, etc., 1953–8).

Smith, Julia, 'Oral and Written: Saints, Miracles and Relics in Brittany, *c.* 850–1250', *Speculum* 65 (1990), pp. 309–43.

Southern, Richard W., *Western Society and the Church in the Middle Ages* (Harmondsworth, 1970).

Sprandel, Rolf, *Das mittelalterliche Zahlungssystem nach Hansisch-Nordischen Quellen des 13.–15. Jahrhunderts* (Stuttgart, 1975).

Spufford, Peter, *Money and its Use in Medieval Europe* (Cambridge, 1988).

Stenton, Frank, *The First Century of English Feudalism 1066–1166* (2nd ed., Oxford, 1961).

idem, et al., The Bayeux Tapestry (London, 1957).

Stephenson, David, *The Governance of Gwynedd* (Cardiff, 1984).

Stewart, Ian, 'The Volume of the Early Scottish Coinage', in D. M. Metcalf (ed.), *Coinage in Medieval Scotland (1100–1600) (British Archaeological Reports* 45, Oxford, 1977), pp. 65–72.

Stringer, K. J., *Earl David of Huntingdon, 1152–1219: A Study in Anglo-Scottish History* (Edinburgh, 1985).

idem, 'The Charters of David, Earl of Huntingdon and Lord of Garioch: A Study in Anglo-Scottish Diplomatic', in *idem* (ed.), *Essays on the Nobility of Medieval Scotland* (Edinburgh, 1985), pp. 72–101.

Struve, Karl Wilhelm, 'Die slawischen Burgen in Wagrien', *Offa* 17–18 (1959–61), pp. 57–108.

Suchodolski, Stanislaw, *Początki mennictwa w Europie środkowej, wschodniej i północnej* (Wrocław, 1971) (English summary, pp. 249–57).

idem, Mennictwo Polskie w XI i XII wieku (Wrocław, etc., 1973) (English summary, pp. 144–52).

Suhle, Arthur, *Deutsche Münz- und Geldgeschichte von den Anfängen bis zum 15. Jahrhundert* (2nd ed., Berlin, 1964).

Székely, György, 'Wallons et Italiens en Europe centrale aux XIe–XVIe siècles', *Annales Universitatis Scientiarum Budapestinensis de Rolando Eötuös Nominatae*, sectio historica 6 (1964), pp. 3–71.

Teuchert, Hermann, *Die Sprachreste der niederländischen Siedlungen des 12. Jahrhunderts* (2nd ed., *MF* 70, Cologne and Vienna, 1972).

Thiriet, Freddy, *La Romanie vénitienne au Moyen Age: Le développement et l'exploitation du domaine colonial vénitien (XII–XIV s.)* (Paris, 1959).

Thordemann, B., *Armour from the Battle of Wisby 1361* (2 vols., Stockholm, 1939).

Tidick, Erika, 'Beiträge zur Geschichte der Kirchenpatrozinien im Deutsch-Ordensland Preussen bis 1525', *Zeitschrift für die Geschichte und Altertumskunde Ermlands* 22 (1926), pp. 343–464.

Titow, J. Z., *English Rural Society 1200–1350* (London, 1969).

idem, Winchester Yields: A Study in Medieval Agricultural Productivity (Cambridge, 1972).

idem, 'Some Evidence of the Thirteenth-Century Population Increase', *Economic History Review*, 2nd ser., 14 (1961), pp. 218–24.

Torres Fontes, Juan, 'Moros, judíos y conversos en la regencia de Don Fernando de Antequera', *Cuadernos de historia de España* 31–2 (1960), pp. 60–97.

Tout, T. F., 'The Fair of Lincoln and the "Histoire de Guillaume le Maréchal"', in his *Collected Papers* (3 vols., Manchester, 1932–4) 2, pp. 191–220.

Trawkowski, Stanisław, 'Die Rolle der deutschen Dorfkolonisation und des deutschen Rechts in Polen im 13. Jahrhundert', in Walter Schlesinger (ed.), *Die deutsche Ostsiedlung des Mittelalters als Problem der europäischen Geschichte* (*Vorträge und Forschungen* 18, Sigmaringen, 1975), pp. 349–68.

Turner, Ralph V., *Men Raised from the Dust: Administrative Service and Upward Mobility in Angevin England* (Philadelphia, 1988).

Tyerman, Christopher, *England and the Crusades, 1095–1588* (Chicago, 1988).

Tylecote, R. F., *Metallurgy in Archaeology* (London, 1962).

Usseglio, Leopoldo, *I marchesi di Monferrato in Italia ed in oriente durante i secoli XII e XIII*, ed. Carlo Patrucco (2 vols., *Bibliotheca della Società storica subalpina* 100–101, Turin, 1926).

Victoria County History of Shropshire 2 (London, 1973).

Vlasto, A. P., *The Entry of the Slavs into Christendom* (Cambridge, 1970).

Vogel, Werner, *Der Verbleib der wendischen Bevölkerung in der Mark Brandenburg* (Berlin, 1960).

von Müller, Adriaan, 'Zum hochmittelalterlichen Besiedlung des Teltow (Brandenburg): Stand eines mehrjährigen archäologisch-siedlungsgeschichtlichen Forschungsprogrammes', in Walter Schlesinger (ed.), *Die deutsche Ostsiedlung als Problem der europäischen Geschichte* (*Vorträge und Forschungen* 18, Sigmaringen, 1975), pp. 311–32.

Wade-Martins, Peter, 'The Origins of Rural Settlement in East Anglia', in P. J. Fowler (ed.), *Recent Work in Rural Archaeology* (Bradford-upon-Avon, 1975), pp. 137–57.

idem, 'The Archaeology of Medieval Rural Settlement in East Anglia', in Michael Aston *et al.* (eds.), *The Rural Settlements of Medieval England* (Oxford, 1989), pp. 149–65.

Waley, Daniel, *The Italian City Republics* (London, 1969).

Walsh, Katherine, *A Fourteenth-Century Scholar and Primate: Richard FitzRalph in Oxford, Avignon and Armagh* (Oxford, 1981).

Watson, Andrew M., 'Towards Denser and More Continuous Settlement: New Crops and Farming Techniques in the Early Middle Ages', in J. A. Raftis (ed.), *Pathways to Medieval Peasants* (Toronto, 1981), pp. 65–82.

Watt, J. A., *The Church and the Two Nations in Medieval Ireland* (Cambridge, 1970).

idem, *The Church in Medieval Ireland* (Dublin, 1972).

idem, 'English Law and the Irish Church: The Reign of Edward I', in *idem*, J. B. Morrall and F. X. Martin (eds.), *Medieval Studies presented to A. Gwynn* (Dublin, 1961), pp. 133–67.

Wenskus, Reinhard, *Stammesbildung und Verfassung: Das Werden der frühmittelalterlichen gentes* (Cologne and Graz, 1961).

idem, *Ausgewählte Aufsätze zum frühen und preussischen Mittelalter*, ed. Hans Patze (Sigmaringen, 1986).

idem, 'Das Ordensland Preussen als Territorialstaat des 14. Jahrhunderts', in Hans Patze (ed.), *Der Deutsche Territorialstaat im 14. Jahrhundert* 1 (*Vorträge und Forschungen* 13, Sigmaringen, 1970), pp. 347–82.

idem, 'Der Deutsche Orden und die nichtdeutsche Bevölkerung des Preussenlandes mit besonderer Berücksichtigung der Siedlung', in Walter Schlesinger (ed.), *Die deutsche Ostsiedlung als Problem der europäischen Geschichte* (*Vorträge und Forschungen* 18, Sigmaringen, 1975), pp. 417–38.

Werner, Karl Ferdinand, 'Heeresorganisation und Kriegführung im Deutschen Königreich des 10. and 11. Jahrhunderts', in *Ordinamenti militari in Occidente nell'alto medioevo* (*Settimane di studio del Centro italiano di studi sull'alto medioevo* 15, 2 vols., Spoleto, 1968) 2, pp. 791–843.

White, Lynn, *Medieval Technology and Social Change* (Oxford, 1962).

Wightman, W. E., *The Lacy Family in England and Normandy 1066–1194* (Oxford, 1966).

Wilson, David M., 'Danish Kings and England in the Late 10th and Early 11th Centuries – Economic Implications', in *Proceedings of the Battle Conference on Anglo-Norman Studies* 3 (1980), ed. R. Allen Brown, pp. 188–96.

Wolff, R. L., 'The Organization of the Latin Patriarchate of Constantinople, 1204–1261', *Traditio* 6 (1948), pp. 33–60.

Wrigley, E. A., and R. S. Schofield, *The Population History of England 1541–1871* (Cambridge, Mass., 1981).

Wurm, Helmut, 'Körpergrösse und Ernährung der Deutschen im Mittelalter', in Bernd Herrmann (ed.), *Mensch und Umwelt im Mittelalter* (Stuttgart, 1986), pp. 101–8.

Zatschek, Heinz, 'Namensänderungen und Doppelnamen in Böhmen und Mähren im hohen Mittelalter', *Zeitschrift für Sudetendeutsche Geschichte* 3 (1939), pp. 1–11.

Zdrójkowski, Zbigniew, 'Miasta na prawie Średzkim', *Śląski kwartalnik historyczny Sobótka* 41 (1986), pp. 243–51.

Zientara, Benedykt, 'Die deutschen Einwanderer in Polen vom 12. bis zum 14. Jahrhundert', in Walter Schlesinger (ed.), *Die deutsche Ostsiedlung des Mittelalters als Problem der europäischen Geschichte* (*Vorträge und Forschungen* 18, Sigmaringen, 1975), pp. 333–48.

Zorn, Wolfgang, 'Deutsche und Undeutsche in der städtischen Rechtsordnung des Mittelalters in Ost-Mitteleuropa', *Zeitschrift für Ostforschung* 1 (1952), pp. 182–94.

Index